A Wittgenstein Dictionary

·························· THE ··························
BLACKWELL PHILOSOPHER DICTIONARIES

A Wittgenstein Dictionary

Hans-Johann Glock

First published 1996

Reprinted 1996, 1997, 1999, 2000

Blackwell Publishers Ltd
108 Cowley Road
Oxford OX4 1JF, UK

Blackwell Publishers Inc
350 Main Street
Malden, Massachusetts 02148, USA

British Library Cataloguing in Publication Data
A CIP catalogue record for this book is available from the British Library

Library of Congress Cataloging in Publication Data
Glock, Hans-Johann, 1960–
A Wittgenstein Dictionary / Hans-Johann Glock.
p.   cm. — (The Blackwell philosopher dictionaries)
Includes bibliographical references and index.
ISBN 0–631–18112–1 (hb: alk. paper) — ISBN 0–631–18537–2 (pb: alk. paper)
1. Wittgenstein, Ludwig, 1889–1951 — Dictionaries, indexes, etc.
I. Title. II. Series.
B3376.W563Z83   1996   95–18426
192—dc20   CIP

Typeset in Baskerville on 10/12 pt by Acorn Bookwork, Salisbury, Wilts
Printed and bound in Great Britain by T. J. International Ltd, Padstow, Cornwall

This book is printed on acid-free paper

MEINEN ELTERN

Von mir werden keine neuen Götzen aufgerichtet;
die alten mögen lernen,
was es mit thönernen Beinen auf sich hat

(I erect no new idols;
let the old ones learn
what it means to have feet of clay)

Friedrich Nietzsche, *Ecce Homo*

Alles, was die Philosophie tun kann ist, Götzen zerstören.
Und das heisst, keinen neuen –
etwa in der 'Abwesenheit eines Götzen' – zu schaffen

(All philosophy can do is to destroy idols.
And that means not creating a new one –
for instance as in the 'absence of an idol')

Ludwig Wittgenstein, 'Big Typescript'

Contents

Acknowledgements

I am grateful to their various publishers for permission to use material from the following articles of mine, which develop some ideas in this book at greater length: '*Investigations* §128: Theses in Philosophy and Undogmatic Procedure', in R. L. Arrington and H. J. Glock (eds), *Wittgenstein's Philosophical Investigations* (London: Routledge, 1991); 'Cambridge, Jena or Vienna? – The Roots of the *Tractatus*', *Ratio*, NS 5 (1992); 'Abusing Use', *Dialectica*, 50 (1996); 'Eine ganze Wolke von Philosophie kondensiert zu einem Tröpfchen Sprachlehre', in E. von Savigny and O. Scholz (eds), *Wittgenstein über die Seele* (Frankfurt: Suhrkamp, 1995); 'Externalism and First-Person Authority' (with J. Preston), *The Monist*, 78 (1995); 'Necessity and Normativity', in H. Sluga and D. Stern (eds), *The Cambridge Companion to Wittgenstein* (New York: CUP, 1996); 'On Safari with Wittgenstein, Quine and Davidson', in R. L. Arrington and H.-J. Glock (eds), *Wittgenstein and Quine* (London: Routledge, 1996).

I owe thanks to my colleagues at Reading for their tolerance and good humour. Bob Arrington, John Hyman and Bede Rundle made helpful comments on parts of this book, for which I am grateful. My greatest debt is to Peter Hacker. As my former supervisor, he had more to teach about Wittgenstein than I could possibly have learned. He read drafts of all of the entries, and prevented me from error again and again. Stephen Ryan, the copy-editor, did a wonderful job on a difficult typescript. Finally, I wish to thank Gabi and Sonja for the patience with which they have put up with life under the wretched D-word.

Notes on the use of this book

This book addresses three kinds of readers. Academics working inside or outside philosophy should find explanations of key terms and issues in Wittgenstein's work, and be able to find out what impact it might have on their own. At the end of entries, I sometimes indicate briefly what impact it has actually had, but for detailed information one should consult the items listed in the Bibliography of Secondary Sources. Students working on Wittgenstein or related topics (Frege, Russell, philosophical logic, metaphysics, epistemology, philosophy of mind) should find an account of major exegetical and substantive problems. Wittgenstein scholars should find a state-of-the-art discussion, as well as some new ideas. I have striven for a comprehensive coverage of the topics, but it is synthetic a priori that I have failed.

Readers without prior knowledge of analytic philosophy are strongly advised to read the Sketch of an Intellectual Biography, by way of an introduction. I have tried to avoid formal symbolism, but some of it is inevitable in discussing logical and mathematical issues. The entries concerned are easier to understand with some knowledge of the propositional and predicate calculus. In line with Wittgenstein, I employ the notation of *Principia Mathematica*, although I use parentheses instead of dots as scope-indicating devices, and '$(\exists x)(\exists y)xRy$' instead of '$(\exists x,y)xRy$'. Other technical devices are explained in the entries concerned.

Inevitably, many of the interpretations presented here are controversial. I have tried to state alternative readings which are plausible or widespread. In the end, readers will have to decide for themselves by looking at Wittgenstein's texts. To facilitate further study, I have not only quoted famous passages, but have also provided ample references, including references to the *Nachlass* where it provides significant additional material. I have made liberal use of cross-references, which are indicated by the relevant entry title (or a cognate – e.g., 'determinate'/'determinary of sense', 'grammatical proposition'/'grammar') in small capitals. Terms which do not occur as independent entries can be located from the index.

Unlike other, more distant philosophers in this series, Wittgenstein provides a 'live option' for contemporary philosophers. For this reason I have striven to convey, wherever possible, how his remarks might be attacked or defended. Some commentators suggest that Wittgenstein does not engage in a rational debate with other philosophers, but merely tries to convert them to his point of view. These commentators find his work so out of the ordinary as to be incommensurable with the rest of philosophy. In my view this interpretation is unfounded. Although Wittgenstein's philosophical method is revolutionary in seeking to undermine even the assumptions underlying previous debates, he does so by way of arguments which can be assessed for their soundness. I have therefore stressed not only lines of historical influence, but agreements and disagreements with past and present thinkers.

Another view is that Wittgenstein's remarks often do not present answers to his self-posed questions, or hard-line positions, that they are full of qualifications and investigate rather than affirm or deny. There is some truth in this view. However, since this is a work of reference I have tried to present as clear-cut a position as Wittgenstein's prudent qualifications allow. Perhaps some of the views presented here should die the death of a thousand qualifications, and others the less-protracted death of straightforward refutation. The task of the continuing debate about the nature and merit of Wittgenstein's philosophy is to deliver or parry such blows; and the purpose of this Dictionary is to facilitate that debate.

System of reference and primary sources

Unless otherwise indicated, all references are to pages of the edition cited. I refer to works by Wittgenstein (including *Nachlass*, lectures, correspondence, dictations and works by Waismann derived from Wittgenstein) by the familiar capital-letter system; to works of authors that influenced him by abbreviated titles. I have provided my own translations wherever appropriate. References to the giants of yore follow established systems. References to Kant, for example, are to pages of the first (A) or second (B) edition of the *Critique of Pure Reason*.

Wittgenstein's works

1. Articles and books in order of composition

The date of composition is specified in square brackets where appropriate.

RCL   'Review of Coffey, *The Science of Logic*', *The Cambridge Review*, 34 (1913) 351; reprinted in PO.

NL   'Notes on Logic' [1913], in NB 93–107.

NM   'Notes dictated to G. E. Moore in Norway' [1914], in NB 108–19.

NB   *Notebooks 1914–16* [German–English parallel text], ed. G. E. M. Anscombe and G. H. von Wright, tr. G. E. M. Anscombe, rev. edn (Oxford: Blackwell, 1979).
    Tagebücher 1914–16 (Frankfurt: Suhrkamp, 1984).

GT   *Geheime Tagebücher*, ed. W. Baum (Vienna: Turia & Kant, 1991). These contain remarks from the Notebooks written in a secret code which have been omitted from NB, and are mainly of biographical relevance.

PT   *Proto-Tractatus* [1917, German–English parallel text], ed. B. F. McGuinness, T. Nyberg and G. H. von Wright, tr. D. F. Pears and B. F. McGuinness, with an introduction by G. H. von Wright (London: Routledge & Kegan Paul, 1971).

TLP   *Tractatus Logico-Philosophicus* [German–English parallel text], tr. D. F. Pears and B. F. McGuinness (London: Routledge & Kegan Paul, 1961). References are to numbered sections.

Tractatus Logico-Philosophicus [German–English parallel text], tr. C. K. Ogden and F. P. Ramsey (London: Routledge, 1990). First published 1922.

Logisch-Philosophische Abhandlung, Kritische Edition, ed. B. McGuinness and J. Schulte (Frankfurt: Suhrkamp, 1989). First German edition in *Annalen der Naturphilosophie*, 14 (1921), 185–262.

WV   *Wörterbuch für Volksschulen* (Vienna: Hölder-Pichler-Tempsky, 1926); facsimile reproduction with an introduction by A. Hübner 1977.

RLF   'Some Remarks on Logical Form', *Proceedings of the Aristotelian Society*, suppl. vol. IX (1929), 162–71.

CV   *Culture and Value* [German–English parallel text], ed. G. H. von Wright in collaboration with H. Nyman, tr. P. Winch (Oxford: Blackwell, 1980).

Vermischte Bemerkungen (Frankfurt: Suhrkamp, 1984).

PR   *Philosophical Remarks* [1929–30], ed. R. Rhees, tr. R. Hargreaves and R. White (Oxford: Blackwell, 1975).

Philosophische Bemerkungen (Frankfurt: Suhrkamp, 1984).

PG   *Philosophical Grammar*, ed. R. Rhees, tr. A. J. P. Kenny (Oxford: Blackwell, 1974).

Philosophische Grammatik (Frankfurt: Suhrkamp, 1984).

GB   'Remarks on Frazer's "The Golden Bough"', ed. R. Rhees, *Synthese*, 17 (1967), 233–53; references are to the complete version in PO.

BB   *The Blue and Brown Books* [1933–35] (Oxford: Blackwell, 1958).

EPB   *Eine Philosophische Betrachtung* [1936], ed. R. Rhees, *Schriften* 5 (Frankfurt: Suhrkamp, 1970), 117–237.

CE   'Cause and Effect: Intuitive Awareness', ed. R. Rhees, tr. P. Winch, *Philosophia*, 6 (1976), 392–445; reprinted in PO.

RFM   *Remarks on the Foundations of Mathematics* [1937–44], ed. G. H. von Wright, R. Rhees and G. E. M. Anscombe, tr. G. E. M. Anscombe, rev. edn (Oxford: Blackwell, 1978; 1st edn 1967).

Bemerkungen zu den Grundlagen der Mathematik (Frankfurt: Suhrkamp, 1984).

PI   *Philosophical Investigations* [German–English parallel text], ed. G. E. M. Anscombe and R. Rhees, tr. G. E. M. Anscombe (Oxford: Blackwell, 1958; 1st edn 1953). References are to sections of Part I (except for footnotes), and to pages of Part II.

RPP I   *Remarks on the Philosophy of Psychology* [1945–7, German–English parallel text], volume I, ed. G. E. M. Anscombe and G. H. von Wright, tr. G. E. M. Anscombe (Oxford: Blackwell, 1980).

4

RPP II   *Remarks on the Philosophy of Psychology* [1948, German–English parallel text], volume II, ed. G. H. von Wright and H. Nyman, tr.
C. G. Luckhardt and M. A. E. Aue (Oxford: Blackwell, 1980).
Bemerkungen zur Philosophie der Psychologie (Frankfurt: Suhrkamp,
1984).

Z   *Zettel* [1945–8, German–English parallel text], ed. G. E. M. Anscombe and G. H. von Wright, tr. G. E. M. Anscombe (Oxford:
Blackwell, 1967).

LW I   *Last Writings on the Philosophy of Psychology* [1948–9, German–English
parallel text], volume 1, ed. G. H. von Wright and H. Nyman,
tr. C. G. Luckhardt and M. A. E. Aue (Oxford: Blackwell,
1982).
Letzte Schriften zur Philosophie der Psychologie (Frankfurt: Suhrkamp,
1984).

LW II   *Last Writings on the Philosophy of Psychology* [1949–51, German–English parallel text], volume 2, ed. G. H. von Wright and H. Nyman, tr. C. G. Luckhardt and M. A. E. Aue (Oxford: Blackwell,
1992).

OC   *On Certainty* [1951, German–English parallel text], ed. G. E. M.
Anscombe and G. H. von Wright, tr. D. Paul and G. E. M.
Anscombe (Oxford: Blackwell, 1969).
Über Gewißheit (Frankfurt: Suhrkamp, 1984).

ROC   *Remarks on Colour* [1951, German–English parallel text], ed. G. E.
M. Anscombe, tr. L. L. McAlister and Margarete Schättle (Ox-
ford: Blackwell, 1980; 1st edn 1977).
Bemerkungen über die Farben (Frankfurt: Suhrkamp, 1984).

PO   *Philosophical Occasions* [German–English parallel texts where appro-
priate], ed. J. Klagge and A. Nordmann (Indianapolis: Hackett,
1993). Contains reprinted versions of RCL, RLF, LE, M, LSD,
LPE, CE, LFW, NPL. Unless otherwise specified, these are
cited after the original paginations, which are given in this
anthology.

2. Lectures and conversations

WVC   *Ludwig Wittgenstein and the Vienna Circle* [1929–32], shorthand notes
recorded by F. Waismann, ed. B. F. McGuinness (Oxford:
Blackwell, 1979).
Ludwig Wittgenstein und der Wiener Kreis (Oxford: Blackwell, 1967 and
Frankfurt: Suhrkamp, 1984).

LE   'A Lecture on Ethics' [1929], *Philosophical Review*, 74 (1965), 3–12.

M   'Wittgenstein's Lectures in 1930–33', in G. E. Moore, *Philosophical*

Papers (London: Allen and Unwin, 1959), references are to the reprinted version in PO.

LWL   *Wittgenstein's Lectures, Cambridge 1930–1932*, from the notes of J. King and D. Lee, ed. Desmond Lee (Oxford: Blackwell, 1980).

AWL   *Wittgenstein's Lectures, Cambridge 1932–1935*, from the notes of A. Ambrose and M. MacDonald, ed. A. Ambrose (Oxford: Blackwell, 1979).

LSD   'The Language of Sense Data and Private Experience – Notes taken by R. Rhees of Wittgenstein's Lectures, 1936', *Philosophical Investigations*, 7 (1984), 1–45, 101–40.

LPE   'Wittgenstein's Notes for Lectures on "Private Experience" and "Sense Data" ' [1936], ed. R. Rhees, *Philosophical Review*, 77 (1968), 275–320.

LC   *Lectures and Conversations on Aesthetics, Psychology and Religious Belief* [1938–46], ed. C. Barrett (Oxford: Blackwell, 1966).

LFM   *Wittgenstein's Lectures on the Foundations of Mathematics, Cambridge 1939*, from the notes of R. G. Bosanquet, N. Malcolm, R. Rhees and Y. Smythies, ed. C. Diamond (Hassocks: Harvester Press, 1976).

LFW   'Lectures on Freedom of the Will' [1939], from the notes of Y. Smythies, PO 427–44.

NPL   'Notes for the Philosophical Lecture' [1941], ed. D. Stern, PO 445–58.

LPP   *Wittgenstein's Lectures on Philosophical Psychology 1946–47*, notes by P. T. Geach, K. J. Shah and A. C. Jackson, ed. P. T. Geach (Hassocks: Harvester Press, 1988).

3. Anthologies and collections

Schriften (Frankfurt: Suhrkamp):
Vol. 1 (1960): TLP, NB, PI. Vol. 2 (1964): PR. Vol. 3 (1967): WVC. Vol. 4 (1969): PG. Vol. 5 (1970): BB, EPB, Z. Vol. 6 (1973): RFM. Vol. 7 (1978): LFM. Vol. 8 (1982): RPP I, RPP II.

Werkausgabe (Frankfurt: Suhrkamp, 1984):
Vol. 1: NB, TLP, PI. Vol. 2: PR. Vol. 3: WVC. Vol. 4: PG. Vol. 5: BB, EPB. Vol. 6: RFM. Vol. 7: RPP I, RPP II, LW I. Vol. 8: ROC, OC, Z, CV.

The Wittgenstein Reader, ed. A. J. P. Kenny (Oxford: Blackwell, 1994):
Selections from TLP, BT, PG, BB, LPE, LC, PI, RFM, RPP I & II, Z, OC.

4. Works derived from dictations by or conversations with Wittgenstein

PLP   F. Waismann, *The Principles of Linguistic Philosophy*, ed. R. Harré (London: Macmillan, 1965).

LSP   F. Waismann, *Logik, Sprache, Philosophie*, ed. G. P. Baker and B. F. McGuinness (Stuttgart: Reclam, 1976).

FW   *Dictations to F. Waismann*, ed. G. P. Baker (London: Routledge, forthcoming). References to dictation numbers.

WAM   N. Malcolm, *Ludwig Wittgenstein − A Memoir*, 2nd edn (Oxford: Oxford University Press, 1984; 1st edn 1958).

SDE   R. Rhees, 'Some Developments in Wittgenstein's View of Ethics', *Philosophical Review*, 74 (1965), 17–26.

RR   R. Rhees, 'On Continuity: Wittgenstein's Ideas 1938', in R. Rhees, *Discussions of Wittgenstein* (London: Routledge & Kegan Paul, 1970), 104–57.

RW   R. Rhees (ed.), *Recollections of Wittgenstein* (Oxford: Oxford University Press, 1984).

WC   O. K. Bouwsma, *Wittgenstein: Conversations 1949–1951*, ed. J. L. Craft and R. E. Hustwit (Indianapolis: Hackett, 1986).

5. Correspondence

EL   Letters to Engelmann.
FL   Letters to von Ficker.
ML   Letters to Moore.
OL   Letters to Ogden.
RAL   Letters to Ramsey.
RUL   Letters to Russell.

These letters are quoted by date as specifically as possible. They are collected in the following editions:

Briefe, ed. B. F. McGuinness and G. H. von Wright. Correspondence with B. Russell, G. E. Moore, J. M. Keynes, F. P. Ramsey, W. Eccles, P. Engelmann and L. von Ficker. In German, with original version of Wittgenstein's own letters (when in English) in an appendix; German translations J. Schulte (Frankfurt: Suhrkamp, 1980).

Letters to C. K. Ogden, ed. G. H. von Wright, with an appendix containing letters by F. P. Ramsey, 1923–4 (Oxford: Blackwell/London: Routledge, 1973).

Letters from Ludwig Wittgenstein, with a Memoir by Paul Engelmann, ed. B. F. McGuinness, tr. L. Furtmüller (Oxford: Blackwell, 1967).

Briefe an Ludwig von Ficker, ed. G. H. von Wright and W. Methlagl (Salzburg:

Müller, 1969); Eng. trans., 'Letters to Ludwig von Ficker', ed. Allan Janik, tr. B. Gillette, in *Wittgenstein: Sources and Perspectives*, ed. C. G. Luckhardt (Hassocks: Harvester Press, 1979).
Letters to Russell, Keynes and Moore, ed. G. H. von Wright, Eng. trans. B. F. McGuinness (Oxford: Blackwell, 1974).

6. *Nachlass*

All references to unpublished material follow von Wright's catalogue (G. H. von Wright, *Wittgenstein* (Oxford: Blackwell, 1982), 35ff.). They are by MS or TS number followed by page number. I use the following abbreviation:

BT   The 'Big Typescript' (TS 213), partly in PO 160–99.

The *Nachlass* is kept in the Library of Trinity College, Cambridge. It is available on microfilm/photocopies from Cornell University, the so-called 'Cornell copy'. The full *Nachlass* will be available on CD-ROM from Oxford University Press, edited by the Wittgenstein Archives at the University of Bergen. The early parts of the *Nachlass* are currently being published as the *Wiener Ausgabe/Vienna Edition*, ed. M. Nedo (Vienna/New York: Springer, 1994–). This edition contains the original pagination. In addition to an introduction and concordance volumes, it will comprise the following: vol. 1: MSS 105, 106; vol. 2: MSS 107, 108; vol. 3: MSS 109, 110; vol. 4: MSS 111, 112; vol. 5: MSS 113, 114; vol. 6: TSS 208, 210; vol. 7/1–2: TS 211; vol. 8: TS 209 (PR); vol. 9/1–2: TS 212; vol. 10/1–2: TS 213 (BT); vol. 11: MSS 153a–b, 154, 155.

Works of other authors

Boltzmann

Physics   *Theoretical Physics and Philosophical Problems*, ed. B. McGuinness (Dordrecht: Reidel, 1974).

Frege

Notation   *Conceptual Notation and Related Articles*, tr. and ed. T. W. Bynum (Oxford: Clarendon, 1972).
            Begriffsschrift (Halle: Nebert, 1879).
Foundations   *The Foundations of Arithmetic*, tr. J. L. Austin, 2nd edn (Oxford: Blackwell, 1953; 1st edn 1950).
            Die Grundlagen der Arithmetik (Breslau: Koebner, 1884).
Laws   *The Basic Laws of Arithmetic*, tr. and ed. M. Furth (Berkeley/ Los Angeles: University of California Press, 1964).
            Grundgesetze der Arithmetik (Jena: Pohle, 1893 and 1903).

'Function'   'Function and Concept'.
'Sense'   'Sense and Reference'.
'Concept'   'On Concept and Object'.
'Negation'   'Negation'.
'Thought'   'The Thought'.
'Compound'   'Compound Thought'.
All of these papers are in *Collected Papers*, ed. B. McGuinness (Oxford: Blackwell, 1984). They are cited after the original paginations, which are given in this collection.

Posthumous   *Posthumous Writings*, ed. H. Hermes, F. Kambartel and F. Kaulbach, tr. P. Long and R. White (Oxford: Blackwell, 1979).

Correspondence *Philosophical and Mathematical Correspondence*, ed. B. McGuinness, tr. H. Kaal (Oxford: Blackwell, 1980).

Hertz

Mechanics   *The Principles of Mechanics*, tr. D. E. Jones and J. T. Walley (London: Macmillan, 1899).
Die Prinzipien der Mechanik (Leipzig: Barth, 1894).

James

Psychology   *The Principles of Psychology* (New York: Dover, 1950; 1st edn 1890).

Köhler

Gestalt   *Gestalt Psychology* (New York: Mentor, 1975; 1st edn 1930).

Mauthner

Beiträge   *Beiträge zu einer Kritik der Sprache* (Stuttgart: Cotta, 1901–3).

Moore

Writings   *Selected Writings*, ed. T. Baldwin (London: Routledge, 1994).

Ramsey

Mathematics   *The Foundations of Mathematics and Other Logical Essays* (London: Routledge & Kegan Paul, 1931).

Russell

Principles   *The Principles of Mathematics*, 2nd edn (London: Allen and Unwin, 1937; 1st edn 1903).

Essays   *Philosophical Essays*, 2nd edn (London: Routledge, 1994; 1st edn 1910).

Principia	*Principia Mathematica*, 2nd edn (Cambridge: Cambridge University Press, 1927; 1st edn 1910).
Problems	*The Problems of Philosophy* (Oxford: Oxford University Press, 1980; 1st edn 1912).
'Theory'	'The Theory of Knowledge' [1913], in *The Collected Papers of Bertrand Russell*, vol. 7, ed. E. Eames and K. Blackwell (London: Allen and Unwin, 1984).
External	*Our Knowledge of the External World as a Field for Scientific Method in Philosophy*, rev. edn (London: Routledge, 1993; 1st edn 1914).
Mysticism	*Mysticism and Logic* (London: Longmans, Green, 1918).
Introduction	*Introduction to Mathematical Philosophy* (London: Allen and Unwin, 1919).
'Introduction'	'Introduction' to *Tractatus Logico-Philosophicus* (TLP).
Analysis	*The Analysis of Mind* (London: Allen and Unwin, 1921).
'Limits'	'The Limits of Empiricism', *Proceedings of the Aristotelian Society*, XXXVI (1935–6).
Logic	*Logic and Knowledge*, ed. R. C. Marsh (London: Allen and Unwin, 1956).

Schlick

Papers	*Philosophical Papers*, ed. H. L. Mulder and B. F. B. van der Velde-Schlick (London: Reidel, 1979).

Schopenhauer

World	*The World as Will and Representation*, tr. E. F. J. Payne (New York: Dover, 1966; 1st edn of trans. 1958).
	Die Welt als Wille und Vorstellung (Leipzig: Brockhaus, 1844; 1st edn 1819).

Sketch of an intellectual biography

Ludwig Wittgenstein (1889–1951) was the youngest child of a wealthy and cultured Viennese family of Jewish descent. The Wittgenstein home was a centre of artistic and, in particular, musical life. It provided Ludwig with what he later called his 'good intellectual nursery-training', which consisted of the music of Viennese classicism and a strand of German literature – with Goethe as a figurehead – which rejected the nationalism and faith in progress that characterized the mainstream of European culture in the nineteenth and early twentieth centuries. Wittgenstein was a cultural conservative who felt at odds with the 'spirit of the main current of European and American civilization' (CV 6–7; CV contains Wittgenstein's intermittent reflections on cultural questions). But his intense intellectual passion and honesty prevented him from being nostalgic or parochial. Indeed, he reacted in a highly creative way to certain modern ideas. This becomes clear when we turn to the direct influences on his thinking, which he listed in 1931: Boltzmann, Hertz, Schopenhauer, Frege, Russell, Kraus, Loos, Weininger, Spengler, Sraffa (CV 19). Those which are relevant to his earlier philosophy fall into three groups: the sages, the philosopher-scientists and the philosopher-logicians.

Sages, Scientists and Madmen

The sages were thinkers outside academic philosophy whose work Wittgenstein read as a youngster. Karl Kraus, the formidable cultural critic of the late Habsburg Empire, impressed Ludwig by his insistence on personal integrity. Wittgenstein was also influenced by Kraus's masterful polemical analysis of language. Opponents are literally taken at their word. Their style, sometimes even a single ill-judged sentence, is taken to reveal both their fallacies and their character failings. Kraus's work was part of the so-called 'crisis of language', a general concern with the authenticity of symbolic expression in art and public life. Another expression of this crisis was Mauthner's critique of language. Mauthner pursued a Kantian goal, the defeat of metaphysical speculation. But he supplanted the critique of reason with a critique of language, and his work owed more to Hume and Mach. His method was psychologistic and historicist: the critique of language is part of social psychology. The content was empiricist – the foundations of language are sensations – and the result sceptical. Reason is identical with language, but the latter is unsuited for penetrating reality. Wittgenstein rightly contrasts his own logical 'critique of language' (TLP 4.0031) with Mauthner's, but it was Mauthner (*Wörterbuch der Philosophie* xi) who first identified philosophy with the critique of language.

Weininger, author of the notorious *Sex and Character*, was less a sage than a psychopath. His theatrically staged suicide in 1903 was copied by a number of young men in Vienna, and his influence on Wittgenstein's personal and cultural attitudes was only marginally more benign. He infected Wittgenstein with a misogyny and with doubts about the creative powers of Jews (CV 13, 16–22) which were as foolish as they were noxious. Weininger's most important influence, however, lay in the idea that one has a moral obligation towards oneself to strive for genius, for the intellectual love of truth and clarity. Logic and ethics are ultimately identical, 'they are no more than duty to oneself' (*Sex and Character* 159). This explains both why the *Tractatus* closely links logic and ethics (TLP 6.13, 6.421) and Wittgenstein's abiding view that philosophical mistakes are signs of character defects.

Wittgenstein's first genuinely philosophical position was Schopenhauer's transcendental idealism. He only abandoned it under the influence of Frege's conceptual realism (WAM 5), and even then returned to it in the mystical parts of the *Tractatus*. Schopenhauer started out from a Kantian distinction between the noumenal world, the world as it is in itself, and the phenomenal world, the world as it appears. 'The world is my representation' (*World* I §1), namely what appears to the knowing subject. It is governed by structural features (space, time, causation) which are imposed on it by that subject. But the world as representation is a manifestation of an underlying reality, the world as a cosmic *will*. Schopenhauer also founded an anti-intellectualism which stressed the role of the will against that of the intellect and influenced Nietzsche and Wittgenstein among others. Moreover, Schopenhauer's idealism easily lapses into solipsism, a philosophical temptation against which Wittgenstein later struggled. Finally, he made the notion of representation rather than that of consciousness the focus of transcendental philosophy (*World* I §10), and thereby contributed to Wittgenstein's interest in linguistic representation.

This interest was reinforced by Hertz and Boltzmann. Both were part of a Neo-Kantian tradition of philosopher-scientists who reflected on the nature of science and sought to free it from obscure, metaphysical elements. In *The Principles of Mechanics* (Pref.), Hertz sharply distinguished between the empirical and the a priori elements of mechanics. He explained the possibility of scientific explanation by reference to the nature of representation. Science forms pictures (*Bilder*) of reality, such that the logical consequences of these pictures correspond to the actual consequences of the external affairs it depicts. Its theories are not predetermined by experience, but actively constructed according to formal and pragmatic constraints which Hertz referred to as 'the laws of thought'. The task of a philosophical reconstruction of mechanics is to avoid pseudo-problems, notably concerning the nature of force or electricity, by presenting these a priori elements in a clear and perspicuous way.

Boltzmann was more hostile to Kant. In a Darwinian vein he accused him of having failed to appreciate that the 'laws of thought' are not immutable, but only innate to the individual as a result of the 'experience of the species' (*Physics* 195). But he developed Hertz's attempt to clarify science by reference to models which are not derived from experience, and retained the view that philosophical puzzlement should be resolved by revealing the nonsensicality of certain questions. Hertz and Boltzmann influenced the picture theory of the *Tractatus* as well as its discussion of science. Most importantly, they reinforced a Kantian conception of the task of philosophy that Wittgenstein also encountered in Schopenhauer: in contrast to science, philosophy does not picture reality, but reflects on the 'laws of thought' which underlie such depiction; its task is a critical one; it results not in a doctrine but in the resolution of confusion.

Wittgenstein's initial plan to study with Boltzmann in Vienna was frustrated by the latter's suicide in 1906. Instead, he was sent to study engineering in Berlin. However, he soon found himself gripped by philosophical problems and started his life-long habit of recording philosophical reflections in dated notebook entries. In 1908 he moved to Manchester, where he participated in experiments with kites and in the development of a jet-reaction propeller. There he began to develop an interest, first in pure mathematics, and then in its philosophical foundations. He was introduced to the writings of Frege and Russell and in 1909 tried to solve the main problem then outstanding – the contradiction Russell had discovered in Frege's system. In 1911, he drew up a plan for a philosophical work, which he discussed with Frege. On Frege's advice he went to Cambridge to study with Russell, who by then had become the leading force in these debates. This proved to be a decisive turning-point in Wittgenstein's life. By way of inspiration and opposition, Frege and Russell provide the essential background of his early philosophy, as well as important targets of his later thought.

Frege and Russell

Frege and Russell invented modern formal logic, and thereby altered the landscape of twentieth-century philosophy. Their work responded to a foundational crisis of nineteenth-century mathematics. Frege's *Begriffsschrift* of 1879 was intended to provide the means both for rigorously checking mathematical proofs and for resolving the problem of the status of mathematics. Frege pioneered logicism, the reduction of mathematics to logic and set theory, by seeking to demonstrate the derivability of arithmetic from purely logical concepts and principles of reasoning (*Notation* Pref., §13; *Foundations* §3). In order to pursue this programme, Frege had to overcome the limitations of Aristotelian syllogistic logic. His crucial step was to analyse propositions not into subject and predicate, as Aristotelian logic had done, but into argument and function. The expression '$x^2 + 1$' represents a function of the variable x because its value depends solely on the 'argument' we substitute for x – it has the value 2 for the argument 1, 5 for the argument 2, etc. Frege extended the notion of a function first to expressions like 'the capital of x' (which has the value Berlin for the argument Germany) and then to propositions. 'Caesar conquered Gaul' is analysed not into the subject 'Caesar' and the predicate 'conquered Gaul' but into a function 'x conquered Gaul' to which 'Caesar' supplies an argument. The value of this function is either the True (e.g., if we substitute 'Caesar') or the False (e.g., if we substitute 'Alexander'), depending on whether the resulting proposition is true or false. Thus, concepts like that expressed by 'x conquered Gaul' are treated as functions which map arguments onto truth-values. The simple, atomic formulae of Frege's concept-script are composed of an argument-expression and a concept-word or function-name. The argument-expressions are names of objects, and the concept-words are names of functions. Frege next extended this idea to the logical connectives by means of which molecular formulae are formed. Negation, for example, is a unary function which maps a truth-value onto the converse truth-value (if 'p' is true, '$\sim p$' is false). Sentences are proper names of one or the other of two 'logical objects', the True and the False, and they are the argument-expressions for the function-names that denominate the logical connectives. Finally, 'All Greeks are bald' is analysed not into the subject 'All Greeks' and the predicate 'are bald', but into the complex concept-word 'if x is a Greek then x is bald' and the quantifier 'For all x'. The latter expresses a second-level function which maps concepts (first-level functions) onto truth-values, the True if the concept has the value True for all arguments, otherwise the False. ('Some Greeks are bald' is treated in a parallel manner.)

This apparatus made it possible to provide the first complete axiomatization of first-order logic – including inferences involving multiple generality which are characteristic of mathematical reasoning – and to exhibit mathematical induction as an application of a purely logical law. In *Grundgesetze der Arithmetik*, this system is enriched by the distinction between sense and meaning (*Laws* I §2). In the concept-script, every sentence (formula) expresses a sense, 'the thought' (what is judged), and refers to or denotes a 'meaning', a truth-value. It expresses a thought by virtue of presenting a truth-value as the value of a function for an argument. Each significant constituent of a sentence (apart from the assertion-sign) likewise expresses a sense and has a referent. Proper names express a sense and refer to an object; concept-words express a sense and refer to a concept.

Frege defined numbers (the basic concept of arithmetic) as classes of classes with the same number of members. Alas, this ingenious procedure made unrestricted use of the notion of a set, and therefore led to the paradox of the set of all sets which are not members of themselves. Russell, who had devised the paradox, developed a logical system closely resembling Frege's. He endeavoured to protect logicism from the paradox by means of a theory of types which prohibits formulae which predicate of sets properties which can only significantly be predicated of their members (e.g., 'The class of lions is a lion'). The logical system of Russell's and Whitehead's *Principia Mathematica*, like that of Frege, uses the analogy between the structure of propositions and the function-theoretic structures of higher analysis. However, Russell's conception of a propositional function differed from Frege's notion of a concept, in that its values were not two logical entities like the True and the False, but propositions. As a consequence, Russell denied that sentences name truth-values. Moreover, he repudiated Frege's sense/meaning distinction, and the supposition that there can be truth-valueless propositions. For Frege, in natural languages a sentence of the form 'The F is G' (e.g., 'The King of France is bald') expresses a thought but lacks a truth-value if nothing which is F exists. Russell's theory of descriptions analysed such sentences into a quantified conjunction, namely 'There is one and only one subject that is F, and that object is G'. If nothing which is F exists, this proposition is not truth-valueless, but false. Like Frege, Russell thought of his formal system as an ideal language which avoids the logical defects (indeterminacy, referential failure, etc.) of natural languages. But his interests were wider. He applied the new logical techniques not just to the foundations of mathematics but also to traditional problems of epistemology and metaphysics, and hoped that they would set philosophy as a whole on the secure path of a science.

Tractatus Logico-Philosophicus: the essence of representation

Wittgenstein's ambition was not to develop the formal aspects of the new logic, to provide new proofs or tools, but to elucidate its philosophical implications. First and foremost among these was the question 'What is logic?' It was in this area that he soon became Russell's equal and his remorseless critic. Russell was forced to acknowledge that *Principia* had not clarified the nature of logic. He decided to leave this job to Wittgenstein; but he got more than he bargained for. While Wittgenstein took over important elements of Frege's and Russell's logical systems, and accepted Russell's view that philosophy is identical with logical analysis, his account of logic and philosophy was completely novel. For a brief period Wittgenstein was the rising star of Cambridge, and a member of the self-appointed intellectual elite, the Apostles. But in 1913 he left for Norway, in order to work in solitude on his new theory of logic. He did not then return to Cambridge, but, with the outbreak of World War I, went to Vienna and volunteered for military service. In spite of the exigencies of war service, Wittgenstein continued to work on what is now known as the *Tractatus Logico-Philosophicus*. Having been taken prisoner in 1918, he managed to send the manuscript to England. Russell's support eventually secured its publication in 1921, and a year later in English translation.

The *Tractatus* is one of the great classics in philosophy, and the only philosophical work Wittgenstein published during his lifetime. It marks the point at which the nineteenth-century debate about the nature of logic between empiricism, psychologism and Platonism merges with the Post-Kantian debate about representation and the nature of philosophy. The point of contact is the notion of thought. Both the discussion about the nature of logic and the Post-Kantian discussion about the nature of representation were conducted in terms of the laws of thought. For Wittgenstein, philosophy or logic is concerned with thought by virtue of reflecting on the nature of representation, since it is in thought that we represent reality. At the same time, Wittgenstein gives a linguistic twist to the Kantian tale. Thoughts are neither abstract nor mental entities, but propositions, sentences which have been projected onto reality, and hence can be completely expressed in language. Philosophy draws limits to thought by establishing the limits of the linguistic expression of thought; it delineates the rules which underlie symbolic representation. These rules also explain the nature of logic. For Wittgenstein's predecessors, necessary propositions are true descriptions, either of how people think (psychologistic logic), or of relations between abstract entities (Frege), or of the most pervasive features of the universe (Russell). For Wittgenstein, by contrast, the a priori status of logical propositions is due not to the fact that they describe a peculiar reality, but to the fact that they reflect rules for describing empirical reality. Logic embodies the necessary preconditions of symbolic representation.

Wittgenstein took over from Frege the demand that the sense of a proposition must be determinate, and from Russell the atomistic programme of analysing propositions into their simple elements. But the core of his quasi-transcendental theory of symbolic representation is his picture theory. In clarifying the essence of the proposition, its form and its relation to what it depicts, the theory also elucidates the nature of the world. The essential logical form of language is identical with the essential metaphysical form of reality, because it comprises those structural features which language and reality must share if the former is to be capable of depicting the latter. The

16

world is the totality of facts. The substance of all possible worlds consists of the totality of sempiternal simple objects. The form of a simple object consists in its combinatorial possibilities with other objects. A possible combination of objects is a state of affairs; the existence of such a combination is a fact. The representation of a state of affairs is a model or picture. It must be isomorphic with what it represents, that is, have the same logical multiplicity and structure. Propositions are logical pictures. They are bipolar, capable of being either true or false. In this they reflect what they represent: a state of affairs (combination of objects) either does or does not exist. The logical analysis of propositions yields elementary propositions which are logically independent of each other because their truth depends solely on the existence or non-existence of atomic states of affairs. The ultimate constituents of elementary propositions are unanalysable names which stand for the objects which are their meaning. Their logico-syntactical form (combinatorial possibilities) mirrors the metaphysical form of the objects. The sense of an elementary proposition is the state of affairs it depicts, and is a function of the meanings of its constituent names. The fact that the names in a proposition are arranged as they are says that things are thus-and-so in reality. The essence of a proposition, the general propositional form, is to say 'Things are thus-and-so.' A proposition is true if the objects for which its names stand are combined in a way which matches the way it combines those names.

Elementary propositions combine to form molecular propositions. The logical constants (propositional connectives and quantifiers) are not names of logical objects or functions, but express the truth-functional operations which effect this combination. All possible forms of truth-functional combination can be generated by the operation of 'joint negation' on the set of elementary propositions. All logical relations between propositions are due to the complexity of molecular propositions, the fact that they are the result of truth-functional combination. The propositions of logic are vacuous tautologies. Their necessity reflects the fact that they combine bipolar propositions in such a way that all information cancels out. They exclude, and hence say, nothing, which means that they are senseless (for example, that it is either raining or not raining says nothing about the weather). However, the fact that a certain combination of bipolar propositions says nothing about the world *shows* something about the essence of the world, its logical form. Logic flows from the essential bipolarity of elementary propositions. By contrast to logical propositions, the pronouncements of metaphysics are nonsensical pseudo-propositions. At best, they try to say what could not be otherwise (e.g., that red is a colour). What they seem to exclude (e.g., red's being a sound) contravenes logic, and is hence nonsensical. But the attempt to refer to something nonsensical, even if only to exclude it, is itself nonsensical. What such pseudo-propositions try to *say* is *shown* by the structure of genuine propositions (e.g., that 'red' can combine only with names of points in the visual field). The only necessary propositions which can be expressed are tautologies and hence analytic (their negation is a contradiction).

Wittgenstein combined his logical theory with reflections on mystical themes (ethics, aesthetics, death) which were inspired by his experiences during the war and heavily influenced by Schopenhauer. Indeed, he seems to have adopted a linguistic version of transcendental idealism: what projects sentences onto reality are ostensive acts of a metaphysical self. Like the eye of the visual field, this subject of representation is not itself part of experience; it cannot be represented through meaningful propositions. Like metaphysical truths, the truths of ethics, aesthetics and religion are ineffable. The pronouncements of the *Tractatus* itself are in the end condemned as nonsensical. By outlining the essential preconditions of representation, they lead one to the correct logical point of view, but once this is achieved, one must throw away the ladder which one has climbed up. Philosophy cannot be a doctrine, since there are no philosophical propositions. It is an activity, namely of analysis which elucidates the meaningful propositions of science and reveals the propositions of metaphysics to violate the bounds of sense. Russell's aspiration to introduce scientific method into philosophy is misguided.

Tractatus Logico-Philosophicus is a breakthrough marred by mystery-mongering. Its criticisms of Frege and Russell are powerful and often definitive. Its own account of logical truth is a definite advance, but marred by its link with an ineffable metaphysics of symbolism. That metaphysics is the climax of an atomist and foundationalist tradition of analysis which straddles rationalism, empiricism and Kantianism: the ultimate constituents and the logical structure of language must mirror the metaphysical structure of the world. Through its non-Platonist and non-mentalist conception of thought or representation, the fact that it explains logic by reference to rules for the combination of signs, and its conception of philosophy as the critical analysis of language, it initiated the 'linguistic turn' of twentieth-century analytical philosophy, and the contemporary quest for a theory of meaning for natural languages.

That linguistic turn was a transformation of the Kantian idea that philosophy is a second-order activity which reflects on the preconditions of representing reality, an idea which was totally alien to Frege and Russell. Moreover, Frege and Russell shared the traditional view (held, for example, by Locke and the Port Royal *Logic*) that although there is a rough correspondence between thought and language, the latter distorts the former. They showed some interest in natural languages and occasionally relied on ordinary grammar for constructing their formal systems. But the latter were intended as ideal languages, capable of doing what natural language cannot because it does not mirror the structure of thought (*Notation* Pref.; *Posthumous* 6, 143, 259, 266; *Correspondence* 67–8; *Principles* 42; *Principia* i.2; *Logic* 176, 205). For Wittgenstein, ordinary language disguises logical form but is not logically defective. Properly analysed, it cannot fail to be seen to mirror the structure of thought. For logic is a condition of sense, and ordinary language is capable of expressing every sense. Function-theoretic logic provides not an ideal language but an ideal notation, one which brings out the logical order which underlies all symbolic representation. These ideas are directed explicitly against Frege's and Russell's non-linguistic conceptions of logic. On the other hand, Wittgenstein's revolution could have occurred only after a symbolism had been developed which looked like an ideal notation and appeared capable of solving philosophical puzzles (Russell's theory of descriptions, in particular, seemed to resolve age-old questions concerning existence). Without this inspiration the idea of analysing language would either have remained an empty slogan, or taken the psychologistic course of Mauthner's critique of language.

The wilderness years

Wittgenstein, with engaging modesty, thought that the *Tractatus* had solved all the fundamental problems of philosophy. After its publication he therefore abandoned the subject. On his return from captivity in 1919, he gave away the fortune inherited from his father, not for altruistic reasons, but to break with his past. In 1920 he took up the unlikely vocation of an elementary school teacher in rural Lower Austria. During this time he composed a spelling dictionary for elementary schools (*Wörterbuch für Volksschulen*). But he soon ran into difficulties and became disenchanted. In 1926 he returned to Vienna. He first worked as a gardener in a monastery. Later he designed and supervised the construction of a modernist mansion for his sister Margarete, which was inspired by the anti-decorative style of the Austrian architect Adolf Loos. Wittgenstein never lost touch with philosophy completely. In 1923 he was visited by F. P. Ramsey, a brilliant young mathematician from Cambridge who had played a crucial part in the translation of the *Tractatus*, and was the most perceptive of its readers and critics. Their discussions led to changes in the second edition of the *Tractatus* (1933). Ramsey's main project was the reformulation of the logicist foundations of mathematics on the basis of Wittgenstein's new philosophy of logic. Although the *Tractatus* rejects the logicist programme, Wittgenstein initially seems to have encouraged Ramsey. But in the course of subsequent visits and correspondence he rejected not only some details of Ramsey's reconstruction, but also the very attempt to provide mathematics with a foundation.

In the meantime, the *Tractatus* had come to the attention of the Vienna

19

Circle, a group of scientifically minded philosophers led by Moritz Schlick. It was recognized by some of them (Schlick, Carnap, Waismann) as a turning-point in the history of philosophy. But their grasp of it was partial. The idea that metaphysical pronouncements are nonsensical pseudo-propositions appealed to their anti-metaphysical fervour, and they dismissed the suggestion that there are ineffable metaphysical truths. They harnessed the restriction of philosophy to the analysis of language, in particular of the propositions of science, to their scientistic conviction that science is the only source of knowledge and understanding, a view Wittgenstein himself found offensive. As committed empiricists they welcomed the idea that necessary propositions are analytic, and hence do not express knowledge of reality. Unlike previous versions of empiricism (Mill, Mach) it does justice to their necessity while avoiding both Platonism and the Kantian idea of synthetic a priori truths. Unlike Wittgenstein, they treated as tautologies not only logical propositions but also arithmetical equations. And while for the *Tractatus* the rules of logical syntax mirror the essence of reality, the Vienna Circle saw them as arbitrary conventions governing the use of signs.

Schlick made contact with Wittgenstein, and although the latter did not take part in the weekly meetings of the Circle, he met a select few (Schlick, Waismann, and initially Carnap and Feigl). These discussions, together with the *Tractatus*, were formative influences on the development of logical positivism in the interwar years (they are recorded in *Wittgenstein and the Vienna Circle*). Waismann was commissioned to write a book – *Logik, Sprache, Philosophie* – which would present an accessible account of the *Tractatus*. But due to Wittgenstein's rapid abandonment of his earlier doctrines, the book turned into an account of his evolving views in the early thirties. Due to the strain this imposed, their relationship was terminated in 1934, and the book was published only in 1965 (in English as *The Principles of Linguistic Philosophy*). In the course of these discussions Wittgenstein developed the now notorious principle of verification according to which the meaning of a proposition is the method of its verification. At the same time, he toyed with a phenomenalist version of verificationism. He distinguished three different types of propositions according to whether and how they can be verified. The only genuine propositions are sense-datum statements, which are verified by direct comparison with one's immediate experience. Other empirical propositions are hypotheses, which can never be completely verified but only be made more or less probable. Finally, mathematical propositions are not verified at all, since they neither agree nor disagree with reality. But their sense is given by their proofs.

Return to Cambridge

The discussions with members of the Vienna Circle, and perhaps a lecture

20

delivered by Brouwer (the founder of intuitionist mathematics) in 1928, revived Wittgenstein's interest in philosophy. In 1929 he returned to Cambridge at the instigation of Ramsey, with whom he enjoyed fruitful discussions until the latter's untimely death in 1930. He restarted his habit of recording philosophical reflections and submitted the *Tractatus* as a doctoral thesis – telling his examiners Russell and Moore 'Don't worry, I know you'll never understand it.' Through their support, he was awarded a research fellowship in 1930. He also started giving his famous lecture-courses. Wittgenstein did not lecture in any conventional way, but thought on his feet, as if he were alone, occasionally directing questions at his handpicked audience. His original intention had been to elaborate and modify some of the thoughts of the *Tractatus*. But it soon became clear that a radical rethinking was required. In realizing this he was helped by discussions with the Marxist economist Piero Sraffa, whom he credited with providing him with an 'anthropological' perspective on philosophical problems. This is most evident in his approach to language, which is no longer seen as an abstract system of quasi-transcendental preconditions of representation, but as part of human practice, part of a form of life. Between 1929 and 1933, the so-called 'transition period', Wittgenstein's thought underwent a series of rapid transformations. These changes can be classified under five headings.

Philosophy of logic   The initial point which led to the unravelling of the impressive system of the *Tractatus* was a detail, namely the colour-exclusion problem. Colour statements like '*A* is red' and '*A* is green' are logically incompatible, and hence, according to the *Tractatus*, have to be analysed into logically independent elementary propositions. Now Wittgenstein realized that this cannot be done, and that the same problem arises for all propositions attributing a determinate property out of a determinable range. As a result he abandoned the requirement that elementary propositions are logically independent, holding instead that they form propositional systems of mutual exclusion and implication. This means that there are logical relations which are not determined by truth-functional composition. However, the thesis of independence was the linchpin of the *Tractatus*'s philosophy of logic. Without it, the idea that logic depends solely on the essential bipolarity of elementary propositions collapses. The idea that there is a single propositional form collapses likewise. At best there can be characteristic forms for the members of specific proposition systems (e.g., colour- or length-ascribing propositions).

Metaphysics of logical atomism   At much the same time, Wittgenstein relinquished the ontology of logical atomism. The world does not consist of facts rather than things, since facts are not concatenations of objects, and cannot be located in space and time. This also spells ruin for the *Tractatus*'s correspondence theory of truth: facts are not extra-linguistic items to which a proposition could correspond. The logical atomist notion of indecomposable objects is equally confused. The distinction between simple and complex is not absolute. Standards of complexity must be laid down seperately for each kind of thing, and even then are relative to different purposes.

Picture theory of the proposition   The collapse of logical atomism also under-mines the picture theory of the proposition. If there are no ultimate con-stituents of facts – simple objects – then there are no corresponding constituents of propositions which are simple in an absolute sense. Wittgen-stein also jettisoned the idea that a proposition must have a logical form which it shares with what it depicts. The spell of this idea was broken by an exchange with Sraffa, who presented him with a Neapolitan gesture of con-tempt and asked 'What is the logical form of *that*?' The picture theory was correct to insist on the pictorial nature of propositions, which means that their relation to the fact that verifies them is a logical, not a contingent one. But it went wrong in explaining that logical relation by holding that propo-sition and fact share a logical form, or that a shadowy entity (a possible state of affairs) mediates between them. The mysterious harmony between language and reality is simply a distorted reflection of a linguistic conven-tion, which specifies that 'the proposition that p' = 'the proposition which is verified by the fact that p'.

Metaphysics of symbolism   The guiding principle of the *Tractatus* had been that the rules of language mirror the structure of reality. Wittgenstein now held that language is autonomous. Grammar – the rules of language – is not re-sponsible to empirical reality or to meanings inhabiting a Platonic realm. There is not a single logical syntax shared under the surface between all meaningful sign-systems, but a genuine plurality of forms of representation. Concepts are not correct or incorrect, only more or less useful. While Witt-genstein rejected the idea that grammar has metaphysical foundations, he acknowledged that grammar is subject to pragmatic constraints. But he also embraced a conceptual relativism according to which no form of representa-tion is intrinsically superior to any other. In this he was influenced by the cultural relativism of Spengler's speculative philosophy of history, which ex-tended relativism even to seemingly inexorable disciplines like mathematics (*Decline of the West* ch. II; MS125 31).

Analysis and philosophy   Wittgenstein continued to hold that because of their a priori character, philosophical problems must be clarified by reference to linguistic rules. But he came to reject logical analysis as a means of achiev-ing this clarity. There are no logically independent elementary propositions or indefinable proper names for analysis to terminate with. More funda-mentally, the very idea that analysis can make unexpected discoveries about language is misguided. Language is not a calculus of definite rules hidden below the school-grammatical surface of natural languages. As normative standards of our linguistic practice, grammatical rules must be accessible to the participants. What is required to achieve clarity about conceptual issues is not logical analysis but a description of our linguistic practices, which constitute a motley of 'language-games'.

The result of these transformations was a fundamentally new conception of language, and of the proper procedures of philosophy. It contained many of the ideas of the *Tractatus*, but in a framework which completely changed their significance. Indeed, the *Tractatus* was seen as 'the symptom of a disease', as Wittgenstein wrote in Schlick's copy of the book. Immediately after his return to Cambridge, Wittgenstein decided to write a new book, at first to continue, and later to correct, his earlier work. But he constantly changed his mind and was never satisfied with the result of his efforts. In the course of his labours he frequently selected and pruned remarks from his notebooks, and worked them into more polished and structured manuscripts and typescripts. None of them reached publication in his lifetime, yet some of them mark important stages in the development of his thought. Thus, *Philosophical Remarks*, which he hastily composed out of manuscripts in order to obtain the research fellowship, represents his verificationist phase, when he had abandoned logical atomism but retained the idea of a 'phenomenological' primary language hidden beneath the surface of ordinary language. The 'Big Typescript' (TS 213) is the closest he ever got to a conventional book with chapter headings and a table of contents. It marks the end of the transition period since it already contains his mature conception of meaning, intentionality and philosophy. It is unfortunate that he did not publish it, and even more unfortunate that instead of publishing it posthumously, the literary executors brought out *Philosophical Grammar*, a compilation from parts of the 'Big Typescript' and Wittgenstein's subsequent attempts to rework it.

During 1933–4, Wittgenstein dictated the *Blue Book* to his class in Cambridge. It remains the most accessible of his writings, because it is neither aphoristic (as the *Tractatus* and *Philosophical Investigations*) nor truncated (as his lecture notes) but discursive. It first clarifies the notions of criteria and family resemblance, and contains Wittgenstein's most sustained attack on the methodological solipsism of his verificationist phase. As early as 1932 he had abandoned the view that sense-data propositions provide the foundations of language, or can be verified by comparison with immediate experiences. Between 1934 and 1936 he lectured on private experience and sense-data. This marks the beginning of his interest in philosophical psychology, which crystalized in the private language argument and the idea that first-person present tense psychological statements are avowals rather than descriptions. In 1934–5 he dictated the *Brown Book*, which employs *ad nauseam* the 'language-game method' of discussing fictional linguistic practices. In 1935 he also developed an interest in moving to the Soviet Union to study medicine, an idea which, mercifully, he abandoned after a visit. Wittgenstein detested Russell's pacifism and humanist socialism, while at the same time sympathizing with the hard left in the thirties and forties (perhaps under the influence of Sraffa). In so far as an underlying principle can be detected in his political views, it was a Tolstoyan ideal of a simple life of manual work, coupled with a mild predilection for authoritarian ideologies – Bolshevism, Catholicism – which place individual liberty and well-being below the pursuit of higher principles.

Philosophical Investigations: a cure for the disease of the understanding

After the end of his fellowship, Wittgenstein spent 1936–7 in Norway. He started *Eine Philosophische Betrachtung* – a German redraft of the *Brown Book*. It ends with the words 'this whole attempt at a revision ... is *worthless*' (MS115 292). Immediately afterwards he started those manuscripts which eventually led to the *Philosophical Investigations*, and which he contrasted favourably with the *Brown Book*. But this marks a turning-point more in style and manner of presentation than in method or substance.

About half of Wittgenstein's writings between 1929 and 1944 were on the philosophy of mathematics (the most important of them are collected in *Remarks on the Foundations of Mathematics*) and shortly before he abandoned the topic he stated that his 'chief contribution' had been in the philosophy of mathematics. He gave various lecture-courses on the subject, in one of which (recorded in LFM) he was confronted by orthodox objections from the brilliant logician Alan Turing.

Wittgenstein's conception of mathematics is as original as the rest of his work, and even more provocative. It views mathematics not as a body of truths about abstract entities, but as part of human practice. Wittgenstein rejects logicism, formalism and intuitionism alike, and claims that the very project of providing foundations for mathematics, together with the fear of hidden contradictions which fuels it, is misguided. The *Tractatus* had already indicated that although mathematical equations appear to describe relations between abstract entities they are, *au fond*, rules for the transformation of empirical propositions. From 1929 onwards he developed this suggestion into a radical solution to Kant's problem of how mathematical propositions can seem to hold true of empirical reality in spite of being a priori. The explanation is that they do not describe a super-empirical reality, as Platonism has it, but express rules for the transformation of propositions about empirical reality. Arithmetic is a system of rules for the transformation of empirical propositions about quantities and magnitudes. The propositions of geometry are not descriptions of the properties of space, but rules for the description of the shapes of and spatial relations among empirical objects. A mathematical proof is not a demonstration of truths about the nature of numbers or geometrical forms but a piece of concept-formation: it stipulates a new rule for the transformation of empirical propositions.

Wittgenstein also freed his earlier account of logical truth from the earlier metaphysics of symbolism. He thereby created a form of conventionalism which differed radically from that of logical positivism. Necessary propositions do not follow from meanings or conventions, but are *themselves rules*, norms of representation which partly determine the meaning of words. To a tautology like '$(p \cdot (p \supset q)) \supset q$' there corresponds a rule of inference (*modus ponens*). Analytic propositions and the propositions of metaphysics are not statements about essences but have the role of norms of representation.

The Nazi takeover of Austria in 1938 placed Wittgenstein in a perilous situation, since he did not want to abandon his family. In 1939 he was appointed to succeed Moore in the chair of philosophy. This allowed him to become a British citizen and to travel to Germany and strike a deal with the Nazis to protect his family. In 1941 he volunteered to work as a porter and laboratory technician in Guy's Hospital, London, and in 1943 he joined a team working on the physiology of shock in Newcastle. In 1944 he resumed his professorship, but gave it up in 1947, partly because of his contempt for academic philosophy, partly for reasons of health.

In 1946 he had stopped work on his second masterpiece, Part I of the *Philosophical Investigations*. Although he never finished it completely, it was as complete as he could make it, and he authorized its posthumous publication (in 1953). It was meant to be read against the backcloth of the *Tractatus*. However, its critique applies not just to Wittgenstein's earlier work, but to the whole tradition to which it belongs. It is often indirect, since it confronts not specific doctrines but the presuppositions that inform them. Thus it starts with a quotation from the *Confessions* in which Augustine describes how he learned to speak. Wittgenstein regarded this as expressing a picture of the essence of language which more or less explicitly informs a multitude of philosophical theories: words are names, their meaning is the object they stand for, with which they are correlated by ostension. Sentences are combinations of names which describe how things are. The essential functions of language are naming and describing, and it is linked with reality by means of word–world connections.

Philosophical Investigations rejects this seemingly innocuous picture. Not all words refer to objects, and there is no such thing as *the* name-relation. Moreover, even in the case of referring expressions, it is a misuse of the term 'meaning' to treat their meaning as the object they stand for. The meaning of a word is not an object of any kind, but its use according to grammatical rules. Finally, ostensive definitions do not provide a connection between language and reality: the objects pointed at are samples, which provide standards for the correct use of words and are in that respect part of grammar.

Furthermore, not all words are, or need to be, sharply defined by reference to necessary and sufficient conditions for their application. Analytic definition is only one form of explanation among others. Many philosophically important concepts are united by 'family resemblances' rather than by a common characteristic mark. In particular, propositions are not united by a common essence, a general propositional form. Not all of them describe states of affairs, and even among those that do, one must distinguish different kinds. The meaning of words and the sense of sentences can only be elucidated by attending to their use in the stream of life.

Like Frege, the *Tractatus* had invoked anti-psychologism to dismiss questions of linguistic understanding as irrelevant to logic, while tacitly relying on an obscure mentalist conception of linguistic understanding. Now Wittgenstein recognizes the importance of the concept of understanding, and provides a conception of understanding which avoids both psychologism and materialism. Understanding an expression is neither a mental nor a physical state or process, but an ability. It is displayed in using and explaining the expression correctly, and in responding appropriately to its use by others. Linguistic rules are not abstract entities, logical machines which churn out their applications independently of us. Rule-following is a practice: what conforms with or violates a rule is determined by what we call 'following the rule' or 'going against it'.

In the *Investigations* the discussion of linguistic understanding leads to an examination of mental concepts in general. Running through the mainstream of modern philosophy is the idea that a person can be certain about his inner world of subjective experiences, but can at best only infer how things are outside that inner world. Subjective experience was conceived not only as the foundation of empirical knowledge, but also as the foundation of language: the meanings of words seem to be fixed by naming subjective impressions (e.g., 'pain' means *this*). Wittgenstein's private language argument undermines this assumption. A ceremony of naming can lay down standards for distinguishing between correct and incorrect uses of a term, and hence provide it with meaning, only if the application of the standards can in principle be explained to and understood by others. Hence there can be no private ostensive definition in which a subjective impression functions as a sample. This undermines the picture of the mind as a private domain to which its subject enjoys privileged access by means of introspection, an inner gaze. According to the traditional picture, the private is better known than the public. I can know for certain that I am in pain, but not that others are in pain. Wittgenstein turns this reasoning on its head. We often know that others are in pain on the basis of their behaviour. The behavioural criteria for the application of mental terms are partly constitutive of their meaning. Although those criteria are defeasible, in the absence of defeating conditions it is senseless to doubt whether someone displaying that behaviour is in pain. On the other hand, to say 'I know that I am in pain' is either an emphatic avowal (rather than a description), or a nonsense, since 'knowing' that one is in pain would presuppose that one can be ignorant, mistaken or in doubt about whether one is, which makes no sense.

The *Investigations* transforms rather than abandons the *Tractatus*'s methodological ideas. Philosophy is not a cognitive discipline – there are no propositions expressing philosophical knowledge – and cannot emulate the methods of science. But this is not a form of obscurantism. Wittgenstein stands firmly in the tradition of critical philosophy inaugurated by Kant, although his anthropological stress on human practice and his Schopenhauerian sympathy for an anti-rationalist voluntarism are at odds with Kant's intellectualism. Wittgenstein's methodological views are based on the conviction that, unlike science, philosophy is concerned not with truth, or matters of fact, but with meaning. Philosophical problems evince conceptual confusions which arise out of the distortion or misapprehension of words with which we are perfectly familiar outside philosophy. These problems should not be answered by constructing theories, but dissolved by describing the rules for the use of the words concerned. Hence, if there were theses in philosophy, everyone would agree with them, because they would be truisms, reminders of grammatical rules (e.g., that we tell whether someone is in pain from his behaviour).

Having resigned his chair, Wittgenstein spent the rest of his life with various friends and disciples in Ireland, the USA, Oxford and Cambridge. In some respects his work after the completion of Part I of the *Investigations* marks a break. In *Investigations* Part I mental concepts (intentionality, understanding, thinking) play an important role because of their connection with the main theme, the nature of language and meaning. Now philosophical psychology is discussed in its own right; indeed, between 1945 and 1949 it is the predominant theme of his writings (*Remarks on the Philosophy of Psychology, Last Writings on the Philosophy of Psychology, Philosophical Investigations* Part II) and lectures. Whereas Part I of the *Investigations* is mainly concerned with attacking misconceptions, these works make steps towards a positive overview of mental concepts. But the emerging picture is less clear-cut and more tentative. During his final years, Wittgenstein also worked briefly on colours (*Remarks on Colour*) and, more intensively, on epistemology, in *On Certainty*. This last work is among his finest. As in the area of mathematics and other minds, Wittgenstein tries to show that sceptical doubts about our knowledge of the material world and foundationalist attempts to meet them are equally misguided. To some readers it has seemed that Wittgenstein's work after Part I of the *Investigations* constitutes a separate phase of his work. Yet, these reflections nowhere contradict that earlier work substantially, but rather complement it and extend it to new areas, such as aspect-perception.

Wittgenstein's legacy

Wittgenstein continued working right up to his death (he had cancer and refused surgery). His last words were 'Tell them I've had a wonderful life!' This would be startling as a comment on his personal life, which was dominated by torment and self-obsession. But it is unsurprising as a comment on his philosophical life, which was one of momentous achievements. If, philosophically speaking, the seventeenth century was the age of science, the eighteenth century the age of reason, and the nineteenth century the age of history, our century is the age of logic and language. Logic would have played an important role without Wittgenstein, due mainly to Russell. But it was Wittgenstein who provided a powerful methodological rationale for its role, and who brought language into the equation.

Wittgenstein's main contributions lie in five areas: philosophy of language, philosophy of logic and mathematics, philosophical psychology, epistemology, and philosophical methodology. In each of them his views were original and revolutionary. He eschewed received positions and rejected traditional alternatives (realism/idealism, Cartesianism/behaviourism, Platonism/nominalism), because of his unique ability to bring to light their most fundamental unchallenged presuppositions. In subjecting these assumptions to critical scrutiny he combined dialectical acuity and imaginative analogical thought.

In their different ways, both the *Tractatus* and the *Investigations* are among the few highlights of German philosophical prose. But there are also serious flaws. Because of his aesthetic aspirations Wittgenstein often condensed his insights to the point of impenetrability, and failed to spell out the arguments in support of his claims. Doing so would 'spoil their beauty', he maintained in 1913, to which Russell trenchantly replied that he should acquire a slave to take over this task. Later, Wittgenstein rightly deplored his inability to work his ideas into a sustained line of argument. As a result, his work often pursues conceptual clarity in an obscure fashion, and constitutes a formidable challenge to readers. Some analytic philosophers simply condemn it out of hand, while others, in the belief that interpretation is an integral part of philosophy, welcome it, even if it occasionally makes them feel like slaves. In any event, Wittgenstein's work possesses a scintillating beauty lacking in other analytical philosophers.

Wittgenstein is among a minority of great philosophers who failed to make a significant contribution to practical philosophy. Although his later work may contain the seeds of important insights in moral psychology, his early attempts to make the subject look ineffable (the *Tractatus*, 'A Lecture on Ethics') deserve the label 'transcendental babble' which he applied to moral reflections in general (EL 16.1.18; FL 11.19). To claim, for example, that 'ethics and aesthetics are one' was certainly not a promising start for someone who later vowed to teach us differences.

On the other hand, Wittgenstein may be unique in the history of philosophy in having produced two fundamentally different and self-contained outlooks. The *Tractatus* was the major influence on logical positivism, and, through the mediation of Carnap, on much subsequent philosophy of language, in particular the project of a theory of meaning for natural language. Yet, as we have seen, after his return to philosophy, Wittgenstein himself attacked fundamental assumptions of this project. He also developed the most sustained attack ever on the inner/outer picture of the mind which has dominated modern philosophy since Descartes. In both respects he was a major influence on analytic philosophy between the thirties and seventies, first through the people who attended his lectures, Moore, Wisdom, Malcolm, Anscombe, Rhees and von Wright, then through *Philosophical Investigations* and the subsequent posthumous publications. In particular, he influenced what is known as 'Oxford ordinary language philosophy', especially the work of Ryle and Strawson.

Since the sixties, Wittgensteinian scholarship and interest in his work have flourished. But the influence of Wittgenstein's thought on the mainstream of analytical philosophy has waned. This is due partly to the dominance of Quine's scientific conception of philosophy in the United States, and partly to the fact that the conception of language presented by the *Investigations* lost out to Tractarian theories of meaning complemented by Chomskian linguistics. Finally, Wittgenstein's philosophical psychology was replaced by materialist theories fuelled by neurophysiology and functionalist theories fuelled by computer science. But many of the arguments which are widely agreed to have refuted Wittgenstein's approach in these areas are either based on misunderstanding or inconclusive. Moreover, the gradual rapprochement of analytic and continental philosophy has rekindled interest in his work, which provides much-needed arguments against the reductionist conceptions of human beings which the hermeneutic tradition rightly abhors. Irrespective of such short-term developments, as long as the spirit of critical philosophy is alive, and fundamental conceptual questions are not simply shrugged of by reference to the most recent ideology, science or pseudo-science, Wittgenstein's work, next to that of Aristotle and Kant, will remain a source of inspiration.

A

aesthetics Aesthetics did not lie at the centre of Wittgenstein's philosophical interests; but art, especially music, had a paramount place in his life. While his taste in music and literature tended to be conservative, the house he designed for his sister Margarete in Vienna in 1926 was modernist. Its extreme austerity radicalizes the anti-decorative ideal of the Austrian architect Adolf Loos, whom Wittgenstein at one time admired. By far Wittgenstein's greatest contribution to art, however, is his writing, which is one of the few highlights of German philosophical prose, albeit an exotic one. He had self-professed aesthetic ambitions, and regarded 'correct' style as integral to good philosophizing (CV 39, 87; Z §712). His writing is not discursive, but consists of short and often laconic remarks. Wittgenstein's similes and analogies, and his elusive wit, are reminiscent of Lichtenberg. However, his remarks are not isolated *aperçus*, but part of a philosophical line of thought. In *Tractatus Logico-Philosophicus* they are very dense, and fitted into a complex structure of great architectonic appeal, while *Philosophical Investigations* is more colloquial.

In spite of his personal interest, Wittgenstein's early remarks on aesthetics are cryptic applications of a philosophical system, his version of Schopenhauer's transcendental idealism. 'Ethics and aesthetics are one' (TLP 6.421). This sibylline pronouncement involves three points. Firstly, like logic and ethics, aesthetics is concerned not with contingent matters of fact, but with what could not be otherwise. Hence it cannot be expressed in meaningful (BIPOLAR) propositions, but only shown (NB 24.7.16; TLP 6.13). Secondly, together with ETHICS, aesthetics constitutes the 'higher' realm of *values*. It is transcendent, since values 'cannot lie *within* the world', but are located in a Schopenhauerian metaphysical WILL outside it (TLP 6.41–6.432; NB 2.8.16). Finally, like logic, ethics and aesthetics are based on a MYSTICAL experience, namely marvelling not at *how* the world is, but *that* it is. In doing so, I view the world from the outside, as a 'limited whole'. In addition, ethics and aesthetics involve 'looking at the world with a happy eye', that is, with a Stoic acceptance of facts which are not subject to the will. The 'work of art' is 'the object seen *sub specie aeternitatis*'. This is reminiscent of Schopenhauer's idea that in aesthetic contemplation we escape the domination of the will (of our desires), since our consciousness is filled by a single image. It also links the aesthetic perspective to SOLIPSISM: in viewing the object, or the world, *sub specie aeternitatis* I make it my own (NB 19.9./7.10./8.10./ 20.10.16; TLP 5.552, 6.43, 6.45; cf. *World* I §34).

Wittgenstein's early remarks on aesthetics are important to his mysticism, but shed little light on art. The identification of ethics and aesthetics under the umbrella of ineffable values obscures precisely the kind of conceptual differences he later tried to emphasize. Arguably, neither Schopenhauer nor the early Wittgenstein adds much beyond metaphysical mystery-mongering to Kant's insight that aesthetic appreciation involves 'disinterested contemplation'. Wittgenstein's later discussion yields more palpable results. He abandons the idea that aesthetic value is ineffable, observes that 'the subject (Aesthetics) is very big and entirely misunderstood' (LC 1), and points to four major mistakes:

(a) It is wrong to focus just on a small group of terms like 'beautiful' or 'ugly'. These are used mainly as interjections, and have 'almost a negligible place' in our reaction to works of art or natural beauty. Most of our aesthetic appreciation consists not in simply liking or disliking a work of art, but in understanding or characterizing it. And where we do assess a work of art, it is not so much as beautiful or hideous, as as right or wrong, closer or more distant to certain ideals or standards. Finally, there are 'tremendous' masterpieces, such as Beethoven's symphonies, which set their own standards, and impress us almost in the way spectacular natural phenomena do (LC 1–11; CV 54–5).

(b) It is wrong to neglect the USE of aesthetic expressions in favour of their linguistic form. Aesthetic appreciation evolves from reactions like delight or discomfort. What matters is not so much words as the occasions on which they are used. These occasions in turn are part of an 'enormously complicated situation'. They must be seen against the background of certain activities, and ultimately of a certain culture or even FORM OF LIFE (LC 2). In describing musical taste, for example, one may have to describe the social role played by musical performances. Unfortunately, Wittgenstein did not clarify whether this context consists exclusively of the social role of the artefact, or whether it also includes, for example, the intentions of the artist. What is clear, as in the case of ethics, is that his CONTEXTUALISM has relativistic implications. Although Wittgenstein speaks of 'deterioration' within an artistic tradition, such as German music, aesthetic standards cannot be judged externally. One may not even understand how to appreciate the works of an artistic tradition (e.g., African art) without immersing oneself in the relevant culture (LC 1–11; LW I §§750–3; PI II 230; CE 399).

(c) The most straightforward aspect of Wittgenstein's aesthetics is his application of the idea of FAMILY RESEMBLANCE. He rejects the craving for an analytic definition of aesthetic terms such as 'beautiful', 'art', or 'work of art', and implies that such terms are family-resemblance concepts (LC 10; AWL 35–6; CV 24). There are no conditions which are individually necessary and jointly sufficient for the application of these terms. Their instances are related in a multiplicity of ways, through a 'complicated network of overlapping similarities'. One of the arguments to this effect is fallacious. Wittgenstein notes that terms like 'beautiful' and 'good' are bound up with what they modify – the features which constitute beauty in a face do not do so in a sofa. However, this does not show that 'beautiful' is a family-resemblance concept, but only that, like 'good', it is used attributively rather than predicatively. Wittgenstein's treatment is most convincing with respect to the terms 'art' and 'work of art'. There may be necessary conditions here: art is a human activity and a work of art an artefact. But there is no single condition by virtue of which the artefacts of Beethoven, Beuys, Brecht, Cage, Giotto, Jandl, Praxiteles, Pollock and Warhol qualify as works of art.

(d) Wittgenstein rejects the idea that aesthetics is a branch of psychology, aiming to provide causal explanations of our aesthetic experience. There are three aspects to this position. (i) Wittgenstein rejects causal accounts of artistic value, in particular hedonistic theories which conceive of aesthetic value as a tendency to cause experiences of pleasure or displeasure. He accuses them of what later became known as the 'affective fallacy', namely of confusing the value of a work of art with the psychological effect it has on people. On such accounts, the value of a work lies in its causal effect (the experience it produces). However, that experience might be created by other means, through another work or even a drug. The only way of appreciating a work of art is by experiencing and understanding its intrinsic features; its value is determined not by any causal effects it might have, but by these features, as measured against certain standards. The question 'Why is this beautiful/valuable?' cannot be answered by a causal explanation (M 104–7).

(ii) Wittgenstein insists that the relationship between an aesthetic judgement or impression and its object (the work) is intentional and hence internal, not an external or causal one – a specific case of his general rejection of causal theories of INTENTIONALITY. My judgement that Vaughan Williams' music is primitive is not about the causes of my reactions, which may be anything from neurophysiological events to being prejudiced against English composers. It is about those features which are mentioned in my judgement or in my subsequent explanations of it.

(iii) Wittgenstein claims that aesthetic explanations are neither causal nor subject to experimental checks: 'an aesthetic explanation is not a causal explanation.' This dictum covers not just explaining why something is beautiful or impressive, but any explanation of 'aesthetic impressions'. 'The puzzles arising from the effects the arts have are not puzzles about how these things are caused.' They are not solved by experiment, since the correct answer is the one which satisfies the subject in question (LC 11–18, 21, 28–9). This claim seems to be refuted by stories like that of Soderini, who claimed to be dissatisfied with the nose of the *David*, but had his qualms dissipated after Michelangelo pretended to have altered it. However, the fact that Soderini's dissatisfaction could be removed without any alteration to the nose no more shows that it was *about* something other than the nose, than the fact that my desire for an apple can be removed without my getting an apple (e.g., by a punch in the stomach) shows that it was something other than an apple that I desired (PR 64; *see* INTENTIONALITY). But the story does show that there is a type of aesthetic explanation which is causal, and hence empirical, namely of what makes us react in a certain way, something of which we may be unaware.

However, Wittgenstein's failure to take into account such aetiological explanations does not vitiate his account of ordinary aesthetic explanations, which specify either the object of our aesthetic reactions, or their motives or reasons. They explain our reactions through enhancing our understanding of the work itself. Ordinary aesthetic explanation is descriptive, in a general sense. Apart from straightforward reference to aesthetic standards, this may involve the following. (a) Pointing out analogies between the work under consideration and others: we place the work under consideration side by side with other items. Sometimes these comparisons are synaesthetic (e.g., when Brahms' music is elucidated by reference to Keller's novels). In other cases it is a matter of ASPECT-PERCEPTION, bringing to notice a hitherto unnoticed feature of the work by placing it in a new environment or altering it in a certain way – thus we may come to notice the power of Klopstock's poems when read in a certain metre (LC 4, 32n; PI II 207; RPP I §§32–7). (b) Certain gestures may help us to understand, in particular, great works of art, which cannot be adequately characterized by reference to aesthetic standards. In such situations we often use words in what Wittgenstein calls an 'intransitive' way. We say that the musical phrase has a particular significance, but not as a preliminary to specifying *what* significance it has. This does not mean, however, that its significance is ineffable. Often we manage to bring out features of music through gestures or facial expressions, as happens, for example, when a conductor explains a musical phrase to an orchestra through gesticulations (BB 158, 178–9; PI §523; CV 69–70).

Wittgenstein's most important contribution to contemporary aesthetics has been his application to aesthetics of the idea of family resemblance. Anglophone aesthetics in the twentieth century has been preoccupied with the question 'What is Art?', partly because modern art itself has self-consciously posed this question as a challenge, and partly because the linguistic turn initiated by Wittgenstein put such analytic questions at the heart of the philosophical enterprise. The attempts to answer the question through an analytic definition have generally been viewed as unsuccessful (often they are blatantly circular) and futile. As a result, Wittgenstein's idea of family resemblance has been welcomed as a liberation, an acceptance which has by and large led to the abandonment of attempts to discover the essence of art.

anthropology Wittgenstein made two stimulating, if brief and unpolished, contributions to the methodology of anthropology. One is his discussion of FORMS OF LIFE and of radical translation. The other is his harsh remarks on Frazer's *Golden Bough*. Frazer attempted to explain a rite in classical antiquity – the succession of the King of Nemi – by reference to similar rituals around the world. Wittgenstein raised the following objections to Frazer's procedure (GB 118–33; AWL 33–4; M 106–7): (a) Frazer's collection of data about other rituals does not provide the genetic explanation of the Nemi rite he sought, but rather the raw materials for an OVERVIEW which explains why we find the ritual horrifying by linking it to basic human impulses with which we are familiar; (b) the very attempt to provide a genetic explanation of the rite should be abandoned in favour of describing it; (c) Frazer presents these rites as instrumental, as aiming at the bringing about of certain causal consequences, and hence as based on false empirical beliefs or on proto-science, when in fact they are expressive or symbolic.

Objection (a) is plausible. Nothing but thin analogies and groundless conjectures supports Frazer's genetic account, while the similarities to and differences from other rites do provide a non-genetic type of insight into the nature of the Nemi rite. Objection (b) is more problematic. When Wittgenstein condemns genetic accounts he must have in mind not that they are illegitimate as such, but that they must be distinguished from understanding what ritual acts mean. Moreover, Wittgenstein does not maintain that the only way of understanding what a ritual means is to link it to universal human impulses or emotions. He states explicitly that explanations can make reference to the beliefs of the participants of the ritual (GB 128). But the historical origins of a ritual matter to its meaning only in so far as the participants themselves attach significance to them. The eating of unleavened bread at the Passover Feast is to be understood as an act of commemoration. But what matters to this understanding is not the fact that the children of Israel ate unleavened bread in the desert, but that pious Jews today believe that they did. However, even if one distinguishes understanding what a ritual means from understanding how it came about, it is implausible to hold, as Wittgenstein does, that the latter contributes nothing to the former. Someone who knows how the beliefs and the practices have evolved may well be in a better position to understand their content. Moreover, some ceremonial acts have no expressive, symbolic or instrumental function, but are simply performed because they accord with tradition (e.g., the pacing back and forth of the Proctors at an Oxford degree ceremony). The only kind of explanation of such rituals that can be given is by reference to their origins and to a ritualistic tradition.

As regards (c), Wittgenstein is right to draw attention to the expressive and symbolic nature of many ritual acts. We do not burn effigies or kiss the pictures of loved ones to achieve a certain effect. 'Magic brings a wish to representation; it expresses a wish.' Moreover, 'if the adoption of a child proceeds in such a way that the mother draws it from under her clothes [as is the case among the Bosnian Turks], it is surely insane to believe that an *error* is present and that she believes she has given birth to the child.' Wittgenstein occasionally acknowledges that some rituals are instrumental. But he also insists that *all* magical rituals are symbolic. However, many rituals which we would count as magic aim at producing a certain effect, and are based on superstition, on false beliefs in supernatural mechanisms. Wittgenstein seems to assume that if ritual practices were instrumental, they would be 'sheer stupidity' (GB 119, 125). However, while superstition is irrational, it is not simply stupid, but an expression of pervasive and profound human fears and aspirations.

aspect-perception This term denotes a gamut of interrelated perceptual phenomena. The paradigmatic case is what Wittgenstein calls 'aspect-dawning' or 'change of aspect' (*Aufleuchten eines Aspekts* or *Aspektwechsel*): certain objects, especially schematic drawings – 'picture-objects' (PI II 194; LW I §489) – can be seen under more than one aspect. An aspect dawns on us when we notice such a hitherto unnoticed aspect of the object we are looking at, that is, if we come to see it *as* something different. Thus we may pass from seeing a 'puzzle picture' as a mere collection of lines to seeing it as a face; or from seeing Jastrow's 'duck-rabbit' as the picture of a duck to seeing it as the picture of a rabbit.

Puzzle pictures like the Necker cube briefly appear in the early work. From 1935 onwards, Wittgenstein's philosophy of psychology returns time and again to *seeing-as* (TLP 5.5423; NB 9.11.14; BB 162–79; PI II 193–229;

RPP I & II *passim*; LW I *passim*; LW II 12–17). Between 1947 and 1949, it dominates his work, partly under the influence of Köhler's Gestalt psychology. Wittgenstein's immediate aim was to dissolve the paradoxical appearance of aspect-dawning: when looking at a picture-object we can come to see it differently, although we also see that the object itself remains unchanged. It seems to have changed and yet seems not to have changed (PI II 193–5; LW I §493).

One way of dealing with aspect-dawning is to point out that perceiving alternative aspects is caused by different patterns of eyeball movements. Wittgenstein was aware of such correlations, but denied that they resolve the paradox (PI II 193, 203, 212–16; LW I §795). For even if they explain why the phenomenon occurs, they do not provide a description of it which escapes the paradox. Wittgenstein attached enormous importance to aspect-perception, since he thought that in this phenomenon 'problems about the concept of seeing come to a head' (LW I §172). Presumably this is because it exemplifies in a precise form the concept-saturatedness of perception. We see one and the same thing (e.g., a person's face) but may see it differently (e.g., as placid or anguished).

Wittgenstein's discussion concentrates mainly on Gestalt psychology. According to Köhler, what we perceive immediately is not a mosaic of discrete and unorganized stimuli (dots and coloured surfaces, sounds), as empiricism and behaviourism have it, but *Gestalten*, circumscribed and organized units, such as material objects or groups of objects (*Gestalt* ch.V). We do not see three dots, but see them form a triangle; we do not hear a chaotic array of sounds, but detect a melody. This is close to Wittgenstein in rejecting the reductionist view according to which we construct perceptual objects out of raw data. Unfortunately, Köhler's treatment of aspect-dawning reifies *Gestalten*. He claims that in aspect-perception we do not see one and the same object under different aspects, but rather two different 'visual objects' or 'visual realities' (*Gestalt* 82, 107, 148–53). In his attempt to do justice to the idea that we see the picture-object differently, Köhler thus turns an aspect (*Gestalt*) into a private mental entity. This reification is not just terminological, it is integral to his account of aspect-perception. The two 'visual objects' are said to differ in their organization, which is as much a feature of them as their colour and shape. Accordingly, what changes in aspect-perception is not the colour or shape of the elements of the visual impression, but their organization. Wittgenstein rejects this explanation. It suggests that what changes in cases of aspect-dawning is the way we perceive the (spatial) relationships between the elements of the picture. But this is mistaken. When asked to depict faithfully what we see, that is, the picture-object, before and after an aspect-change, there is no more difference in the organization of the elements than in their shape or colour (although we may go about depicting the object differently). The characteristic of aspect-dawning is precisely that no specific feature of the visual field changes. The alleged change in organization cannot be specified, which means that Köhler's 'organization' could only refer to ineffable features of a private object, which the PRIVATE LANGUAGE ARGUMENT excludes as chimerical (PI II 196–7; RPP I §§536, 1113–25; LW I §§444–5, 510–12).

An alternative to the 'Gestalt' explanation is that what has changed is our interpretation, not of a private impression, but of the object perceived. This raises a question which dominates Wittgenstein's discussion, namely whether noticing an aspect is a case of seeing or of thinking. Wittgenstein's verdict on this issue is ambivalent. His first point is that types of aspect-perception differ according to the degree of thinking involved (PI II 207–12; LW I §§179, 530, 582–8, 699–704; RPP I §§1, 70–4, 970; RPP II §§496, 509). At one end lie 'conceptual' aspects like those of the duck-rabbit, which cannot be expressed solely by pointing to parts of the picture-object, but require possession of the relevant concepts. At the other, lie 'purely optical' cases, such as the 'double cross' ✤, in which we can express our seeing of the aspect by following certain lines of the picture-object, without using concepts (but even here concepts like background and foreground seem involved).

His second point is that the concept of seeing an aspect lies between that of seeing, which is a state, and that of interpreting, which is an action. It is closer to the latter in the following respects (PI II 212; RPP I §§27, 169; RPP II §§544–5; LW I §§451, 488, 612):

the 'optical' or 'visual' picture remains the same, as we have seen;
aspect-seeing, unlike most cases of seeing, is subject to the will: although we may not always succeed in noticing an aspect or keeping it in focus, it always makes sense to try to do so, and we often succeed;
in noticing an aspect of the conceptual kind we do not just focus on properties of the object perceived, but realize certain INTERNAL RELATIONS between it and other objects, relations of similarity and dissimilarity such as those between two human faces.

Aspect-perception is closer to seeing in the following respects (PI II 203–4, 212; RPP I §§8, 1025; RPP II §§388, 547):

there is no possibility of being mistaken about seeing an aspect;
aspect-seeing is a state; in particular it has 'genuine duration', that is, it has a beginning and an end which can be clocked, can be interrupted, etc.;
there is no more direct expression of the experience than the report of aspect-perception 'I see it *as* a rabbit', that is, there is no sharp contrast between the 'interpretation' and the uninterpreted data.

It may seem that Wittgenstein creates an artificially stark contrast between seeing and thinking by restricting the latter to interpreting, to conjecturing what a picture represents (RPP I §§8–9, 13, 20; RPP II §390; PI II 193, 197, 212; LW II 14). But the paradox of aspect-dawning does not depend on such a narrow conception of thinking. I may know about the duck-rabbit picture, and think 'One can see a rabbit here', without being able to *see* it.

Wittgenstein suggests that the paradox trades on an equivocation: what I see in the ordinary sense has not changed, while what I see in the sense of 'seeing' closer to thinking has. Given the extent to which he has laboured the paradox, this solution is more a whimper than a bang. Nevertheless, it features important insights. Reports of aspect-dawning are not descriptions, either direct or indirect (interpreting), of an inner experience which accompanies ordinary perception, but AVOWALS, spontaneous reactions to what we see. Moreover, what changes in aspect-dawning is not what we perceive, or its 'organization', but our attitude to it, how we react to it and what we can do with it. Suddenly, we copy or explain the puzzle picture differently, change the way we play a piece of music or recite a poem (PI II 197–8, 208; RPP I §982; LC 1–11). One important thing we do in noticing an aspect is placing what we perceive in another context; we detect new connections or draw fresh comparisons. This is why changing the context of an object may alter our perception of it (PI II 212; RPP I §1030; LW I §516).

Wittgenstein illustrates aspect-seeing through 'aspect-blindness', the inability to experience aspect-dawning (PI II 213–14; RPP II §§42, 478–9, 490; LW I §§492–3, 778–84). An aspect-blind person could apply a new description to a picture-object, use, for example, the schematic drawing of a cube as a picture of a three-dimensional object. But he would not experience this as seeing something differently, experiencing a jump in aspect, and would not recognize the incompatibility with treating it as a two-dimensional complex of three parallelograms. His defect is one not of sight but of imagination.

A special kind of aspect-blindness is 'meaning-blindness', the inability to experience the meaning of a word (PI II 175–6, 210; RPP I §§189, 202–6, 243–50, 342–4; cp. James's 'soul blindness', *Psychology* I ch. II). This does not reinstate the idea that the meaning of a word is a mental phenomenon which accompanies UNDERSTANDING. Instead, Wittgenstein claims that words have a 'familiar physiognomy': they are associated with other words, situations and experiences, and can assimilate these connections. Thus one may feel that names 'fit' their bearers. And words turn into mere sounds if these connections are severed, e.g. when they are mechanically repeated several times (PI II 214–15, 218).

Experiencing meaning underlies the 'secondary sense' of terms: some people are inclined to say things like ' "e" is yellow', ' "u" is darker than "i" ' or even 'Tuesdays are lean, Wednesdays are fat.' This secondary sense

(a) differs from the primary sense: obviously 'e' is not yellow in the sense in which flowers are – it cannot be compared with a sample of yellow; (b) presupposes the primary sense: it can only be explained by reference to the primary one, but not vice versa; (c) is not a matter of ambiguity or of metaphor: we can disambiguate 'bank' by introducing a new term and can paraphrase metaphors, but we cannot express secondary senses in any other way (PI II 216; LW I §§797–8). Secondary sense also explains sylleptic ambiguity: the fact that we speak of deep sorrows and wells, of plaintive cries and melodies, etc.

The meaning-blind person uses and explains words correctly, but has no 'feel' for their physiognomy, a lack which is comparable to the lack of a musical ear. For this reason, he is barred from important forms of AESTHETIC discourse, or from understanding puns.

Some passages of Wittgenstein declare that the importance of aspect-perception lies in its connection with experiences of meaning, while others insist, correctly, that such experiences are not essential to the concept of meaning (PI II 214; LW I §784 vs. RPP I §358; RPP II §§242–6). A tempting explanation of Wittgenstein's obsession with the topic is that for him aspect-perception is integral to *all* perception. This seems to be supported by his distinction between aspect-dawning and 'the continuous seeing of an aspect'. Yet Wittgenstein denied that seeing-as is typical of all experience. Seeing-as requires a contrast between two different ways of perceiving an object, but under normal circumstances it makes no sense to say that, for example, one sees the cutlery *as* a knife and fork (PI II 194–5). Accordingly, Wittgenstein confines continuous aspect-perception to objects like pictures. Here no special circumstances are needed for a contrast between relating to what is perceived either as the depiction of something else, or as an object in its own right.

It is precisely by denying that all perception is aspect-perception that Wittgenstein rejects the empiricist myth of the given, the idea that what we perceive immediately are raw stimuli, which we then interpret as something else (RPP I §§1101–2; Z §§223–5). Typically, we do not just hear noises, but words and melodies, do not just see colours and shapes, but material objects, not just bare bodily movement, but human BEHAVIOUR infused with attitudes and emotions. What is constitutive of ordinary perception is that aspect-perception is *possible*: under special circumstances we react to words as sounds, or human behaviour as mere bodily movement. But while it is always possible to describe what one perceives in terms of sounds, or colour and shape, it does not follow that any other description is indirect or inferred. On the contrary, it is easier to describe a person's face as 'sad', 'radiant' or 'bored', than to describe it in physical terms. We know the conclusions of the alleged inference, not its premises. Neural stimuli may feature in a causal explanation of perception and understanding, but are not raw data from which we construct objects or linguistic meaning.

assertion   *see* BELIEF

Augustinian picture of language   *Philosophical Investigations* starts with a quotation from the *Confessions* (I/8) in which Augustine describes how he learned language as a child. Wittgenstein first mentions this passage in the 'Big Typescript' (BT 25-7; see PG 57). From the *Brown Book* onwards he used it as the starting-point of what was to become the *Investigations*. This marks a break in the manner of presentation of his later work. It demands explanation, since the passage is part of Augustine's autobiography, not of his reflections on language. The reason Wittgenstein gave for using the quotation is that it stems from a great and clear thinker, and thus displays the importance of what he refers to as 'Augustine's conception of' or 'description of language' (PI §§1–4; EPB 117). This suggests that he treated Augustine's view not as a full-blown theory of language, but as a proto-theoretic paradigm or 'picture' which deserves critical attention because it tacitly underlies sophisticated philosophical theories. The claims which *Investigations* §1 extracts from the passage are:

(a)   every individual word has 'a meaning';
(b)   all words are names, i.e. stand for objects;
(c)   the meaning of a word is the object it stands for;
(d)   the connection between words (names) and their meanings (referents) is established by ostensive definition, which establishes a mental association between word and object;
(e)   sentences are combinations of names.

Two consequences are spelled out subsequently:

(f)   the sole function of language is to represent reality: words refer, sentences describe (PI §§21–7);
(g)   the child can establish the association between word and object only through thinking, which means that it must already possess a private language, in order to learn the public one (PI §32; *see* PRIVATE LANGUAGE ARGUMENT).

Accordingly, the Augustinian picture comprises four positions: a referential conception of word-meaning; a descriptivist conception of sentences; the idea that OSTENSIVE DEFINITION provides the foundations of language; and the idea that a language of THOUGHT underlies our public languages.

Wittgenstein was the first to subject this position to sustained criticism. One of his strategies in *Investigations* §§1–64 is the use of fictional LANGUAGE-GAMES, invented forms of communication. Thus, the language of the builders (PI §§2, 6, 8) seeks to display the Augustinian picture as 'a primitive idea of how language functions' or an 'idea of a language more primitive than ours'. Even that, however, is too generous, as can be seen from his other objections (matched here to the claims listed above): (a) There are so-called syncategorematic expressions (articles, demonstrative pronouns, connectives like 'if ... then') which are meaningful only within a context. (b) The Augustinian claim is modelled solely on proper names, mass nouns and sortal nouns. It ignores verbs, adjectives, adverbs, connectives, prepositions, indexicals and exclamations (PG 56; BB 77; PI §27). (c) Even in the case of noun-phrases which can be said to name or stand for something, one must distinguish between their meaning and what they stand for. 'When Mr N.N. dies one says that the bearer of the name dies, not that the meaning dies' (PI §40). There are two parts to this objection: (i) if referential failure due to the referent's ceasing to exist rendered a referring expression meaningless, propositions like 'Mr N.N. died' could not make sense; (ii) identifying the meaning of a word with its referent is a category mistake, namely of confusing what a word stands for with its meaning: the referent of 'Mr N.N.' can die, but not its meaning (AWL 44). (e) One must distinguish a proposition like 'Plato was the pupil of Socrates and the teacher of Aristotle' from a mere list of names like 'Socrates, Plato, Aristotle'; only the former says something, and thereby makes a 'move in the language-game' (PI §22). (f) The Augustinian picture runs counter to the 'multiplicity of language-games'. In addition to describing there are not just questions and commands but 'countless' other kinds (e.g., telling jokes, thanking, cursing, greeting, praying) (PI §23). Nor is describing the highest common factor of these various linguistic activities.

Some have held that the Augustinian picture is an all-pervasive philosophical illusion, the principal target not just of Wittgenstein's philosophy of language but also of his philosophy of psychology and of mathematics. Others have maintained that it is too implausible to be his major target, or the source of so many philosophical positions. Wittgenstein nowhere suggests that the Augustinian picture is the *only* source of philosophical confusion; but he maintains that complex philosophical edifices are often based on simple pictures or assumptions. In fact, the referential conception of word-meaning has played a prominent role in semantics since Plato. It is not confined to the absurd suggestion that all words are proper names which have material objects for their meanings, but includes the very idea of 'meanings', entities correlated with the sign (as in the scholastic tag 'unum nomen, unum nominatum'). Wittgenstein accuses even nominalism of being committed to the Augustinian picture, because it accepts that all words either name something or name nothing, and settles for the second alternative, in order to avoid commitment to abstract entities. The Augustinian picture may also grant that there are distinct types of expressions, while insisting that they all stand for or signify something, and that the differences are simply due to the differences between the types of objects signified. By the same token it may insist that the differences between various uses of sentences are due to their describing different types of facts (PI §§24, 383; PLP 143, 407).

These elaborations of the referential conception lie behind mentalist and Platonist conceptions of meaning, which postulate non-material entities to play the role of meanings. The mentalist version goes back to Aristotle, and influences modern linguistics via de Saussure's distinction between *signifiant* and *signifié*. It has been rampant in British empiricism ever since Locke claimed that all words have their meaning in virtue of standing for ideas. Russell's theories of meaning are variations on this mentalist theme. 'Words all have meaning in the simple sense that they are symbols which stand for something other than themselves' (*Principles* 47). Russell moved away from this extreme version of the Augustinian picture in the theory of descriptions: expressions like 'the present King of France' are analysed as 'incomplete symbols' which do not refer to an object. At the same time, he condones claim (e): fully analysed propositions are combinations of 'logically proper names' – names which stand for objects that could not fail to exist, and hence are immune to referential failure. According to his 'principle of acquaintance', these names are demonstratives like 'this' which refer to sense-data. Throughout his career, Russell maintained that words have meaning by virtue of an ostensive association with private contents of experience. Moreover, even when, under Wittgenstein's impact, he ceased to regard sentences as combinations of names, he remained committed to the idea that the facts which sentences express are 'complexes', that is, con-catenations of simple objects (*Logic* 200–3; *Problems* 79–80; *Principia* i.43). Russell never abandoned the Augustinian picture. Instead he provided it with a line of defence: although the surface of language may not correspond to the picture, its ultimate elements, to be revealed by LOGICAL ANALYSIS, do.

The Platonist idea that meanings are not private ideas but abstract enti-ties beyond space and time is prominent in Bolzano, Meinong and Frege. Frege diverges from the Augustinian picture in three respects. Firstly, he sharply distinguishes between 'proper names' ('the morning star'), and con-cept-words ('is a planet'). Secondly, according to Frege's 'context-principle' a word has a meaning only in the context of a sentence (*Foundations* §§60–2, 106). This overcomes the semantic atomism of claim (a): a sentence can be meaningful without every individual word's being associated with a material or mental entity. That numerals have a meaning (which is an abstract object) is evident from the contribution they make to the truth-values of sen-tences in which they occur. Thirdly, Frege distinguishes between the sense (*Sinn*) and the meaning (*Bedeutung*) of expressions, i.e. their referent ('Sense'; *Laws* I §2).

This two-tier model of meaning, familiar from Mill's distinction between connotation and denotation, avoids the problem of referential failure without postulating logically proper names, since an expression without a 'meaning' can have a sense. But in other respects it remains wedded to the Augustinian picture. Frege's dichotomy incorporates claim (c): 'the word "meaning" is being used illicitly', namely for the thing that corresponds to the word (PI §40). Moreover, in his ideal language every expression (apart from the assertion-sign) not only expresses a sense but refers to a meaning. Worse, 'senses' are themselves abstract entities inhabiting a Platonic 'third realm' ('Thought' 68–9). In this respect they merely add to the number of entities the Augustinian picture assigns to words. Finally, although concept-words differ from proper names, they are still names, namely of abstract entities (functions); so are mathematical and logical symbols, and even sentences, which name either one of two 'logical objects', the True and the False.

The *Tractatus* moves further away from the Augustinian paradigm. It rejects both the idea that LOGICAL CONSTANTS (propositional connectives, quantifiers) are names of entities, and the ensuing view that the propositions of LOGIC are descriptions of some kind of reality. It also insists that a PRO-POSITION is not a name of anything, but a sentence-in-use, a propositional sign in its projective relation to the world. Saying is not naming. Using Frege's distinction, Wittgenstein claims that only propositions have a 'sense', and only names have a 'meaning'. At the same time, the *Tractatus* holds that all constituents of fully analysed propositions are names. The elementary propositions of which complex propositions are formed are 'a nexus, a concatenation, of names' (TLP 3.201f., 4.22f.). It tries to avoid claim (e) by insisting that propositions, unlike lists of names, are FACTS: they have a structure (LOGICAL FORM), which, along with the meaning of their constituent names, determines their sense. However, like Frege, the *Tractatus* explicitly condones claim (c): 'A name means an object. The object is its meaning' (TLP 3.203). Finally, the PICTURE THEORY is based on the idea that the only meaningful propositions are those that describe possible states of affairs.

All this suggests that many august semantic theories lie in the target-area of the *Investigations'* attack. That attack is completed by Wittgenstein's alternative: the meaning of a word is its USE; for *some* expressions, that use is to refer to an object, and they can be explained by pointing at their referent (PI §43). Many critics of this alternative revert to elements of the Augustinian picture. Thus it has been claimed that what matters about the use of a word so far as its meaning is concerned, is precisely what it stands for or signifies. Furthermore, the axioms of contemporary truth-conditional semantics correlate singular terms with objects, and predicates with ordered sets of objects. Finally, it is generally accepted that although the *Investigations* rightly insisted against the *Tractatus* that there are different types of speech acts, even an imperative or a question contains a descriptive element, its sense (a thought or assumption), which must be distinguished from its 'force'.

In his discussion of BELIEF, the later Wittgenstein challenges this sense/

force distinction. Whether or not his attacks are successful, the Augustinian picture is not a straw-man. Equally, however, there is no 'guilt by association': a semantic theory cannot be attacked simply for containing 'Augustinian ideas', since there are important connections between meaning and reference. This also goes for the influence of the Augustinian picture in areas other than language. Reification is a paradigmatic 'Augustinian' temptation. If all nouns are names, psychological expressions must name mental objects, events, processes or states; mathematical and logical terms must name abstract entities. Platonism and Cartesianism postulate separate ontological realms which are inhabited by the alleged referents of abstract nouns like numerals or of mental terms like 'pain' and 'understanding'. There is no doubt that this move is a recurrent target of Wittgenstein's philosophy of mathematics and of psychology. He also challenges the seemingly self-evident claim that mathematical propositions and first-person psychological utterances 'describe' abstract or mental objects. At the same time, the attack on the Augustinian picture does not finish off these venerable positions. It shows only that it is misguided to insist that words *must* refer, or sentences describe, not that the expressions at issue actually fail to do so. Moreover, while the Augustinian picture is one possible reason for adopting these positions, there are other, and often stronger reasons, such as the objectivity and inexorability of mathematics, or the indubitability of AVOWALS.

autonomy of language, or arbitrariness of grammar These terms indicate the idea that GRAMMAR, the linguistic rules which constitute our conceptual scheme, is arbitrary, in the sense that it does not pay heed to any putative essence or form of reality and cannot be correct or incorrect in a philosophically relevant way. This provocative claim is directed against linguistic foundationalism, the view that language should mirror the essence of the world. One version of this is the search for an ideal language, like that of Leibniz, Frege and Russell, which is supposed to mirror the structure of thought and reality more accurately than ordinary language (*Posthumous* 266; *Logic* 185–234, 338).

The *Tractatus* rejects the idea that natural language could be logically flawed, but embraces an alternative version of linguistic foundationalism. Any language capable of depicting reality must be governed by LOGICAL SYNTAX, which is a 'mirror-image of the world' (TLP 6.13). Its rules must match the structural features of reality: the LOGICAL FORM of names must mirror the essence of the objects they stand for. At the same time, 'logic must take care of itself' (TLP 5.473). The SAYING/SHOWING distinction prohibits a doctrine like Russell's theory of types which justifies logical syntax by reference to reality: any proposition that purports to justify logical syntax must be meaningful, and hence presupposes logical syntax. Yet, the extralinguistic foundations of logic *show* themselves, in the logical form of elemen-

45

tary propositions and in the fact that certain combinations of signs are TAUTOLOGIES (TLP 6.124). Finally, while the superficial features which distinguish different languages are arbitrary, there is only one 'all-embracing logic which mirrors the world', common to all sign-systems capable of picturing reality (TLP 5.511; see NM 108–9).

That the *Tractatus* contains a foundationalist 'mythology of symbolism' (PG 56; Z §211) is confirmed by subsequent comments. After 1929, Wittgenstein initially insisted that unlike games, grammar is *not* 'arbitrary', because it has to mirror the multiplicity of facts; and that 'the essence of language is a picture of the essence of the world', albeit not in propositions, but in grammatical rules (LWL 8–10; PR 85). Gradually he came to hold that the apparent essence of reality is nothing but a 'shadow of grammar'. Grammar constitutes our FORM OF REPRESENTATION, it determines what counts as a representation of reality, and is not itself responsible to reality (PG 88, 184; PI §§371–3). There are three major aspects to this autonomy.

(a) Grammar is self-contained, not responsible to extralinguistic reality. (i) Wittgenstein attacks the idea that there is a MEANING-BODY behind a sign, a non-linguistic entity – its meaning – which determines how it can be used correctly. Grammatical rules do not somehow follow from 'meanings', they partly constitute them. Signs as such don't have meanings; we give them meaning by adopting certain standards of linguistic correctness, by explaining and using them in a certain way (BB 27–8).

(ii) There is a natural view, explicit in empiricism and implicit in the *Tractatus*, that OSTENSIVE DEFINITIONS forge a link between a word and its extralinguistic meaning, thus grounding language in reality. Wittgenstein now argues that the samples used in ostensive definitions are part of grammar, in that they function as standards for the correct application of words, as do colour samples for colour-words.

(iii) Wittgenstein rejects the idea that the rules of LOGICAL INFERENCE can be justified either by empirical facts or through model-theoretic proofs.

(iv) A powerful challenge to the idea of the self-containedness of grammar is the Lockean idea of 'real essences', revived by Kripke and Putnam. When we found that certain substances that used to be called 'gold' because they satisfied superficial criteria have a different atomic structure from gold, we did not conclude that gold does not always have the atomic number 79, but distinguished between real gold and, for example, fool's gold. Consequently, the real meaning of words is determined not by the rules we adopt, but by the 'real nature' of the things referred to, which science discovers. Wittgenstein anticipated this line of argument. We sometimes change the CRITERIA for the applications of words. But this amounts to conceptual change sparked off by an empirical discovery, not to a discovery of 'the real meaning' (Z §438). Putnam objects that this ignores the fact that we now know more about gold than before. Wittgenstein could reply that we know more about gold, that is, about the atomic consistency of a certain stuff, without knowing more about the *meaning* of 'gold'. The latter is determined by our EXPLANATION of meaning, which specifies criteria that must be fulfilled by anything we call 'gold'. And we distinguish between UNDERSTANDING the term and having expert chemical knowledge. But even if science does not discover meanings, we, for good reasons, change certain concepts in accordance with its findings, and to this extent language is not autonomous. One might further claim that the new concept is simply correct, since it corresponds to objective features of a stuff (gold). However, that stuff has an indefinite number of objective properties. These *could* all be used to define different concepts, which may be more or less useful, or have more or less explanatory power. But that is not a matter of corresponding to reality.

(b) Grammatical rules cannot be justified. Even if grammatical rules cannot be justified by reference to reality, might they not be justified in the same way as strategic or technical rules, by reference to their purpose or function? Wittgenstein resists this (PG 184–5, 190–4; PI §§491–6; Z §§320–2; MS165 106; BT 194–5). We can justify the rules of an activity like cooking by reference to its goal, with cooking the production of tasty food, since that goal can be specified independently of the means by which it is attained. But we cannot justify the rules of language by reference to a goal like communication, since the relationship between language and communication is conceptual, not instrumental. A sound-system which does not fulfil the purpose of communicating is not a worse language, but no language at all. (Note, however, that this sits uneasily with Wittgenstein's simultaneous insistence that language cannot be defined as a means of communication since it is a FAMILY-RESEMBLANCE concept.)

Wittgenstein also provides a quasi-Kantian argument against any attempt to justify grammar by reference to facts. We cannot invoke facts in support of grammatical rules without expressing them in language. Hence, to justify a grammatical rule could only mean to support it by adducing a PROPOSITION. But any such proposition is expressed in some language, and therefore presupposes a certain grammatical framework. There is no such thing as an extralinguistic or preconceptual perspective outside any grammar from which we could justify a given grammatical system (*see* TRUTH). This confronts the foundationalist with a dilemma. Either the grammar of the supporting proposition is identical with that of the rule to be justified. In that case the justification is circular. Or the supporting sentence belongs to a different grammatical system. This would avoid circularity, but only at the cost of incommensurability. A different grammatical system defines different concepts, hence a statement in a different system can neither justify nor refute grammatical propositions of our system. We cannot justify the grammar of our colour-words by claiming that there *are* precisely four primary colours which objectively resemble each other, because the concept of similarity upon which this move depends is part of the grammar we seek to justify. The foundationalist could only provide a conceptually independent justification, and thus avoid the first horn of the dilemma, if he could allude to the possibility of a fifth primary colour and deny that this possibility is realized. But this lands him upon the second horn, since the possibility of a fifth colour is precisely excluded as nonsensical by our rules. Each form of representation creates its own concepts and thus lays down its own standards of what it makes sense to say, which means that justification and what is to be justified would pass each other by (PR 54–5; PG 97, 114; LWL 83).

(c) Alternative forms of representation are not irrational in an absolute sense. It seems obvious that certain essential features of language are superior to any genuine alternatives. Wittgenstein rejects even this modest suggestion, by reference to various alternative norms of representation (e.g., deviant ways of counting, calculating and measuring). 'One symbolism is in fact as good as the next; no one symbolism is necessary' (AWL 22, see 63, 117; RFM 38, 91–4, 105–6; LFM 201–2; RR 121–2). The rationale for this view is that every form of representation provides a framework for dealing with 'recalcitrant' experiences without having to surrender the form of representation itself (AWL 16, 39–40, 70). Prefiguring Kuhn's idea of a scientific paradigm, Wittgenstein illustrates how one could hold on to Newton's first law of motion come what may. If a body does not rest or move with a constant motion along a straight line, we postulate that some mass, visible or invisible, acts upon it.

Alternative forms of representation are possible even in mathematics. It is possible to adopt '$12 \times 12 = 143$' as a norm of representation (LFM 97). It has been objected that a community which did so would have to count in a manner which its members would recognize as mistaken. But to say that they *must* have made a mistake is to adopt *our* norm of representation '$12 \times 12 = 144$'. For them, by contrast, something must have gone wrong when they count 144 objects. This may appear unconvincing: when these people count twelve groups of twelve objects they will get 143 only by leaving an object out. However, they could hold on to their norm of representation without appearing to themselves to have committed such a mistake, by assuming that things arranged in twelve groups of twelve increase in number by one whenever they are counted. Moreover, their allegiance to their form of representation does not differ in kind from our allegiance to our own. If it turned out that whenever we count twelve groups of twelve things we get 143, we would not abandon '$12 \times 12 = 144$', but look for explanations elsewhere. However, such *ad hoc* assumptions would not work for numbers we can count at a glance, and this is one factor which restricts the possibility of alternative forms of representation.

According to a naturalist interpretation, Wittgenstein's alternative techniques are not meant to be intelligible, but meant to illustrate that it is a contingent fact that we speak and act as we do. Wittgenstein himself, however, claimed that divergent concepts become 'intelligible' if we imagine 'certain very general facts of nature to be different' (PI II 230; RPP I §48; RFM 91, 95). Indeed, some of his examples are no less intelligible than the medieval practice of measuring by the ell. What is unintelligible according to Wittgenstein is only the idea of changing our form of representation while retaining our present concepts. But this reply seems to confront a dilemma. Either alternative techniques make for different concepts, in which case Wittgenstein is not entitled to speak of alternative forms of, for example, measuring. Or the alternative technique counts as a form of measuring because it shares with our techniques a certain function (e.g., of allowing the fitting together of building-blocks), in which case our techniques are clearly superior. To this Wittgenstein would reply that such functional constraints are themselves conditional on certain needs and interests. Alternative techniques may be inferior as means of achieving *our* ends. But a pre-technological community which is only interested in measuring cloth can get by with ells, irrespective of the fact that the lengths of people's arms vary. The basis of calling this a form of 'measuring' lies in the fact that it plays an analogous role in their form of life.

Nevertheless, Wittgenstein acknowledges that there are limits to revising our form of representation. On the one hand these are conceptual. While our concepts of counting, measuring, etc. are flexible enough to accommodate certain variations, there is a much tighter link between the 'laws of logic' and notions like 'reasoning', 'thinking' and even 'proposition' or 'language' (RFM 80, 89–95, 336; LFM 201–2, 214). A practice which does not conform to the rule for the *modus ponens* simply does not qualify as inferring. And a system which allows the derivation of a contradiction does not count as an alternative logic. However, this does not jeopardize the autonomy of grammar. For these limits are set not by Platonic entities, as Frege had it, or by a 'METALOGICAL' obligation to avoid contradictions, as the logical positivists thought, but by our concepts, by what we call 'inferring', 'reasoning', or '(a system of) rules' (PG 111, 304; WVC 199–200; AWL 4). And the rules for the use of these terms pay no more heed to reality than those of other words; rather, a practice which does not conform to them would be unintelligible to us, and would not count as a language (note the parallels with Davidson's argument against the idea of an untranslatable language).

There are also pragmatic constraints. Norms of representation cannot be metaphysically correct or incorrect. But given certain facts – biological and socio-historical facts about us and general regularities in the world around us – adopting certain rules can be 'practical' or 'impractical' (AWL 70). Provided that the world is as it is, people who employed alternative scientific paradigms, ways of calculating or measuring for purposes similar to ours, would have to make adjustments which would eventually collapse under their own weight. Drastic changes in certain facts could render certain rules not only impractical but even inapplicable (RFM 51–2, 200; RPP II §§347–9; *see* FRAMEWORK).

The autonomy of language does not amount to an 'anything goes' relativism. Grammar is not arbitrary in the sense of being irrelevant, discretionary, easily alterable or a matter of individual choice. Language is embedded in a FORM OF LIFE, and is hence subject to the same restrictions as human activities in general. The idea of the autonomy of grammar is provocative. Yet its ultimate rationale is a grammatical reminder: we call propositions true or false, but not concepts, rules or explanations. A unit of measurement is not correct or incorrect in the way that a statement of length is. Grammatical rules can be correct in the sense of conforming to an established practice, or of serving certain purposes. But Wittgenstein has made out a powerful case against the idea that they have to mirror a putative essence of reality.

avowal This term was introduced into philosophy by Ryle, but it is also a common translation of Wittgenstein's *Äußerung* or *Ausdruck* (alternatives being 'expression', 'manifestation', 'utterance'). Wittgenstein characterized some uses of first-person present tense psychological sentences as avowals. Negatively, this indicates that they are not descriptions or reports of private mental entities encountered in an inner realm. Positively, Wittgenstein characterizes avowals as expressive in the way in which a gesture or frown expresses or manifests emotions, attitudes, etc. They are partial substitutes for, and learnt extensions of, natural expressions of the mental, such as cries, smiles or grimaces. Sensation-words 'are connected with the primitive, the natural, expressions of the sensation and used in their place. A child has hurt himself and he cries; and then adults talk to him and teach him exclamations and, later, sentences. They teach the child new pain-behaviour' (PI §244). This is not armchair learning-theory but a claim that logically the function of avowals is akin to that of non-verbal manifestations.

This idea is crucial to Wittgenstein's rejection of the INNER/OUTER picture, and developed out of his break with the PICTURE THEORY, according to which all meaningful propositions express a thought and represent how things are. The view that all meaningful propositions are descriptive survived in the VERIFICATIONISM of the transition period, which insists that a proposition that cannot be conclusively verified lacks sense. Wittgenstein concluded that only sense-datum statements which describe immediate experience are genuine PROPOSITIONS: only they allow of conclusive verification by being directly confronted with experience. Accordingly, verification means something different in the first-person case

(1) I am in pain

from what it means in the third-person case

(1') N.N. is in pain

which is verified by reference to N.N.'s BEHAVIOUR.

In 1932, Wittgenstein realized that verification applies only to cases like (1'), which is verified by reference to behavioural CRITERIA, not to cases like (1). There are no intelligible answers to the question 'How do you know that you have a pain?' (M 98–9; LSD 13; Z §436). (a) 'Because I feel it' will not do, since there is no difference between feeling a pain and having a pain. For one cannot have a pain and not feel it, or feel a pain one does not have. Consequently, the answer amounts to 'I know I have a pain because I have it', which is vacuous. (b) 'By introspection' presupposes that one can 'look to see whether one has it', which does not make sense, for there is no such thing as perceiving or misperceiving one's pain.

As a result Wittgenstein detects a fundamental difference between psychological and other predicates. There is rough logical parity between

(2) I weigh over 100 kg

and

(2') H.G. weighs over 100 kg.

By contrast, there is a logical asymmetry between (1), which is an avowal, and (1'), which is a description. Unlike descriptions, avowals: (a) do not allow of verification, for there is no such thing as my 'finding out' that I have a sensation or intend to go to London, or of my 'perceiving' or 'recognizing' my sensations or experiences; (b) do not allow of significant error, ignorance or doubt; there is no room for misidentifying their subject (*see* I/SELF) or for misapplying their predicates: 'I thought I had a pain, but it turned out to be an itch, and it was Sarah's, not mine' is nonsense; (c) do not express knowledge claims (Z §§472, 549; PI §§290, 571; LPE 319; *see* PRIVACY).

Occasionally Wittgenstein suggests that avowals are not cognitive because they are not descriptions; sometimes he intimates that they are not descriptions because they do not express knowledge. Ultimately, both claims are based on the idea that there is a grammatical link between epistemic concepts and the concept of description (RPP I §572; Z §549; LW I §51). Genuine knowledge is possible only of what can be described; genuine descriptions or assertions involve the exercise of perceptual capacities, and the possibility of observation (examination), justification and (dis-)confirmation.

Some readers of *Philosophical Investigations* §§243–315 have detected a painful emphasis on spontaneous expressions of pain. Even if (1) resembles an expression like 'Ouch', this does not seem to be the case for psychological terms which are not connected with a specific behavioural manifestation, such as 'thinking'. But Wittgenstein's overall treatment does not in fact suffer from a 'one-sided diet' of examples (PI §593). Moreover, Wittgenstein acknowledges that any type-sentence can, in suitable contexts, be used non-expressively, to make cool reports or explanations. Thus, a sentence like (1), or an utterance like 'I am afraid', could be an expression, a report (e.g., to a doctor) or an explanation (e.g., of one's trembling hands) (PI II 187–9). However, this concession invites the allegation that Wittgenstein is guilty of a speech-act fallacy. The meaning of 'pain' must be the same whether it occurs in avowals like (1), or in more complex cases, in which the sentence does not serve to express a pain. The expressive role of some first-person present tense psychological utterances seems due not to the meaning of the words involved, but to the use to which they are put in the simple cases on which Wittgenstein focuses. But Wittgenstein can reply: 'if "I'm afraid" is not always something like a cry of complaint and yet sometimes is, then why should it *always* be a description of a state of mind', as the inner/outer dualism implies? (PI II 189; RPP I §633). He does not claim that psychological terms are ambiguous, that, for example, 'pain' has a different meaning in (1) from the one it has in (1′), but that (1) and (1′) employ the term differently, are part of different linguistic techniques, and that the expressive use of psychological terms is, in their first-person present tense application, the standard one (RPP I §693; LW I §§874–5, 899).

Wittgenstein places excessive weight on the distinction between expressive and descriptive uses. A single utterance can fulfil both functions: an utterance of (2) can both state one's body weight and express remorse. Moreover, although 'I believe that *p*' is not a description, it is often a report rather than a spontaneous manifestation; it may say what my long-held convictions are. Nevertheless, Wittgenstein is right to hold that psychological reports are typically not based on inner observation or recognition of private phenomena (RPP II §§176–7; LW I §51; PI §§274, 291–2; Z §434; *see* INNER/ OUTER). Moreover, they are parasitical upon genuine expressions of a pre-linguistic kind (PI §§244, 290): unless certain forms of behaviour naturally counted as manifestations of sensations, beliefs, emotions, etc., our mental vocabulary would not have the meaning it does. This connection semantically characterizes, for example, sensation-terms. Although (2) may be used to express remorse, that possibility depends on contingent assumptions which are extrinsic to the meaning of 'weigh over 100 kg'. By contrast, 'pain' would no longer be the name of a sensation if avowals like (1) did not have a 'particular function in our life' which is analogous to that of natural expressions of pain (LPE 301; LSD 35; RPP I §313; Z §§532–4). What distinguishes avowals from other utterances is the way they are linked to non-linguistic forms of behaviour.

A final objection is that (1) is a basis for truth-functional operations like conjunction, and can, moreover, function as a premise in a valid inference, for example

(3)   I am in pain; therefore someone is in pain.

Both points indicate that (1) is capable of being true or false, and is in that sense descriptive. Furthermore, there is logical symmetry between avowals and descriptions: (1), uttered by me now, says exactly the same as (1') said by you now, if I am N.N. And there are logical relations between the simple cases on which Wittgenstein focuses, and complex cases. One defence of Wittgenstein is that such functions and relations can involve uses of words which are definitely not descriptive. From N.N.'s saying 'Off with his head!' we can infer something about N.N.'s state of mind (RPP I §463). However, this is inadequate: what we draw an inference from here is not the statement itself, but the fact that the speaker made it. By contrast, (1) appears in inferences in its own right. (3) makes sense; 'Ouch; therefore someone is in pain' does not. This is due to the fact that (1), unlike exclamations, is true or false.

Fortunately, Wittgenstein grants that there are differences between first-person psychological utterances and natural expressions (LPE 301, 318–20; LSD 11; LW I §898). The former are articulate, that is, grammatically composed of subject and predicate; can be used descriptively, and appear in non-expressive contexts; allow of logical and tense transformations; and can be true or false. But at the same time Wittgenstein insists that these similarities to descriptions do not entail that avowals are straightforwardly descriptive. As regards the symmetry between (1) and (1'), he would argue that although their status is the same for the purposes of formal LOGIC, which is concerned only with entailment, that is, transformations preserving truth-value, it need not for that reason be the same for the purposes of philosophical GRAMMAR. 'Being true' amounts to something different – has a different grammar – in the case of avowals: their truth is guaranteed by truthfulness (PI II 222), since they are not liable to mistake or error, only to insincerity. Furthermore, although the sense of a proposition is not identical with the method of its verification, 'whether and how a proposition can be verified' is a contribution to its grammar (PI §353, II 224–5), which means that the grammar of (1) differs from that of (1'). Wittgenstein's point is that although avowals may be called descriptive, they lack conceptual connections which characterize ordinary descriptions (PI §§290–2; RPP I §572). He concludes that the inner/outer picture is mistaken to think that we 'read off' descriptions of our sensations, desires, thoughts, etc. from inner facts.

Finally, Wittgenstein recognized that with respect to first/third-person asymmetry, psychological concepts form a spectrum of cases. At one end lie sensations like pain, followed by intentions, thoughts, etc. Here there is no such thing as being mistaken or finding out, and typically no room for description. Somewhere in the middle lie emotions and states of mind with genuine duration. They are typically avowed, but it is possible to find out that I am in love or angry from my reactions. Similarly, I can describe the course of my anxiety or fear as it waxes or wanes (PI §§585–8; RPP II §§156, 722; LW I §43). But although here there is room for genuine self-knowledge and error, which may sometimes rest on (mis-)perception or (defective) observation, the problem is typically self-deception, a mistake of the will, not of the intellect. At the other end of the spectrum are psycho-pathological terms. I may (although I need not) be unqualified to decide whether I am neurotic.

B

behaviour and behaviourism   Modern philosophy has been dominated by an INNER/OUTER dualism which distinguishes between the physical world containing matter, energy and tangible objects, including human bodies, and the private world of mental phenomena. Behaviourism is a twentieth-century reaction to this position. It holds that attributing mental states, processes or events to people really amounts to making statements about their actual behaviour or dispositions to behave. Behaviourism comes in three versions: *metaphysical* behaviourism denies that there are mental phenomena; *methodological* behaviourism insists that psychologists should not invoke them in explaining behaviour, since they are not intersubjectively accessible; *logical* behaviourism claims that propositions about the mental are semantically equivalent to propositions about behavioural dispositions – thus

(1)   Helga is sad

might be translated as

(1′)   Helga is speaking in a low monotone, and her head is drooping.

Wittgenstein has often been suspected of holding some version of behaviourism, and been placed alongside Ryle. His attitude to methodological behaviourism is ambivalent. He claims that psychology, unlike philosophy, has the task of investigating the causal mechanisms which link stimulus and response. But this goes hand in hand with a 'hermeneutic' distinction between understanding and explanation which implies that human action cannot be made intelligible – seen as meaningful – through the CAUSAL explanations of science (e.g. PLP ch. VI). UNDERSTANDING requires reference to things which methodological behaviourism rejects – desires, beliefs, moods, emotions, etc. His philosophy is also at odds with metaphysical behaviourism. The early work presupposes that there is a language of THOUGHT which consists of mental elements that can be studied by psychology. Moreover, his first discussion of behaviourist ideas, those expressed in Russell's account of INTENTIONALITY in *The Analysis of Mind* (chs III, XII), is critical. He accuses them of mistaking the internal relations between an expectation and its fulfilment, a symbol and its meaning, which are normative, with the external relations between stimulus and response, which are a matter of contingent fact.

Wittgenstein's relationship to logical behaviourism is more complex. He never gave a behaviourist account of the first-person case. But a behaviourist analysis of third-person psychological propositions is perhaps implicit in the *Tractatus* (*see* BELIEF), at least Wittgenstein thought so in 1932 when he accused Carnap of plagiarism in developing logical behaviourism under the title 'physicalism'. Such an account is explicit in the methodological SOLIPSISM of the transition period, which sharply distinguishes between genuine 'propositions', which can be verified by reference to primary experiences, and third-person psychological propositions, which are mere 'hypotheses', to be analysed in terms of behaviour. This position combines a 'no ownership' analysis of first-person psychological propositions with a behaviourist analysis of the third-person case (*see* I/SELF; PRIVACY). The official rationale for it was provided by VERIFICATIONISM (WVC 49–50, 244; PR 88–95). If the meaning of a proposition is the method of its verification, the meaning of third-person psychological propositions like (1) is given by the behavioural evidence we have for the mental phenomena (e.g., Helga's sadness). For we cannot verify those phenomena by reference to the subject's private experiences. Consequently, to ascribe mental phenomena to others is to talk of their behaviour. Wittgenstein also suggests that (1) has the same sense as (1'), since both are confirmed by the same experiences. But even a verificationist might resist this reductionist conclusion, on the grounds that there is possible evidence (not necessarily available) which sets apart (1) and (1') (e.g., Helga's laughing merrily when she is unobserved).

During the thirties, Wittgenstein became increasingly critical of behaviourism. (a) He rejected the idea, to be found in Carnap's logical behaviourism, that first-person psychological propositions can be analysed into propositions about one's own behaviour, to be verified by self-observation. It does not make sense to verify a proposition like 'I am sad' by observing one's own posture and behaviour (PR 89–90; Z §539). Wittgenstein later claimed that by and large such propositions are not descriptions at all, let alone descriptions of behaviour, but AVOWALS, expressions of the mental. Such avowals have a role similar to that of expressive behaviour, but they are not *about* behaviour. To moan is not to say 'I moan', to cry out 'I am in pain' is not to say 'I am manifesting pain-behaviour' (PI §244, II 179; LSD 11; LPE 296; RPP I §287).

(b) Against metaphysical behaviourism Wittgenstein stressed that it is essential to the grammar of mental terms, even of sensation-words relatively closely tied to behaviour, that someone can be in pain without manifesting it, or that one can pretend to be in pain without being so. There cannot be a 'greater difference' than that between pain-behaviour with and pain-behaviour without pain. At the same time, the PRIVATE LANGUAGE ARGUMENT implies that the idea of pain as a private entity is a 'grammatical fiction' (PI §§304–11) imposed on us by the AUGUSTINIAN PICTURE OF LANGUAGE which suggests that words must refer to a 'something', which in the case of sensation-words is an inner something.

(c) While behaviourism rejects the Cartesian picture of the mind as a private mental theatre, it accepts the attendant conception of the body as a mere mechanism, and of human behaviour as 'colourless' physical movements. Wittgenstein occasionally tended towards such a picture (PR ch. VI; BB 51–2), but came to realize that it is flawed. The behavioural manifestations of most mental phenomena are extremely diverse. We can recognize Helga's behaviour as expressing sadness only if,we already approach it 'from the point of view of sadness' (PR 89). This means that we do not, by and large, infer psychologically relevant descriptions of human behaviour from austere physical ones. For we often know the conclusions of such alleged inferences without knowing their premises. It is easier to describe Helga as 'sad' or 'bored' than to describe her features or movements in physical terms (RPP I §§1066–8, 1102; LW I §§766–7; Z §225).

(d) By a similar token, it is wrong to think that a HUMAN BEING is a body. Rather, it requires a shift in perspective analogous to that involved in ASPECT-PERCEPTION to view a human being as a physiological mechanism, and human behaviour as mechanical movement (PI §420, II 178). For this reason, Wittgenstein would not go along with Ryle's analysis of mental concepts in terms of dispositions to behave. We can only ascribe mental concepts to creatures with certain abilities. And, unlike dispositions, abilities are (i) confined to sentient creatures and (ii) not actualized automatically given certain conditions (one need not exercise an ability).

(e) When Wittgenstein speaks of the behavioural manifestations of the mental, 'behaviour' includes not just facial expressions and gestures, but also what people do and say, and the occasions for the use of mental terms. These form a highly complex syndrome. What counts as a manifestation of sadness on one occasion, may not on another (RPP I §§129, 314; Z §492). The relationship between the mental and behaviour is much more complicated than behaviourists suppose.

At the same time, Wittgenstein's later philosophy of psychology retains points of contact with logical behaviourism. It rejects the dualist account of the mental as inalienable and epistemically private. It accepts, albeit as an empirical fact, that language-learning (and thereby the possession of a complex mental life) is founded on brute 'training' (*Abrichtung*), rather than genuine EXPLANATION, and presupposes natural patterns of behaviour and reaction, to be activated by certain stimuli. And it claims that the ascription of psychological predicates to other people is *logically* connected with behaviour.

However, that logical connection is not one of logical equivalence between propositions (namely psychological and behavioural ones). Rather, it takes two forms. First, it only makes sense to ascribe mental phenomena to creatures who can manifest the mental in their behaviour. 'Only of a living human being and what resembles (behaves like) a living human being can one say: it has sensations; it sees; is blind; hears; is deaf; is conscious or unconscious' (PI §281). Second, our mental terms would not mean what they do if they were not bound up with behavioural criteria. The resulting position undermines both behaviourism and dualism. Mental phenomena are neither reducible to, nor totally separable from, their bodily and behavioural expressions. The relationship between mental phenomena and their behavioural manifestations is not a causal one to be discovered empirically, through theory and induction, but a criterial one: it is part of the concepts of particular mental phenomena that they have a characteristic manifestation in behaviour (LPE 286; LSD 10). And it is part of mental concepts in general that they have some such manifestation. We would have no use for these expressions if they were not bound up with behavioural CRITERIA. If we came across human beings who used a word which lacked any connection with pain-behaviour and the circumstances in which we display it, we would not translate it as 'pain'. The idea of super-spartans who are in constant agony without showing it is as incoherent as describing as soulless human beings who behave exactly like us (LPP 281). 'The human body is the best picture of the human soul' (PI II 178). We are inclined to think of mental episodes as given, and of the expression as secondary, as mere symptoms through which we may come to know the mind. But Wittgenstein makes out a strong case for thinking that the intelligibility of mental terms presupposes the possibility of behavioural manifestations. Ascribing THOUGHTS, for example, makes sense only in cases where we have criteria for identifying thoughts, which means that thoughts must be capable of being expressed.

belief Wittgenstein's earliest discussion of belief arises from his objections to Russell's theories of judgement. Initially, Russell had held a dual-relation theory, according to which a belief is a dual relation between something mental – a subject or an act of belief – and a 'proposition', an objective entity that exists whether or not it is believed. *Tractatus* 5.54f. dismisses this theory as violating the extensionalist principle that when one proposition occurs in another one, as according to the dual-relation theory 'p' does in the proposition 'A believes that p', it can do so only as the basis of truth-functional operations, which 'p' does not in 'A believes that p' (for the truth of the latter is not a function of that of the former) (*see* GENERAL PROPOSITIONAL FORM). Both Wittgenstein and Russell also came to reject it for a less dogmatic reason. In

(1) A believes/judges that p

what A believes is not an object, a fact. (1) does not presuppose that there *is* something to be believed; it may be true even if no fact corresponds to '*p*' (NL 95; *Problems* 72–3). In response to this problem, Russell developed his multiple-relation theory of judgement (*Essays* ch. VII; 'Theory' 110): Othello's belief that Desdemona loves Cassio is not a dual relation between him and a proposition, but a multiple relation between him and the constituents of the proposition – Desdemona, love and Cassio. On this account, the occurrence of the judgement does not entail that the relation of love obtains between Desdemona and Cassio.

According to Wittgenstein, this ensures the possibility of false judgements only at the unacceptable price of allowing nonsensical judgements. The correct analysis of (1) must 'show that it is impossible for a judgement to be a piece of nonsense' (TLP 5.5422), '*p*' must be a meaningful BIPOLAR proposition (RUL 6.13; NL 103). By splitting the proposition into its constituents, Russell fails to guarantee the preservation of logical form between the constituents of the judgement, and hence allows a judgement like 'the knife is the square root of the fork' (similarly, Bradley complained that Russell ignores the unity of judgement).

Tractatus 5.542 presents an analysis of belief intended to avoid both the appearance that the proposition *p* here occurs in a non-truth-functional way; and the possibility of judging nonsense. Wittgenstein's solution is to incorporate the propositional form in ascriptions of belief. Thus, (1) is of the form

(2) '*p*' says *p*.

Like (2), (1) correlates not a fact – *p* – and an object – the subject *A* – but two facts, the depicted fact, *p* (assuming that *p* is a fact), and the thought-constituting fact, '*p*'. It does so through correlating their components, namely the elements of thought with objects in reality. (1) means that in *A* there is a mental fact which pictures the fact that *p*. Only composite things with an articulate structure consisting of elements correlated with objects can say or picture something. This implies that there is no unitary subject '*A*', no soul-substance, but only a complex array of mental elements (TLP 5.5421; *see* SOLIPSISM).

This analysis guarantees the meaningfulness of what is judged by insisting that it is not a complex of objects which can be combined in any old way, but a FACT in which objects hang together subject to their combinatorial possibilities. But it replaces Russell's inchoate notion of a relation between a mind and the uncoordinated terms of judgement with the obscure idea that 'thinking the sense of *p*' projects THOUGHT onto reality (TLP 3.11). Moreover, it is prima facie unclear how *Tractatus* 5.542 avoids the problem of non-truth-functional occurrences. (2) can be understood in three different ways. If what appears in quotation-marks is a description of 'accidental' features of the propositional SIGN, (2) would always be false, since without a METHOD OF PROJECTION signs cannot depict anything. Alternatively, (2) might

59

express an external relation between two facts: the fact that the speaker thinks or means such-and-such and the fact that p. In that case it is a bipolar proposition, but its truth-value is determined not by that of 'p', but by an empirical relationship between the fact that p and a mental fact. Finally, the relation between the two facts might be internal, namely, if the description in quotation-marks includes a method of projection, that is, identifies 'p' as precisely the proposition that says that p. But in that case (2) would be necessarily true, and therefore its truth-value would again not be a function of that of 'p'. Moreover, by virtue of expressing an internal relation, (2) would be a pseudo-proposition which tries to say what can only be shown by the proposition p. None of these alternatives allows for 'p' to occur truth-functionally in (2), or, consequently, in (1). The last preserves the extensionality thesis in so far as it does not violate the principle that propositions occur in *genuine* propositions only as the bases of truth-functional operations, but does so at the price of branding belief ascriptions as pseudo-propositions. Waismann later suggested that the analysis should be confined to the first-person case 'I believe that p' for which it was first developed (NM 119). But it is hard to see how this avoids the aforementioned problems.

Wittgenstein's second discussion of belief starts out from Frege's and Russell's ideas about assertion (*Notation* §§2–3; *Laws* I §5; 'Function' 22; *Correspondence* 79; *Principles* 35; *Principia* 8, 92; 'Theory' 107). Both distinguished in an assertion the act of asserting from what is asserted, the proposition or thought. One of their reasons was the need to distinguish the occurrence of a proposition 'p' when it is not asserted, as in '$p \supset q$', from its occurrence on its own, when it is (the so-called 'Frege point'). For this purpose, Frege introduced the assertion-sign '$\vdash$' to express the act of judging something to be true. Every line in his logical system has the form

(3) $\vdash p$

where '$-p$' (involving the horizontal 'content-stroke') expresses the mere thought without judging it to be true, while the vertical 'judgement-stroke' signals the act of assertion which takes us from a thought to a truth-value. In Frege's system, all inferences proceed from asserted propositions to asserted propositions, and one can make inferences only from true propositions. Having abandoned the idea that all judgements are of subject-predicate form, he claimed that '$\vdash$' (meaning 'it is a fact that') is the 'common predicate of all judgements'. Russell took over the assertion-sign to add the force of 'it is true that' to the unasserted proposition; he held that true propositions have the quality of being asserted in a non-psychological, logical sense.

In 1911, Wittgenstein seems to have held that the only things which exist are 'asserted' (i.e., true) propositions, which are facts. By the time of 'Notes on Logic', however, he insisted that the assertion-sign is logically irrelevant (NL 95–6; TLP 4.023, 4.063f., 4.442). It indicates merely the psychological fact that the author holds the proposition to be true; it does not belong to the proposition: (a) one can draw inferences from *false* propositions (Frege and Russell ignored this, presumably because their axiomatic conception of LOGIC focuses on proof, which requires true premises); (b) neither 'is true' nor 'is a fact' is the 'verb' of propositions, the formal predicate they all have in common; for what is asserted through these verbs must already have a sense, that is, be a proposition.

As a result, Wittgenstein claims against Frege and Russell that logic is exclusively concerned with the *unasserted* proposition, which shows how things stand if it is true. However, this claim is inaccurate. For it is part of Wittgenstein's account that only the asserted proposition *says* something, namely *that* things stand as the unasserted proposition shows them to stand. This is required not just by the Frege point but also because the early Wittgenstein seems to have accepted that an unasserted proposition can be common to the assertion that *p*, the question of whether it is the case that *p*, the command to make it the case that *p*, etc. (TLP 4.022; NB 26.11.14; MS109 249; BT 149). Wittgenstein later returned to this idea (PI §22, 11n; BT 208; RFM 116; Z §684; PLP 302–3). He ascribes to Frege the idea that that part of a declarative sentence which expresses an 'assumption', that is, the thing that is asserted, functions like a *sentence-radical*. The assumption, or thought, is the descriptive content of what is asserted, but can also be a component of other, non-assertoric speech acts. It might be represented by '–*p*' in '?–*p*' for sentence-questions and '!–*p*' for commands, as well as '⊢*p*' for assertions. It has been claimed that *Philosophical Investigations* uses this idea to accommodate non-descriptive uses of language within the semantics of the *Tractatus*: the PICTURE THEORY provides an adequate account of the sentence-radical, but needs to be complemented by a theory of 'semantic mood' to account for the uses of sentences in different language-games. In fact, however, the later Wittgenstein rejects the idea that assertoric utterances can be analysed into assumption plus assertion. He also rejects the idea that different speech acts share a common propositional content, and that all propositions contain descriptions. If sound, his arguments also undermine contemporary distinctions between sense and force, and thereby threaten truth-conditional semantics, which relies on the possibility of isolating in non-assertoric speech acts a descriptive component (propositional content) capable of being true or false (*see* AUGUSTINIAN PICTURE OF LANGUAGE). There are four points of attack.

(a) The Fregean theory imposes contradictory demands on that part of a declarative sentence which is supposed to express the mere assumption or thought. On the one hand, it must *not* be a complete sentence, since it must lack assertoric force, as does the noun-phrase 'that *p*' in

(3′)   It is asserted that *p*.

On the other hand, it *must* be a complete sentence, since the assumption/

thought is the sense of a sentence, not of a noun-phrase. Consequently, there is no such thing as a sentence-radical, fit to express the sense of a declarative sentence but unfit to express assertoric force. Assertion is not something added to a proposition.

(b) One cannot characterize the concept of a proposition, what is true or false, independently of that of assertion. But to this Frege could reply that the non-assertoric occurrence of propositions in, for example, '$p \supset q$' shows that the concept of a proposition is at best linked to the *possibility* of assertion.

(c) The assumption that p must be common to '$?-p$' and '$\vdash p$'. According to Wittgenstein, '$?-p$' concerns the same assumption as '$?-{\sim}p$', since both questions can be answered by either '$\vdash p$' or '$\vdash {\sim}p$'. This implies, however, that the assumption that p is the same as the assumption that ${\sim}p$, which is absurd.

(d) '$\vdash$' does not signify a component of an assertion, or a mental activity which gives the utterance its assertoric force. It merely serves as a punctuation-mark which indicates the beginning of the sentence. And what gives an utterance assertoric force is not an accompaniment, but the way it is used by the speaker. But these observations are compatible with the Frege point, the use of '$\vdash$' to distinguish between the occurrences of 'p' in '$\vdash p$' and '$\vdash (p \supset q)$'.

The idea that assertion is a mental process which effects the transition from a mere assumption to a declarative utterance is further attacked in the discussions of 'Moore's paradox' from the 1940s (ML 10.44; PI II 190–2; RPP I §§470–504; RPP II §§277–83; *Writings* ch. 12). Moore had observed that while we often do not believe something which is true, it is 'absurd' to say

(4) It is raining, but I don't believe it.

Wittgenstein rejected Moore's suggestion that this absurdity is of a psychological nature. He claimed that utterances like (4) are senseless, and show something about the logic of assertion. For one thing, they indicate a further problem with the Fregean analysis. Moore's paradox shows that 'I believe that it is raining' has a similar logical role to the simple assertion 'It is raining.' At the same time, the 'assumption' that it is raining is not the same as the assumption that I believe this to be so, which concerns myself, not the weather. If these two observations are expressed in accordance with the Fregean analysis, we get:

(a) '$\vdash p$' has a similar logical role to '$\vdash \mathrm{Ib}p$'
(b) '$-p$' has a dissimilar role to '$-\mathrm{Ib}p$'.

While (a) implies that the assumption contained in '$\vdash p$' is the same as that in '$\vdash \mathrm{Ib}p$', (b) implies that it is not. Moreover, (b) suggests that the assertion 'I believe that p' cannot be split up into an assumption and an expression of belief, because 'I believe' cannot be eliminated without altering the assumption itself. Consequently, the step from '$-p$' to '$\vdash p$' cannot be one of adding assertoric force to a common assumption.

A second implication of Moore's paradox is that belief is not a phenomenon which we observe in ourselves. If 'I believe that . . .' described in phenomenal terms something about the speaker, whether about his brain, mind or behaviour, (4) would not be paradoxical. For there could be no inconsistency between describing how things are with me (my mind/my brain) and describing the weather. The role of 'I believe that p' is that of expressing the belief that p. This is also a role of simply uttering 'p', which is why there is an inconsistency between avowing 'p' and disavowing the belief that p. I may report rather than AVOW my long-held convictions. But I do not describe them, since such reports commit me to a claim, which no mere description could (RPP I §§715–16; *see* INTENDING AND MEANING SOMETHING).

On such grounds, Wittgenstein attacks the neo-Humean position of James and Russell, according to which belief is a feeling of approval towards a proposition (*Psychology* II ch. XXI; *Analysis* 250–2). Although feelings may accompany my beliefs, they are neither necessary nor sufficient. And although 'to believe' is a static verb, it no more signifies a mental state such as a feeling than a mental act or process. Belief is neither something one does, nor something one undergoes or is in. Unlike genuine mental processes or states, beliefs lack 'genuine duration' (PI §§571–94, II 193–229; RPP I §§596, 710, 832–6; *see* PHILOSOPHICAL PSYCHOLOGY). Expressions of belief are less determinate and characteristic than those of emotions, which is why dispositional theories of belief fail. But the concept of belief is internally linked with what people *would* (sincerely) say they believe, and how they would act in certain circumstances. (*See also* CERTAINTY.)

bipolarity According to the principle of bipolarity, every proposition must be capable of being true, *and* capable of being false. This principle, which Wittgenstein was the first to espouse, differs from the weaker principle of bivalence, according to which every proposition is either true or false. Represented symbolically (along lines Wittgenstein condoned in 'Notes dictated to Moore' but later rejected), the principle of bivalence reads $(p)(p \vee {\sim}p)$, while the principle of bipolarity comes out as $(p)(\Diamond p \cdot \Diamond {\sim}p)$. From early on, Wittgenstein held that bipolarity is the essence of the proposition (RUL 5.9.13; NL 94–9, 104; NM 113). The term derives from a metaphor: a proposition, like a magnet, has two poles, a true one and a false one. It is true if things are as it says they are, false if they are not. The starting-point of this idea is Frege's view that names and propositions alike have 'sense' and 'meaning', the meaning of a proposition being one or the other of two 'logical objects', the True and the False. Initially, Wittgenstein followed Frege in claiming that propositions have a MEANING, that is, stand for something, just as names do. But he maintained that this meaning is not a truth-value, but the FACT which corresponds to the proposition in reality. The 'meaning' of 'p' is identical with that of '$\sim p$', since the fact that makes it true that p is the same fact that makes it false that $\sim p$, and vice versa. But the negation-sign reverses the *sense* of the proposition: capitalizing on the ambiguity of the German *Sinn* (sense or direction), one can say that if it is a fact that p, then the true pole of p points towards reality, and so does the false pole of '$\sim p$'. What 'p' depicts is precisely what '$\sim p$' depicts, only the latter says that this is *not* how things stand.

Bipolarity marks a fundamental contrast between NAMES, which stand for things, and PROPOSITIONS, which depict a possible state of affairs and can be negated. This led the *Tractatus* to claim that only propositions have a sense and only names a meaning. In order to understand a name one must know its referent, but in order to understand a proposition one need not know whether it is true or false. What we understand in the case of a proposition is its 'sense', that is, both what would be the case if it were true and what would be the case if it were false. Consequently, the proposition is internally related to its negation, somewhat as

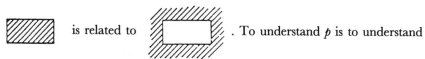

To understand p is to understand its negation (NL 97, 101; NB 14.11.14; TLP 3.144, 3.221).

The idea that it is essential for propositions to be bipolar contrasts with Frege and Russell, and not just because they treated propositions as names (of truth-values and complexes respectively). Frege went wrong, not only in treating truth and falsity as objects which are named by some propositions, namely those which do not suffer from truth-value gaps, but in ignoring that a proposition is essentially connected with *both* truth-values. For him, there is no closer connection between a true proposition and the False than between that proposition and any other object (e.g., the number 7). To be sure, that p is true entails that $\sim p$ is false; but Frege fails to realize that it is no coincidence that negation operates in this way, but something which arises from the very nature of the proposition p itself. Russell was closer to the *Tractatus* in that he insisted on bivalence, and treated truth and falsity as properties rather than objects. But he gave the impression that it is a contingent fact that all propositions possess one of these properties. By contrast, Wittgenstein insisted on bipolarity rather than bivalence, and treated this as an essential condition of a proposition's ability to represent reality (NL 104; TLP 6.111–6.126, 6.21f.).

According to the principle of bipolarity, a propositional sign (*Satzzeichen*) only has a sense if it determines a possibility which the world either satisfies or not. This has the astonishing consequence that logic, mathematics and metaphysics do not consist of propositions. There can be no propositions which are logically necessary, since they could not possibly be false, and there would be no gap between understanding their sense and recognizing their truth (cp. TLP 3.04f., 4.024). The truths of logic are TAUTOLOGIES, limiting cases of meaningful empirical propositions, namely propositions with zero sense. Metaphysical propositions are nonsensical. At best, they try to say what can only be shown, the form of bipolar propositions. MATHEMATICAL propositions are 'pseudo-propositions', they do not depict anything, but are rules which license inferences between empirical propositions. The TRUTH-TABLE presentation of propositions provides an ideal notation which makes perspicuous the logical structure of all languages, because it shows that propositions have essentially two poles (T and F). It also shows how the necessary propositions of logic flow from this essential bipolarity, by displaying how in certain combinations the truth/falsity of elementary propositions cancels out. This shows something about the structure of the world, namely that it consists of mutually independent states of affairs (TLP 4.121, 6.12, 6.124; NM 108–11).

The logical positivists seized on bipolarity, and the ensuing treatment of logical necessity, in order to exclude synthetic a priori truths. But Wittgenstein himself later rejected the principle of bipolarity as part of a 'mythology of symbolism' (PG 56; Z §211). In the *Tractatus*, propositions must be bipolar because they depict states of affairs which either obtain or fail to obtain. However, that facts either obtain or fail to obtain is not a metaphysical feature of reality, but merely part of what we call a fact or state of affairs. Equally, TRUTH and falsehood belong to our concept of propositions, but this is no metaphysical revelation, it merely means that we call propositions what we also call either true or false (FW 55; PI §§136–7). Propositions are indeed typically bipolar in that their truth excludes a possibility. But the concept of a proposition is a FAMILY-RESEMBLANCE concept. There is no warrant for restricting the concept to descriptions of possible states of affairs. Indeed, not even all empirical propositions are straightforwardly bipolar – the *Weltbild* propositions of *On Certainty* could not simply turn out to be false (*see* CERTAINTY).

'The negation of nonsense is nonsense' (RAL 2.7.27). Wittgenstein later relaxed this bipolar conception of NONSENSE by allowing that at least some negations of nonsense, like 'Nothing can be red and green all over', are GRAMMATICAL propositions. But the dogmatic principle soldiers on in some parts of his later work: the claim that I cannot know that I am in pain, because I could not be wrong, rests partly on the assumption that there is no knowledge without the possibility of ignorance or error, and the suggestion that 'I' is not a referring expression on the assumption that referring presupposes the possibility of referential failure. However, in these arguments Wittgenstein also pursues a more promising line. Rather than insist dogmatically that the negation of a nonsense must itself be a nonsense, he points out the *difference* between such propositions and propositions which express a cognitive claim because they exclude possibilities that can be described intelligibly, such as 'Nothing can be fatty and healthy' (*see* I/SELF; PRIVACY).

C

calculus model Between 1929 and 1933, Wittgenstein compared speaking a language to operating a logical or mathematical calculus (PR ch. XX; BT 25, 142; PG 57, 63). The analogy serves different purposes.

(a) In speaking a language we operate, in thought, a complex system of exact rules. The propositions of ordinary language can be definitely analysed into elements of such a calculus (RLF; LWL 117).

(b) The meaning of a word is its place in the symbolism, it is determined by rules which lay down its correct USE. Equally, to understand a sentence is to see it as part of a system without which it would be dead. 'The role of a sentence in the calculus is its sense' (PG 130, see 59, 172; LWL 28, 37; BB 5, 42).

(c) Grammar is not a causal mechanism. The rules of a calculus specify not what the probable result of employing a word will be, but what sort of operation has been performed (PG 70).

(d) Speaking a language is an activity (PG 193; WVC 171–2), just as a calculus is something we operate.

It has been maintained that Wittgenstein never abandoned the calculus model. What is correct is that his later remarks continue to recycle material from the early thirties which compares language with a calculus in order to bring out points (b)–(c) (e.g. PI 14n, §§559, 565; MS130 214). But these points are also expressed in the comparison of language with a game, in particular that of chess. Although the term 'LANGUAGE-GAME' is first used as equivalent to 'calculus' (PG 67), the fact that it replaced the latter by the time of the *Blue* and *Brown Books* indicates a shift in Wittgenstein's conception of language. What remains is the idea that language is an activity governed by rules. What alters is Wittgenstein's conception of these rules: the rules of GRAMMAR resemble those of a game like hide-and-seek more than they do those of formal calculi. Finally, *Philosophical Investigations* explains the calculus model as the view that 'if anyone utters a sentence and *means* or *understands* it he is operating a calculus according to definite rules' (PI §81). Wittgenstein states two things about this view, that he previously held it and that it is mistaken.

Sometimes the calculus model is presented as the conception of language which Wittgenstein held between the idea of logical syntax and that of grammar. The analogy only emerges in the transition period, but the idea of a language with precise rules goes back to Leibniz's plan for a *characteristica universalis*. It was given a boost by Frege's and Russell's development of logical calculi governed by a definite list of formation and transformation rules. In their case the model was held to apply only to an 'ideal language'. By contrast, the *Investigations*' characterization fits de Saussure's conception of *langue* as an abstract system of rules which underlies *parole*, the use of ordinary language on particular occasions, and the *Tractatus*'s account of LOGICAL SYNTAX as a system of rules for the meaningful combination of signs which governs *all* symbolisms, including natural languages. These rules

> are comprehensive and definite (TLP 5.4541): for any possible combination of signs, they determine unequivocally whether or not that combination makes sense, and, if so, what sense it makes, this sense being itself 'determinate', namely a specific configuration of objects which must obtain for the proposition to be true (TLP 3.23f.; *see* MEANING);
> constitute a highly complex system which is concealed by the school-grammatical surface of language, and has to be discovered by LOGICAL ANALYSIS;
> govern human speech, although its speakers are not aware of them: 'Human beings have the ability to construct languages capable of expressing every sense, without having any idea how each word has meaning or what its meaning is – just as people speak without knowing how the individual sounds are produced' (TLP 4.002, see 5.5562; RLF 171).

The *Tractatus* is committed to the view that speaking a language is operating a calculus of hidden rules. After his return to philosophy, Wittgenstein claimed that this calculus does not reflect the essential nature of reality, but is AUTONOMOUS. He also realized that ELEMENTARY PROPOSITIONS cannot be logically independent. Propositions are compared with reality not individually, like pictures, but in groups, like the graduating marks of a ruler. Establishing that *x* is 3 m long *ipso facto* establishes that it is not 5 m long. Equally, seeing that a point in the visual field is red implies *ipso facto* that it is neither blue nor yellow nor green, etc. He concluded that propositions form 'proposition systems' (*Satzsysteme*), that is, sets of propositions such that their members exclude each other not because of their truth-functional complexity but because of the concept-words occurring in them (WVC 63–4, 78–89; PR ch. VIII; cp. TLP 2.15121). These systems of mutual exclusion are at the same time LOGICAL SPACES of possibilities: 'black' is another mark on the same ruler as 'red', but '5 m long' is not; the visual point could be black, yet it could not be 5 m long (PR 75–7).

Accordingly, logical syntax is even more complicated than previously thought, which prompted Russell's complaint that *Philosophical Remarks* would make 'mathematics and logic almost incredibly difficult'. By the same token, analysis makes even more startling discoveries – for example, that all propositions contain expressions for real numbers. Appearances notwithstanding, natural languages are logico-syntactical systems. They consist of formation and transformation rules and assignments of meanings to the indefinables (which correspond to the 'axioms' of logical systems). These jointly determine the sense of every well-formed sentence. Together with the appropriate facts they also determine their truth-values unequivocally.

Wittgenstein quickly realized that the idea of proposition systems has only a narrow range of application, namely to determinates (5 m long, red) of a determinable (length, colour); and even there it ignores the fact that not all determinates of a determinable share the same combinatorial possibilities (*see* COLOUR). Gradually, he also came to attack the picture of language as a system of precise and rigid rules. For one thing, linguistic rules are not DETERMINATE in the sense of Frege and the *Tractatus*. They allow for borderline cases, and do not invariably dictate for every conceivable circumstance whether or not a combination of signs is NONSENSICAL. The same holds for games: there are no rules for how high one throws the ball before serving, yet this does not mean that tennis cannot be played (PI §§68, 83; OC §139). Indeed, the idea of an activity which is bounded by inexorable rules in all of its aspects is absurd, since there are indefinitely many such aspects. Moreover, for any game there are countless bizarre possibilities which cannot be budgeted for in advance. The rules of tennis are none the worse for failure to specify what happens if the ball is caught by a pelican flying by (PI §§80, 84–7; Z §440; PLP 76–80).

This insight transforms the *Tractatus*'s insistence that 'all the propositions of our everyday language, just as they stand, are in perfect logical order' (TLP 5.5563). Ramsey had condemned this as a piece of 'scholasticism'. Wittgenstein concurred by referring approvingly to Ramsey's remark that 'logic is a normative science' (*Mathematics* 269; PI §81). This reference emphasizes the contrast between the clear, strict rules of logical calculi and the fluctuating and vague rules of ordinary language (BT 248). It does not acknowledge that ordinary language should, if possible, approach formal calculi, as ideal-language philosophers like Frege, Russell and Carnap would have it; Wittgenstein continues to reject the idea that ordinary language is logically inferior to the formal languages of logic. Instead, it means that we must not project the 'crystalline purity' of formal calculi onto ordinary language by dogmatically insisting that complete order is hidden beneath a disorderly surface (PI §§98–108). Formal calculi do not reveal the 'depth-grammar' of language. Their only legitimate philosophical role is as objects of comparison (PI §131; BB 28; MS116 80–2). They help us to achieve an OVERVIEW of our grammar by way of similarity and contrast.

The most important element of truth in the calculus model concerns points (c) and (d) above. Wittgenstein insists that a 'rule doesn't act at a distance. It acts only by being applied' (BB 13–14; PG 80–1). When I *follow* a rule by Φing, rather than merely act *in accordance with* a rule, the rule is part of my reason for acting as I do (*see* RULE-FOLLOWING). This means that rules must somehow be involved in the process of explaining, justifying, applying and understanding. For they have their normative status only in virtue of being used as standards of correctness by us. Rules do not exist independently of the use speakers make of rule-formulations, their 'esse est applicari'. In order to bring out this point Wittgenstein clarified rule-following by reference to calculations in which the rule plays a visible part, such as consulting rule-books or calculating according to a schema (WVC 168–71; PG 99–101; PLP 124–8).

At the same time, Wittgenstein had to acknowledge that most instances of rule-following, including calculations, do not involve (overt or mental) consultation of rule-formulations, just as competent chess-players rarely consult the rules (WVC 153–4; LWL 48, 83, 101; PG 85–6, 153; PI §§54, 82–3; RFM 414–22; PLP 129–35). A possible reaction is to insist that in such cases the agent *would* explain or justify his Φing by reference to the rule-formulation (PI §§82–3). Rules have potential actuality. However, Wittgenstein came to realize that even this does not hold inevitably. 'For not only do we not think of the rules of usage ... while using language, but when we are asked to give such rules, in most cases we aren't able to do so. We are unable clearly to circumscribe the concepts we use; not because we don't know their real definition, but because there is no real "definition" to them'. He concluded that regarding it as guided by definite or explicit rules is a 'one-sided way of looking at language' (BB 25; PG 68).

This gradual abandonment of the calculus model creates various tensions in Wittgenstein's mature work. For one thing, why should one adopt this one-sided perspective of cataloguing grammatical rules? Some passages suggest that PHILOSOPHY sometimes 'makes up' or 'lays down' definite rules where there are none, or accentuates aspects of linguistic use, namely for the purpose of counteracting specific distortions of the concepts concerned (AWL 47–8; BT 416; Z §467; RPP I §§51–2). Others insist that any filling in of conceptual contours is itself a distortion (RPP I §§257, 648).

Moreover, even at a time when he was still comparing language to a calculus, Wittgenstein castigated as 'hellish' Moore's idea that only logical analysis shows us what, if anything, we mean by our propositions (WVC 129–30). More generally, he rejected the idea which united Frege, Russell and the *Tractatus*, that analysis can make 'deep' or 'unheard of' *discoveries*; there are, he insisted, no surprises in grammar (WVC 77; LWL 16–17; BT 418–19, 435–6; PG 114–15, 210; MS109 212; MS116 80–2). 'What is hidden, is of no interest to us' (PI §§126–8). This is justified if grammatical rules are evident in the explanations speakers *would* give when asked. However, that fails to be the case, not just for the FAMILY-RESEMBLANCE concepts at issue in *Blue and Brown Books* 25, but also, for example, for the difference between 'almost' and 'nearly', the use of the definite article or of the subjunctive, and the sequence of tenses in conditionals. Wittgenstein would accept examples as adequate EXPLANATIONS. But in these cases, even they may not be forthcoming. Consequently, in so far as language is governed by GRAMMATICAL rules, these are not simply open to view, but need to be made explicit (in line with Ryle's distinction between 'knowing how' and 'knowing that'). Wittgenstein is right that this is not a matter of gathering new information – as competent speakers we have all the information we need. But it is a matter of elicitation and reflection, and may involve trial and error.

Ironically, questioning one side of the calculus model, the idea that we constantly consult rule-formulations, leads one to another, the idea of discoveries. But Wittgenstein's attack retains critical potency against positions which combine both ideas. This holds of Wittgenstein's own early position, and for some contemporary theories of meaning for natural languages in philosophy (Davidson, Dummett) and linguistics (Chomsky). These theories are committed to the view that we have tacit knowledge of a complex system of formation and derivation rules which is hidden below the surface of language as presented by school-grammar. Meaning and understanding a word consist in operating this calculus; but since we are not aware of such calculations, they must be subconscious, and occur at high speed.

Against this, Wittgenstein shows that UNDERSTANDING does not require any such calculations. The causes of my speaking and understanding include high-speed neural processes unknown to me, but this does not hold of my *reasons* for applying or understanding words in a certain way. Although the rules reconstructed by philosophical grammar may not play a role in our practice of applying and even explaining words, it is assumed that speakers are capable of recognizing certain formulations as expressions of the rules they are following. What is important is that they should recognize these formulations not just as accurate descriptions of patterns of linguistic behaviour, but also as expressing standards by which they distinguish correct and incorrect employments of words. For example, speakers who may be incapable of explaining the terms 'automatically' and 'inadvertently' will recognize that a certain form of behaviour can satisfy the latter term without satisfying the former.

Even this potentiality is absent in the case of the rules invoked by theories of meaning. Indeed, the arcane apparatus of the latter is unintelligible to many competent speakers. The inference from 'She kissed him in the garden' to 'She kissed him' is recognized by people who are incapable of even learning the quantificational rules through which theories of meaning explain its validity. This means that such rules are in no sense standards of

71

the correct use of our words (RFM 414–22; MS129 79). The line between rule-following and acting in accordance with a rule has been blurred.

Wittgenstein is right to insist that rules cannot be hidden in the sense that we are denied access to them, or transcendent, incapable of playing a role in our practice. However, he fails to show that we cannot make discoveries of some kind. Instead, he makes out a case for thinking that these will reveal language to be structured not by logical calculi, but by the diverse and complex patterns and subtle nuances highlighted by ordinary language philosophy.

causation Wittgenstein's early account of causation has both a negative and a positive side. Negatively, he follows Hume in rejecting the idea of causal necessity. There is only one kind of necessity, namely logical necessity; 'outside logic everything is accidental.' This means that there is 'no causal nexus' to justify an inference from the existence of one situation (*Sachlage*) to that of another. Hence, too, there is no 'compulsion' that one thing should happen because another has happened, and we cannot *know* future events (TLP 5.135–5.1362, 6.3, 6.36311–6.372; PT 5.0442f.; NB 15.10.16; *see* INDUCTION). Positively, Wittgenstein explains the role of causation in SCIENCE through a Neo-Kantian account of natural or causal laws. Like other so-called 'fundamental' laws of science, the 'law of causality', according to which every event has a cause, is not a law, but 'the form of a law'. This means that it is neither a law of logic, nor an empirical generalization, nor a synthetic a priori proposition (*see* INDUCTION). Indeed, it is not a proposition at all, since it tries to say what can only be shown. What it indicates is a certain 'form of description' which is crucial to scientific theorizing (TLP 6.321f.). Descriptions which connect events in a non-lawlike manner are excluded from science. To characterize something as an event is to imply that it is explicable by reference to *some* (often unknown) causal law. Causation itself is a formal concept. It characterizes not reality, but the 'network' of an optional FORM OF REPRESENTING reality, such as Newtonian mechanics (TLP 6.33–6.341, 6.36f., 6.362).

Wittgenstein's later thoughts on causation, assembled mainly in 'Cause and Effect: Intuitive Awareness' (see also LC 13–15; BT 406–7), move away from the empiricism of the negative account, while developing the conventionalist themes of the positive account. He continues to hold the Humean view that causal relations are external, that is, obtain between logically independent events (see PI §220; Z §296), and to elucidate causation by reference to causal explanations. But he now focuses on the way we establish causal connections in everyday life, and the results challenge crucial aspects of the Humean position.

Firstly, he rejects a uniform nomological account of causation. There is an irreducible variety of 'prototypes' of causal connections: (a) impact (collision of billiard balls); (b) traction (pulling a string); (c) mechanisms like clocks, which combine (a) and (b); (d) human reactions to sensations or emotions (being hit on the head or frightened by someone's facial expression); (e) statements which are based on observing regular successions of events. Since Wittgenstein stresses both the variety of cases and the fact that we use the same word, he arguably regards 'cause' as a FAMILY-RESEMBLANCE concept. He denies not only that the Humean paradigm (e) is the only prototype of causation, but also that it is the fundamental one. The 'cause-effect language-game' of everyday life is rooted not in observation or experimentation, but in a practice, which in turn is based on certain primitive reactions. For example, we react to a painful blow by pointing to someone and saying 'He did it' (CE 409–10, 416–17, 420, 433).

Secondly, according to Hume we can never directly observe a causal connection, but only a succession of events; consequently our causal statements must be based on observing a regular sequence of parallel events and are always provisional, subject to refutation by subsequent observations. Wittgenstein follows Russell in holding that there are causal relations which we know immediately, while rejecting the idea that this is based on intuition (CE 409, 431; LC 22). Recognizing the most basic forms of causation, especially those involving direct physical contact, (a)–(d), does not depend on observing constant regularities or on experiments; we directly observe one thing acting upon another, and know the cause immediately, though not infallibly. Both immediate and non-immediate connections are paradigmatic cases of what we call a causal nexus, and constitutive of the idea of causation. While rejecting Hume's empiricism, Wittgenstein makes the claim that the principle of causality, 'Every event must have a cause', is not a synthetic a priori truth, as Kant thought, but a disguised rule of GRAMMAR (AWL 16). If this means that our grammar simply rules out as nonsensical the expression 'uncaused event', it is wrong. But one might argue that it is a norm of representation of classical mechanics that it always makes sense to *look* for the cause of an event, even if no plausible candidate is in sight.

Wittgenstein also challenges a more general dogma which unites empiricists and rationalists, namely that all causes must be necessitating: whenever an effect occurs in one case but not in an apparently similar case, there must be relevant further differences. Wittgenstein, by contrast, denies that in the case of two apparently identical plant seeds which produce different kinds of plants there *must* be a difference in the seeds underlying these different dispositions. The insistence that there must, is not based on an insight into the actual nature of things, but amounts to adhering to a norm of representation – instead, we could treat the *origin* of the seeds, irrespective of their physical structure, not just as the basis for a prediction ('Seeds from a type-A plant will produce type-A plants'), but also as a genuine explanation, that is, add '... *because* they are from type-A plants'. He even suggests that it would be better to adopt such a norm in place of our current one (Z §§608–10; CE 410–11, 433–4).

One might concede that there is nothing unintelligible in supposing that there is no structural difference between the seeds, but insist that looking for such a difference come what may is a Kantian regulative principle, which is constitutive of scientific investigation and perhaps of rational thought. Here it is important to separate several issues. Wittgenstein is right to reject the idea that all dispositional qualities must be explicable in terms of structural properties of the objects manifesting them. For this could not apply to the ultimate constituents of matter, which, by definition, have no components and hence no structural properties. Wittgenstein is also right in claiming that the idea of necessitating causes is an optional norm of representation. Indeed, there are areas of science that operate with non-necessitating causes, notably quantum-mechanics. However, as Wittgenstein himself acknowledges, his treatment of the seed example upsets our conceptions of causality, since it urges us to accept explanations by reference not just to non-necessitating causes, but also to phenomenal properties (concerning the origin of the seeds). Accepting such explanations is on a par with accepting astrological explanations backed by statistical evidence. It amounts to abandoning a norm of representation – 'Causal explanations must ultimately be structural, not phenomenal' – which may not be justifiable by reference to an 'essence of reality' (*see* AUTONOMY OF LANGUAGE), but which has been definitive of scientific explanation since the seventeenth century.

Wittgenstein's idea of non-necessitating causes has been taken up by Anscombe. The claim that there is an irreducible variety of types of causation and that the notion of a cause is rooted in action rather than observation is reminiscent of Collingwood's idea of a cause as a 'lever', a condition under the control of human agents by means of which they can bring about or prevent certain other conditions. Von Wright has defended the stronger claim, suggested by Wittgenstein, that the interventionist notion of 'cause' is not only genetically but also logically prior to the one based on observation, since it alone affords the means of distinguishing between mere concomitance and a genuine causal connection.

A central feature of Wittgenstein's later reflections is that causal explanation is only one way of answering the question 'Why?', and that reasons must be distinguished from causes. He blames the ubiquitous temptation of assimilating the two on the fact that reasons, like Humean causes, are general, and on the impression that in the first-person case we are aware of our reasons as causes 'seen from the inside' (BB 15; see PG 228; PI §378; PLP 119–22). He makes a few points to distinguish the reasons for believing that p or for Φing from the causes, often in the context of criticizing Freud's view of psychoanalytic explanations as causal (though unfortunately without developing them at any length).

(a) The concept of a reason is that of a step in reasoning, which is a transition from one assertion or thought to another: 'Giving a reason is like giving a calculation by which you have arrived at a certain result' (BB 14–15; RFM 39; AWL 4–5; LC 21–2; PI §§489–90). This need not mean that I actually passed through a certain process, but includes justifications *ex post actu*, which invoke steps I could have taken. The difference between asking for the cause and asking for the reason is like that between asking 'What mechanism has taken you from A to B?' and asking 'By what route did you come from A to B?' Reasons, unlike causes, play a justificatory role. Moreover, in some cases the relationship between a reason and what it is a reason for is INTERNAL, that is, (partly) constitutive of the relata, like the relationship between the premises and the conclusion of a LOGICAL INFERENCE (deductive argument), or between a rule and its correct application (*see* RULE-FOLLOWING).

(b) We must typically *know* our reasons, and the criterion for what a person's reasons are is what that person sincerely avows them to be. (The Freudian conception of 'unconscious reasons' modifies the concept of a reason, but still insists that ascribing unconscious reasons is subject to the patient's consent.) Unlike causes, reasons for one's behaviour are not discovered by one on the basis of evidence (AWL 5, 28, 37–40; BB 57–8; LC 18, 23–5; PG 101; PI §§475, 487–8; LPP 23).

(c) While chains of causes go on indefinitely, reasons come to an end. Even where there are chains of reasons, these peter out. But this does not open the door to SCEPTICISM; it is part and parcel of the concept of justification (BB 14; PI §§217, 485).

Wittgenstein's distinction between reasons and causes is at odds with a causal conception of the mind, according to which mental phenomena are the inner causes of outward behaviour. Part of this picture is a causal conception of intentional action, for which human behaviour is explained by reference to efficient causes – acts or events which take place either in a private mental realm (the soul) or, more plausibly, in the brain. Wittgenstein, by contrast, holds that intentional behaviour is explained teleologically, by reference to an agent's reasons (beliefs, intentions, wants). Unlike efficient causes, reasons do not necessitate action: if the agent could do no other he would not act intentionally. This view stands in the tradition of the hermeneutical distinction between the explanation (*Erklären*) of the natural sciences and the understanding (*Verstehen*) of the social sciences. It was developed by Anscombe, who, unlike Wittgenstein, claimed explicitly that the link between an action and the reason for action is always internal, and hence not causal; and by Winch, who linked it to the methodology of the social sciences. Their position has been forcefully criticized by Davidson. Starting out from the Wittgensteinian idea that logical relations are *de dicto*, that is, due to the way we describe things, he argues that reason and action may be logically related under some descriptions, but not others, which leaves open the possibility that, besides being linked internally, they are events related by causal laws. Moreover, what else could explain the difference between something's being *a* reason for an action, and something's being *the* reason why it was performed, if not that only the latter was causally efficacious in bringing about the action? Davidson concludes that although we explain action by reference to reasons (beliefs and desires) these are causes and are identical with neurophysiological phenomena. According to Wittgenstein, on the other hand, the correlation between mental and neurophysiological phenomena is merely contingent; it is not logically necessary that the mental life has causal roots (*see* INNER/OUTER). He also denied that beliefs and desires are mental states with genuine duration, which implies that they cannot be identical with neural states (*see* PHILOSOPHICAL PSYCHOLOGY).

Wittgenstein intimates a way of resisting Davidson's 'what else?' argument (PI §487; AWL 5; LC 22–3). We distinguish *the* reason for Φing from other reasons by reference not to the presence of a causal connection, but to the context of the action, notably to what reasons have previously weighed with the agent in similar circumstances. Indeed, there need not be a pre-established connection between the action and the reason. Often it is only the agent's sincere avowal which determines why he did it, although sometimes the context provides grounds for rejecting such avowals as based on self-deception (contextualist elements are also central to Wittgenstein's attacks on causal conceptions of the WILL). However, even if correct, this argument does not rule out that *some* mental concepts are causal. When I say that I clenched my teeth because of the stabbing pain in my neck, I do not give reasons for the clenching, I give a causal explanation.

certainty Many of Wittgenstein's discussions have implications for epistemology. But it was only during the last year and a half of his life that he tackled the topic in a direct and sustained way. The resulting notes have been published as *On Certainty*. They were never polished or revised, let alone completed, and hence contain numerous hesitations, occasional inconsistencies and much inconclusiveness. But they also possess a thematic unity absent from most of Wittgenstein's later work.

On Certainty's inspiration was Moore's defence of common sense. Moore maintained that there are empirical truths which one can know with certainty, for example, that one is a human being, that the object one is pointing to is one's hand, and that the earth has existed for many years. Moore thought that these 'common sense' propositions are founded on evidence, although we often cannot tell what it is, and that they entail that there is a mind-independent world, and thereby refute scepticism. Wittgenstein thought that Moore had drawn attention to an important class of propositions. He granted that one can be *certain* of these truisms, but denied that one *knows* them. He granted that 'I know that p' where p is a Moore-type proposition can have an everyday use in exceptional circumstances (OC §§23, 252–62, 347–50, 387, 412, 423, 433, 526, 596, 622; *Writings* chs 3, 9–10). But this is not Moore's point, since it does not provide a reply to scepticism. Moore's use ignores that in 'normal linguistic exchange' (OC §260, see §§58, 243; PI II 221) we reserve 'I know' for cases in which

(a)   it also makes sense to speak of believing or making certain;
(b)   there is an answer to the question 'How do you know?';
(c)   one is prepared to give compelling reasons for one's claim.

Requirement (b) does not mean that we must actually be able to answer the question, only that there is an answer in principle. Nor does it commit Wittgenstein to the view that all knowledge rests on evidence. The question 'How do you know?' can equally be answered by specifying the perceptual faculty through which one has informed oneself of something. Wittgenstein occasionally suggests that we can talk of knowledge only where, (i) there is a logical possibility of being mistaken or ignorant, and (ii) that possibility has been ruled out by the application of 'clear rules of evidence'. But he also states that 'I know how it is = I *can* say how it is, and it is as I say it is', which implies that I *can* know in the absence of these conditions (LW II 49, 58; OC §§243, 250, 483–4, 564, 574–6).

Another of Wittgenstein's points is that Moore's assurance that he knows that he has two hands does not ensure that he does know, for while avowals, like 'I believe' or 'I am certain', guarantee belief or certainty, 'I know' as an expression of a conviction of knowledge does not guarantee knowledge, only that one thinks one knows (LW II 89; OC §§12–15, 21, 137, 180, 489). The certainty involved here is what Wittgenstein calls 'subjective certainty', a feeling of unshakable conviction. But he also suggests that objective certainty, which is not a mental state, but signifies the inconceivability of doubt or of one's being mistaken, belongs to a different category from knowledge (OC §§54–6, 193–4, 308; LW II 88). Wittgenstein does not substantiate this claim, but may nevertheless have a point against Moore. The use of 'I know' outside its normal context invites the sceptical question of how this has been settled. Moore seems to make a 'presumptuous' and 'unconditional' claim, that nothing could prove him to be wrong. But 'I know' seems not to tolerate such a 'metaphysical emphasis' (OC §§21, 251, 425, 481–2, 553–4). Like Austin, Wittgenstein suggests that empirical knowledge claims are defeasible: even if they are well justified, there can be no metaphysical guarantee against their turning out to be wrong.

On the other hand, this does not license scepticism. Doubt requires grounds. But the mere imaginability of not-p is no ground for doubting that p (OC §§4, 122, 323, 458, 519). This is obvious if imaginability signifies the logical possibility of not-p, which obtains by definition for contingent propositions. But the Cartesian sceptic will claim that our being deceived by a malignant demon is an *epistemic* possibility, that is, consistent with what we know. But that suggestion in turn requires a rationale, and the only rationale for the malignant demon hypothesis is its logical possibility. The Cartesian sceptic validly infers from the possibility that I shall turn out to be wrong the possibility that I do not know. But he is wrong to infer from the latter that I do not know ($\Diamond \sim p \supset \Diamond \sim Kap$ but not $\Diamond \sim Kap \supset \sim Kap$). In cases in which my well-supported claim turns out to be right, I *did* know. The possibility of 'I thought I knew' does not count against the possibility of 'I know' (OC §12).

Wittgenstein sometimes concedes Moore's use of 'I know' and concentrates on the crucial point, namely the contrast between these uses and ordinary empirical knowledge claims (OC §§288, 397, 520, 552). Moore's propositions play a 'peculiar logical role in the system of our empirical propositions'. They constitute the 'scaffolding' of our thoughts, the 'foundations' of our language-games, the 'hinges' on which our questions and doubts turn, our 'world-picture', 'the inherited background against which [we] distinguish between true and false' (OC §§94–5, 136, 211, 308, 341–3, 401–3, 614, 655). Hinge propositions are empirical in that their negation makes sense. But the possibility of their being false is restricted by the fact that our whole system of beliefs depends on our ready acceptance of them. Doubt concerning them is infectious, and does not fit with anything else we believe.

Among the world-picture or hinge propositions listed by Moore and Wittgenstein one can distinguish four types (OC §§4, 118, 207, 281–4, 291–3, 327, 555–8, 567, 599, 618). The first are trans-historical: they stand fast for any sane person – for example, 'The earth has existed for a long time' and 'Cats don't grow on trees.' The second change with time: they were originally discovered and supported by evidence, but, once established, occupy a pivotal role in relation to others, such as that there is a brain in the human skull or that water boils at 100° C. In addition to these impersonal hinge propositions there are two types of personal cases: generally applicable propositions about which each person is certain for himself, such as 'I have two hands' and 'My name is N.N.'; and person-specific propositions which are part of my subjective world-picture, for example that I have spent most of my life in Germany.

Wittgenstein makes a variety of claims about hinge propositions. (a) They are (*mutatis mutandis* in the last case) certain not just for individuals, but for everybody, unlike for example the claim that in a certain part of England there is a village called so-and-so (OC §§100–3, 462).

(b) I might, in special circumstances, be wrong about hinge propositions, but that would mean that I am deranged rather than merely mistaken. Politicians on a campaign tour are often mistaken about where they are, but if they did not know where they usually live, that would be an aberration. I might be confused about my own name, but if this happened to a majority, the language-game with proper names could not be played (OC §§71–5, 156, 303–5, 579, 628).

(c) Hinge propositions of the trans-historical kind are not based on investigation and are not supported by evidence (OC §§103, 138), because there are no more fundamental propositions on the basis of which they could be believed. There is evidence for these propositions in the sense that they could be defended by offering certain considerations. But these are not my reasons for holding the belief, because they are not better known to me than the conclusion, although they might do that for people with a different set of beliefs. We have geological and evolutionary evidence, for example, for

(1)   The world has existed for a billion years

but not for

(2)   The world has existed for a hundred years.

Although (1) entails (2), it does not support it. For the evidence in its favour presupposes (2): although it is not directly derived from it, that evidence, along with the whole discourse of geological evidence, would collapse without (2).

(d) Wittgenstein also suggests that the sense of hinge propositions like (2) is less clear than that of empirical propositions like (1) because it is unclear with 'what ideas and observations' they belong (PI II 221–2). However, unlike 'I know that I am in pain', to which he links it (2), many hinge propositions exemplify Gricean conversational implicatures, since their negation is not nonsensical. Although in normal conditions hinge propositions are too obvious to be informative, and are not held by us on the basis of evidence, their conventional sense specifies what evidence we could use. A king who believed that the world started with him would have to be *converted* to our world-view (OC §§92, 422), but it is clear what we would use to effect the conversion (photographs, written testimony, etc.).

(e) By far Wittgenstein's most important claim about hinge propositions is that they can be neither justified nor doubted, since their certainty is presupposed in all judging (OC §§308, 494, 614). One of his points is that doubt cannot stand at the beginning of the LANGUAGE-GAME. If a child were immediately to doubt what it is taught, it could not learn certain language-games. But the point is not just either genetic or pragmatic – due to our human condition we must begin with non-doubting. The suspicious pupil is not displaying admirable caution, but simply fails to participate in our epistemic practice, and hence to raise a genuine doubt. Doubt only makes sense within a language-game. By extending doubt to the hinges on which the language-game turns, the SCEPTIC is sawing off the branch on which he is sitting. Doubt presupposes not only the possibility of certainty, but that many things *are* certain. Our language-games can only be played against a relatively permanent backdrop of certainties (OC §§115, 150, 283, 472-7).

One line of argument here is holistic: we must hold certain things certain in order to question others. This leaves open the possibility that individual hinge propositions should turn out to be wrong. Indeed, commentators have felt that Wittgenstein's inclusion of 'I know that I have never been to the moon' (OC §§106-11, 286, 662-7) shows that he overestimated how central hinge propositions are to our web of beliefs. But as we have seen, Wittgenstein acknowledges that some hinge propositions may loose their status. Moreover, to suppose now that Wittgenstein in 1951 might have been to the moon is not the same as for Wittgenstein in 1951 to suppose that he had been there. The latter raises unmanageable questions about how he should have escaped the earth's gravitational field, etc.

Whether the revision of a hinge proposition will lead to a collapse of our web of beliefs partly depends on whether we are dealing with a *change* of natural processes, or a *discovery*. Certain scientific discoveries would not prevent us from engaging in most of our language-games, but would merely change the discipline concerned. But what 'if something *really unheard-of* happened', for example, that now cows stood on their heads and laughed and spoke (OC §§512-18)? Wittgenstein intimates (with Austin) that this would not so much show that I did not know that this is a cow as show that what used to be a cow has changed into something else. Unheard-of events do not so much falsify our claims as lead to a breakdown of our concepts. In some cases this change would be restricted to particular concepts. But if natural regularity broke down, our practice of making knowledge claims might lose its applicability altogether.

Wittgenstein grants the possibility of unheard-of events, or of my suddenly being contradicted from all sides. Some have detected in this a kind of meta-scepticism. This seems borne out by Wittgenstein's idea that we cannot know the truth of hinge propositions, or at any rate would have to qualify any claim to such knowledge by 'so far as one can know these things', and by his claim that it 'is always by favour of Nature that one knows something' (OC §§420, 503-5, 623). But his point is merely that it is a contingent fact that nature is such that we can operate with certain concepts like knowledge. He even leaves open whether we could continue our language-games even if these FRAMEWORK conditions changed (OC §§516, 619). The mere logical possibility of unheard-of events does not license Humean *Angst* that chaos might break out at any moment, since unheard-of events are excluded by natural necessity (although at the ultimate, micro-physical level what is naturally necessary is a matter of brute fact – *see* CAUSATION).

Wittgenstein occasionally spoke of hinge propositions as providing the foundations of our rational thought (OC §§162–7, 401–2). But these foundations do not serve as a basis for other beliefs in the sense in which axioms underpin theorems. We don't deduce other truths from them, but rely on them as a 'background' for our rational arguing. The 'foundation-walls are carried by the whole house', that is, they owe their special status to the fact that they underlie the linguistic institution of argument (OC §§246–8, see §§94, 153, 204). Indeed, the ultimate foundations of our knowledge are not beliefs, but forms of behaviour.

According to Wittgenstein, the certainty of a belief consists in its role within our framework of beliefs. A belief is certain if it can be appealed to in order to justify other beliefs but does not itself stand in need of justification. Descartes would protest that this does not answer the sceptic, since the latter doubts whether these beliefs *should* play that role. However, that challenge presupposes that our practices must reflect the essence of reality, which runs counter to the AUTONOMY OF LANGUAGE.

On Certainty's most important achievement was to provide the cue for an epistemology socialized (which the sociology of knowledge claims to have taken up). Neither the knowledge of a culture, nor even that of any of its members, can be derived from the perceptual experiences of an individual. The accumulated knowledge of a culture is a collective achievement – an idea shared by Hegelians, Marxists and pragmatists. None of us can survey, let alone master, that totality (OC §§161, 288–98). Learning is based on accepting the authority of a community, and even adults have to take many things on trust (OC §§170, 374–8, 509; Z §§413–16). But this does not deny the possibility of critical thought. By accepting many things, we can participate in epistemic activities which allow us to rectify some of our beliefs, occasionally even parts of our world-view (OC §§161–2). Unlike Quine's epistemology naturalized, Wittgenstein's epistemology socialized makes this point without reducing belief-formation behaviouristically to a matter of stimulus and response.

colour This provides an illustration of the atomistic ontology of the *Tractatus*. Wittgenstein makes three points:

(a) There are internal relations between colours, relations which cannot fail to hold between them, for example that white is lighter than black (TLP 4.123).

(b) 'Being coloured' (along with space and time) is a 'form of objects'. Every 'visual object' (visible object) is in a 'colour-space', that is, it must have *some* colour (just as every object must have some spatio-temporal location); this is one of its essential 'internal properties' (TLP 2.0131, 2.0251; PT 2.0251f.; *see* LOGICAL FORM).

(c)   Ascriptions of different colours to a point in the visual field are inconsistent.

      (1)   *A* is red

necessarily excludes

      (2)   *A* is green (blue, yellow, etc.).

Such 'colour-exclusion' – (c) – is an apparent counter-example to the *Tractatus*'s claim that all necessity is LOGICAL, a consequence of the truth-functional complexity of molecular propositions. Wittgenstein tries to deal with this difficulty by showing that (1) and (2) can be analysed as logical products which 'contradict' each other (e.g., (1) as '$p.q.r$'; (2) as '$s.t.{\sim}r$'). He toyed with two lines of analysis. The first invokes physics and claims that on analysis (1) and (2) imply logically incompatible propositions about the velocity of particles (TLP 6.3751; NB 16.8./11.9.16). A more straightforward version suggests that on analysis they respectively entail something like '*A* reflects mainly light of 620 nm' and '*A* reflects mainly light of 520 nm.'

The second line of analysis involves the idea that colours like red are composed of simpler elements – unanalysable shades of colour. (1) and (2) are analysed into propositions which ascribe a certain 'quantity' of red and green respectively to *A*, plus a supplementary clause stating 'and nothing else', which means that their conjunction is a contradiction (MS105; RLF; PR ch. VIII; BT 473–85).

Unfortunately, as Ramsey detected, both analyses only push the problem one step back (*Mathematics* 279–80). The resulting propositions once more exclude each other; they ascribe one out of a range of incompatible specifications, a determinate of a determinable. Worse, Wittgenstein realized that such propositions as (1) and (2) cannot be constructed out of simpler ones, ascribing degrees of a quality, since logical conjunction cannot reduplicate the effect of adding degrees. If (1) ascribes to *A*, for example, 3 degrees of R,

      (1*)   *A* is 3R

it cannot be analysed as

      (1**)   *A* is 1R.*A* is 1R.*A* is 1R

since (1**) is simply equivalent to '*A* is 1R'. Nor can it be analysed as

      (1***)   *A* is 1R.*A* is 2R.*A* is 3R

for (1***) contains the analysandum; and '*A* is 3R' means either '*precisely* 3R', in which case it *excludes* the other conjuncts, or '*at least* 3R', in which case it *entails* the other conjuncts. Colour-exclusion thus led Wittgenstein to realize that statements of degree cannot be analysed to yield ELEMENTARY PROPOSITIONS which are logically independent.

His response was to abandon that requirement, and thereby logical atomism, which suggests that the *Tractatus* had conceived of unanalysable shades of colours as objects, and of elementary propositions along the lines of (1*). The result is the idea of a 'proposition system': propositions of degree are compared with reality not individually, but all at once, like the graduating marks of a ruler; (1) at a stroke determines that *A* is neither green nor blue, etc. (WVC 63–4; PR 108–11). Secondly, there are non-truth-functional logical relations: (1) and (2) do not 'contradict', they 'logically exclude', each other (*see* TRUTH-TABLES). By this token,

(3) Nothing can be red and green all over

is neither analytic nor empirical (cp. 'Nothing can be white and a metal'), nor synthetic a priori, as Husserl suggested. We are not prevented from imagining a counter-example by the transcendental structure of the mind; rather, nothing would count as red and green all over. (3) is a GRAMMATICAL proposition, that is, it expresses a rule that excludes as nonsensical a certain combination of words (WVC 67–8; PR 78–9), namely '*A* is red and green all over.'

In his *Remarks on Colour* (1950–51), Wittgenstein extended this idea. The INTERNAL relations noticed earlier are part of a whole 'mathematics', 'geometry' or 'logic' of colour (ROC III §§3, 63, 86, 188) which must be distinguished from its physics. *Tractatus* 2.0232 was wrong to imply that determinates of a single determinable share all combinatorial possibilities. Thus Wittgenstein asks, 'Why is it that something can be transparent green but not transparent white?' And he insists that such questions cannot be answered by physical or psychological theories, for they concern not causal properties of colours, for example that red things emit light of 620 nm, or irritate people, but their internal properties. He also resists the attempt to answer them by reference to facts which lie between science and logic, as with Goethe's 'phenomenological' theory of colours (ROC I §§19, 22, 39–40, 53, 70–3, II §§3, 16, III §§81–2, 229; WAM 125). He would also reject the solution offered by scientific realism (*see* AUTONOMY OF LANGUAGE): to be both transparent and white is impossible, since to be transparent is to *transmit* most incident light, while to be white is to *reflect* most of it, not because of grammar or empirical fact, but of metaphysical necessity. But no theory of light transmission or reflection is part of our colour concepts. To reflect most incident light is not part of the explanation of 'white', and not an internal property: we would not stop calling clean snow 'white' if measurement revealed that it transmits or absorbs most light.

Wittgenstein himself elucidates the incompatibility between white and transparent through 'rules of appearance' governing the use of visual terms. First, something white behind a coloured transparent medium appears in the colour of the medium (we may know it to be white, but have to use the medium's colour in representing how it appears); something black appears black. Consequently, a putative 'white transparent medium' makes white appear white, black appear black, that is, behaves like a *colourless* medium, which is absurd (ROC I §20, III §173). Second, any coloured medium darkens the appearance of what is seen through it. For a putative white medium to do so, it would itself have to be dark, that is, not white (ROC I §30).

Wittgenstein elucidates other seemingly phenomenological features, for example that there cannot be a reddish-green, and the contrast between pure and mixed colours, by reference to standard representations of colour (colour-octahedron, -circle, -charts), which he characterizes as arrangements of grammatical rules (LWL 8, 11; PR 51, 75, 276–81). This is linked to the crucial role of OSTENSIVE DEFINITION: we explain, justify and criticize the use of our colour vocabulary by reference to samples: 'This colour (pointing at a chart or a ripe tomato) is red.' Grammatical propositions about colours reflect normative connections we set up through our employment of colour samples. For example, we use the ordered pair of a black and a white patch also as a paradigm of 'lighter' and 'darker', to exclude as nonsensical the claim that *this* white patch is darker than *this* black one (RFM 48, 75–6).

The role of ostensive definition explains other features of colour-terms.

(d)   They are not defined lexically (a point the *Tractatus* distorted by holding that objects cannot be 'described') but through samples (PG 89–90, 208–9).

(e)   Primary colours like red are simple not in the metaphysical sense of Tractarian OBJECTS, but in that our form of representation *treats* them as simple elements of mixed colours, and does not provide a method of analysing them (RPP I §§605–9).

(f)   The blind or colour-blind do not have the colour concepts of the normally sighted (ROC I §§9, 13, 77, III *passim*; RPP I §602; LW II 24–6, 61, 74–9). The reason for this is not that they lack a certain private experience – the PRIVATE LANGUAGE ARGUMENT undermines the idea that colours are subjective in that each individual might mean something different by 'red' in spite of explaining and applying it in the same way (inverted spectrum). Rather, it is due to the fact that they lack the perceptual abilities to participate fully in our language-game with colour-terms. A colour-blind person might know that the top light of a traffic-light is red, but could not know it by simply looking at the light and saying 'This is red.'

consciousness   Wittgenstein's early philosophy involved a form of SOLIPSISM, according to which reality is identical with life, and life with 'consciousness', that is, my current experience, with the striking result that in death, when consciousness ends, 'the world does not change but stops existing.' This echoes Schopenhauer, who had claimed that the world is my representation, and that the concept of representation coincides with that of consciousness. Although Wittgenstein abandoned his Schopenhauerian metaphysics after the *Tractatus*, in his VERIFICATIONIST phase he continued to hold that 'All that is real is the experience of the present moment' (M 102–3; see NB 11.6./24.7./2.8.16; TLP 5.621, 6.431; *World* I §§1, 10, II ch. 1). From 1932 onwards, however, Wittgenstein came to criticize not only this exotic solipsism of the present moment, but also the INNER/OUTER picture of the mind as a private realm which has dominated philosophy since Descartes. 'The picture is something like this: Though the ether is filled with vibrations the world is dark. But one day man opens his seeing eye, and there is light' (PI II 184). Consciousness is conceived as the ray of light which illuminates our private mental episodes, an inner glow which, in James's words, marks 'the chasm' separating mind from matter, the foundations of empirical knowledge from what we can at best infer (LPE 296–7; *Psychology* I 134–6). In his mature later work, Wittgenstein raised several objections against this idea of an inner 'world of consciousness' (LW II 21, 74; PI §§412–27; LPE 320).

(a) The view that the content of consciousness or experience is entities to which only I have access is challenged by the PRIVATE LANGUAGE ARGUMENT, which denies that the idea of such private 'thuses' and 'thises' makes sense (RPP I §§91, 109, 896).

(b) Far from consciousness being known through infallible introspection, there is no such thing as perceiving or encountering one's own consciousness. If after an accident I tell a doctor 'I am conscious', I do not report the result of having observed my mind, but simply signal that I have regained consciousness, something I could equally well have done by saying 'Hello!' (PI §§416–17; Z §§396, 401–2).

(c) Partly for this reason, it is misguided to seek the essence of consciousness through turning one's attention towards one's own consciousness. What is needed is an investigation of how the word 'consciousness' and its cognates are used.

(d) Such an investigation reveals that 'consciousness' does not refer to a phenomenon (state or process) occurring inside us. The alleged ontological split between the physical world and the world of consciousness is merely a categorial difference drawn in our language, namely between those things which are sentient, that is, capable of perceiving and reacting to their environment, and those which are not. That healthy HUMAN BEINGS are conscious (or that they see, feel and hear) is a grammatical proposition, and the suggestion that human beings who behave just as we do might in fact be automatons is absurd (PI §§281–4, 420; Z §395; RPP II §§14, 19, 35; LW II 78).

(e) If this is correct, there is no 'unbridgeable gulf between consciousness and brain-process', and no unsolvable metaphysical mystery about consciousness (PI §412; BB 47). Although it makes no sense to attribute consciousness to the brain or its parts, and although consciousness is not a process which takes place in the brain, there is nothing paradoxical about a neurophysiological event, whether it be an electrical stimulation of the brain, or the squeezing of the eyeball, producing certain experiences (e.g., a flash of light in the visual field). Equally, there is no metaphysical mystery about the fact that only creatures with a central nervous system of a certain complexity are conscious, although there are scientific puzzles here which Wittgenstein did not address, for example, why and in what way capacities for sensation and volition presuppose certain neurophysiological mechanisms and processes, and how these capacities emerged in the evolutionary process.

constructivism   *see* GENERAL PROPOSITIONAL FORM; MATHEMATICAL PROOF; NUMBERS

contextualism   This doctrine holds that in the explanation of meaning, judgements, sentences or propositions take priority over concepts or words. It is implicit in Kant (B92–3), who held that the sole function of concepts is to be employed in judgements, and Bentham, who gave a contextual definition of grammatical particles like 'if' or 'but', that is, explained them by paraphrasing the sentences in which they occur. Frege insists on the primacy of judgements (thoughts) over concepts: rather than constructing judgements out of concepts (like traditional logic), he derives the latter from analysing the former. This idea underlies his famous 'context principle': never 'enquire after the meaning of a word in isolation' and 'Only in the context of a proposition do words mean something' (*Foundations* x, §§60–2, 106; see *Posthumous* 15–16, 253). This principle has three implications. Firstly, a sufficiency condition: for a word to have meaning it suffices that it play a part in expressing a judgement. This allowed him to insist, against psychologism, that for a sentence to be meaningful, it is not necessary for every individual word to be associated with an idea. Secondly, compositionalism: the meaning of a word is its contribution to the content of sentences in which it occurs, because the latter is composed of the meanings of its constituents (similarly, for Russell a proposition is the value of a propositional function). Finally, a restrictive condition: only in a sentence which expresses a judgement have words a real logical 'content', for only there do they (partly) determine the validity of inferences.

When Frege divided content into 'sense' and 'meaning', he regarded the sense and the meaning of a sentence as determined respectively by the senses and meanings of its constituents. But he rejected the legitimacy of contextual definitions, and never adapted the context principle to the distinction (*Posthumous* 255–6; 'Sense' 35–6; *Laws* II §66). The *Tractatus* does this, but in a modified form. Whereas Frege distinguished between the 'saturated' names of objects (e.g., 'Paris') and the 'unsaturated' names of functions (e.g., 'is the capital of France'), Wittgenstein insists that all names are unsaturated, that is, have meaning only in coordination with others. Moreover, he denies that propositions have MEANING, and that NAMES have sense. 'Only the proposition has sense. Only in the context of a proposition has a name meaning' (TLP 3.3, see 3.314). Two rationales for this 'restrictive principle' concerning names can be detected. The explicit one (TLP 2.0121–2.0131; PT 2.0122) derives from the isomorphism between language and reality postulated by the PICTURE THEORY. As regards their combinatorial possibilities, names behave like the objects they stand for. It is essential to OBJECTS that they are concatenated with other objects in facts: an object cannot occur on its own, but stands in determinate relationships with other objects (*see* LOGICAL SPACE). In going proxy for objects, names do the same, hence they are part of FACTS of a special kind, namely propositions. What depicts the fact that *a* stands in the relation *R* to *b* is not a mere list of signs, but the fact that '*a*' stands to the left and '*b*' to the right of '*R*' (TLP 3.1431f.; *see* ELEMENTARY PROPOSITION).

The implicit rationale is provided by the compositionalism of the *Tractatus*. In line with a (possibly independent) suggestion by Frege, it seeks to explain the 'creativity of language', the fact (first noted by von Humboldt) that we can understand propositions which we have never heard before (TLP 3.318, 4.02–4.03; NL 98, 104; *Posthumous* 225, 243; *Correspondence* 79). The *Tractatus*'s solution has been widely accepted by contemporary philosophers of language. All that is needed to understand an unlimited number of propositions is knowledge of the primitive expressions (names), and their combinatorial rules. To understand a proposition is to understand the meanings of its constituents plus its LOGICAL FORM, that is, the manner of its composition (contemporary theories add that the rules of composition are recursive, and hence allow the formation of an infinite number of sentences). At the ultimate level, the sense of an elementary proposition is a function of its constituent names, that is, both of their meanings – the objects they represent – and of their logical form, their combinatorial possibilities. By the same token, the role of names is to contribute to the determination of the sense of elementary propositions. Alas, both rationales show at best that names must be capable of occurring in propositions, not that they have meaning only when they actually occur in propositions, as the restrictive principle requires.

Wittgenstein later rejected both the idea that PROPOSITIONS must consist of function and argument, and compositionalism generally. The sense of a proposition is not determined exclusively by the meanings of its constituents and the mode of their combination, but depends at least partly on its role, on how it is used on a particular occasion of utterance. UNDERSTANDING the components and mode of composition of a sentence may be a necessary condition for understanding it, but it is not sufficient. Given our method of determining time by reference to the sun's zenith, 'It is 5 o'clock on the sun' of itself makes no sense (PI §§350–1; BB 105–6; RPP II §§93–4). We could stipulate a sense, but that is not the same as calculating it from the sentence's components and mode of composition. Moreover, logical form and status are given by grammatical form only in so far as a given type-expression form is *canonically* used for a certain purpose. And the standard purpose of a type-sentence may be at odds with what its linguistic form suggests. It is common practice to give orders with declarative or interrogative sentences ('I'd like you to shut the door', 'Would you shut the door?'), or to ask questions with imperatives ('Tell me what you think!'). Whether a sentence is a GRAMMATICAL proposition, that is, typically expresses a linguistic rule, depends on its role or function within our linguistic practice: 'War is war' is typically not used to express the law of identity. Finally, on a given occasion a form of words may serve a non-canonical purpose – as with a rhetorical question. This depends on how the speaker uses it on that occasion, and is evident from how he would explain or defend his utterance, and what responses he would admit as relevant (PI II 221; LW I §17; MS131 141–2; *see* INTENDING AND MEANING SOMETHING).

This functionalist account of sense removes an objection to the idea that first-person psychological statements like 'I am in pain' are AVOWALS rather than descriptions or reports, namely that they must have the same (descriptive) sense as third-person statements ('H.G. is in pain'), since they combine equivalent components in the same way (LW I §44). It also means that whether a combination of signs is NONSENSE is no longer decided by reference to general rules alone, but also depends on the circumstances in which the expression functions (PI §489; OC §§229, 348–50, 433); and it supports Wittgenstein's warning that focusing on the form of expressions rather than their use leads to philosophical confusion (LC 2; AWL 46; PI §§10–14). Finally, it challenges an assumption of truth-conditional semantics, namely that sentences have literal meanings determined only by their components and logical form.

Wittgenstein continued to condone the general idea of the primacy of propositions over their constituents. However, the rationale is novel. What gives meaning to words is no longer their being embedded in a logical form, but their being incorporated in a language-game (*see* USE). 'A word has meaning only as part of a sentence' (PI §49). Taken at face value this is wrong. When I address someone, or paint 'WC' on a door, I have not made a meaningless utterance, or written down a meaningless mark. But with occasional exceptions (PR 59), Wittgenstein explains his dictum in a way which acknowledges that individual words can mean something without actually occurring in a proposition. What he insists on is that a word must be capable of occurring in propositions, and that such occurrences of words are semantically primary. He reaches this conclusion through the following (implicit) steps.

(a) A proposition is the minimal unit by which a move is made in the language-game: only propositions can say something. There are no half-propositions in the sense in which there is half a loaf of bread (BT 1; PG 44).

(b) Naming an object is no more a move in a language-game than putting a piece on the board is a move in chess. Naming presupposes a sentential context in that it is essentially a 'preparation' for sentential use (PI §49; PLP 13–14, 199, 318–20).

(c) A name can be used in isolation only if there is a LANGUAGE-GAME in which such moves are made: 'WC' would not be a label if we did not talk about lavatories.

(d) Understanding a word implies *inter alia* knowing how to use it in sentences.

The kernel of truth in Frege and the *Tractatus* is that the meaning of a word is determined by how it can be used within sentences. But it does not follow that the word has a meaning only in the context of a sentence. On the contrary, it is the *individual word* which has such a use and hence a meaning. If it is clear what role a word would play in a proposition, it has a meaning whether or not it actually fulfils that role.

This position naturally leads to an extension of contextualism to the idea that sentences have meaning only within the context of a whole language (*see* FORM OF LIFE). A proposition can be a *move* only in the context of the whole 'game of language'. 'To understand a sentence means to understand a language' (PI §199; see PG 172; BB 5; LW I §913). This semantic holism is reminiscent of Quine and Davidson. Taken literally, it implies that one cannot understand any part of a language unless one understands every part, which ignores that we have to learn a language by segments, and that there are degrees of understanding. On a charitable interpretation, it means that one cannot credit someone with understanding just one sentence and nothing else. For a proposition is a sign in a system, one possible combination of words among, and in contrast with, others. Hence, understanding a proposition is part of the 'mastery of a technique' (PI §199; PG 63, 152–3). It involves both the ability to employ a word in some other contexts, and knowledge of some of the logical links between the given sentence and others. 'Light dawns gradually over the whole' (OC §§141–2). We do not learn everything at once, but our grasp of each part is complete only once we have mastered the whole. Thus understood, semantic holism explains rather than ignores the fact that there are degrees of understanding.

contradiction   For Wittgenstein, a contradiction like '$p . \tilde{} p$' is on a par with a TAUTOLOGY like '$\tilde{} (p . \tilde{} p)$' in that it is not nonsensical but senseless, because it says nothing. By contrast, the law of contradiction is not the vacuous '$\tilde{} (p . \tilde{} p)$', but a rule which prohibits an expression like '$p . \tilde{} p$'. What logicians are afraid of are not contradictions *per se*, which have a legitimate role, notably in *reductio ad absurdum* arguments, but violations of this rule, for example a failure to withdraw a postulate which implies a contradiction. There is no such thing as a contradictory rule, since it could not tell one what to do, and a contradictory proposition is no more a move in the language-game than placing and withdrawing a piece from a square is a move in chess (WVC 130–1, 176, 199–200; PG 128–9, 305; AWL 4; LFM 209, 212–14, 223; RPP I §44; RPP II §290).

Wittgenstein's remarks on the consequences of contradictions for the foundations of mathematics are self-consciously provocative. He does not tolerate, let alone promote, contradictions. However, he regarded as superstitious the sceptical fear that there might be 'hidden' contradictions which, like a germ, might infect the whole body of mathematics unbeknownst to us, and consequently he rejected the idea which underlies Hilbert's META-MATHEMATICS that such contradictions should or could be precluded in advance by consistency proofs (WVC 119; RFM 204–19, 254–6, 370–8, 400–1, 410; LFM 7–8, 67, 209–30). A hidden contradiction is not an unnoticed contradiction, that is, one which is explicit in a set of rules, and has merely been overlooked, or one which can be generated according to an established method (WVC 120, 143, 174–5, 208; LFM 226). Rather, it is one which is added to the system by a new, unforeseen type of construction – such as the construction of statements like 'X is a member of itself.' According to this distinction, Russell did not discover an existing contradiction in Frege's calculus, but invented a way of constructing a contradiction, and thereby modified that calculus. Nothing forces us to accept this kind of modification. We can decide that the path leading to the contradiction is not a proper derivation within the system. The rules we have operated commit us only to what can be generated through their straightforward application, not to what can be added. Equally, no meta-mathematical discovery could produce a system immune to the possibility of such constructions. Certainty of this kind could only be achieved by a 'good angel' (RFM 378; LFM 221–4; *see* MATHEMATICAL PROOF).

When a contradiction is constructed or detected, it does not show that everything we did before was wrong. A contradiction is harmful only if it brings the application of the calculus to a halt. Thus, if it were suddenly noticed, because, say, the vice-president turns up for the first time, that certain statutes made inconsistent demands on the seating of the vice-president at state banquets, this would not show that what we did previously was wrong (LFM 210). By the same token, it is difficult to see how our basic arithmetic could be overturned by recherché discoveries in mathematical logic, a difficulty which lends support to Wittgenstein's suggestion 'that Frege's and Russell's logic is not the foundation of arithmetic anyway' (LFM 228; WVC 149; RFM 400-1). However, Wittgenstein himself insisted that an expression like 'Φ and do not Φ in situation X' is not what we call a rule (PG 305). Hence, one should add that in the case of our unnoticed contradiction there was something wrong before it was revealed in our practice, not with what we did, but with the statutes, namely that they did not provide coherent guidance on the seating of the vice-president. Equally, an arithmetic which did not prohibit division by 0 would be inadequate even before someone started dividing by 0.

Even if one accepts Wittgenstein's ideas about unnoticed and hidden contradictions, some of his remarks on what to do once a contradiction comes to light are problematic.

> One might say 'Finding a contradiction in a system, like finding a germ in an otherwise healthy body, shows that the whole system or body is diseased.' – Not at all. The contradiction does not even falsify anything. Let it lie. Do not go there. (LFM 138)

This is like saying that we can avoid trouble with the statutes about seating arrangements simply by refraining from having state banquets; it defies the purpose of the rule system. In other passages, Wittgenstein takes a more plausible line: when we discover a contradiction, remedial action is called for, but it can always be provided, notably through *ad hoc* stipulations like Russell's, which prohibit expressions like 'X is a member of itself.' Thus, the main problem with contradictions is that anything would follow from a contradiction, but we can avoid this by making it a rule that no conclusions should be drawn from a contradiction (WVC 132; RFM 208, 373-7; LFM 209-10, 219-28).

Waismann and Turing protested that this only cures the symptoms, since an inconsistent system will create indefinitely many contradictions. In reply it has been argued that we can only derive indefinitely many contradictions by (tacitly) drawing inferences from a contradiction, which would mean that Wittgenstein's rule would prevent the derivation of contradictions. But Wittgenstein himself acknowledged that the contradiction can be contained only if we can survey the system, which means that ultimately the solution to the emergence of a contradiction is to disentangle ourselves from the confusions engendered by our own rules. Once we have done so, the straightforward solution is to modify the system, for example, by declaring one of two conflicting rules obsolete (RFM 209; PI §125; LFM 210).

Wittgenstein also rejected Turing's suggestion that bridges might collapse as the result of a hidden contradiction in our mathematics (LFM 210-21). If a bridge collapses, either our physics is wrong, or we have made a mistake in the calculations. Strictly speaking this is wrong, because in an inconsistent system someone might argue '$p . \neg p$; *ergo* $2 \times 2 = 369$' and use that result in constructing a bridge. But Wittgenstein is right that we would not call this calculating, and that the real problem here is not the contradiction, but the drawing of such absurd conclusions.

Wittgenstein's general attitude towards the fear of hidden contradictions also inspires his ill-famed discussion of Gödel's first incompleteness theorem (RFM 116–23, 383–9). The theorem states that for any axiomatic system S adequate to formalize arithmetic – such as that of *Principia* – there is at least one well-formed formula which cannot be proven in this system. The technique used in reaching this result is to translate meta-mathematical statements about the provability in S into arithmetical statements, which are themselves part of S. On that basis we can prove within S an arithmetical statement 'P' which represents within S the meta-mathematical statement 'P is not provable in S', or, more vividly, 'I am unprovable.' But if S is consistent, P is true (no false proposition can be proven), and hence unprovable.

Wittgenstein did not impugn the validity of the proof, but only the interpretation of 'P' as saying of itself both that it is unprovable and that it is true. One of his arguments is that this interpretation is paradoxical, since for 'P' to be *true* in S is for it either to be an axiom of S or to have been *proven* from those axioms. Critics have also detected another line of argument, namely that Gödel's interpretation of 'P' is untenable because it is on a par with the liar's paradox. This would ignore that in Gödel's proof no single self-referential statement like 'I am false' occurs; rather, we have two versions of the same proposition in two different systems, one version is true but unprovable in S, the other is true and provable in the meta-mathematical system M. However, Wittgenstein's real point is precisely that there cannot be two versions of the same mathematical proposition in two different systems, since a mathematical proposition has sense only as part of a particular proof-system. According to him, Gödel's proof has in fact constructed two *different* propositions, one of which – 'P' in S – is unprovable, while the other – 'P is unprovable in S' – is true but part of M, and hence has no sceptical implications. Neither line of argument evidences the egregious technical incompetence of which Wittgenstein has been accused. But both presuppose his view that a sentence is a meaningful mathematical truth only if it has been derived within a particular system of MATHEMATICAL PROOF. Without independent reasons for this view, Wittgenstein's attack on Gödel is question-begging, since Gödel's interpretation implies precisely that there is a gap between mathematical meaning and truth on the one hand, and mathematical proof and provability on the other.

conventionalism   *see* FORM OF REPRESENTATION; LOGIC; MATHEMATICAL PROOF

criteria   These are ways of telling whether something satisfies a concept X, or evidence for something's being an X. Although used by Plato, the term has achieved philosophical prominence only through Wittgenstein's later work. It has been treated as a technical term, in spite of its modest frequency and the fact that there is only one passage which defines it. For the most part, Wittgenstein's use of the term is in line with the ordinary one. But sometimes he specifies that criteria provide a special kind of evidence. The root of this idea lies in a distinction of his VERIFICATIONIST phase (WVC 97–101, 159–61, 210–11, 255–6; PR 94–5, 282–6; LWL 16, 66; M 55–61; PG 219–23). A 'genuine' PROPOSITION must be conclusively verifiable by reference to reality, which leaves as candidates for genuine propositionhood only sense-datum propositions that describe immediate experience. Statements about material objects or the experience of others cannot be so verified, and are mere 'hypotheses'. They are not strictly true or false, and not propositions in the same sense as 'genuine' ones, but rather rules for the construction of such propositions. Those propositions which give evidential support to hypotheses are called 'symptoms'. Thus, the different views of a material object support hypotheses about the material object itself; the resulting hypotheses explain our previous experiences and predict future ones ('If viewed from a different angle, the object will look like this'). The relation between hypothesis and evidential symptom falls short of entailment: symptoms never conclusively verify or falsify a hypothesis, they only make it more or less probable. For the evidential support is defeasible: the addition of further propositions to the set of symptoms may make the hypothesis less plausible. Moreover, a hypothesis can always be upheld or abandoned by adopting auxiliary hypotheses. Which course we take depends on considerations of simplicity and predictive power. That relation is nevertheless 'grammatical' or 'logical': what symptoms render more or less probable what hypothesis is determined a priori, not through experience (induction).

Wittgenstein later realized that while his candidate 'genuine propositions' do not in fact allow of verification, since they are not descriptions but AVOWALS, his so-called 'hypotheses', humdrum propositions like 'The table is round' or 'She has a toothache', are not rules or laws, and *can* sometimes be conclusively verified. As a result, the relation between a hypothesis and its evidential symptoms was replaced by that between a proposition and its 'criteria' (first in his Cambridge lectures of 1932–3: AWL 17–19, 28–35, 59–62). Like symptoms, criteria are grounds or reasons fixed by grammar, not experience. But there are also differences between the earlier and the later relation. (a) The relata of the criterial relation are characterized diversely: 'phenomena', 'facts' and 'propositions' are criteria of 'sentences', 'statements', 'phenomena', 'facts', 'knowledge', 'assertions', 'concepts' and 'words'. Ultimately, these variations are terminological; they express a single idea in a formal (linguistic) or material mode, and by reference to propositions or concepts. The basic point is that certain phenomena or facts license the application of certain words. (b) Criteria can conclusively verify a proposition (see below). (c) They may be unique, although many concepts have multiple criteria.

In the *Blue Book*, Wittgenstein gives an explicit explanation which reverses his initial terminology (BB 24–5). 'Symptoms' are now defined as empirical evidence; they support a conclusion through theory and induction. By contrast, a 'criterion' q for a claim that p is a ground or reason for the truth of p, in virtue not of empirical evidence, but of grammatical rules. It is part of the meaning of 'p' and 'q' that q's being the case – the satisfaction of the criterion – is a ground or reason for the truth of 'p'. An inflamed throat is a symptom of angina; the presence of a particular bacillus is the 'defining criterion'.

Commentators have sometimes given the impression that for Wittgenstein the use of all propositions and concepts is governed by criteria. In fact, he stated that avowals and concepts which are defined through OSTENSIVE DEFINITION (e.g., colour predicates) are not subject to criteria. The same might hold for FAMILY-RESEMBLANCE concepts. On the other hand,

> expressive behaviour is a criterion for third-person psychological utterances;
>
> performances are criteria for potentialities, powers and abilities (notably applying and explaining a word correctly are criteria for UNDERSTANDING it);
>
> scientific concepts like angina are governed by criteria, although these often fluctuate (see below);
>
> mathematical concepts are governed by 'defining' criteria (having three sides is *the* criterion for a plane figure's being a triangle);
>
> MATHEMATICAL PROOFS are criteria for mathematical truths, and the result of an arithmetical operation is a criterion for its having been carried out (RFM 319) (if you do not get 144, you have not squared 12); and
>
> applying count-nouns requires 'criteria of identity' (*see* PRIVATE LANGUAGE ARGUMENT).

The idea of criteria has three distinctive and problematic features:

(a) Criteria determine the meaning of the words they govern. What connects meaning and criteria is verification (AWL 17–19, 27–8; PI §353): to explain one's criteria for something's being F is to specify how 'a is F' is verified. The meaning of 'F' is not necessarily *given* by specifying the criteria: 'being in pain' does not mean 'screaming in circumstances of injury'. Nonetheless, the criteria *determine* (at least partly) the meaning of 'F'. To specify the criteria for 'F' is to specify rules for the use of 'F', and hence (partially) to explain its meaning. Criteria are 'fixed by grammar', 'laid down by language' and in that sense a matter of 'convention' (AWL 28–9; BB 24, 57; LPE 293; PI §§322, 371).

Accordingly, the relation between concepts and their criteria is INTERNAL. It makes no sense to say, for example, 'Here is pain, and there is behaviour – it just happens that they are associated' (LPE 286; LSD 10). It also means that a change in criteria is a conceptual change, a change in the meaning of words: that q is a criterion for being F is partly constitutive of the concept of being F. Thus, mathematical proofs are concept-forming, since they lay down new criteria for applying, for example, numerals. And scientists often change the meaning of words under the impact of empirical findings, for example when they discover that one phenomenon from a certain cluster causes the others (as in the case of angina where the bacillus causes the symptoms) or allows of precise measurement (Z §438).

Criteria have since been invoked, firstly to combat scepticism about other minds, and secondly to develop an anti-realist theory of meaning, which, in contrast to the alleged realism of the *Tractatus*, is based on assertability-conditions rather than truth-conditions. The latter application is unfaithful to both the early (*see* VERIFICATIONISM) and the later Wittgenstein, whose conception of PHILOSOPHY rules out theories of meaning; and, as we have seen, only *some* uses of language are subject to criteria.

Distortions apart, Wittgenstein's treatment of criteria has come in for powerful criticism. Radical empiricists like Quine deny that there is such a thing as conceptual evidence or internal relations. Others have claimed that criteria cannot be a matter of convention: no one has ever stipulated that behaviour should express pain, and no one could decide otherwise. Proponents of a realist semantics like Putnam add that the criteria we use to establish whether something is, for example, a case of angina are only crude ways of detecting a natural kind. What 'angina' means is determined by the ultimate scientific theory about the matter (*see* AUTONOMY OF LANGUAGE). By that token, the idea that cases in which scientists adopt new criteria for the application of a term like 'angina' amount to cases of conceptual change is wrong because it implies that we are no longer talking about the same thing. Arguably, however, Putnam's objections illustrate an important lesson of Wittgenstein's account, namely that there is a 'fluctuation in grammar between criteria and symptoms' (PI §354, see §79). The logical status of certain relations may change from being criterial to being symptomatic, and it may do so as a result of empirical discoveries (this lesson was reinforced by Wittgenstein's work on shock during the war). Scientific concepts are typically held in place by several criteria, and we can abandon some of them while retaining others. That is why we are not simply talking about a completely different phenomenon. Nevertheless, to alter the criteria is to alter how we explain and employ, for example, 'angina', and hence amounts to a modification of our concept.

(b) Criteria are ways of telling how one knows something. To specify the criteria for the truth of 'p' is to characterize ways of verifying 'p', of answering the question 'How do you know?' (AWL 17–19, 28; BB 24–5, 51, 57; Z §439; LPE 293; PI §§182, 228). In line with his earlier conception of symptoms, Wittgenstein sometimes refers to criteria as 'evidence'. This is misleading, because it suggests that 'p' is logically independent of 'q', whereas the relationship is in fact an internal one, yet it does rightly suggest the defeasibility of (some) criteria (see (c) below). But it is important to stress that criteria differ from necessary and sufficient conditions not just by virtue of being (in some cases) defeasible but also in that they must be features which can be invoked to justify the application of a term. There may be necessary and sufficient conditions which do not satisfy this condition. Thus, Wittgenstein claimed that being bivalent is necessary and sufficient for being a proposition, but not an independent feature by which we could recognize something as a proposition (*see* PI §136; BIPOLARITY).

(c) The criteria for some words are defeasible. This legal term is not used by Wittgenstein, but it indicates the special nature of criterial evidence. In some cases, a criterion is a logically sufficient condition, or even a necessary and sufficient condition, for something's being X: the presence of a certain bacillus for angina, having three sides for being a triangle. In other cases the criterial relation does not amount to entailment, but shares a feature of inductive evidence: it need not be decisive, because it can be undermined by further evidence. Whether or not criteria conclusively support p may depend on the circumstances. If Susan screams 'It hurts' and writhes on the floor, this is a criterion for her being in pain; but if she is rehearsing for a play, it will not confirm that she is suffering. Such defeasibility cannot be avoided by claiming that a criterion q is a necessary constituent of a sufficient condition which includes those circumstances which, together with the fact that p, entail that q. For there is no definite list of such circumstances, and even if there were, it is not part of our explanations of psychological terms, and hence not part of their meaning (Z §§117–22).

Defeasibility threatens to open the flood-gates to scepticism about other minds. For all our criterial evidence, we may be wrong in our inferences from it about Susan's state of mind. It has therefore been suggested that criteria for psychological terms should not be considered as evidential (in an inferential sense). If we see her screaming and writhing, we do not infer (consciously or unconsciously) that she is in pain from behavioural evidence, we simply register her agony. This interpretation is in line with Wittgenstein's attempt to avoid the INNER/OUTER picture of the mind as something hidden for which we have merely evidence. The answer to the question 'How do you know she was in pain?' is simply 'I *saw* her writhing in agony.' Like straightforward observations of material objects, this does not adduce evidence, but specifies a perceptual capacity which directly shows us how things are. This perceptual model makes our relation to other minds less open to sceptical challenge, while still allowing for the possibility of error. It also acknowledges that what we observe is not colourless movements described in neutral, physical terms, but *pain*-BEHAVIOUR. On the other hand, it does not work for cases like 'Helga intends to go to London.' Here, the answer to the question 'How do you know?' is not simply 'I saw her', but, for example, 'She told me, and later bought a ticket.'

In any event, Wittgenstein accuses the sceptical challenge of ignoring the internal relation between psychological concepts and behavioural criteria, and thereby distorting the concepts involved. The fact that criterial evidence is defeasible does not entail that it is actually defeated in a particular case. Any challenge in a particular case must point out defeating conditions, but these are themselves defeasible, and quickly peter out (RPP I §137): there is no more room for doubt once it turns out that Susan has broken her leg during the rehearsal (*see* SCEPTICISM). The possibility of lying and pretence does not overturn this verdict. For one thing, the very concept of pretending to be in pain is parasitic upon the concept of being in pain; it makes sense only because there are manifestations of pain which are not subject to pretence, such as the grimace of an infant. Moreover, there are criteria for pretending no less than for being in pain. One can't pretend to be distraught while throwing oneself off the roof. Doubt in such circumstances betokens not caution, but misunderstanding or distortion of the concepts involved. In such circumstances, we can know, and be certain, and a 'proof' or 'guarantee' is provided by behavioural criteria (PI §§246, 249–50, II 181, 222–9; LPE 293; Z §§570–1).

Wittgenstein's last writings question the idea of criterial support as decisive grounds. There can be no *proof* of third-person ascriptions of emotions, and we may often be unable to decide whether someone is, for example, annoyed. But this does not hold for sensations, and does not rehabilitate scepticism. For this 'indeterminacy' and 'unpredictability' is constitutive of some of our concepts of the inner. Moreover, often those who are closely acquainted with a person can make even the most subtle emotional ascriptions with certainty, without being able to specify conclusive criteria, since their evidence is 'imponderable', that is, consists of a syndrome of behaviour, context and previous events (PI II 227–8; LW II 70, 87, 90–5). Criteria are neither the linchpin of a new semantics nor *the* wonder weapon against scepticism about other minds. But they signify conceptual connections between psychological concepts and behaviour which are unwisely ignored by adherents to the inner/outer picture of the mind.

D

determinacy of sense Frege had postulated that a concept must have 'sharp boundaries', that is, that its definition must 'unambiguously determine, as regards any object, whether or not it falls under the concept' (*Laws* II §§56–64; *Posthumous* 155). A concept without a precise definition is not a genuine concept. One rationale behind this is the principle of bivalence: every sentence must be determinately true or false. Another is that Frege treats concepts as functions, and a mathematical function is defined only if its value is stipulated unequivocally for every argument. Finally, for Frege the sense of a complex expression is a function of the senses of its constituents, which means that indeterminacy is contagious. To avoid vagueness, a definition must be complete: it must determine for any object whether or not it falls under the concept, whatever the facts.

Wittgenstein imbibed Frege's ideal of determinacy of sense and the demand for completeness of definition. But whereas for Frege and Russell the vagueness of natural language is a defect which must be avoided by an ideal language suitable for scientific purposes, for the *Tractatus* it is a surface phenomenon, that is, a phenomenon which analysis reveals to be merely superficial. Many sentences of ordinary language appear vague or ambiguous. However, this vagueness 'can be justified' – ordinary language is in good logical order. Although a proposition may leave certain things open, if so it must be determinately indeterminate, that is, it must be settled what precise range it leaves to the facts. 'The watch is lying on the table' leaves open the precise location of the watch. But it must define absolutely sharply what possible locations it can occupy. Hence, LOGICAL ANALYSIS reveals it to be a statement to the effect that there are two objects of such-and-such a kind which stand in one out of a variety of possible spatial relations to each other. Even this may create problems, since it might be unclear what precisely counts as lying on the table. Nevertheless, Wittgenstein insists that what I mean by uttering that sentence *on a specific occasion* must always be perfectly sharp. The implications of a given proposition 'must be settled in advance' by its sense (TLP 3.24, 5.156; NB 7.9.14, 16.–22.6.15; PT 3.20101–3.20103). Determinacy of sense is a precondition of there being any sense at all.

Wittgenstein shares Frege's commitment to bivalence: 'A proposition must restrict reality to two alternatives: yes or no' (TLP 4.023; FW 55). But that commitment is in turn derived from the PICTURE THEORY: the sense of a proposition is a state of affairs, that is, a possible configuration of simple elements. But such a configuration is something absolutely precise: either it exists, or it does not. A proposition must be determinate because there must be a precise configuration of simple elements which either verifies or falsifies it. The logical requirement that the sense of propositions be determinate mirrors the metaphysical nature of facts, and implies that the analysis of all propositions terminates with logically proper NAMES which stand for indestructible simple OBJECTS. A proposition can depict a precise configuration of elements only if its ultimate constituents stand in a one-to-one correlation with these elements. Otherwise, the FACT that its ultimate constituents are combined in a certain way does not depict a specific combination of things.

After the *Tractatus*, Wittgenstein's attitude to indeterminacy changed. He abided by the conviction that 'all the propositions of our everyday language, just as they stand, are in good logical order' (TLP 5.5563). 'Ordinary language is all right' (BB 28; PI §98). But his conception of that order changed radically, as he abandoned the idea that speaking a language is operating a CALCULUS according to definite rules. Not only is it incoherent to suppose that every aspect of language must be governed by rules, it is equally misguided to insist that the rules that do operate must preclude the possibility of vagueness under all conceivable circumstances. At first, he held fast to the idea that the logical order of language mirrors the structure of reality, while modifying his atomistic ontology. Inexactness or vagueness, he argued, is an intrinsic property of certain objects and experiences. It distinguishes, for example, the geometry of the visual field from Euclidean geometry, and is essential to memory images and some visual experiences. The 'inexact' terms of ordinary language are best suited to express exactly the 'blurredness' of what we experience (WVC 55–6; PR 260–3; PLP 208–11).

Philosophical Investigations is often seen in the same light, namely as maintaining that vagueness is an essential feature of language. Thus understood, it has been a major inspiration behind attempts to construct a logic of vagueness. However, Wittgenstein's mature treatment of the topic (PI §§75–88, 98–107) does not promote vagueness; it merely resists the dogmatic demand of determinacy of sense, that is, the insistence that the *possibility* of doubt or disagreement about the application of an expression must be eliminated. Equally, Waismann's influential term 'open texture' rejects not exactness, but the demand that inexactness should be impossible (although on the basis of VERIFICATIONIST ideas Wittgenstein had repudiated by the time of the *Investigations*). Not all concepts are actually vague, and though most empirical concepts allow of borderline cases, they do not thereby become useless, an idea Hart extended to legal concepts in order to combat legal formalism and rule-scepticism.

Wittgenstein rejects the assumptions behind the demand for determinacy. Bivalence and BIPOLARITY are optional features of language. Moreover, vagueness is not necessarily contagious, as the compositionalism of Frege and the *Tractatus* insisted. A claim that the river bank is overgrown by plants is not indefinite because biologists may puzzle over whether to classify certain micro-organisms as plants or animals. A resolution of such puzzles through a sharp definition of 'plant' would not sharpen our understanding of every sentence in which the word occurs; it would introduce a new concept (BT 69, 250; MS115 41).

Far from insisting on the desirability of vagueness, Wittgenstein insists that 'inexact' and 'incomplete' are terms of reproach, 'exact' and 'complete' terms of praise. But he takes Frege and the *Tractatus* to task for distorting the ideal of exactness.

(a) There is no single ideal of exactness. The contrast between exact and inexact is relative to a context and a purpose (e.g., whether we are measuring our distance to the sun or the length of a table) (PI §§88, 100; BT 249–50). An inexact definition is not one which fails to meet the elusive ideal of determinacy, but one which fails to meet the requirements of understanding in a given context.

(b) No EXPLANATION could avert all possibility of indeterminacy, since no system of rules can budget for the countless bizarre possibilities in advance (PI §§80, 84–7).

(c) Although vagueness is a defect, a proposition with a vague sense still has a sense, just as a vague boundary still is a boundary. If there is only one gap in an enclosure, it is determined that there is only one way out (a fly-bottle is a trap, although there is a way out). If I tell someone 'Stand roughly there', accompanied by pointing at a particular spot, some actions will count as complying with the order, and others not, although there may be borderline cases. For a concept to be useful, all that is required is that it is defined for some cases, so that some things would definitely fall under it, and others definitely would not. The Sorites paradox arises out of the failure to recognize that this absence of precise bounds is constitutive of perfectly useful concepts like 'heap': the order to make a heap is clear, although the order to make the smallest heap which still counts as such is not (PI §§68–71, 79, 88, 99; PR 264; PG 236–40). 'Heap' is not the kind of concept to which one can apply mathematical induction. By the same token, names need not be analysable into a set of uniquely identifying descriptions to have a use, and a FAMILY-RESEMBLANCE concept like 'game' does not cease to be a concept by failing to be defined analytically.

(d) One might respond in the spirit of the *Tractatus* that although the rules may allow a certain degree of elasticity, that degree must itself be determinate: there may be borderline cases, but it must be exactly determined what counts as such a case. However, this idea leads to a vicious regress. If we try to make the limits of an area more precise by drawing a line, that line has a breadth. If we try to avoid this by using the colour-edge of the line, the only way of determining what counts as overlapping this exact boundary is to draw another line, etc. (PI §88; Z §§441–2).

E

---

elementary proposition (*Elementarsatz*) Traditional grammar regarded subject-predicate sentences like 'Mary is blond' as simple. Logical atomism, by contrast, used modern logic to show that such propositions are 'molecular', that is, truth-functions of simpler propositions, just as '$p.q$' and '$p \supset q$' are truth-functions of 'p' and 'q'. 'Atomic' or 'elementary' propositions are 'the simplest' propositions into which all others can be analysed but which cannot themselves be analysed into simpler propositions (RUL 8.12; NL 95–7; NM 111). For Russell, the foundations of knowledge also provide the foundations of linguistic meaning. According to his empiricist 'principle of acquaintance', every proposition which we can understand must consist of names which refer to sense-data with which we are acquainted. A proposition is meaningful only if all of its real constituents stand for something, and only the existence of sense- and memory-data is immune to Cartesian doubt. 'This is white', referring to a present sense-datum, is about 'as simple a fact as one can get hold of', but Russell did not rule out that the analysis of propositions might 'go on forever' (*Logic* 198–202).

The possibility of openended analysis was unacceptable to the early Wittgenstein. His quasi-Kantian theory of symbolism left the actual 'composition' of elementary propositions to the 'application of logic': only future analysis could reveal the composition and logical forms of elementary propositions (TLP 5.557). But he insisted 'on purely logical grounds' (TLP 5.5562) that there must be elementary propositions to ensure that the analysis of propositions terminates, that the sense of propositions is determinate, that no truth-value gaps should occur, and that whether a proposition has sense should not depend on empirical facts. Elementary propositions form the basis of all linguistic representation (*see* GENERAL PROPOSITIONAL FORM), and hence the core of the PICTURE THEORY. Wittgenstein does not decide what propositions are unanalysable, but specifies, more rigorously than Russell, the conditions they have to fulfil. They must be:

(a) Logically independent. No two elementary propositions can either be inconsistent with or entail each other. If 'p' entails 'q', its sense contains that of 'q', that is, analysis must reveal 'q' to be one of the truth-functional components of *p*. Equally, if '*p*' contradicts '*q*', it entails, and hence 'contains', '~*q*'. In both cases '*p*' is complex, not elementary (TLP 4.1211, 4.211, 5.134, 6.3751). This requirement was fuelled by the idea that molecular propositions are truth-functions of elementary ones, which presupposes that in a TRUTH-TABLE each elementary proposition can be assigned a truth-value independently of all others.

(b) Pictures. They depict a 'state of affairs', assert the existence of a certain combination of OBJECTS. If they are true, that state of affairs exists, it is what Russell called an 'atomic fact' (TLP 4.21).

(c) A 'nexus' or 'combination' of names. A fully analysed proposition consists exclusively of logically proper NAMES 'in immediate combination', which go proxy for simple objects. Elementary propositions depict states of affairs by combining the names in a way which corresponds to a possible combination of objects (TLP 4.22f.).

(d) Intrinsically positive. Condition (b) implies that all elementary propositions depict, truly or falsely, a 'positive fact', namely the existence of a state of affairs. They say that something is the case, that objects are combined in a certain way, rather than that something is not the case (TLP 4.021–4.023). And condition (a) implies that if '*p*' is elementary, '~*p*' cannot be, since the two are contradictories. A false elementary proposition is not the negation of a true one, but rather depicts a different, and non-existent, combination of objects (TLP 2.06, 4.022; RUL 19.8.19).

(e) Capable of being false in only one way. Propositions about complexes (e.g., '$\Phi(aRb)$') can be false either if the complex does not exist (i.e., if *a* does not stand in the relation *R* to *b*), or if it lacks the property attributed to it (Φ). An elementary proposition, by contrast, excludes exactly one possibility, namely that the objects named by its constituents are not arranged the way the latter are in the proposition (TLP 4.25f.).

Some commentators hold that Wittgenstein was deliberately non-committal about any other features of elementary propositions, since they are inessential to the transcendental deduction of their existence. But Wittgenstein inherited other ideas about the nature of propositions from Frege and Russell, notably that they are composed not of subject and predicate, but of function and argument (TLP 3.141, 3.318, 5.47). Russell maintained that the simples named by the constituents of atomic propositions comprise not just 'particulars', but also 'qualities' like colours, and 'relations'. Wittgenstein initially rejected this view, holding that a proposition like 'Socrates is human' is not of the form *Fa*, but to be analysed as 'Socrates' and 'something is human', and that objects are not of different logical types (RUL 1.13; NL 100, 107). He abandoned the former claim (*see* GENERALITY), and his *Notebooks* state explicitly that 'relations and properties are *objects* too' (NB 16.6.15, see 21.6.15; NM 112).

Nominalist interpreters maintain that the *Tractatus*, by contrast with the *Notebooks*, treats properties and relations as logical forms, not objects; elementary propositions are logical networks sprinkled with names of particulars. They have adduced four arguments. The first is that the *Tractatus* indicates that signs for properties and for individuals are of different logical types, and employs different styles of variables for them (TLP 3.323f., 5.5261); Wittgenstein would not have failed to mention that there are two distinct types of *objects*, consequently the difference is one between names (which stand for objects) and other signs. *But* through the claim that they have different LOGICAL FORMS Wittgenstein did sort objects into distinct categories of different combinatorial possibilities. He may have thought it superfluous to state explicitly that the most general distinction is between individuals, properties and relations, given Russell's similar position.

The second is that *Tractatus* 2.0251 states that 'Space, time, and colour (being coloured) are forms of objects.' *But* what are here called forms of objects are not determinate properties (spaces, times, colours), but determinables like being coloured (see TLP 2.0131). Rather, that the *Tractatus* speaks of such determinables as 'formal properties', and also of 'formal relations', suggests that there are also non-formal properties and relations (TLP 4.122). Finally, since an object's form comprises its possibilities of combining with other objects, *Tractatus* 2.0251 and *Proto-Tractatus* 2.0251f. imply that visual objects combine with colours, and hence that colours are objects.

The third argument is that the comparison of propositions with spatial arrangements (TLP 3.1431, 4.012, 4.016, 4.0311) suggests that in an ideal notation properties and relations are displayed not through function-signs, but through spatial properties of names standing for particulars: 'fa' is expressed by '$\overset{a}{v}$' and '$\phi(x,y)$' as '$\overset{x}{y}$'. It has been objected that this would imply, contrary to the *Tractatus*, that the depth-structure of propositions must be expressed in writing. Yet the nominalist proposal is committed only to the possibility of replacing function-signs by relations (spatial or temporal) between signs. But it does ignore that neither the indefinite number of possible properties and relations, nor their different logical multiplicities, can be displayed through discernible configurations. To avoid this difficulty, it has been suggested that relation-signs *occur* in elementary propositions yet without being *names*. But this contradicts condition (c): the only components of elementary propositions are names.

Lastly, it is pointed out that the *Tractatus* holds that, 'Instead of "The complex sign 'aRb' says that a stands to b in the relation R", we ought to put, "*That* 'a' stands to 'b' in a certain relation says *that aRb*"' (TLP 3.1431f.). But this passage is directed not against the idea that relations are objects but against Russell's claim that 'aRb' is the name of a complex in which both relata are in turn linked to the relation *R*. According to Wittgenstein, objects combine in states of affairs not with the aid of further links, but directly, like links in a chain. The components of states of affairs stand in a determinate relation to each other (*aRb* is not identical with *bRa*) without any logical glue. The representation of this is possible because PROPOSITIONS are facts. What represents the relation between *a* and *b* in '*aRb*' is not '*R*' as such, but *that* it occurs between '*a*' and '*b*'. The real component of '*aRb*' that signifies that relation is not '*R*', which looks like the proper names '*a*' and '*b*', but '*xRy*', which is a *relation*-name (see NL 96–8; TLP 2.03f.).

That some names stand for properties and relations is further suggested by three points. First, it is the only way of reconciling two claims about elementary propositions: that they are a nexus of names – (c) – and that they consist of function and argument. Secondly, according to *Tractatus* 4.24, elementary propositions are functions of names and have the form fx, $\phi(x,y)$, etc. Thirdly, *Tractatus* 4.123 speaks of shades of colours as objects, at least in an extended use of the term. The realist interpretation is further supported by Wittgenstein's subsequent discussions of the *Tractatus*. Most notably, in a lecture Wittgenstein unequivocally stated that the objects of *Tractatus* 2.01 include properties like colours and spatial relations (LWL 120; see RLF; WVC 220; PG 199–201; TS220 §109; MS127 1.3.44). Moreover, he ascribes to the *Tractatus* the view that a property is an object which can enter into combinations with individuals (GB 134; BT 433–4; BB 17).

The *Tractatus*'s failure to provide examples of elementary propositions is due less to agnosticism than to the difficulties Wittgenstein encountered (in the *Notebooks*) in trying to square his preconceptions about simplicity with his logical specifications. Nevertheless, hints in the *Tractatus*, as well as in previous and later writings, indicate that analysis proceeds in the direction of the phenomenally given (sensory impressions). States of affairs are instantiations or co-instantiations of properties like colours and (spatial) relations at spatio-temporal points or points in the visual field. A point in the visual field stands in a 'colour-space': it must have *some* colour, and combines with a particular colour, like two links in a chain without any additional relations (TLP 2.0131; NB 3.9.14, 6.–7.5.15; PG 211). 'Some Remarks on Logical Form' makes the picture concrete: take your visual field, flatten it and put a grid across. Elementary propositions use the coordinates to refer to a point in the visual field, and ascribe to it a shade of colour (a system reminiscent of PI §48; see also ROC I 61–2, III 58, 149), for example,

(1)   *A* (the spatial point with coordinates x,y) is red.

Accordingly, objects are *minima sensibilia* (NB 7.5.15): particulars like spatial points, ultimate perceptual qualities such as shades of colours, tones and smells and simple spatial relations.

105

One objection against this interpretation is that the OBJECTS of the *Tracta-tus* must be indestructible, common to all possible words. But unlike Russell's sense-data, Wittgenstein's candidates are not fleeting mental episodes. They are not temporary, and might appear to be *sempiternalia* the existence of which is metaphysically, not just epistemically, guaranteed. Red complexes and sense-data can be destroyed, but, according to the position *Investigations* §§46–59 ascribes to the *Tractatus*, the colour red cannot. The same might be thought of spatio-temporal points: while such a point might fail to have a certain colour, it could not fail to exist. That Wittgenstein extends sempiternality to points in the visual field can be explained by reference to his SOLIPSISM, which insists that the world is what is given to a transcendental subject of representation.

A second objection is that *Tractatus* 6.3751 states that a proposition like (1) is incompatible with, for example, 'A is green' and hence *not* elementary. Wittgenstein thought that (1) can be analysed as a logical product of elementary propositions which entails that A is not green, and seems to have envisaged that the resulting elementary propositions ascribe to A either unanalysable shades of colour, or light of a certain wavelength. In 1929 he realized that this programme is hopeless. The resulting propositions again exclude each other (if A is dark red it cannot be light red, if it only emits light of 620 nm it cannot also emit light of 520 nm). The reason is that like (1) they ascribe to an object one out of a range of incompatible specifications, a determinate of a determinable colour, velocity, electrical charge, pressure, etc. And there is no way of analysing such propositions into simple ones which would satisfy the requirement of logical independence (*see* COLOUR). Wittgenstein's reaction was to abandon not the idea that elementary propositions involve phenomenal qualities, but the insistence on the logical independence of elementary propositions, and with it logical atomism (RLF; PR ch.VIII; MS 105) (Russell had always been less rigorous in this respect, and hence less troubled by colour-exclusion). Elementary propositions may exclude each other. What is compared with reality is never a single proposition, but a 'proposition system': (1) at a stroke determines that A is neither green nor blue, etc. (WVC 63–4; PR 109–12).

In any event, Wittgenstein came to believe that nothing could satisfy his specifications for elementary propositions. Take another candidate with which he had toyed (NB 29.10.14, 20.6.15), propositions which ascribe a spatio-temporal location to physical simples.

(2)   The material point P is in place x, y, z at time t

excludes P's being in any other place, and hence again is not elementary. It has been suggested that the problem is avoided by propositions which simply combine spatial and temporal coordinates:

(2′)   x,y,z,t.

This suggestion honours condition (a), since (2′) implies nothing about other spatio-temporal points. However, it violates (b). (2′) by itself is a merely the *name* of a point. To turn it into a picture of a state of affairs which states that a mass-point exists at a certain spatio-temporal point, one has to add a quantified provision: 'There is a mass-point...' That is, (2′) itself is not a proposition. Without reference to qualities and relations nothing can be *said*, and most qualities and relations are determinates of a determinable. Consequently, even if one can construct logically independent propositions, it is improbable that one can analyse ordinary propositions into such propositions.

With the demise of logical atomism, elementary propositions lose their 'earlier significance' (PR 111). However, the notion soldiers on for a while with the idea that the only genuine propositions are sense-datum propositions that describe immediate experience. This position is closer to Russell than to the *Tractatus*, in that it makes semantic primitiveness turn on epistemic primitiveness, and it influenced logical positivism's idea of an observation-sentence. Wittgenstein later rejected it (*see* PRIVATE LANGUAGE ARGUMENT). He also claimed that propositions are simple only in the relative sense that within a given grammatical system there are no provisions for their truth-functional analysis (PG 211), as with the colour-propositions of *Investigations* §48.

ethics Ethics occupies a peculiar role in Wittgenstein's thinking. He attached overarching personal importance to questions of moral value. Yet, his written treatments of ethics are brief and obscure, while his views on language have had a strong, albeit intermittent and diffuse, influence on analytic moral philosophy. Wittgenstein's personal moral outlook was egocentric and contemplative. In this he was shaped by Schopenhauer and by Weininger's *Sex and Character*, which proclaimed that 'logic and ethics are fundamentally the same, they are no more than duty to oneself' (159). One has a moral obligation to strive for logical clarity. The SAYING/SHOWING distinction of the *Tractatus* gives substance to the first part of Weininger's slogan: only the empirical propositions of science are meaningful, since they picture contingent states of affairs (truly or falsely). What Wittgenstein calls the 'higher' (TLP 6.42, 6.432), all areas of value, share with the logical structures of language the fate of being ineffable; they cannot be said, they can only be shown. Ethics, aesthetics and logic are linked by virtue of being 'transcendental': while everything factual is 'accidental', they try to express what could not be otherwise, the 'preconditions of the world' (NB 24.7.16; TLP 6.13, 6.421).

However, unlike the logical structure of language, ethical value is not even shown by any meaningful propositions, although it may be shown in actions, attitudes or works of art (EL 9.4.17). Ethics is not just transcendental, it is 'transcendent'. Values 'cannot lie *within* the world', which 'itself is neither good nor evil'; their 'bearer' is a Schopenhauerian metaphysical WILL outside the world (TLP 6.41–6.43; NB 2.8.16). Wittgenstein resolves an inconsistency between two Schopenhauerian ideas, namely that moral redemption lies in denying the will and that compassion, an exercise of the will, is essential to morality, by adopting a Kantian distinction between good and bad willing (NB 21./24./29.7.16; TLP 6.43; *World* II chs XLVII–XLIX). Equally Kantian is the view that the consequences of an action are ethically irrelevant, unlike the spirit in which it is performed. But Wittgenstein's rationale is Spinozistic rather than Kantian. He identifies being good with being happy, being bad with being unhappy (NB 8./29./30.7.16). Reward and punishment are crucial to ethics, but 'reside in the action itself' (TLP 6.422). The reason is that the will is causally impotent. Good or evil willing cannot change the facts, but only the 'limits of the world', namely the 'attitude of the subject to the world'. A good will is its own reward because it looks at the world with 'a happy eye', accepts whatever happens with equanimity (TLP 6.43; NB 20.10.16). This Stoic attitude is the ethical result of the MYSTICAL capacity to view the world *sub specie aeternitatis*, which is also essential to art. 'Ethics and aesthetics are one' not just because they are ineffable, which is merely a precondition for their identity, but because both are based on a mystical attitude which marvels at the existence of the world, and is content with its brute facts (TLP 6.421, 6.45; NB 7./8.10.16).

Wittgenstein maintained that the 'point' of *Tractatus Logico-Philosophicus* was an ethical one, namely to delimit 'the Ethical' from within, by 'remaining silent about it' (FL 10./11.19). However, the structure and composition of the *Tractatus* suggest rather that the mystical passages owe their existence to Wittgenstein's experiences during the war, and were grafted onto a logical trunk (the connection being provided by the saying/showing distinction). This is confirmed by the fact that ethics plays only a minor role in Wittgenstein's subsequent rethinking of the *Tractatus*. Most notable is 'A Lecture on Ethics' of 1929, which elaborates the idea that ethics is ineffable. It expands Moore's definition of ethics as the enquiry into what is good, in order to accommodate everything that has value and concerns the meaning of life, including aesthetics. Again following Moore, Wittgenstein distinguishes a trivial or *relative*, from an ethical or *absolute* sense of terms of appreciation. The relative sense simply implies satisfaction of certain standards, as in 'You play tennis well.' By contrast, the absolute sense is elusive, since no factual statement can ever be or logically imply an absolute judgement of value such as 'You ought to behave decently.' Wittgenstein invokes three experiences to shed light on absolute value. The first is the mystical experience of wonder at the existence of the world. The second is the feeling 'I am safe, nothing can injure me, whatever happens.' This Stoic thought is notorious from

Socrates and Kierkegaard. In Wittgenstein's thought it follows from the logical independence of world and ethical will: just as the latter cannot influence the former, the world cannot harm a virtuous person. For goodness lies in the eye of the beholder, in meeting the afflictions of life in a happy spirit. In this sense, the world of the happy, that is, virtuous, person differs from that of the unhappy one (NB 29.7.16; TLP 6.43). The final experience is that of guilt, which Wittgenstein explains as God's disapproving of one's conduct. In the same vein, he rejects the 'rationalist' claim that 'God wills the good because it is good' in favour of 'Good is what God demands', on the grounds that this reveals the inexplicability of the good, and its independence from facts (WVC 115).

These three points deliberately explain the obscure – absolute value – by the more obscure. The last one makes ethics parasitic on RELIGION, only in order to insist that ethics cannot be explained. Moreover, it falls foul of an elenctic argument in Plato's *Euthyphro* which is close to Wittgenstein's own procedure: we wouldn't call murder 'good', even if it were demanded by God. And Wittgenstein himself acknowledged that the first two amount to a misuse of expressions like 'safe', 'existence' or 'wondering'. Making a virtue of necessity, he radicalizes Moore's claim that 'good' is indefinable: ethics is deep precisely because it inevitably transgresses the limits of language. Fortunately, this is wrong: while judgements of absolute value like 'One ought to keep promises' may not be factual, they are neither nonsensical nor mystical in the way Wittgenstein envisages. Indeed, his insistence on the ineffable nature of ethics is explicitly stipulative: 'I would reject any significant description [of ethics] *ab initio*, on the ground of its significance.' Behind this stipulation lies the conviction that language can express only facts, which restricts significance to factual description (LE 7–9, 11–12; WVC 68–9).

This credo, part of the PICTURE THEORY, is later abandoned. It may be 'impossible' to describe what ethical (and aesthetic) appreciation consists in, but the reason lies in CONTEXTUALISM: we must focus not on the appearance of ethical terms, which resembles that of other words, but on their specific role within our whole culture (LC 2, 7–8). The ethical *shows* itself no longer in mystical attitudes of a solipsistic self, but in social patterns of action. As a result, sibylline pronouncements on the indefinability or ineffability of ethical terms give way to (underdeveloped) investigations into their use (RPP I §160; AWL 34–6). One result of this investigation is that the 'meaning of "good" is bound up with the act it modifies' (a good lie is different from a good deed). Wittgenstein concludes that 'good' is a FAMILY-RESEMBLANCE term. But his argument establishes only that 'good' is used attributively rather than predicatively (a good liar is not necessarily good *tout court*).

It is doubtful whether different things are termed 'good' because of overlapping similarities. That 'good' has a single ethical role in spite of different standards of application is suggested by ideas which survive from the transition period. Crucial to ethics is its contrast with factual propositions and scientific theories. In spite of itself, 'A Lecture on Ethics' does explain that contrast, at least partially, namely by reference to the action-guiding nature of ethical judgements. While there is a logical gap between factual judgements and decisions to act, ethical judgements express directly the grounds or attitudes on which we act. This ties in with two later observations (LC 2; AWL 35). Firstly, ethical terms replace and extend natural reactions (gestures, facial expressions) of approval and disapproval. Secondly, their 'grammar' is determined not only by the object they modify, but also by the reasons a person offers for applying them.

Wittgenstein draws relativistic conclusions from these observations (SDE 23–4; *see* FORM OF LIFE). Ethical judgements are not responsible to reality, and do not contradict each other in the way empirical propositions do. They express the reasons on which we act, and can be justified only within an ethical system, such as Christian ethics. Like grammar, these systems are AUTONOMOUS. Each one of them sets its own standards of justification, since it involves a distinct array of moral concepts. Christian and secular ethics employ terms like 'good' with different meanings, which means that their claims are mutually incommensurable. This is not to say that divergent judgements are 'equally right', or 'right from their own standpoint', but only to say that to make them is to 'adopt' a certain framework of action and justification, which itself cannot be justified. The question of whether Christian or secular ethics itself is right 'does not make sense'.

Wittgenstein mentions one problem with his relativism, the thought that it might destroy the '*imperative* in morality'. He can allow for commitment in the 'first person' (SDE 23; WVC 116–17; CV 60), since ethical judgements express the basis on which an individual intends to act. However, he cannot allow for the idea of moral obligations that bind all individuals, independently of their personal outlook. We can condemn actions demanded by other ethics only from within our own system. If it is impossible to establish the moral superiority of that system, we lack any justification for interfering with such acts, although this is precisely what our own system would bid us do. Wittgenstein's discussion of the laws of logic suggests a strategy for alleviating this problem, namely that there are conceptual limits on what we call 'an ethics'. Unfortunately, this runs counter to his claim that even Goering's remark 'Right is whatever we like' expresses 'a kind of ethics' (SDE 25). But the fact that this slogan expresses the basis on which Goering acted is not enough to sustain Wittgenstein's assessment. The point is not that Goering's outlook is unintelligible, as some Wittgensteinians have suggested, but that it is a paradigm of immorality, not of an alternative ethics.

The logical positivists took over Wittgenstein's early claim that ethics is nonsensical, because unverifiable, while dropping the idea of its paramount importance. His later stress on non-descriptive uses of language influenced both emotivism and prescriptivism. Ironically, he has also been invoked by contemporary cognitivists, who claim that all indicative sentences, including moral ones, make claims to truth. This suggestion is at odds with his view that the similarity in linguistic form disguises logical differences between moral and descriptive propositions (see SDE 24). But he shares the cognitivists' idea that moral discourse cannot be disqualified as less objective than scientific discourse.

explanation Although the *Tractatus* drew a sharp contrast between PHILOSOPHY and empirical SCIENCE (NL 106; TLP 4.111ff.), it can be seen as providing quasi-scientific explanations. Just as science explains the behaviour of macroscopic objects by reference to their microscopic structure, so the *Tractatus* explains the ability of ordinary language to depict reality by reference to its hidden LOGICAL SYNTAX. This fact lies behind Wittgenstein's later exhortations that philosophical explanations be replaced by descriptions of grammatical rules (PI §§109, 126, 496). Attempts to explain the INTENTIONAL relation between language and reality by reference to logico-metaphysical or mental mechanisms are spurious. Genuine CAUSAL explanations are of course legitimate, but their place is in the hypothetico-deductive sciences.

Wittgenstein's philosophy aims at a kind of understanding, yet one which does not require discovering new evidence or hidden causal processes, but is achieved by an OVERVIEW which organizes familiar phenomena in a new way. One kind of explanation Wittgenstein provides pinpoints the sources of philosophical confusions, but he intimates that unlike the diagnostic explanations of medicine, such explanations are not causal. He detected various similarities between his philosophical therapy and psychoanalysis: (a) both try to bring out a patient's repressed worries; (b) the ultimate standard for articulating these worries is that the patient should recognize them; (c) they involve a fight against the will as well as the intellect; (d) the disease can only be cured after it has run its course (AWL 37–40; PI §§133, 254–5, 599; BT 407–10; PG 382; LC 18, 23–5, 43; Z §382).

A far more important role in his later work is played by explanations of meaning. These are not causal explanations of *why* we use a certain term, or of what the (perlocutionary) effects of using it are on particular hearers, but explanations of how we use it, that is, they specify rules for its correct use (PI §§120, 491–8). Such grammatical explanations are not, therefore, incompatible with the idea that philosophy describes linguistic rules. Unlike causal explanations, which in principle can go on for ever, such explanations come to an end. We cannot explain (save perhaps in the causal sense), for example, why locutions like 'I was going to Φ' need not be based on evidence. It is a characteristic philosophical mistake to look for a further explanation here, when 'we ought to look at what happens as a "proto-phenomenon"

111

(Urphänomen)' and simply to note '*this language-game is played*' (PI §§654–5; Z §§314–15; RFM 102–3; RPP I §889).

Wittgenstein claims that it is fruitful to investigate how a word is taught. But this is not because he is engaging in armchair learning-theory (LC 1–2; Z §412). Even his claim that teaching through explanations presupposes certain fundamental linguistic skills is not an empirical genetic theory, but conceptual: explanations are correlates of requests for explanations of, or of unclarities about, meaning, and hence presuppose a certain degree of linguistic understanding on the part of the learner, for example the ability to ask for the meaning of a word (PI §§6, 27; PG 62; PLP 126). Wittgenstein's only contingent observation is that we are not born with such abilities, but acquire them through 'training' (*Abrichtung*) or 'drill'. He also makes a pedagogic claim which is reminiscent of his observation that even doubt presupposes the recognition of some authority: educators should keep in mind that training provides the foundation of explanation, as it does for rule-following or calculation (Z §419; PI §§5, 86, 157–8, 189, 198, 206, 441; LFM 58–60, 182–8; *see* FRAMEWORK). Training does not presuppose understanding, but only patterns of reaction on the part of the trainee. A child will look in the direction in which one points, while a cat will look at the pointing finger. Wittgenstein also claims that the order of teaching is a necessary condition for any logical priority between concepts: 'seems *F*' cannot be logically prior to 'is *F*' if it must be taught later (PI §§143–6; AWL 102; Z §§414–15).

Historical and physiological facts about how we are taught to speak are philosophically irrelevant, what matters is *what* is taught (LWL 38; BB 12–14; PG 41, 66, 70). In teaching, what we explain is the meaning of words. An explanation of meaning, unlike mere drill or a drug which induces understanding, is normative, it provides a standard for the correct use of a term. In this respect explanations *are* linguistic rules, a point which makes plausible Wittgenstein's idea that language is structured by GRAMMAR, a system of rules (PG 191; TS228 §34). Equally important are the consequences for Wittgenstein's elucidation of the notion of meaning. Meaning is what is explained by an explanation of meaning. This allows one to sidestep the misbegotten search for *the meaning* of a term '*X*', an entity of some kind (a MEANING-BODY), in favour of an investigation of the way '*X*' is explained (PG 59, 69; BB 1; PI §560; AWL 48–9), and emphasizes the normative nature of meaning: what explanations of meaning explain is the *correct* USE of '*X*'.

It also links explanation with linguistic understanding. The meaning of '*X*' is what one understands when one understands its explanation (BT 11; PG 60). Both explanation and use are criteria of UNDERSTANDING a word. To understand '*X*' is not only to be able to use it correctly, but to be able to answer the question 'What does "*X*" mean?' Wittgenstein's remarks on the conceptual connections between meaning, explanation and understanding sound trivial, as they should, being grammatical reminders. But if correct, they have significant philosophical implications. For one thing, they imply that neither the meaning of a word, nor our understanding of it, can outstrip our ability to explain it (PI §75). A speaker may understand more than he explains, but not more than he is able to explain. This would rule out the CALCULUS MODEL, according to which the meanings of words and our understanding of them are determined by hidden rules of which we are ignorant.

However, the claim that understanding parallels explanation must itself be qualified. Thus, Wittgenstein recognized that in exceptional circumstances the two criteria of understanding can come apart: someone may be able to apply 'X' correctly, without being able to explain it at all. Moreover, it is quite common that we can only give defective explanations for certain terms, notably those which have to be explained for different contexts, like prepositions or conjunctions. This is not always a sign of carelessness or lack of linguistic self-consciousness: a satisfactory explanation of such terms requires thorough elicitation and reflection. Wittgenstein tended to ignore this point; however, it does not follow that the correct explanations can be such that competent speakers uncoached by philosophers would not even recognize them, as is the case with the logicists' definition of numbers as sets of sets and many explanations given by contemporary theories of meaning. Frege's idea that we can discover that the real meaning of a word differs radically from the meaning we have given it in our explanations is incoherent (BB 27–18; *Foundations* vii).

The philosophical tradition is inimical to this suggestion. Since Plato it has been assumed that the only adequate or legitimate explanation of a term is an analytic definition, which analyses it into a conjunction of characteristic marks, preferably *per genus et differentiam*. Thus, Frege treats definition as logical analysis into 'marks' (*Merkmale*) which together make up the definiendum. He relaxed the initial requirement by allowing for definitions which use expressions of generality instead of marks (e.g., in case of 'prime number'), but insisted that definitions must specify necessary and sufficient conditions for the application of a word (*Foundations* §§53, 104; 'Concept'). For Russell, definitions are symbolic abbreviations constructed out of primitive (i.e., unanalysable) ideas (*Principles* 27, 429; *Principia* i.1, 91), and a similar idea is at work in the *Tractatus*'s conception of LOGICAL ANALYSIS.

Plato also suggested that we cannot find out anything about X unless we possess an analytic definition of X. Accordingly, such definitions must stand at the beginning of a philosophical system, an idea embraced by the rationalists. Kant demurred, because he felt that stringent definitions can at best be the result, not the starting-point, of philosophical inquiry. But the conception of what constitutes a philosophically adequate explanation remained unchallenged until Wittgenstein's later work: 'I cannot characterize my standpoint better than by saying that it is opposed to that which Socrates represents in the Platonic dialogues' (TS302 14; PG 120–1). Socrates was right to ask, for example, 'What is virtue?', but wrong to reject partial explanations or explanations by exemplification or analogies. There may be reasons for restricting 'definition' to explanations of a certain kind. But it is wrong to hold that the meaning of 'X' or the content of our understanding of it is equivalent to such a definition (PI §75).

Forms of explanation are diverse, analytic definition is only one of them. Other legitimate forms of explanation are OSTENSIVE DEFINITION, paraphrase, contrastive paraphrase, exemplification, series of examples, etc. These ordinarily accepted explanations are not defective or incomplete. Examples, in particular, 'are decent signs, not just rubbish or hocus-pocus' (PG 273). Not only are some terms inaccessible to analytic definition, notably COLOUR-terms and FAMILY-RESEMBLANCE terms; the idea that philosophically adequate explanations must be complete in the way that such definitions are complete is misguided to begin with. The function of such explanations is to remove or avert misunderstandings which do or would actually occur without them, not all conceivable misunderstandings (PI §88). This does not mean that a correct explanation is simply one which actually results in understanding. However, it does mean that a correct explanation of 'X' need not cover all the circumstances in which it can be used, but only discriminate relevant circumstances in which 'X' can and cannot be used. The concept of completeness is purpose and circumstance relative. An explanation is complete if it can be invoked as a standard for the correct application of a term in normal contexts. An explanation of 'thinking' need not predetermine whether or not fish think, an explanation of number (*pace* Frege) need not tell us that Caesar is not a number (Z §§114–18; BT 60–9; *Foundations* §56).

Wittgenstein here conflates what an adequate explanation must include and what it must convey. An explanation of 'thinking' need not mention fish or imply anything about them, but it must indicate possible grounds for deciding whether or not they think. Equally, an explanation of number need not mention Caesar, but must indicate the category difference between numerals and the names of people. At the same time, Wittgenstein is right to insist that no explanation can forestall the mere possibility of misunderstanding or doubt (PI §§80, 84–7). An explanation is adequate if it establishes an agreed pattern of application relative to a certain set of FRAMEWORK conditions. For example, our criteria of personal identity combine bodily continuity, memory and character-traits. If these no longer coincided, the term 'person' would disintegrate. But that logical possibility does not render our present explanation of 'person' inadequate (BB 62).

F

fact 'The world is everything that is the case. The world is the totality of facts, not of objects.' The famous beginning of the *Tractatus* is the climax of a realist tradition which assigned importance to facts as mind-independent constituents of the world. Frege, Moore, Russell, and Wittgenstein in 1911 combined this motif with a (partly terminological) idiosyncracy: they identified facts with 'true' or 'asserted propositions'. But Russell and Wittgenstein soon came to understand facts as what makes propositions true (if they are true). Like Moore, Russell treated a fact as a complex of entities ('concepts' or 'terms') which subsists timelessly, regardless of whether it is thought by anyone: the fact that Socrates is mortal consists of the philosopher and the property of being mortal. In his atomistic period, he analysed the world into 'atomic facts' consisting of simple 'individuals', which comprise 'particulars', their qualities and relations (*Principles* ch. 4; *Logic* 178–89; *Writings* ch. 1).

At first, Wittgenstein maintained that the MEANING of a proposition '*p*' is the fact that corresponds to it in reality, the fact that *p* if it is true, the fact that ~*p* if it is false. Later, he abandoned this idea. Only NAMES have a meaning, the absolutely simple 'objects' they stand for. Propositions do not, since they do not stand for anything, but describe; and what a proposition describes, a fact or situation, can be expressed only by a proposition, something which can be prefixed by a that-clause. In spite of occasional lapses (NB 6.10.14, 30.5.15), Wittgenstein urged against Moore and Russell that neither a proposition nor what it represents is a 'complex' (TLP 3.14ff.; NL 98, 107). Complexes are mere combinations of objects, and are denoted by definite descriptions; they include what we ordinarily think of as objects (TLP 2.0201, 3.24; NB 23.–24.5./15.6.15). Like complexes, but unlike OBJECTS, facts are composite, composed of simples (*aus einfachen Teilen zusammengesetzt*; NB 17.6.15; see TLP 3.21, 4.032). Propositions are themselves facts, not mere lists of names: what symbolizes in '*aRb*' is not the complex of signs, but the *fact that* '*R*' occurs between '*a*' and '*b*' with '*a*' to the left and '*b*' to the right. By the same token, facts in general are distinct from complexes of objects: the fact that *a* stands in the relation *R* to *b* is distinct from the complex (*aRb*) – *a*'s standing-in-the-relation-*R* to *b* – which is itself a constituent of a fact like Φ(*aRb*). The broom consists of the broomstick fixed brush, but it is a component of facts – e.g., the fact that the broom stands in the corner – rather than itself being a fact. A fact or state of affairs cannot be identified by listing its components, but only by specifying the determinate way in which these are connected, its 'structure'. Whereas the complex (*aRb*) is the same as the complex (*bRa*), the fact that *aRb* differs from the fact that *bRa*; looking at the Necker cube we can perceive two distinct facts with the same constituents (TLP 2.032, 3.1432, 5.5423).

Russell sometimes follows Bradley in holding that the components of the relational fact *aRb* need to be bound together by further relations relating *a* and *b* respectively to *R*; at other times he maintains that what unites them is a logical form – *x*Φ*y* ('Theory' 80–8, 97–9). Wittgenstein's distinction of facts and complexes renders both suggestions superfluous. The LOGICAL FORM of a fact is not one of its constituents. *aRb* and *bRa* have the same constituents but are different facts. A two-place relation needs only two monadic objects – *a* and *b* – and a diadic one – *xRy* – to constitute a state of affairs, not two further relations to link each object with the relation between them. In a state of affairs, objects fit into one another, like links in a chain, without any logical glue.

According to the PICTURE THEORY, a proposition represents its sense, a state of affairs, which may or may not obtain, depending on whether the proposition is true or false (TLP 2.201ff., 4.021f., 4.031). There is a terminological unclarity here. 'What is the case, the fact, is the existence (*Bestehen*) of states of affairs. A state of affairs is a combination (*Verbindung*) of objects' (TLP 2f.; note that the literal translation of *Bestehen* is 'obtaining', and that single-object states of affairs are excluded by definition). In a letter to Russell, Wittgenstein stated that a state of affairs (*Sachverhalt*) is what corresponds to a true elementary proposition (e.g., '*p*'), while a fact (*Tatsache*) is what corresponds to a true molecular proposition (e.g., '*p . q . r*') (RUL 19.8.19); and he approved of Ogden's corresponding translation of *Sachverhalt* as 'atomic fact'. Nevertheless, 'state of affairs' is the literal translation, and does not beg exegetical questions. For there is also evidence that the difference between states of affairs and facts is the difference between what is possibly and what is actually the case. The *Tractatus* applies the terms 'possible' and 'non-obtaining' to states of affairs and situations (*Sachlagen*), but never to facts (TLP 2.012ff., 2.06, 2.202f., 3.11). At the same time, facts are more complex than states of affairs (TLP 2.03ff., 4.2211): a fact (its structure) consists of a plurality of states of affairs (their structures). Therefore the following distinction has been suggested: a fact is the existence of a set of states of affairs $(S_1 \ldots S_n)$; a state of affairs is a possible combination (concatenation/ arrangement) of objects corresponding to an elementary proposition; a situation is a possible arrangement corresponding to a molecular proposition. However, while some passages support the suggestion that situations are the molecular equivalent of states of affairs, others belie it (TLP 2.11, 2.201f. vs.

2.012ff., 2.034). In view of Wittgenstein's own pronouncements, one should therefore treat the distinction between states of affairs and facts as one between the elementary and the complex. Alas, this would render his position inconsistent. The sense of a proposition, what it depicts, is a state of affairs or situation (TLP 2.201ff., 4.02ff.; NB 2.10./2.11.14). A state of affairs is a *possible* combination of objects which exists if the proposition is true, and does not if it is false, otherwise the sense of a proposition would depend on its being true. On the other hand, to speak of possible or non-obtaining facts runs counter to ordinary usage. By itself this would not matter, since *Philosophical Grammar* explicitly rejects this terminological restriction (PG 301–3; see also FW 55). But it is also incompatible with the *Tractatus*'s own statement that a fact is *something which is the case* (TLP 1ff.). Wittgenstein's letter ignores that states of affairs must be potentialities, facts actualities.

Perhaps this is due to his operating with two different concepts of a fact. Initially, a fact is the *obtaining* of a state of affairs. But the *Tractatus* also distinguishes between a 'positive fact' as the obtaining and a 'negative fact' as the *non-obtaining* of states of affairs (TLP 2.06; NL 97–9). However, this does not remove the aforementioned difficulty, since a negative fact – the fact that such-and-such is not the case – like a positive fact, is an actuality.

Worse, there is an additional unclarity. The *Tractatus* defines the world as the totality of obtaining states of affairs, reality as the obtaining and non-obtaining of states of affairs, but also claims 'The sum-total of reality is the world' (TLP 2.04, 2.06, 2.063). Together, these passages seem to identify the set of positive facts with the set of positive and negative facts. One might try to resist that conclusion by pointing out that the world is identified with the totality of obtaining states of affairs, while reality could be a *subset* of the totality of obtaining and non-obtaining states of affairs. But even this subset must include non-obtaining states of affairs, which are not part of the world.

At any rate, the structure of reality is implicated in that of the world (TLP 1.12, 2.05). Objects cannot occur on their own, but must enter into combinations with other objects. A list of all positive facts therefore mentions all objects. Moreover, objects have not only external properties (of being actually combined with other objects in facts), but also internal properties, the capacity of being combined with other objects in possible states of affairs. Every object contains within its nature all the possibilities for its entering into combination with other objects. This means that the totality of objects, which is given with the totality of obtaining states of affairs (= world), determines the totality of possible states of affairs (= reality). Indeed, if even a single object a is given, *all* objects are given (TLP 2.011–2.014, 5.524). For the nature of a will determine for all other objects whether or not they can be combined with a.

Although the *Tractatus* distinguishes between positive and negative facts, the facts that ELEMENTARY PROPOSITIONS depict the existence of are always positive facts, namely the obtaining of a state of affairs (RUL 19.8.19). By combining names in a certain way, an elementary proposition says, truly or falsely, that something is the case, that objects are combined in a certain way, rather than that something is not the case (TLP 4.022). Consequently, the negation of a true elementary proposition is not a false elementary proposition, but a false molecular proposition, while a false elementary proposition depicts a non-obtaining combination of objects.

This approach solves a problem about negative facts and propositions. It seems that what corresponds to the negative proposition 'Blood is not green' must be blood's not being green, which in turn consists in its being red or blue or yellow. Along such lines, Schlick reasoned that negative propositions are essentially ambiguous and hence defective. Russell, by contrast, rightly rejected the idea of analysing '~*Fa*' as 'There is a proposition "*Ga*" which is true and incompatible with "*Fa*"', and hence grudgingly accepted negative atomic facts as part of the ontological zoo (*Logic* 209–14). Wittgenstein avoided Schlick's confusion by distinguishing between *p*'s not being the case and what is the case instead of *p*: 'not-*p*' does not mean the same as 'anything else, only not *p*'. But he also insisted that '~*p*' does not refer to a different reality from '*p*': it is the same fact which verifies one of them and falsifies the other (NL 94–6; NB 4.11.14; TLP 4.0621f.).

Wittgenstein's ontology of atomic facts can be illustrated as follows: *a–d* are objects of one type (individuals), *E–H* of another (properties), shaded areas are actual combinations (obtaining states of affairs), unshaded areas possible but non-obtaining combinations:

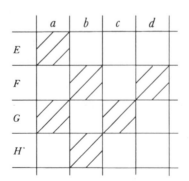

Just as elementary propositions are logically independent, so are the atomic facts and states of affairs they depict. The obtaining or non-obtaining of a state of affairs must neither preclude nor entail the obtaining or non-obtaining of any other (TLP 1.2f., 2.061f.; NB 28.11.16) – *F*'s being combined with *b* neither precludes nor entails *F*'s being combined with *a* or *b*'s being combined with *H*. Accordingly, what corresponds to the negative fact that ˜*Fa* is not that objects *a* and *F could* not be combined because of *G* and *a*'s being combined, but simply that they *are* not so combined. A complete description of the 'world', of the totality of positive facts, is given by listing all elementary propositions and specifying which of them are true (TLP 4.063, 4.26). No two members of this list will be logically incompatible, and none will be the negation of any other. We do not require any propositions involving the negation-sign. One and the same reality corresponds to a proposition and its negation, and that reality is always a concatenation of objects, that is, a positive fact.

This model underlies the idea that the world is the totality of facts rather than things. Some have understood this as a novel, dynamic ontology, based on the idea that we perceive the world not as composed of disconnected bits, but as being ordered according to that-clauses. But the *Tractatus* is not concerned with how we perceive reality. Its ontology is part of a theory of symbolic representation. The world is primarily what is being represented in language. That the world is the totality of facts means that in order to represent the world we have to depict facts. In that sense, the world cannot consist of, that is, be identified with, objects, since the latter are common to all possible worlds.

Although Wittgenstein's later reflections on facts rarely engage with the details of the *Tractatus*, they suggest that this ontology of representation is based on a misconception of facts (PG 199–201; PI §48; MS127 1.3.44). Wittgenstein reiterates and elaborates the distinction between facts and complexes. A complex (e.g., a flower) is a spatial object composed of spatial parts smaller than the whole (e.g., stalk and bloom). The spatial relations between the component parts are not themselves components of the complex: a chain is composed of its links, not of its links plus their spatial relations. The same goes for the properties of a complex: a red circle consists of parts, but it does not consist of redness and circularity. These observations may be directed against the *Tractatus*, although it is unclear whether the latter is committed to treating redness as a component of a complex. On the other hand, Wittgenstein clearly criticizes the *Tractatus* for speaking of facts and states of affairs as composed of constituents (*Bestandteile*), as 'combinations' or 'configurations' of objects (TLP 2.01f., 2.0271–2.03). The fact that the circle is red is not a combination of a circle and redness, the fact that the book is on the table is not composed of the book, the table and the relation of being on. Consequently, facts are not formed by objects as a chain is by its links. Unlike complexes, facts are not spatio-temporal occupants of the world (they have no spatial location and cannot move). For this reason it is also misleading to conceive of propositions as describing facts, states of affairs or situations (cp. TLP 3.144, 4.016, 4.023). Rather, in *stating* a fact, for example that the broomstick is stuck into the brush, one can describe a *complex*, namely the broom, which is a space-occupant. Similarly, one cannot point at a fact, but only point out a fact. One can point at a complex, but that is not to point out that its components are related in a certain way. The *Tractatus* wrongly assimilated facts to constituents of the world. The world is the totality of things, not of facts, although a description of the world consists of statements of fact. This undermines not only logical atomism, but also any correspondence theory of TRUTH, such as the one of the *Tractatus*, which treats facts as worldly items to which our propositions correspond.

family resemblance (*Familienähnlichkeit*) The term occurs in Nietzsche (*Beyond Good and Evil* §20). Another possible source is Nicod's discussion of various types of resemblances (*Geometry in the Sensible World* 55ff.). Wittgenstein first uses it in 'Big Typescript' §58, which reprimands Spengler for sorting cultural epochs dogmatically into families (*Gattungen*) rather than acknowledging that these epochs can be classified variously according to different family resemblances. In this capacity, the notion is part of Wittgenstein's general resistance to dogmatism (BT 259–60; EPB 158), and linked to the idea that an OVERVIEW constructs connecting links between the phenomena it describes. It also occurs briefly in his discussion of ASPECT-PERCEPTION: to recognize a family resemblance between different faces is the dawning of an aspect (PI II 193, 210; RPP II §§551–6; LW I §692).

The notion is crucial to Wittgenstein's attack on essentialism, the view that there must be something common to all instances of a concept that explains why they fall under it (PG 74–5), and that the only adequate or legitimate EXPLANATION of a word is an analytic definition which lays down necessary and sufficient conditions for its application, entailing that, for example, explanations by reference to examples are inadequate. Wittgenstein condemns this 'contemptuous attitude towards the particular case' as based on a misguided 'craving for generality' (BB 17–18). The *Tractatus* had succumbed to this craving in trying to delineate the essence of symbolic representation, and in particular in its doctrine of the GENERAL PROPOSITIONAL FORM, according to which all propositions depict possible states of affairs and are of the form 'Things are thus-and-so.' By contrast, *Philosophical Investigations* §§1–64 elucidates the concepts of language and of a proposition with the help of a series of language-games. Wittgenstein's interlocutor complains that although Wittgenstein has nattered on about language-games, he has not stated what a language-game is, and has therefore failed to explain the essence of language (PI §65). Wittgenstein pleads guilty to the charge, but rejects the underlying demand on the grounds that there is no essence of language, but only different phenomena related in various ways.

He illustrates this first by reference to the notion of a game, because of the antecedent comparison of language to a game (PI §§66–7). When we '*look and see*' whether all games have something in common, we notice that they are united not by a single common defining feature, but by a complex network of overlapping and criss-crossing similarities, just as the different members of a family resemble each other in different respects (build, features, colour of eyes, etc.). What holds the concept together and gives it its unity is not a 'single thread' running through all cases, but, as it were, an overlapping of different fibres, as in a rope (BB 87; PG 75). This can be illustrated as follows:

GAMES

		A	B	C	D	E	F	G
F	1	————————			————		————
E								
A	2		————————————		————		
T								
U	3	———		————————————			
R	4	———	———		————————		
E								
S	5		————————			————————	

Wittgenstein does not maintain that games have nothing in common – he refers to them as 'procedures', and it is manifest that they are all activities. But this falls short of a definition, since there are many activities which are not games. The claim is that there is no set of conditions which all and only games satisfy, and hence no analytic definition of 'game' in terms of necessary and sufficient conditions. Wittgenstein presents this finding as 'the result' of an examination (PI §66; TS302 14). But he has only argued for it by counter-examples to some plausible definitions. He is therefore open to the charge that, with persistence, 'game' can be analytically defined, for example, as a rule-guided activity with fixed objectives that are of little or no importance to the participants outside the context of the game. It could be claimed that such a definition does not merely sharpen our concept through a stipulation, a possibility Wittgenstein concedes (PI §69), but captures how we already use 'game' (it also captures the German *Spiel*, but not *spielen* (playing), which covers activities without fixed rules or objectives, such as throwing a ball in the air).

These qualms about the claim that games have no common defining characteristics leave intact the more modest claim that they *need not* have any such thing in common (BB 25, 86–7; BT 16–20, 86–7; PG 74–6; PLP 180–90). This suffices to resist the essentialist position that there must be an analytic definition. Even if such a definition could be provided, it would not be constitutive of the meaning of our word 'game', since the latter can be, and has been, explained by reference to examples, not to such a common characteristic. But this fall-back position also faces objections. One is that our concept of a game *is* explained by reference to a common property, it is just that this property is the *disjunction* of all the resemblances which link members of the family of games. But this objection is a mere 'playing with words' (PI §67). Unlike the suggested analytic definition, it does not provide a standard for the correct use of 'game' other than the overlapping similarities stressed by Wittgenstein. Moreover, it does not distinguish the case of 'game', in which the resemblances are themselves recognizably related, and which therefore can be applied to an open class of new cases, from artificially constructed disjunctive concepts (e.g., of being either a member of parliament or a cane toad).

The more serious objection is that the notion of a family-resemblance concept is incoherent. The proper conclusion to draw from the fact that we explain 'game' in a variety of different ways, is that it is not a univocal term, but has *different*, albeit related, meanings. Wittgenstein seems to have rejected this suggestion, by insisting that, for example, in the case of 'understanding' we do not have a family of meanings, but family resemblances within a *single* concept (e.g., PI §§531-2). Against him one might invoke his own idea that the meaning of a word is its use, and that diversity of USE entails diversity of meaning. We apply 'game' to different pairs of instances on diverse grounds. Indeed, Wittgenstein himself intimates that a term is ambiguous if and only if in one and the same context it can make for both a true and a false statement (BB 58). Yet, on the account just given, saying for example that the Olympic Games are games can be true or false depending on the rationale applied. Wittgenstein replies to such qualms by noting that there need not be any justification for including something under the concept: 'a transition can be made from anything to anything' (PG 75-6). But while it is correct that no particular concept-formation is forced on us, we distinguish between ambiguous and univocal terms, and between a new empirical application of a term and an extension of a concept, and we do this precisely on the grounds of whether or not the new application is licensed by the original explanation.

Wittgenstein could accept this and still insist that 'game' differs from a genuinely ambiguous terms like 'light' or 'bank' which lack the overlapping similarities that allow one to speak of *the* concept of a game or number (PI §§67-71; PG 75). One might insist that we must distinguish three different cases – univocality, family of meanings, as with 'game', and ambiguity – since to reduce the second case to the first stretches the notion of univocity beyond breaking-point. However, Wittgenstein could reply that the question of what constitutes identity or difference in meaning or concepts cannot be answered by criteria which are as hard and fast or context-independent as the maxim 'same concept, same marks' suggests (PI §§547-70).

Wittgenstein himself occasionally suggests that family-resemblance concepts evolve around one or more 'centres of variation', paradigmatic cases such as football in the case of 'game', to which we relate other cases on different grounds (EPB 190). This would bring his conception close to Gasking's idea of a 'cluster-concept', although he would reject the suggestion that we apply 'game' to non-central instances on the basis of complex calculations concerning their differentially weighted resemblances to these core cases.

Even if an analytic definition can be provided for 'game', there remain other candidates, such as 'art' or 'romanticism', which seem impervious to such attempts. This is part of the reason why Wittgenstein's notion has had such a tremendous impact on discussions of the question 'What is art?' in AESTHETICS. Similar considerations would apply to labels such as 'science', 'politics', 'law'. Wittgenstein also treated as expressing family-resemblance concepts terms which are even more specific than 'game', such as 'reading', 'comparing' and even 'chair' (PI §164; BB 86–7; PG 118).

It has been suggested that the notion of family resemblance is supposed to provide a general solution to the problem of universals: against nominalism, it points out that different instances have more in common than merely being called 'F'; against realism, that what they share is just their being F, not an additional common property. But this proposal distorts the idea of common property: being F is not a property by virtue of which something qualifies as being F (although it may be a property by virtue of which something qualifies as being G, etc.).

In any event, Wittgenstein did not propound the view that *all* concepts are family-resemblance concepts. His account suggests rather that at least some of the branches of a family-resemblance concept are united by necessary and sufficient conditions. This is obvious in the case of Wittgenstein's other paradigm of a family-resemblance concept, namely that of a NUMBER. The various types of numbers – natural, rational, real, complex, etc. – are not defined by a common property. Indeed it would even be mistake to suppose that the natural numbers are simply a subset of the signed integers, since positive rational integers are subject to different rules – we can subtract 9 from 5 if we are operating within the signed integers, but not if we are operating within the natural numbers. We are dealing with a family tree which can be variously extended. But each such extension (e.g., the introduction of real numbers) is precisely defined (PG 70; PI §135; for a similar idea see Russell, *Introduction* 63–4). Equally, there are analytic definitions for some scientific (PLP 93–4, 183) and legal concepts.

Family-resemblance concepts are not the only ones which do not fit the essentialist model. Others are colour concepts, and concepts like 'high' and 'deep': 'blue' refers to a range of shades, but there is no feature which all of these have in common by virtue of which they are blue (BB 130–7; PI §§380–1). But Wittgenstein's main concern is with two other types of concepts. Some passages suggest that psychological concepts, notably that of UNDERSTANDING, are family-resemblance concepts (e.g. BB 19–20, 32–3, 115–25, 144–52; PI §§236, 531–2; Z §26). However, this view recedes into the background. Perhaps Wittgenstein realized that what is united by over-lapping similarities here are the forms of behaviour on the basis of which we ascribe such terms to others, and that this does not entail that the terms themselves are family-resemblance terms.

The other group are the formal or categorial concepts of the *Tractatus*, in particular 'proposition' and 'language' (PI §§65–8, 108, 135, 179; BT 60–74; PG 112–27). Wittgenstein claims that no analytic definition will fit these terms. For these are not technical terms, but terms of ordinary language, which in their ordinary use refer to a variety of different but related phe-nomena. Any analytic definition of such terms would be stipulative, and would not remove the philosophical puzzles, which arise out of our ordin-ary, unsanitized concepts (BB 25–8; PG 119–20).

Some readers have felt that abandoning the quest for analytic definitions or for accounts which subsume phenomena under general principles is at odds with the very idea of rational investigation. But as Aristotle has taught us, one should not treat any topic with greater systematicity than it allows. In so far as Wittgenstein's methodological maxim 'I'll teach you differences!' is based on Butler's motto 'Everything is what it is, and not another thing', it is unassailable (RW 157; PR 196; LC 27). However, it is just as dogmatic to deny uniformity where it exists as to insist on it where it is absent.

first/third-person asymmetry   *see* AVOWAL; INNER/OUTER; PRIVACY

form of life (*Lebensform*)   A work by Spranger bears the title *Lebensformen*, but this refers to types of individual character. Wittgenstein's term, by con-trast, stresses the intertwining of culture, world-view and language. He may have picked up this idea from Spengler (*Decline of the West* I 55), but it has a long tradition in German philosophy (Hamann, Herder, Hegel, von Hum-boldt). Although the term occurs only half a dozen times in Wittgenstein's published work, it has given rise to a multitude of misinterpretations, partly due to his nonchalant use. The term 'language-game' is meant to highlight that 'the *speaking* of language is part of an activity, or of a form of life' (PI §23; *see* RFM 335; MS119 148). Like speech-act theory, Wittgenstein stresses that speaking is a rule-guided *activity*. But he goes further by holding that our LANGUAGE-GAMES are 'interwoven' with non-linguistic activities, and must be understood within this CONTEXT. This holds not just for our actual speech-patterns. Indeed, the best argument for Wittgenstein's claim that the non-linguistic context is essential to understanding linguistic activities is that fictitious language-games can only be properly assessed if one tells a story about how they fit in with the overall practice of the fictitious community.

'To imagine a language means to imagine a form of life' (PI §§7, 19). In *Blue and Brown Books* 134, to imagine a language is equated with imagining a 'culture'. Accordingly, *a* form of life is a culture or social formation, the totality of communal activities into which language-games are embedded.

At the same time, Wittgenstein also speaks of form*s* of life. 'Instead of the unanalysable, specific, indefinable: the fact that we act in such-and-such ways, e.g. *punish* certain actions, *establish* the state of affairs thus-and-so, *give orders*, report, describe colours, take an interest in the feelings of others. What has to be accepted, the given – one might say – are facts of life// forms of life' (RPP I §630; MS133 54). This passage has been invoked to show that a form of life *is* a language-game, and that there are countless forms of life, just as there are language-games. But even leaving aside the singular use noted above, the facts of life listed are not uniformly language-games. Rather, facts of life are the specific patterns of behaviour which together constitute *a* form of life.

'It is characteristic of our language that the foundation on which it grows consists in steady forms of life, regular activity. Its function is determined *above all* by the action which it accompanies' (CE 404). These remarks shed badly needed light on the famous 'What has to be accepted, the given, is – so one could say – *forms of life*' (PI II 226). In the *Tractatus*, the foundations of language were provided by 'unanalysable' sempiternal OBJECTS, whose essences – combinatorial possibilities – are supposed to determine, in an ineffable way, the LOGICAL SPACE of possible situations, and thereby set unalterable limits to what it makes sense to say. Now Wittgenstein holds that in so far as language has foundations, they are provided not by metaphysical atoms (see PR 72), but by shifting patterns of communal activity.

The idea that forms of life provide the foundations of language has been elaborated in two opposite directions. On a *transcendental* reading, the notions of a language-game and of a form of life take the place of the (quasi-)transcendental preconditions of symbolic representation in the *Tractatus*. However, even if our communal practice is a precondition of our language-games, this does not amount to a justification (transcendental deduction) of that practice (although the fact that language requires the context of a practice may reveal certain sceptical doubts to be nonsensical). Furthermore, although the conditions of sense laid down by GRAMMAR antecede matters of fact decided by reality, the point of the notion of a form of life is precisely to de-transcendentalize that contrast by acknowledging that grammar is an integral part of human practice, and hence subject to change.

The opposing interpretation is *naturalistic*. It is often held that our form of life is part of our inflexible biological human nature which rigidly determines how we act and react. This might be supported by reference to Wittgenstein's claim that he provides 'remarks on the natural history of human beings' (PI §415). However, Wittgenstein's naturalism is anthropological rather than biological. Ordering, questioning, recounting, chatting are 'as much a part of our natural history as walking, eating, drinking, playing' (PI §25). These activities, as well as those already quoted, are cultural activities, forms of social interaction. Again, measuring, and even mathematics and logic, are 'anthropological phenomena' which are part of our 'natural history' (RFM 352–3, 356, 399; RPP I §1109). This natural history is the history of cultural, language-using creatures. We must distinguish forms of life from the common human nature onto which they are grafted (*see* FRAMEWORK). Wittgenstein (like Marxism and pragmatism) stresses not our inflexible biological outfit, but our historical practice.

Equally, it has been suggested that there is really only *one* form of life for human beings, that different forms of life are simply unintelligible to us: it is indeed a contingent fact that we speak and act as we do; and we may even be in a position to appreciate that it is logically possible to have different forms of life; but human nature prevents us from understanding these alternative forms of life themselves. This is at odds with Wittgenstein's insistence that different FORMS OF REPRESENTATION become intelligible against the background of *different forms of life*. Measuring with elastic rulers (RFM 38, 91–4) is no different from measuring by the ell. It makes good sense for a community with concerns different from ours. To be sure, there is a difference between recognizing that people measured by the ell in the Middle Ages and imagining that we could revert to this technique now. Such a change would involve fundamental changes in our techniques, our technology and hence our goals and values. But it is not unintelligible; we can understand what is involved, even though it does not appeal to us. Different forms of representation are intelligible given different training or different purposes (Z §§352, 387–8). Even the idea that they must fulfil something we recognize as a relevant purpose is merely a prejudice of our instrumental form of life (see RPP I §49; RFM 95).

As regards linguistic practices, Wittgenstein embraces not a naturalist determinism, but a cultural relativism (e.g. MS109 58), which follows from the conceptual relativism of the AUTONOMY OF LANGUAGE. The latter denies merely that our forms of representation are subject to metaphysical standards, a putative essence of reality, not that they may be subject to pragmatic standards. However, it· is based on the idea that each form of representation lays down its own standards of rationality, which implies that even pragmatic justifications are internal to particular language-games. Hence, criticizing a 'language-game' from the outside can never be a matter of rational argument, but only of 'persuasion' (OC §§92, 262, 608–12; *see* CERTAINTY). Note, however, that language-game relativism should not be Wittgenstein's final word. Within the framework of a form of life it is possible to justify or reform particular language-games – a grammatical proposition like 'One cannot know the future' might be justified by the unreliability of our predictions (LW I §188), or reformed if their reliability improved drastically. What cannot be so criticized is the linguistic practice (form of life) as a whole.

Like other relativists, Wittgenstein studiously ignores the objection that his position is self-refuting because it is implicitly committed to the claim that it itself is correct in a way it explicitly rejects. Unlike other relativists, Wittgenstein might have a reply. His points about the immanence of justification and doubt do not *apply* epistemic terms in a way limited by the practice concerned. They are grammatical remarks, reminders of the way these words are used in this practice. As such they aspire to be correct in a way which transcends different practices – they could be made by a philosopher who engages in a different practice. But this is compatible with acknowledging that there is no necessity about engaging in a particular language-game. Wittgenstein can be a conceptual relativist, but not a philosophical one.

Wittgenstein can be accused of ignoring the fact that in justifying, for example, our scientific world-picture against a community that predicts the future on the basis of oracles (OC §609), we can draw on certain universal values, such as due respect for experience and successful prediction. If it turns out that meteorology is better at predicting the weather, a community which persistently sticks to oracles can be accused of instrumental irrationality. However, this does not mean that they *must* abandon their practice, since their adherence may express different priorities. Another possibility which Wittgenstein himself mentions is that we may be able to claim that our world-view encompasses theirs and is hence richer (OC §286). But in other respects our scientific and technological world-view may actually be impoverished.

Perhaps Wittgenstein never came to explore the rational limitations to relativism because he increasingly stressed the naturalistic limitations. He regards his certainty that there is, say, a chair over there 'not as something akin to hastiness or superficiality, but as a form of life ... as something that lies beyond being justified or unjustified; as it were, as something animal' (OC §§358–9). But he adds '(That is very badly expressed and probably badly thought as well).' What is inflexible are not forms of life in the sense of social practices, but some of their constituent activities or facts of nature. We could not stop taking an interest in people's pain (LW II 43). 'Language ... is a refinement, in the beginning was the deed. First there must be a firm, hard stone for building ... *Afterwards* it's certainly important that the stone can be trimmed, that it's not *too* hard' (CE 420; CV 31). The point is not so much that human nature is immutable as that language in general and reasoning in particular are rooted in forms of behaviour which are neither rational nor irrational, but antecede questions of rationality (OC §§204, 475).

127

Anticipating the current debate about radical translation, Wittgenstein briefly discussed the 'ethnological point of view' or 'anthropological method' which we adopt when coming to understand an (actual or invented) alien community (CV 37; SDE 25). Like Quine and Davidson, he insists that there are minimum requirements which a form of linguistic behaviour must meet in order to be intelligible to us. According to their 'principle of charity', interpretation presupposes that we can treat the aliens' beliefs as by and large true. Wittgenstein concurs partly. 'If language is to be a means of communication there must be agreement not only in definitions but also ... in judgements' (PI §242). But while the principle of charity stresses the second point, it discards the first. By maximizing agreement in opinion, it puts the cart (truth) before the horse (meaning). By and large, we must understand what people say in order to judge whether they are speaking the truth. Sharing a language is 'not agreement in opinions but in form of life' (PI §241; see RFM 353). By the same token, understanding an alien language presupposes convergence not of beliefs, but of patterns of behaviour, which presuppose common perceptual capacities, needs and emotions: 'The common behaviour of mankind is the system of reference by means of which we interpret an unknown language' (PI §206; see RFM 414–21; EPB 149).

This explains Wittgenstein's puzzling remark that 'If a lion could talk, we could not understand him' (PI II 223). On one reading, this means that we could not understand a lion who utters English sentences like 'I'm not interested in you, I've just had an antelope', which is obviously false (although one might, following Austin, question whether such a talkative creature could count as a lion). On a charitable reading, it means that if lions had a *feline* language of complex growls, roars, etc., we could never come to learn it. Why? Because their form of life, and their behavioural repertoire, are so alien to us. We could not make head or tail of their facial expressions, gestures and demeanour. Moreover, our ability to interact even with a tame lion is strictly limited. For related reasons we 'could not find our feet' with a community of human beings who give no expression of feeling of any kind, and we would be completely at a loss with spherical Martians (Z §390; LC 2–3; see also RPP II §568; LW I §190; MS137 13.11.48).

The need for convergence in form of life has yet unexplored implications for ethics. It might be used to justify the idea that our obligations towards living human beings are of a different kind from those towards animals, simply because our ability to interact with animals, to share ideas, responsibilities and aspirations with them, is so severely restricted.

Wittgenstein's form of life contextualism became more pronounced with time. He claimed that to describe human action we need to describe not just what '*one* man is doing *now*, but the whole hurly-burly of human actions', the 'way of living' of which an individual action is part (Z §567; RFM 335–6). Sensation-terms like 'pain' are applied to others on the basis of straightforward behavioural CRITERIA. By contrast, moods and intentional attitudes (hope, pretence, grief, INTENDING, RULE-FOLLOWING) cannot be ascribed simply on the basis of an individual's momentary behaviour, but require a certain surrounding. This 'context' is provided not by certain mental accompaniments, but by (a) the subject's abilities; (b) the 'whole history of the incident', by what went on before and after; (c) the social surroundings, that is, the existence of certain language-games in the subject's linguistic community. For example, a baby moving a chess-piece does not count as playing chess, nor is a baby capable of pretending. One can be in pain for a split second, but not for so brief an instant expect someone, or be in grief. And one can intend to play chess only if the technique of the game exists (PI §§200, 205, 250, 337, 583, 643–4; BB 147; RPP II §631; LW I §§859–76; LW II 26–47; Z §99).

After *Philosophical Investigations* Part I, Wittgenstein expressed this by saying that such terms refer to 'patterns in the weave of our life' (*Lebensmuster*) (PI II 174, 229; LW I §§862–9, 942, 966; LW II 42–3, 55–6, 84; Z §§567–9). The complexity of this weave explains why some third-person psychological judgements are uncertain. The possibility of disagreement about the emotions of others reflects an indeterminacy which is constitutive of some of our psychological terms. That indeterminacy in turn is due to communal patterns of behaviour: mental concepts must be elastic and flexible because human behaviour, and our reaction to it, is diverse and unpredictable (RPP II §§651–3; LW I §§206–11; LW II 24–5, 61–4, 72, 84–95). We cannot make subtle emotional ascriptions on the basis of simple criteria, but need to take into account the context and previous events. This is often possible only if one is acquainted with the person concerned, and has intimate knowledge of human nature.

form of representation (*Form der Darstellung*) In the *Tractatus*, this is the external 'standpoint' from which a picture represents its subject (TLP 2.173f.; *see* LOGICAL FORM). Closer to Wittgenstein's later notion is the Hertzian idea that different scientific theories are guided by different 'forms of describing the world' (*Formen der Weltbeschreibung*). The later Wittgenstein extends this idea beyond SCIENCE. A 'representational form' is a way of looking at things, a kind of *Weltanschauung* (PI §122). This idea encompasses one's approach to philosophy, which in Wittgenstein's case is guided by the attempt to provide an OVERVIEW of grammar. By contrast, the world-picture (*Weltbild*) of *On Certainty* is the inherited background of our scientific and everyday reasoning. Like a 'mythology', it can itself be altered not through reasoning, but only through a conversion (OC §§92, 94–7, 167, 262, 612).

Similarly, Wittgenstein characterizes GRAMMAR, the system of rules which provide standards for the correct use of words, as our 'method' or 'form of representation' (M 51; OC §§61–2; PI §§50, 104, 158). 'That one proposition is true and another false is no part of grammar. What belongs to grammar are all the conditions (the method) necessary for comparing the proposition with reality. That is, all the conditions necessary for the understanding (of the sense)' (PG 88). In virtue of determining what combinations of signs make sense, and hence count as candidates for truth – 'the *kind of statement* we make about phenomena' (PI §90) – grammar itself is not subject to empirical refutation. Logic is 'antecedent' to the correspondence between 'what is said and reality' (RFM 96).

This provides the key to Wittgenstein's later account of logical necessity. As in the *Tractatus*, he resists the Platonist view of necessary propositions as part of a super-physics of the abstract which differ from empirical propositions merely by describing more abstract objects. He also rejects the empiricist reduction of necessary propositions to empirical generalizations (*see* INTERNAL RELATIONS). The contrast between them is even greater than traditionally assumed. Empirical propositions can be said to describe possible states of affairs, but necessary propositions cannot be said to describe necessary states of affairs. For their role is normative rather than descriptive. They function as, or are linked to, 'grammatical propositions', sentences which are typically used to express grammatical rules. A grammatical proposition like

(1)   Black is darker than white

is a 'norm of description' or of 'representation' (RFM 75–6; AWL 16; OC §§167, 321). It lays down what counts as an intelligible description of reality, establishes internal relations between concepts ('black' and 'white') and licenses transformations of empirical propositions (from 'Coal is black and snow is white' to 'Coal is darker than snow').

Grammatical propositions antecede experience in an innocuous sense (PR 143; LWL 12; AWL 90). They can be neither confirmed nor confuted by experience. (1) cannot be overthrown by the putative statement 'This white object is darker than that black object', since the latter is a nonsensical combination of signs. This antecedence to experience renders intelligible the apparently mysterious 'hardness' of necessary propositions and internal relations (PI §437; RFM 84; PG 126–7). To say that it is logically impossible for a white object to be darker than a black one is to say that we would not *call* an object both 'white' and 'darker than a black object'. Given our rules, it makes no sense to apply both terms to one and the same object at the same time. Wittgenstein explains logical necessity through the distinction between sense and nonsense drawn by our norms of representation.

As in the *Tractatus*, Wittgenstein emphasizes the differences between various kinds of necessary propositions. He holds on to his earlier account of logical propositions as TAUTOLOGIES (AWL 137–40; LFM 277–81). But he no longer condemns other necessary truths as pseudo-propositions. Arithmetical equations, geometrical propositions and analytic propositions are grammatical rules (see respectively WVC 156; PG 347; RFM 363 and WVC 38, 61–3; LWL 8, 55 and PI §251). Metaphysical propositions, if they are not merely nonsensical, typically *mask* grammatical rules (BB 35, 55; AWL 65–9; Z §458). Their linguistic appearance is that of statements of fact, but their actual role is that of grammatical propositions.

Unlike their predecessors (rules of LOGICAL SYNTAX), grammatical rules are 'conventions' (*Übereinkunft, Konvention*). Although they are rarely subject to decisions their function, if not their history, is that of conventions (PI §§354–5; AWL 89–90, 156–7; PG 68, 190). Grammar is AUTONOMOUS, it reflects neither the essence of reality nor an inflexible human nature (*see* FRAME-WORK). Accordingly, Wittgenstein's account of logical necessity is conventionalist. However, it differs substantially from the conventionalism of the logical positivists. Their goal was to develop a form of empiricism that could account for logical necessity without either reducing it to empirical generality, lapsing into Platonism or admitting synthetic a priori truths. Necessary propositions, the positivists argued, are a priori, but do not amount to knowledge about the world. For, with the help of the *Tractatus*, it seemed that all necessary propositions could be seen as analytic, true solely in virtue of the meanings of their constituent words. Logical truths are tautologies which are true in virtue of the meaning of the LOGICAL CONSTANTS alone, and analytical truths can be reduced to tautologies by substituting synonyms for synonyms – thus 'All bachelors are unmarried' is transformed into 'All unmarried men are unmarried', a tautology of the form '$(x)((fx . gx) \supset gx)$' the truth of which follows from the meaning of the logical signs involved. Necessary propositions are true by meaning or convention. They either are themselves conventions (definitions) or follow from such conventions.

Wittgenstein's distinction between grammatical and empirical propositions deviates from the logical positivists' analytic/synthetic distinction in four respects. (a) Many of his grammatical propositions do not fit into even the most generous list of analytical truths. The reason is that Wittgenstein had realized that there are non-truth-functional logical relations (PR 105–6), and hence necessary propositions like (1) which are not analytic in the sense of the *Tractatus* and the Vienna Circle. (b) The analytic/synthetic distinction is set up in terms of the forms and constituents of type-sentences. But whether an utterance expresses a grammatical proposition, that is, is used to express a linguistic rule, depends on its role on an occasion of utterance, on whether in the particular case it is used as a standard of correctness. For example, 'War is war' is not typically used to express the law of identity (PI II 221; WVC 153–4; PR 59; AWL 64–5; BT 241). (c) The distinction involves the idea that the truth of necessary propositions is a *consequence* of the meaning of their constituents. According to Wittgenstein, necessary propositions *determine* rather than follow from the meaning of words, since they are partly constitutive of the meaning of the constituent terms (*see* MEANING-BODY). (d) By explaining the status of necessary propositions by reference to their normative rather than descriptive employment, Wittgenstein rejects the view that they are a special kind of truths, one whose source is meaning or convention instead of experience. Notably, if tautologies are degenerate propositions which do not say anything, a point the logical positivists accepted, in what sense could they be true?

These differences are brought out by the fact that Wittgenstein contemplates using the label 'synthetic a priori' for, firstly, mathematical propositions, presumably because they *can* be used descriptively as well as normatively ('$25^2 = 625$' can be used as a prognosis of what result people will get when they square 25, though it is in fact used as a criterion for having performed that operation – RFM 318–19, 327–30); and secondly, grammatical propositions which cannot be explained through the predicate calculus – 'There is no reddish-green' or '"Above" has five letters', for example (RFM 245–6, 336). Kant's idea that mathematical and metaphysical propositions are synthetic a priori expresses an insight: the fact that they seem to anticipate reality requires an explanation. The Viennese account of all necessary propositions as truths which say nothing leaves them without a role. In repudiating the separation of necessary propositions from their application, Wittgenstein takes up Kant's problem. But he insists that necessary propositions are a priori precisely because they are not *about* anything and hence not synthetic (WVC 67, 77–8; LWL 79; PLP 67–8). The role of necessary propositions for empirical discourse is that of norms of representation which provide guidelines for 'channelling' (dealing with) experience (RFM 240, 324–5, 387). 'Whenever we say that something must be the case, we are using a norm of expression'; a logical connection 'is always a connexion in grammar' (AWL 16, 162; RFM 64, 88).

While Wittgenstein's conventionalism avoids the difficulties of the Viennese version, it faces serious ones of its own (*see* MATHEMATICAL PROOF). Even sympathetic commentators like Waismann have felt that the claim that necessary propositions are rules ignores that the former are *about* numbers, colours, lengths, sensations, etc., not words; and that the former but not the latter can be said to be *true* (PLP 66–7, 136–7). However, Wittgenstein could grant that necessary propositions are not in fact rules while insisting that they resemble rules in that they 'play the role of norms of description' (RFM 363; LFM 55, 256) – they license transformations of empirical propositions. Moreover, his point is that for a necessary proposition to be about something and to be true is *toto caelo* different from what it is for an empirical proposition to be so (AWL 154; LFM 114, 250–1; PI §251). The role of a grammatical proposition like 'All bachelors are unmarried' is not to make a true statement of fact about bachelors but to explain the meaning of 'bachelor'. We do not verify it by investigating the marital status of people identified as bachelors, and its denial displays not factual ignorance but linguistic misunderstanding. Most importantly, it excludes not a genuine possibility, but only a NONSENSICAL form of words.

Even if Wittgenstein's conventionalism is not wholly satisfactory, his distinction between grammatical and empirical propositions not only escapes Quine's celebrated attack on the analytic/synthetic distinction, but also helps to undermine Quine's empiricist assimilation of necessary and empirical propositions. Because of (c), it avoids what Quine calls the 'myth of the museum', the idea that abstract entities (logical forms or meanings) force us to hold on to certain propositions come what may; and because of (d) it is not committed to the idea of 'truth by convention'. Moreover, Wittgenstein can accommodate Quine's holistic picture of a web of beliefs according to which even 'necessary propositions' can be abandoned to preserve other beliefs. Indeed, he himself advocated such a holism during his VERIFICA- TIONIST period: 'hypotheses', that is, all propositions going beyond what is immediately given to the senses, cannot be conclusively verified or falsified, because recalcitrant evidence can be accommodated by auxiliary hypotheses (PR 285–90). This may have influenced Carnap's holism in *The Logical Syntax of Language*, and hence, indirectly, Quine's own. During the transition period, Wittgenstein did not extend this revisability to necessary propositions, and he later dropped the empiricist myth of unconceptualized sense- experiences. But the holistic picture survives in *On Certainty* (OC §§94–6, 512–19). Moreover, his functional conception of grammatical rules, according to which an expression is a rule if it is employed as a standard of correct use, implies that the logical status of sentences can change according to our way of using them. Empirical propositions are 'hardened' into rules (RFM 325, cp. 192, 338–9), while rules lose their privileged status and are abandoned. For example, the sentence 'An acid is a substance which, in solution, turns litmus-paper red' lost its normative status (acids now being defined as proton-donors) and turned into an empirical statement which holds true of most, but not all, acids. Conversely, the statement 'Gold has 79 protons' was originally an empirical discovery but is now partly constitutive of what we mean by 'gold'.

Unlike Quine, but like Carnap, Grice and Strawson, Wittgenstein insists that this is compatible with a dynamic distinction between necessary and empirical propositions. The abandoning of grammatical propositions can be motivated by theoretical considerations ranging from new experiences to simplicity, fruitfulness or sheer beauty. But it is distinct from the falsification of a theory. There is no such thing as the falsification of a grammatical proposition. For its normative status means that the proposition itself is (partly) constitutive of the meaning of its constituent terms (BB 23, 56; AWL 40). After such a revision, it makes sense to use words in ways which were previously excluded as nonsensical.

(2)   Nobody under the age of 10 is an adult

is a grammatical proposition which partly determines whom we call an adult. If we were to allow a statement like

(3)   Jane's three-year-old daughter is an adult

because, for example, she has amazing intellectual capacities, we would not have falsified (2). For allowing (3) amounts to instituting a new way of using 'adult', and this introduces a new concept. Consequently (2) and (3) would not contradict each other, since 'adult' means something different in each case.

Scientific concepts are typically held in place by more than one explanation. In cases where several phenomena (fever, presence of virus) are found together in association with a particular disease, the only way to distinguish between CRITERIA and symptoms may be a decision (BB 25). 'The fluctuation in grammar between criteria and symptoms makes it look as if there were nothing at all but symptoms' (PI §354, cp. §79; Z §438). But with respect to specific experiments, it is often possible to decide whether or not particular statements are used normatively or empirically. To deny this would be to deny that one can distinguish, with respect to a particular measurement, between the role of the ruler and the role of the object measured (PI §50). Indeed, a collection of beliefs can only be woven into a web if certain propositions are not merely abandoned with greater reluctance than others, but play a different role, namely that of establishing logical connections between different beliefs (this is of a piece with Lewis Carroll's insight into the need to distinguish between the axioms and the rules of inference of a formal system).

Wittgenstein anticipated Quine's assimilation of necessary propositions to well-entrenched beliefs (presumably because he saw it as the inevitable consequence of Russell's and Ramsey's empiricist conception of mathematics) but claimed that it ignores 'the *deep* need for the convention' (RFM 65, 237).

> [I]f there were only an external connection no connection could be described at all, since we only describe the external connection by means of an internal one. If this is lacking we lose the footing we need for describing anything at all – just as we can't shift anything with our hands unless our feet are planted firmly. (PR 66)

If all the norms of representation concerning, for example, 'bachelor' were transformed into empirical propositions this would mean that all of the following sentences could be rejected: 'Bachelors are unmarried men', 'Bachelors are human beings', 'Bachelors are made of flesh and blood.' Under these circumstances anything at all could be called 'bachelor', since there would be no reason to deny that anything falls under the concept. Consequently, the use of this term would have become totally arbitrary, that is, the term itself would have become senseless. Correspondingly, if we surrendered the grammatical rules governing the use of all our words, these words would lose all meaning. Of course, our habit of uttering words might continue: a communal phonetic babbling without rules is conceivable. But it would resemble speaking in tongues more than a 'language' (PI §§207, 528). If anything can be said, nothing can be meaningfully said.

There is an important parallel between Wittgenstein and Quine. Both characterize logical truths not in terms of their form or structure, but by reference to linguistic behaviour. But unlike Quine's reductionist behaviourism, Wittgenstein views language as essentially guided by norms. It is this normativist conception of language which allows him to make sense of, rather than to reject, the notion of logical necessity.

formal concepts   *see* SAYING/SHOWING

framework   One of the principles of Wittgenstein's early philosophy was the autonomy of sense: whether a proposition makes sense must not depend on another proposition's truth (NM 117; TLP 2.0211). Language is a self-contained abstract system governed by rules of LOGICAL SYNTAX. Recognizing the importance of the surroundings of language is a major achievement of Wittgenstein's later reflections. His first step is to radicalize the *Tractatus*'s CONTEXTUALISM: a word has meaning only as part of a LANGUAGE-GAME, which itself is part of a communal FORM OF LIFE. The second is a kind of naturalism. Our linguistic and non-linguistic activities are conditioned by certain 'facts of nature'. Our concepts rest on a 'scaffolding of facts' in that different facts of nature would make intelligible different 'concept-formations' (PI II 230; RPP I §48; Z §§350, 387–8). In this context Wittgenstein distinguishes three elements:

(a)   the GRAMMATICAL rules which constitute a language-game like that of measurement;

(b)   the application of these rules in empirical propositions (specific measurements);

(c)   the framework or 'scaffolding' which allows us to operate the language-game.

> Disputes do not break out ... over the question whether a rule has been obeyed or not ... That is part of the scaffolding from which our language operates ... [Human beings] agree in the *language* they use. That is not agreement in opinions but in form of life. If language is to be a means of communication there must be agreement not only in definitions but also

... in judgements. This seems to abolish logic, but does not do so. It is one thing to describe methods of measurement, and another to obtain and state results of measurement. But what we call 'measuring' is partly determined by a certain constancy in results of measurement. (PI §§240–2; see OC §156)

This passage can be rendered consistent if 'agreement ... in form of life' is not exhausted by agreement in definitions/judgements (i.e., opinions), but includes 'a consensus of action', of applying the same technique (LFM 183–4). The idea that language requires agreement in judgements as well as definitions *would* abolish logic, if communal consensus determined whether or not a particular measurement is correct. This is why Wittgenstein insists that what counts as the correct application of rules (an accurate measurement) is determined by the rules themselves, which are our standards of correctness; the definition of 'correct measurement' is not 'what people agree on'. These rules specify neither the results of particular measurements – (b) – nor that there is general agreement in applying them – (c) (RFM 322–5, 359–66, 379–89, 406–14; Z §§319, 428–31; *see* RULE-FOLLOWING; TRUTH). Nevertheless, without such agreement, the rules would 'lose their point' (PI §242; RFM 200); a technique which did not produce such consensus would not be called 'measuring' (according to Wittgenstein, therefore, in this exceptional case the rules themselves *do* include a reference to consensus).

The required consensus in application is less stringent for emotion-terms, for example (LW II 23–4; PI II 224–8), and minimal for essentially contested terms like 'corrupt'. Moreover, communal agreement is not the only framework or background condition for playing certain language-games. Thus, our concepts of measures work only in a world with relatively stable rigid objects; but this is not laid down in the rules of, for example, metric measurement. What Wittgenstein calls 'facts of nature' play the same role (although sometimes by allowing consensus). These facts fall into three groups:

General regularities concerning the world around us. Objects do not vanish or come into existence, grow or shrink, etc., in a rapid or chaotic manner (PI §142).

Biological and anthropological facts concerning us. Our perceptual capacities allow us to discern such-and-such colours (Z §§345, 368; PLP 250–4), our memory permits calculations of a certain complexity (MS118 131), our shared patterns of reaction allow us to teach (AWL 102; LFM 182) – OSTENSIVE DEFINITION, for example, presupposes that human beings look not at the pointing finger (as cats do), but in the direction in which it points.

Socio-historical facts concerning particular groups or periods. Our ways of speaking express practical needs and interests (RFM 41, 80–1) shaped by history.

Given these facts, certain forms of representation will be 'practical' or 'impractical' (AWL 70). Provided that the world is as it is, people who employed alternative ways of calculating or measuring for purposes similar to ours would have to make tedious adjustments. By the same token, drastic changes in these facts could render our rules inadequate in this pragmatic sense. They might not only become impractical but even be inapplicable (PI §569; RFM 51–2, 200). If objects constantly and unpredictably vanished or sprang into existence, our language-game of counting would loose its 'point' or become 'unusable'. So too would our colour-concepts if objects constantly changed their colours at random.

The rules of tennis do not include that it is to be played at Earth-gravity. But tennis would be pointless on the moon (every serve would be an ace) and could not be played on Jupiter. Although the framework conditions do not determine what the rules of the language-game are, they partly determine what language-games are played. Hence they impose limits on the possibility of adopting different grammatical rules (*see* AUTONOMY OF LANGUAGE). 'Yes, but has nature nothing to say here? Indeed she has – but she makes her voice audible in another way. "You'll surely run up against existence and non-existence somewhere!" But that means against *facts*, not concepts' (Z §364). The way we speak is part of human practice, and hence subject to the same kinds of factors that determine human behaviour in general. However, these facts of nature do not provide a naturalistic justification of our grammar. A change in the framework conditions would render our rules not incorrect (false to the facts) but pointless or obsolete (PG 109–10; Z §§366–7; RPP II §§347–53).

Wittgenstein would not even concede that given such-and-such framework conditions we are causally forced to adopt specific language-games (Z §351). The relative stability of the material world is a condition for measurement, but does not force us to adopt the metric system (that is a prerogative of the EC Commission). Similarly, common colour discriminatory abilities and the relative constancy of the colours of things are framework conditions of any colour grammar, but these are compatible with widely differing colour grammars among the various languages of mankind. This is at odds with the idea that the right, or perhaps just inevitable, rules are those which we find natural. Wittgenstein acknowledges that we find certain rules 'natural' (AWL 67; LFM e.g. 183, 243), but adds that this is relative to people and circumstances; it is not biologically fixed, but malleable, for example through education (Z §387; PI §§595–6).

Framework conditions impose causal constraints: they partly explain why we do not go down one road, but not why we go down another. One may feel nevertheless that acknowledging them pollutes philosophical descriptions of grammar with causal EXPLANATIONS. Wittgenstein himself claims to supply 'remarks on the natural history of human beings' (PI §415); while elsewhere he disavows such ambitions:

> Our interest certainly includes the correspondence between concepts and very general facts of nature. (Such facts as mostly do not strike us because of their generality.) But our interest does not fall back upon these possible causes of concept-formation. We are not doing natural science; nor even natural history – since we can also invent fictitious natural history for our purposes. (PI II 230; see RPP I §48)

The last remark does not, however, keep philosophy free of causal hypotheses, since such hypotheses could connect fictitious background conditions with fictitious concept-formations. More promising are Wittgenstein's attempts to distinguish his kind of natural history from natural science. Sometimes they leave unclear how his natural history differs from straightforward grammatical remarks, for example when he suggests that it includes such propositions as 'Grasshoppers cannot read or write', although not 'Human beings think, grasshoppers don't' (RPP II §§14–25). Equally, for Wittgenstein it is a conceptual point that people with different discriminatory capacities could not have our COLOUR-concepts. In other passages, however, his kind of natural history clearly concerns 'empirical', that is, contingent facts, for example that human beings modify their concepts in response to experience (Z §352). Unlike grammatical reminders they do not remind us of the linguistic rules we follow; instead, they remind us of facts about ourselves. But these empirical facts are not arcane, a topic of scientific hypotheses. The natural history of measurement is not a branch of applied physics about how best to measure something under certain conditions. Rather, it assembles empirical facts in a way that makes intelligible or unsurprising the one point which matters to philosophy: that if certain contingent framework conditions changed, we would find alternative procedures plausible or useful, and our actual procedures impracticable or pointless (RPP I §§950–1109; LW I §§207–9; see OVERVIEW). Physics might tell us that a change in certain laws of nature would lead objects to grow or shrink constantly and chaotically. But it does not take physics to appreciate that under such circumstances measuring sizes would become pointless. The relevant facts go unnoticed precisely because they are so familiar and general – a 'miss the wood for the trees' effect (PI §129, II 230; RPP I §§46, 78).

This theme recurs in *On Certainty*. Wittgenstein there discusses the empirical common-sense truisms which Moore had claimed to know for CERTAIN. He treats them as world-picture or hinge propositions: although they are empirical, that is, state contingent facts, they could not simply turn out to be false, since this would remove the background against which we distinguish true and false. *On Certainty* occasionally speaks of these propositions as a 'scaffolding' or 'framework' of our thought, and, like *Philosophical Investigations*, states that 'the possiblity of a language-game is conditioned by certain facts' (OC §§211, 617). Nevertheless, the points behind the notions of facts of nature and hinge propositions differ in principle: if facts of nature were different, specific language-games would change; if we could not be certain of some hinge propositions, our entire web of beliefs would collapse. There is an overlap between the two categories: if certain 'unheard-of events' (OC §513) were to occur, for example, objects grow or shrink constantly for no apparent reason, this would not only shake our system of beliefs but, as we have seen, render pointless or impracticable specific language-games. But uncertainty about some other hinge propositions (e.g., the spherical nature of the earth) would affect not so much specific language-games as forms of representation within a specialized scientific discourse.

Wittgenstein claims that hinge propositions, like facts of nature, go unnoticed because they form part of the background of our language-games. They are 'withdrawn from circulation' and 'shunted onto an unused siding', and 'lie apart from the road travelled by enquiry' (OC §§88, 210). Some commentators have concluded that hinge propositions are ghostly phenomena because they are abstract, ineffable and transcend our linguistic practice, thereby violating the idea that meaning is use. However, the very point of speaking about hinge propositions is that they play a special role in our linguistic practice (OC §§94–8, 152, 248). Moreover, *On Certainty* holds only that hinge propositions *are*, by and large, not stated, not that they cannot be stated. Wittgenstein's point is that 'if they are ever formulated', they are exempt from doubt (OC §88). It has also been claimed that *On Certainty* revives the *Tractatus*'s SAYING/SHOWING distinction and that hinge propositions are ineffable, that is, can only show themselves in our practice. But one passage invoked in this context merely raises the possibility, and the other ends by stating that 'that's not how it is' (OC §§501, 618). What is correct is this. Wittgenstein tentatively suggested that to say, with Moore, that we *know* hinge propositions creates confusion because it invites sceptical doubts, and is hence at odds with our treating them as certain, which shows itself in the way we act (e.g. OC §§7, 466). But this is not to say that it creates confusion or fuels scepticism to draw attention to these propositions, as long as one does not mistake them for ordinary empirical claims. Like the structure of Husserl's 'life-world', facts of nature and hinge propositions are not ineffable, but special: their role is too basic to be easily noted.

G

general propositional form (*allgemeine Satzform*) Wittgenstein's early philosophy seeks to determine the nature of representation and of what is represented, the world. It does so by establishing the essence of the proposition. Various types of propositions differ in their logical forms, and these are to be discovered by the application of logic. But these possible forms have something in common which is established a priori. That a form of words can constitute a proposition is not a matter of experience, but implicit in the rules of LOGICAL SYNTAX. The general propositional form is the essence of the proposition, the necessary and sufficient conditions for something to be a proposition in any 'sign-language' (*Zeichensprache*). Since language is the totality of propositions, the general propositional form also provides features which unite all languages, in spite of their superficial differences. It is the only LOGICAL CONSTANT, 'the one and only general primitive sign in logic', since all logical operations, and hence all logical propositions and inferences, are given with the very idea of a BIPOLAR elementary proposition (TLP 4.001, 5.47ff.; NB 22.1./5.5.15, 2.8.16).

'The general propositional form is: Things are thus-and-so (*Es verhält sich so und so*)' (TLP 4.5). This formula is not restricted to true propositions. The general propositional form is the colloquial equivalent of a 'propositional variable' (TLP 4.53; OL 27, 30). It is the most general propositional variable, the one which corresponds to the 'formal concept' of a proposition (*see* SAYING/SHOWING). Its range of values is not a particular type of proposition – '*fa*', '*fb*', etc. – but the totality of propositions. Far from being vacuous, the formula indicates that propositions must be logically articulate (composed of function and argument), and must depict possible states of affairs, that is, be descriptive.

In the first instance, the formula applies to ELEMENTARY PROPOSITIONS. But according to the *Tractatus*, all propositions derive their representational character from such elementary propositions. The totality of propositions is determined by the totality of elementary propositions (TLP 4.51–5.01; RUL 8.12). An essential part of the doctrine of the general propositional form is the *thesis of extensionality*: 'A proposition is a truth-function of elementary propositions. (An elementary proposition is a truth-function of itself)' (TLP 5).

140

The parenthesis alludes to the fact that in the TRUTH-TABLE notation every elementary proposition is expressed as a truth-function (conjunction) of itself and a tautology involving all other elementary propositions (e.g., '$p.(q \vee \sim q)$, etc.'). The first clause states that the truth of any proposition is dependent solely upon the truth of the elementary propositions into which it can be analysed: 'propositions occur in other propositions only as the bases of truth-operations' (TLP 5.54). Consequently, the *Tractatus* has to explain away the numerous *intensional contexts* of natural languages, such as the embedding of a proposition in the scope of an intentional verb (in indirect speech or ascriptions of propositional attitudes), causal explanations, scientific laws and modal propositions. It does so with varying degrees of implausibility, either by reducing these occurrences to extensional ones, as in the case of CAUSAL explanations and ascriptions of BELIEF, or by denying that they constitute genuine propositions, as in the case of SCIENTIFIC laws and modal proposi- tions (*see* LOGIC).

As a result of extensionalism, *Tractatus* 6 equates the general propositional form with the 'general form of a truth-function': $[\bar{p}, \bar{\xi}, N(\bar{\xi})]$. This formula specifies a series of propositions (the values of the most comprehensive pro- positional variable) not through simply listing them (as in 'p, q, r') or through a propositional function, as in the case of the quantifiers, but through a 'formal series' the members of which are ordered by a 'formal law' which establishes internal relations between them (TLP 4.1252, 5.501). It does so through a reiterable operation (TLP 5.23–5.3), one which can be applied to its own results (TLP 5.251). Applying O to a one gets $O'a$, by repeating the operation one gets $O'O'a$, and so on – as in 2, 4 $(2+2)$, 6 $(2+2+2)$, etc. Such a series is determined by its first member and by the operation that produces the following term out of the preceding one (TLP 4.1273). It is expressed as $[a, x, O'a]$ – a is the first term, x an arbitrary term, $O'a$ the form of x's immediate successor.

Truth-functional operations are reiterable, and hence create a formal series expressed through an analogous ordered triple. $\bar{p}$ is the first member. It is not a truth-function of elementary propositions ('$p.q.r$'), but a list of all elementary propositions (p, q, r, etc.). '$\bar{\xi}$' signifies not a random selection of propositions, as Russell's Introduction claims, but a set of propositions which has been constructed out of the initial set, and which may include elemen- tary as well as molecular propositions ('¯' indicates not generality, but that ξ 'represents', that is, lists, all of its values – TLP 5.501). $N(\bar{\xi})$ is the result of applying the operation of joint negation to $\bar{\xi}$. The operation N is a general- ized version of the diadic truth-operator 'neither p nor q', known as the Sheffer stroke '$p \downarrow q$', from which it differs in that it operates on an arbitrary number of propositions (this is important since the *Tractatus* is agnostic about the number of elementary propositions) to yield a single proposition, the joint denial of them all. In the truth-table notation the Sheffer stroke is expressed as '(FFFT)(p,q)', N as '(- - - - T)(....)', with the right-hand brackets indicating an arbitrary selection of n propositions, and the left-hand brackets a truth-table with $2^n - 1$ F's omitted (TLP 5.5). In other words, the result of applying N to $\bar{\xi}$ is true only if all the members of $\bar{\xi}$ are false. For example, '$N(p,q,r)$' is equivalent to '$\sim p . \sim q . \sim r$'.

By specifying the general propositional form in this way, Wittgenstein espouses a constructivist claim. Every proposition is 'a result of successive applications to elementary propositions of the operation $N(\bar{\xi})$' (TLP 6.001; see NL 94, 102–3). The truth-functional connectives employed by Frege and Russell – '$\sim$', '$\supset$', '$.$', '$\vee$' – are not just interdefinable, but can all be reduced to the Sheffer stroke, and hence to N (TLP 5.1311, 5.42, 5.441). (M, a generalized version of the other Sheffer stroke '$p \uparrow q$', namely 'either not p or not q, etc.', serves the *Tractatus*'s purposes equally well – RUL 19.8.19.) Sheffer had shown that '$\downarrow$' is 'expressively adequate' for the propositional calculus, capable of expressing all truth-functions of arbitrarily many truth-arguments. The same holds, *a fortiori*, for the generalized version N. For example, all 16 truth-functions of two elementary propositions, the starting-point of a formal series, can be generated through a process which starts as follows: 1. $N(p,q)$ $[\sim(p \vee q)]$, 2. $N(N(p,q))$ $[(p \vee q)]$, 3. $N(N(p,q), N(N(p,q)))$ $[\sim(\sim(p \vee q) \vee (p \vee q))]$ (contradiction), 4. $N(N(N(p,q), N(N(p,q))))$ $[\sim\sim(\sim(p \vee q) \vee (p \vee q))]$ (tautology). However, if we apply N to that last result, or even to any combination of the previous results, no new truth-function is created. To get any further we have to bring into play a new proposition, by applying N to 'p' and 'q' individually, then to the resulting '$\sim p$', '$\sim q$'; and so on. This suggests that Wittgenstein's procedure does not result in a formal series: it generates all the truth-functions of 'p' and 'q', but not in a single definite order. Furthermore, if the initial set of elementary propositions is infinite, Cantor's diagonal proof that $2^{\aleph_0} > \aleph_0$ promises to specify an infinite subset of elementary propositions which cannot be generated through Wittgenstein's procedure (but note that Wittgenstein rejects Cantor's proof; *see* NUMBERS).

The operation N is stretched even further by the task of constructing all general propositions. Like propositional logic, quantification theory results from the application of the same truth-functional operation. It differs merely in the way in which the base of N is specified, namely by a propositional function. If $\bar{\xi}$ has as its members all the values of the propositional function fx, that is, the set of propositions 'fa, fb, fc, etc', then '$N(\bar{\xi})$' is the joint denial of all these propositions, '$N(fx)$', and hence equivalent to '$\sim(\exists x)fx$'. If we apply N to that result, we get '$(\exists x)fx$'. If $\bar{\xi}$ has as its members all the values of $N(fx)$, then '$N(N(fx))$' is '$(x)fx$', and '$N(N(N(fx)))$' is '$\sim(x)fx$'. This preserves the unity of propositional and predicate logic: '$\sim p$', '$\sim(p \vee q)$' and '$\sim(\exists x)fx$' are all expressed through the same operation, as '$N(p)$', '$N(p,q)$', '$N(fx)$'.

It has been alleged that this notation is expressively inadequate, incapable of generating all formulae of first-order quantification theory. This inadequacy emerges in the case of multiply general formulae such as '$(\exists x)(y)fxy$' in which the variables of the propositional function are bound by distinct quantifiers. Thus, formulae are generated from the propositional variable 'fxy', which has as its values 'faa', 'fab', 'fac', 'fba', etc. Applying N to this delivers the joint denial of these propositions, '$N(fxy)$', which is equivalent to '$\sim(\exists x)(\exists y)fxy$', and applying N to that proposition delivers '$N(N(fxy))$', that is, '$(\exists x)(\exists y)fxy$'. Unfortunately, any further application of N will simply take us back and forth between equivalents of these two formulae (a similar deadlock results if we start from the propositional variable $\sim fxy$). The problem is not due to the employment of a single operator N. '$M(fxy)$' is equivalent to '$\sim(x)(y)fxy$', '$M(M(fxy))$' to '$(x)(y)fxy$', but then the flip-flop starts again. What is needed is rather a way of operating separately on the two argument-places of the propositional function. This can be done through enriching the N-operator by a variable-binding device. Thus, if one employs '$Nx(fx)$' to indicate the joint denial of all propositions resulting from substituting names for the variable x, the previous stumbling-block '$(\exists x)(y)fxy$' can be expressed as '$N(Nx(Ny(Nfxy)))$', which translates as '$\sim(x)\sim(y)\sim\sim fxy$'.

While such an expressively adequate notation is not explicit in the *Tractatus*, it is compatible with what *Tractatus* 5.501 says about the stipulation of values for a propositional variable. However, it expresses '$(\exists x)fx$' as '$N(Nx(fx))$' $\equiv$ '$N(N(fa, fb, fc,$ etc.$))$', and '$(x)fx$' as '$Nx(N(fx))$' $\equiv$ '$N(N(fa), N(fb), N(fc),$ etc.$)$'. In the first case, a single operation N is applied to a possibly infinite class of propositions, and then N again to the result. In the second, N is applied to each of the members of that class, and then N again to the result. Now, it seems that this final operation presupposes the prior execution of (possibly) infinitely many steps, and has no immediate predecessor. This would infringe the *Tractatus*'s demand that all truth-functions be 'results of the successive application of a finite number of truth-operations' (TLP 5.32). This objection is held to be on a par with the point that the truth-tabular decision procedure cannot be applied to quantification over infinite domains. But Wittgenstein was well aware of this, and his treatment of GENERALITY precisely avoids the need to go through an infinite number of steps, by specifying the bases through propositional functions. And the original objection ignores that what counts are not the individual operations, but the *stages* of truth-functional construction, of which there are just two in our case: starting with an elementary proposition 'fa' we apply N once to yield '$N(fa)$', which in turn delivers the propositional function $N(fx)$. Applying N to all values of this function yields '$Nx(N(fx))$'.

Although the *Tractatus*'s constructivism is not obviously inadequate, it is open to other objections. It does not provide the unitary explanation the *Tractatus* sought, since the modified N-operator occurs both with and without a variable, as in '$N(Nx(fx))$'. Wittgenstein himself later pointed out that specifying the base of operations through a propositional function means something entirely different in the case of infinite domains. In that case, the 'and so on' which is equivalent to the notion of successive operations cannot be replaced by a list but indicates a new type of operation. To reduce logic to a single operation is both impossible and superfluous. Since logical constants do not represent logical objects anyway, we do not need to reduce their number to minimize our ontological commitments. The *Tractatus's* motive for the reduction is the attempt, following Frege, to avoid piecemeal definitions of the logical constants (TLP 5.45f., 5.46; NL 99, 105; *Laws* I §33, II §§56–67, 139–44): in order to define them as they apply not just to elementary propositions (e.g., in '$\sim p$'), but also to propositions which already contain constants ('$\sim(p.q)$', '$\sim(\exists x)fx$'), one would have to introduce one connective in advance of the others, with the result that one could not draw on the latter in defining the former. But this problem can be avoided either through recursive definitions, as in model theory, or by granting, as does the later Wittgenstein, that signs like '$\sim$' and '.' may operate in slightly different, albeit analogous, ways in different areas.

Wittgenstein's later self-criticism focused not on his logical constructivism, but on the very idea of a general propositional form. 'This is how things are' looks like the general propositional form because it is used as a sentence-schema which picks up the reference to an antecedent sentence. Although it does not itself say something true or false, it sounds like an English sentence, it consists of subject and predicate. This indicates that our concept of a proposition is in one sense determined by a *Satzklang*, and hence by the rules of sentence-formation in a given language. But this does not provide the logico-semantic essence sought by the *Tractatus*. And the idea that all propositions say that such-and-such is the case is only a confused way of saying that a proposition is whatever is true or false (expresses a thought/fact, can be the object of a propositional attitude), that is, is an argument of the truth-functional calculus (PLP 288–98, 372). But Wittgenstein's redundancy theory of TRUTH implies that this provides neither a metaphysical insight into the essence of propositions nor an independent test of propositionhood, since our concept of truth and falsehood is itself part and parcel of our concept of a proposition (PI §136; PG 124). To be sure, whether a sign-combination counts as a proposition is a matter of grammar, not experience, but the rules governing the term 'proposition' are neither sharp nor inflexible.

Wittgenstein also came to reject the thesis of extensionality, noting that it characterizes the propositional calculus, but not ordinary language. Moreover, the idea that all propositions are, or contain, a description is part of the misleading AUGUSTINIAN PICTURE OF LANGUAGE. Questions, commands, threats, warnings and exhortations are *Sätze* (this term, unlike 'proposition', is not confined to indicative sentences). And many propositions, notably GRAMMATICAL propositions, MATHEMATICAL propositions, and AVOWALS, have the form of indicative sentences, but, Wittgenstein argues, a non-descriptive role. *Philosophical Investigations* intimates that a PROPOSITION could be explained as a move in the language-game. But even that explanation fails to cover tautologies and contradictions (which don't say anything). For such reasons, the *Investigations* also rejects the very quest for a definition of 'proposition'. The concept of a proposition is a FAMILY-RESEMBLANCE concept. It is explained through examples. What holds together questions, commands, observation sentences, first- and third-person psychological propositions, logical propositions, mathematical equations, laws of physics, is not a single common essence, but a web of similarities and analogies. It is possible to define sharply one type of proposition, for example, tautologies. Indeed, the doctrine of the general propositional form defines the propositions of the propositional calculus as formulae which are either bases or results of truth-functional operations. But this no more shows that 'proposition' is not a family-resemblance concept, than the fact that one can give sharp definitions of particular types of numbers shows that 'number' is not a family-resemblance concept.

generality Frege's invention of a notation for quantification was crucial to the development of modern logic. It allowed for the formalization of statements involving multiple generality, which are essential to mathematical definitions (e.g., of a continuous function) and proofs (e.g., of number-theoretic theorems) (*Notation* §§11–12; *Laws* I §§8, 21–2). Frege analysed 'All Greeks are bald' not into a subject 'all Greeks' and a predicate 'are bald', but into a complex one-place function-name, 'if x is a Greek, then x is bald', which is bound by the universal quantifier 'For all x'. Just as 'x is a Greek' is the name of a first-level truth-function mapping objects onto truth-values (the True for Socrates, the False for Caesar), so this quantifier is a variable-binding, variable-indexed 'second-level function' which maps first-level functions onto truth-values – thus the universal quantifier has the value F for the argument 'x is a Greek' (for not everything is a Greek), T for '$x = x$' (everything is identical with itself). A 'general' proposition asserts that a function $\Phi(x)$ has the value T for all arguments. 'Existential' propositions are not general in this sense, but negations of general propositions. Thus, 'Some Greeks are bald' comes out as 'Not for all x, if x is a Greek, x is not bald.' But like 'all', 'some' (which corresponds to *existence*) is a second-level concept, the one which has 'falling within it' all first-level concepts which have at least one object 'falling under' them (*Foundations* §53; 'Function' 26–7; 'Concept' 199–202). Russell followed a similar line. He treated existence as 'a property of a propositional function', but replaced Frege's cumbersome notation: '$(x)fx$' means that the propositional function fx is true in all instances, '$(\exists x)fx$' that it is true in at least one instance. The quantifiers, like the propositional connectives, are names of 'logical constants', objects of which we have logical experience (*Principia* *9; *Logic* 228–41; *External* 64–7; *Introduction* ch. XV).

145

Wittgenstein praises the variable-binding apparatus '(x)' and '$(\exists x)$' for having the 'mathematical multiplicity' required to express generality (TLP 4.04ff.; NB 23.10.14). It signifies what is being generalized, by showing which part of its scope varies and which is constant, thereby distinguishing between, for example, '$(x)fx$' (quantification over individuals) and '$(\Phi)\Phi x$' (quantification over properties). It has a determinate scope, which allows one to distinguish, for example, truth functions of general propositions like '$(x)fx \supset (x)gx$' from general propositions involving a complex function like '$(x)(fx \supset gx)$'. Finally, it allows for one variable to fall within the scope of another, which makes it possible to express multiple generality, and to distinguish '$(x)(\exists y)xRy$' (e.g., 'For every natural number there is a greater one') from '$(\exists y)(x)xRy$' (e.g., 'There is a natural number which is greater than all others').

At the same time, Wittgenstein rejects Russell's assimilation of '$(\exists x)fx$' to 'fx is possible', because the former can be false even if sentences of the form 'fx' express a logical (and indeed an empirical) possibility (TLP 4.464, 5.525). More importantly, he attacks the idea that quantifiers are NAMES of LOGICAL CONSTANTS, logical entities of some kind. The quantifiers no more stand for second-level concepts or properties than '.' or '$\vee$' for relations between propositions. Moreover, the arguments of quantifiers, what they operate on, cannot be names (of first-level concepts), since they must be capable of being true or false. This is shown by the fact that '$(x)fx$' can be negated not just externally, '$\sim(x)fx$', but also internally, '$(x)\sim fx$', a point highlighted by Wittgenstein's T/F notation (*see* TRUTH-TABLES). Frege and Russell fail to do justice to the fact that the understanding of general (i.e., universal) or existential propositions presupposes an understanding of ELEMENTARY PROPOSITIONS, since the sense of the former is a function of that of certain elementary propositions, and hence has to be explained by reference to them (TLP 4.411; NL 106).

'$(x)fx$' and '$(\exists x)fx$' express 'truth-functions', but those functions are not things of any kind, but operations, namely of forming a logical product or sum. The quantifiers differ from propositional connectives solely in the way in which the base of the operation is specified, namely not through listing these propositions, as in '$(p.q) \vee r$', but through a 'propositional variable' – Russell's propositional function – 'fx'. Such a variable is a 'logical prototype'; it collects all the propositions of a certain form, since its values are all those propositions we get by substituting a name for the variable, that is, fa, fb, fc, etc. (TLP 3.315–3.317, 5.501, 5.522). Russell maintained that the *Tractatus* 'derives' '$(x)fx$' from the logical product of its instances, '$fa.fb.fc...$', and '$(\exists x)fx$' from the logical sum, '$fa \vee fb \vee fc...$' ('Introduction' xv–xvi). And Ramsey held that Wittgenstein's approach explains why 'fa' entails '$(\exists x)fx$' and '$(x)fx$' 'fa', while Frege's explanation of '$(\exists x)fx$' as 'f has application' – a statement of the form $A(f)$ – does not (*Mathematics* 153–4). Ironically, *Tracta-*

146

tus 5.521 *blames* Frege and Russell for adopting this very approach (neither Frege nor Russell did so explicity, although *Principia* I *59 comes close), and *Philosophical Grammar* blames the early Wittgenstein (PG 268). The riddle's solution is that the *Tractatus* attacks only the way in which Frege and Russell linked generality to logical sum and product; while the later Wittgenstein questions this link itself.

The *Tractatus* makes two points against Frege and Russell (TLP 5.1311, 5.523; NB 3.11./24.11.14, 2.12.16). (a) They confused two facts about the universal proposition $(x)fx$: that it is a truth-function of *all* of its instances, and that it is true just in case *all* the members of that set are true. The former is the generality which $(x)fx$ *shares* with $(\exists x)fx$, namely that it is a truth-functional operation on all the values of a propositional function (fa, fb, fc, etc.). It is expressed not by the quantifiers but by the 'argument', that is, by the *pattern* '$x\ fx$', while '( )' and '($\exists$)' differentiate the truth-functional operations performed on the values of the propositional function. (b) They *derived* the quantifiers from conjunctions and disjunctions. This is inadequate, since the conjuncts/disjuncts involved are themselves instances (values) of the propositional function; they already contain generality – 'fa' is equivalent to '$(\exists x)(fx . x = a)$' (TLP 5.47) – and hence cannot be used to explain it. Moreover, they leave the relationship between general propositions and their instances unexplained.

By clarifying that relation, Wittgenstein avoids some difficulties which confront the straightforward identification of '$(x)fx$' with '$fa . fb . fc \ldots$' and of '$(\exists x)fx$' with '$fa \lor fb \lor fc \ldots$' The first is that one can understand a general proposition without ever having heard of a, b or c. Many Americans believe that all communists are evil, without being able to name a single communist. 'The world can be completely described by means of fully generalized propositions' (TLP 5.526; NB 17./19.10.14; PG 203–4). Nevertheless, a connection with a logical product remains: *some* statement of the form '$fa . fb . fc \ldots$' must be equivalent to the universal proposition, and this is why I know that, for example, '$\sim fa$' is incompatible with '$(x)fx$', whether or not I have heard of a. Wittgenstein's account does justice to both points, since it specifies the propositions involved through a propositional variable, and not by enumerating them, which would require the use of particular names.

This also avoids a second problem. One can analyse '$(x)fx$' into a specific conjunction '$fa_1 . fa_2 \ldots fa_n$' only if the number of objects in the universe is finite. Even quantifying over a finite domain, for example, 'Everything in this room is radioactive', is equivalent to a specific logical product like 'The cup is radioactive . the table is radioactive' only if one adds the rider 'and there is nothing else in the room', which in turn can be expressed as a specific logical product only if the universe does not contain an infinite number of objects. This would make the explanation of quantification depend on an 'axiom of finitude', and is incompatible with the *Tractatus*'s insistence that there are 'no privileged numbers in logic': it is an empirical matter, settled by the 'application of logic', how many objects there are (TLP 4.128, 4.2211, 5.453, 5.553). The *Tractatus* avoids that problem since it does not list the elementary propositions which form the basis of the truth-functional operation, and therefore does not use a specific list of names. However, this in turn creates a problem detected by Ramsey (*Mathematics* 59–60, 153–5): since completely generalized propositions do not refer to any specific objects, it seems that they might allow more play to the facts than do the totality of elementary propositions – contrary to *Tractatus* 5.5262. If the world only contains a finite number of objects, we could construct a general proposition which contains more distinct variables than there are objects. Take the statement

(1) There are at least three individuals with some property.

In Russellian notation this comes out as

(1′) $(\exists x)(\exists y)(\exists z)(\exists\Phi)(\Phi x . \Phi y . \Phi z . x \neq y . x \neq z . y \neq z)$.

But in a world in which there are only two individuals, Wittgenstein's account of generality seems to turn (1′) into a contradiction. If we substitute 'f' for 'Φ', 'a' for 'x' and 'b' for 'y' and 'z' (in our model-world no other individual constant is available), we get

(1*) $fa . fb . fb . a \neq b . a \neq b . b \neq b$

a contradiction because of the last conjunct (by the same token, 'There is at least one individual' and 'There are at least two individuals' come out as tautologies). Ramsey's solution was to accept this consequence: statements about the number of objects in the world are either tautologies or contradictions. The *Tractatus*, by contrast, classifies such propositions as nonsensical (TLP 4.1272, 5.535; NB 9.10.14). It can do so because it forgoes the use of the IDENTITY-sign and analyses (1) as

(1″) $(\exists x)(\exists y)(\exists z)(\exists\Phi)(\Phi x . \Phi y . \Phi z)$.

Substitution into that proposition will not yield a contradiction. Nevertheless, our commitment to objects in fully general propositions cannot outstrip the number of objects, because the propositional function Φx will not have values other than fa and fb, that is, there will be no other propositions for truth-functions to operate on, which means that propositions employing more variables than x and y have no application and are hence meaningless. The number of objects in the universe, which Russell's axiom of infinity tried to state, will be *shown* by the number of names employed by an ideal notation, which in turn determines the number of variables that can be meaningfully introduced.

Wittgenstein later detected flaws in the idea that, since '$(x)fx$' entails 'fa', it must amount to the simultaneous assertion of all propositions of the form 'fx'. That idea assumes that there is a totality of propositions of that form which is both well-defined and, although not actually enumerated, capable of being enumerated. Both assumptions, he later claimed, are unjustified.

(a) The *Tractatus* has been criticized for failing to realize that the truth-tabular decision procedure cannot be extended to the predicate calculus, since it cannot be applied to infinite logical sums or products. But in fact the *Tractatus* explicitly restricts that procedure to cases 'in which no sign of generality' occurs (TLP 6.1203). However, it does assume that the logical operations apply in the same way to a list of propositions and to the values of propositional functions. This holds for cases in which the class defined by the propositional function is closed, such as the primary colours or the tones of the octave. Here a list of names can be given in response to the question '*Which objects are f?*', and this list need not be followed by a cut-off clause, 'and these are all', since, for example, the idea of a fifth primary colour is excluded as nonsensical by our grammar. 'In this picture I see all the primary colours' is shorthand for 'I see red.I see green.I see blue...' The dots here are 'dots of laziness' (LWL 15–16, 89–90; AWL 5–6; M 88–90; PR 117; PG 268–88; PI §208).

However, this does not hold for *infinite* classes: no matter how far the conjunction '2 is even.4 is even.6 is even...' is extended, it never captures the sense of the arithmetical 'all', which is given not through an enumeration or any other description, but through a rule of construction, namely mathematical induction (WVC 45, 51–3, 82; LWL 13–14; PR 150–1, 193–205; PG 432; BB 95–8). As a result, Wittgenstein, like the finitists (his pupil Goodstein and Skolem), refuses to express general claims about infinite domains through Russellian quantifiers and maintains that in such domains we cannot state that there is an x which is f without stating a rule for specifying which x is f. By the same token, universal statements about such domains are never true accidentally (as 'All men are mortal'), but always by virtue of a rule of construction.

The *Tractatus*'s treatment is also inapplicable in cases in which the number of possibilities is not so much infinite as *indeterminate*. The *Tractatus* had insisted that while a proposition can leave something undetermined, it cannot be an incomplete picture: what it leaves open must be specified, by the presence of a disjunction of possibilities (TLP 5.156; NB 16.6.15).

(2) There is a circle in this square

leaves open how the circle is placed within the square, but does so by specifying that it occupies one of all the possible positions within the square. Wittgenstein later saw that this is mistaken, not only because there is no definite number of positions, but because the different positions 'are not mentioned at all'. We do not verify (2) by going through every point. (2) is best expressed through *unbound* variables which make clear that it does not talk about a totality of possibilities, but is indeterminate (WVC 38–41; PG 257–67).

(b) The *Tractatus*'s account implies that a logical sum and product can be formed on any propositional function. However, once it is recognized that the elementary propositions of form *fx* may not be logically independent, the possibility of one type of operation no longer guarantees that of another type: thus, it makes sense to say '(∃x)(x is the colour of A)' but not '(x)(x is the colour of A)', since 'A is red' is incompatible with 'A is green', etc. Equally, while '(∃x)(x is a circle . x is within the square)' makes sense, '(x)(x is a circle . x is within the square)' does not. More generally, what makes sense in *some* cases need not make sense in *all* cases. Wittgenstein diagnosed that the *Tractatus*'s account of generality was based on the mistaken view that somehow any quantified proposition could be analysed into some logical product or sum. But his critique is not confined to the *Tractatus*. The quantifiers of the predicate calculus suggest that expressions of generality are topic-neutral. Wittgenstein, by contrast, now claims that every propositional system has its own rules of generality, and of the entailment between '(x)fx' and 'fa'. 'There are as many different "alls" ' as there are types of propositions (PG 269; see LFM 262–70; LPP 51).

grammar According to the early Wittgenstein, 'distrust of grammar is the first requisite of philosophizing' (NL 106). For the 'school-grammatical' form of propositions disguises their LOGICAL FORM. The latter is revealed by an ideal notation which follows the rules of LOGICAL SYNTAX, or 'logical grammar' (TLP 3.325; see *Logic* 185, 269). Subsequently, Wittgenstein used the term 'grammar' to denote both the constitutive rules of language and the philosophical investigation or tabulation of these rules (WVC 184; LWL 46–8; BT 437; PI §90). Throughout his career he continued to use the term 'logic' or 'logic of language' (*Sprachlogik*) in the same two capacities (PI §§38, 90–3, 345; RPP I §1050; LW I §256; OC §§56, 501, 628), on the understanding that logical questions are really grammatical (Z §590), that is, concern rules for the use of words.

Wittgenstein also speaks of 'the grammar of' particular words, expressions, phrases, propositions/sentences, and even of the grammar of states and processes (BB 24; PI 18n, §187 – BB 1, 109; PI §660 – BB 70 – BB 51–3; PI §353 – PI §572; PG 82). But properly speaking, it is the corresponding linguistic expression which has a grammar, namely a certain way of being used. 'Grammatical rules' are standards for the correct use of an expression which 'determine' its meaning: to give the meaning of a word is to specify its grammar (M 51; PG 62–4; OC §§61–2; LWL 34–9). 'Correct' here does not mean 'true', since one can use a term in accordance with linguistic rules without saying something true. But a term is not used meaningfully if it is applied to objects to which it could not apply truly. Equally, to deny that a term applies to paradigmatic instances in a clear situation is to display misunderstanding. The sense of a proposition is determined by its place in the grammatical system, in that the latter determines its logical relations with other propositions (PG 152–3). The grammar of a language is the overall system of grammatical rules, of the constitutive rules which define that language by determining what it makes sense to say in it (PR 51; LWL 46–59; PG 60, 133, 143; PI §496). Unlike its predecessor logical syntax, grammar is not universal – different languages have different grammars. But the grammar of an individual word like 'understanding' *is*, in so far as other languages have equivalent words.

The idea of grammar draws attention to the fact that speaking a language is, among other things, to engage in a rule-guided activity. Some have maintained that Wittgenstein did not subscribe to this normativist conception of language, and that his comparison of language to rule-following activities is a misleading heuristic device which betokens a school-masterly attitude. This view may be motivated by his qualms about the idea of logical syntax as an arcane system of hidden rules. But Wittgenstein did not abandon the idea that language is rule-governed, he clarified it, comparing language no longer to a calculus but to a game (*see* LANGUAGE-GAME). Unlike these analogies, the idea that language is rule-governed is not just a heuristic device. Understanding a language involves mastery of techniques concerning the application of rules (*see* RULE-FOLLOWING). And Wittgenstein continued to stress the link between language, meaning and rules: 'following according to the rule is FUNDAMENTAL to our language-game' (RFM 330; see BT §45; OC §§61–2).

To assess Wittgenstein's normativist picture of language, one must appreciate that his conception of rules is a functional one. Whether a sentence expresses a grammatical rule depends on its role or function within our linguistic practice. Wittgenstein distinguishes between 'empirical propositions' and 'grammatical propositions', sentences which are typically used to express a rule (e.g. PI §§251, 458; AWL 31, 105–6; RFM 162). This distinction is not based on linguistic form – a grammatical proposition need not be a meta-linguistic statement about how an expression is to be used. What counts is whether we *use* it as a standard of linguistic correctness. The contrast between grammatical and empirical propositions is one between the *rules of* our language-games, and *moves in* our language-games made in accordance with these rules (e.g. PI §49; OC §622). The 'truth' of a grammatical proposition consists not in stating how things are, but in accurately expressing a rule. Grammatical propositions must be distinguished from empirical statements to the effect that a community follows certain linguistic rules, for example, 'All Englishmen use these signs in this way' (AWL 154; SDE 24), and from propositions about the FRAMEWORK conditions which make rules practicable. For they are used normatively, to explain, justify and criticize uses of words.

Grammatical rules in this sense comprise not just school-grammatical or syntactical rules, but also EXPLANATIONS of meaning (PG 68, 143; M 69; PR 78). What counts as an explanation of meaning is again a matter of function, not form. Such rules include (a) definitions, whether in formal ('"Bachelor" means "unmarried man"') or material mode ('Bachelors are unmarried men'); (b) analytical propositions ('All bachelors are unmarried'); (c) colour-charts and conversion-tables (BB 4; LFM 118); (d) OSTENSIVE DEFINITIONS (BB 12, 90); (e) explanations by exemplification (PI §§69–79); (f) expressions of the 'geometry' of colour like 'Nothing can be red and green all over' (PR 51–2; LWL 8); (g) propositions of arithmetic and geometry (WVC 38, 61–3, 156; PR 143, 170, 216, 249; LWL 8, 55; PG 319, 347; RFM *passim*; *see* MATHEMATICS).

Wittgenstein's normativist conception of language contrasts sharply with Quine's and Davidson's claim that the notion of a rule presupposes rather than explains that of language. Less radically, one may protest that even in Wittgenstein's extremely liberal sense rules are not prominent in our linguistic practice. Here it is important to note that Wittgenstein did not insist that rules are essential to learning a language (LW I §968). What counts is solely whether our acquired practice can be characterized as rule-governed, where this does not require that we actually consult the rules (LWL 48; PG 153; PI §§82–3) but only that we *could* explain, criticize and justify our uses of words by reference to rules (*see* CALCULUS MODEL), and do so when the occasion demands it. Rules in Wittgenstein's liberal sense play a role in a host of pedagogic and critical activities, some of which are institutionalized (education, dictionaries): the teaching of language, the explanation of particular words, the correction of mistakes, the justification of uses, the acquisition of higher linguistic skills.

One might retort that this role is necessarily derivative. Grammatical rules may distinguish between correct and incorrect use, but do not determine either. For the rule is of no account unless it codifies existing practice, that is, the prevailing practice. This reduces the difference between correct and incorrect to that between conformity and nonconformity. Against this, Wittgenstein rightly insisted that to use 'X' correctly does not mean the same as to use 'X' as most people do (RFM 406; Z §431). There is no incoherence in the idea that a majority should commit linguistic mistakes (although in most cases to use 'X' correctly is to use it as most people do). Moreover, although there may be grey areas, there is a difference between regularities in linguistic behaviour and linguistic norms. While some deviations from ordinary patterns are unusual (using 'sobriquet' instead of 'nick-name') or inappropriate (referring to policemen as 'cops' in court), others are linguistic mistakes – syntactic slips, malapropisms, wrong choices of words (but not all of these amount to a meaningless use of words, as Wittgenstein sometimes seems to suggest).

What is correct is that explicating and tabulating those grammatical rules which are relevant to philosophy is not just secondary to linguistic practice, but involves a 'one-sided perspective' on language (PG 68; BB 25), one which emphasizes certain features of our practice. Wittgenstein's PHILOSOPHY adopts this perspective. It keeps the 'account book of language' and consists of grammatical 'investigations', 'notes', 'analyses', 'remarks' or 'reminders' (*Erinnerungen*) (PI §§89–90, 127, 199, 232, 392, 496, 574; PG 60). It reminds us of the way we use words. One reason for doing this is that '*Essence* is expressed in grammar'; grammar determines 'what kind of object something is' since it specifies what can be meaningfully said about it – 'Green is a colour' is a grammatical proposition (PI §§371–3; PR 118; PG 463–4; BB 19; LSD 20). Empirical investigations into the physical nature of an object or stuff X presuppose the grammar of 'X', since the latter determines what counts as X. The answer to the Socratic 'What is X?' is given not by inspecting essences (abstract or mental objects), but by clarifying the meaning of 'X', which is given by the rules for the use of 'X' (PI §383). More generally, while metaphysics seeks to discover necessary truths about the essential structure of reality, according to Wittgenstein the apparent structure of reality is nothing but a 'shadow' of grammar: he explains the special status of logically necessary propositions through the idea that their role is normative rather than descriptive. Grammar constitutes our FORM OF REPRESENTATION, it lays down what counts as an intelligible description of reality, and is hence not subject to empirical refutation.

Even if one accepts these claims, one may feel with Moore that Wittgenstein's liberal use of 'grammar' disguises the fact that philosophy must be concerned with rules which are more fundamental than those of school-grammar (M 69; LWL 97–8). Wittgenstein denies that there is such a difference between the two types of grammar. Both deal with rules for the use of words, and there is no difference between 'contingent' and 'essential' rules, 'both kinds of rules are rules in the same sense. It is just that some have been the subject of philosophical discussions and some have not.' Philosophical grammar is special not in dealing with special rules, but in its aim, namely of resolving philosophical problems. It differs from school-grammar or linguistics merely in that (a) it is not concerned with exactness or comprehensiveness for its own sake; (b) it pays no attention to the history of language or genetic problems in general; (c) its observations concern features that are often shared by many languages (although they no longer concern the logical structure of all possible symbolisms); (d) it has a wider, functional conception of grammatical rules (AWL 31, 96–7; BT 413; PG 190; PI II

230; Z §§464–5). Indeed most of the rules which interest philosophy, for example, 'One cannot know that *p* unless it is true that *p*', do not concern the grammarian, but that is because his purposes are not those of the philosopher. However, one may grant the differences of purpose, while insisting that they point towards fundamentally different kinds of rules. Thus Moore insisted that philosophically relevant rules, like 'Nothing can be red and green all over', exclude the inconceivable, while what children learn at school, for example, 'You don't say "Three men was in the field" but "Three men *were* in the field"', has nothing to do with philosophy. Reportedly, Wittgenstein replied that this example indeed has nothing to do with philosophy, since here all is perspicuous. But what about 'God the Father, God the Son and God the Holy Ghost *were* in the field or *was* in the field?'

This rejoinder is inadequate. For we can easily distinguish the 'perspicuous' school-grammatical problem from the philosophical problem: the decision whether to employ the singular or the plural form would become trivial if the problems concerning the Trinity could be intelligibly resolved. It remains tempting to hold that if the latter is a grammatical problem at all, it concerns rules of a different kind (viz., concerning 'God' and 'person'). Nevertheless, one should grant Wittgenstein that there is a spectrum of grammatical rules ranging from the philosophically insignificant ('The words "north-east of" must be followed by a noun-phrase in the accusative') over borderline cases ('The words "north-east of" must be followed by a terrestrial place designation except "North Pole" or "South Pole"') to philosophically relevant cases ('The words "it is true that…" should not be used with an adverb of time') (PLP 135–7).

Wittgenstein himself distinguishes between the 'depth grammar' and 'surface grammar' of words (PI §664). Traditional philosophy goes wrong by focusing on the latter, that is, the immediately evident (auditory or visual) features of words, at the expense of their overall USE, which is like classifying clouds by their shape (LC 2; AWL 46; PI §§10–14; Z §462). The surface grammar (sentence structure) of 'I have a pain' is the same as that of 'I have a pin', that of 'expectation' is that of a state (PI §§572–3) and that of 'to mean' is that of an action verb like 'to say' (*see* PHILOSOPHICAL PSYCHOLOGY). But their depth grammar is altogether different: the words have different combinatorial possibilities, and the propositions are different moves in the language-game, with different logical relations and articulations. But it would be wrong to think that this indicates a contrast between fundamentally different kinds of grammatical rules, for example perspicuous ones violation of which produces *patent* school-grammatical nonsense, and complex rules violation of which produces *latent* philosophical nonsense. Disregard for depth grammar yields patent nonsense like 'I meant her passionately'; grammatical investigations check whether philosophical positions lead to such nonsense (PI §464). The metaphor of depth is misleading, since it suggests that depth grammar is discovered through logical or linguistic analysis, as in the *Tractatus* or Chomsky. The contrast is not between the surface and the 'geology' of expressions, but between the local surroundings which can be taken in at a glance, and the overall geography; that is, use of an expression. Moreover, Wittgenstein insisted that (apart from being more difficult to recognize) most metaphysical propositions are NONSENSE in the same sense as humdrum violations of grammar and that grammar is *flat*, that is, that there are no METALOGICAL rules or concepts which are logically more fundamental than others.

On Certainty explicitly raises the question of whether 'rule and empirical proposition merge into one another' (OC §309). Three possible grounds for a positive answer can be detected. One is that some propositions which have the *form* of empirical propositions are among the hinges on which our language-games turn. Another is that we can imagine circumstances in which certain sentences turn from grammatical propositions into moves of the language-game. Finally, 'there is no sharp boundary between propositions of logic and empirical propositions.' But Wittgenstein adds that this 'lack of sharpness *is* that of the boundary between *rule* and empirical proposition' and due to the fact that the concept of a proposition is itself vague (OC §§56, 82, 318–20, 622). That a division is not 'sharp' does not mean that it is unworkable. Moreover, the first two possible grounds are accommodated in Wittgenstein's functional conception of grammatical rules: the logical status of a sentence is due not to its linguistic form, but to the way it is used, and can hence change: 'any empirical proposition can be transformed into a postulate – and then becomes a norm of description' (OC §321). It is true that Wittgenstein suspects this statement to be reminiscent of TLP (in fact it recalls PR 59). But what he means is that it would be dogmatic to insist that *any* proposition could change its logical role, since the revisability of our form of representation is restricted. The famous metaphor of the 'river-bed of thoughts' distinguishes between 'the movement of the waters on the river-bed' (changes in empirical beliefs), 'the shift of the bed itself' (conceptual changes brought about by adopting new grammatical rules), and the 'hard rock' of the river-bank which is not subject to alteration (OC §§95–9). The last includes propositions of logic which partly define what we mean by thinking, inferring, language, while the shifting sand of the bank consists of propositions which we could use either normatively or descriptively. The only significant concession of *On Certainty* to the view that there is no boundary between empirical and grammatical propositions, namely that even among empirical propositions some (e.g., 'The earth has existed for over a hundred years') must be CERTAIN, is more damaging to rationalism than to Wittgenstein's earlier views (OC §§401–2, 558; WAM 70–5). In contrast to necessary propositions, the reason is not that their negation is excluded as nonsensical by a specific grammatical rule, but rather that abandoning them would undermine our whole system of beliefs.

H

human being 'Only of a living human being and what resembles (behaves like) a living human being can one say: it has sensations; it sees; is blind; hears; is deaf; is conscious or unconscious' (PI §281, see §§282–7, 359–61). Wittgenstein is aware that we apply some psychological terms to inanimate objects like dolls, but maintains that this is a 'secondary use', since it involves endowing these objects with the behavioural capacities of human beings, as in a fairy-tale. In Wittgenstein's work one can detect two interrelated rationales for this famous claim. One is that there is a conceptual rather than merely empirical connection between psychological terms and certain forms of BEHAVIOUR. One can meaningfully ascribe THOUGHTS only to creatures that are in principle capable of manifesting them. *Mutatis mutandis*, sensation-names and perceptual verbs can be applied only to sentient creatures who react to their environment and can display pleasure and pain, that is, to animals, although this is a matter of degree (PI §284). The second rationale is that such expressions make sense only as part of the complex weave of a form of life: 'The concept of pain is characterized by its particular function in our life … we only call 'pain' what has *this* position, *these* connections' (Z §§532–3). On one understanding, there is a tension between the stress on behavioural CRITERIA and the FORM OF LIFE contextualism. For, the latter seems to imply that in a community of people who display, say, pain-behaviour just as we do, but do not react to it with sympathy, 'pain' would not have the same meaning. On the other hand, the two are compatible if the context of a form of life is needed because without it certain forms of expressive behaviour would be unintelligible (although this does not hold of pain-behaviour).

If Wittgenstein's restriction of experiential predicates to sentient creatures is correct, it makes no sense to ascribe psychological terms either to a non-corporeal soul-substance, as Cartesianism does, or to the human body or one of its parts, as materialist theories, in particular mind-brain identity theories, do, or to a machine, notably a computer, as cognitive science and functionalism do. Although most contemporary philosophers accept the first corollary, they would maintain that the second two have been overtaken by science, which informs us that the mind is the brain, and which has constructed computers which are capable of playing chess or performing complex calculations. However, the issue is far from straightforward.

Bodies Wittgenstein's dictum implies that a human being cannot be identified with a body, but *has* a body. Saying 'Carter's body is in pain' instead of 'Carter is in pain' would amount to a shift in grammar (PI §283; BB 73). This points in the direction of Strawson's claim that a human being or person is neither a Cartesian soul nor a body, nor a composite of the two, but a distinct type of thing to which both physical and mental predicates apply, and which can be said to have rather than be a body. The conclusion is supported by the fact that substituting body-referring expressions ('Carter's body') for personal names *salva significatione* and *salva veritate* is possible only for non-psychological predicates (as in 'Carter is sun-burnt all over', but not in 'Carter intends to go to London' or 'Mary loves Carter').

Parts of the body We apply psychological expressions metaphorically or metonymically to parts of the body, for example in 'She has a generous heart' or 'My hand hurts.' But it is noteworthy that in the latter case we comfort the sufferer, not the hand (PI §286; Z §§540–1). Equally, 'My brain is numb' means 'I can't think.' But it is nonsense to say either of a person's mind or of his brain that it has a toothache, sees the sunset, intends to go to London. It is equally nonsensical to say, using the terms with their standard meaning, that a brain classifies or compares, asks questions, and answers them by constructing theories. Nothing a brain can intelligibly be said to do (e.g., emitting electric impulses) could constitute thinking, etc. Such things are regularly said about the brain by psychologists, neurophysiologists and philosophers, and that use could be seen as a legitimate extension or technical use of psychological vocabulary, but it needs to be explained. This is done by those who apply epistemic terms to the brain only in the purely technical sense of communication theory. But often such applications surreptitiously trade on our non-technical use of epistemic terms, which are tied to human behaviour, or they boil down to the claim that the processes which are thought to license such applications are correlated with experiences as a matter of empirical fact (thus Wittgenstein held that localizing thoughts in parts of the brain uses the expression 'locality of thought' in a different sense (BB 7)). If this is correct, explaining the mental capacities of human beings through applying mental terms to the brain where they cannot have their standard meaning is a homunculus fallacy, on a par with postulating a little man within our brain.

Computers We speak of computers as calculating and playing chess. Wittgenstein, by contrast, suggested that to say of a machine that it thinks is a

157

category mistake, not because thinking is an occult process in a mental realm (BB 47; PG 106), but because manipulating symbols is by itself not sufficient for thinking or understanding (in this respect his reasoning parallels Searle's celebrated Chinese Room argument). Manipulating symbols counts as calculating or inferring only if it is a normative rather than merely mechanical activity. It must be possible to distinguish between a prediction that such-and-such a result will be obtained and judging a result to be *correct*. While machines can act in accordance with rules, provided they are properly programmed and functioning, only human beings (or creatures who 'resemble' – behave like – them, which 'machines' as thought of here do not) are capable of following rules, and hence of calculating, etc. For only they are capable of justifying or correcting their proceeding by reference to the rule (*see* RULE-FOLLOWING).

This reasoning underlies Wittgenstein's remark: 'Turing's "machines". These machines are *humans* who calculate' (RPP I §1096). Turing had sketched the notion of a machine which would compute number-theoretic functions by analogy with human beings. Wittgenstein's point is that what Turing machines do counts as genuine calculating only if it is performed by human beings. For although such human beings would presumably be calculating mechanically, that is, without consulting rules, they would be capable of calculating non-mechanically, they could invoke rules or recognize mistakes (RFM 234, 257–8, 382, 422; LFM 36–9; RPP I §560).

A natural objection is that computers of a certain complexity can do the same: when asked why they produce a certain result they cite the relevant rules, and they could be programmed to commit and rectify mistakes. And the problem about Turing machines being too mechanical for calculation seems taken care of by the so-called 'Turing test', according to which whether or not a computer can think depends on whether or not the answers it gives on a screen are indistinguishable from those a human being might type out. Answers which could pass that test would have to be unpredictable and non-wooden. The Turing test is in line with Wittgenstein (and in conflict with Searle) in so far as it decides on whether or not computers think by reference not to their internal constitution (being made of silicon rather than carbohydrates), but to their capacities, what they can do. But Wittgenstein's dictum implies that the test is mistaken to treat the appearance of symbols on a screen as a form of behaviour which could display thought. Typing out symbols counts as 'thinking' and 'calculating' only for a creature to whom we can ascribe a wider range of psychological attributes (RPP I §563). It is plausible to hold that neither experiences nor emotions can be ascribed to a machine which merely reacts to the pushing of keys in accordance with a programme. But this by itself does not preclude one's talking here of thought or calculation. The ultimate rationale for Wittgenstein's position is that rule-following requires the doing of things *for a reason*, which is possible only for a creature which possesses conation and a will, that is, can take an interest in things and pursue goals. None of this holds of a computer, even if it passes the Turing test. However, this would not rule out ascribing psychological attributes to science-fictional android robots who move about, react to their environment, talk and solve problems, feel pleasure and pain, etc. But such robots would no longer count as machines.

I

I/self There are three traditional theories concerning the first-person pronoun. According to Cartesianism it refers to a soul-substance attached to the body; according to Humean theories it can refer only to a bundle of mental episodes, since no such unitary substance is encountered in introspection; according to Kantianism it signifies the transcendental unity of apperception, a formal feature of all judgements, namely that they can be prefixed by 'I think'. Wittgenstein imbibed these options through Schopenhauer's Kantianism and Russell's Humeanism. Both rejected the Cartesian soul-substance, but retained various 'selves'. Schopenhauer turned the transcendental unity of apperception into the idea that the subject of experience cannot itself be experienced (*World* II ch. 41). Russell first thought of 'I' as the logically proper NAME of a self we know by acquaintance, then as the mere grammatical subject of psychological predication known by description (*Problems* 27–8; 'Theory' 36–7).

'The I, the I is what is deeply mysterious' (NB 5.8.16). Wittgenstein transposed the perplexities of Humeanism and Kantianism onto a linguistic plane. Thus, the transcendental SOLIPSISM of the *Tractatus* involves removing the first-person pronoun from the analysis of BELIEF-sentences like 'I think that *p*'. The immediate reason is the Humean idea that the I is not found in experience. But the deeper rationale is Kantian. Whatever we experience could be otherwise. By contrast, it is a priori that the experience I now have is *my* experience, or that this visual field is *my* visual field. Hence I cannot ascribe experiences to myself in BIPOLAR propositions. The subject of experience does not just happen to elude introspection, it could not be encountered in experience, since its connection with experience is not a posteriori.

The idea that 'I' can be eliminated from our language survived the transition from transcendental to methodological solipsism. A 'phenomenological' language which refers to subjective experiences is semantically basic; but the experiences of this language have no owner (*see* PRIVACY). Following Lichtenberg, instead of 'I think' we should say 'It thinks', as in 'It rains' (WVC 49–50; M 100–1; PR 88–90). The reason is not that 'thinking' is a feature-placing predicate like 'raining', but that it is logically impossible for anybody else to have what I have when I have a pain, since no one else could have a pain which *I* could encounter. Accordingly, 'I have a toothache' is analytic; it is senseless to say that *I* as opposed to someone else has the pain. In first-person present tense psychological utterances 'I' is redundant.

The eliminability of 'I' is illustrated by a fictional language with a despot at its centre. When the despot has a toothache, he (and everybody else) does not say

(1)   I have (He has) a toothache

but simply

(1′)   There is a toothache.

However, when someone else – N.N. – has a toothache, everybody, including N.N., says

(2)   N.N. is behaving as the Centre behaves when there is a toothache.

Wittgenstein claims that this Lichtenbergian language makes perspicuous what is essential to our form of representation. But as regards anybody other than the Centre, this language differs sharply from ours: (a) it precludes others conjecturing that N.N. has a pain not manifested in his behaviour; (b) it makes N.N.'s report subject to error, since it is possible to mischaracterize one's own behaviour; (c) because (2), unlike (1), is based on behaviour, 'pain' is ambiguous; *real* pain could be attributed only to the Centre. The methodological solipsist might respond that each one of us employs a mono-centred language which is adequate for its centre. But even for the centre such a language is inadequate. 'I' occurs not just in propositions like (1), but also in introductions like 'I am N.N.' or propositions like 'I am not N.N.', which cannot be reproduced in the mono-centred language. Wittgenstein later tried to accommodate these points by abandoning the simple elimination of 'I' in favour of distinguishing between its use 'as subject' in propositions like (1) and its use 'as object' (BB 66–7; see M 100–3; PR 86) in propositions like

(3)   I have broken my arm.

Unlike (1), (3) is not immune to doubt or error. Accordingly ,'I' is either essentially redundant – as in (1) – or refers to my body – as in (3).

Wittgenstein never came back to this 'dual-use' view, and it is flawed in several respects. Although in uttering (3), I may be in doubt or error, this cannot arise from misidentification. To be sure, in a rugby-scrum I might mistake my arm for yours, but I do not misidentify myself, or mistake myself for you. Moreover, the dual-use view implies that a first-person proposition like

(4)   I am writing a letter

must be analysed into a proposition about bare bodily movements, plus an infallible first-person experiential proposition, for example about volitions. Later, Wittgenstein realized that this distorts both the subject and the predicate of such utterances. (4) does not ascribe a 'colourless' bodily movement, but a human action which is infused with rather than accompanied by intentions (*see* BEHAVIOUR AND BEHAVIOURISM). Equally, its subject is not a body, but a HUMAN BEING. 'I' and 'this body' are interchangeable *salva veritate* in propositions like (3), but they are not even interchangeable *salva significatione* in propositions like (4). This does not mean that 'I' is ambiguous, but simply that its function and that of 'this body' are analogous for part of their range, but diverge elsewhere.

This rules out the materialist alternative to traditional accounts, according to which 'I' refers to a body or one of its parts, for example the brain. But the fact that 'I' does not refer to a body does not entail that it refers to an entity (ego, soul, self) attached to the body. For Wittgenstein, it is nevertheless essential to our use of 'I' that it is emitted by creatures that *have* a body – on the Kantian grounds that there are no criteria of identity for soul-substances (AWL 24, 62; BB 69; LPE 300, 308). The obvious alternative is Strawson's suggestion that the first-person pronoun refers neither to a body, nor to a self, nor to a bundle of mental episodes, but to a 'person', a living creature with special mental capacities. Obviously, 'I' is no more the proper name of a person than 'here' is the name of a place (LPE 298; PI §410). Equally, it does not mean the same as 'the person who is now speaking', since it cannot be substituted *salva veritate* in 'The person who is now speaking is the headmistress.' Nevertheless, it seems that its meaning is given by the rule that 'I' refers to the person that uses it. In spite of his focus on human beings, Wittgenstein questioned this proposal, and occasionally flatly rejected it: 'It is correct, although paradoxical, to say: " 'I' does not refer to (*bezeichnet*) a person" ' (MS116 215; LPE 283).

This claim that 'I' is not a referring expression cannot be defended by reference to the idea that first-person psychological utterances are AVOWALS rather than descriptions. Its use is not confined to avowals, and referring is not tied to description ('God save the Queen!'). A possible defence is the suggestion that 'I am N.N.' is not an identity statement, on the grounds that it is not verified like ordinary identity statements ('This is Lewis Carroll'), and is typically used to introduce oneself. However, 'I am N.N.' can be used to affirm an identity (e.g., when I find out that I have been nicknamed 'N.N.'), which means that 'I' remains a candidate for referring.

Wittgenstein himself focuses on a different line of argument, which develops a kernel of truth in his previous accounts (PI §§398–411; BT 523). There are substantial differences between, on the one hand, the first-person pronoun and, on the other, person-referring expressions such as proper names, descriptions, personal pronouns, and demonstratives ('this', 'that').

(a) 'I' does not allow of referential failure: (i) 'I' cannot mischaracterize that which the speaker intends to talk about; (ii) as we have seen, I cannot mistake myself for you, but only ascribe to myself something that applies to you; (iii) when I utter 'The present King of France is bald', the grammatical subject does not apply to anything, but there is no such risk in uttering 'I'-sentences. For these reasons, an amnesiac can use 'I' correctly without knowing whether he is speaking of N.N. or the Φer. What he needs to know is only that he is speaking about *himself*, and this he is assured of by virtue of knowing that it issues from *his* mouth. In contrast to other personal pronouns, using 'I' does not presuppose the possibility of identifying the referent through a name or description, or through a deictic gesture.

However, instead of concluding that 'I' is not a referring expression, one might conclude that it is a *super-referring*-expression, one guaranteed against referential failure. One could compare ordinary referring to shooting an arrow at a bull's-eye on a wall, which one may hit or miss. In these terms, the use of 'I' is analogous not to a magic arrow that always hits its target, as a completely unambiguous set of names or definite descriptions might be, but to drawing a bull's-eye around an arrow already stuck in the wall. The idea of hit or miss has no place, and this marks a logical difference from ordinary referring expressions.

(b) For the user himself, 'I' does not identify someone, in the sense of singling out someone from a group of people or things, although its use may enable *others* to identify someone. 'I don't choose the mouth which says "I have toothache"' (LPE 311; MS220 25). It might be objected that I single myself out from others, for example, in confessing that *I* and no one else broke the vase. But this is a case not of identifying oneself, but of drawing attention to oneself; for it does not specify *who* it is – N.N., the Φer – that broke the vase. One might reply that it does so in the same way in which deictic expressions do. However, to say 'I' is not thereby to point at anything, it is more akin to raising one's arm. 'I' signifies the point of origin of the system of deixis, not a point on the deictic graph (BB 67–8; LSD 33; BT 523).

Ultimately, the question of whether 'I' is a referring expression depends on what one makes of the term 'referring', an issue Wittgenstein did not sufficiently discuss. It seems clear that 'I', as well as 'you', 'she', etc., may be used to refer to a single person. And in uttering 'I broke the vase' I tell you who did it. Just like 'H.G.', 'I' helps determine the sense of propositions in which it occurs, and it does so by determining whom the proposition is about. It makes that contribution in a way which differs from that of other referring expressions. But this might best be expressed by saying that 'I' is a degenerate case of a referring expression, just as tautologies are degenerate cases of propositions.

identity (the same)   This concept played an important part in the logicist programme of reducing arithmetical equations to logical propositions, and for this reason '=' was introduced into logic by Frege to denote a binary truth-function governed by special axioms (*Laws* I §§4, 7, 47). This created a puzzle. If statements like

(1)   The morning star is the evening star

express a relation, is it one between objects, or between the names which represent them? In 'Sense and Reference', Frege rejected the second option (adopted in *Notation* §8), on the grounds that if (1) were about signs it would not express proper knowledge, since the connection between a name and its object is arbitrary. The first alternative, however, seems to imply that (1) is equivalent to

(2)   The morning star is the morning star

which is an instance of the traditional 'law of identity' – every object is identical with itself. But unlike (2), (1) is informative, it expresses an empirical discovery. In response, Frege distinguished between two aspects of an expression's content, its 'MEANING', that is, the object it stands for, and its 'sense', the mode of presentation of its meaning. 'The morning star' and 'the evening star' mean the same object – Venus – but present it in different ways, which is why (1) differs from (2).

Like Frege, Russell used '=' to formalize count-statements. While he rejected the sense/meaning distinction, his theory of descriptions actually elaborates Frege's gnomic solution to the puzzle of non-trivial identity statements (*Logic* 39–56; *Principia* I 66–71). That NAMES like 'the morning star' have sense can only mean that they are abbreviations of definite descriptions, for example, 'the planet visible in the morning sky'. On this basis, (1) can be analysed as making three substantial claims: there is exactly one planet visible in the morning sky; there is exactly one planet visible in the evening sky; whatever planet is visible in the morning sky is also visible in the evening sky. Identity statements of the form 'a = the F', for example

(3)   Scott is the author of *Waverley*

come out as '$(\exists x)(fx . (y)(fy \supset x=y) . x=a)$', or, more simply,

(3') $fa . (y)(fy \supset y=a)$

Wittgenstein followed Frege and Russell in holding that 'is' and its cognates in natural language are ambiguous between identity (as in (1)), predication ('Socrates is mortal') and existence ('There is a God'). Throughout his career, he diagnosed this as a cause of confusions such as the Hegelian paradox of 'identity in difference' (TLP 3.323; RCL; LWL 4; PG 53; PI §558) and suggested that these might be forestalled through a notation which replaces 'is' respectively through '=', '∈' and '(∃x)' (TS220 §99). This is the only exemplification of a method envisaged in *Philosophical Investigations* §90, namely of dissolving philosophical problems through a new notation. But it is not in line with the early work, which bans '=' from the ideal notation as part of its flight from LOGICAL CONSTANTS. Like quantifiers and propositional connectives, '=' is already present in elementary propositions, since '*fa*' says the same as '(∃x)(*fx . x = a*)' (TLP 5.47; NM 117). However, 'Identity of object I express by identity of sign, and not by using a sign for identity. Difference of objects I express by difference of signs' (TLP 5.53; NB 29.11.14). While ordinary language often employs several names for a single object and the same name for different objects, an ideal notation uses a different sign for every object. Just as the existence of an object is shown in language by the use of a name (TLP 5.535), identity is shown by the use of the same name. One motive for this strategy is the *Tractatus*'s insistence that all necessity is truth-functional (*see* LOGIC). Apparent necessary truths like '*a = a*' or '(*x*)*x = x*' cannot be reduced to TAUTOLOGIES (RUL 17.10.13), and hence must be treated as 'pseudo-propositions'. A possible justification for this treatment runs like this:

P_1 Any meaningful proposition can be understood without knowing whether it is true (TLP 4.024).

P_2 One cannot understand two names without knowing whether they refer to the same object or to two different objects (TLP 4.243, 6.2322).

C   If '*a*' and '*b*' are names, '*a = b*' cannot be meaningfully expressed; like '*a = a*' or '(*x*)*x = x*' it is a pseudo-proposition (TLP 5.534).

Even if one waives the suspicion that P_1, a consequence of the principle of BIPOLARITY, is dogmatic, P_2 obviously does not hold for ordinary singular terms. It does hold, however, for the logically proper names postulated by the *Tractatus*. In their case, '*a = b*' is either necessarily true or necessarily false. Since it is not molecular, it cannot be a tautology, and must hence be nonsensical.

Another line of thought underlies the claim that 'to say of *two* things that they are identical is nonsense, and to say of *one* thing that it is identical with itself is to say nothing at all' (TLP 5.5303). According to Quine, this ignores that identity statements can be true and non-trivial because different singular terms can refer to the same thing. In fact, Quine's point reinforces the

Tractatus. Proposition (1) does not talk about signs, but the knowledge it expresses is also expressed by

(1′) 'The morning star' and 'the evening star' name one and the same stellar body.

(1) only has a role because we can refer to a single object through different singular terms. This role becomes obsolete in a symbolism in which every thing has its own unique name: all propositions of the form '$a = b$' would be incorrect, and those of the form '$a = a$' pointless (NB 5.–6.9./11.11.14). That notation is superior because it avoids the suggestion that identity is a relation like 'x loves y', albeit one that every thing has to itself, but to no other thing. That this is mistaken becomes clear if one looks at the statement 'Only a is f'. The Russellian paraphrase of this is the second conjunct of (3′), that is, '$(y)(fy \supset y = a)$'. But 'what this proposition says is simply that *only* a satisfies the function f, and not that only things which have a certain relation to a satisfy the function f. Of course, it might then be said that *only* a did have this relation to a, but to express that, we should need the identity-sign itself' (TLP 5.5301). The last sentence draws attention to the fact that Russell's analysis cannot clarify the nature of the alleged relation between a and b in '$a = b$', since the problematic sign reoccurs in the second conjunct of the analysans. That clause amounts to the claim that there is at most one f, which is best expressed by

(3*) $\sim(\exists x)(\exists y)(fx . fy . x \neq y)$.

No such paraphrase is available for a genuine relation like 'x loves y'. Whereas the basic use of such relational expressions is in unquantified propositions like 'a loves b', '$=$' is explained by reference to its occurrence within the scope of a quantifier. This suggests that the sign itself is part of the apparatus of quantification, which is the point of Wittgenstein's analysis (NB 29.11.14, 12.5.15). Identity and difference of names indicates identity and difference of objects – 'fab'. $\sim a = b$' is simply 'fab', '$fab . a = b$' simply 'faa' (or 'fbb'). Equally, if one adopts Wittgenstein's convention for reading the quantifiers, then identity and difference of variables indicates that the same or different names must be substituted. Accordingly, (3′) can be written as

(3#) $fa . \sim(\exists x,y)(fx . fy)$

Other uses of '$=$' can be treated along the same lines (TLP 5.531–5.533):

English	Russell	TLP
There are at least 2 things which are f	$(\exists x)(\exists y)(fx . fy . \sim x = y)$	$(\exists x)(\exists y)fx . fy$
Somebody loves himself	$(\exists x)(\exists y)(fx . fy . x = y)$	$(\exists x)fxx$
Somebody loves somebody	$(\exists x)(\exists y) xRy$	$(\exists x)(\exists y)xRy \vee (\exists x)xRx$

If anything is f, it is a	$(x)(fx \supset x = a)$	$(x)(fx \supset fa) . \sim (\exists x)(\exists y)(fx . fy)$
There are at most 2 things which are f	$(x)(y)(z)((fx . fy . fz) \supset$	
	$(x = y \lor x = z \lor y = z)$	$\sim (\exists x)(\exists y)(\exists z)(fx . fy . fz)$
Precisely one thing is f	$(x)(y)(fx \supset x = y)$	$(\exists x)fx . \sim (\exists x)(\exists y)fx . fy$

This removal of '=' has far-reaching consequences. (a) The *Tractatus* does not deny that ordinary identity statements like (1) and (2) make sense. They involve signs of complexes, which are analysed into a description of their simple components. But this LOGICAL ANALYSIS does not employ '='; it indicates the identity of simple objects through using the same name. (b) Frege's axioms governing identity are pseudo-propositions (TLP 5.534); at best they try to say something which shows itself in the logical structure of ordinary discourse. (c) The problems created by Russell's axiom of infinity (the claim that there is an infinite number of objects in the universe) cannot arise. For claims about how many objects there are, in contrast to claims about how many objects of a particular kind F there are, cannot even be formulated (*see* GENERALITY). By the same token, that a simple object a exists cannot be expressed by '$(\exists x)(x = a)$'. (d) Mathematical equations are pseudo-propositions. They do not say anything about the world, but equate signs which are equivalent by virtue of rules governing reiterable operations (TLP 6.2ff.).

Identity played a major role in Ramsey's attempt to improve the logicism of *Principia*. He followed Wittgenstein's criticism of Russell's definition of identity, namely that it implies the principle of the identity of indiscernibles, that is, that two objects cannot have all their qualities in common (*Principia* *13.01; TLP 5.5302; *Mathematics* 30–1). Unfortunately, like Russell and Wittgenstein he ignored the question of whether these qualities are to include spatio-temporal location, an inclusion which would make the principle plausible. At the same time, Ramsey tried to retain identity in a way which accommodates the *Tractatus*, arguing in effect that true identity statements are tautologies and false ones contradictions. In reply, Wittgenstein insisted that a false identity statement involving logically proper names is nonsensical rather than contradictory, and that the same holds for true identity statements, since the negation of a nonsense is itself a nonsense (RAL 2.7.26, 7./ 8.26).

After abandoning the idea that only truth-functional necessity is expressible, Wittgenstein allowed necessary propositions involving identity. However, he continued to deny that identity statements describe a peculiar relation in which everything stands to itself. Although this is not evident from their form, statements of the type '$a = b$' have the role of GRAMMATICAL propositions: they express substitution rules which license transformations of empirical propositions, for example from 'Φa' to 'Φb', and exclude certain propositions as nonsensical, for example '$\Phi a . {\sim}\Phi b$'. Thus a mathematical proposition like '$12 \times 12 = 144$' licenses the inference from 'There were 12 rows of 12 chairs' to 'There were 144 chairs.' Equally, an identity statement like (1) licenses the inference from 'The morning star is a planet' to 'The evening star is a planet', and excludes 'The morning star is a planet but the evening star isn't.' Such statements can be informative because given our criteria for understanding singular terms it is possible for someone to know what the morning star is, and what the evening star is, without knowing that they are identical. The role, if not the form, of (1) is that of a rule for the use of words. This casts doubt on Kripke's claim that (1) is a posteriori but *necessary*: the discovery (1) expresses is a contingent fact, namely that a single object satisfies two descriptions, or is the bearer of two names. What could be said to be necessary, but would be a priori, is the identity of a thing with itself.

Even that, however, presupposes the legitimacy of propositions of the form '$a = a$' (the law of identity), which Wittgenstein continued to question. '$a = a$' looks like a genuine truth because its negation strikes us as obviously false, and is the result of applying the substitution rule '$a = b$' to itself. But like 'Everything is identical with itself' or 'Everything fits into its own shape', '$a = a$' is degenerate. The 'partners' of the apparent relationship are not independent. Wittgenstein maintains that it would make sense to say that a is identical with itself only if it could fail to be so, which is impossible since '$a \neq a$' is a nonsense, and so is trying to distinguish something from itself. Accordingly, '$a = a$' is 'nonsense', a 'perfectly useless proposition' (PI §216; LFM 26–7, 200, 282–3; RFM 89, 404; BT 412; MS119 49).

Whether or not this holds true in general, Wittgenstein does show that the identity of an object with itself does not provide us with an absolute paradigm of what counts as 'doing the same' in RULE-FOLLOWING. What counts as doing the same is determined only relative to the rule, and hence the notion of doing the same cannot provide an independent standard: whether my saying '6' after '2, 4' counts as doing the same depends on whether I follow the series $y = 2x$ or the series $y = x^2$. There is no single, context-free or purpose-independent way of determining what counts as doing the same. More generally, talk about identity makes sense only relative to a practice which lays down techniques for establishing how many things one is dealing with, and whether or not something encountered now is the same as something encountered earlier. These criteria differ with the kind of thing at issue. For material objects it is spatio-temporal continuity, for persons a mixture of spatio-temporal continuity, memory and character-traits (PG 203; LFM 263; BB 55, 61–2). Wittgenstein coined the term 'criterion of identity', but the idea that talking about objects of a certain kind requires such criteria goes back to Locke (*An Essay concerning Human Understanding* II.16, 27) and Frege (*Foundations* §§62–9). It is used in the PRIVATE LANGUAGE ARGUMENT, in the Kant–Strawson attack on the notion of an immaterial substance, and by Quine ('No entity without identity!').

imagination The British empiricists held that the only contents of the mind are ideas or perceptions, which are understood as mental images, and are differentiated merely by differing degrees of intensity. Kant criticized this imagist conception by distinguishing between intuitions (sensations) and concepts, which are non-pictorial, and by insisting that to possess a concept is not a matter of having a mental image, but of being able to apply a rule. But Kant remained wedded to the imagist orthodoxy in so far as the rules he postulated are rules for constructing mental images. The later Wittgenstein not only denied that our mental life in general is based on having mental images (*see* MEMORY; THOUGHT/THINKING; UNDERSTANDING), but challenged the imagist conception of the imagination itself. According to that conception, imagination is a case of non-sensory perception, of seeing with the mind's eye: when we imagine something, we have an image which is just like a physical picture, except that it is private rather than public.

Like other opponents of the imagist position, such as Reid, Sartre and Ryle, Wittgenstein did not deny the existence of mental imagery (*Bilder, Vorstellungen*), or that we can see things with the mind's eye (e.g. PI §§6, 57, II 177; RPP I §§111–19, 359, 726, 1050; RPP II §§224–39, 511; LW I §§92, 135, 315–17, 729, 794, 808; LW II 12, 19). Instead, he made four other claims.

(a) 'One ought to ask, not what mental images (*Vorstellungen*) are or what happens when one imagines something, but how the word "imagination" (*Vorstellung*) is used' (PI §370). For the essence of imagination is nothing but its GRAMMAR.

(b) Investigation of that grammar reveals that the applicability of the word 'imagination' is not restricted to cases in which mental images cross my mind. It is possible that people should be able to imagine things, and to express what they imagine in writings or drawings, without seeing anything before their mind's eye. Indeed, no mental event or process need happen when one imagines something (RPP II §§66, 144; Z §624; *see* PHILOSOPHICAL PSYCHOLOGY).

In one respect, Wittgenstein's critique of imagism does not go far enough. Although he often uses 'to imagine' (*sich vorstellen, sich denken*) in a non-perceptual way, for example when he speaks of imagining a hypothesis, an explanation or a language (PI §§6, 19; LW I §§292, 341, 722, 777; Z §§98, 148, 440, 571), he maintains that it is essential to imagining that it employs concepts of sense perception (RPP I §885). But it makes sense to imagine things which it makes scant sense to perceive or picture to oneself (e.g., Rosa Luxemburg's last thoughts or that there are perfect numbers). It follows that not all cases of imagining could involve mental imagery.

(c) Even when mental images are involved in imagination, their nature is misunderstood by the imagist tradition. Mental images are not like physical pictures, only private. 'A mental image (*Vorstellung*) is not a picture' (PI §301; RPP II §§63, 112; Z §621; LPE 285; PR 82). It lacks definite boundaries, and is not subject to the criteria of identity for material things. We ascribe mental images to others on the basis of AVOWALS and BEHAVIOUR, that is, on what the subject says or draws when asked, while in the first-person case we employ no criterion at all. What the subject imagines, what the inner picture is of, is determined by what he says it is of, that is, there is first-person authority in respect of mental images (PI §§377–8; LW I §811). We do not 'recognize' our mental images, nor can we observe or inspect them (PI §§379–82; RPP II §885; Z §632). The language-game of imagining starts not with a private entity which is then described, but with the expression of what one imagines. A mental image is not a private entity, but the way we imagine something, just as a visual impression is the way we organize what we see (LW I §§440–3).

(d) Correspondingly, the imagist tradition misunderstood the relationship between imagination and perception. 'The *tie-up* between imaging and seeing is close; but there is no *similarity*' (Z §625). Any description of what is perceived can be used to describe what one imagines (although, as we have seen, the reverse does not hold). But identical descriptions are used differently in these contexts. Perceiving and imagining are categorially distinct (RPP II §§69–70, 130–9; Z §§629–37). (i) The difference between visual images and visual impressions is not merely a matter of vividness, as Hume thought (*A Treatise of Human Nature* I.i.3). It is unclear what standards of vividness Hume invokes. But one may be able to imagine something more clearly than one can see it. Furthermore, it makes no sense to wonder whether one is imagining or perceiving, although it makes sense to wonder whether one is hallucinating or perceiving (RPP II §§96, 142; Z §621; LPP 313–14). (ii) While looking or hearing inform one about how things are in one's environment, imagining does not (RPP II §63; Z §§621, 627). (iii) Unlike perceiving and hallucinating, imagining is subject to the will. Thus, one can try to 'banish' mental images in a way that one cannot visual impressions, and one can be surprised by what one sees but not (in the same way) by what one imagines (Z §§621, 627, 632–3). By the same token, imagining is creative rather than receptive, and hence closer to depicting than to seeing or hallucinating (RPP I §§111, 653; RPP II §§80–92, 115). (iv) Wittgenstein links imagination to ASPECT-PERCEPTION: seeing X as Y often involves imagining X as Y (PI II 193–229; RPP II §543).

induction Throughout his career Wittgenstein rejected two paradigmatic defences of inductive reasoning against Hume's attack: the suggestion that it is covertly probabilistic, and the invocation of a principle of the uniformity of nature. While the *Tractatus* adopts a Humean scepticism about inductive reasoning, the later writings reject both scepticism about induction and foundationalist attempts to vindicate it. In the *Tractatus*, observations on induction (TLP 6.3f., 6.363–6.36311) are linked to the discussion of SCIENCE. Induction is a procedure, namely of 'accepting as true the *simplest* law that can be reconciled with our experiences'. It has only a psychological justification; 'there are no grounds for believing that the simplest eventuality will in fact be realized.' For the 'law of induction', according to which nature is uniform – will carry on the way it has in the past – is a 'proposition with a sense', and therefore has no logical justification. Everything outside logic, in the domain of empirical science, is 'accidental'. In particular, CAUSATION is neither a real nor a necessary connection between events. Consequently we cannot *know* that the sun will rise tomorrow. For reasoning yields knowledge only if the premises are known to be true and entail the conclusion; but the existence of one situation never entails the existence of another. Knowledge requires certainty, which is a limiting case of probability, that is, restricted to tautologies. But if p is a tautology, so is 'A knows that p' (TLP 2.012, 4.464, 5.135–5.1362, 6.36311; PT 5.0444); it would be more in line with Wittgenstein's account of TAUTOLOGIES to claim that A knows that p is nonsensical, since in that case there is nothing to be known).

Like causation, probability (TLP 5.1, 5.15–5.156; NB 8.–9.11.14; PT 5.0932) is not a real nexus between events, nor is it a special logical constant peculiar to probability propositions. It is a relation between propositions, as in 'r gives to s the probability pr(r,s)'. The *Tractatus* provides a *logical* account of probability as a relation between the structures of propositions which can be displayed through TRUTH-TABLES. It elaborates Laplace's classical definition of probability as a ratio of the number of possibilities which are favourable to the occurrence of an event and the number of overall possibilities. Like Bolzano it drops from the definition the requirement that the possibilities be equally likely. The degree of probability which proposition 'r' gives to proposition 's' is the ratio of the number of truth-grounds of 's' that are also truth-grounds of 'r' to the number of truth-grounds of 'r'. The 'truth-grounds' or 'range' of a proposition are the truth-possibilities of its arguments that make it true, those rows of its truth-table in which it has a T. For example, '$p \, . \, q$' has the truth-ground (TT), and '$p \lor q$' has the truth-grounds (TT), (FT), (TF):

p q	$p \cdot q$
T T	T
F T	F
T F	F
F F	F

p q	$p \vee q$
T T	T
F T	T
T F	T
F F	F

If T_r is the number of T's for 'r', and T_{rs} the number of T's for 's' where 'r' also has a T, then $\mathrm{pr}(r,s) = T_{rs}/T_r$. Consequently: (a) if '$r$' and '$s$' are logically incompatible, the number of truth-grounds they share is 0, and hence $\mathrm{pr}(r,s) = 0$; (b) if all the truth-grounds of 's' are also truth-grounds of 'r', then $\mathrm{pr}(r,s) = 1$, that is, 's' follows from 'r' (this is the probability that '$p \cdot q$' gives to '$p \vee q$'); (c) if 's' is either a tautology or a contradiction, then for all non-contradictory propositions 'r', $\mathrm{pr}(r,s)$ equals 1 or 0 respectively (these are 'limiting cases of probability', TLP 5.152); (d) if neither 's' nor '$\sim s$' follows from 'r', then $0 < \mathrm{pr}(r,s) < 1$ (depending on their inner constitutions), thus '$p \vee q$' gives to '$p \cdot q$' the probability $1/3$; (e) if 'r' and 's' are logically independent ELEMENTARY PROPOSITIONS, $\mathrm{pr}(r,s) = 1/2$.

Wittgenstein's account delivers the axioms of a standard a priori probability calculus. Its main problem, as for all logical theories, is to reconcile such a priori propositions with contingent statistical observations. (e) suggests, implausibly, that knowing the truth of any elementary proposition 'r' gives us as much reason to expect another, 's', to be true as to expect 's' to be false. (Only if 's' is a molecular proposition can its probability relative to the set of propositions known to be true differ from $1/2$, since certain possibilities may be ruled out.) Successive draws from an urn containing an equal number of black and white balls (after each of which the ball is returned) will show that, as the draw continues, the number of black balls drawn gradually approximates to that of white balls drawn. This does not confirm the a priori judgement that the probability of drawing a white ball is $1/2$, but rather that relative to the 'hypothesized laws of nature', and to the initial conditions of the experiment, the two events are equipossible, that is, that a condition for the application of the probability calculus is satisfied (TLP 5.154). This is an empirical matter, since there might be an unknown physical link between the colour of objects and their propensity to be drawn.

The probability calculus of the *Tractatus* collapsed with the doctrine that there are logically independent elementary propositions, but it influenced Ramsey, Waismann and Carnap. The insight that there is a difference between a priori judgements of probability and empirical statistical judgements is elaborated in *Philosophical Remarks* (ch. XXII) and the 'Big Typescript' (BT §§32–3; see PG 215–35; WVC 93–100; PI §§482–4). It *seems* that a priori probability judgements are confirmed by statistical observations about the relative frequency of alternative outcomes in a limited series of experiments. Attempts to construe inductive reasoning as a form of probabilistic reasoning in which observations of past regularities render a prediction probable trade on this illusion. Statistical observations, for example that in the past 20 per cent of smokers have died of lung cancer, may lead to an inductive extrapolation which assigns a certain probability to N.N.'s dying of lung cancer. One cannot, however, assign a probability to the induction itself. Further experience may confirm that the initial regularity continues, but this merely confirms the specific extrapolation, which is itself an inductive hypothesis, not the method of induction as such. Consequently, probability cannot vindicate induction. Probabilistic reasoning amounts either to statistical extrapolations (the smoker case) which are themselves inductive, or to applications of a calculus (the urn case) which presuppose rather than explain natural regularities and their continuation.

Both the invocation of the law of induction and of probability try to vindicate induction by assimilating it to deduction. Against this, Wittgenstein insists that nothing in logic can license an inference from a previously observed regularity to a universal generalization or a prediction. His later treatment (PI §§466–90; OC *passim*) elaborates on the futility of trying to vindicate induction. (a) Russell's and Ramsey's pragmatist proposal that induction is justified through its usefulness is awry. 'Thinking has been found to pay' itself exemplifies the pattern of reasoning it is supposed to vindicate (PI §§467–9; OC §§130–1; cp. 'Limits' 148; *Mathematics* 245). (b) The law of induction is merely empirical, and hence open to the same disconfirmation which threatens particular inductions (OC §499). (c) It plays no role in our reasoning. We do not make a blanket assumption that what has happened in the past must happen again. Nor does empirical reasoning fit the deductive pattern of logical inference. We must distinguish between 'This is a fire, so it will burn me', the truth of which depends on contingent regularities, and 'This is a fire, fire always burns, so this will burn me', the validity of which depends not on reality but on a rule of inference (PI §§472–3; RFM 40, 397). (d) If our empirical reasoning were deductive, this would only relocate the problem from the empirical inference 'This is a fire, so it will burn me' to the generalization 'Fire always burns', which rests on exactly the same empirical grounds as the direct empirical inference (PI §479; OC §134).

The *Tractatus* had concluded that inductive reasoning could not yield certainty and hence knowledge. Now Wittgenstein emphatically claims that we do know that the sun will rise tomorrow, and can be certain that we shall get burnt if we put our hand in the fire. This CERTAINTY is not a non-empirical limiting case of probability, nor based on an assumption like the principle of the uniformity of nature. 'It is our *acting* which lies at the bottom of the language-game' of inductive reasoning (OC §§204, 273, 298, 613–19; PI §§472–4). Our activities are informed by the collective experience of a community bound together by science and education. They are ultimately founded on our primitive reactions to the regularities of the world. One's belief that one will be burnt is of a piece with the *fear* of being burnt, which is caused by the experience of having been burnt. In the absence of causal regularities, inductive reasoning would become irrational only in the sense that it would lose its point, because one could never predict what was going to happen next.

There is a naturalist streak in these observations. Unlike naturalism, however, Wittgenstein denies that our natural reactions vindicate either induction or inductive scepticism (PI §§475–83; OC §§128–9, 295–6). While experience provides 'a hundred reasons' for our specific predictions (PI §478), it does not provide grounds for the practice of taking relevant experiences as grounds for prediction (OC §§130–1). But the demand for such grounds is itself absurd, so that inductive scepticism gets no hold here. Wittgenstein's attack on inductive scepticism resembles that of Strawson, but is less clear. Inductive reasoning is not *a* method for predicting the future which may be more or less adequate, it defines what it is to make rational predictions. We call a prediction 'reasonable' precisely if it is supported by previous experience. On a more specific level, it is a grammatical proposition that making a transition from a specific kind of evidence to a certain conclusion is rational. 'A good ground is one that looks *like this*' (PI §483). If the sceptic replies that our patterns of reasoning themselves are inadequate, because these regularities have only been observed in the past, he ignores that there can be no such thing as *now* having evidence from the *future* (although we can have evidence *for* future events) (OC §275). The sceptic's point cannot be that there are good reasons for empirical beliefs, only past experience is not one of them. Instead, he simply refuses to call information about the past evidence for the future. But this could at best be a recommendation for a terminological shift. Because of the AUTONOMY OF LANGUAGE, Wittgenstein maintains that the sceptic's new rules for using the term 'reason' cannot be metaphysically superior to ours. And in pragmatic respects they are inferior, since they remove the vital distinction between conclusive, good and weak evidence.

inner/outer (*Innen/Außen*; *Inneres/Äußeres*) This contrast first appears in the middle thirties, features prominently in Wittgenstein's work after 1945, and is the main theme of his last manuscripts on philosophical psychology (RPP II §§170, 335, 643–4, 703–4; LW I & II *passim*). It characterizes the dualism of the mental and the physical. We find it natural to distinguish between the physical world containing matter, energy and tangible objects, including human bodies, which is public, and the human mind, a private world hidden behind our behaviour. And we think that each individual has a privileged access to his own mind, while our access to the minds of others is indirect, based on observations of their behaviour, and at best uncertain. Wittgenstein regards this as a 'picture' which is embedded in our language. Its roots lie in the fact that we apply mental predicates to others, but not to ourselves, on the basis of behavioural CRITERIA, something 'external'. However, outside philosophy the distinction between the mental and the physical does not coincide with this dichotomy of inner and outer: we regard toothache as *physical* pain, to be contrasted with mental suffering (LPE 278–83; LSD 118).

The inner/outer picture informs not just Cartesian dualism, but the mainstream of modern philosophy, including rationalism, empiricism and Kantianism. Even Frege, who insisted that what we think – 'thoughts' – are abstract entities in a 'third realm', accepted the traditional contrast between the 'second realm' of material objects and the first realm of 'ideas' which are the private properties of individuals: I cannot have your pain and you cannot have my sympathy ('Thought' 68–75). Idealism and phenomenalism dispense with the physical world, but cleave to the image of the mind as a private immaterial theatre to which we have immediate access. BEHAVIOUR-ISM, by contrast, reduces the mental to human behaviour, which it describes in purely physical terms. Finally, materialism rejects the Cartesian conception of the mind as an immaterial substance, but concludes that it must be a material substance, thereby replacing the mind/body dualism with a *brain/ body* dualism, in which the brain takes on the role of the inner. These positions question one half of the dichotomy, but not the contrast itself. They ignore that we describe human behaviour not as mere bodily movement, but *ab initio* in terms of our mental vocabulary, for example as jumping for joy or chuckling with glee. The mental is neither a fiction, nor hidden behind the outer. It infuses our behaviour and is expressed in it (LSD 10–11, 134–5; PI §357, II 178, 222–3; LW II 24–8, 81–95).

Wittgenstein's attack on the inner/outer dichotomy is often accused of reducing the inner to the outer, and thereby ignoring the most important aspects of human existence. Ironically, Wittgenstein in turn accuses the inner/outer conception of mistakenly assimilating the mental to the physical. It construes the relationship between mental phenomena and mental terms 'on the model of' material 'object and designation', and thereby turns the mind into a *realm* of mental entities, states, processes and events, which are just like their physical counterparts, only hidden and more ethereal (PI §§293, 308, 339; BB 47, 64, 70). Like Platonism, this tendency is fuelled by the AUGUSTINIAN PICTURE OF LANGUAGE, which suggests that all words stand for objects, and all sentences describe something – if not physical entities, then entities of a different kind. Wittgenstein's PRIVATE LANGUAGE ARGUMENT shows that the idea of private entities, and hence of the mind as an inner theatre, is incoherent. Wittgenstein also questions the assumption which unites dualism, materialism and behaviourism, namely that first-person present tense psychological utterances are descriptions or reports – if not of a soul, then of the brain or of behaviour. He claims that in fact they are typically AVOW-ALS, expressions of the inner which are in some respects analogous to natural reactions, gestures, grimaces, etc.

Along with the attack on the inner realm goes a challenge to the idea that self-knowledge is based on introspection, inward perception which is direct and infallible. The Cartesian idea of an infallible faculty of perception is mystifying. But it is equally awry to think of introspection as fallible, in the vein of James (*Psychology* I 189–90) and contemporary anti-Cartesians. For most mental phenomena, it does not even make sense to suppose that their subject misperceives them or mistakes them for something else. The possibility of a gap between its seeming to be so and its being so which characterizes perception is absent. Moreover, there is no meaningful answer to the question 'How do you know that you are in pain?' I do not observe, perceive or recognize my own sensations or experiences, I simply have them (LPE 278–80; LSD 111–12; MS160 61). Philosophical talk of 'introspection' or an 'inner sense' is metaphorical, and once more projects onto the mental features of the physical. There is an innocuous use of the term 'introspection'. We sometimes observe or describe our own state of mind, not in avowing a toothache, but in special cases of self-reflection: 'I dreaded her arrival all day long. On waking up I felt ... Then I remembered...' But in such cases we do not operate a mysterious inner sense, we simply note more or less skilfully, and over a period of time, how our thoughts, feelings and moods change. In contrast to observing the outer, such observation often alters the mental phenomena in question (PI §§585–7, II 188, 220–1; RPP I §§466–7; RPP II §§156, 177, 722–8; LW I §§975–9; LPP 235).

As a result, Wittgenstein turns on its head the idea of epistemic PRIVACY, according to which only I can know that I am in pain, while others can at best surmise it. Because there is no such thing as misperceiving one's own pain, or being mistaken about it, to say that I know that I am in pain is either a nonsense, or an emphatic assertion that I *am* in pain. At the same time, in the ordinary sense of 'know' others can, and often do, know that I am in pain. It is also misleading to claim that such knowledge is 'indirect': the sufferer does not know directly or indirectly of his being in pain, he suffers it, and for us there is no more direct way of knowing than by seeing him moan and writhe. In such cases we do not *infer* – draw the conclusion – that he is in pain, we *see* that he is suffering. Nevertheless, one might hold, I cannot see the pain itself, only the behaviour which expresses it. But this is like saying that I cannot see sounds or hear colours. It indicates only a categorial distinction between mental and behavioural terms, not that statements involving the former are always inferred from those involving the latter (PI §246; LSD 13; LW I §§767, 885).

It is tempting to protest that the mind is hidden in that there is always the possibility that others are lying or pretending. This shows that our third-person judgements are fallible. It does not establish the sceptical conclusion that, in a particular case, we are or could always be mistaken. Lying, deceit and pretence are parasitic on sincere avowals of the inner: pretending to be in pain is not behaviour without mental accompaniment, but behaviour plus something, a dishonest purpose, say, that makes sense only in a language-game in which sincerity can often be taken for granted. Nor is pretence possible in all cases, for example when someone falls into a fire and screams with pain (LSD 10; LPE 318; PI §§249–50, II 179–80, 229; Z §§570–1).

At the same time, the complex thoughts and feelings of some people may be enigmatic to us, even if they do their best to reveal them. This is due to the 'imponderability of the mental' (PI II 227–8; LW II 63–7, 87–93). Ascriptions of subtle emotions are not just defeasible, but may require close personal acquaintance or even be undecidable. But rather than reinstate the idea of an iron ontological curtain between the inner and the outer, these points reinforce the link between the mind and behaviour. For the occasional uncertainty of our judgements reflects an indeterminacy in our concepts, which in turn is due to the complex nature of our FORM OF LIFE. That the occasions for the use of some mental terms constitute a highly complex syndrome is due to the fact that human behaviour is unpredictable, and our reactions to it diverse and culturally relative.

The materialist version of the inner/outer dichotomy is more plausible than the mentalist one, since it invokes not a mysterious ontological realm, but an essential part of our body. Nevertheless, Wittgenstein's later work challenges many versions of materialism. His insistence that mental predicates can be applied only to living organisms, in particular HUMAN BEINGS, is incompatible with the view that it is the brain which thinks, feels or is conscious, but also with functionalism, the view that mental states are functional states of a machine. His PHILOSOPHICAL PSYCHOLOGY shows that our mental concepts do not amount to a primitive scientific theory which could be dispensed with in favour of something more up-to-date, as eliminative materialism envisages.

Nevertheless, it seems plausible that mental phenomena are inner causes of outward behaviour, and must hence be identical with neurophysiological phenomena, that is, brain-processes or -states. However, even if one grants this CAUSAL conception of the mind, it does not follow that psychological statements describe neurophysiological phenomena. If Wittgenstein is right, first-person present tense psychological utterances are by-and-large not descriptions of anything, let alone the brain. Less controversially, what little I know about my brain is based on fallible evidence, but that I have certain sensations, intentions, beliefs, etc., is neither subject to error, ignorance or doubt, nor based on evidence or observation of any kind.

177

That one cannot substitute 'I am in pain' for 'my C-fibres are firing' in 'I can doubt whether my C-fibres are firing' points to a category difference between mental and neurophysiological concepts. However, 'I can doubt whether...' constitutes an intensional context. Hence this failure of substitutability is compatible with a token-token identity theory like Davidson's anomalous monism, which claims merely that each *individual* mental phenomenon must be identical with an individual neurophysiological event, even though we are ignorant of what neurophysiological events correspond to what mental ones. Nevertheless, Wittgenstein would reject this view. He does not deny that a brain of a certain size and complexity is a precondition for the possession of mental capacities, and that some mental phenomena (e.g., perceiving a flash of light) are correlated with specific neurophysiological processes (PI §§376, 412). But he denies that there *must* be a universal parallelism between the mental and the physical, even at the level of tokens. 'No supposition seems to me more natural than that there is no process in the brain correlated with ... thinking; so that it would be impossible to read off thought-processes from brain-processes.' For although my spoken thoughts may be correlated with a series of impulses going out from the brain, this order might proceed 'out of chaos' (Z §§608–11). According to Wittgenstein, the mental does not supervene on the physical: there need not be any neurophysiological difference between someone who speaks thinkingly and someone who does not, just as there need not be any physiological difference between seeds producing different plants. This stance is problematic, since it amounts to denying that there must be a causal explanation of mental processes. It may not violate any logico-metaphysical necessities, but it is incompatible with a highly successful regulative principle of the neuro-sciences. At the same time, Wittgenstein gives strong reasons to suppose that many mental phenomena, notably understanding, believing, INTENDING AND MEANING SOMETHING, are categorially distinct from events, processes and states, since they lack the temporal properties ('genuine duration', datability) of the neural states and goings-on they are supposed to be identical with.

Moreover, even where neurophysiological phenomena are, as a matter of empirical fact, correlated with mental phenomena, they are neither necessary nor sufficient for the latter. Their presence does not entail that of mental phenomena (whatever the reading of the EEG, I am not in pain unless I feel that I am). And it is logically possible that mental phenomena are present not just without neurophysiological accompaniments of a specific kind (I can be in pain without any significant reading on the EEG), but without any neurophysiological accompaniments whatsoever: 'it is imaginable that my skull should turn out empty when it was operated on' (OC §4; see PI §§149–58; BB 118–20; RPP I §1063; *see also* UNDERSTANDING). This specifically does *not* mean that we could doubt that normal human beings have brains, since this is one of the hinge propositions which could be relinquished only at the price of a disintegration of our belief-system (*see* CERTAINTY). It means rather that there is no conceptual connection between neurophysiological mechanisms and mental phenomena. Neurophysiological concepts play no role in our explanation and application of mental terms: third-person uses of mental terms are based on behavioural criteria, first-person uses are not based on any criteria, let alone neurophysiological ones, although a belief in a general connection between neurophysiological and mental phenomena is part of our world-view (**BB** 47).

intending and meaning something The later Wittgenstein discusses not only the *logical* mysteries surrounding INTENTIONALITY, but also the *mental* side of intentional verbs like BELIEVING that *p*, intending to Φ and meaning a particular object *x*. The last two are discussed in the final two parts of *Philosophical Investigations* Part I (PI §§629–60 & 661–93, respectively). This is no coincidence, since they are both linked to voluntary powers and obscured by misconceptions of the WILL, the discussion of which occupies the preceding sections. While intending had not received philosophical attention since Bentham, meaning something was important to Wittgenstein's early work. The *Tractatus* held that a propositional sign '*Fa*' is projected onto a state of affairs in virtue of being accompanied by a proposition in the language of thought. It is part of this METHOD OF PROJECTION that by '*a*' I mean a particular object. This is why among the subjects running through the *Investigations* is not only *Bedeutung*, the conventional meaning of a word in a language, but also *Meinen*, what a speaker means by a word on a particular occasion of utterance (PI 18n, §§22, 33–5; 81, 186–8, 358, 504–13, 592).

For the later Wittgenstein, whether I intend or mean something, and if so what, is determined neither by thought-processes nor by ostensive acts. Intentional verbs do not signify *phenomena* – acts, activities, events, processes or states, whether in the mind or in the brain. 'If God had looked into our minds he would not have been able to see there whom we were speaking of' (PI II 217). The first argument for this astonishing claim is that intentional verbs do not belong to those logical categories, since they lack 'genuine duration' (*see* PHILOSOPHICAL PSYCHOLOGY). It may seem as if meaning something is the act of directing one's attention towards it. But no such act need be involved. If *A* simulates being in pain and says 'It will stop soon', he can be said to mean the pain, even though there is no pain on which he could focus his attention. Meaning something is no more a mental activity than rising in price is an activity of butter (PI §§666–7, 693).

Wittgenstein's second argument is familiar from his treatment of UNDERSTANDING. Mental or physical processes or states are neither necessary nor sufficient for believing, intending or meaning something. There may be empirical correlations between such phenomena and intentional attitudes.

179

They may inform a psychologist about my 'unconscious' intentions. But they do not determine the content of intentional attitudes, what I think, intend or mean. *Pace* James and Russell (*Psychology* I 253–4; *Analysis* ch. XII), there are no feelings or experiences which characterize intentional attitudes. Even if one grants, as Wittgenstein does, that intentions might be accompanied by characteristic feelings, these feelings are not the intentions they accompany (PI §§591, 646, II 217; Z §33). As regards meaning something by what one said, the temptation to postulate feelings is fuelled by confusing it with meaning what one said. But not even the latter need involve feelings (e.g., of sincerity): 'I meant what I said' does not report the result of self-observation, but affirms one's willingness to stand by one's utterance. Normally, we associate feelings with some expressions. But such feelings are neither necessary nor sufficient for the expressions' making sense (BB 10–11; PI II 217; RPP I §232; *see* ASPECT-PERCEPTION).

Intentional attitudes are not tied to mental images or words crossing one's mind. My long-standing intentions could not consist in pertinent images or words constantly crossing my mind. Equally, when I utter a sentence like

(1)   Napoleon was impetuous

(meaning the victor of Austerlitz) a mental image might cross my mind, but it need not. Moreover, even if I mean Napoleon I, an image of his nephew may cross my mind, simply because the former always reminds me of the latter. Finally, I can mean someone without knowing what he looks like. In that case, even if an image crosses my mind, it could not possibly determine whom I meant (PI §§663, 680, II 175–6; PG 103; BB 39–40, 142; RPP I §§226–33). It is equally implausible to insist that I can mean Napoleon I only if words like 'the victor of Austerlitz' cross my mind. One might claim that to mean Napoleon I is at any rate to think of him. But while 'I meant...' is sometimes equivalent to 'I thought of...', it is not always (PI 33n, §690, II 217). I might make an absent-minded remark about Napoleon I while thinking about Napoleon III. By the same token, James was wrong to suggest that the entire thought must already be present in my mind for me to mean something by an utterance (PI §337; Z §1; LW I §§843–4; *Psychology* I ch. IX).

A tempting objection is that although mental images are never necessary or sufficient, and although no thought is necessary, verbal thoughts of a certain kind are sufficient for meaning something: if, while uttering 'Napoleon', the words 'the loser of Sedan' cross my mind, I must mean Napoleon III. In reply, Wittgenstein points out that (irrespective of whether it is uttered) even the 'most explicit' expression determines what one means only if it in turn is intended to identify the person meant (PI §641). But it need not be, since it could be part of a recital, or a slogan crossing one's mind. More fundamentally, mere phenomena, whether processes or states, whether physiological or mental, are necessarily insufficient to determine one's intentional attitudes – this is the kernel of truth in the *Tractatus*'s invocation of acts of meaning. 'It is not the picture which intends, but we must intend something by it.' But if this intending in turn is a mere 'process', 'phenomenon' or 'fact', it is no less dead than the picture (Z §§236–8; PG 143–4, 148; RPP I §215). 'For no *process* could have the consequences of meaning' (PI II 218). That I mean Napoleon I has the consequence that my utterance *counts* as one about Napoleon I. It commits me to a certain claim, which in turn licenses subsequent moves in the language-game. Such normative consequences cannot follow from a description of my mind, brain or behaviour. Similarly, a description of states or processes does not have the same consequences as the claim that I intend to Φ. It does not characterize my Φing as the exercise of a voluntary power for which I can be held responsible (Wittgenstein draws the same lesson from 'Moore's paradox'; *see* BELIEF).

Wittgenstein's denial that intentional attitudes are states or processes of the subject is one source of contemporary externalism, the view that what *A* thinks is at least partly determined by facts 'external' and possibly unknown to *A*, namely his relation to his physical (Putnam) or social (Burge) environment. Some early passages suggest that intentional attitudes are a matter of certain phenomena in the right kind of surrounding (e.g. BB 147). But in his mature work Wittgenstein explicitly denies that meaning something refers to a 'family of mental and other processes' (Z §§9, 26). Instead, he mentions three CRITERIA we use to ascribe intentional attitudes.

(a) AVOWALS. *A*'s intention need not be evident from anything crossing his mind, but is displayed by the expression of his intention, and the same is true of his meaning something. He can be credited with intending to Φ, or with having meant Napoleon I, if this is what he avows, either then or later, provided that there are no grounds for questioning his sincerity (Z §§3, 9, 53; PI §452; PG 103; BB 161; RPP I §§579–80).

(b) Explanations. What *A* means is evident from how, if the occasion arises, he explains, justifies or elaborates his utterances, what consequences he derives from them, what replies and reactions he accepts as pertinent (PG 40–5; Z §24).

(c) Context. Whom *A* meant by (1) may depend on the topic of the conversation, on *A*'s background, and especially on about whom he had a reason to speak.

Unlike externalism, this account respects first-person authority, the fact that, by and large, I cannot be mistaken about what I intend or mean. *A* does not ascribe intentional attitudes to himself on the basis of these criteria, he avows them. While others may cast doubt on the wisdom of his intentions, or the pertinence of his remark about Napoleon I, they cannot intelligibly accuse him of being mistaken, but only of being dishonest (PI §§587, 679; Z §§22, 53). What matters about the context here are only facts of which *A* is aware. And these contextual criteria can be defeated by sincere avowals and explanations. Even if the conversation is about Napoleon III, *A* means Napoleon I if he sincerely says so.

This is in line with Wittgenstein's functional conception of sense. The content of an utterance does not simply depend upon the constituents and structure of the type-sentence, it depends also on how a token of that type-sentence is USED on a particular occasion (PI II 221). This in turn is a matter of the 'intention' of the speaker. But these intentions are not the bringing about of certain (perlocutionary) effects in the audience, as for Grice, nor constituted by mental accompaniments of the utterance. By contrast to a recent trend, Wittgenstein does not explain linguistic meaning, or even speaker's meaning, by reference to the intrinsic intentionality of the mind (LW I §§17, 37). It is the ability of human agents to avow, explain and elaborate on what they believe, intend and mean which underlies intentional attitudes. We cannot mean whatever we wish by whatever signs we use, simply by performing a mental act (PI 18n, §§508–10, 665; Z §6). However, this is not to dispute that there is such a thing as speaker's meaning. The cases involved – meaning 'The weather is fine' by 'a b c d', or 'It's warm here' by 'It's cold here' – are not ordinary cases of speaker's meaning. They do not involve the resolution of indexicals, ambiguity or contextual unclarity, but are deviations from ordinary use. Even this is not impossible. 'A word has the meaning someone has given to it' (BB 28; PI §665). But it requires not a mental act, nor even just a simple avowal, but an explanation of the rules according to which these words are used on this occasion.

Wittgenstein agrees with externalism that we cannot simply avow any intentional attitudes whatever. While the context cannot show that *A* is mistaken about what he believes, intends or means, it can render certain avowals and third-person ascriptions unintelligible. Contextual features do not determine the content of intentional attitudes directly, as externalism says they do, but they determine the range of intentional attitudes which can be ascribed. One can be in agonizing pain for a split second, irrespective of the setting, since it can be displayed in characteristic pain-behaviour. But one cannot, for example, expect something for a split second, irrespective of the setting, since an expectation 'is embedded in a situation from which it arises' (PI §581). Moreover, one can intend to perform, or will, only what is, or what one believes to be, within one's power (see PI §§614–16). Finally, intentions are embedded in human customs and institutions. One can intend to play chess only if the practice of playing the game exists (PI §§205, 337). For one can intend to Φ only if one can display or execute this intention. In the case of complex intentions this in turn presupposes a social and historical context, since otherwise the relevant actions and utterances do not count as expressions of the intention. Such a setting is not required for the intentions to drink, run or go to sleep (as some externalists have it), since these can be displayed in pre-conventional, non-linguistic behaviour. However, all but the most basic human intentions require the weave of a social and historical FORM OF LIFE.

Whereas externalism holds that intentional attitudes are relational rather than intrinsic, Wittgenstein holds that they are potentialities rather than actualities. In one place he distinguishes them from states of consciousness as 'dispositions' (Z §72; RPP II §57), which would render his position close to that of Ryle. But although someone who intends to Φ is disposed (i.e., inclined) to Φing, this is not equivalent to having a disposition to Φ (RPP II §178). For one has to find out what one's dispositions are through noting how one is prone to react in certain circumstances. But one does not have to find out that one intends to Φ. And one may have an intention (e.g., to burst out angrily) without having a corresponding disposition, and vice versa. More importantly, dispositions are inevitably realized given certain circumstances (see AWL 91). Intentional attitudes rest on *abilities* rather than dispositions.

One might sum up Wittgenstein's position as follows:

A means N.N. by uttering 'x' at t_1 =
had A been asked at t_1 whom he meant, and been inclined to answer honestly, he would have answered 'N.N.'

But Wittgenstein rejects any analysis in terms of necessary and sufficient conditions: 'the error lies in saying that meaning consists in something' (Z §§16, 26, see §680; PI §§335, 678). His reasons emerge from the peculiar way in which he approaches the subject, namely through retrospective self-ascriptions like 'I was going to say ... at t_1' or 'When I said ... at t_1, I meant...' One idea of his is that these do not just *report* a pre-existing connection (between an incipient action and an intention, an utterance and its referent), but *draw* such a connection (PI §§682–3; similarly PI §487 for explanations of actions). Yet this is plausible only if the initial action or utterance was indeterminate, for example when, without explicit deliberation, I start drawing a head (Z §§8, 32).

Wittgenstein's second line is more promising. If intending/meaning something consisted in a certain fact (intrinsic or relational, actual or dispositional), then remembering having intended/meant something must consist in remembering this fact. But retrospective self-ascriptions are not based on remembering a certain (counterfactual) fact. We don't say 'I meant/intended ... because, had you asked me, I would have said...', but the other way around: 'Had you asked me, I would have said..., because I meant/intended...' They do not depend on recollecting either the 'details' of the situation or 'the whole story' but are nonetheless 'semi-verifiable'. They do not enjoy the complete authority of avowals at t_1. Others may correct me by reference to 'details of the situation'. But none of these pieces of evidence *is* the remembered intention, since my memory does not rest on such evidence. Others pronounce on what I intended by inference from details, or by interpreting the situation, but I do not. If I did, I could not possess the certainty I often have. Retrospective self-ascriptions are not reports of any type of fact, but 'memory-reactions' (PI §§343, 636, 638; MS116 301).

intentionality This is the directedness of the mind towards an object, which may or may not exist. The term was introduced by Brentano (*Psychologie vom Empirischen Standpunkt* II.1.v), who maintained against the Cartesian tradition that intentionality rather than consciousness is the distinguishing feature of the mental. The problem of how thought and language can relate to reality, be about something, goes back at least to Democritus. But it was Plato who formulated the puzzle of intentionality: How can one think what is not the case? For if it is not the case, then it does not exist, and what does not exist is nothing. But to think nothing is not to think anything at all (*Theaetetus* 189a; see PI §518).

The early Wittgenstein sought to explain how one part of reality, a propositional sign consisting of mere sounds or marks, can represent another, a fact 'outside in the world' (NB 27.10.14). Like Plato, he was exercised by the 'mystery of negation' – we can think '*how* things are *not*' – and by the puzzle that false thoughts represent even though what they represent is not a fact and hence does not even exist. 'If a picture presents what-is-not-the-case ... this only happens through it presenting *that* which is *not* the case. For the picture says, as it were, "*this* is how it is *not*" and to the question "How is it not?" just the positive proposition is the answer' (NB 3.11.14; FW 24). The propositions p and $\sim p$ do not signify different entities: it is the same fact which verifies one of them and falsifies the other (NL 94–6; NB 4.11.14; TLP 4.064). He linked this to a third puzzle, namely of how thought can 'reach right up to reality' (TLP 2.1511f.). If my thought is true, what I think must be identical with what is the case, but if it is false, it cannot be; yet the content of my thought is the same in both cases.

The PICTURE THEORY develops a solution to these interrelated puzzles. (a) The possibility of falsehood and the mystery of negation. No fact need correspond to the proposition as a whole, but something must correspond to each of its elements (NAMES), namely an element (object) of the situation it depicts (AWL 110). Moreover, it must share with that situation a LOGICAL FORM: the names must have the same combinatorial possibilities as the objects they stand for. Given the appropriate METHOD OF PROJECTION, the fact that the elements of the picture are related to each other in a determinate way represents a specific configuration of objects.

(b) *Reaching right up to reality*. The antinomy is avoided by holding that, whether or not my thought is true, its content is one and the same possibility, which is actualized in the first case but not in the second. *What I think* is the 'sense of the proposition', the 'state of affairs' depicted, a possible combination of objects (TLP 3:11, 4.021). The possibility of that combination is guaranteed by the proposition which 'contains' it (TLP 2.203, 3.02; NB 5.11.14), because the combinatorial possibilities of names mirror those of objects. The world only decides whether or not the place in LOGICAL SPACE determined by the proposition is filled.

On his return to philosophy, Wittgenstein abandoned not just logical atomism, the idea that the possibility of representation rests on the existence of sempiternal OBJECTS, but also the idea that representation presupposes an agreement in form between a proposition and a possible state of affairs. He continued to discuss the relationship between propositions and facts, but now as a special case of intentionality, the 'harmony between thought and reality' which obtains equally between beliefs, expectations, desires, etc., and what verifies or fulfils them (PI §429; PG 142–3, 162–3; LWL 24). The reason for this widening lies in his exposure to the causal theories of intentionality of Ogden and Richards (*The Meaning of Meaning*) and especially Russell. According to the behaviourist account in *The Analysis of Mind* (chs I, III, XII), a conscious desire is accompanied by a true belief as to its 'purpose', that is, the state of affairs which will bring quiescence, the cessation of discomfort. Such beliefs rest on inductive evidence concerning what sort of state has in the past removed what sort of discomfort. Accordingly, a desire is a feeling of discomfort which causally generates a 'behaviour cycle' terminating in quiescence or pleasure. One knows what one desires just as one knows what others desire, namely by inferring it from past patterns of behaviour. Russell also distinguished the 'objective' of a belief from 'what is believed'. The latter, like the believing, must consist of present occurrences in the believer, irrespective of the objective. The 'objective' of my belief that Caesar crossed the Rubicon is a past event. However, 'what I believe' cannot be the actual event that makes the belief true, since the latter has long since passed. Instead, it is a related event occurring now in my mind; otherwise, how could I say what I *now* believe?

Russell connects a thought and what satisfies it through a *tertium quid*: my belief is verified if I recognize its objective, my desire is fulfilled if I have a feeling of satisfaction. As Wittgenstein pointed out, this implies that 'if I wanted to eat an apple, and someone punched me in the stomach, taking away my appetite, then it was this punch that I originally wanted.' To avoid this absurd consequence, Wittgenstein invokes a key element of his earlier 'picture conception' (PR 64; see LWL 9; FW 97; TLP 4.014, 4.023, 4.03).

The relation between a thought and what satisfies it is not causal but INTER-NAL, that is, constitutive of the relata. My belief that *p* could not be made true by any fact other than that *p*, whatever feelings that fact may produce in me. Equally, 'I should like an apple' does not mean 'I want whatever will quell my feeling of nonsatisfaction and believe that an apple will do the trick' (PI §440; PG 134).

Wittgenstein also attacks the very question of how I know what I think. In saying that I want, say, an apple, I am stating *what* I want, not predicting or conjecturing that an apple will quell a feeling of nonsatisfaction. Nor do I read off what I want or believe from introspecting a mental state or process; rather, I give *expression* to my belief or desire. *Pace* Russell, I cannot be mistaken about the content of my wish, and do not find out what it is I wish (PI §441; BB 22). One can say 'I don't know what I want.' But typically, these are cases not of ignorance (I have a determinate wish but don't know what it is) but of indecision (I haven't made up my mind). However, we also say, for example, 'I am longing for something, but don't know what', and such locutions underlie Freud's idea of discovering our unconscious beliefs and desires. Wittgenstein tries to defuse this locution by claiming that it is equivalent to an 'intransitive' use of 'longing' – 'I have a feeling of longing' – and merely displays a preference for a certain form of representation (BB 22–3, 29). But although a transitive use plus a disclaimer of knowledge may express an objectless mood or emotion, it often does more than this, for it often avows ignorance, not of the intentional object, but of the *cause* of one's emotional state. It is equivalent to 'I don't know what would make me content at present.' Wittgenstein rightly distinguished intentional relations from causal ones, but ignored that what fuels psychoanalysis is not just those cases where there is the possibility of vacuous reformulation through a modified intentional idiom, but causal and, more generally, hypothetical uses of our existing intentional idiom. Sometimes we find out what we desire by noticing our reactions (RPP II §3), and this provides a starting-point for Freud's idea of unconscious desires.

During the early thirties (esp. PG chs VII–IX) Wittgenstein provided an account of intentionality without invoking a 'pre-established' logico-metaphysical isomorphism (BT 189). The eventual upshot was *Philosophical Investigations* §§428–65, which is highly condensed and conceals the background of his discussion. The basic idea is that puzzles about intentionality are metaphysical shadows of humdrum grammatical rules. 'Like everything metaphysical, the harmony between thought and reality is to be found in the grammar of the language' (PG 162; Z §55). The belief that *p* is made true by the fact that *p*, my wish for *x* is fulfilled by the event of my obtaining *x*, the order to Φ by Φ-ing; if it is false that this is red, then this is not red – but these are not metaphysical truths about the relation between thought and reality, they are GRAMMATICAL rules which lay down how the expression of thoughts can be transformed into statements about what verifies, falsifies or fulfils them (PG 162; PI §§136, 429, 458): 'The proposition that p' = 'the proposition which the fact that p makes true'; 'The expectation that p' = 'the expectation which will be fulfilled if p'; 'It is false that p' = '$\backsim p$'; 'The order to Φ' = 'the order which is executed by Φ-ing'. Such rules also determine what is *called* 'the proposition that p', 'the expectation that p', etc., and thereby establish connections between the concepts of proposition, expectation, etc., and those of fact, fulfilment, etc. The grammar of 'expectation' is such that expectations are individuated by what would fulfil them, and such that the expression of expectations involves a clause that can be converted into a description of their fulfilment (PR 66–9; PG 150). This is not a harmony between a thought and a situation, but between one proposition and another. 'It is in language that an expectation and its fulfilment make contact' (PI §445; PG 140).

This point is concealed by the idea that an expectation as such is something 'unsatisfied' because it is the expectation of something 'outside the process' of expectation (PI §438), and similarly for other types of thoughts. It is a grammatical truth that a belief is a belief that something is the case, an expectation an expectation that something will be the case, and that whether or not a belief is true or an expectation fulfilled is decided by how things were, are or come to be. Nevertheless, the metaphor of satisfaction is misleading. That my thought is 'unsatisfied' does not mean that I *feel* unsatisfied until it is 'satisfied'; moreover, I may feel dissatisfied by the satisfaction of my wish, if it is disappointing (PI §441; BB 22). One might drop the notion of satisfaction, while insisting that thoughts are directed at something extra-mental which *fits* them, just like a piston fits a cylinder (PI §439). However, the physical relation of fitting is external: a cylinder can be identified without specifying the piston which fits it. The analogy might mean that the same mathematical description applies to both cylinder and piston. But then it merely restates the idea that the expression of my expectation fits the statement of its fulfilment in that the same form of words occurs in both (PI §429; PR 71; LWL 33; PG 134). There are not two events here, my expecting him (which might be thought to consist, say, in my pacing up and down) and his coming, which stand in a mysterious relation of fit. Rather, 'the expectation that p' and 'the expectation which will be fulfilled if p' are two ways of referring to the same expectation. These points dissolve the puzzle about how a thought, something I have here and now, can be about something which is far away and in the future or past (PI §428; PG 136). Given the order to Φ, one can say what will fulfil that order. But if we say that it anticipates the future by ordering what will later happen, we must add: or does not happen (PI §461), which tells us nothing about the future.

The idea that thoughts bridge a gulf in space and time is one motive behind 'surrogationalism', the view, shared by Russell and classical empiricism, that thought must contain a surrogate of its (often distant and non-existent) object, a representation of what is thought. Surrogationalism is also fuelled by a dilemma: on the one hand, thoughts are individuated by their content; on the other, they cannot *contain* what is thought because the latter is a possibly remote situation; hence, it seems, they must contain a surrogate of it. But this violates the *Tractatus*'s insistence that the proposition 'reaches right up to reality'. For it implies that even when the proposition is true, what actually obtains or transpires is not exactly the same as what one believed, wanted or remembered, but only something similar to it, a paler shadow (in this vein Hume – *An Enquiry concerning Human Understanding* II.11 – claimed that the vivacity of the idea I have when I remember something never reaches that of the original impression). But there is a difference between expecting something only similar to what actually transpires, for example a light red patch instead of a standard red patch, and expecting exactly what happens. And this is not a matter of comparing an actual event with a mental duplicate: ' "The report was not as loud as I had expected" – "Then was there a louder bang in your expectation?" ' (PI §§442–3).

In the *Tractatus* what is thought *is* the state of affairs which obtains if it is true. Still, that state of affairs is a 'shadow of the fact' which mediates between the thought and the fact – albeit a perfect one. It has the same form as the fact, and merely lacks the latter's existence. 'It is as if an event even now stood in readiness before the door of reality and were then to make its appearance in reality – like coming into a room' (PG 137; see LWL 30; BT 104; BB 31–2, 36–7; PI §§519–21; TS302 7–8, 11–12; FW 57). In sum, the proposition determines a possible fact, while reality determines whether it is actualized. But in fact this boils down to the idea that if a proposition makes sense, it is clear what would verify it, whether or not it is true (PI §461). It does not require an intermediary. The temptation to postulate such a shadow derives from the very idea of thought having a 'content'. The content of a thought is simply what is thought, namely that *p*. Contents are not intermediaries but logical constructions, projections of that-clauses. Their reification confuses, for example, '*A* believes that *p*' with '*A* believes *B*.' In the latter case we have an *object-accusative*, two relata must exist, one to believe, and one to be believed. The former, by contrast, involves a disguised *intentional-accusative*. What we believe is *that p*. Here 'believe' does not express a genuine relation, since it can apply without there being two relata – *that p* may not be a fact. The second relatum cannot be furnished by a possible state of affairs, since this implies that what *A* believes is one thing (a fact) if *p* is true, but another (a state of affairs) if *p* is false.

Wittgenstein's PHILOSOPHICAL PSYCHOLOGY rejects Brentano's influential idea that intentionality is the hallmark of the mental, on the grounds that it is absent not just from sensations and feelings, but also from objectless moods and emotions (a view he shares with Heidegger). His discussion of intentionality illustrates that philosophical clarifications are as complex – and, occasionally, as contrived – as the knots which they untie (Z §452). The reward is a demystified picture which undermines the views of Plato, Russell and the *Tractatus*, and challenges the contemporary view of intentionality as a relation between a subject and a 'content', and the idea of a direction of fit between thoughts and reality.

internal relations   These are relations which could not fail to obtain, since they are given with or (partly) constitutive of the terms (objects or relata), such as white's being lighter than black. Equally, an internal property is a property which a thing could not fail to possess, because it is essential to its being the thing it is (TLP 4.122–4.1252; NM 116–17). The internal or essential properties of an OBJECT are its LOGICAL FORM, they determine its combinatorial possibilities with other objects (TLP 2.01231, 2.0141). Wittgenstein picked up this term from Russell (*Principles* 221–6, 447–9; *Essays* 139–46; *External* ch. II; *Logic* 333–9). Russell, following Moore, had insisted against Bradley that there are external, non-essential relations. Wittgenstein did not participate in this debate, but announced that the 'vexed question' whether all relations are internal is 'settled' once we realize that an internal relation between two situations is expressed by an internal relation between the propositions depicting them (TLP 4.125f.). Internal relations are not genuine relations at all, since they cannot be meaningfully expressed by a proposition. They are *structural* relations, namely between propositions, or between propositions and the states of affairs they depict (TLP 4.014). They show themselves if these propositions are properly analysed. Thus, the internal relation between the numbers 1 and 2 shows itself in the fact that the latter succeeds the former in a formal series. Equally, the internal relations of LOGICAL INFERENCE between propositions, for example between a proposition about a complex and propositions about its components, are due to the truth-functional composition of the relata, and show themselves if the latter are properly analysed (TLP 3.24, 5.131, 5.2f.). This also reveals that there *are* external relations, since not all propositions are truth-functionally related. Indeed, there *must be* external relations, namely between different ELEMENTARY PROPOSITIONS (atomic states of affairs), for these are logically independent.

Although Wittgenstein later abandoned the idea that all logical relations are truth-functional, he continued to speak of logical relations as 'internal' (PG 152–3; RFM 363–4; PI II 212). His abiding concern was to insist that empirical and necessary propositions differ 'categorically' (M 86–7; LWL 9, 56–7; CE 443). Science ascribes properties and relations which can be verified or falsified empirically. Causal relations in particular can only be established empirically, by observation and induction (PI §169). Such properties and relations are contingent, and the corresponding statements, such as '$g = 9.81$ m/sec^2', 'Tom Tower is 25 m high' and 'Radioactivity causes cancer', are corrigible. Even if these relations are *physically* necessary, the corresponding propositions could in principle be refuted by new experiments or observations. By contrast, logic, mathematics and philosophy are concerned with propositions which are *logically* necessary and hence a priori. In their cases, refutation is not extremely improbable, but inconceivable, as with '$p \supset p$', '$2 + 2 = 4$' and 'White is lighter than black' (AWL 18; cp. TLP 5.1362, 6.1231f., 6.3ff.). The explanation is that these relations are internal: two colours which do not stand in the relation mentioned, simply are not white and black (RFM 75–6). It is impossible, therefore, to find out that these relata do not stand in that relationship. Wittgenstein castigated empiricism, notably Russell's account of intentionality, for assimilating internal to external relations. Internal relations are not limiting cases of external ones. Necessary propositions are not well-confirmed inductive generalizations, as Mill and, occasionally, Russell suggested (PR 64; LWL 79–80; 'Limits'). Otherwise, the negation of a necessary proposition could be true, with the absurd consequence that on some distant planet, exceptionally, white might be darker than black.

Wittgenstein came to favour the terms 'grammatical relations' or 'grammatical connections' over 'internal relations' (M 87). GRAMMATICAL relations are not relations which we establish by examining the relata, since we could not identify the relata independently of the relations. The relata are not really connected by a relation of 'fit', as that between a piston and a cylinder, but 'belong' with each other (PI §§136, 437–9, 537). Like everything metaphysical, internal relations are to be found in grammar. They are creatures of our practice, since they are effected by the way we identify things, for example by the fact that we *call* 144, and nothing else, the square of 12 (Z §55; PG 160–1; LFM 73–85; RFM 88; *see* MATHEMATICAL PROOF). Wittgenstein makes two interrelated points about grammatical relations. One is that they cannot be underpinned or explained by postulating mediating links between the relata. This is directed against for example the *Tractatus*'s invocation of a 'sense' to mediate between a proposition and the fact which verifies or falsifies it, Russell's invocation of feelings of satisfaction to mediate between a desire and what fulfils it (*see* INTENTIONALITY), and the invocation of an interpretation to mediate between a rule and its application (*see* RULE-FOLLOWING). Such moves lead to a dilemma: either that link is itself internally related to both of the relata, in which case it engenders a regress, or it is only externally related, in which case it reduces the internal relation to an external one. I do not need to add an interpretation in order to understand an order: unless any such interpretation called forth by the order is the right one, it hinders rather than aids understanding; but if it is the *right* one, the order was already determinate without it (LWL 30–6, 56–9; PG 47; WVC 154–7). Secondly, there is no such thing as justifying or doubting an internal relation. Since the relation is (partly) constitutive of the relata, one cannot coherently deny that it obtains without ceasing to talk about those relata. Consequently, a sceptic cannot meaningfully deny that the relation obtains. At most, he could reject the practice which treats the two as internally related.

K

kinaesthesis This topic exercised Wittgenstein in his latest works on PHILOSOPHICAL PSYCHOLOGY (PI II 185–6; LPP 17, 36, 72–92, 135, 157–8, 195, 202–20, 236, 256, 277–9, 309–23; RPP I §§382–408, 452, 698, 754–98, 948; RPP II §§63, 147; Z §§477–83, 498, 503; LW I §§386–405; LW II 16–17), presumably because it is an exception to his claim that the INNER is typically not an object of knowledge (*see* AVOWAL; PRIVACY). He conceded that we can *know* the positions of our limbs: my assertion that my fingers are intertwined in a certain way is fallible and correctible by others. What he denied is a view held by psychologists like James (*Psychology* II chs XX, XXIII) and Köhler (*Gestalt* 127–8), namely that this knowledge is based on kinaesthetic sensations (he also rejected the related idea that I am informed about the location of sensations by certain of their features). I could infer the location of limbs from bodily sensations, for example, if a characteristic rheumatic pain always accompanies a certain position of my limbs (LPP 78). Yet, typically, we know the position of our limbs without recourse to sensations or any kind of observation. (a) Genuine sensations have duration and intensity; such sensations rarely accompany kinaesthetic knowledge (RPP I §§386, 771, 783; Z §478; LPP *passim*). (b) It is wrong to suppose that kinaesthetic knowledge must rest on something. Even if it is causally dependent upon specific neurophysiological phenomena, these need not be sensed: we can tell the direction of a sound because of the difference in effect on our two ears, but that difference is not sensed (PI II 185; LPP 90). (c) The empirical fact that a disruption of afferent nerves results in loss of both kinaesthesis and sensations does not establish that sensations are essential to the concept of kinaesthesis. Wittgenstein also claims that what results is not simply an absence of sensations, but a specific sensation of deprivation (RPP I §§406, 758).

L

language-game (*Sprachspiel*)   From 1930 onward, Wittgenstein compared axiomatic systems with chess. This analogy stems from the formalists, who treated arithmetic as a game played with mathematical symbols. It was castigated by Frege, who saw only two alternatives: either arithmetic is about mere signs, or it is about what the signs stand for. Wittgenstein rejects this dichotomy. Arithmetic is no more 'about' ink marks than chess is about wooden pieces. But that does not mean that either numerals or chess-pieces go proxy for anything. Rather, the 'meaning' of a mathematical sign, like that of a chess piece, is the sum of the rules that determine its possible 'moves'. What differentiates applied mathematics and language from chess and pure mathematics is merely their 'application', the way in which they engage with other (linguistic and non-linguistic) activities (WVC 103–5, 124, 150–1, 163, 170; MS166 28–9; *Laws* II §88; *see* NUMBERS).

The term 'language-game' is the result of Wittgenstein's extending, from 1932 onwards, the game analogy to language as a whole. It first occurs in TS211 578 (see also BT 201; PG 62, often cited as the first occurrence, is later, deriving from MS114). Initially, it is used interchangeably with 'calculus'. Its point is to draw attention to various similarities between language and games, just as the calculus analogy highlighted similarities between language and formal systems.

The starting-point of both analogies is that language is a rule-guided activity. (a) Like a game, language has constitutive rules, namely those of GRAMMAR. Unlike strategic rules, these do not determine what move/utterance will bring success, but rather what is correct or makes sense, and thereby define the game/language. (b) The meaning of a word is not an object it stands for, but is determined by the rules governing its operation (LWL 43–5, 59; AWL 3, 30, 44–8, 120, 151; PG 59; *see* MEANING-BODY). We learn the meaning of words by learning how to use them, just as we learn how to play chess, not by associating the pieces with objects, but by learning how they can be moved (*see* USE). (c) A proposition is a move or operation in the game of language; it would be meaningless without the system of which it is a part. Its sense is its role in the unfolding linguistic activity (PI §§23, 199, 421; PG 130, 172; BB 42). As in the case of games, what moves are possible depends on the situation (position on the board) and for each move certain responses are intelligible while others are excluded.

The game analogy gradually replaces the calculus analogy. This signifies Wittgenstein's abandonment of the CALCULUS MODEL, according to which these rules constitute a rigid, precise and definite order hidden behind the motley appearance of language. As part of the same development, chess is joined by less rigid games, such as ring-a-ring o' roses, as an object of comparison with language. Moreover, by turning to language-games, Wittgenstein switched attention from the geometry of a symbolism (whether language or calculus) to its place in human practice. He used the term in four different capacities, which (roughly) in turn occupy centre-stage.

Teaching practices   Language-games are first explained (in BB 17) as 'ways of using signs' which are simpler than those of everyday language, 'primitive forms of language', with which 'a child begins to make use of words'. This view evolves into the idea of a language-game as a 'system of communication' by which children 'learn' or are 'taught' their native language (PI §7; BB 81). The fact that many words are taught by pointing at an object is one reason for thinking that their meaning is the object pointed at; conversely, by investigating our teaching practices, Wittgenstein draws attention to the fact that the relation between a name and its object is not monolithic (PI §§8–18). Equally, how the meaning of words like 'pain', 'dream' or 'beautiful' is, or might be, learnt sheds light on the (often non-descriptive) role of our propositions involving those terms (PI §244; LC 1–2).

Teaching practices are important to Wittgenstein, not because he engages in armchair speculations about the 'hypothetical history' of our subsequent linguistic practice (he condoned the logical possibility of innate linguistic skills), but only in so far as they display distinctive features of the subsequent use of the words, in particular EXPLANATIONS which continue to play a role as standards of correctness (BB 12–14; PG 188). While language-games are primitive forms of language, they are supposed to be 'complete' (AWL 101; BB 81; PI §§2, 18), in the sense in which for Wittgenstein the rational numbers are not just an incomplete subset of the real NUMBERS. Teaching practices, by contrast, are fragments of our language. This may be one reason why they recede in favour of fictional language-games.

Fictional language-games   These are hypothetical or invented linguistic practices of a simple or primitive kind. Such 'clear and simple language-games' serve as 'objects of comparison' (PI §130, see §§2–27). They are supposed to shed light on our own more-complicated language-games by way of bringing into sharp relief some of their features. Wittgenstein envisages at least two ways in which this might happen. One is to build up our complicated discourse with terms like 'truth', 'assertion', 'proposition', etc., out of more-primitive language-games. This approach dominates the *Brown Book*, which discusses a string of fictional language-games, without providing any philosophical stage-setting, or weaving them into any line of argument. Mercifully, this monolithic language-game method had receded by the time of *Philosophical Investigations*.

Another strategy is to use language-games as part of a *reductio ad absurdum* argument. This constructs language-games which correspond to the understanding of certain concepts underlying a certain philosophical theory, and points out the contrast with our actual language-games and concepts. For example, a language-game is set up in which 'knowing' and 'understanding' are used to refer to states of consciousness with genuine duration, in order to point out that we do not use them in this way. In the *Investigations*, Wittgenstein employs language-games to unmask the *Tractatus*'s doctrine of 'simples', and its method of analysis (PI §§48, 60–4). The most famous example of this tactic is the language-game of the builders in *Investigations* §2 (to which complications are added subsequently): it consists of four words, 'block', 'pillar', 'slab' and 'beam'. These are called out by a builder A, while B, his assistant, brings him the stone which he has learnt to bring at each call. This 'primitive language' is supposed to fit the AUGUSTINIAN PICTURE OF LANGUAGE, according to which all words are names of objects. Its obvious point is that our language includes many uses of words besides those of naming or calling for an object (PI §3).

Wittgenstein conceives of this tedious interaction, together with the teaching which precedes it, as a 'complete primitive language', 'the whole language of a tribe' (PI §§2, 6; BB 77). Even sympathetic readers have protested that although a language might have a limited vocabulary, the builders' practice fails to qualify as one, because, firstly, their utterances lack syntactic structure, secondly, they do not engage in conversation and, thirdly, the interaction does not provide for a difference between meaningful and nonsensical employments of the vocabulary. The first point assumes, against Wittgenstein, that there can be no one-word sentences (*see* PROPOSITION). The second would count equally against the idea of a group of soliloquists (PI §243), but does not hold water in either case: actually being used in communication is not a precondition of language-hood; and in any case the builders *could* use their vocabulary to pass stones between them. The third point would disqualify the builders from speaking a language by Wittgenstein's own lights. Whether it applies depends on whether B's reactions differentiate between A's making a practical mistake, like calling out for a stone which is unavailable, and A's making a linguistic mistake, that is, employing the vocabulary in nonsensical ways, for example by saying 'Block, Block!' *Investigations* §6 describes the teaching as a process of stimulus-response conditioning, and hence does not provide room for this distinction. But §7 does, in so far as 'naming' the stones is supposed to set up standards for the correct use of the terms. Wittgenstein also recognizes that for this practice to count as even 'a rudimentary language' the builders must not behave 'merely mechanically' and must be part of a form of life similar to our's (Z §99; MS165 94–6).

Linguistic activities   Although he continued to claim that for the purposes of understanding our own concepts, 'nothing' is more important than the construction of fictitious ones (LW I §19), Wittgenstein makes less use of fictional language-games after the *Investigations*. Instead, he focuses more on actual linguistic activities, and describes them against the background of our non-linguistic practices. In the same vein, *Investigations* §23 provides a list of speech acts: giving orders, describing the appearance of an object, asking, swearing, constructing an object from a description, etc. Elsewhere, Wittgenstein adds more-complex activities such as lying, telling stories, reporting dreams, confessing a motive, and forming and testing hypotheses. He also includes modes of discourse, such as making inductive predictions, talking about physical objects or sense-impressions, and ascribing colours to objects (PI §§249, 363, 630, II 180, 184, 224; Z §345). He also speaks of 'the language-game with' (i.e., the use of) words such as 'game', 'proposition', 'language', 'thought', 'read' and 'pain' (PI §§71, 96, 156, 300).

Commentators have complained that Wittgenstein gives no criteria of identity for language-games. But there is no fundamental difficulty here. Wittgenstein distinguishes linguistic activities at different levels of generality. What counts as the same activity (e.g., whether one needs to distinguish telling a story from telling a joke) depends on the level concerned, and on all levels there will be borderline cases. More problematic is that Wittgenstein uses his list of language-games to illustrate that there are 'countless kinds of sentences' (PI §23). One might reasonably object that while, for example, 'Are you with me?' can be *used* to ask a question and to issue a reprimand, types of sentences are distinguished by their grammatical moods only (declarative, imperative, interrogative), and that this distinction not only cuts across Wittgenstein's (questions occur in fairy-tales and scientific theory-construction), but is more fundamental. Wittgenstein is on safer ground in claiming that there is an irreducible 'multiplicity of language-games' (PI §§23–4), ways of employing words which differ in philosophically significant respects. The diverse functions of language cannot be reduced to description or representation, as the *Tractatus*'s doctrine of the GENERAL PROPOSITIONAL FORM had it. Like 'game', 'language' is a FAMILY-RESEMBLANCE word: there is no single defining feature which all games have in common, including the games we play with words (PI §65).

Stressing the motley of language is one use to which Wittgenstein puts actual language-games. Another is the claim that PHILOSOPHICAL confusion arises from crossing language-games (see RFM 117–18), that is, from using the words of one language-game according to rules of another. Yet another is that like all games, language-games are AUTONOMOUS; they are not responsible to external goals, unlike an activity like cooking (PG 184–5; Z §320).

Against this game analogy it has been objected that games are subject to pragmatic standards: they can be improved according to whether they entertain us, take too much time, etc. But similar points apply to language-games like greeting or measuring. Another objection is that games, unlike linguistic activities, are trivial. Yet some games play a more important role in our lives than certain linguistic flourishes.

Language as a game   There is a point at which the analogy does break down. Unlike games, the fragments of our linguistic practice are interrelated (e.g., ordering and obeying), and form part of an overall system. Wittgenstein describes this by comparing language to an 'ancient city' (PI §18; the analogy occurs in Boltzmann, *Physics* 77 and Mauthner, *Beiträge* I 26): its centre, everyday language, is a maze of crooked streets, while its most recent additions, specialized idioms like those of chemistry or mathematics, constitute suburbs with straight and uniform lines. Moreover, he also employs the term 'language-game' to signify this overall system. Thus, he speaks of 'the whole language-game' and 'the human language-game', 'our language-game' (BB 108; OC §§554–9). Indeed, it is through this use of the term that he makes his most important point: 'I shall also call the whole, consisting of language and the actions into which it is woven, the "language-game"' (PI §7).

It is the way in which linguistic activities are interwoven with, and embedded in, our non-linguistic practices, which makes them less trivial than games. The linguistic activities of the builders are as crucial to their lives as measurement and inductive reasoning are to ours. The language-game with 'pain' is interwoven with ways of verifying third-person pain ascriptions, but also with commiseration, etc. Our language-games are embedded in our FORM OF LIFE, the overall practices of a linguistic community. Because of this connection with practice, word-games like Scrabble would not count as language-games for Wittgenstein. This idea comes more and more to the fore in Wittgenstein's writings. Whereas at first words have meaning within a proposition, and the game they are used in, he later said that 'words have meaning only in the stream of life' (LW I §913). The techniques of employing them are part of our natural history. But Wittgenstein never identified the notion of a language-game with that of a form of life. Language-games are 'part of', embedded in, a form of life (PI §§23–5). There is also a growing emphasis on the idea that our language-games are not subject to justification, but rooted in our natural reactions and activities (RPP I §916; RPP II §453; OC §§402–3, 559).

Wittgenstein's neologism has been widely accepted, and extended ('the language-game of science' or 'of religion'). Dummett has compared verifying a proposition to winning at chess (although Wittgenstein repudiated that suggestion with respect to mathematical propositions – PG 289–95). Hintikka has used games of seeking and finding to provide a semantics for quantifiers.

logic Logic studies the structural features which distinguish valid from invalid arguments. The watershed in its development was the complete axiomatization of the predicate calculus in *Begriffsschrift*. Frege pioneered logicism, the reduction of mathematics to logic, by seeking to demonstrate the derivability of arithmetic from purely logical concepts and principles of reasoning. He overcame the limitations of syllogistic logic by exploiting an analogy between concepts and mathematical functions to analyse propositions into argument-expressions and function-names instead of subject and predicate. Frege's system was axiomatic: all the truths of the predicate calculus can be derived as theorems from its 'basic laws' according to rules of inference. Frege understood the axioms not as analytic consequences of arbitrary definitions, but as self-evident truths about abstract entities like numbers, concepts and relations which are certified by a 'logical source of knowledge'. These axioms 'contain', in undeveloped form, all the theorems which can be derived from them according to rules of inference (*Notation* §13; *Laws* II App.; *Posthumous* 267–79). Frege's logicism foundered on the set-theoretic paradox discerned by Russell, who then tried to escape it through his theory of types. The system of *Principia* also uses (a somewhat different) function-theoretic analysis, and is axiomatic. Russell was not clear about what validated these axioms. He wavered between arguing that they are inductively validated by the truth of their deductive consequences, and holding (with Frege) that they are self-evident truths known by logical intuition (*Principia* I 12, 59; *Problems* 81; 'Theory' 156–66). But what gives them their necessary status, he could not explain. Another weakness was that to avoid the paradoxes he had to rely on the axiom of infinity ('The number of objects in the universe is infinite'), which looks empirical and cannot even be known to be true.

   Young Ludwig likened the development of function-theoretic logic to the scientific revolution in the seventeenth century (RCL). He took over – and transformed – important elements of Frege's and Russell's logical systems. Moreover, he followed Russell in identifying philosophy with the logical analysis of propositions (TLP 4.003f.). But his 'philosophy of logic' departed radically from his predecessors'. With considerable chutzpah he includes their work under the label 'the old logic', and castigates them for having failed to clarify the nature of logic (TLP 4.1121, 4.126; NL 93; NM 109). At the turn of the century, there were three accounts of logical truths. According to psychologistic logicians like Boole and Erdmann, they describe how human beings (by and large) think, their basic mental operations, and are determined by the nature of the human mind. Against this, Platonists like Frege protested that logical truths are objective, and that this objectivity can be secured only by assuming that their subject-matter – thoughts and their structure – is not private ideas in the minds of individuals, but abstract entities inhabiting a 'third realm' beyond space and time. Finally, Russell held that the propositions of logic are supremely general truths about the most pervasive features of reality, a view reminiscent of Aristotle's conception of metaphysics as the most general science (*Laws* I Pref.; *Principles* 3–9, 106; *External* 189–90; 'Theory' 97–101).

Wittgenstein eschews all three alternatives through a 'reflective turn' in the tradition of Kant. Kant distinguished between 'formal logic', which abstracts from the objects of knowledge, and 'transcendental logic', which investigates preconditions of thinking about objects. The former consists of analytic a priori truths. But there are also synthetic a priori truths in mathematics, metaphysics and the a priori elements of science. They hold true of experience (are synthetic) without being made true by experience (are a priori), because they express necessary preconditions of the possibility of experience. Wittgenstein picked this idea up from Schopenhauer and Hertz, who explained the a priori elements of science by reference to structural features of the way we represent objects. The *Tractatus* extends this idea to the analytic truths of formal logic, while rejecting the idea of synthetic a priori truths. Necessary propositions are neither statements about the way people actually think, nor about the most pervasive features of reality, nor about a Platonist *hinterworld*, but reflect the conditions for the possibility of empirical representation. In contrast to Kant, these conditions no longer reside in a mental machinery. Logic investigates the nature and limits of *thought*, because it is in thought that we represent reality. But it does so by drawing limits to the 'linguistic expression of thought' (TLP Pref.). These limits are set by LOGICAL SYNTAX, the system of rules which determines whether a combination of signs is meaningful. Logical syntax antecedes questions of truth and falsity. It cannot be overturned by empirical propositions, since nothing which contravenes it counts as a meaningful proposition. The special status of necessary propositions is not due to the abstract nature of their alleged referents, for there are no LOGICAL CONSTANTS or logical 'objects'. They are not statements about objects of any kind, but reflect 'rules of symbolism' (TLP 6.12ff.).

The nature of this link varies with the type of necessary proposition. Mathematical equations are pseudo-propositions. They do not say anything about the world, but equate signs which are equivalent by virtue of rules governing reiterable operations (TLP 6.2ff.). Metaphysical propositions are nonsensical. They either covertly violate logical syntax (traditional metaphysics) or, like the pronouncements of the *Tractatus* itself, try to say what can only be shown, the essential structures of reality, which must be mirrored by the linguistic rules for depicting reality but cannot themselves be depicted (TLP 3.324, 4.003, 4.12ff., 6.53f.). The only *expressible* necessity is that of logical propositions, which are analytic, that is, TAUTOLOGIES (TLP 6.1ff., 6.126ff.). And they too say nothing about the world, since they combine empirical propositions in such a way (according to rules governing truth-functional operations) that all factual information cancels out (TLP 6.121).

From this linguistic perspective, the *Tractatus* criticizes Russell's statistical view of modality, according to which a propositional function is possible if it is 'sometimes true'. For '$(\exists x) fx$' can be false even if it is logically or physically possible for something to be f. Moreover, that '$(\exists x) fx$' is capable of being true presupposes that 'fa' makes sense, that is, that 'fx' is logically possible. Modal notions are crucial not just to distinguishing logical from empirical propositions, but also to characterizing the latter as bipolar – they *can* be true and *can* be false. However, the modal status of a proposition – whether it is a tautology (necessary), a contradiction (impossible) or bipolar (possible) – cannot be expressed by a meaningful bipolar proposition (it is not a *contingent* feature) but shows itself in its structure (TLP 2.012ff., 4.464, 5.525; *Introduction* 165; *Logic* 231; *see* SAYING/SHOWING).

Logic, then, comprises the most general preconditions for the possibility of symbolic, and in particular linguistic, representation – it is a 'logic of representation' (TLP 4.015). This means that there is no such thing as a logically defective language. Logic is a condition of sense, and there is no halfway house between sense and nonsense. The systems of *Begriffsschrift* and *Principia* are not in better logical order than ordinary language, as Frege and Russell held, they are simply better at revealing that order. However, even in that capacity they are marred by their axiomatic presentation, which evinces what for Wittgenstein are misconceptions about the nature of logic. For this reason, he questioned all three elements of the 'old', axiomatic logic – axioms, theorems and logical inference.

Logical theorems need not be derived from axioms; they are vacuous tautologies, which can be recognized as true 'from the symbol alone', by calculating their logical properties, and hence without comparing them to reality or deducing them from other propositions (TLP 6.113, 6.126). This fact contains 'the whole philosophy of logic' because it also casts doubt on the axiomatic conception of axioms and rules of inference. There are no logical truths which are essentially 'primitive' and contain an infinite number of essentially 'derived' theorems. All 'propositions of logic are of equal status', namely tautological; they all say the same, namely nothing. Indeed, the TRUTH-TABLE notation shows that, for example, '$\sim(p . \sim p)$', '$p \vee \sim p$' and '$p \supset p$' are merely different ways of expressing one and the same tautology – $(TT)(p)$. Similarly, the fact that logical constants like '$\sim$', '$.$' or '$\supset$' are interdefinable shows that they are not primitive signs. Moreover, axioms cannot be justified by appeal to their self-evidence, since the truth of a proposition does not follow from the fact that it is self-evident to us (TLP 5.1363, 5.42f., 6.127f.). Although neither tautologies nor contradictions say anything, that a certain combination of signs is tautological or contradictory shows something about the logical relations between propositions. For example, that '$(p \cdot (p \supset q)) \supset q$' is a tautology (and its negation a contradiction) shows that 'q' follows from 'p' and '$p \supset q$', and thereby provides 'the form of a proof' (TLP 6.12ff.). The rules invoked by Frege and Russell are neither necessary for nor capable of justifying LOGICAL INFERENCE.

Wittgenstein also casts doubt on the traditional idea that logic is topic-neutral, that the laws of thought 'are everywhere the same' (*Foundations* Introd.; *Posthumous* 128). The *Tractatus* accepts that the logical operators apply equally to all types of propositions (an assumption Wittgenstein later questioned – *see* GENERALITY), but denies that the rules of inference apply equally to empirical and non-empirical disciplines. Proof *by* logic deduces a bipolar proposition from given premises. Proof *in* logic, on the other hand, does not discover new truths about anything, it is merely the recognition of yet further empty tautologies. It proves not the truth of a proposition, but that a certain combination of signs is a tautology or an equation, and hence part of logic or mathematics (TLP 6.1263; NM 108–9). It has been suggested that this means that logical and MATHEMATICAL PROOF cannot exemplify the same pattern of inference as scientific reasoning. But deriving Fermat's theorem from the conjunction of the Tanayama–Weil conjecture with the fact that the latter implies the former, obviously exemplifies *modus ponens*. If proof in logic amounts to transforming propositions through the application of truth-functional operations (TLP 6.126), this applies equally to transforming '$\sim(p \cdot \sim p)$' into '$\sim p \vee p$' (which are tautologies) and to transforming '$\sim(p \cdot q)$' into '$\sim p \vee \sim q$' (which are not). If it amounts to a truth-tabular calculation that a proposition of the form '$\Phi \supset \Psi$' is a tautology (TLP 6.1203), this is done irrespectively of whether 'Φ' and 'Ψ' are themselves tautologies or bipolar propositions. A tautology must correspond to a proof in logic just as to a proof by logic. *Tractatus* 6.126ff. suggests that the difference lies in the fact that proof in logic is superfluous, since the tautological nature of a proposition will be evident in a perspicuous notation – but so will the internal relations between empirical propositions which underlie proof by logic. What sets proof in logic apart is not a special pattern (logic provides all patterns of proof), but that the acceptability of the conclusion does not depend on either reality or the truth of a set of premises.

'Logic must take care of itself' (TLP 5.473f.; NB 22.8./2.9./8.9.14). This idea attacks Russell's attempt in the theory of types to justify the rules of logic by reference to the meanings of signs. But although there is no doctrine like the theory of types which could justify logic, the latter is ineffably grounded in reality. Logic rests on nothing, save the essential nature of propositions – their BIPOLARITY: the fact that in certain combinations (tautologies) this bipolarity cancels out shows the 'formal' properties which language must share with reality in order to depict it. Logic does not presuppose any logical facts or experience of logical objects. But it does presuppose that 'names have meaning and elementary propositions have sense', that is, that propositions are bipolar pictures; and it is linked to the MYSTICAL experience 'that the world is', namely that there are indestructible simple OBJECTS which give NAMES their meaning (TLP 5.552f., 6.12, 6.124, 6.13).

Wittgenstein later came to think that logic does not rest on ineffable foundations (*see* AUTONOMY OF LANGUAGE). He also abandoned the idea that logic is confined to tautologies or truth-functional relations. He first recognized that statements like 'Nothing can be red and green all over' are legitimate and logically necessary without being analytical in the sense of the *Tractatus*, and even contemplated calling such propositions synthetic a priori. He allowed for logical relations which fall short of entailment (*see* CRITERIA) and claimed that AVOWALS are not subject to logical operations in the same way as empirical descriptions. Finally, he noted *vis-à-vis* Moore's paradox that logic excludes as 'inadmissible' not just contradictions like '$p.\sim p$' but also 'It is raining, but I do not believe it' (*see* BELIEF). According to Wittgenstein, there are serious gaps in a 'pure logic' which concentrates exclusively on the rules and relations codified by formal systems like the predicate calculus; he states and that 'logic isn't as simple as logicians think it is' (ML 10.44; RPP I §§488–9). The *Tractatus* was right in linking logic to language: logic provides us with 'norms of representation', rules for transforming symbols, for passing from premises to conclusions. But it ignored a host of rules which Wittgenstein included in his later notion of GRAMMAR. He continued to use the term 'logic', but with the proviso that it includes all the constitutive rules of our language-games (OC §§56, 501, 628). Wittgenstein's non-formal conception of logic challenges current formal semantics, which is itself indebted to the *Tractatus* and the Vienna Circle.

Although the *Tractatus*'s conception of logic was entwined with a dubious metaphysics of symbolism, most of its criticisms of Frege and Russell do not presuppose the latter. By linking logic to rules of symbolism, Wittgenstein gave it a novel 'linguistic' orientation. The claim that logical propositions are tautologies was adopted by the logical positivists, for whom it provided a means of doing justice to the necessity of mathematics and logic without lapsing into Platonism or recognizing synthetic a priori truths. But the Vienna Circle ignored the *Tractatus*'s idea that logical necessity derives from metaphysical structures shared by language and reality, and held instead that necessary propositions are true by virtue of arbitrary linguistic conventions. It was only later that Wittgenstein himself adopted a (radically different) version of conventionalism (*see* FORM OF REPRESENTATION).

logical analysis This is the process of identifying the components of a proposition, thought or fact, and the way in which they are combined (its LOGICAL FORM). It gained impetus through Frege's invention of the predicate calculus. Frege's 'concept-script' was an instrument for the derivation of arithmetic from purely logical concepts and principles of reasoning. But it was also supposed to free 'thought' from the tyranny of words bemoaned since Plato (*Notation* Pref.; *Posthumous* 6–7, 253, 269–70). Ordinary language conceals the logical relations and articulations of concepts and propositions, is rife with ambiguity and vagueness, and contains vacuous singular terms which lead to propositions without a truth-value like

(1)   The present King of France is bald.

Russell pursued a similar logicist goal, but as part of a wider, Cartesian project. He tried to justify our scientific views by first analysing them, and then reformulating them in a 'logically perfect language' which would give fewer hostages to scepticism. The theory of descriptions allowed him to avoid Meinongian entities like the round square, and to maintain, against Frege, that the principle of bivalence holds even for propositions like (1), which is analysed into a conjunction that is false rather than truth-valueless, if there is no present King of France, namely 'There is one and only one object that is the present King of France, and that object is bald.' It also suggests that the grammatical form of subject and predicate conceals the logical form of propositions, and allowed Russell to pursue the project of empiricist reductionism through logical rather than psychological analysis. Logical atomism seeks to analyse propositions into atomic propositions which refer to sense-data. Inspired by this programme, Russell identified philosophy with the logical analysis of propositions (*External* chs II–III; *Mysticism* 108–9, 148–9).

Wittgenstein took over the idea that philosophy is logical analysis and credited the theory of descriptions with having shown that the apparent logical form of propositions differs from their real one. He concluded that 'distrust of grammar is the first requisite for philosophizing', since grammar engenders philosophical confusions (NL 106; see RUL 11.13; TLP Pref., 3.323f., 4.003f.; WAM 57). However, while ordinary language 'disguises thought', it is not logically defective, as Frege and Russell had supposed. It is capable of 'expressing every sense' (TLP 4.002), and must hence conform to LOGICAL SYNTAX. What is needed is not an ideal language, capable of expressing things ordinary language cannot express, but an ideal *notation* which displays the logical structure already present in ordinary propositions. The symbolisms of Frege and Russell go some way to providing a logically perspicuous notation (TLP 3.325). This is why, in spite of divergent conceptions of analysis, there is considerable agreement in detail.

Frege arguably countenanced the possibility of alternative analyses (*Corre-*

spondence 10; *Notation* §10). By contrast, the logical atomism of Russell and Wittgenstein is committed to the idea that there are definite constituents of propositions. Nevertheless, Wittgenstein prevaricated on this issue. He considered both the possibility that ordinary material objects might be the basic referents of language, and the possibility that analysis might go on for ever. Eventually, he decided that analysis must go beyond ordinary material objects, but also come to a definite end. Although a proposition of the form '*aRb*' can initially be seen as the value of different propositional functions (e.g., of '(ξ)*a*' or '(ξ)*Rb*'), it has 'one and only one' complete analysis, which is not arbitrary (cp. TLP 3.25, 3.3442; NB 17.6.15 with 3.9./8.10.14, 14.6.15).

Like Russell, Wittgenstein never worked out exactly how ordinary propositions were to be analysed; he did not even provide examples of elementary propositions or their elements. Nevertheless, two basic ideas are clear: (a) according to the doctrine of the general propositional form, all meaningful propositions are truth-functions of logically independent ELEMENTARY PROPOSITIONS; (b) the latter consist of logically proper names, which cannot be further analysed since they stand for absolutely simple OBJECTS (TLP 3.201ff., 4.22f.; NB 12.10.14).

Reasonably clear also is the direction analysis should take, and its Russellian tools. The first step is to analyse into singular propositions all propositions which we would ordinarily recognize as in some sense complex. Thus, general propositions like 'All swords have a sharp blade' yield singular propositions like

(2)   Excalibur has a sharp blade.

Such propositions contain complex concept-words such as 'has a sharp blade' which, following Frege, are analysable into their characteristic 'marks' (*Merkmale*), the necessary and sufficient conditions for their application (TLP 4.126; OL 28–9), for example

(2′)   Excalibur has a blade . Excalibur is sharp.

According to *Tractatus* 3.24, ordinary singular terms, including proper names like 'Excalibur', are 'contractions' of a 'symbol for a complex' into a 'simple symbol'. They can be treated along the lines of the theory of descriptions: thus, 'Excalibur' is replaced by a definite description – e.g., 'King Arthur's sword' – which in turn is paraphrased as an incomplete symbol through quantifiers and concept-words:

(2*)   There is one and only one *x* which is King Arthur's sword that *x* has a blade . that *x* is sharp.

(2*) contains the vague predicate 'sharp', and that conjunct might therefore be analysed into a disjunction of determinate possibilities, for example 'that

204

x cuts through armour $\lor$ x cuts your hand when you touch it $\lor$ ...' Given that Wittgenstein's version of the theory of descriptions avoids the sign of IDENTITY, the following line of analysis emerges:

$$\Phi e \equiv \Phi(\iota x)fx \equiv (\exists x)(y)((fy \equiv (y = x)) . \Psi x . (\Omega_1 x \lor \Omega_2 x \lor \ldots))$$
$$\equiv (\exists x)(fx . \Psi x . (\Omega_1 x \lor \Omega_2 x \lor \ldots)) . \sim(\exists x)(\exists y)(fx . fy).$$

For commentators who claim that NAMES are mere 'dummies' which do not distinguish one object from another, analysis comes to an end with such formulae containing quantifiers and variables; the substitution of names for bound variables adds nothing: 'The world can be completely described by means of fully generalized propositions, i.e. without first correlating any name with a particular object. Then, in order to arrive at the customary mode of expression we need simply say, after an expression like "There is one and only one x such that...": and this x is a' (TLP 5.526; NB 17./ 19.10.14). However, even if the world can be described completely through general propositions, there must be names, because only they go proxy for particular objects: a general description does not entail that it is a specific thing which is the only one to have a certain property (NB 31.5.15). Moreover, general propositions like (2*) cannot be the terminus of analysis. For: (a) they are truth-functions of, and presuppose, elementary propositions (TLP 4.411, 5, 6ff., 6.124); (b) the Russellian analysis preserves bivalence at the price of ambiguity: (2*) can fail to be true in two ways: either if Arthur had no sword, or if that sword does not have a sharp blade; (c) Arthur's sword is a complex, something we ordinarily denote by a singular term but which actually consists of parts into which it must be analysed (NB 7./20./ 23.5./20.6.15).

At this point, one must switch to what Wisdom later called 'new level analysis', one which takes us to things of an ontologically more basic kind. The *Tractatus* intimates two lines such an analysis could take. 'Every statement about complexes can be resolved into a statement about their constituents and into those propositions that describe the complexes completely.' The latter say that 'the complex exists', namely by stating that its constituents are so related as to form the complex. A complex consists, for example, of a's standing-in-the-relation-R to b. A proposition which ascribes a property to it – '$\Phi(aRb)$' – comes out as '$\Phi a . \Phi b . aRb$' (TLP 2.0201, 3.24; NL 93, 101; NM 111; NB 5.9.14; PI §60). If $\sim aRb$, then the analysandum does not lack a truth-value, but is false. Thus,

(3)   Excalibur is in the corner

is analysed into

(3')   The blade is in the corner . the hilt is in the corner . the blade is fixed in the hilt.

205

However, this analysis confronts problems concerning propositions like (2). Most properties of the complex, including a specific weight, shape and size, are not properties of its parts. This problem can only be avoided either by treating these properties as constituents of the complex, an absurd idea, with which Wittgenstein seems to have toyed (*see* FACT), or by analysing all discourse into propositions which ascribe physical properties to ultimate physical particles.

The second line of analysis intimated by the *Tractatus* is phenomenalist: all propositions containing GENERALITY are analysed into conjunctions or disjunctions of possibilities. Thus, an existential proposition like 'There is one and only one sword of King Arthur' is analysed into a logical sum of elementary propositions, '$p_1 \lor p_2 \lor p_3 \ldots$' The disjuncts jointly exhaust the possible experiences which would make it the case that there is a complex like King Arthur's sword.

It is unclear how either the physicalist or the phenomenalist line is to be pursued. How, for example, are sensory modalities other than sight to be accounted for (presumably, public space would have to be constructed out of visual, auditory and tactile space)? Furthermore, in the TRUTH-TABLE notation every elementary proposition is represented as a truth-function of all others, namely as a conjunction of itself and a tautology involving all other elementary propositions. Consequently, a fully analysed ordinary proposition is a long truth-function of elementary propositions, in which *all* elementary propositions, and hence *all* names, occur. The fully analysed proposition is much more complicated than the unanalysed proposition with which it is supposed to be equivalent. In order to understand the sense of humdrum propositions like (3), we have to know either Excalibur's ultimate material constituents, or what phenomenal states would make it the case that Excalibur exists. This makes the understanding of a proposition depend on knowledge of (recherché) empirical facts. It sits uneasily with the idea that there are no surprises in logic (TLP 6.125f., 6.1261), and threatens the idea that sense antecedes matters of fact. Unsurprisingly, therefore, the *Notebooks* had wavered between holding that a fully analysed proposition contains as many names as there are ultimate elements in the state of affairs depicted (a view shared by Moore) and holding that it contains as many as the speaker knows to be there (NB 12./20.10./18.12.14, 18.6.15; *Principia Ethica* 8).

The *Tractatus* sweeps these problems under the carpet. Its SAYING/SHOWING distinction prohibits descriptions of the logical form of propositions. Accordingly, logical analysis is no longer supposed to result in a doctrine, as in 'Notes on Logic', but is a critical *activity*, namely of showing on the one hand that empirical propositions are meaningful, and how they represent what they do, and on the other that metaphysical propositions are nonsensical, since they violate logical syntax (TLP 6.53–7). Yet, the *Tractatus* itself does not engage in the analysis of specific propositions (with the exception of perfunctory attempts to fit recalcitrant cases, like propositions about BELIEFS and COLOURS, into its general framework). Instead, it provides the general framework for this activity, by sketching the GENERAL PROPOSITIONAL FORM, features a proposition must possess to represent reality. Thus, we can know 'without further ado' that all propositions can be analysed into truth-functions of elementary propositions consisting of simple names. By contrast, it leaves to the 'application of logic', that is, the analysis of actual proposi-tions of natural language, the task of answering questions like what objects are simple? what propositions are elementary? are there relations with twenty-seven terms? (TLP 5.55ff.). The possible forms of elementary proposi-tions depend on the possible combinations of objects, which we cannot list prior to future analysis. It is not a matter of experience, but it is a matter of future discovery. We have the capacity to form meaningful sentences, but are ignorant of what their real meaning is, and of how they signify (TLP 4.002, 5.5562; NL 100).

In 1929, Wittgenstein stressed even more that we need to discover the logical form of propositions. He claimed to have found out, for example, that elementary propositions must contain real numbers (RLF 163–6, 171; WVC 42–3). Yet, it was left to Carnap's *Logische Aufbau der Welt* to pursue (unsuccessfully) this programme. Wittgenstein himself soon ques-tioned not only the atomistic model of analysis into ultimate constituents, but the idea itself: the quasi-transcendental theory of features that language must possess, 'dogmatically' ignores the reality of language (WVC 182–3); the quasi-empiricist project of applied logic ignores the difference between chemical and logical analysis. Moreover, it is based on Moore's 'hellish idea' that it takes analysis to find out what our humdrum propositions mean (LWL 34–5, 90; M 114; WVC 129–30; PI §§60–4). Even if we could dis-cover Excalibur's ultimate constituents, this would contribute to our knowl-edge of its physical make-up, but not to our understanding of the sense of (3).

Wittgenstein now holds that there are not only no 'surprises' but also no 'discoveries' in logic or GRAMMAR, since he rejects the idea that speakers have tacit knowledge of a complex CALCULUS or arcane logical forms (WVC 77; LWL 16–17; PG 114–15; PI §§126–9). A 'correct logical point of view' (TLP 4.1213) is achieved not through a quasi-geological excavation, but through a quasi-geographical OVERVIEW, which displays features of our lin-guistic practice that lie open to view. In so far as it is legitimate, analysis amounts either to the description of grammar, or to the substitution of one kind of notation by another, less misleading one (though the only example of the latter method is in his treatment of identity) (PR 51; WVC 45–7; BT 418; PI §§90–2; TS220 §98).

Wittgenstein's early conception of analysis as discovering the underlying structure of natural languages, shorn of its logical atomism, has become one of the sources of modern semantics through the mediation of Carnap's *Logical Syntax of Language*. His recantations have been instrumental in bringing an end to reductive analysis in both its atomistic and its empiricist version. Nowadays, the term 'analysis' often signifies no more than the elucidation of conceptual connections. But most analytical philosophers insist that although analysis may not reduce propositions, it still discovers their logical form and content. In doing so, they should confront Wittgenstein's arguments against the calculus model and against the assumption that what is said on a given occasion is determined solely by the logical forms and constituents of type-sentences (*see* CONTEXTUALISM).

logical constants   These are symbols which indicate the logical form of propositions. In the predicate calculus, these are the propositional connectives '~', ' ∨ ', '.' and '⊃', and the quantifiers '(x)' and '$(\exists x)$'. Russell, who coined the term, used it more widely for all the fundamental concepts of logic, including 'relation', 'set' and 'truth'. For Russell, logic describes the most general aspects of reality. It catalogues the logical forms of facts by abstracting from the material components of non-logical propositions. The symbols which survive this process are names of 'logical indefinables' or 'logical constants'. These denote 'logical objects' with which we are acquainted through a 'logical experience' or 'intuition'. Two groups can be distinguished, namely the 'logical forms' of atomic facts, and the logical objects which allegedly correspond to propositional connectives and quantifiers. Just as elementary propositions are names of 'atomic' complexes, so the connectives and quantifiers by means of which molecular propositions are formed name constituents of 'non-atomic' complexes (*Principles* xv, 8–11; 'Theory' 80, 97–101).

Frege did not speak of 'logical constants'. But like Russell he conceived of fundamental logical notions, especially the distinction between concepts and objects, as denoting ontological categories (*Foundations* Introd.; 'Function' 31), and of propositional connectives and quantifiers as names of truth-functions. Just as ordinary concepts map objects onto truth-values, so negation is a concept (unary function) mapping a truth-value onto the converse truth-value, and conditionality a binary function mapping a pair of truth-values onto a truth-value. Finally, the quantifiers are variable-binding, variable-indexed second-level functions which map concepts (first-level functions) onto truth-values. Thus, 'x conquered Gaul' has the value T for Caesar, so that 'Caesar did *not* conquer Gaul' maps the truth-value T onto F, while 'There is an x such that x conquered Gaul' maps the first-level concept 'x conquered Gaul' onto T. For Russell, propositions are not names of truth-values (but of complexes), hence truth-functions map atomic propositions (or propositional functions like 'x conquered Gaul' in the case of quantifiers) onto molecular propositions.

Like Russell, Wittgenstein includes among the 'logical constants' not just the connectives and quantifiers, but also the identity-sign '=' and the logical forms of elementary propositions. The idea that 'there are NO *logical* constants' stands at the beginning of his philosophy of logic, and it is the 'fundamental thought' of the *Tractatus* that the ' "logical constants" are not representatives; that there can be no representatives of the *logic* of facts' (TLP 4.0312, 5.4–5.47; RUL 22.6.12; NB 25.12.14). The signs of logic are not names of logical entities, whether Russell's logical objects or Frege's genuine functions. By the same token, the propositions of logic are not statements about entities, they describe neither abstract features of empirical reality nor a Platonic *hinterworld*, but are vacuous TAUTOLOGIES which reflect rules for the combination of signs.

At first, Wittgenstein expressed the idea that logical constants do not represent by saying that they are all 'copulae', a kind of cement which holds together the material components of propositions, and which remains when the latter have been abstracted away (RUL summer 1912–1.13). Later, he separated the discussion of the LOGICAL FORMS of elementary propositions from that of other logical constants. The main target of the former is Russell, of the latter Frege. Both are accused of hypostatizing referents for logical propositions because of failing to see that PROPOSITIONS are not names. Against Frege in particular he insists that the signs 'F' and 'T' no more refer to logical objects than do brackets, but merely indicate the truth-possibilities of propositions (TLP 4.441; NL 107). 'xRy' signifies a relation between objects – '$p \lor q$' does not signify an analogous relation between propositions (TLP 5.44, 5.46f.; NL 98–101; NM 116). Propositional connectives do not name functions; they express 'truth-operations' by means of which we generate molecular propositions out of elementary ones. The truth-value and the sense of the results of such operations *are* a function of the truth-values and senses of their bases. But the operations do not name relations between propositions, they express internal relations between the structures of propositions by showing what has to be done to a proposition to make another out of it (e.g., that '$p \lor q$' has to be negated to obtain '$\sim p . \sim q$') (TLP 5.2–5.25, 5.3; NB 17.8./29.8./22.11.16).

Wittgenstein adduces several arguments against Frege. (a) If connectives were function-names, their argument-expressions would have to be proper names of objects. But the arguments of truth-functions are propositions, which are totally distinct from names (TLP 4.441).

(b) If the True and the False were objects, then Frege's method for determining, for example, the sense of the negation-sign would break down (TLP 4.431). Thus, provided that 'p' has the same truth-value as 'q' (e.g., T), '$\sim p$' would have the same sense as '$\sim q$', since both express the thought that the True falls under the concept of negation. But obviously '$\sim p$' and '$\sim q$' have different senses, just as 'p' and 'q' do.

(c) In contrast to genuine function-signs such as 'x is red', nothing in reality corresponds to '$\sim$'. A false proposition does not correspond to a negative fact which includes an object called 'negation'; there is *no* fact that corresponds to it. The only effect of '$\sim$' is to reverse the truth-value of a proposition. Although 'p' and '$\sim p$' have opposite senses, both mention the same configuration of the same objects. They can be contrasted without a separate sign, by reversing the truth-poles – 'T p F' vs. 'F p T' (TLP 2.01, 4.0621, 6.1203).

(d) A function cannot be its own argument, one cannot substitute the function 'ξ is a horse' in the argument-place of 'ξ is a horse'; whereas the result of a truth-operation can be the basis of that same operation (TLP 5.251).

(e) Since a function assigns one object to another, '$\sim\sim p$' would have to be about negation as an object, and hence to say something different from 'p' (TLP 5.44). By the same token, infinitely many propositions, '$\sim\sim p$', '$\sim\sim\sim\sim p$', etc., would follow from a single proposition p, which is absurd (TLP 5.43).

(f) Only operations, not functions, can cancel each other, or vanish: $\sim\sim p = p$ (TLP 5.253f., 5.441; NB 24.1.15; PT 5.0022).

(g) '$\sim$', '$\supset$', '$.$', '(x)', '$(\exists x)$', etc. are interdefinable ($\sim(\exists x)\sim fx \equiv (x)fx$, $(\exists x)(fx . x = a) \equiv fa$); hence they neither are 'primitive signs', as Frege's and Russell's axiomatic systems assumed, nor denote different types of functions (TLP 5.42, 5.441).

The last point applies to the quantifiers as well as to the connectives, and the *Tractatus* adds other arguments to extend the rejection of logical constants to quantification (*see* GENERALITY) and IDENTITY. With the exception of (b), these criticisms apply to Russell as well as Frege. But some of them can in turn be questioned. It has been claimed that (e) and (f) assume that 'p' and '$\sim\sim p$' have the same sense, which goes through on Wittgenstein's conception of sense as the state of affairs depicted, but not on Frege's, since 'p' and '$\sim\sim p$' present the same truth-value in different ways, just as '$2 + 2$' and '2^2' present the same number in different ways. However, this assumption is reasonable. For 'p' and '$\sim\sim p$' *say the same*, whether or not this conforms with Frege's notion of sense; indeed, Frege himself concedes that '$p \supset q$' expresses the same thought as '$\sim(p . \sim q)$' ('Compound' 40–6).

Point (d) may also be questioned; it does not compare like with like. Indeed a function cannot be its own argument, but an operation cannot be its own basis either – one cannot multiply multiplication. Moreover, just as an operation can be applied to its own result, some functions can take as their arguments one of their own values, and this holds true precisely for truth-functional connectives, which have truth-values for both arguments and values. Similarly, some functions, for example $f(x) = (-1)x$, cancel out: applied to the argument 1 it yields the value -1, for the argument -1 it yields the value 1. However, Wittgenstein could reply that this is due to the fact that multiplication fits Frege's conception of a function no better than negation. Whereas it is clear how certain *activities* can cancel each other, it is unclear how this can be done by adding to a sentence the name of an entity (a function). Wittgenstein here relies on (c), the general point that the role of propositional connectives is not to refer, but to transform propositions.

Wittgenstein tries to curb the temptation to hypostatize referents for logical terms by removing them from his ideal notation. All truth-functional operations are reduced to a single one, joint negation, which Wittgenstein thought capable of generating, from elementary propositions, all meaningful propositions. But even the sign for joint negation – '$N(\bar{\xi})$' – does not appear in the ideal notation, since the latter presents all propositions through TRUTH-TABLES, without using any propositional connectives (TLP 4.44, 5.101): instead of '$p \supset q$' simply '(TTFT)(p,q)', instead of both '$\sim\sim p$' and 'p' simply '(TF)(p)'. This idea is extended to quantified propositions by treating them as logical sums or products; and identity is expressed not through a special sign, but through using a unique sign for every object.

At the end of this purge, only one logical constant remains, the GENERAL PROPOSITIONAL FORM which all propositions have in common, namely that they are pictures which state how things stand. That logical constant is given with the bare notion of an ELEMENTARY PROPOSITION. The logical operations add nothing since they are reducible to the operation of joint negation, that is, to conjunction and negation. Being essentially bipolar, every proposition is connected with both truth and falsity, and hence with negation, while the possibility of asserting more than one proposition contains the idea of conjunction. All logical operations are already contained in an elementary proposition, 'fa', since the latter is equivalent to '$(\exists x)(fx . x = a)$'. Logic is a fall-out from the essence of representation, since LOGICAL INFERENCES and logical propositions (TAUTOLOGIES) arise out of the truth-functional complexity of propositions, which in turn is the result of applying truth-operations to bipolar elementary propositions (TLP 5.441, 5.47ff.; RUL summer 1912; NB 5.11.14, 5.5.15).

Wittgenstein's non-referential account of logical operators was accepted first by the logical positivists, and later generally. But that acceptance was mainly based on a general abhorrence of abstract entities, not on his specific arguments or his vision of a constant-free notation. He himself abandoned the latter. But he extended the insight into the non-referring role of logical terms to other signs in his attack on the AUGUSTINIAN PICTURE OF LANGUAGE. That attack also undermines the idea that the meaning of a word is what it stands for, and thereby removes the need to express the insight that logical operators do not refer by saying that they have no meaning (TLP 6.126). Wittgenstein also questioned the claim that the predicate calculus provides adequate explanations of ordinary terms like 'not', 'and', 'all', 'if ... then'

(LWL 52–3; PG 55; RFM 41–3; RPP I §§269–74; Z §677; PLP 105), a point elaborated by Strawson. Their meaning is determined not by formal stipulations but by the way we explain and use them in everyday life, and they can be explained through examples or even ostensively.

logical form The logical form of a proposition is its structure as paraphrased by formal logic for the purpose of revealing those features which matter to the validity of arguments in which it occurs. The idea goes back to Aristotle's invention of logical formalization through the use of variables. The term 'logical form' was introduced in the nineteenth century. But it only gained wide currency in the wake of Frege's invention of the predicate calculus, which replaces the idea that all propositions consist of subject and predicate with a complex function-theoretic analysis and suggests that there are many different types of propositions, which differ in their structure or form. Russell was the first to draw methodological conclusions from this idea. Philosophy is logical analysis, it studies the logical form of propositions. Since there is a fundamental identity of structure between propositions and the facts they represent, making an inventory of the logical forms of propositions will reveal the essential structure of reality (*External* ch. II, 212–13; *Mysticism* 75; *Logic* 197, 216–17, 234, 331). Russell combined these influential ideas about the importance of logical forms with idiosyncratic views about their nature. Their discovery proceeds through abstraction from nonlogical propositions. The expressions which survive this process are variables and 'logical constants'. Among the latter, along with propositional connectives and quantifiers, are names of 'pure' or 'logical forms'. Thus, 'Plato loves Socrates' yields '$x \Phi y$'. These forms are completely general facts – in our case 'Something is somehow related to something' or 'There are dual complexes.' Under Wittgenstein's influence, Russell came to deny that logical forms are 'entities' we can name. But he continued to treat them as 'logical objects' with which we are acquainted through a 'logical experience' akin to our acquaintance with the taste of pineapple (*Principles* xv, 3–11, 106; 'Theory' 97–101, 113–14, 129–31).

Wittgenstein initially accepted that philosophy is the doctrine of logical form. He credited Russell's theory of descriptions with showing that the real logical form of propositions differs greatly from their apparent (school-grammatical) one, and concluded that 'distrust of grammar is the first requisite of philosophizing' (NL 106; TLP 4.0031). He also retained the idea that the structure of propositions can be revealed by abstracting from their material components. If we replace all 'constituents' of 'Plato loves Socrates' by variables we reach a 'logical prototype' – '$x \Phi y$' – which displays the logical form of all those propositions that describe a dual relation (TLP 3.315–3.317; NL 93, 104). While the GENERAL PROPOSITIONAL FORM is shared by all propositions, types of propositions are distinguished by their logical form.

At the same time, Wittgenstein claimed that Russell had imposed inconsistent demands on these logical forms: they had to be both facts expressed by propositions, that is, capable of being negated ('There are dual relations'), and objects designated by names ('the dual relation'). As Wittgenstein trenchantly remarked, they were to combine 'the useful property of being compounded', the hallmark of propositions and FACTS, with the 'agreeable property' of being simple, which for logical atomism is the privilege of OBJECTS (NL 100–101, 104, 107). Wittgenstein's general target was the idea, shared by Russell and Frege, that logical signs are names of LOGICAL CONSTANTS, arcane entities which provide the subject-matter of LOGIC (NL 98). As regards logical forms, he insisted that they are not objects of any kind. At first, he characterized them as 'copulae', the logical network or cement which holds together the material components of propositions and remains behind when these have been abstracted away (RUL summer 1912, 1.13). Later, he insisted that the form of a proposition is not a separate object, but determined by the forms of its constituents.

This idea is tied up with the PICTURE THEORY. A proposition is a picture which models reality, truly or falsely, by virtue of the relationship between its elements representing the relationship between the elements of the situation. Such a picture possesses two essential features, firstly a METHOD OF PROJECTION connecting the elements of the model with the elements of the situation it represents, and secondly structural features which it must share with reality in order to depict the latter. Wittgenstein referred to this shared structure as the 'form of a picture', or its 'logical form' (NB 20./25./ 29.10.14). In the *Tractatus* he distinguished several notions:

(a) The 'structure' of a picture is the conventionally determined way in which its elements must be arranged in order for it to model the way in which the elements of the situation are related (TLP 2.032, 2.15). By definition, this structure is possessed only by the picture.

(b) Something possesses the 'pictorial form' (*Form der Abbildung*) required to depict a particular situation if it is possible to arrange its elements in a way that mirrors the relationship between the objects of that situation; that is, pictorial form is the possibility of that arrangement, which means that it must be shared by picture and situation (TLP 2.15– 2.172).

(c) 'Logical form' is what any picture, of whatever pictorial form, must share with what it depicts (TLP 2.18ff.). The picture must have the same logico-mathematical multiplicity as the situation (TLP 4.032– 4.0412, 5.474f.; Wittgenstein attributes this notion to Hertz, see *Mechanics* §418), that is (i) it must have the same number of elements as the situation has objects, and (ii) these elements must share the combinatorial possibilities of the objects they stand for.

(d)   The 'representational form' (*Form der Darstellung*) is the external 'stand-point' from which the picture represents its subject (TLP 2.173f.), the method of representing which differs in different media. While pictor-ial form and logical form are what *A* must have in common with *B* in order to picture it, representational form is what distinguishes them, preventing *A* from being a mere duplicate of *B*.

Consider the law-court model of a traffic accident which inspired the picture theory (NB 29.9.14). The form of that model includes the spatial relationships between the toy pram and the toy lorry; it does not include relationships which play no role in the conventions of depiction, like that between their weights. The three-dimensional nature of the model is part of its pictorial form; it guarantees that spatial relationships between the toys can represent spatial relationships between lorry and pram. But so can two-dimensional relationships between the elements of a drawing. Here we have two pictures of the same state of affairs with different representational forms, that is, in different media. Both media involve features (e.g., size and colour of the elements) which distinguish the picture from what it depicts. Neither the two-dimensionality of the drawing nor the three-dimensionality of the model is part of the logical form, since logical form must be common to all pictures of the same state of affairs, irrespective of their representational form. This logical form would not be shared with the acci-dent by, for example, a single, stationary ball, which lacks the logical multi-plicity required to depict it. Equally, the spatial arrangement of notes in a score is part of its representational form, it is not shared by the music. By contrast, the possibility of ordering distinct elements along two parameters is shared not just by music and score (and hence is part of the score's pic-torial form) but by the music and *any* representation of it (e.g., a digital recording), and it is hence part of the score's logical form. Whatever has pictorial form also has logical form. While not every picture is, for exam-ple, spatial, every picture must be a 'logical picture', that is, possess a logi-cal form. A THOUGHT is a logical picture *par excellence*: its *only* pictorial form is logical form, which means that it requires no particular medium of depiction (TLP 2.181–2.19, 3).

Not just pictures and what they depict have a logical form, but also their constituents – NAMES and objects. Indeed, the logical form of a proposition is determined by that of its constituents (NB 1.11.14; TLP 2.0233, 6.23). Just as the form of propositions and facts is the possibility of a certain structure, that of their constituents is the possibility of their entering into certain com-binations. The form of a name is what it has in common with all other names of the same logico-syntactical category, its combinatorial possibilities, which are represented by the variables of which those names are values. The combinatorial possibilities of a name mirror those of the object it stands for, and thereby show something about the structure of reality (TLP 2.012ff.; NB 16.8.16). An object has both internal (structural/formal) and external properties. Its external properties consist in its being combined with whatever other objects it happens to be combined with. Its internal properties consist in the possibility of its combining with some objects to form states of affairs, and the impossibility of its combining with other objects (TLP 2.0141, 4.123). Each of these combinatorial possibilities is *a* form of an object, and essential to it. Their totality is *the* (logical) form of the object – the logical equivalent of the chemical valency, which determines the combinability of elements. Thus, being coloured is a form of visual objects, space and time forms of all objects (TLP 2.0251; PT 2.0251f.). It is an internal property of a visual object *not* to have a pitch, but to have *some* colour (and vice versa for a note), an external property to have, for example, the colour red. It is an internal property of all objects, including sounds, to have some spatio-temporal location (although presumably sounds would be located in auditory rather than visual space), an external property to have specific spatio-temporal coordinates.

The form of an object A determines for every other object whether or not A can combine with it. This is why if even a *single* object A is given, *all* objects are given – they are all part of A's form (TLP 5.524). It is also why objects constitute the 'substance of the world', that which 'subsists' independently of what is the case, this substance being 'both form and content'. It is content since, independently of what the facts are, the only elements of facts are the indestructible objects. It is form since, through their own forms, the totality of objects determines what states of affairs (combinations of objects) are possible. This fixed order of possibilities, which is equivalent to LOGICAL SPACE, is common to all possible worlds, and the *Tractatus* calls it the 'form of the world' (TLP 2.021–2.0271). Just as each proposition must share its logical form with the state of affairs it depicts, so language, the totality of propositions, must share with what it depicts *the* logical form, 'the form of reality' (TLP 2.18 – apparently equivalent to the 'form of world'). The harmony between language and reality which makes representation possible is the logico-pictorial isomorphism, the structural identity, between what represents and what is represented. According to the SAYING/SHOWING distinction, however, the logical form shared between language and reality cannot itself be represented in meaningful bipolar propositions: an object could not lack its combinatorial possibilities, or a fact its logical form, without ceasing to be that particular object or fact. Instead, that, for example, red is a colour shows itself in the logico-syntactical behaviour of 'red' in empirical propositions (TLP 3.262, 3.326). The form of an object is not itself an object, but rather its internal properties. It is represented not by a name, but by formal concepts – 'function', 'NUMBER', 'colour', 'sound'. A formal concept does not denote an arcane entity of which we could have a logical experience, it is in effect a variable which we understand as soon as we understand the signs which are its values (TLP 4.126–4.12721). A logico-syntactical category is nothing but an abstraction from the distinctive role of certain signs within empirical propositions.

Wittgenstein's later work abandons the idea that LOGICAL ANALYSIS discovers the hidden logical form of language, but continued to reject the reification of logico-linguistic forms (*see* MEANING-BODY).

logical inference   This is the derivation of a proposition, the conclusion, from a set of other propositions, the premises, which entail the conclusion. One of the tasks of formal LOGIC is to investigate the rules which codify such inferences by specifying that propositions of a certain structure entail propositions of another structure. Thus, *modus ponens* states that all inferences of the form

(1) p; if p then q; *ergo* q

are valid. To each rule of inference corresponds a logical truth, in our case

(2) $(p \cdot (p \supset q)) \supset q$.

Frege and Russell constructed axiomatic systems in which the truths of the first-order predicate calculus are derived as theorems from a handful of axioms through the use of a couple of inference-rules (notably *modus ponens* and a principle of substitution). Their formal systems (but not all of their informal discussions) distinguish between 'axioms' and 'rules of inference' (a difference whose importance had been demonstrated by Lewis Carroll): 'logical laws' or 'laws of thought' do not describe how people actually think (*pace* psychologism) but how they must think to think truly, and are based on correct descriptions of logical objects and relations (*Laws* I xvff., §§14–25, 47–8; *Posthumous* 128, 145–6; *Problems* 40–50).

Throughout his career, Wittgenstein questioned this picture of the 'rules of deduction' or 'laws of inference'. The *Tractatus* distinguishes sharply between logical propositions and valid inferences. The former are not propositions about logical entities and relations, as Frege and Russell maintained, but TAUTOLOGIES. (2) says nothing, since it combines its constituent propositions in such a way that all information cancels out. *A fortiori*, it does not say that one proposition follows from others. However, *that* (2) is a tautology makes clear that q follows from p and $p \supset q$, and thus provides the 'form of a proof' – *modus ponens* (TLP 6.1201, 6.1221, 6.1264; NM 108–9, 114, 117). This solves a puzzle which exercised Frege, namely how laws of logic can differ, in spite of the fact that they can be derived from each other and seem 'almost without content' ('Compound' 50). Although (2) *says* the same as, for example, '$(p \lor p) \supset p$', namely nothing, they *show* something different, since the fact that the former is a tautology differs from the fact that the latter is a tautology.

'Every proposition of logic is a *modus ponens* represented in signs' (TLP 6.1264): if Φ entails Ψ, then $\Phi \supset \Psi$ must, on analysis, turn out to be a tautology. All logical propositions say the same – nothing – and hence are equivalent. Axiomatic logic is wrong to distinguish primitive axioms and derived theorems. Moreover, it claims to prove the truth of logical propositions by applying rules of deduction to axioms. Wittgenstein protests that this ignores the difference between proof *by* logic and proof *in* logic: 'a logical proof of a proposition that has sense and a proof *in* logic must be two entirely different things' (TLP 6.1263; NM 109).

(1′)   If the stove is smoking, the chimney is out of order; the stove is smoking; *ergo* the chimney is out of order

deduces the truth of an empirical conclusion from that of the premises. By contrast,

(3) $(p.(p \supset q)) \supset q \equiv (\neg q.(p \supset q)) \supset \neg p$

proves not so much the truth of a proposition (a tautology cannot strictly speaking be true, since it says nothing) as that a certain sign-combination *is* a tautology, and hence part of logic. It does so without reference to any axioms, simply by calculating 'the logical properties of symbols' (NM 108–9; TLP 6.126). Unfortunately, the *Tractatus* provides conflicting accounts of this process. *Tractatus* 6.126 describes it as one of 'constructing' or 'producing' a tautology out of others through successive applications of truth-functional operations. This description fits the axiomatic procedure better than it does the truth-tabular decision procedure of *Tractatus* 6.1203, which does not derive one tautology from another, but calculates whether a proposition has the truth-value T for all 'truth-combinations' of its components.

Perhaps the explanation is that the *Tractatus* does not reject one proof-procedure, the axiomatic, in favour of another, but only the idea that any proof-procedure establishes truths about logical entities rather than displaying rules for the use of the truth-functional operators (TLP 6.126). In any event, at the deepest level, the *Tractatus* proposes to dispense with logical proof altogether. All meaningful propositions are truth-functions of logically independent ELEMENTARY PROPOSITIONS, and can be expressed through the TRUTH-TABLE notation. In this notation (1) can be written down as an array of three truth-tables. Each row of these truth-tables represents a different 'truth-possibility', a possible combination of truth-values of p and q. In the following abbreviation, the truth-value of each proposition for the four truth-possibilities are indicated by a quadruplet of T's and F's.

(1*)   (TFTF)(p,q) [p]; (TTFT)(p,q) [$p \supset q$]; *ergo* (TTFF)(p,q) [q].

217

The sense of a sentence is given by its 'truth-conditions', its assignment of truth-values for each truth-possibility of its arguments. Those possibilities that make a sentence true are its 'truth-grounds'. That 'q' follows from 'p' and '$p \supset q$' means that all truth-possibilities which are truth-grounds of *both* of the first two propositions – namely the first truth-possibility – are *also* truth-grounds of the last. Nowhere does a T occur for both of the premises and an F for the conclusion, that is, it is logically impossible that the premises should all be true and the conclusion nevertheless false – the definition of entailment (TLP 4.431, 5.101–5.1241). By contrast,

(4) $(TTFF)(p,q)$ [q]; $(TTFT)(p,q)$ [$p \supset q$]; *ergo* $(TFTF)(p,q)$ [p]

is a fallacy (that of asserting the consequent), since there is a truth-possibility (the second one) in which both premises are true and the conclusion false.

Accordingly, all entailment arises out of the complexity (truth-functional composition) of propositions (elementary propositions have no genuine entailments). Russell recognized that this constitutes 'an amazing simplification of the theory of inference' ('Introduction' xvi), but failed to appreciate the radical implications. Entailment is an INTERNAL RELATION between propositions. But rules of inference cannot justify such relations, they are indeed superfluous (TLP 5.13–5.132; NL 93, 100; NM 108–9). Firstly, one cannot justify an inference like (1′) by reference to (1): the latter is a mere schema which turns into a proposition only through substituting meaningful propositions for its sentence-letters, thus producing another inference of the same form, which cannot justify the initial one. Secondly, (1) cannot be justified by reference to the fact that (2) is a tautology. That (2) is a tautology and that (1) is valid are two aspects of one and the same structural relation between premises and conclusion; neither of them provides an independent justification of the other (such a justification cannot be provided for internal relations in general, since the relata cannot be identified without presupposing that the relation obtains). That (2) is a tautology, or that 'p' and '$p \supset q$' entail 'q', cannot even be meaningfully said, since these are internal properties of the propositions concerned, which *show* themselves in an adequate notation that displays their structure (*see* SAYING/SHOWING). In such a notation we would be able to recognize all logical properties and relations by inspecting *empirical* propositions. Ascertaining that (2) is a tautology would be unnecessary; we could dispense both with tautologies and with the truth-tabular decision procedure for recognizing them (TLP 6.122, 6.1262).

However, in 1929 Wittgenstein realized that it is not always possible to analyse molecular propositions as truth-functions of elementary ones, since there are non-truth-functional logical relations. He retained the idea that entailment is an internal or 'grammatical' relation between premises and conclusion; but realized that not all such relations are captured by truth-tabular containment. What holds generally is merely the (traditional) point that the conclusion of an inference does not add new information to the premises (PLP 371; WVC 92). Moreover, rules of inference are neither non-sensical nor superfluous. They are GRAMMATICAL rules, norms which license the transformation of propositions. Every grammatical rule can be employed as a rule of inference, and we invoke such rules constantly in explaining, justifying and criticizing such symbolic transformations. As before, rules of inference are distinguished from tautologies. Unlike (2), which says nothing, ' "$(p.(p \supset q)) \supset q$" is a tautology' is a paradigm which states that transformations of a certain type are legitimate. Equally, the law of contradiction is not the vacuous '$\sim(p.\sim p)$', but a rule which excludes as nonsensical the logical product '$p.\sim p$' (WVC 131; AWL 137–40; RPP I §44; RPP II §732; Z §682).

The earlier view that such rules are superfluous seems due to the idea that the internal relations between propositions flow from the nature of the logical operations by means of which they are constructed (TLP 6.124), which Wittgenstein now rejects. Acknowledging rules of inference or logical relations between propositions is now seen to be on a par with under-standing molecular propositions and the logical operators. Rules of inference do not *follow* from the meaning of the logical operators, they are partly con-stitutive of the latter. *Modus ponens*, the law of excluded middle, and the law of contradiction are also partly constitutive of the concepts of a proposition, and of inferring. In this sense they *are* laws of thought: a practice which does not conform with them, for example one based on (4) or on Prior's round-about inference ticket, does not count as reasoning (RFM 39–41, 89, 397–8; LFM 277–8; *see* AUTONOMY OF LANGUAGE).

The *Tractatus*'s truth-tabular definition of entailment influenced model theory, which conceives of an inference as a formal relation between the truth-conditions of propositions. Wittgenstein later reverted to the more nat-ural idea of inferring as something people *do*, while insisting that.it is not a private mental process (*see* THOUGHT/THINKING) but one of transforming sym-bols according to rules. Wittgenstein's abiding conviction that 'logic must take care of itself' (TLP 5.473) is at odds with model-theoretic attempts to justify rules of inference. One suggestion from this quarter is that such rules must be 'sound', that is, must not permit one to infer false conclusions from true premises. Against this, Wittgenstein claims that there is a difference between empirical and logical inferences (RFM 40, 397). The validity of 'The stove is smoking, so the chimney is out of order' depends on the truth-values of empirical propositions – if the chimney is in order, we abandon that inference. (1') is not amenable to such refutation. If the chimney is in order, we blame not (1'), but one or both of the premises. (1') is not a state-ment about reality, but a transformation of signs according to a norm of representation. Finally, model theory has been invoked to justify rules of inference by reference to the semantical definitions of the logical constants.

This project is incompatible with Wittgenstein's rejection of MEANING-BODIES, and with his claim that proofs in logic establish not a true description of the world, but the tautological nature of a combination of signs. *If* these claims can be sustained, they reinstate the Aristotelian idea that logical laws cannot be justified without circularity, since they are presupposed in all reasoning.

logical necessity   *see* FORM OF REPRESENTATION; LOGIC

logical space (*logischer Raum*)   The term originates in Boltzmann's generalized thermodynamics, which treats the independent properties of a physical system as defining separate coordinates in a multidimensional system the points of which constitute the 'ensemble of possible states'. The *Tractatus* does not define the term 'logical space', but clearly it there refers to the ensemble of logical possibilities. Logical space stands to 'reality', the existence and non-existence of states of affairs (TLP 2.05), as the potential to the actual. The term conveys the idea that logical possibilities form a 'logical scaffolding' (TLP 3.42), a systematic manifold akin to a coordinate system. The world is the 'facts in logical space' (TLP 1.13), since the contingent existence of states of affairs is embedded in an a priori order of possibilities. There are several dimensions to the analogy between space and the ensemble of logical possibilities.

(a) A 'place' (*Ort*) in logical space is determined by a 'proposition' (TLP 3.4–3.42), which here means an ELEMENTARY PROPOSITION. It is a possible state of affairs, which corresponds to the two 'truth-possibilities' of an elementary proposition – being true or being false (TLP 4.3ff.). For n propositions there are 2^n truth-possibilities, that is, possible combinations of truth-values. If there are only two elementary propositions, p, q, then there are four such truth-possibilities, ways the world can be, which are represented by the rows of a TRUTH-TABLE.

$$
\begin{array}{cc|}
p & q \\
\hline
T & T \\
F & T \\
T & F \\
F & F \\
\end{array}
$$

(b) Just as the existence of a point in geometrical space is guaranteed independently of whether it is occupied or empty, namely by its coordinates, so a place in logical space, the possibility of a state of affairs, is guaranteed by the existence of its component objects, independently of whether or not that state of affairs exists (TLP 3.4–3.411). A point in the visual field is surrounded by a 'colour-space', that is, it must have *some* colour, a note *some* pitch, an object of touch *some* hardness (TLP 2.0131), and so on for all determinables. Objects must fill some region of logical space, that is, realize some actuality in the space of possibilities, but it is an empirical matter what place they actually fill.

(c) This analogy extends to the idea of filling space. A place in logical space is taken up or filled if the state of affairs exists. By the same token, a proposition can leave to the facts a 'range' (*Spielraum*) to fill, namely those parts of logical space (possible states of affairs) which are compatible with its being true (TLP 4.463, 5.5262). Any proposition divides the whole of logical space into those truth-possibilities which agree, and those which disagree with it. Tautologies leave to reality 'the whole' of logical space, while contradictions 'fill' the whole of logical space, since they are true or false, respectively, whatever the facts. The range a molecular proposition leaves to the facts is determined by its 'truth-conditions', which is a partitioning of the set of truth-possibilities into those which make it true, its 'truth-grounds', and those which make it false. The number of truth-grounds of a proposition provides a measure of its range, and thereby of its probability (TLP 4.463f., 5.101; *see* INDUCTION).

(d) Finally, just as space is the field within which material objects move, logical space is a field of possible change, namely for the changing configurations (combinations) of objects in facts (TLP 2.0271f.). And just as material objects have a shape, which determines their possibility of movement, the objects of the *Tractatus* have a LOGICAL FORM, the possibility or impossibility of their combining with other objects in a state of affairs (TLP 2.011– 2.0141, 2.0251).

It might be thought that the places in logical space include not just all possible (existing and non-existing) states of affairs, but also their negations, since *Tractatus* 4.0641 states that the 'negating proposition determines a logical place *different* from that of the negated proposition'. But the negating proposition '$\sim p$' determines a logical place by describing it as 'lying outside' that of 'p', which means that it really determines a logical range (see (c)) consisting of all possible states of affairs except p.

Tractatus 4.463 speaks of logical space as 'infinite'. This can be understood as claiming that there must be infinitely many states of affairs or objects (TLP 2.0131). It has further been held that this is necessary in order to ensure the logical independence of elementary propositions: if object A can combine only with a finite number n of objects, that it is not combined with $n - 1$ of these objects entails that it is combined with the remaining object. But what entails an elementary proposition p_n here is a *molecular* proposition of the form '$\sim p_1 . \sim p_2 . \ldots . \sim p_{n-1}$'. Moreover, Wittgenstein declares that it is an open question, perhaps to be solved by the 'application of logic', whether there are infinitely many states of affairs and objects (TLP 4.2211, 5.55ff.), and this is in line with his idea that logic must not depend on contingent facts. Finally, it seems that his account of the GENERAL PROPOSITIONAL FORM is successful only if the number of elementary propositions is finite (TLP 5.32).

It is implied by (b) that among objects there are no 'bachelors', that is, that all of them are *actually* combined with at least one other object. This is taken for granted by most commentators, but can be disputed by reference to *Tractatus* 2.013: 'Each thing is ... in a space of possible states of affairs. This space I can imagine empty, but I cannot imagine the thing without the space.' This suggests that all places of logical space might be empty because no state of affairs exists. However, under such circumstances there would be no propositions (which are themselves facts), and hence no linguistic representation. Moreover, if the spaces which surround objects are analogous to a colour-space, each object must combine with at least one object from that space: a point in the visual field must have *some* colour (TLP 2.0121, 2.0131). It would seem, therefore, that the possibility of bachelors is incompatible with the notion of logical space after all.

It follows that there is mutual dependence between objects and logical space. On the one hand, objects depend on logical space, since it is essential to them to have a location within it. On the other, objects structure logical space, since their form determines their combinatorial possibilities. The nature of every individual object determines the totality of states of affairs in which it can occur, hence objects in general 'contain the possibility of all situations' (TLP 2.012, 2.0123, 2.014). Moreover, since the form of any object determines whether or not it can combine with any other object, if even a single object is given, all objects, and hence the whole of logical space, are given (TLP 2.0124, 5.524). This helps to explain *Tractatus* 3.42: 'A proposition can determine only one place in logical space: nevertheless the whole of logical space must already be given by it.' The immediate reason, alluded to in the following parentheses, is that an elementary proposition already contains all logical operations, since it can be expressed as a truth-function of itself with a tautology involving all other elementary propositions (see TLP 5.47). This means that depicting any single state of affairs involves mentioning all possible states of affairs, that is, the whole of logical space. The underlying reason why this is the logically adequate way of expressing elementary propositions is that the possibility of any single state of affairs, via the forms of its constituent objects, determines what other states of affairs are possible.

This has the unpalatable consequence that understanding one thought requires understanding them all. It is the myth that there is, as Wittgenstein later put it, an 'a priori order of the world', 'the order of *possibilities*' shared by world and thought (PI §97). He came to hold that what is logically possible is determined by the FORM OF REPRESENTATION we adopt, not by the essence of immutable objects, MEANING-BODIES, which impose a certain order on our linguistic practices. At the same time, Wittgenstein continued to use the idea of geometrical space to illustrate that a logical possibility can be actualized or not, and that a possibility of a certain logical kind can be actualized only by something internally related to it (e.g. PR 71, 111, 216–18, 252–3; PI §671; RPP II §64).

The *Tractatus*'s technical apparatus (truth-possibilities, range, etc.) influenced model theory and possible world semantics through Carnap's notion of an 'L-state', and the theory of probability through Waismann and Carnap.

logical syntax   Logical syntax or 'logical grammar' (TLP 3.325) is the system of rules for the use of signs which, according to the early Wittgenstein, lies hidden behind the surface of language and needs to be discovered by LOGICAL ANALYSIS. Logic is traditionally thought to codify patterns of valid inference. This connection with rules was given further impetus by the development of axiomatic systems which distinguish between axioms and the rules of inference that lay down what formulae can be inferred from what other formulae. Moreover, Russell's theory of types invoked logical rules to avoid the set-theoretic paradoxes. It introduced a distinction between sentences which are either true or false, and sentences which are meaningless or absurd, although they may be impeccable as regards vocabulary and (school-grammatical) syntax. A string of signs like 'The class of men is a man' is not false but nonsensical, since it violates logical rules (similarly, in Husserl's *Logical Investigations* 'logical grammar' comprises rules which a combination of words must respect in order to be even in the running for truth).

The idea that meaning or sense antecedes the contrast between truth and falsity lies at the heart of Wittgenstein's conception of LOGIC. The 'rules of logical syntax' are 'sign-rules' (*Zeichenregeln*) (TLP 3.3ff., 6.02, 6.124–6.126; NM 109; RUL 11.13). They determine whether a combination of signs makes sense, and fall into four groups:

intra-propositional ones for combining simple names within elementary propositions (these are roughly the rules of the theory of types);

rules for the definitions of names of complexes, which introduce abbreviatory symbols;

extra-propositional ones for combining elementary propositions by truth-functional operators (these are linked to TAUTOLOGIES and LOGICAL INFERENCE);

rules for reiterable operations which result in a 'formal series' (*Formenreihe*), such as the series of natural integers.

Logical syntax cannot be refuted by experience, since nothing which contravenes it counts as a meaningful proposition. So-called 'necessary' propositions are not statements about a special kind of object, but reflect the rules for representing objects in bipolar propositions. This is why philosophical problems, which are a priori, are to be resolved by reference not to reality, but to these rules. Philosophical theories are typically nonsensical rather than false, since they are based on violations or misunderstandings of logical syntax (TLP 4.002ff.).

Ordinary language engenders such confusions, because it 'disguises thought' (TLP 4.002): its school-grammatical surface conceals the underlying logical structure. But it is not logically defective, as Frege and Russell had supposed. There are no more or less logical languages. Any language, any sign-system capable of representing reality, must conform to the rules of logical syntax. Natural languages are capable of expressing every sense. Consequently, their propositions are 'in perfect logical order' just as they are; 'they are not in any way logically *less correct* or less exact or *more confused* than propositions written down ... in Russell's symbolism or any other "Begriffsschrift". (Only it is easier for us to gather their logical form when they are expressed in an appropriate symbolism.)' (OL 10.5.22; TLP 5.5563; NB 17./22.6.15). To be sure, many sentences of ordinary language appear vague or ambiguous. But this vagueness is determinate and conceals that they contain general propositions. Any specific employment of such sentences is analysable into a disjunction of possibilities, and hence does not violate the principle of bivalence (TLP 3.24, 5.156; NB 7.9.14, 16.–22.6.15; *see* DETERMINACY OF SENSE; GENERALITY). Equally, ordinary language allows the formulation of nonsensical pseudo-propositions, and conceals the logical form of propositions: quantifiers look like proper names ('nobody') or predicates ('exists'), ambiguities lead to philosophical confusions ('is' functions as copula, sign of identity and existential quantifier), and formal concepts like 'object' look like genuine concepts. However, to guard against such deception we need, not an 'ideal language' supposedly capable of expressing things natural languages cannot express, but an 'ideal notation' or 'sign-language' (*Zeichensprache*). Such a notation is 'governed by *logical* grammar – by logical syntax' (TLP 3.325); it displays the hidden logical form of ordinary propositions.

> The idea is to express in an appropriate symbolism what in ordinary language leads to endless misunderstandings ... where ordinary language disguises logical structure, where it allows the formation of pseudo-propositions, where it uses one term in an infinity of different meanings, we must replace it by a symbolism which gives a clear picture of the logical structure, excludes pseudo-propositions, and uses its terms unambiguously. (RLF 163)

As Ramsey pointed out, Russell was mistaken in holding that the *Tractatus* is concerned with a 'logically perfect language' ('Introduction' vs. *Mathematics* App.).

The *Tractatus* also disagrees with another aspect of Russell's position. The theory of types *states* that certain kinds of symbols cannot be sensibly combined because of their meanings, that is, because they stand for certain kinds of entities ('logical types'). Wittgenstein protests that assertions like ' "The class of lions is a lion" is nonsensical' are themselves nonsensical, since they refer to the meaning of a proposition in order to exclude the latter as meaningless. Equally, there are no BIPOLAR propositions about the logical type of a symbol, for example ' "Green" is not a proper name', since that already presupposes that one understands the mentioned symbol. Fortunately, a theory of symbolism need not talk about meanings, since the type of a symbol shows itself in the use of the SIGN. This is why the *Tractatus* speaks of logical *syntax*: the rules of logic are exclusively concerned with the combination of signs and make no reference to meaning, that is, semantics (TLP 3.33ff., 6.126; NM 109–10).

The idea that philosophy describes logical syntax without talking about what signs stand for (meanings) influenced Carnap's *Logical Syntax of Language*, which tried to avoid the conclusion that logical syntax is ineffable through the distinction between 'material' and 'formal mode' (*see* SAYING/SHOWING). The idea of categorial rules determining the combinatorial possibilities of signs inspired Ryle's doctrine of category mistakes. Wittgenstein himself continued to hold that the bounds of sense are drawn by linguistic rules. But he no longer restricted logico-linguistic rules to syntax, since he recognized that the meaning of a word is not a MEANING-BODY. For a while he continued to hold on to a CALCULUS MODEL, according to which the rules of natural languages are hidden behind the surface. From 1931 onwards he abandoned that idea, and with it the term 'logical syntax' in favour of 'GRAMMAR'.

M

mathematical proof Platonists regard mathematical proof as a means for discovering truths about an independently existing mathematical world. Wittgenstein rejects this view of mathematics as 'the natural history of mathematical objects'. According to him, the mathematician is an inventor rather than a discoverer (RFM 99, 111, 137–8; LFM 22, 63–8, 82–4, 101). This by itself is neither as original nor as outlandish as his followers and detractors have made it out to be. Although the Platonist view is intuitively plausible, it has been attacked by philosophers since Aristotle and by constructivist mathematicians since Kronecker. What sets Wittgenstein's conception of proof apart is its link with the idea that mathematics is normative.

From the very beginning, Wittgenstein distinguished sharply between proof *by* LOGIC and mathematics, and proof *in* logic and mathematics. Proof by logic or mathematics, for example in engineering, derives the truth of an empirical conclusion from the truth of empirical premises according to what for Wittgenstein are rules for the transformation of signs. By contrast, a proof in logic or mathematics does not so much deduce the truth of one proposition from that of another, as establish *that* a certain combination of signs is a tautology or an equation, that is, belongs to logic or mathematics respectively. To say that a necessary proposition like '2 + 2 = 4' is true is not to say that it conforms to a necessary fact in a Platonic realm, but to say that it *is* a mathematical proposition; i.e., part of our FORM OF REPRESENTATION (for Wittgenstein there is strictly speaking no such thing as a *false* mathematical proposition, since propositions like '2 + 2 = 5' are not part of our form of representation). '2 + 2 = 4' lays down what counts as an intelligible description of reality and functions as a rule of empirical inference (e.g., 'I made two pies, and then another two, hence I made four pies overall'). By the same token, the negation of a mathematical proposition, for example, '2 + 2 ≠ 4', corresponds to a NONSENSICAL transformation of empirical propositions (e.g., 'I made two pies, and then another two, hence I did not make four pies overall') (TLP 6.113, 6.2321; PR 250–1; AWL 200; PG 373, 392). Such a proposition has no role within empirical reasoning, although it has a role *within* MATHEMATICS, but only as part of proofs by *reductio ad absurdum*. To prove that a mathematical proposition is true is to incorporate it as a GRAM-

226

MATICAL proposition among the 'paradigms of language' (RFM 50, 162–4, 169; LFM *passim*).

During the transition period, Wittgenstein added to this normativist conception the idea that the sense of a mathematical proposition is given by its proof. It is the method of calculation which determines the sense of a proposition of the form '$a \times b$', and hence of a numerical identity like '$25 \times 25 = 625$' (WVC 79; PG 370). This is analogous to the claim that the sense of an empirical proposition is given by its method of VERIFICATION. However, to check a mathematical proposition by calculation or proof is not to conduct an experiment (RFM 51–9, 65–75, 192–201, 364–6, 379–98; LFM 36–9, 71–5, 85–109, 128–30). In the case of verifying an empirical proposition we can be surprised by brute facts. By contrast, knowing how to prove (or disprove) a theorem is to know that one *must* get a certain result, and that a different result is simply unthinkable. A mathematical proof lays down an INTERNAL RELATION, namely between performing a certain operation and getting a certain result (AWL 185–91, 214, 223; RFM 221, 309–10, 363): it establishes, for example, that only an operation with the result 144 counts as (is called) squaring 12. Equally, once we understand how it can be decided whether an angle can be trisected by compass and ruler, we know that nothing could count as trisecting an angle by compass and ruler. By contrast to empirical propositions, the route to a mathematical proposition cannot be described without arriving at the destination: there is no gap between knowing how to verify it, and knowing *whether* it can be verified (LFM 64).

Wittgenstein realized that this threatens to undermine the existence of mathematical 'problems', that is, questions which have not yet been solved (PR 170–5). In response, he distinguished between, on the one hand, propositions and questions for which there is an established method of proof or calculation, that is, which are part of a 'proof system', and on the other, those for which there is not. The former can be understood without having the solution. Thus, the question 'What is 61×175?' has a clear sense, even if no one has ever performed this multiplication, because all we have to do is apply an established set of rules. By contrast, mathematical theorems which we do not know how to decide (e.g., Goldbach's conjecture) lack such sense (AWL 8, 197–8; PG 366, 377; see below).

Even if mathematical equations function as norms of representation in empirical discourse, the question is whether Wittgenstein's account of the logical connections between different equations can do justice to pure mathematics, the inferential aspect of mathematics. This problem also faced the conventionalism of the Vienna Circle, who claimed that necessary propositions are themselves either rules (axioms and definitions), or propositions the truth of which follows from these conventions. As Quine showed, this position is flawed, since it leaves unexplained the necessity by which the theorems follow from the stipulated conventions. According to Dummett, Wittgenstein developed an alternative to this moderate conventionalism, one which does not presuppose non-conventional relationships of entailment. This 'full-blooded conventionalism' holds that the logical necessity of any statement is always the *direct* expression of a linguistic convention, to which the previously established conventions do not commit us. It seems that conventionalism either has to rely on the notion of logical consequence, a metaphysical surplus-necessity, or distorts the deductive nature of mathematics and the compelling force of its proofs.

This interpretation is right to point out that for Wittgenstein mathematical theorems are not true by virtue of conventions, but themselves rules (*see* MEANING-BODY). And he considers a community which has 'applied mathematics without pure mathematics', that is, accepts mathematical propositions as norms of representation without deriving them from others – roughly the state of mathematics before it was axiomatized by the Greeks (RFM 232–4). But he also recognized that in our mathematics we do not simply stipulate the theorems. The result of a calculation is a rule and yet 'not simply stipulated but produced according to rules', namely of inference (RFM 228; see LFM 101, 166). If it were otherwise, we would not need techniques of calculation or proof.

Moreover, in line with the idea of proof systems, Wittgenstein distinguished between the 'necessity of the whole system', and the 'necessity in the system', which links axioms and their consequences (LFM 142–9, 241). This corresponds to the difference between proofs which extend an existing proof-system, like the introduction of multiplication in $\mathbb{Z}$, the set of signed integers, and mere 'homework', proofs and calculations which merely apply an already established technique, for example a multiplication in $\mathbb{N}$, the set of natural numbers, that has not yet been performed (PR 187; LFM 69, 238; RFM 313). In the former cases, there is no logical necessity. Expansions or changes of a system of proof are not predetermined by the existing rules (RFM 268–70). For by applying the old technique in a new area we change the concepts involved (we extend the meaning of 'multiplication' by giving sense to ' -2×-3'). These are new concept-formations, which may be subject to certain standards (e.g., of a pragmatic or aesthetic kind), but to which there are genuine alternatives, as is shown by the debates about the introduction of negative integers and of infinitesimals.

By contrast, when we apply an established system, the results are predetermined. It might seem that this simply takes us back to moderate conventionalism: we have an arbitrary choice in selecting a certain system of rules (e.g., between Euclidean and Riemannian geometry), but are logically compelled within the system we choose (just as a traveller has a choice between several trains, but can no longer change direction once he has boarded a particular one). However, Wittgenstein's discussion of RULE-

FOLLOWING undermines this picture of logical compulsion. The proof does not grab us by the throat and carry us to the conclusion once we have granted the axioms and rules of inference. At any point, we can do and say whatever we want (within the limits of physical laws). It is just that we would not *call*, for example, '1,500 × 169 = 18' a multiplication. The logical necessity within the system boils down to the applicability of certain expressions. Someone who does not acknowledge a proof or calculation within an established system 'has parted company with us' (RFM 60; LFM 106).

This distinction preserves the idea that in mathematics we know as much as God does (LFM 103–4): within the system we can compute anything, and outside the system there is no fact of the matter. However, even if Wittgenstein avoids the spectre of a non-conventional surplus-necessity, his position faces several problems. For one thing, he does not stick to the distinction between the necessity within, and the non-determined extension of, a proof system, perhaps because of his occasional flirtations with a kind of rule-scepticism. Thus, he claims that any expansion of an irrational number is an extension of mathematics, in spite of the fact that there is an established technique (RFM 266–7). Furthermore, he suggests that in a 'proof I have won through to a *decision*', perhaps even in the case of proofs within a system (RFM 163, 279, 309; LFM 109, 124–5).

Even if one rejects the idea that a proof expresses cognition of facts in a Platonic realm, this is misleading in that one does not decide to be convinced by an argument. But perhaps the decision Wittgenstein has in mind is not whether to accept the proof (having constructed a proof, we cannot resist the conclusion without ceasing to calculate), but whether to adopt the conclusion as a norm of representation. Having established a theorem in Euclidean geometry, we are still at liberty to employ or reject it for the purposes of terrestrial navigation. In this case, talk of 'decision' might be compatible with Wittgenstein's insistence that while a proof does not 'compel' us in the sense of a logical machine, it 'guides' or 'convinces' us, much in the sense in which for Leibniz reason inclines but does not compel (RFM 161, 187, 238–9).

The need for persuasion lies also at the heart of Wittgenstein's claim that proofs must be 'surveyable', that is, perspicuous. We must be able to see the connections, since these connections are not an extrinsic means for recording a brute fact about a Platonic realm, but an integral part of the conclusion. Mathematical proofs which go beyond the straightforward application of an established proof system do not discover existing connections between concepts, they establish these connections. In their case, objectivity cannot mean that getting a particular result is a criterion for having applied the proof system, but only that the extension of the system is surveyable (RFM 150–1, 158–9, 166, 170–5, 187, 248–9; PG 330–1). However, the question is whether the conviction which a proof must carry lies in the fact that it spells out implications of our axioms and definitions which exist prior to any attempt to construct the proof, and whether we may refuse to accept the proof without being irrational. As regards the first part of the question, Wittgenstein's negative answer is based on the idea that the result of a mathematical proof is concept-formation. It modifies existing concepts by linking them with concepts with which they were hitherto unconnected and providing us with new CRITERIA for the application of its constituent terms. Thus, once we accept the proof of Pythagoras' theorem, having a hypothenuse the square over which is identical with the sum of those over its two cathetes becomes a necessary condition for something's being a right-angled triangle. However, if the proof modifies the concept of a right-angled triangle, it cannot be driven by the *unmodified* concept. It has been replied that this last point is trivial, provided that the new criteria will always coincide with the old ones ('including an angle of 90°'): whenever we judge a figure to be a right-angled triangle by the new criteria, we should also have been justified to judge it to be a right-angled triangle by the old criteria. If this is the case, the proof modifies concepts only in the sense of unfolding the commitment to the new criteria already implicit in the existing concept. But this can only mean that understanding the term 'right-angled triangle' is incompatible with rejecting Pythagoras' theorem. But prior to accepting the proof, understanding that term did not require acceptance of any statements concerning the squares over hypothenuse and cathetes. Yet Wittgenstein's own conception is also problematic: to say that each new conceptual connection modifies the meaning of 'right-angled triangle' is at best a stipulation, and one which stretches our concepts beyond breaking-point when we are told that 'each new proof in mathematics widens the meaning of "proof"' (AWL 10, see 116–17; PG 374; cp. RFM 440).

It has been argued that even radical extensions of mathematical systems are bound by some kind of logical entelechy: our concept of addition is already implicit in the concept of counting. A teacher who counts as we do but has not yet adopted our technique of addition is already implicitly committed to, for example, '$7 + 5 = 12$'. If she counts seven girls and five boys, and then thirteen children altogether, she must have made what by her own lights is a counting mistake. Wittgenstein has been defended on the grounds that saying that she *must* have made a mistake already imputes our criterion, which results from accepting '$7 + 5 = 12$'. This is correct, but compatible with the idea that we know that the teacher either commits what she would accept as a mistake, or does not count in our sense, since she regularly takes one pupil twice. The teacher could adopt a new norm of representation which differs from ours, but only by making cumbersome and unreasonable assumptions, for example that although she always gets the result 12, one pupil constantly vanishes on counting (*see* AUTONOMY OF LANGUAGE).

Wittgenstein does not deny that there are constraints on the acceptance of proofs, notably those of a pragmatic or aesthetic kind (RFM 370; LFM 82). But it is fair to say that he does not illuminate their workings. This holds in particular for those proofs which neither are simple calculations nor extend mathematics in a substantial way, but constitute the bread and butter of mathematical research.

A final problem for Wittgenstein is the claim that we do not understand mathematical questions or propositions such as Goldbach's conjecture in advance of having decided them. This conclusion is inevitable if we combine the idea that in mathematics there is no gap between knowing how to prove a proposition and knowing whether it can be proven, with the dogmatic assertion that grasping the sense of a mathematical proposition involves knowing how it can be proven. It is usually dismissed out of hand by an equally dogmatic invocation of compositionalism: we understand what the terms 'even number', 'prime' and 'sum' mean, hence we must understand Goldbach's conjecture, that every even number greater than 2 is the sum of two primes. However, Wittgenstein showed that understanding the components of a proposition and their mode of combination is not a sufficient condition for understanding it (see CONTEXTUALISM). Another objection, originating in Waismann, is that without some understanding, we could not even set out to look for a proof. Wittgenstein anticipated this objection, and claimed that the creative mathematician understands the proposition which he does not yet know how to prove only in the sense in which a composer understands a theme he wants to integrate into his composition, namely in that he has an inkling of the techniques to be employed (RFM 314–15, 370). What Wittgenstein ignores is the straightforward point that a mathematician, unlike a toddler, understands Goldbach's conjecture in the sense of knowing how it would operate as a norm of representation, that is, he knows what it would be to accept it as an axiom, whether or not he knows how to prove it as a theorem.

mathematics An interest in mathematics initially led Wittgenstein from engineering to philosophy. Almost half of his work between 1929 and 1944 is in this area; and shortly before he abandoned work on it he claimed that his 'chief contribution' had been in 'the philosophy of mathematics'. Whereas his discussions in the early and transition period include highly technical details, he later concentrates on questions which can be illustrated by reference to elementary arithmetic (LFM 13–14). Exegesis and evaluation of his contributions (both early and late) are still at a rudimentary stage. Wittgenstein's claims about mathematics are often baffling, and have been accused of containing definite technical errors. But on closer scrutiny the alleged errors turn out to be philosophical challenges to cherished assumptions about the nature of mathematics. On the other hand, while these challenges are ingenious and radical, they are controversial and often problematic.

Mathematics provided Wittgenstein's gateway into philosophy, but he quickly moved on to the nature of logic and representation. His treatment of mathematics emerged relatively late (NB 17.8./21.11.16) and occupies only two brief passages in the *Tractatus*'s discussion of non-empirical would-be propositions (TLP 6.02–6.031 & 6.2–6.241). Nevertheless, the *Tractatus* contains profound objections to Frege's and Russell's logicism. Logicism is the attempt to reduce mathematics to logic. It aims to provide mathematics with a secure foundation, and to show against Kant that mathematical propositions are not synthetic a priori but analytic, in that their proof relies exclusively on logical axioms and definitions (*Notation* Pref., §13; *Foundations* §§3–4). The concepts of mathematics can be defined in terms of logical concepts; its propositions can be derived from logical principles through logical deduction.

The *Tractatus* challenges logicism in several respects: (a) its SAYING/SHOWING distinction rejects Russell's attempt to avoid the set-theoretic paradoxes through the theory of types; (b) it challenges the axiomatic conception of LOGIC according to which there are more- and less-fundamental necessary truths (axioms and theorems respectively), and thereby the idea that deriving mathematical propositions from logical axioms grounds them in something more certain or evident; (c) it criticizes the logicist definition of NUMBERS, and submits a constructivist alternative, according to which the natural numbers represent stages in the execution of a logical operation.

Just as numerals do not stand for abstract objects, mathematical equations do not say anything about a Platonist world. Rather, they equate signs which are equivalent by virtue of rules governing reiterable operations (TLP 6.2ff.). Like the TAUTOLOGIES of logic, the equations of mathematics say nothing about the world, but 'show' its 'logic', presumably because they display the structure of truth-functional operations. However, while tautologies are 'senseless' propositions, equations are 'pseudo-propositions', on a par with the nonsensical pronouncements of metaphysics (TLP 6.2–6.22). It may seem that the reason for this discrimination lies in the fact that the *Tractatus* eliminates the IDENTITY-sign from its ideal notation. But this is not the whole story, since that ideal notation equally represents truth-functional relations without LOGICAL CONSTANTS. The real difference is that tautologies are limiting cases of meaningful empirical propositions. Equations are not, and unlike vacuous tautologies, they seem to be saying something. However, according to the saying/showing distinction, the 'identity of meaning' (here taken in a non-Fregean sense) between, for example, the signs '2 × 2' and '4', that is, the fact that they can be substituted for each other, cannot be asserted by a meaningful proposition, it must be seen from the expressions themselves (TLP 6.23ff.), although only if they are properly analysed, which in the case of complex equations would require substantial calculations.

'[I]n real life, a mathematical proposition is never what we want. Rather, we make use of mathematical propositions *only* in inferences from propositions that do not belong to mathematics to others that likewise do not belong to mathematics. (In philosophy the question, "What do we actually use this word or this proposition for?" repeatedly leads to valuable insights.)' (TLP 6.211). This passage contains the seeds of Wittgenstein's later account of mathematical propositions. After 1929, Wittgenstein abandoned the saying/showing distinction, and, as a result, no longer treated mathematical equations as pseudo-propositions. Instead, he followed his own recommendation and examined the role of mathematical propositions in empirical reasoning. This sets his account apart from traditional discussions of necessary truths, which are preoccupied with questions like 'What is the source of necessary truths?' and 'How can we come to know them?' Wittgenstein, by contrast, is concerned with the prior question of what it is for a proposition to be necessarily true. And he answers that question by looking at how these propositions are actually used, what their role is.

In doing so, he takes up a profound problem which had been ignored by logicism, and which defies the Platonist picture according to which mathematical propositions are truths about a separate ontological realm of abstract entities, but which had been detected by Kant. Mathematical propositions appear to be synthetic a priori; they do not rely on experience, but nevertheless seem to hold true of the objects of experience, that is, of the material world rather than a Platonic *hinterworld*. Wittgenstein takes seriously the empiricist position, explicit in Mill and implicit in Russell and Ramsey, according to which mathematical propositions are well-confirmed truths about the most pervasive aspects of material reality, because it is based on a hard-nosed 'realism' which avoids both arcane abstract entities (Platonism) and arcane mental structures (Kant's pure intuitions). But he rejects it, because he recognizes that 'no experience will refute' mathematical propositions. If we put two apples into a bucket and add another two, but find only three apples on emptying the bucket, we conclude not that, exceptionally, $2 + 2 = 3$, but that one apple must have vanished (AWL 197; RFM 325). We can use an equation like '$25^2 = 625$' descriptively, for the purpose of predicting what result people will get when they square 25. But in fact we use it normatively, to lay down what result people *must* get, if they have squared 25: the result is a criterion for having performed the operation concerned: if you do not get 625, you must have miscalculated, that is, you have not squared 25. 'Calculation is not an experiment' (TLP 6.2331; see AWL 185–91; RFM 221, 308–10, 318–19, 327–30, 359–63, 392–3).

This provides the key to Wittgenstein's own account. Mathematical propositions describe neither abstract entities nor empirical reality, nor do they reflect the transcendental workings of the mind. Their a priori status is due to the fact that, in spite of their descriptive appearance, their role is a normative one: nothing which contravenes them counts as an intelligible description of reality: 'There are $2 + 2$, that is, 3 apples in the basket' is nonsensical (RFM 363, 425, 431; LFM 55; *see* FORM OF REPRESENTATION). Mathematical propositions are rules of GRAMMAR, 'paradigms' for the transformation of empirical propositions. Arithmetic equations do not describe relations between abstract entities, but are norms for describing the numbers of objects in the empirical world, that is, substitution rules. '$2 + 2 = 4$' licenses one to pass from 'There are two pairs of apples in the bucket' to 'There are four apples in the bucket.' By the same token, an inequation like '$4 > 3$' permits the characterizing of a quartet as larger in number than a trio, and precludes 'This trio is larger in number than that quartet' (WVC 62, 153–7; PR 143, 170, 249; PG 347; RFM 98–9, 163–4; MS123 98). Geometrical propositions are rules for describing the shapes of and spatial relations among objects, and for the use of words like 'length', 'equal length', etc. They also set up ideals or norms for describing a measurement as accurate (WVC 38, 61–3, 162–3; PR 216; LWL 8, 55; PG 319; RR 127; LFM 256; PLP 44). 'The sum of the angles of a triangle is $180°$' specifies that if figure A is a triangle, its angles must add up to $180°$.

The idea that mathematical propositions are norms of description correctly explains applied mathematics, by identifying the role of mathematical propositions within empirical discourse. It should ensure Wittgenstein's place in the philosophy of mathematics, even if his account of how we arrive at such norms in pure mathematics is inadequate (*see* MATHEMATICAL PROOF). It separates his position from the established schools of twentieth-century philosophy of mathematics, which are united by the idea that mathematical propositions refer to some kind of reality, whether physical signs (formalism), mental processes (intuitionism) or abstract entities (logicism).

Logicism Like logic, mathematics moves within the rules of our language, and is hence unassailable by experience. Nevertheless, Wittgenstein retained the idea that there is a difference between the tautologies of logic, which say nothing, and hence cannot express a rule, and mathematical propositions, which themselves express rules (RFM 98–9; WVC 35, 106–7, 218–19; PR 126; AWL 146–8; LFM 272–85). The logical positivists ignored this distinction, and hence believed that Wittgenstein's account merely added to logicism the idea that mathematical propositions are tautologies.

Intuitionism Wittgenstein, influenced by Schopenhauer and Spengler, shared the anti-intellectualist outlook of Brouwer's intuitionism, and the idea that mathematics rests on human activity. But he rejected the idea that this activity is non-linguistic and mental, and rests on a 'basic intuition'. He agreed with Brouwer that the law of excluded middle does not apply to 'Four consecutive 7's occur in the expansion of π.' But his point was that there is no such thing as *the* expansion of π – an actual infinity – only an unlimited technique for expanding π, and hence expansions of π up to *n* places (WVC 71–3; PR 146–9; AWL 140, 189–201; PG 451–80; RFM 266–79; PI §§352, 516; PLP 391–6). Moreover, he rejected Brouwer's and Weyl's idea that such sentences are meaningful, yet undecidable because they transcend our recognitional powers. Instead, he argued, in a VERIFICA-TIONIST vein, that a mathematical proposition which is undecidable in principle does not have a third truth-value (undecidable) but is senseless, and that the law of excluded middle partly defines what we mean by a PROPOSITION (PR 176, 210; AWL 139–40; PG 458; LFM 237; PI §136). However, if Wittgenstein is right that we are dealing with a FAMILY-RESEMBLANCE concept here, this claim might have to be restricted, for example to propositions of mathematics or of the predicate calculus (*see* BIPOLARITY).

Formalism Unlike some nominalists or formalists, Wittgenstein is not com-mitted to the claim that mathematical propositions are really about signs: '2 + 2 = 4' is neither about signs (inscriptions or sounds), nor about how people use signs. Yet, although it is not a meta-linguistic statement, it is used as a rule for the use of signs. Wittgenstein tries to eschew both formalism and Platonism by insisting that what distinguishes a mathematical symbol from an empty sign, just as what distinguishes a chess-piece from a piece of wood, is not that it describes abstract entities and relations, but that it has a rule-guided use within our linguistic practices (WVC 103–5; LFM 112; RFM 243; RR 128; *see* LANGUAGE-GAME). This by itself does not set his position apart from those formalists who claim that mathematics is a rule-guided game with signs. However, for Wittgenstein 'it is essential to mathe-matics that its signs are also employed in *mufti*. It is the use outside mathe-matics, and so the *meaning* of the signs, that makes the sign-game into mathematics' (RFM 257, see 232, 258–60, 295, 376). This does not mean that all parts of mathematics must have direct empirical application, but only that those which do not must be connected with parts that do. There is no pure mathematics without *some* applied mathematics. Mathematics *would* be just a game if it did not play a role within our empirical reasoning.

Wittgenstein not only disagrees with these different schools, but also ques-tions the whole enterprise to which they are alternative contributions, namely of providing mathematics with secure foundations. He makes two basic points. One is that the attempts to ground mathematics, and in parti-cular Hilbert's META-MATHEMATICS, fail, since they simply produce further mathematical calculi. The other is that the fear of the sceptical threat posed by CONTRADICTIONS and antinomies of the kind Russell detected in Frege's system is a 'superstition' (WVC 196; RFM 120–2). It cannot be overcome, by constructing logical symbolisms – this is the 'disastrous intrusion' of logic into mathematics – but only dissolved, by philosophical clarification (RFM 281, 300).

Wittgenstein distinguishes sharply between mathematics, which changes our conceptual scheme by deriving new norms of representation (e.g., equations), and philosophy, which simply describes the evolving conceptual scheme. According to *Philosophical Investigations* §§124–5, philosophy 'leaves mathematics as it is'. It is concerned not with the technical cogency of the calculations and proofs, but only with the 'prose' with which mathematicians surround them, the philosophical descriptions they give of their significance (WVC 149; PG 369, 396; RFM 142; LFM 13–14). However, in other passages Wittgenstein acknowledges that this distinction between mathematical equations and philosophical prose is artificial. Without their prose context, many proofs in mathematical logic and set theory would be mere games with symbols. If Wittgenstein is right that this context is bedevilled by metaphysical confusions, this may not change the proofs, but it should change our '*attitude* to contradiction and to consistency proofs'. It should make mathematicians 'abandon' as uninteresting, for example, transfinite set theory, and should slow down the growth of new formal systems (RFM 213; CV 1–2; LFM 103; PG 381–2). Wittgenstein's much-discussed 'non-revisionism' boils down to the idea that while technical advances in mathematical logic may create new philosophical problems they cannot solve them, since these problems require conceptual clarification (PI §125; RFM 388). Another contribution to the philosophy of mathematics is Wittgenstein's anthropological perspective on mathematics as part of the natural history of mankind, and the idea that mathematics is a family of activities for a family of purposes (RFM 92–3, 176, 182, 399).

meaning (*Bedeutung*)   This concept occupies a central role in Wittgenstein's work, because of his abiding conviction that philosophical problems are rooted in language. His later work invokes and elucidates the everyday notion of linguistic meaning (*see* USE). His early discussion is a metaphysical reflection on the nature of symbolic representation, and evolves from a technical dichotomy between 'sense' and 'meaning' adapted from Frege. Frege was not concerned with all aspects of the meaning of expressions, for example not with their 'colouring', the mental associations they evoke, but only with those which bear on the validity of arguments in which they occur, their logical 'content'. In his mature system he distinguished two aspects of content: sense (*Sinn*) and meaning (*Bedeutung*). In an ideal language every sentence expresses a sense, the thought (what is judged), and refers to a meaning or referent, a truth-value, the True or the False. It expresses a thought by presenting a truth-value as the value of a function for an argument. Each significant constituent of a sentence also expresses a sense and has a referent. Proper names express a sense and refer to an object, concept-words express a sense and refer to a concept. This distinction explains both how an expression may fail to refer without being senseless, and the non-trivial nature of IDENTITY statements like 'The morning star is the evening star': although the two expressions mean the same object, their sense or 'mode of presentation' differs ('Sense' 25–36; *Laws* I §2; *Correspondence* 63; *Notation* §§2–8).

Initially, Wittgenstein accepted the idea that propositions have a meaning (*Bedeutung*), while rejecting other aspects of Frege's position (NL 94–104; NM 112–13). Neither the sense nor the meaning of a proposition is an object. The meaning of '*p*' is not its truth-value, but the fact that corresponds to it in reality, that *p* if it is true, that ~*p* if it is false. PROPOSITIONS differ from names. They are BIPOLAR – capable of being true and capable of being false – which is precisely to say that they have a sense. To understand a name is to know what it refers to, but to understand a proposition one need not know whether it is true or false, but only what would be the case in either event.

The *Notebooks* sharpen this contrast by gradually abandoning the idea that propositions have a meaning (NB 20.9./2.10./26.10./2.11.14). As a result, the *Tractatus* maintains that names have a meaning but no sense, while propositions have a sense but no meaning (TLP 3.142, 3.203, 3.3). (The *Tractatus* also employs the terms 'meaning' and 'sense' non-technically (e.g. TLP 5.02, 5.451, 6.521), a fact which has misled some commentators.) The sense of a proposition is 'what it represents', namely a possible 'state of affairs' or 'situation', an arrangement of objects which may or may not obtain, depending on whether the proposition is true or false. The proposition *shows* its sense, 'how things stand *if* it is true. And it *says that* they do so stand' (TLP 4.022, see 2.201ff.; *see also* SAYING/SHOWING). The sense of a proposition is neither an object that corresponds to it, a Fregean thought, nor the mode of presentation of a truth-value, but a possibility, a potential combination of objects which need not be realized.

Sense antecedes the facts: in order to decide whether a proposition is true, its sense must be determined; to understand its sense we need not know its truth-value, but only 'what is the case if it is true' (TLP 4.024, 4.061–4.063; NB 24.10.14; *Laws* I §32). This idea goes back to Frege, and lies at the heart of modern truth-conditional semantics. The sense of a truth-function of '*p*' is a function of the sense of '*p*'. Negation, for example, reverses the sense of the proposition. '*p*' and '~*p*' have 'opposite sense', even though one and the same reality corresponds to them: a single fact verifies one of them and falsifies the other (TLP 4.0621, 5.122, 5.2341; NL 95, 105; NB 6.5.15). The sense of a 'molecular' proposition is given by its 'truth-conditions', that is, by determining for each of the possible combinations of truth-values among its constituents (elementary propositions) whether it comes out as true or as false in a TRUTH-TABLE: '$p.q$' is true if both 'p' and 'q' are true, false if either or both are false (TLP 4.431). An ELEMENTARY PROPOSITION cannot have truth-conditions in this sense. But it can have 'truth-grounds', and to understand them is to know what is the case if it is true (TLP 5.101–5.121). To know what is the case if a molecular proposition is true is to know what elementary propositions make it true, to know what is the case if an elementary proposition is true is to know what possible combination of objects corresponds to the way its elements are combined. There is a condition which an elementary proposition must satisfy to be true, namely that it depicts objects as being combined in the way they actually are.

The sense of an elementary proposition is determined by the meanings of its simple 'constituents', that is, NAMES (TLP 3.318, 4.026f.). In order to understand an elementary proposition, we need to know what OBJECTS its constituent names stand for. 'A name means an object. The object is its meaning' (TLP 3.203, 3.22). This is a straightforward version of the AUGUS-TINIAN PICTURE OF LANGUAGE which Wittgenstein later rejected: the meaning of a name is the object which it 'represents' (*vertreten*); meaning (*bedeuten*) is a one-to-one relationship between names and objects. The *Tractatus*'s position here has been defended on the grounds that it employs a technical notion, and that the *Bedeutung* of a name is its semantical role, the contribution it makes to the sense of a proposition. However, that technical use precisely *identifies* the meaning of a word with what it stands for. And a name contributes to the sense of a proposition by 'going proxy' for an object. The very 'possibility of propositions' is based on this relation: unless a name has been associated with an object, propositions in which it occurs will lack a sense (TLP 4.0311f., 5.473, 6.53). This is no aberration, but essential to the PICTURE THEORY: a proposition can be false yet have a sense only because, although no fact corresponds to it as a whole, it consists of elements which are correlated with elements of reality.

It is more plausible to defend the *Tractatus* by claiming that, as in *Philosophical Investigations*, the meaning of names is determined by their use: what objects they stand for depends on their logical syntax, the way they behave in propositions. The *Tractatus* indeed condones a version of 'Occam's Razor': signs which have no 'logico-syntactical employment', no role in representing reality, are meaningless; two signs with the same employment mean the same (TLP 3.326ff.; NB 23.4.15). Moreover, it is correct that one can learn the meaning of a name from its use in propositions. But for the propositional sign to have a sense in the first place it must be projected onto reality by the mind. And although Wittgenstein speaks of the METHOD OF PROJECTION as the 'application of the propositional sign', this in turn is identified with a mental activity, 'the thinking of its sense' (PT 3.13; TLP 3.11). The speaker thinks a mere propositional SIGN onto a possible state of affairs.

And to do that, he must correlate its elements with the elements of the state of affairs depicted.

The *Tractatus*'s discussion of meaning and sense was an important step in the development of semantics. It features important insights: the denial that LOGICAL CONSTANTS stand for something, and the contrast between propositions and names; and prefigures others: the importance of linguistic use. But it remains wedded to mistakes: a referential conception of meaning, and the idea that a proposition's sense must be DETERMINATE.

meaning-body (*Bedeutungskörper*) Wittgenstein uses this term to characterize the idea that behind each sign there is a non-linguistic entity, its meaning, which determines how it is to be used correctly. According to this view, a word is analogous to a single painted surface of an otherwise invisible glass-body with a certain geometrical shape (e.g., a cube or pyramid). The combinatorial possibilities of the visible surface depend on the shape of the body behind it. Similarly, grammatical rules are seen as the geometry of meaning-bodies. We can derive the rules for the use of a word from its meaning, since the latter is a (concrete, abstract or mental) entity which determines the combinatorial possibilities of the word (PG 54; AWL 50–1; PLP 234–7). Grammatical rules are not AUTONOMOUS, but responsible to the 'true' or 'real' meaning of the sign involved, something outside language which can be discovered through LOGICAL ANALYSIS.

Such a view is prominent in Frege, who thought that he had for the first time revealed the true meaning of number-words, and insisted, against the formalists, that the rules for the use of mathematical symbols must 'follow from what they stand for', their meanings (*Foundations* Introd.; *Laws* II §§91, 136). It can also be detected in the early Wittgenstein, who thought that the identity '$\sim\sim p = p$' *mirrors* 'the fact that double negation is an affirmation' (NB 4.12.14), which in turn is an aspect of the essential BIPOLARITY of the proposition. On the other hand, one of the ideas behind the *Tractatus*'s SAYING/SHOWING distinction was that we cannot derive the rules governing the use of a sign from its meaning, since the sign does not have a meaning in advance of these rules.

Wittgenstein later directed this idea against Frege's Platonism, the *Tractatus*'s metaphysics of symbolism and the mentalism of James (*Psychology* I 245–6; see also *Analysis* 252), for whom the meaning of a logical term like 'not' is a feeling (e.g., of rejection) which we associate with it (PG 58; BT 42). His arguments also threaten the seemingly innocuous claim of logical positivism that the truth of tautologies follows from the TRUTH-TABULAR definitions of the logical connectives, and the attempt of model theory to show that our rules of inference follow from the semantical definitions of the logical constants. All these positions derive what for Wittgenstein are GRAMMATICAL propositions or rules from meanings.

239

Against this idea, Wittgenstein adduces two interrelated arguments. Firstly, while a rule can logically follow from another rule (that 'Betty' is written with a capital 'B' follows from the rule that all proper names are written with a capital), it is unclear how it could follow from a meaning (PLP 236). Secondly, necessary propositions do not *follow* from the meanings of signs or from linguistic conventions, they partly constitute them. For to abandon a necessary proposition is to change the meanings of at least some of its constituent signs.

> Grammar is not accountable to any reality. It is grammatical rules that determine meaning (constitute it) and so they themselves are not answerable to any meaning and to that extent are arbitrary. (PG 184, see 52–3, 243–6; AWL 4; RFM 42; LSD 20).

Rules of inference, for example, determine the meaning of the logical constants, rather than proceed from them. Whether a specific transformation of symbols is licensed or not is one aspect of the correct use and hence of the meaning of the terms involved. That we use '$\sim\sim p = p$' as a rule of inference contributes to the meaning of '$\sim$'. Without that rule, the sign would not have the meaning it has. And if the rule were changed, if we accepted instead '$\sim\sim p = \sim p$', the meaning of '$\sim$' would change correspondingly. Accordingly, the rules of inference cannot correspond or fail to correspond to the meaning of, for example, negation. Someone who passes let us say from '$\sim\sim p$' to '$\sim p$' does not follow a false rule of negation, but has given a different meaning to '$\sim$' (PI 147n; RFM 398).

There are three problems with these arguments. One is mentioned by Wittgenstein himself, namely that questions of identity and difference of meaning are more complex than they allow (PI §§547–59). If two people use 'not' in the same way except that one of them uses double negation emphatically and the other as equivalent to assertion, we would not say that they employ 'two species of negation'. For we would not say that 'not' means something different for each of them in 'Do not enter the room.' On the other hand, we would say that it does mean something different in 'I ain't done nothing' (RFM 104). Questions of synonymy are context-dependent. Secondly, to say that '$\sim\sim p = p$' follows from the truth-tabular definition of '$\sim$' can be understood innocuously as the contrapositive of Wittgenstein's own claim. From Wittgenstein's claim that if we alter the rule we alter the meaning, it follows that if we do *not* alter the meaning we get the rule. Thirdly, although we could use '$\sim$' according to either '$\sim\sim p = p$' or '$\sim\sim p = \sim p$', it would be inconsistent to combine *our* truth-tabular explanation of it with the second rule. For in that case we would say that the truth-table has been misunderstood. By Wittgenstein's own lights, the truth-tabular explanation is a rule, and to accept '$\sim\sim p = \sim p$' is a criterion for having misunderstood that rule, because one is not applying to '~p' the same operation (that of reversing the truth-value) that has been applied to 'p'.

To the last point, Wittgenstein replies 'Who says what "the same thing" is' (LFM 180, see 81–2; RFM 102–6; FW 57–8). What he has in mind is that the rule follows from the explanation only if it is understood that in the truth-table the place of 'p' can be taken by '~p' (that we apply negation as in '~(~p)' and not as in '(~~p)'). Accordingly, '~~$p = p$' is not determined by the truth-table definition alone, but only in conjunction with this second rule. Since there is no comparable rule in natural languages, nothing determines how to understand 'I ain't done nothing' (LFM 184). But this leaves the first two objections. It seems that 'The rules determine the meaning' is as wrong as 'The meaning determines the rules.' Understanding the truth-tabular explanation and acknowledging '~~$p = p$' are simply INTERNALLY RELATED aspects of one and the same practice of using '~'. The truth-table would mean something different in a practice in which '~~$p = p$' were rejected. They are simply two different rules of our practice and both of them are constitutive of that practice.

This leaves intact the original case against meaning-bodies. Signs as such don't have meanings. There are no entities from which the use of a sign 'flows', or which force us to use, for example, the truth-table one way or another. We give meaning to signs by explaining and using them in a particular way; and by employing them differently we can change their meanings (BB 27–8; AWL 50–1, 131–2; *see* RULE-FOLLOWING). The rules we adopt are neither correct nor incorrect. This chimes in with Quine's claim that the logical positivists' idea that necessary truths are true by virtue of meaning is based on the 'myth of the museum', the idea that there are abstract or mental entities – meanings or logical forms – which force us to hold on to a certain form of words come what may. But unlike Frege and the *Tractatus*, the logical positivists and model theory could replace talk of meanings by talk of explanations. Yet, if rules and explanations are different aspects of one and the same practice, one cannot understand the explanation and then see what rules follow from it. Rather, to understand the explanation *is* to acknowledge the rules.

memory The traditional view is that memory is a storage system, a piece of wax (Plato) or a store-house of ideas (Locke) which contains previous impressions or experiences, or at least their traces (Aristotle). According to this picture, when I remember a thing or an event X, I retrieve a mental image of X and parade it before my mind's eye; when I recognize X, I notice that my current impression of X fits with a mental image derived from a previous experience of X. The difference between a current and a remembered experience is then held to lie either in the greater vivacity of the former (Hume, *A Treatise of Human Nature* I.1.v), or in a feeling of familiarity accompanying the latter (James, *Psychology* I ch. XVI; Russell, *Analysis* ch. IX).

The later Wittgenstein condemned this conception of memory and recognition as 'primitive' (BB 165). His reflections were inspired by James and Russell, although Augustine's *Confessions* (ch. X) may also have played a role. For one thing, Wittgenstein rejected the idea that memory essentially involves mental images. Although mental images may accompany my remembering *X*, they are neither necessary nor sufficient. Moreover, even in cases in which mental images cross my mind, I do not read off what happened from the images. When I remember, say, having wished to Φ or having meant so-and-so, or what a perfect number is, I do not and cannot read off what I remember from any mental image (PI §§645–51; RPP I §468).

Even if *X* is something that can be pictured, having a mental image of *X* does not guarantee remembering. As imagists like James realized, the image would still have to be certified as a representation of something past. *Pace* James, however, this cannot be explained by a special feeling of familiarity or 'pastness'. Firstly, I would in turn have to recognize, that is, remember this feeling. Secondly, I can connect a feeling with the past only if I discover that it is regularly associated with memories as opposed to other kinds of experience; but I would need to rely on my memory to make this correlation. It takes memory to tell me whether what I experience is the past. Finally, connecting such a feeling with the past presupposes having a concept of the past, but that concept is in turn learnt by remembering. More generally, remembering *X* cannot be explained as the occurrence of a 'memory-experience', since memory is presupposed in linking experiences to the past. Remembering has 'no experiential content', that is, nothing that happens while I remember is the remembering (PI §§595–6, II 231; LW I §837; Z §662). Although characteristic mental experiences or processes may accompany remembering, they do not constitute it. This reasoning underlies Wittgenstein's denial that remembering is a mental process or experience, and that there is a uniform connection between remembering and what is remembered (PI §§305–8; PG 79–80).

Even if one abandons the imagist conception, one may agree with Aristotle (*On Memory* 450a–b) that I can remember *X* only if the original experience of *X* has left some physiological trace in me. This idea of memory traces was accepted, for example, by James, and developed by Köhler, who held that the brain must contain a physiological record which is isomorphic with the recorded experience (*Gestalt* 210–11). Wittgenstein attacked Köhler's reasoning (RPP I §§220, 903–9; Z §§608–13). For one thing, he pointed out that when we remember we do not read the past event off a neurophysiological trace: unlike a written record, such a trace has no symbolic content.

For another, he questioned Köhler's plausible assumption that the remembered events cannot have a present effect – the remembering – unless they continued to exist in some way. According to Wittgenstein, there might be a psychological regularity, a causal relation between the experience and the remembering, to 'which no physiological regularity' corresponds. This is to deny that there must be a psychophysical parallelism and thereby, by Wittgenstein's own admission, to challenge our conceptions of CAUSALITY.

On the other hand, Wittgenstein tacitly accepts the idea that the connection between the remembered event and the remembering must be causal to begin with. Although this assumption is shared by the currently dominant causal theory of memory, it can be questioned on Wittgensteinian grounds. I remember X now *because* I experienced X earlier, but the 'because' here seems a GRAMMATICAL one: it is part of our concept of memory that unless I had experienced X, I could not possibly remember X. By contrast, that there is a causal connection between experience and remembering seems to be a scientific discovery.

Wittgenstein disputes the view of recognition as the matching of an object or a current sense-impression with a stored mental image (PI §§596–610; PG 179–82; BB 84–8, 165; RPP I §1041). Firstly, recognition need not involve a mental image of what is recognized. Secondly, even if a mental image of X does accompany recognizing X, it cannot explain it, for one would in turn have to recognize that the image is an image of X. Thirdly, it is wrong to hold that a process of recognition takes place whenever we perceive familiar things: when I enter my study, I neither recognize my desk, nor fail to recognize it.

This last claim has been attacked along Gricean lines: the fact that we do not say that I recognized the desk does not imply that I did not. But it is incumbent upon Griceans to show that the fact that we would not speak of recognition in such cases is due to general pragmatic maxims rather than to semantic features pertaining specifically to the term 'recognize' (*see* WILL).

Wittgenstein's attack on the idea that stored representations are essential to memory and recognition pertains not just to the imagist tradition, but also to the idea of representations in the brain which ranges from Köhler to Marr. His claim that nothing need have occurred when I remember X was elaborated by Malcolm, who holds that to remember X is simply to have experienced or learnt X, and not to have forgotten it, and that the causal connection between experience and remembering is a contingent fact rather than part of the concept of remembering.

metalogic/-mathematics/-philosophy Wittgenstein declares the rejection of such 'meta-disciplines' to be a 'leading principle' of his philosophy (PG 116). It is part of his anti-foundationalist conception of philosophy and is directed against the idea that philosophy is needed to either justify or explain our ordinary (i.e., non-philosophical) uses of language. The idea that we cannot know anything unless we have answered the question 'What is knowledge?' is as absurd as thinking that we cannot spell at all unless we have completed a meta-investigation into the spelling of 'spelling' (PI §121; TS219 10). By the same token, there are no '*essential problems* in philosophy' which must be solved before anything else can be done. While different problems have a special importance at particular stages in the history of philosophy, none of them are intrinsically fundamental (BT 407; CV 10; RPP I §1000). This is the 'real discovery' in philosophy, because it 'makes me capable of stopping doing philosophy when I want to' without leaving everything 'hanging in the air' (PI §133; BT 431–2). There are several aspects to this idea.

Meta-mathematics Hilbert used this term to refer to his programme of establishing the consistency of mathematics by making mathematical proofs the topic of another mathematical calculus. Wittgenstein's rejection of meta-mathematics is directed not just at Hilbert's programme (WVC 120–1, 133–6; PR 180), but more generally at any attempt at providing foundations for mathematics, including the original logicist programme of reducing it to logic (AWL 12–13, 68; PG 296–8; LFM 260–2, 271–2). Wittgenstein rejects this idea through a simple regress argument. Both meta-mathematics and the logical systems of Frege and Russell are themselves nothing but further calculi, more MATHEMATICS 'in disguise'. Indeed, they are less basic than standard arithmetic, since they are remote from our mathematical practices and presuppose a grasp of standard arithmetic. 'They are no more the foundation of mathematics for us than the painted rock is the support of a painted tower' (RFM 378).

Metaphilosophy Nowadays this simply refers to philosophical methodology. The term was introduced by Lazerowitz, to indicate a non-philosophical discipline which explains the nature of philosophy by combining Wittgensteinian and Freudian ideas. Ironically, Wittgenstein himself took the traditional line that the nature of philosophy is itself a philosophical problem, and explicitly rejected the idea of metaphilosophy: 'One might think: if philosophy speaks of the use of the word "philosophy" there must be a second-order philosophy. But it is not so: it is, rather, like the case of orthography, which deals with the word "orthography" among others without then being second-order' (PI §121; see LSP 25). He relates this to the idea that ordinary language, including ordinary, non-philosophical employments of specialized languages, is fundamental to philosophy. Philosophical problems concern expressions which already have a non-philosophical use (RPP I §550). This would be granted by ideal language philosophers like Carnap. However, they blame philosophical problems on the ambiguity and vague-

244

ness of ordinary language, and try to resolve them through the introduction of artificial calculi in which these problems cannot be formulated. But if the problems arise from ordinary concepts, their resolution must clarify those concepts. As Strawson put it: artificial concepts can cast light on these difficulties only if their relation to our ordinary concepts is understood, which presupposes an accurate understanding of the latter. This by itself will achieve the desired resolution, if Wittgenstein is right in claiming that philosophical problems arise not out of deficiencies of ordinary language, but out of its misuse or misconstrual in philosophical reflection – when 'language idles' (PI §§38, 89).

Introducing a new notation may remove possible sources of philosophical error: we may curb the temptation for Hegelian confusions about 'identity in difference' by adopting a notation which replaces 'is' by either '=' or '∈' (PI §90; TS220 §99; *see* IDENTITY). But this presupposes that our 'is' in fact expresses both identity and predication. Introducing new grammatical rules plays a (limited) role in clarifying the old ones. But unless we have achieved the latter, we will not be able to cope with the new problems which any novel notation will create. New notations, whether formal languages or fictional LANGUAGE-GAMES, are useful mainly as *'objects of comparison … to throw light on the facts of our language by way not only of similarities, but also of dissimilarities'* (PI §130, see also §§2–64).

Metalogic Carnap's *Logical Syntax of Language* ascribes the origin of this term to the Warsaw logicians. At present, it is used to refer to second-order reflections about logic (e.g., proofs of soundness and completeness). Wittgenstein himself uses this term – mainly in the 'Big Typescript' (BT 3, 16, 205, 282, 285–6). Logic determines what is necessary, but there is no metalogic which makes logic necessary. We cannot step behind the distinction between sense and nonsense drawn by logic (PG 126–7). Wittgenstein also denies that there are metalogical concepts. This has been presented as directed against the view that psychological concepts like understanding or meaning denote mental phenomena which give language its meaning. While this interpretation fits some passages (Z §284; BT 1; MS110 189–91; MS116 16), it is too narrow. Wittgenstein uses the term 'metalogical' for non-psychological concepts (BT 412; PG 101) and maintains that all concepts which philosophy uses in describing ordinary language are themselves ordinary.

> When I talk about language … I must speak the language of every day. Is this language somehow too coarse and material for what we want to say? *Then how is another one to be constructed?* – And how strange that we should be able to do anything at all with the one we have! In giving explanations I already have to use language full-blown (not some sort of preparatory, provisional one) … (PI §120)

245

This is directed firstly against the *Tractatus*, which had already insisted that philosophy elucidates ordinary language, but had assigned an extra-ordinary status to the concepts used to do so. According to the SAYING/SHOWING distinction, 'proposition', 'name', 'function', etc., are 'formal concepts' which cannot even be meaningfully employed. The price formal concepts pay for being taken off the index in the later philosophy, is that their legitimate use is as 'low' and 'homely' as that of ordinary 'material' concepts (PI §§97, 108–9; PG 121). It is also directed against James's idea that ordinary concepts are too coarse to describe mental phenomena, partly because the latter slip by too quickly (PI §§436, 610; PG 169; *Psychology* I 195, 251), and against the idea that a 'phenomenological' language referring to sense-data is semantically primary (*see* VERIFICATIONISM).

Wittgenstein supports his view that there are no more-fundamental or more-refined artificial concepts for philosophy to rely on with a regress argument. In elucidating ordinary concepts (e.g., 'red', 'I'), philosophy may use technical terms like 'colour-predicate', 'indexical' or 'language-game', as well as terms like 'foundations' or 'philosophy'. But if the terms employed in philosophical clarification were part of a meta-symbolism, there would be a need for a further clarification in yet another language, and so on. We would end up with an 'infinite hierarchy' (LFM 14) of meta-languages, the equivalent of the regress of justification we encountered with respect to meta-mathematical calculi. Artificial languages cannot be constructed in a vacuum. At least some of their expressions have to be explained in terms which are already familiar, ultimately those of ordinary language, 'which must speak for itself' (BT 1; PG 40; PI §§5–6; Z §419). With respect to many purposes, ordinary language is inferior to technical idioms. But it is the semantic bedrock: through acquiring ordinary language we acquire the ability to learn and explain new and technical terms. There is no semantic exit from this language, either upwards into a hierarchy of meta-languages, or downwards to reality (*see* OSTENSIVE DEFINITION). We come to it not through another language, but through training in basic linguistic skills (*see* EXPLANATION).

It has been claimed that for Wittgenstein grammar is *flat*: there are no rules or concepts which are more fundamental than others. Wittgenstein's rejection of metalogic actually suggests that the concepts of ordinary language *are* fundamental in that we cannot 'get behind' them (PG 244). We cannot describe our practice of following rules in more basic terms than the rule-formulations of the participants. Those who do not understand those formulations cannot be enlightened through a 'preparatory' language, but can only be taught to participate (RFM 330, 392–3; Z §§310–19).

At the same time, Wittgenstein did cast doubt on the idea that there are 'categories', general concepts which signify basic structures of language and provide the sole topic of philosophy. His reflections on COLOUR-terms show that words belonging to the same category do not share all their combinatorial possibilities; thereby prefiguring later objections to Ryle's definition of categories as classes of expressions which can be substituted for each other *salva significatione*. Nevertheless, Wittgenstein shared Ryle's aspirations: the grammatical differences he sought to teach us are category differences in a loose sense (RPP I §793; RPP II §§7, 690; Z §86). Moreover, his idea that concepts like 'thinking', 'inferring', etc., impose conceptual limits on alternative grammars parallels the Kantian idea that categorial concepts are constitutive of the concept of experience or of a conceptual scheme (*see* AUTONOMY OF LANGUAGE).

However, Wittgenstein's attack on metalogical concepts rightly points out that categorial concepts like 'experience', 'act', 'event', 'state' or 'process' are not semantically prior: understanding them is not a precondition of understanding other concepts. Rather, they are devised in philosophy, in order to characterize the logical role of classes of non-categorial terms (see PLP 103–6). Moreover, categorial terms do not provide a sharply defined basis for philosophy. 'These extremely general terms have an extremely blurred meaning. They relate in practice to innumerable special cases, but that does not make them any *solider*; no, it rather makes them more fluid' (RPP I §648). It is precisely for this reason that they are so prone to cause philosophical confusion.

Finally, Wittgenstein explicitly renounced the idea, subsequently championed by Dummett, that the philosophy of language is the foundation of philosophy. We do not have to clarify concepts like 'language', 'meaning' or 'grammar' before we can clarify, for example, ethical concepts. For we can describe the grammar of 'virtuous' or 'duty' without relying on a description of the grammar of 'meaning'. But Wittgenstein *is* committed to regarding some concepts as fundamental in a methodological sense, since he maintains, for example, that PHILOSOPHICAL problems are based on *conceptual* confusions arising from misconstruing the *meaning* of words (LWL 61; M 51, 114; AWL 31).

method of projection According to the PICTURE THEORY, a proposition can depict a state of affairs only if its elements, NAMES, 'correspond' to, that is, 'stand' or 'go proxy for' (*vertreten*), the elements of the latter, OBJECTS (TLP 2.13f., 3.22, 4.0311f.). The 'correlations' between the elements of the picture (thought, proposition) and the elements of the situation it represents are the 'pictorial relation' (*abbildende Beziehung*). These correlations are like 'feelers' extending from the picture's elements, through which the picture itself reaches right out to reality, that is, depicts a particular combination of objects (TLP 2.1513ff.). Wittgenstein also uses the term 'pictorial relation' for the relation which obtains between picture and situation as a whole rather than between their elements (TLP 4.014). In this use it seems equivalent to a 'method of projection', 'comparison', or 'depiction' (*Projektions-/ Vergleichs-/ Abbildungsmethode*), or a 'manner of representation' (*Darstellungsweise*). Earlier, he had contrasted method of projection and pictorial relation (NM 112). Even if the elements of picture and situation have been correlated, it remains to be determined which relations between the names are part of the picture's 'structure', that is, have symbolic significance in that they determine what the proposition depicts. Equally, the fact that its elements are related in specified ways (that it has a certain 'structure') only depicts a specific state of affairs if these elements stand for specific 'things'. Accordingly, a picture consists of structure plus pictorial relation; that is, of two relations, one between its elements, and one between the latter and reality. We can represent a specific accident (which may or may not have occurred) with the aid of toy cars and dolls only if we lay down both what toy corresponds to what actual thing, and which relations between the toys represent actual relations between objects (e.g., their spatial relations, but not those between their weights). In subsequent writings, 'method of projection' includes both structure and pictorial relation, that is, everything required to compare a propositional sign with a specific situation (NB 30.10.–1.11.14; TLP 3.11–3.13). The idea is inspired by geometrical projection, which includes everything needed to transform one figure (the proposition) into another (the depicted situation).

'A proposition includes all that the projection includes, but not what is projected. Therefore, though what is projected is not itself included, its possibility is. A proposition, therefore, does not actually contain its sense, but does contain the possibility of expressing it ... A proposition contains the form, but not the content, of its sense' (TLP 3.13, see 3.34). The proposition does not 'contain its sense', the possible state of affairs, firstly because a configuration of signs cannot contain the configuration of things which it represents, and secondly because, if the proposition is false, there will be no such configuration to contain. What strictly speaking contains the 'possibility of expressing' the sense is not the proposition, which *does* express it, but the 'propositional sign'. It does so because it shares a LOGICAL FORM with the situation it depicts, it has the same logico-mathematical multiplicity (TLP 4.04) according to the conventions of LOGICAL SYNTAX.

These conventions determine only the combinatorial possibilities of names, and thereby the logical form of the propositional sign. But the SIGN as such does not depict; to become a *symbol* it must be given a content through a method of projection. The method of projection is the 'application of the propositional sign'. Correlating signs and reality is something we do. This prefigures the later view that what endows signs with meaning is not a correlated entity but their USE. Alas, the early Wittgenstein gives this idea a mentalist gloss: the application of the propositional sign, and hence 'the method of projection', is 'to think the sense of the proposition' (*das Denken des Satz-Sinnes*) (TLP 3.11; PT 3.12f.). When we use a propositional sign with understanding, as a model of reality, we have to think its sense into it, that is, we have to think of the situation depicted. Consequently, a continuous process of thinking and meaning accompanies and underlies every meaningful use of signs. While thinking is a process, a thought is not. Nor is it an abstract entity, as in Frege. It is a psychic fact: '*A* thinks that *p*' means that there is a psychic fact (involving *A*) the constituents of which are correlated with the constituents of *p*. These psychical constituents correspond to the words of language.

> I do not know what the constituents of a thought are, but I know *that* it must have such constituents, which correspond to the words of language. Again, the kind of relation of the constituents of thought and of the pictured fact is irrelevant. It would be a matter of psychology to find it out ... The psychical constituents have the same sort of relation to reality as words. (RUL 19.8.19; see TLP 4.1121, 5.542).

'Thinking is a kind of language' (NB 12.9.16), a thought is a proposition in the language of thought. Although, under the pretext of anti-psychologism, the *Tractatus* relegates to empirical psychology the question of what the constituents of thoughts are, it incorporates the mentalist idea that it is the mind which gives meaning to language. Representation requires an isomorphism between three different systems: language (propositional sign), thought (proposition-in-thought) and reality (state of affairs) (see AWL 112; PI §96).

What projects the psychic elements of thought onto reality? According to one interpretation this question is misguided: unlike perceptible linguistic propositions, thoughts are intrinsically representational. This might be part of their being 'logical' pictures (TLP 3), and would explain why 'the proposition represents the situation, as it were, off its own bat' (NB 5.11.14). On the other hand, it implies that the constituents of thought have precisely *not* 'the same sort of relation to reality as words'. It also conflicts with the idea that meaning is conferred on signs by our conventions (TLP 3.322, 3.342, 6.53). The meanings of the 'primitive' elements of language must be explained to us. However, since such signs are unanalysable, that is, cannot be defined, that explanation must be by other means. The *Tractatus* says that they can be explained through 'elucidations', but also that the understanding of these presupposes that their meanings are known (TLP 3.263, 4.026). It is therefore probable that, although the *Tractatus* does not mention OSTENSIVE DEFINITION, it is acts of meaning that link a name with a particular object, and thereby create the pictorial relation. '*By* my correlating the components of the picture with objects, it comes to represent a situation and to be right or wrong.' 'I know what I mean; I mean just THIS' (NB 26.11.14, 22.6.15, see 31.5./20.6.15; TLP 2.1511). Such acts cannot be performed by the empirical self, which is merely a complex of the psychic elements that are to be correlated with objects; they must hence be acts of the 'metaphysical' or 'willing' subject. The ineffable metaphysical subject invoked by SOLIPSISM 'sets limits to language' by infusing words with life, a Schopenhauerian idea Wittgenstein later criticized (TLP 5.631, 5.641; NB 4.8./ 9.11.16; PG 143–4; MS165 9–11).

In the *Tractatus* there is an unresolved tension between the invocation of acts of meaning and the idea of intrinsically representational thoughts. Wittgenstein later rejected both alternatives. The PRIVATE LANGUAGE ARGUMENT shows that signs cannot be explained through private ostensive definitions. He also criticized the 'old conception of the proposition' (MS165 86), shared by Moore, namely that propositions, unlike sentences, are immune to misinterpretation. Treating THOUGHTS as self-interpreting signs simply replaces a question about indisputable capacities of sign-language (*Zeichensprache*) with a mystery about the capacities of a postulated language of thought. If a word in this language is supposed to endow spoken words with meaning, it must itself have symbolic content. But in that case 'it would for us just be another sign' which itself stands in need of a method of projection. This holds not just for thought constituents, but for any 'object *co-existing* with the sign', whether mental images, sense-data or Fregean senses (BB 5; see PG 40). Associating the word 'cube' with the mental image of a cube does not determine its correct application, since that representation must itself be applied, and could, through a suitable geometrical projection, be applied to a pyramid (PI §139; *see* RULE-FOLLOWING).

The picture theory seems to accommodate this point, since the pictorial relation or projection is itself an integral part of the picture, partly constitutive of its being a specific picture (TLP 2.15ff.; NB 15.10.14). But this confuses the method of projection, which cannot be part of a picture, with the lines of projection (PI §141; PG 213–14). Even picture plus projection-lines (the 'feelers' linking names and objects) leaves open various methods of application, since they do not have their use laid up within them. A mental image of two cubes connected by projection-lines can license the application of 'cube' not only to a cube but also to a quadrangular prism. Nothing short of the application itself determines the projected situation. But to say that a situation is completely determined by the application of the picture relinquishes the core of the picture theory, namely that a proposition can picture 'off its own bat' since it is a logical form infused with content by a method of projection. What projects signs onto reality is our using them according to GRAMMATICAL rules (BB 4; PR 77–9, 85; PG 132; PI §§430–3).

mind and machine   *see* HUMAN BEING

mind/body   *see* INNER/OUTER

mysticism   This is traditionally defined as the experience of a union with God or the universe. Throughout his life, Wittgenstein was attracted to unorthodox religious figures (Tolstoy, Kierkegaard, Tagore). But his only notable treatment of mysticism is in the early work, and linked to his logico-metaphysical system. While 'the mystical' was extremely important to Wittgenstein, it is not the essential core of the *Tractatus*. Mystical themes appear only in 1916, but then immediately dominate the *Notebooks*. This happened under the influence of experiences during World War I, which led him to read Tolstoy's *Gospel in Brief*, and to re-read Schopenhauer. Wittgenstein grafted mystical themes onto a logical trunk. However, it is no coincidence that he did so. Initially, what cannot be said but only shown are the 'logical properties of language'. But the SAYING/SHOWING distinction invites extension to the mystical. It promises a handle for contrasting the empirical propositions of science with not just LOGIC and metaphysics, but also 'the higher', the realm of value – ETHICS, AESTHETICS and RELIGION. Moreover, the mystical is the traditional archetype for something ineffable, something which 'cannot be put into words' but 'shows itself' (cp. NM 108 & TLP 6.522). Finally, the link with mysticism keeps what is of ultimate importance, the realm of value, safe from the encroachment of science, albeit at the price of rendering it ineffable. At the same time, there are differences between logic and the mystical. What logical propositions try to say is shown by empirical propositions. But there are *no* genuine propositions which show, for example, ethical value – although it is plausible to suppose that ethical value is shown by peoples' actions and attitudes, as in Tolstoy's story 'The Three Hermits', which Wittgenstein admired.

In line with, and possibly influenced by, Russell's *Mysticism and Logic* (ch. X), the mystical is characterized as inexpressible (an idea Wittgenstein, but not Russell, extended to metaphysics), yet also as involving the following:

(a)   'the problem of life', which remains untouched even if all scientific problems have been solved (TLP 6.43ff., 6.52f.);

(b)   a 'contemplation' or 'feeling' of the world *sub specie aeternitate*, that is, from the outside, as a 'limited whole' (NB 7.10.16; TLP 6.45);

(c)   the claim that ethics and aesthetics are based on accepting the world (NB 20.10.16; TLP 6.42–6.43);

(d)   the idea that death is unreal (TLP 6.43ff.).

In the context of the *Notebooks* and the *Tractatus*, these familiar mystical *topoi* take on a new character. (a) is related to the idea that the answer to the problem of life is God, who is identified with 'the meaning (*Sinn*) of life' and of the world (NB 11.6./8.7.16; TLP 6.521). It has been suggested that *Sinn* is here used technically, as that which is depicted by propositions (*see* MEANING). But this is wrong. Firstly, that technical notion applies only to propositions, not to either life or the world. Secondly, although the *Sinn* that God provides lies not in specific moral or spiritual values, it is ethical in nature, since it consists in the 'vanishing of the problem' of life, namely as the result of happily accepting the world as it is – (c).

Another possible link between the mystical and logical doctrines is that the *Tractatus* seems to identify God with the GENERAL PROPOSITIONAL FORM, since both are characterized as 'how things stand' (NB 1.8.16; TLP 4.5, 5.471f.). However, the general form of the proposition is '*This* is how things stand', which does not always refer to an actual fact (not all propositions are true) but to a possible state of affairs. By contrast, God is identified with the world understood as 'fate', something independent of our will, which suggests that He is identical with how things actually are, as a matter of brute fact. Finally, God, the meaning of life and of the world, also transcends that world, since He 'does not reveal himself *in* the world' (NB 8.7.16 vs. TLP 6.41, 6.432). This could only mean that God is identical not with *how* the world actually is, but with *that* it is.

Whether or not Wittgenstein's various claims can be made to cohere, the last one links up with (b), the core of his mysticism. 'Not *how* the world is, is the mystical, but *that* it is ... The feeling of the world as a limited whole is the mystical feeling' (TLP 6.44f.). Accordingly, the *Tractatus* directly characterizes the mystical through three features:

it is the paradigm of what is 'inexpressible' and shows itself;
it is the content of an attitude, 'experience' or feeling;
it is the existence of the world.

How the world is, what the facts are, can have no value, and is part of the problem of life, not of its solution. What is relevant to the higher is only 'that the world is'. Here there is an indisputable link between mysticism and logic, since this is also the content of the quasi-experience presupposed by logic: not the 'How' of the world, but its 'What': 'that something *is*' (TLP 5.552f.). This 'experience' must concern not the truth of a contingent existential proposition, but the existence of the 'substance of the world', the totality of simple OBJECTS. This is not to say that it is expressed by a list of what simple objects, states of affairs or elementary propositions there actually are, which is part of the 'application of logic', not its precondition (TLP 5.55ff., 6.124). By contrast, the 'experience' at issue must be possessed by anybody who understands propositions in their unanalysed form, not as a conscious mental episode, but as something implicit in one's thought. What is required is simply the knowledge that *there is* a totality of simple objects, and of existing states of affairs, and that the essence or general form of propositions is to say how things are. To know this is to know that the world has limits, which might be described as knowing the world as a limited whole.

The contemplation of the world *sub specie aeternitatis* as existing and as a limited whole unites logic, ethics and aesthetics as 'transcendental' 'conditions of the world' (NB 24.7./7.10./20.10.16; TLP 6.13, 6.421). But only the last two involve (c), which cannot be milked out of Wittgenstein's metaphysics of symbolism. Taking the world's existence for granted may be a logical precondition of thinking, and a reflective logician might be filled with wonder at this existence. But being content with the world, with how things are, distinguishes the good from the evil will, and the happy from the unhappy life.

Wittgenstein combines this idea with his peculiar version of SOLIPSISM. Because life (the transcendental self) and world are one, the world of the happy, that is, virtuous, man differs from that of the unhappy one (NB 29.– 30.7.16; TLP 6.43). The world 'waxes and wanes' as a whole according to whether the transcendental self is capable of finding meaning in it, that is, whether it accepts it in a cheerful spirit, or perceives it as a hostile place. The other side of the solipsistic coin is that no part of the world, and no fact, has a privileged status. This is in the first instance directed at Schopenhauer's idea that my own body is an embodiment of the WILL. But it also ties in with the fact that Wittgenstein bases a Stoic moral ideal on a mystical experience: 'I am safe, nothing can injure me, whatever happens.' Just as the will cannot influence the world, the world cannot harm a virtuous man. For goodness is in the eye of the beholder, in his meeting the afflictions of life in a happy spirit.

Wittgenstein's solipsism is also crucial to (d). It implies that time is a transcendental feature imposed by the metaphysical self, which is why at death the world 'comes to an end'. At the same time Wittgenstein subscribes to the venerable idea that eternal life belongs to those who live in the present (TLP 6.431ff.). Happiness is attained by forsaking both fear and hope. The way to escape the temporal character of human existence is to be content with how the world is, which is beyond the control of the human will (TLP 6.373f.).

The early Wittgenstein manages to link traditional mystical themes with his metaphysics of symbolism and his solipsism. Unfortunately, the construction is obscure, and there is a noticeable break between the idea that the existence of the world is presupposed by logic – (b) – and the moral salvation involved in accepting the world as it is – (c) and (d). This fact may explain why the later Wittgenstein neither developed nor criticized his earlier mysticism. By contrast, many commentators have detected various similarities between Wittgenstein's work (early and late) and mystical themes, notably in Kierkegaard and Zen-Buddhism.

N

names Names entered the philosophical limelight with Mill's *System of Logic* (bk. I). Mill applied the label not just to proper names and common nouns, but also to descriptions, abstract nouns and adjectives. At the same time, he held that proper names like 'Aristotle' have a 'denotation', their bearer, but no 'connotation', since they do not imply an attribute. For Frege, propositions are composed of names of objects and names of concepts. Unlike Mill, he ascribed to ordinary proper names not just a 'meaning', their bearer, but also a 'sense', which may differ from speaker to speaker: for some the sense of 'Aristotle' is given by the description 'the pupil of Plato', for others by 'the teacher of Alexander the Great' ('Sense' 27). Russell took this line one step further. His logical atomism was guided by the 'principle of acquaintance', according to which every meaningful proposition must consist of expressions which refer to things with which we are acquainted. Like definite descriptions ('the present King of France'), ordinary proper names do not fulfil this condition. The theory of descriptions therefore claims that the latter are really abbreviated descriptions. Definite descriptions, in turn, are 'incomplete symbols', which do not refer to anything. Sentences of the form 'The *F* is *G*' are analysed into conjunctions of three propositions: there is at least one thing which is *F*; there is at most one thing which is *F*; that thing is *G*. If nothing satisfies the description, such sentences do not lack a truth-value, as Frege had it, but are simply false (*Problems* ch. 5; *Introduction* ch. XVI). Such incomplete expressions have meaning only because they are defined through signs which cannot be defined further but are directly linked with elements with which we are acquainted. These are 'real' or 'logically proper names', which are ensured against referential failure and provide the foundations of language (*Logic* 168, 194–201, 270). They stand for 'simples' (particulars, qualities and relations) and have the following features: (a) their meaning is an object the existence of which is not open to doubt, and to which neither existence nor non-existence can be attributed; (b) they resist logical analysis, and are in that sense 'simple symbols'; and (c) to understand a logically proper name involves no knowledge by description, only acquaintance with its meaning. From Russell's empiricist perspective, signs which satisfy these conditions must refer to sense- or memory-data, the existence of which cannot be doubted. The only logically proper names for particulars are 'this' or 'that', when used to refer to a mental entity with which the speaker is acquainted at that moment, and for properties the only logically proper names are colour-terms like 'white'.

The young Wittgenstein further developed Russell's programme of LOGI-CAL ANALYSIS. For him too, ordinary proper names are abbreviations of descriptions. The latter are treated in accordance with a modified theory of descriptions, the resulting existential propositions analysed as disjunctions of elementary propositions (*see* GENERALITY), which are finally analysed into semantic atoms which are names of simple 'objects'. He did not share Russell's empiricist preconceptions about what these OBJECTS must be like. He was concerned primarily with showing that there must be unanalysable signs if language is to be capable of representing reality: the PICTURE THEORY requires that there should be simple elements of propositions which correspond to the indivisible elements of reality. Nevertheless, what Wittgenstein calls 'simple signs' or simply 'names' (TLP 3.2ff.) have to fulfil specifications similar to those of Russell's logically proper names.

(a) They 'go proxy for' (*vertreten*), 'mean' (*bedeuten*), 'signify' (*bezeichnen*) an object, which is their 'meaning' (*Bedeutung*) (TLP 2.131, 3.203, 4.0312). However, the requirement on these objects is not epistemological (immunity from Cartesian doubt) but ontological: it must be impossible for them not to exist. Consequently, a name cannot be inserted into the argument-place of 'x exists', since the result would not be a BIPOLAR proposition.

(b) Signs which signify complexes are abbreviations (of definite descriptions, or disjunctions in the case of properties) and disappear in logical analysis (TLP 3.24). By contrast, names are 'primitive' (TLP 3.26f.). This does not mean that they are simple *qua* sounds or inscriptions, but that they cannot be further analysed or defined. They are directly correlated with objects, without the mediation of descriptions.

(c) The only descriptions of objects are propositions which say something *about* them, namely that they are combined with certain other objects, that is, which state their 'external properties', but these do not tell us *what* an object is, that is, its internal properties, which specify what other objects it *can* combine with (TLP 2.023ff., 3.221). To understand a name is to grasp its LOGICAL FORM, its combinatorial possibilities, which mirror those of the object it deputizes for. Its meaning must be explained to us, though the only means of explanation mentioned by the *Tractatus* is by 'elucidations', propositions which contain the sign, and hence presuppose that it is understood (TLP 2.0123f., 3.263, 4.026; *see* OSTENSIVE DEFINITION). Wittgenstein relegated to psychology the question how the correlation between name and object is effected (*see* METHOD OF PROJECTION).

There are also important differences between Russell and the *Tractatus*.

Like Russell, Wittgenstein speaks of names as having 'meaning on their own' (TLP 3.261). But because of his CONTEXTUALISM, this means only that they relate to reality directly, not that they have meaning in isolation, outside propositions. Moreover, Wittgenstein detects a lack of rigour in Russell's account of simplicity, because Russell uses as logically proper names symbols which we have to *treat* as simple because no analysis is currently available. For Wittgenstein, names, and the objects they stand for, are *intrinsically* simple, and differ absolutely from complexes (NL 100–1; NB 26.4./21.6.15; *Logic* 198, 244–6; *see* ELEMENTARY PROPOSITION). The price for this rigour is Wittgenstein's refusal to provide examples of simple signs or objects. Irrespective of this reticence, the *Tractatus* is committed to rejecting Russell's idea, condoned in the *Notebooks* (NB 16.6.15), that 'this' is a name. For that implies that the meaning of a name changes on every occasion of its use, and hence that every token of 'this' is a different name. The *Tractatus*, by contrast, insists that a name is a type, the class of token-expressions which refer to one and the same object (TLP 3.203, 3.3411; NL 102).

In this respect, Wittgenstein's later discussion of indexicals like 'this' (PI §38; BT 523ff.; BB 109) continues his earlier work. The enterprise is a different one, however. Russell's claim that 'this' is the only 'genuine name' is countered by reference not to the transcendental requirements on simple signs, but to the actual workings of ordinary proper names. On the one hand, there are similarities between indexicals and names: both are singular terms, and both can occur in ostensive definitions – one can answer the question 'What colour is your bike?' by saying either 'This colour' (pointing to a sample) or 'Green'. On the other hand, although there are diverse types of names (of people, places, colours, directions, numbers, etc.), an indexical like 'this' differs from them all in at least two respects: firstly, it cannot be explained ostensively (partly because its referent is a function of the context of its use); secondly, to refer, it requires accompaniment by a deictic gesture.

Other claims of *Philosophical Investigations* include the *Tractatus* in their target-area. The meaning of a name cannot be identified with its bearer (*see* AUGUSTINIAN PICTURE OF LANGUAGE). Furthermore, there is no such thing as *the* name-relation (PI §§15, 37; BB 172–3). Labels are connected with their bearers by being attached to them, but the use of personal names is more complicated, and this holds even more of abstract names like numerals. The connection between a name and its bearer is neither mysterious, nor inexorable or independent of the way we explain and employ names (*see* OSTENSIVE DEFINITION). Wittgenstein also notices a point generally ignored by philosophers, namely the importance proper names have for their bearer's sense of identity (GB 125–6; MS131 141).

Investigations §79 criticizes the 'abbreviation theory' espoused by Russell and presupposed by the *Tractatus*. The meaning of a proper name is not a *single* description which its bearer, if there is one, must uniquely satisfy. Firstly, since different speakers associate different descriptions with a name, this would lead to Frege's predicament, namely that the name and sentences in which it occurs have different meanings (senses) for different speakers. Secondly, although we may explain 'Moses' through a description, we do not treat that description as a definition. If it turns out that such a description, for example, 'the man who as a child was taken from the Nile by Pharaoh's daughter', does not apply to anybody, we would not conclude that Moses did not exist, or retract propositions about him as false, as the theory of descriptions has it, but provide an alternative description.

Some have interpreted this as a 'cluster theory' according to which the meaning of a name is a cluster of uniquely identifying descriptions, such that the bearer is whatever satisfies most or a weighted proportion of them. *Investigations* §79 indeed suggests a modification of the abbreviation theory in the light of the idea of FAMILY RESEMBLANCE: the traits we use to explain 'Moses' form a loose family in which many clusters can take on the role of being defining characteristics. But it does not commit Wittgenstein to the underlying assumption that the meaning of names is determined by descriptions, which runs counter to two other ideas of his (BT 253; PLP 71; TS211 494): (a) *no* definition, however complex, captures what we mean by 'Moses', since any one could be rejected in certain circumstances – we do not use names rigidly, in conformity with definitions laid down in advance; (b) there are various CRITERIA for understanding proper names: giving descriptions is not the only one, nor is it the only way of explaining names, which can also be done through ostension or introduction – 'That is the Tower', 'I am H.G.'

This last point also implies that 'no-meaning theories' (Mill, Kripke) are wrong to sever names from descriptions completely. Giving a description is one criterion, albeit defeasible, of knowing who Moses was. Nor is it clear that the connection between name and bearer established by a baptism has the unique role Kripke claims for it, rather than featuring among many possible explanations, as *Investigations* §79 suggests – 'the man who lived at that time and place and was then called "Moses".' Finally, Kripke is wrong to suggest that someone who says 'Moses was a seventeenth-century Dutch genre-painter' must make a false statement about Moses, provided that he has picked up the term through a communicative chain leading back to the baptism. On the other hand, the later Wittgenstein makes an assumption rightly questioned by no-meaning theories, namely that proper names have a meaning which is explained by explaining who their bearer is. Only some names have a meaning other than an etymological one. And even in those cases, the meaning does not determine whom or what the name stands for: 'Instant Plumbing' might be the name of the slowest company in town.

naturalism   *see* FORM OF LIFE; FRAMEWORK

necessity   *see* FORM OF REPRESENTATION; LOGIC

negation   *see* BIPOLARITY; FACT; LOGICAL CONSTANTS

nonsense   For Frege, a first-level concept like 'is a planet' is a function which maps objects onto truth-values. Any object can be the argument of any first-level function; there are no ranges from which arguments have to be taken. (Similarly, truth-functions admit as arguments not just propositions but any object.) 'The number 7 is a planet' is on the same footing as 'The sun is a planet', namely simply false. But 'is a planet is a planet' ($f(fx)$') is ill-formed, because the argument-place of the outer 'f' must be filled by a saturated sign, the name of an object. Although Frege introduced a hierarchy of propositional functions, he did not operate with a systematic distinction between sense and nonsense ('Function' 17–21; 'Concept'; *Laws* I §§21–5). Russell's theory of types, by contrast, introduced a systematic distinction between statements which are true or false and statements which are meaningless, although they may be impeccable as regards vocabulary and syntax (*Principia* II).

(1)   The class of lions is a lion

is not false, as Frege had it, but 'meaningless', since it predicates of a class what can only be predicated of individuals.

The early Wittgenstein took up this idea in a way which placed the notion of nonsense – in the sense of 'meaningless' rather than 'obviously false' or 'pointless' – at the centre of logic. Whether a proposition is true is determined by how things are. LOGIC is concerned with the prior question of what strings of signs are propositions capable of representing reality at all (truly or falsely). He combined this with Kant's idea that philosophy is a critical activity which draws the bounds between legitimate discourse (notably, the 'debatable sphere of science' – TLP 4.11ff.) and illegitimate speculation (notably, metaphysics). The *Tractatus* aims

> to draw a limit to thought, or rather – not to thought, but to the expression of thoughts: for in order to be able to draw a limit to thought, we should have to find both sides of the limit thinkable (i.e. we should have to be able to think what cannot be thought). It will therefore only be in language that the limit can be drawn, and what lies on the other side of the limit will simply be nonsense. (Pref.)

While Kant draws limits to knowledge, Wittgenstein draws limits to meaningful discourse.

(a) Logic is concerned with thought, because it is in thought that we represent reality. But THOUGHTS are neither abstract nor mental entities; they are sentences-in-use, propositional signs in their projective relation to the world. Consequently, thoughts can be completely expressed in language, and logic can draw limits to thought by establishing the limits of the linguistic expression of thought.

(b) These limits *must* be drawn in language. By definition, what lies beyond them cannot be thought, and hence – by (a) – cannot be *said*. 'Thought can never be of anything illogical, since, if it were, we should have to think illogically' (TLP 3.03, 5.473, 5.61). This is impossible since logic comprises the necessary preconditions of thought. Consequently, the limits of thought cannot be drawn by propositions talking about both sides, but only from the inside (TLP 4.113ff.). This is done by LOGICAL SYNTAX, the system of 'sign-rules' (*Zeichenregeln*) (TLP 3.32–3.34, 6.02, 6.124ff.; NM 109; RAL 11.13) which determine whether a combination of signs is capable of representing a possible state of affairs and hence amounts to a proposition.

(c) These rules cannot be expressed in meaningful propositions. For such expressions would state necessary properties of symbols, and hence would not be BIPOLAR: they would not exclude a genuine possibility, and hence could not express what they are meant to exclude. We cannot refer to something illogical like the class of lions being a lion by means of a meaningful expression. Hence any attempt to exclude it as logically impossible is itself nonsensical. The bounds of sense cannot be *said* in philosophical propositions, but *show* themselves in the logical form of non-philosophical propositions. Accordingly, the *Tractatus* seems committed to classifying expressions as follows:

(i)   Only the bipolar propositions of science are *meaningful* (TLP 4.11–4.116, 6.53).

(ii) TAUTOLOGIES and contradictions are *senseless*, that is, have zero sense.

(iii) The sentences of traditional metaphysics are *nonsensical*. They are based on 'misunderstandings' of logical syntax, which they violate in a way brought out by logical analysis (TLP 3.323f., 4.003, 6.53). This idea is retained in *Philosophical Investigations* §464: many metaphysical propositions are 'latent nonsense' which GRAMMATICAL investigations unmask by bringing out the 'patent nonsense' they imply.

(iv) The pronouncements of the *Tractatus* are *not* based on a misunderstanding of logical syntax, but rather express insights into its workings. In doing so, however, they try to say what can only be shown. They are 'pseudo-propositions' which can be seen as *illuminating nonsense* (TLP 4.12ff., 5.534f., 6.54f.; NB 20.10.14; *see* SAYING/SHOWING).

The *Tractatus* features two accounts of nonsense. One is that the non-sensicality of

(2)   Socrates is identical

is a matter of deprivation, that is, due to the fact that we have failed to give 'identical' any adjectival meaning. But if we lay down such a meaning, stipulating, for example, that 'is identical' means 'is human', then we are dealing with two different symbols. If a proposition 'has no sense, that can only be because we have failed to give a *meaning* to some of its constituents' (TLP 5.4733, see 5.473, 6.53). Indeed, it has been suggested that according to the *Tractatus* no part of (2) means what it does in a meaningful proposition. This would follow from a literal interpretation of the work's CON-TEXTUALISM: a word (name) has meaning only in the context of a proposition with a sense, which implies that no part of (2) has a meaning.

At the same time, the *Tractatus* espouses a form of compositionalism: the sense of elementary propositions is determined by the meanings of their constituent NAMES, that is, by what objects they stand for. Objects have a LOGICAL FORM, which is their possibility of entering into certain combinations with other objects. Objects, and derivatively their names, fall into different logical categories: a point x,y in the visual field must have a colour, and cannot have a pitch. In the case of a meaningful proposition, to grasp the meaning and logical form of its names is to grasp the possible combination of objects it depicts (NB 1.11.14; TLP 3.318, 4.02–4.03), while in the case of (2) or

(3)   Point x,y is C-flat

it is to grasp that this combination of names does not depict a possible combination of objects precisely because the constituents have incompatible meanings. (3) amounts to what Ryle (inspired by the *Tractatus*) called a 'category mistake'.

Wittgenstein's later work undermines both sides of the antinomy. Contextualism is correct only in so far as the meaning of a word is determined by how it can be USED within propositions. It does not follow that it lacks meaning outside propositions: it is precisely the type-word on its own which has such a use, and hence a meaning. Compositionalism regards the meaning of a word as an associated entity which determines the combinatorial possibilities of the word. Although we can talk nonsense, that is, combine words in ways excluded by their meanings, we cannot think nonsense, because we get stuck in trying to associate a sense with what results (*see* MEANING-BODY). However, while 'The rose is red' *would* be nonsense if 'is' there meant the same as in '2 × 2 is 4', the reason is not that 'is' is associated with two different entities only one of which fits into this context. Rather, grammar licenses the substitution of '=' in the latter, but not in the former. This is not a consequence of 'is' having two meanings, but rather

260

partly constitutive of its having a different meaning or use in these two contexts. Nonsense results if a combination of signs is excluded by grammar, either through an explicit rule (e.g., 'Nothing visible can have a pitch'), or merely by the absence of any rule for the use of an aberrant form of words, as with (2). The fact that we could stipulate a use for (2) does not show that it previously had a sense. We may be prevented from pursuing a path not just by obstacles across it, but also by the path itself coming to an end (PG 53–4; PI §558, II 175–6; RPP I §§43, 246; PLP 39, 237).

Moreover, Wittgenstein criticizes compositionalism for holding that making sense is a feature of type-sentences, and determined simply by their form and constituents. For him (as for Ryle), it is uses of words on a particular occasion which have or lack sense. Whether an utterance makes sense, and what sense it makes, is not determined exclusively by its linguistic form, but depends also on the circumstances under which the utterance is made and also on the previous communication between speaker and hearer (PI §489, II 221; OC §§212, 229, 348–50, 433). Whether an utterance of 'This is green' involves a category mistake depends on whether it is used to refer to a number or an apple. A type-sentence like 'I see Armstrong in the south-west corner of that room' can be used to make a perfectly intelligible statement, but it can also be used in a nonsensical way, for example if Armstrong is floating in a space-ship between Jupiter and Neptune, or if I am sitting blindfolded in my office. Conversely, saying 'I feel water 10 feet down' does not make sense if the speaker has just dug a small hole into which he reaches his arm, but would make sense if he were holding a long probing device. The bounds of sense are not drawn once and for all by an inexorable system, but are circumstance-relative and allow of borderline cases (AWL 21; BB 9–10; Z §328).

Detecting nonsense in philosophy is no longer a matter of invoking a canonical system of rules detected by LOGICAL ANALYSIS (TLP 6.53). It is done through a critical dialogue which Wittgenstein later referred to as an 'undogmatic procedure' (WVC 183–6; see PR 54–5; BT 424–5). Persistent misinterpretations notwithstanding, Wittgenstein refrains explicitly from criticizing philosophical positions merely for employing words in ways that differ from our ordinary ones (RPP I §548; RPP II §289; LPP 270). He himself introduces technical terms where convenient. He also recognizes that new experiences (scientific or poetic) are often expressed through apparently nonsensical phrases. But he would insist that this is possible only because, in response to the new experience, a new employment of familiar words is explained. One cannot alter the bounds of sense simply through fiat, by uttering hitherto prohibited or vacuous forms of words. Rather, one needs to lay down rules for the use of that form, and display its application. Wittgenstein's ambitious claim is that it is constitutive of metaphysical theories and questions that their employment of terms is at odds with their explanations and that they use deviant rules along with the ordinary ones. As a result, traditional philosophers cannot coherently explain the meaning of their questions and theories. They are confronted with a trilemma: either their novel uses of terms remain unexplained (unintelligibility), or it is revealed that they cross language-games by using incompatible rules (inconsistency), or their consistent employment of new concepts simply passes by the ordinary use – including the standard use of technical terms – and hence the concepts in terms of which the philosophical problems were phrased (PR 55–6; AWL 27; PI §191; RFM 118; LPP 7; *see* SCEPTICISM).

The later Wittgenstein abandons the saying/showing doctrine. Necessary propositions other than tautologies are not pseudo-propositions. Yet, their role is that not of empirical descriptions, but of grammatical rules (*see* FORM OF REPRESENTATION). They exclude not a genuine possibility, but only a nonsensical sign-combination. To substantiate this radical claim, Wittgenstein relies on a bipolar principle of sense (RAL 2.7.27): the negation of a meaningful proposition must also be meaningful. Yet the 'negation of an a priori proposition' is not false (in the sense of depicting an unrealized possibility) but nonsensical (PI §§251–2; AWL 208). Frege argued the contraposition: although it is nonsensical to *assert* the negation of a logical truth, such propositions are false, since their own negation is undeniably true ('Compound' 50). Wittgenstein advances three considerations for his position:

(a) One cannot think or believe a contradiction, for example that things are not identical with themselves. This is not due to the limitations of our powers of imagination, as Frege suggested. Nothing could even count as an attempt to imagine such a thing. To deny the law of identity is a criterion not of extraordinary powers of imagination, but of either a misunderstanding of or a deviant use of the expression 'identical with' (PG 129–30; RFM 89–90, 95; PI §109; *Laws* I xvii). However, one can hold beliefs which *turn out* to be contradictory, that is, cannot be spelled out coherently, as is the case with most philosophical theories.

(b) That a necessary falsehood cannot possibly be true means that nothing counts as its being true. This implies, however, that one cannot specify what the proposition asserts or means. Accordingly, the 'possibility' excluded by necessary truths cannot be specified by the meaningful use of signs (AWL 139–43, 165–6).

(c) Our reaction to attempts to specify what it would be for a necessary falsehood (e.g., 'This is green and yellow all over') to be true shows that we exclude ('withdraw from circulation') a certain combination of words (PI §§498–500; RPP II §290).

Were we to find something which we described as green and yellow [all over] we would immediately say this was not an excluded case. We have not excluded any case at all, but rather the use of an expression. And what we exclude has no semblance of sense. (AWL 63–4)

What such necessary propositions exclude is a move within a language-game, just like 'There is no castling in draughts' (Z §134). The difference between logically necessary and logically impossible is not akin to that between true and false but is that between a rule of expression and a use of words which that rule excludes as nonsensical. Grammatical propositions do not make statements, not even, like Kant's synthetic a priori principles, about the limits of human knowledge. They do not identify 'limits of human understanding' which one could transcend in order to describe them. Instead, they set the 'limit(s) of language', establish what it makes sense to say from within (CV 15; WVC 68; BT 406–8; PI §119; BB 65). Beyond these bounds lie not unknowable things in themselves, but only nonsense.

One might resist this conclusion by arguing that the falsehood of a necessary proposition is after all conceivable or imaginable. Thus, it has been argued that fairy-tales or Escher's drawings portray a logical impossibility. Wittgenstein anticipated this move. There is a use of 'I can't imagine...' which is an alternative way of asserting logical impossibility (Z §253; PI §§395–7). But the bounds of sense are not determined by the scope of our imagination (as Hume maintained – *A Treatise of Human Nature* I.ii.2). That one can conjure up images in conjunction with a form of words is neither necessary nor sufficient for its making sense (LWL 94; PG 128–9; PI §512; Z §§247–51, 272–5; MS116, 65–6). To establish whether an expression (tale/drawing) makes sense, one must investigate how it is constructed (Escher's drawings violate rules of pictorial representation) and whether it has an application in the language-game.

Wittgenstein also denies that there is a logical difference between gibberish like 'Ab sur ah' and philosophically relevant nonsense like 'No one can have my thought.' He admits that 'the word "nonsense" is used to exclude different things for different reasons', but insists that 'it cannot be the case that an expression is excluded and yet not quite excluded – excluded because it stands for the impossible, and not quite excluded because in excluding it we have to think the impossible.' The only difference between ordinary and philosophical nonsense is that between *patent* nonsense which causes no confusion since we recognize it immediately by the 'jingle of words', and *latent* nonsense, 'where operations are required to enable us to recognize it as nonsense' (AWL 64; PI §§464, 524; LWL 98). There is no halfway house between sense and nonsense. This conflicts with Chomsky's suggestion that, for example, 'Colourless green ideas sleep furiously' is syntactically well-formed but 'semantically anomalous'. Wittgenstein would reject this position, and more generally the semiotic triad of syntax, semantics and pragmatics: semantic anomalies are *not* propositions, since they cannot be used to perform a move in the language-game; their lacking sense is precisely a matter of what semioticians would regard as mere pragmatics, namely the absence of an established use.

numbers Numbers play a crucial role in Wittgenstein's abiding rejection of logicism, the reduction of mathematics to logic. Since all other branches of mathematics can be build up from arithmetic, the logicist project boils down to defining the concept of a natural number in set-theoretic terms, and to deducing the principle of mathematical induction from logical principles. Although Frege regarded numbers as abstract objects, he effectively defined numbers as classes of classes with the same number of members. The number 2 is the class of pairs, the number 3 the class of trios, and so on. This definition is not circular, since numerical equivalence between two classes can be defined through the notion of a one-to-one correlation. Two classes are equivalent if each member of the first can be correlated with a different member of the other class leaving none over. The number 0 is defined as the class of classes equivalent to the class of objects which are not identical with themselves, that is, as a class which contains only the null-class, $\{\emptyset\}$. The number 1 is defined as the class of classes equivalent to the class whose only member is 0, $\{0\}$; the number 2 as the class of classes equivalent to the class whose only members are 0 and 1, $\{0, 1\}$; etc.

Frege's ingenious procedure presupposes that classes are capable of being members of other classes. In that case, it makes sense to ask of each class whether or not it is a member of itself. As Russell noticed, this leads to the paradoxical notion of the class of all classes which are not members of themselves: if it is a member of itself, then it is not a member of itself, and vice versa. In order to prevent the paradox, Russell introduced his theory of types. It prohibits saying of a class what can only be said of its members, namely that it is a member of such and such a class. Given this prohibition, the series of natural numbers cannot be constructed in Frege's manner. The number 1 would be of higher logical type than 0, since it has 0 as its member, and in that case the set $\{0, 1\}$ cannot be used to define the number 2, since entities of different type cannot be members of the same class. Russell overcame this difficulty by defining 1 as the class of all classes equivalent to the class whose members are the members of the null-class plus an object not a member of that class. The number 2 is defined as the class of all classes equivalent to the class whose members are the members of the class used to define 1 plus an object not a member of that defining class. In this way, the natural numbers can be defined one after another, but only if there is an infinite supply of objects. This forced Russell to introduce the axiom of infinity, according to which the number of objects in the universe is not finite.

Russell's *ad hoc* use of axioms like those of infinity, of reducibility and of multiplication or choice to prop up logicism was the first target of Wittgenstein's critique. These axioms are unsuitable for grounding mathematics in logic, since they are at best contingently true, and at worst nonsensical. How many objects there are cannot be determined by logic (RUL 11.–12.13; NB 9.10.14; TLP 5.535, 5.55, 6.1232f.; PR 167; RFM 283, 400). He also criticized the logicist definition of the natural numbers. In later writings, he claimed that the idea of a one-to-one correlation cannot explain the concept of number. Whether there is a one-to-one correlation (e.g., between two sets of strokes) need not simply be self-evident. And our criterion for deciding such questions is precisely whether these sets have the same *number* of elements (PG 331; PR 125–6, 281; AWL 148–9; LFM 152–68).

Wittgenstein's early criticism concerns a different point. Given the relation between a number n and its immediate successor $n + 1$, Frege and Russell defined what it is for any number to follow n in the series of natural numbers, just as given 'y is a child of x' one can define 'y is a descendant of x'. Ordinarily we would explain 'descendant' by 'a person's children, the children of his children, the children of the children of his children, *and so on*'. However, Frege and Russell felt that the 'and so on' needed to be eliminated (*Introduction* 20–1; *Foundations* §§18, 79–80). To this end, they introduced the notion of a hereditary or ancestral property, as one which belongs to a person if it belongs to a person's parents. We can then define 'y is a descendant of x' as 'y is a child of some person who has all the hereditary properties of x'. However, while a descendant of x must have all the properties which are hereditary in the family started by x, it is logically possible for someone to possess all these properties without being a member of the family. Frege and Russell sought to overcome this difficulty by claiming that one of the properties hereditary in the family is precisely the property of 'being a descendant of x', with the consequence that anybody who has all the hereditary properties must be a member of the family. By this token, 'n is a natural number' can be defined as 'n is identical with 0 or has all the hereditary properties of 0', and the principle of mathematical induction turns into a logical truism: if P is a hereditary property of 0, then P belongs to everything which has all the hereditary properties of 0.

Like Poincaré, the *Tractatus* rejected this procedure as circular (TLP 4.1273), presumably because in defining 'y is a descendant of x' through the notion of a hereditary property it treats being a descendant of x as itself a hereditary property. Wittgenstein later suggested to Waismann (*Introduction to Mathematical Thinking* ch. 8) that it is equally circular to try to establish the principle of mathematical induction through an inductive definition of natural number. To try to define natural numbers in such a way that the principle of mathematical induction can be derived as a tautological consequence is to fail to appreciate that the principle is itself a criterion for a property's being true of *all* numbers, and hence partly constitutive of the meaning of the term 'natural number'. The same reasoning informs Wittgenstein's discussion of Skolem's inductive proof of the associative law of addition (PG 397–424; PR ch. XIV): it is misleading to think that a proposition about all natural numbers can be *proven* by the principle of induction – $P(1)$, and $P(c)$ entails $P(c+1)$, *therefore* P holds for all numbers; for the principle *defines* what it is for P to hold of all natural numbers, hence it does not provide an independent method for establishing such a claim.

The *Tractatus* treats 'number' not as a material concept which applies to some but not all abstract objects (Frege) or classes of classes (Russell), but as a formal concept, like that of a proposition, which is presented by a special style of variable (TLP 6.022f.). Like 'proposition', the formal concept 'number' is expressed through a 'formal series', a series whose members are ordered by an INTERNAL RELATION and are produced by a reiterable operation: 'x, $\Omega'x$, $\Omega'\Omega'x$, $\Omega'\Omega'\Omega'x$, and so on' (TLP 4.1252, 5.23ff.). We 'arrive at numbers' as follows (TLP 6.02f.). We define 'x' (the starting-point of the series) as '$\Omega^{0}{}'x$', and the successor of any given member '$\Omega'\Omega^{n}{}'x$' as '$\Omega^{n+1}{}'x$'. This allows us to rewrite the series as '$\Omega^{0}{}'x$, $\Omega^{0+1}{}'x$, $\Omega^{0+1+1}{}'x$, $\Omega^{0+1+1+1}{}'x$, etc.' and to state the general form of an operation as '$[\Omega^{0}{}'x, \Omega^{n}{}'x, \Omega^{n+1}{}'x]$'. Finally, we derive the integers: $1 := 0 + 1$; $2 := 0 + 1 + 1$; $3 := 0 + 1 + 1 + 1$; etc.

The 'general form of an integer' (TLP 6.03) (which parallels the GENERAL PROPOSITIONAL FORM) is $[0, \xi, \xi + 1]$. This suggests that Wittgenstein simply provides an inductive definition of the integers which takes for granted the notions of 0 and of the successor of a number which logicism tried to explain. In fact, however, it is crucial to his account that numbers are not the results of a *mathematical* operation (adding 1) on *numerals*, but fall-outs from *logical* operations on *propositions*. 'A number is the exponent of an operation' (TLP 6.021). Numbers correspond to stages in the construction of molecular propositions out of elementary ones through truth-functional operations. This is why mathematics is a 'logical method' (TLP 6.2, 6.234). However, unlike logicism, Wittgenstein does not regard logic as more basic than mathematics. In the margins of Ramsey's copy of the *Tractatus* he wrote 'the fundamental idea of math is the idea of *calculus* presented here by the idea of *operation*. The beginning of logic presupposes *calculation* and hence number'. Two is simply the number of times an operation must be reiterated to produce an expression of the form '$\Omega'\Omega'x$'. This may appear circular: in order to define numbers it refers to the application of the operation a certain *number of times*. But according to the *Tractatus*'s SAYING/SHOWING distinction, we need not invoke the number here: the stage of the formal series that '$\Omega'\Omega'x$' represents *shows* itself in the structure of that expression (properly analysed). In any event, it remains possible to explain the general notion of number by reference to the idea of successive applications of an operation. This notion in turn hinges on the idea of 'and so on'. While the logicists unsuccessfully tried to eliminate this idea, the *Tractatus* makes it central to mathematics. Both Russell and Ramsey portrayed the *Tractatus*'s account of mathematics as too restrictive ('Introduction'; *Mathematics* 17) because it is confined to elementary numerical equations. However, its failure to deal with transfinite cardinals is not a lacuna, but rather a consequence of its constructivist approach. Numbers are the exponents of operations which cannot take one beyond the finite.

Wittgenstein always rejected both the formalist and nominalist tendency to identify numbers with numerals and the Platonist contention that numerals stand for abstract objects (TLP 4.241, 6.232; WVC 34, 103–5; PR 129–30; PG 321; PI §383). Numbers are what numerals signify, but the meaning of numerals is given not by abstract entities, but by the rules for their use. Any sentence containing a numeral can be translated into a sentence representing the application of an operation. An equation like '$2 \times 2 = 4$' can be written as '$\Omega^2{}'\Omega^2{}'x = \Omega^4{}'x$' – repeating the twofold application of an operation twice is equivalent to its fourfold application (TLP 6.231, 6.241). Arithmetic equations do not talk about numbers, they work with numbers. A number-statement like 'There are two apples in the basket' is not about four objects (the two apples, the basket and the number 2), but rather indicates that an operation can be performed on the apples in the basket, namely taking out one ($\Omega'x$) and taking out another ($\Omega'\Omega'x$).

Wittgenstein later abandoned the *Tractatus*'s 'nebulous introduction of the concept of number by means of the general form of an operation' (PR 131), and treated 'number' as a FAMILY-RESEMBLANCE concept. But he retained the idea of numbers as the product of a technique. As a result, he rejected the notion of the actual infinite. That the series of integers is endless means not that it refers to an abstract totality, but that the possibility of repeating the operation '$+1$' is unlimited. The idea of infinity derives from the idea of an unlimited technique of sign-construction which can be continued indefinitely. A finite class is given by a list of its members, an infinite class is given by a law of construction, the principle of induction (TLP 6.1232; PR 140, 160–7; PG 461; BB 95–8; RFM 138; PI §208).

Although Wittgenstein's account is constructivist, it does not amount to finitism, let alone strict finitism. It is not driven by epistemological worries about our capacity to apprehend infinite totalities. The proper explanation of numbers does not take into account the feasibility of operations for human beings. The impossibility of running through all natural numbers is logical, not biological: there is a grammatical rule which rules out the expression 'the greatest natural number' as nonsensical. Moreover, Wittgenstein does not deny that there are infinite classes, but the difference between them and finite classes is not just one of size, but also a categorial one, between an enumerable list and an unbounded operation (RFM 142; PR 148).

This idea underlies his accusation that set theory presents the difference between finite, infinite and transfinite sets as a difference in magnitude (WVC 228; PR 164–5, 211–22; PG 460–71; RFM 125–42). Both Dedekind's definition of infinity and of real numbers on the one hand, and Cantor's proof that the rational numbers are denumerable, that is, can be paired off with the natural numbers ($\mathbb{N}$), while the real numbers ($\mathbb{R}$) are not, use the notion of a one-to-one correlation to establish the cardinality of infinite sets. Given that procedure, Cantor shows that the cardinality of $\mathbb{R}$ is greater than that of $\mathbb{N}$. But, as Wittgenstein points out, that procedure has a clear sense only with respect to finite classes. Cantor's diagonal method does not establish that $\mathbb{R}$ lacks an independently defined property, having a one-to-one correlation with a given set, but extends the notion of one-to-one correlation to infinite classes. What Cantor shows is that one can order rational numbers in a way which is precluded for real numbers. But it is only through a piece of concept-formation which we need not accept that he reaches the conclusion that there is a hierarchy of hitherto unknown mathematical entities – the transfinite cardinals.

O

object (*Gegenstand*) Wittgenstein uses this term, along with the more explicit 'simple object' and 'simple', for the ultimate constituents of reality (TLP 1.1–2.0272, 4.1272; NM 111; NB 3.9.14, 9./11.5.15; there is no evidence that he contrasted 'object' and 'thing' (*Ding, Sache*)). Objects are essentially simple, while 'complexes' (e.g., ordinary material objects) are combinations of simples. Objects form the 'substance of the world': since all change is the combination or separation of objects, they themselves are unchanging, and indestructible. Objects have both INTERNAL properties, their combinatorial possibilities with other objects, and external properties, being combined with whatever other objects they happen to be combined with (TLP 2.01ff.). The logical atomism of Wittgenstein and Russell seeks these elements through LOGICAL ANALYSIS. It holds that all propositions can be revealed to be truth-functions of atomic propositions, which in turn consist of unanalysable NAMES. Objects are what these constituents of fully analysed propositions stand for. They cannot be 'described', that is, defined, but only named. This guarantees that they do not generate any necessary connections between atomic propositions: 'The broom is in the corner' can be logically incompatible with 'The mop is on the table', since mop and broom are complex, and hence could share a common element – the handle (TLP 3.2ff.).

Russell pursued this analysis to the point where, for empiricism, the foundations of language and of knowledge coincide. The existence of sense- and memory-data is immune to doubt, which ensures that propositions about them are immune to referential failure. Therefore the 'principle of acquaintance' states that we can understand propositions only if we are directly aware of the simple 'individuals' they stand for. These include not just 'particulars', sense-data to which we refer through an indexical like 'this', but also 'qualities' and 'relations'. Russell gave 'This is white' as an example of an atomic proposition, but confessed that for all he knew 'analysis could go on forever' (*Logic* 193–203, 270; *Problems* ch. 5).

Wittgenstein considered and rejected this possibility (NB 3.9./8.10.14). For his logical atomism was inspired not by empiricist epistemology, but by a quasi-Kantian theory of symbolism which explores the necessary preconditions of representation. By his own admission, when Wittgenstein wrote the

269

Tractatus he was incapable of producing an example of a simple object or an unanalysable name. Determining the 'composition' of elementary propositions was left to future analysis. But on 'purely logical grounds' it could be known that 'analysis must come to an end': there *must* be elements of reality on the one hand and of THOUGHT and language on the other, if the latter are to represent the former (NB 14.–17.6.15; TLP 4.221, 5.55ff.; RUL 19.8.19; AWL 11; WAM 70). That objects are postulated by a theory of symbolism does not mean that their existence and nature are a matter of linguistic convention (as some interpreters hold); indeed, that theory insists that the LOGICAL FORM of names must mirror the combinatorial possibilities of the objects they deputize for. Nor does it mean that anything whatsoever might turn out to fulfil the role of simples. The *Notebooks* try hard to provide an example of an object, and even the more agnostic *Tractatus* indicates the direction in which to look. Arguably, ELEMENTARY PROPOSITIONS contain names not just for particulars, but also for properties and relations; they describe, for example, the colours and shapes of specks in the visual field, and their spatial relations to other such specks. Objects are objects of acquaintance, not sense-data but their unanalysable constituents. The closest one gets are *minima sensibilia* (NB 7.5.15): particulars like spatial points, ultimate perceptual qualities such as shades of colours, tones and smells, and simple spatial relations. Unlike Russell's sense-data, they are not temporary; they are apparent *sempiternalia* which are metaphysically, not just epistemically, guaranteed: red complexes and sense-data can be destroyed, the colour red, or points in space and time, cannot; and they are incomplete: they must combine with each other into changing combinations – i.e., facts (*see* CONTEXTUALISM).

Wittgenstein's main point remains that there must be objects if representation is to be possible. The basic idea is a regress argument going back to Plato. Ordinary signs are explained through definitions. But the 'chain of definitions must have an end', since defined signs signify via the signs that serve as their definition. Consequently, there must be signs which relate to objects not through definitions (descriptions) but directly, by *naming* them (NB 9.5.15; TLP 3.26f.). Existential and universal propositions are analysable into disjunctions or conjunctions of elementary propositions from which all molecular propositions derive their sense (*see* GENERALITY). These elementary propositions consist solely of names. They combine these in a way which, given a suitable METHOD OF PROJECTION, represents a possible combination of the objects the names stand for. No existing state of affairs need correspond to a proposition as a whole. But unless each name were correlated with an object, its MEANING, the proposition could not depict a possible state of affairs. Representation requires a one-to-one correlation between the elements of propositions and those of possible states of affairs (TLP 4.031f., 5.123).

Thus, the PICTURE THEORY implies that names 'pin' propositions onto reality. But as Wittgenstein realized, it does not imply that their referents must be simple or indestructible – they could be ordinary objects like books (NB 31.5.14.–15.6.15). A variety of (often implicit) considerations led him to stronger conclusions:

(a) Complexity. The idea of a simple is 'contained' in that of a complex which can be analysed (decomposed). There are complexes; any complex consists of simpler parts; *ergo* there must be non-complex objects (NB 15.6.15; TLP 2.02ff.).

(b) The form of the world. The world has a fixed LOGICAL FORM which determines what is logically possible but is itself determined by the possibility of things occurring in states of affairs. If all things were complex, that is, destructible, the world's logical form, and hence what is logically possible, could change (TLP 2.012ff.).

(c) Autonomy of sense. Whether a proposition has a sense must not depend on the truth of another proposition stating that something or other happens to exist, for that would make logic dependent upon contingent fact. But if the words occurring in a proposition designated only complexes and not (ultimately) simples, what corresponds to them might be destroyed. In that case, they would lack meaning, since nothing would correspond to them. Therefore, for the proposition to have a sense it would have to be true that the corresponding complexes happen to exist, which contradicts the autonomy of sense (TLP 2.0211; NM 117).

To some, this argument has seemed incompatible with Wittgenstein's rejection of truth-value gaps: a sentence with a sense must be either true or false. A complex consists of, for example, a's standing-in-the-relation-R to b. A proposition ascribing a property to it – '$\Phi(aRb)$' – comes out as '$\Phi a . \Phi b . aRb$' (TLP 2.0201, 3.24; NB 15.5.15; *Principles* 466). If $\sim aRb$, then the analysandum does not lack a truth-value, but is false. It is not the sense, but rather the truth of a proposition which depends on the existence of complexes. *But*, it has a sense only if the propositions of the analysans do – the sense of a complex proposition is a function of that of its constituents. And these propositions are senseless unless they ultimately consist of names for simples: if 'a' were further explained through descriptions only, its referring to something, and hence the sense of 'aRb', would depend on facts.

(d) Determinacy of sense. 'The requirement that simple signs be possible is the requirement that sense be determinate' (TLP 3.23). Precisely why is less determinate, but there are three possible lines of thought:

(i)   Unless analysis terminates by correlating unanalysable symbols with simple objects, the sense of a molecular proposition, its truth-conditions, is not settled in advance; we would not know, for example, how to continue the analysis of '$\Phi(aRb)$', and hence what it entails (NB 18.6.15; PT 3.20101ff.).

(ii) Unless the constituents of reality are sharply defined, a proposition could not restrict reality 'to two alternatives: yes or no' (TLP 4.023). There would not be a precise configuration of simple elements which either verifies or falsifies it.

(iii) A proposition about a complex is indeterminate in that it can fail to be true in more than one way: its elements can be combined in a way which does not correspond to an existing state of affairs, or, since they are not logically proper names, they can fail to refer. This does not mean that such a proposition is logically deficient; for what it leaves open is itself determinate. But this indeterminacy cannot run all the way through to the elementary propositions into which propositions about complexes can be analysed (TLP 5.156; NB 16.–17.6.15).

After his return to philosophy, Wittgenstein realized that he had built a metaphysical mythology on a logical basis: in so far as the needs which objects were meant to satisfy are genuine, they do not require necessary existents. Argument (a) is invalid. That a complex consists of simpler parts does not entail that there are parts which cannot be further analysed: analysis might go on for ever. Equally, it is fallacious to move from the truism, 'Every complex is made up of simples' to the controversial, 'There are simples of which every complex is made up.' Moreover, the distinction between simple and complex does not have an absolute sense; one and the same thing can be regarded as simple or complex, depending on the standards we employ (PI §§47–8). For example, the squares of a chessboard are simple for the purpose of the game, but might be glued together from triangular half-squares. Indeed, for some purposes something can even be seen as composed of two components greater than itself, as with the composition of forces in mechanics.

It has been replied that not all standards of simplicity need be of equal standing; some things might be intrinsically simple, notably the ultimate constituents of matter. However, that would be physical simplicity, established by experiments. What Wittgenstein is now rejecting is the idea that there is absolute logical simplicity, required by the possibility of representation, independently of experience. In some cases (e.g., pure colours), there may be no customary or natural standards of complexity, but this must not be confused with the presence of absolute criteria of simplicity (PG 211; PI §59; Z §338). And even if there were intrinsic simples, these would have to be sempiternal only if the *Tractatus* were right in assuming that all change is mere recombination of elements.

As to consideration (b), Wittgenstein's later idea of the AUTONOMY OF LAN-GUAGE denies that there is a fixed order of logical possibilities – LOGICAL SPACE: what is logically possible is determined not by the putative metaphysical atoms, but by linguistic rules (PI §97). By the same token, however, there is a kernel of truth to line (c). The sense of a proposition is prior to its truth: in order to decide whether a proposition is true, its sense must be determined (to ascribe a property F to an object a, it must be settled when something can be identified as a and what counts as being F); whereas to understand its sense we need not know its truth-value, but only 'what is the case if it is true' (TLP 4.024, 4.061f.; NB 24.10.14; PG 184–5). But to hold that this priority requires necessary existents amounts to an argument like

P_1 Necessarily: if 'aRb' makes sense, it necessarily makes sense.

P_2 Necessarily: if 'aRb' makes sense, a exists.

C   Necessarily: if 'aRb' makes sense, a necessarily exists.

This is valid in some systems of modal logic, but both premises are false. There is no necessity about certain forms of words having sense. And P_2 is mistaken in assuming that a proposition has a sense only if every one of its constituents stands for an object; most words have meaning without standing for something, and even referring expressions like 'Excalibur' do not lose their meaning if their referent is destroyed (PI §§39–44).

At the same time, there are expressions the meaning of which seems to be tied to the existence of objects, namely those which can only be explained through OSTENSIVE DEFINITION. In so far as the needs which simples were intended to satisfy are genuine, they are fulfilled by the samples by reference to which we explain colour-, sound- and smell-words, as well as many measures. Like simples, these samples can be described only by specifying their external properties, not through their internal properties. But what this amounts to is the lexical indefinability of, for example, colour-terms. What looked like metaphysical atoms are instruments of our form of representation. Samples are simple in that their existence is presupposed, not by language as such, but by particular language-games. Ostensively defined terms would indeed loose their meaning if all possible samples by reference to which they can be explained did not exist. But this does not go towards vindicating (c). While the sense of an empirical proposition must not depend on its *own* truth, it depends on a rule, and the possibility of explaining the rule can depend on the truth of *another* proposition stating the existence of samples, or our ability to use them. *Philosophical Investigations* considers the reply that at least the samples presupposed in ostensive definitions must be indestructible, since otherwise we could not describe a world in which everything destructible is destroyed, which would derogate from the independence of grammar. But from the fact that it is possible to describe such a state of affairs, it does not follow that this must be possible in that state of affairs itself (WVC 43; AWL 120; PG 208–9; BB 31; PI §§48–57).

In consideration (d), (i) is right to claim that the logical implications of propositions should be settled in advance of experience. However, this does not require the existence of sempiternal simples, but only an established pattern of EXPLANATION. Wittgenstein also now criticizes the assumption behind (ii), namely that the sense of a sentence must be DETERMINATE, which itself seems based on the image of a world of distinct facts. But even if it were correct, it would not entail simplicity: the example of the number-line shows that there is no incompatability between determinacy and infinite divisibility. The same applies to (iii): many propositions can fail to be true in either of these ways, without being the worse for it.

The later Wittgenstein ignored a second kernel of truth in the *Tractatus*'s account, namely the idea of non-descriptive referring. Simples were meant to be 'what we can speak about *no matter what may be the case*' (PR 72). If all referring took place through descriptions, it would require that there is one and only one thing satisfying the description. But Donnellan has shown that genuinely referring uses of singular terms do not depend on this condition: one can sometimes refer to a bright young thing as 'the old fool'. However, this requires not simples, but a shared understanding between speaker and hearer about who is meant on this occasion.

operation   *see* GENERAL PROPOSITIONAL FORM; LOGICAL CONSTANTS; NUMBERS; TRUTH-TABLES

ostensive definition   An ostensive definition is an explanation of the meaning of a word as in 'This is an elephant' or 'That colour is called "red".' It typically involves three elements: a demonstrative, 'This is…', 'That is called "…"'; a deictic gesture ☞ (pointing); and a sample, the object pointed at. The expression was first used in Johnson's *Logic* (1921), but the idea itself is much older. There is a venerable position, Wittgenstein called it the AUGUSTINIAN PICTURE OF LANGUAGE, according to which language has a hierarchical structure. Some expressions are 'definables', that is, they can be explained through lexical definitions. However, such definitions only connect the definiendum with other words, the definiens. Hence it seems that there must be 'indefinables', simple expressions which are the terminus of lexical definitions and must be connected with objects in reality through some kind of ostension (BB 1). This picture is prominent in Locke (*An Essay concerning Human Understanding* III.4), where the objects are mental – 'simple ideas', and a similar picture is at work in Russell, for whom logically proper NAMES stand for individuals with which we are acquainted.

The *Tractatus* is equally committed to the idea that names, the simple constituents of propositions which cannot be analytically defined, stand in a one-to-one correlation to simple objects. How, precisely, this correlation is effected is left for psychology to determine. What is clear is that names are related to objects directly, without the mediation of descriptions. Consequently, names cannot be explained through definitions. But they can be explained through 'elucidations ... propositions which already contain the primitive signs. So they can only be understood if the meanings of those signs are already known' (TLP 3.263). This is puzzling, because the meaning of a primitive sign will be explained through the employment of a proposition containing it, which itself can only be understood if one understands the term explained. Perhaps the point is that we learn the meaning of names by learning how to employ them in propositions. Accordingly, elucidations would simply be elementary propositions in which the name occurs. But this is incompatible with the idea that names, *unlike* propositions, need to be explained and given meaning in the first instance (TLP 4.026–4.03). Moreover, although Wittgenstein's early work does not mention ostensive definition, it intimates that the METHOD OF PROJECTING names onto objects consists of acts of ostension, of meaning *this*. Accordingly, in line with a suggestion by Russell (*Principia* 91), elucidations are propositions of the form 'This is A' which explain by describing.

That, at any rate, was Wittgenstein's view after his return to philosophy. His discussions with the Vienna Circle seem partly responsible for their interest in ostensive definitions. For the logical positivists, ostensive definitions were a means of injecting empirical content into a formal, uninterpreted calculus (e.g. *Papers* I 219–20). Wittgenstein moved in the opposite direction. Commenting on Waismann's attempt to summarize the *Tractatus*, he denied that an ostensive definition (*hinweisende Erklärung*) provides a 'connection between language and reality', and later claimed that for this reason 'language remains self-contained and autonomous' (WVC 209–10, 246; PG 97; AWL 87). This is a startling claim. But Wittgenstein does not deny that we, for the most part, talk about language-independent things; he denies only that the latter constitute the meanings of our words, and hence that there are *semantic* connections between language and world. Empirical propositions refer to language-independent items and are verified or falsified by the way things are. But this distinguishes them from ostensive definitions. One must distinguish the use of a sentence of the form 'This is A' to make an empirical statement from its employment in giving an ostensive definition (PR 54–5; PG 88). The latter does not 'describe' the object pointed at as A, either truly or falsely, but defines what counts as being A. An ostensive definition cannot simultaneously be a description, just as the juxtaposition of a ruler with a rod cannot simultaneously constitute a measurement of the rod and a calibration of the ruler. From this perspective, the elucidations of the *Tractatus* are a logical mongrel between an ostensive definition of a name 'A', and an empirical proposition employing that name to depict a state of affairs.

Ostensive definitions have the same normative function as other types of GRAMMATICAL explanation. They determine what counts as the correct application of signs. For this reason, they are part of grammar (*Sprachlehre*), not of the empirical application of language. More precisely, they function as substitution rules which license the substitution of a demonstrative together with a gesture indicating a sample for the definiendum. They specify that anything which is *this* can be characterized as being *A*. An ostensive definition of red, for example, entitles one to pass from 'My bike is this☞ colour' to 'My bike is red' (PR 78; PG 88–91, 202; BB 12, 85–90, 109). Language remains autonomous because the samples used in ostensive definitions are part of grammar (PI §16; PR 73). This claim does not amount to a stipulative extension of the concept of language. Rather, it reminds us of the fact that samples function as standards for the correct use of words, and thus have a normative role analogous to that of grammatical propositions. We explain 'Red is this☞ colour', and subsequently criticize misapplications of the term by reference to the sample we pointed at.

The normative role of samples also lies behind Wittgenstein's claim that the standard metre cannot be said to be (or not to be) one metre long (PI §50). *Qua* sample, the object belongs to the means of representation and cannot be described in empirical propositions. One and the same object may function now as a sample, now as an object described as having the defined property; but the normative and the empirical roles are mutually exclusive inasmuch as what functions as a norm of description cannot simultaneously be described as falling under that norm; it might be the subject of a subsequent measurement, but not as long as it is a canonical sample, as was the case with the standard metre bar. Consequently, Kripke was right to claim that the standard metre – this particular rod – might have had a length other than one metre, but wrong to conclude that it therefore makes sense to state the length of the standard metre in metres, as long as that unit of measurement is defined by reference to that rod. What one can say is that the rod which actually served as the standard metre might not be used as a canonical sample, which opens up the possibility of measuring it, but against a *different* standard.

Wittgenstein also uses ostensive definition to resolve a puzzle which exercised the logical positivists, namely of how to explain the necessary status of statements like 'Nothing can simultaneously be red and green all over', or 'Black is darker than white' (RFM 75–6). Such propositions cannot be derived from explicit definitions and the laws of logic alone, that is, they are not analytic. But neither are they synthetic a priori descriptions of the essential natures of colours. Rather, they are rules for the use of COLOUR-words which are part of our practice of explaining and applying these words by reference to samples. Their necessity amounts to this: what we employ as a sample of red we do not employ as a sample of green; and a black patch may serve not only to explain what 'black' means, but also, in conjunction with a white patch, as an explanation of what 'darker than' means.

Even if one accepts that samples are part of grammar, it is natural to suppose that ostensive definitions of 'indefinables' provide the ultimate explanations of our words, and thereby the foundations of language. Wittgenstein rejects this claim (BB 1; BT 256–7; *see* AUTONOMY OF LANGUAGE). For one thing, whether something functions as a sample is not a matter of its essential nature, but of human choice. Samples determine the meaning of signs only because we use them as standards of correctness. What determines the correct use of the explanandum is not the sample, but the way we use it for the purpose of explanation and correction. For another, not all words can be defined ostensively, for example not 'today', 'not', 'but' or 'perhaps' (BB 77), not to mention 'relic' or 'justice'.

Moreover, ostensive definitions do not provide an *inexorable* grounding of our words (PI §§27–36; LPP 427). 'An ostensive definition can be variously interpreted in *every* case' (PI §28). There are several reasons for this. (a) The deictic gesture can be misunderstood completely – thus a pupil might react as cats do, namely look at one's hand rather than in the direction pointed (PI §185). (b) An ostensive definition requires a stage-setting, the logico-grammatical 'post' or category of the definiendum must be known (PI §§30–1, 257), that is, it must be clear whether we are pointing at a colour, a length, a shape, a number, etc. (c) We need a method of application: acquaintance with its bearer counts for nothing, unless we master the general use of a word, since the use of a word does not flow from the object pointed at (*see* MEANING-BODY). A single connection can justify divergent patterns of behaviour (PG 80). In this respect Wittgenstein has been supported by Quine. However, for Quine ostensive definitions play only a causal role in language acquisition by establishing dispositions to verbal behaviour. For Wittgenstein, they have a continuing normative role in guiding our practice. The normative trajectory of an ostensive correlation is established by a practice of correction and justification by reference to the sample.

The impossibility of providing mental equivalents for these features, especially for (c), rules out the possibility of private ostensive definitions, and hence of a PRIVATE LANGUAGE. By a similar token, Augustine is wrong to suppose that language acquisition is merely a matter of establishing a mental association between word and object, since this presupposes the possession of a degree of linguistic understanding, because of (b). At the same time, there is a kernel of truth in the idea that ostensive definitions are primary. To someone who is ignorant of either term, the explanation ' "Carnadine" means "red" ' is less useful than 'Carnadine is this colour' (PG 89–90; RPP I §609), precisely because the latter provides him with a sample for the application of the term. More importantly, ostension is an essential ingredient of the basic linguistic training which precedes full-blown EXPLANATIONS, whether ostensive or lexical. This is no coincidence, since we need to present the child with paradigms to which the words apply, and often teach words through direct exemplification ('That's☞ a banana').

This point is not necessarily inimical to Wittgenstein's account. Wittgenstein stressed that the fact that ostensive definitions can be misunderstood does not mean that they are illegitimate, since this does not set them apart from other kinds of definitions. Indeed, Wittgenstein argued that ostensive definitions can be applied to a greater range of terms than is generally acknowledged, including numerals (PI §§28–9). Furthermore, some expressions, notably colour-terms, can be defined only ostensively (something similar holds for smells, tastes, textures and sounds). This marks a kernel of truth in the *Tractatus*'s myth that indestructible OBJECTS are presupposed by language. Such terms can be explained only if suitable samples exist. One could point at a green object and say, 'This is not red.' But this is not an ostensive definition of either 'red' or 'not red' (PG 89–92, 136; PI 14n; BT 49–51), since such a green object cannot be used as an object of comparison which would license our saying of, say, yellow or blue things that they are not red. If all red objects suddenly turned green, the term 'red' would not lose its meaning straightaway, as the *Tractatus* had it. But the technique of applying it in, for example, 'Remember those red sunsets?' would slowly die out. Such observations suggest that contemporary truth-conditional theories of meaning are wrong simply to ignore ostensive definitions, which they do in spite of the fact that their axioms relate individual constants to objects ('a' refers to a). This means that they leave unexplained what it is for a singular term or name to stand for an object.

overview (*Übersicht*) Wittgenstein's use of this term and its cognates has been variously rendered (e.g., as 'survey' or 'surview'), and this has cloaked the pervasiveness and importance of the concept in his work. The need for surveyability (*Übersichtlichkeit*) of first principles was announced by Frege. But Wittgenstein's idea that an overview of grammar provides a remedy for philosophical confusion is inspired more by Hertz, who held that problems concerning concepts like force are not to be answered by providing new scientific information or definitions, but to be dissolved by a clearer understanding of existing information and definitions (*Mechanics*, Introd.). Boltzmann suggests, furthermore, that such dissolution is to be achieved by a system in which the analogies or models that underlie science are presented in a surveyable fashion (*Physics* 5–6, 75, 167).

Wittgenstein first introduced the term in the context of methodological reflections on ANTHROPOLOGY (GB 130–3). He claimed that the collection of facts concerning rituals around the world in Frazer's *Golden Bough* provides not the genetic explanation of the King of Nemi ritual which Frazer sought, but instead a different kind of illuminating synopsis of the data. He contrasts the method of 'developmental hypothesis' with two other ways of assembling the data, namely providing a 'schema', and arranging the facts in a 'perspicuous representation'. Both are part of the 'morphological method' of Goethe and Spengler (MS110 256; PLP ch. IV). Goethe's plant-morphology uses a fictional primordial plant as an archetype by reference to which the morphology of all plants can be understood. Spengler emulates Goethe by comparing cultural epochs to families and claiming that cultures have archetypal life-cycles. While Wittgenstein acknowledges Spengler's influence, he accuses him of dogmatism (CV 14–19, 26–7). Instead of insisting that cultures must conform to his scheme, he should have treated these 'archetypes' (*Urbilder*) or 'ideals' (*Vorbilder*) as 'objects of comparison': they do not characterize the phenomena but determine a possible scheme for viewing them.

What is common to these thinkers is the idea that there are forms of understanding other than the causal explanation of the deductive-nomological sciences; and that one can shed light on a diverse multitude of phenomena without discovering anything new, by arranging what is already known in a way which clarifies the links or interconnections. Wittgenstein thought of this methodological idea as a world-view competing with the scientistic one. He applied it to AESTHETICS (LC 29) and MATHEMATICS. But his main use of it is in philosophical methodology.

A main source of our failure to understand is that we do not survey (*übersehen*) the use of our words. Our grammar is lacking in perspicuity (*Übersichtlichkeit*). A perspicuous representation (*übersichtliche Darstellung*) produces this understanding which consists in 'seeing connections'. Hence the importance of finding and inventing *intermediate cases*. The concept of a perspicuous representation is of fundamental significance for us. It earmarks our form of representation, the way we look at things. (Is this a 'Weltanschauung'?) (PI §122; see GB 133; BT 417; PR Pref.; CV 7; *see also* FORM OF REPRESENTATION)

This idea is heir to the *Tractatus*'s vision of the 'correct logical point of view' (TLP 4.1213). Both provide remedies for our 'failure to understand' grammar or LOGICAL SYNTAX (the rules of language) and hence for the resulting philosophical confusions. The *Tractatus* tried to achieve this aim by an ideal notation which provides a perspicuous representation of the logical forms of propositions without SAYING anything about them, namely through the graphic means of TRUTH-TABULAR notation (TLP 4.31, 5.101, 6.1203). However, to represent a proposition in this notation presupposes that it has been analysed. While LOGICAL ANALYSIS delves beneath the appearances of language, the later Wittgenstein seeks a correct logical point of view by logical geography rather than logical geology (AWL 43; LFM 44). Grammatical rules are not hidden, but lie open to view in our linguistic practice (*see* CALCULUS MODEL). However, they are not perspicuous (PR 51; PI §122). Although as competent speakers we have mastered the grammar of our language, we are prone to misunderstand, distort or ignore certain differences between expressions, or logical connections between propositions, in the course of philosophical reflection.

Wittgenstein detects various roots of such philosophical confusion: (a) phenomenological features both of language-use, where we associate familiar words with specific feelings (*see* ASPECT-PERCEPTION) and mistakenly conclude that they constitute the meanings of these words (PI II 174–6, 181–3, 214), and of solitary philosophical reflection, for example, a tendency to focus manically on a particular phenomenon to the exclusion of others (PI §§38, 593); (b) a 'craving for generality' (BB 17–18) which inclines us towards a uniform account of FAMILY-RESEMBLANCE concepts such as 'proposition'; (c) the emulation of science which makes us try to answer problems (e.g., the mind/body problem) through explanatory theories instead of dissolving them through grammatical reminders; (d) the mesmerizing influence of inclinations of reason, notably the 'quest for the unconditioned' (Kant), the tendency to dig ever deeper or to look for a reality behind the phenomena without recognizing when to stop (Z §314; RFM 102–3; RPP I §889); (e) analogies in the surface GRAMMAR of logically distinct expressions (e.g., between numerals and names, or 'speaking' and 'meaning'); (f) the tendency to project features of one language-game onto another (e.g., of discourse about material objects onto our psychological idiom); (g) pictures embedded in language (e.g., that things go on 'in our heads').

Wittgenstein claimed that a whole 'mythology' is laid down in our language (GB 133; BT 433–5; PI §§422–6; OC §90; MS110 184). He ascribed this idea to Paul Ernst, but the term itself occurs rather in Nietzsche, who preceded Wittgenstein in claiming that grammatical structures may mislead us into metaphysical illusions (*The Wanderer and his Shadow* §11; *Beyond Good and Evil* §§16–34). Such mythologies may be harmless or even fruitful in non-philosophical discourse, but need to be checked in philosophy, since they obscure conceptual connections. To curb these temptations, an 'overview' presents a segment of grammar pertinent to a given philosophical problem in a detailed and perspicuous way (PI §122). It is an enumeration or arrangement of grammatical rules/propositions.

Recently, this interpretation has been challenged on the grounds that, in spite of this professed importance, there is only one labelled instance of a perspicuous representation in Wittgenstein's *oeuvre*, namely the colour-octahedron, which is characterized as a '*perspicuous* representation of grammar' (PR 51–2). The solution of the problem is thought to lie in the idea that perspicuous representations do not consist of grammatical propositions which could take the place of grammatical explanations, but are 'second-order' descriptions of grammatical rules. The colour-octahedron does not lay down rules for the use of colour-words, it depicts these rules. Accordingly, there is no dearth of perspicuous representations: any description of grammar qualifies, and so do the simple language-games which Wittgenstein used as 'objects of comparison'.

However, while an object of comparison (archetype, ideal) may contribute to the provision of a perspicuous representation, it cannot constitute one by itself, because it is supposed to 'throw light on the facts of our language by way not only of similarities, but also of dissimilarities' (PI §§130–1, see §§2–21; BB 77–9; CV 14, 26–7): we cannot represent the rules of chess through describing draughts, although the latter may help us to understand the former. The idea that perspicuous representations are on a different level from grammatical propositions is equally untenable. 'The colour-octahedron *is* grammar, since it tells us that we can speak of a reddish blue, but not of a reddish green, etc.' (PR 75; see LWL 8). This means that perspicuous representations do consist of grammatical propositions (not of 'second-order' descriptions).

One might nevertheless insist that for Wittgenstein there can be incompatible ways of articulating grammatical rules which are of equal merit. The purpose of a perspicuous representation is not to display grammar as it is, but to bring about a Gestalt-switch by highlighting a new aspect of the use of our words. Perspicuous representations do not purport to be exclusive or even correct, they aim only to remove the influence of certain disquieting aspects of grammar, in the hope of allaying philosophical puzzlement: 'Look at it this way . . . , if that doesn't calm you down, look at it that way . . .' The consequence of such grammatical aspect-perception is a philosophical relativism prominent in Waismann, who claimed that philosophy should proceed through developing 'grammatical models', invented language-games (PLP ch. IV). The idea is not to make statements about the 'reality of language', but to let these models speak for themselves. We place them next to ordinary language and say 'Just look at that!' No one can agree or disagree with this procedure, since these models do not assert anything.

However, Waismann (*How I see Philosophy*) developed these ideas in opposition to Wittgenstein. The latter recognized that an overview establishes 'an order' in our understanding of language which is purpose-relative (namely to the resolution of specific problems), not '*the* order' (PI §132; TS220 §107). There are different articulations of the same grammatical rules – the colour-octahedron could be replaced by a list of combinatorial rules ('There is no such thing as a reddish green; there is such a thing as bluish green, etc.'). And some of them may use different objects of comparison. But none of this implies that there is no fact of the matter as to what the grammatical rules are or what it makes sense to say. Indeed, Wittgenstein's complaint against dogmatism is that it distorts our 'actual language' (PI §107) by projecting onto it features of the object of comparison. This presupposes that one can fail to do justice to the grammatical facts. The reply to the dogmatic 'This is how it has to be!' is 'Look and see' the 'application of a word as it really is' – not to make one up by concocting grammatical models (PI §§66, 112; MS111 82). The alternative to dogmatism is not relativism, but 'the quiet weighing of linguistic facts' (Z §447).

The notion of an overview suggests that there is a sense in which Wittgensteinian philosophy can be systematic. Indeed, Wittgenstein provided two different 'classifications of psychological concepts' (RPP I §895; RPP II §§63, 148; Z §472). He also envisaged a 'genealogical tree' (*Stammbaum*) for them – as for number concepts, presumably as a way of showing how, for example, the system of natural numbers can be extended into that of signed integers (RPP I §722; *see* PHILOSOPHICAL PSYCHOLOGY). These overviews do not aspire to 'precision'. But Wittgenstein envisaged a 'complete overview of everything which can create unclarity' (Z §§273, 464). This need not mean that there is a 'totality' or 'complete list of rules' for our language: the notion of '*all* rules' is dubious even for a single term, since clear criteria of identity exist only for codified rules (e.g., those of chess) (MS157a 108; TS220 92). But it suggests that overviews of particular segments of grammar can be as comprehensive as one pleases.

Accordingly, there can be progress in mapping conceptual landscapes and resolving particular problems. But this is compatible with Wittgenstein's claim that philosophy is open-ended (Z §447; BB 44). Like the expansion of π, philosophy can get better, without ever getting nearer to completion. The reason is that even a global overview of grammar cannot provide a panacea for philosophical puzzles. Firstly, the language in which they are rooted changes, thereby creating new problems, as happened with the development of the new physics, of formal logic and of computers; secondly, there is not a definite number of ways of getting confused. 'There is not *a* philosophical method, though there are indeed methods, like different therapies' (PI §133). Philosophy cannot terminate if, as Kant and Wittgenstein suggest, the fascination with philosophical problems is part of the human condition (BT 422–4). Some passages intimate that this tendency might itself be eradicated by cultural change (RFM 132; CV 86–9). But unlike post-modern prophets of the demise of philosophy such as Rorty, Wittgenstein provides no clues as to what such a change would amount to.

The final question is whether the construction of overviews constitutes a positive aim of Wittgensteinian philosophy. Often Wittgenstein states the aim of philosophy in purely negative terms, namely 'to show the fly the way out of the fly-bottle' by making philosophical problems '*completely* disappear' (PI §§309, 133; see AWL 21; BT 425; CV 43). But why should one do philosophy at all if it only gets rid of errors it itself has created? One answer

282

is that philosophy is of value because of 'the philosopher in us' (TS219 11): the temptation to conceptual confusion is not confined to professional philosophers. But this leaves us with Ryle's famous question of what a fly would miss that never got into the fly-bottle. Here we must appreciate that philosophy should dissolve our urge to ask philosophical questions, not by whatever means (e.g., a knock on the head), but through an understanding of their nature and sources. A fly which never got into the bottle would lack not only the ability to extricate itself from similar holes, a kind of know-how, but also the conceptual clarity which Wittgenstein regarded as an end in itself (PI II 206; PR Pref.; CV 7). Whether one regards a successful overview as interesting in its own right, as Strawson does descriptive metaphysics, or merely as an aspect of philosophical critique is a matter of intellectual temperament. Even if philosophy does not contribute to human knowledge, it contributes to human understanding.

P

phenomenology   *see* VERIFICATIONISM

Philosophical Investigations (*Philosophische Untersuchungen*, 1953)   This is the *summa* of Wittgenstein's later philosophy, just as the *Tractatus* was the *summa* of his early work. Ever since his return to Cambridge in 1929, Wittgenstein had tried to compose a book crystallizing his new ideas. Some 200 remarks of the printed text stem from the 'Big Typescript' of 1933. However, the work which eventually resulted in *Philosophical Investigations* started in 1936–7, after Wittgenstein had abandoned *Eine Philosophische Betrachtung*. Genetically speaking, *Investigations* Part I falls into three parts. The first, §§1–189, stems from the 'Early Version' (TS220). Wittgenstein offered this to Cambridge University Press in 1938, but withdrew it within a month. Subsequently, he made several attempts to complete this trunk. The first addition (TS221, a version of *Remarks on the Foundations of Mathematics* Part I) is contemporaneous with the 'Early Version' and concerns mathematics. The second attempt took place in 1943, when Wittgenstein submitted a (now lost) typescript to the Press. It is probable that it also included a discussion of mathematics, since this was the main topic of Wittgenstein's manuscripts up to 1943. This might explain why the Preface, written in 1945, still mentions 'the foundations of mathematics' as one of the topics discussed. In the third attempt, the 'Intermediate Version' of 1944 (TS242), Wittgenstein replaced the mathematical continuations by §§189–421. The final sections, §§422–693, were added in 1945/6 (from TS228). Wittgenstein undertook minor revisions on up to 1950, and left the book for posthumous publication.

By and large, the *Investigations* avoids the sibylline pronouncements of the *Tractatus*. The prose is lucid and non-technical. Nevertheless, four factors make it difficult to understand (apart from the fact that its content often runs counter to 2,500 years of philosophizing). The first is the aphoristic and often ironic style, which is reminiscent of Lichtenberg and Nietzsche. Wittgenstein's remarks resonate, they provide a trajectory of thought, but leave it to the reader to develop it. Secondly, in sharp contrast to the *Tractatus*, the *Investigations* evolves around a dialogue between Wittgenstein and an interlocutor whose confusions he tries to resolve. This dialogical structure allows Wittgenstein to explore all the temptations and false leads presented by a topic. Usually, the interlocutor's interventions are marked by inverted commas. But one occasionally faces the task of determining who speaks (Wittgenstein or the interlocutor).

Thirdly, the numbered sections lack a linear structure, and there are no formally indicated chapters. The Preface states that Wittgenstein had abandoned his plan of writing a more conventional, textbook-style work (this might refer to the *Blue* and *Brown Books* and *Eine Philosophische Betrachtung*) and claims that the book travels 'over a wide field of thought criss-cross in every direction'. Partly, this is 'connected with the very nature of the investigation', which has to elucidate from various perspectives concepts which are themselves interlinked. But it is also due to a self-acknowledged failure on Wittgenstein's part to rein in his thoughts, which often proceed by leaps and bounds.

Fourthly, the *Investigations* rarely identifies its targets. As a result, some readers have complained that Wittgenstein seems to be exorcizing views no one has ever held. Partly, this is due to his attempt to formulate the fundamental assumptions and pictures which inform whole strands of philosophical thinking. But, like the lack of a linear structure, it is also due to his idiosyncratic method of composition. The *Investigations* is the result of a constant revision of typescripts based on first-draft manuscripts. This involved inserting new remarks copied out from other drafts, pruning away others, rearranging the order of remarks, curtailing particular remarks, and changing specific phrases or words. These processes had a tendency to condense the remarks. The text became stylistically more polished, but often less intelligible. Wittgenstein dropped phrases, explanations or illustrations which are illuminating or even essential for understanding a passage, and have to be reconstructed from the *Nachlass* (e.g. 46n, §§144, 373, 559).

The *leitmotif* which unites the various themes of *Investigations* Part I is language and linguistic representation. This had already been the core of the *Tractatus*, and the Preface states that the book should be seen 'by contrast with and against the background of' the *Tractatus*, which it criticizes for containing 'grave errors'. The book starts with a quotation from Augustine, in which Wittgenstein detects a simple picture that lies behind misconceptions about language since Plato, but which he links in particular with Frege, Russell and the *Tractatus*. Part I ends with a discussion of meaning something, which warns against regarding it as a mental activity or process. Unlike the *Tractatus*, the *Investigations* pursues the connections between linguistic meaning and psychological concepts, notably those of UNDERSTANDING and THOUGHT, and volitional concepts like WILLING and INTENDING AND MEANING SOMETHING. It is mainly for this reason that it turns to issues in the philosophy of mind, such as the private language argument. (These take on a life of their own in the PHILOSOPHICAL PSYCHOLOGY after *Investigations* Part I.)

In spite of its fragmentary appearance, *Investigations* Part I displays more argumentative structure than is commonly assumed. One can even divide it into 'chapters', continuous stretches of text devoted to a specific cluster of issues:

§§1–64: the AUGUSTINIAN PICTURE OF LANGUAGE, notably in the *Tractatus*'s and Russell's logical atomism

§§65–88: the attack on the *Tractatus*'s and Frege's ideal of the DETERMINACY OF SENSE

§§89–133: the nature of PHILOSOPHY, and LOGIC'S quest for an ideal language

§§134–42: the GENERAL PROPOSITIONAL FORM and the nature of TRUTH

§§143–84: linguistic understanding and the concept of reading

§§185–242: RULE-FOLLOWING and the FRAMEWORK of language

§§243–315: the PRIVATE LANGUAGE ARGUMENT

§§316–62: thought and thinking

§§363–97: IMAGINATION and mental images

§§398–411: the first-person pronoun 'I' and the nature of the self

§§412–27: CONSCIOUSNESS

§§428–65: INTENTIONALITY – the harmony between language and reality

§§466–90: INDUCTION and the justification of empirical BELIEFS

§§491–546: GRAMMAR and the bounds of sense

§§547–70: IDENTITY and difference of linguistic MEANING

§§571–610: mental states and processes: expectation, belief

§§611–28: the will

§§629–60: intending

§§661–93: meaning something.

Part II of *Philosophical Investigations* (TS234) is part of the work on philosophical psychology which preoccupied Wittgenstein after the completion of *Investigations* Part I. On the basis of conversations with Wittgenstein in 1948, the editors of the *Investigations* report that Wittgenstein intended to suppress a good deal of §§491–693, and to work into its place material from Part II. But although these parts of Part I are less polished than the preceding sections, it is not easy to see how they could have been supplemented by material from Part II, or how the latter could have been grafted onto Part I. Wittgenstein never made any attempts to do so, and in many respects Part II, especially the discussion of ASPECT-PERCEPTION, moves off in fresh directions.

philosophical psychology Themes from philosophical psychology – intentionality, thinking, understanding – play an important role in Wittgenstein's later work because of their connection with linguistic meaning. However, he also had an intrinsic interest in psychology (in 1912 he conducted experiments on the psychology of music), and after 1943 his main work was in philosophical psychology, independently of its connection with language.

One important cue for his discussion of the nature of psychology and of psychological concepts in *Remarks on the Philosophy of Psychology* was provided by Köhler's *Gestalt Psychology*, which he read in 1947. Köhler explained the difficulties of psychology by reference to its being a 'young science', which still has to follow physics in replacing qualitative observation by quantitative measurement. Wittgenstein rejected this diagnosis (PI II 232; RPP I §§1039, 1093). The difficulties of psychology are akin to those of set theory rather than infant physics. They are due not to an absence of adequate instrumentation, a lack of quantitative concepts or a deficiency of mathematical technique, but to conceptual confusion. Although Wittgenstein denied that there *must* be a universal parallelism between the mental and the physical (*see* CAUSATION; INNER/OUTER), he does not reject experimental psychology or the study of the neurophysiological causes and prerequisites of mental phenomena and abilities. His point is that the experimental methods 'pass by' the philosophical problems, and that the latter can impede genuine advances in psychology.

Köhler preceded eliminative materialism in envisaging the possibility of replacing our ordinary psychological statements and concepts by neurophysiological ones. Wittgenstein could have no qualms about empirical psychology introducing technical terms like 'unconditioned reflex'. However, he would insist that this will not solve the philosophical problems arising from our ordinary psychological concepts (*see* METALOGIC). Moreover, for the most part 'the concepts of psychology are just everyday concepts ... not concepts newly fashioned by science for its own purpose, as are the concepts of physics and chemistry.' But in any case, ordinary language does not contain a primitive *theory* ('folk psychology') which has been superseded by science, as eliminative materialism has it, but only *concepts* like thinking, perceiving, imagining (RPP II §62; Z §223). These concepts do not incorporate a theory, since they do not predict anything and can be neither true nor false. Instead, they are presupposed by empirical theories and define the topics of psychology. In order to establish correlations between, for example, perception and neurophysiological processes, it must be clear what counts as the subject's perceiving something, which is determined by the GRAMMAR of common-or-garden terms like 'seeing' and 'hearing'. We can modify our psychological concepts, and have done so (e.g., by incorporating the Freudian idea of the unconscious). Nevertheless, Wittgenstein complains that it is unclear what sorts of discoveries would make possible Köhler's envisaged replacement (MS130 1.8.46). Moreover, even if we can establish pervasive correlations between mental and physical phenomena, we could not abandon our mental concepts in favour of neurophysiological ones without ceasing to be human. Although we employ these concepts *inter alia* to explain

287

human behaviour, such explanations are not CAUSAL like those of the nomo-logical sciences, but teleological. If we explained human behaviour as neces-sitated by efficient causes, we would no longer treat it as intentional action, which presupposes that the subject is guided by reasons. Moreover, unlike neurophysiological concepts, our psychological concepts are not exclusively or even primarily used to explain, predict and control behaviour. Their functions are as diverse as human life (RPP II §35): we use them to express our thoughts, emotions and attitudes, to commiserate, encourage, condemn. These functions are essential to our life, and none of them could be served by neurophysiological concepts.

Another inspiration for Wittgenstein's philosophical psychology was James's encyclopaedic *Principles of Psychology*, which he regarded as a 'rich source' of philosophical problems and confusions (MS124 291; MS165 150–1). In contrast to Köhler's reductionism, James was a follower of Wundt's introspective psychology. He treated introspection as an unproblematic 'looking into one's own mind', although he diverged from the Cartesian tra-dition by admitting it to be fallible. As a result, he tried to establish the nature of experience, thinking and the self through observing his own 'stream of thought', that is, the sequence of his mental episodes (*Psychology* I 185–90, 301, ch. IX). James represents what Wittgenstein called 'the old conception' of psychology as a science which observes objects, states and processes 'in the psychical sphere, as does physics in the physical'. But this parallel is, he thought, misleading. Whereas the physicist observes the phe-nomena he explains, the psychologist observes the *behavioural expressions* of the mind (PI §571; TS229 §1360). According to Wittgenstein's attack on the INNER/OUTER picture of the mind as a private realm concealed to others, this does not mean that the subject has a more direct access to mental phenom-ena by means of introspection. First-person present tense psychological state-ments are typically AVOWALS, not descriptions or reports based on observation, fallible or infallible. Moreover, inner and outer are inextricably linked. *Pace* mentalism, third-person psychological propositions can be based on what people do and say, since characteristic forms of behaviour are CRITERIA of the mental. *Pace* behaviourism, we do not infer such propositions from descriptions of mere bodily movement but describe human behaviour *ab initio* in mental terms.

Even without the idea that the mind is PRIVATE, known only to the sub-ject, the introspectionist method is awry. In line with the empiricist tradition, it reduces all mental phenomena to mental episodes, things which cross our mind, like feelings, sensations, images and words. In line with Kant, Witt-genstein criticized 'the reduction of everything to sensations or images' and the temptation to 'hypostatize feelings where there are none' (LPP 80; PI §598). Intentional verbs like THINKING, BELIEVING or WILLING do not signify *phenomena*, goings-on or states which could be detected by me, or God, looking into my mind (PI II 217; Z §471; RPP II §§3, 31–5, 75–7, 130–3; LW II 17–18, 74–6). The only describable 'happenings' which are relevant to the meaning of these verbs involve overt behaviour; they do not signify mental or neurophysiological activities, processes or states.

Wittgenstein advances two arguments in favour of this claim. One is that inner goings-on are neither necessary nor sufficient for INTENDING AND MEANING SOMETHING. The other is that mentalists and materialists have misapplied such categorial terms to the mental. There are mental activities (e.g., calculating in the head), events (e.g., hearing a gunshot) and processes ('undergoings') (e.g., having mental images or impressions), and 'mental states' or 'states of consciousness' (e.g., moods – anxiety, fear, cheerfulness – or occurrent emotions). But there is a 'category difference' between these phenomena and intentional attitudes (Z §86, see §§72–85; PI 59n, §§165, 308, 339, 572–3; RPP I §§648, 836; RPP II §§43–57, 63, 148). Intentional attitudes are not acts or activities, since most of them are not subject to the will (one cannot decide to, or order others to, believe or intend something) and even those which might be, like meaning something, cannot be performed more or less successfully (PI §§674–81; Z §§51–2). Nor are they non-voluntary events or processes: they cannot occur, take place or go on in time, or be slowed down, reversed or left unfinished. For example, it makes no sense to say '*While* I meant...', referring to a particular period of time. And although '*When* I said "Napoleon", I meant the victor of Austerlitz' refers to a particular time, namely that of the original utterance, nothing need have gone on at that time over and above the utterance (PG 103).

Although from the point of view of school-grammar, intentional verbs are static rather than progressive, they do not signify states. States are things one is in, but I am not currently in a state of intending to go to London or of believing that Napoleon was impetuous. At any given time, I believe or intend indefinitely many things, but I am not in indefinitely many different mental states. Wittgenstein's opponents might respond that they use 'mental state' as a technical term, to refer to all mental phenomena. But according to Wittgenstein, intentional attitudes differ from real 'states of consciousness' by virtue of lacking what he calls 'genuine duration' (Z §§45–7, 81–2; RPP I §836; RPP II §45). This means that they

(a)   cannot take a course, that is, unfold in different ways;
(b)   cannot be spot-checked or observed continuously;
(c)   cannot be clocked by a stop-watch;
(d)   are neither interrupted by a break of consciousness or a shift of attention, nor endure continuously.

This verdict can be questioned. Concerning (a) and (b), one can point out that intentions can be more or less strong, that is, possess an observable dimension along which they can vary without losing their identity. But arguably this is not an inherent property of the intention, analogous to the persistence or intensity of a feeling, but concerns rather the manner in which one cleaves to it. One might hold against (c) that we can measure the time between the inception of an intention and its lapse, or realization. But it is implausible to hold that all intentions or beliefs can be clocked in this way. Moreover, according to (d), even those which can, lack other temporal qualities of states. My belief that Napoleon was impetuous has not lasted continuously for ten years, but nor has it lapsed every time I have fallen asleep only to be resumed on waking. One can believe something inter-mittently. Yet this is not to be interrupted in one's believing – as one's state of anxiety may be interrupted by distractions – but to vacillate in one's beliefs. It has been objected that (d) uses the notion of a state of conscious-ness, and hence cannot, without circularity, demarcate such states from intentional attitudes. But the point is simply that a state is something which can be interrupted, whereas intentional attitudes cannot. Wittgenstein's demarcation can be upheld only if all these different features are brought to bear.

Accordingly, we cannot establish the essence of, for example, thinking by watching ourselves while we think. The essence of mental phenomena, those features which they could not fail to possess, is determined by GRAMMAR, the rules for the correct use of mental terms. And in the case of many mental terms these rules do not even refer to anything which crosses our mind. Therefore philosophy should analyse mental concepts not through introspec-tion, but by describing the use of words (PI §§314–16, 371–3, 383–4).

Later, Wittgenstein envisaged a 'genealogical tree' which would show how different types of psychological concepts add new joints (types of moves) to our language-games. He also tried to provide a classification of psychological concepts or phenomena which, while not necessarily precise, would provide a philosophically illuminating OVERVIEW (RPP I §§722, 836, 895; Z §464). This classification suggests that psychological verbs are characterized by first/third-person asymmetry, and can be treated as referring to mental epi-sodes or experiences (*Erlebnisse*).

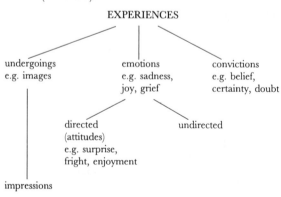

EXPERIENCES

undergoings	emotions	convictions
e.g. images	e.g. sadness,	e.g. belief,
	joy, grief	certainty, doubt

directed   undirected
(attitudes)
e.g. surprise,
fright, enjoyment

impressions

Convictions like belief, certainty or doubt lack genuine duration. Undergoings (images and impressions) have both genuine duration and intensity. Emotions have duration, a typical mimetic expression, but lack a bodily location (unlike sensations). They colour our thoughts – one can think sadly or anxiously.

This classification is problematic: the categories are not clearly demarcated; treating experiences as the *summa genera* is incompatible with the denial that convictions are goings-on; and first/third-person asymmetry does not characterize all the terms we usually classify as mental, notably not dispositional ones like 'neurotic' or 'intelligent'. Wittgenstein's second attempt (RPP II §§63, 148) is more promising.

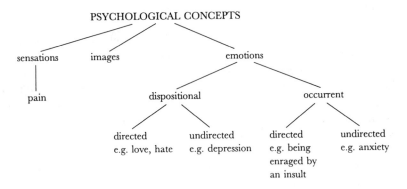

The former category of undergoings (*Erfahrungen*) is divided into 'sensations' (*Sinnesempfindungen*), which have genuine duration, admit of simultaneous occurrence, degrees and qualitative mixtures, and inform us about the material world, and 'images', which do not and are subject to the will. Emotions are characterized by genuine duration and typical feelings. They are divided into directed emotional dispositions (e.g., loving or hating), undirected emotional dispositions (e.g., depression), undirected occurrent emotions (e.g., anxiety) and directed occurrent emotions (e.g., being enraged by an insult).

This classification incorporates important insights, but is still inadequate. It fails to distinguish between sensations and perceptions, even though the former but, following Wittgenstein, not the latter have a location in the body. And its categories do not accommodate thinking, consciousness or volition. Although such defects might be overcome, there is a seemingly insuperable difficulty. Even if the domain of the psychological can be demarcated, psychological concepts will not form a neat Porphyrian tree, as long as they are characterized along different parameters.

Wittgenstein neither explicitly renounced the idea of such a typology, nor did he make further attempts to perfect it. Instead, he tried to clarify the logical category of mental concepts by distinguishing them from each other individually, through various parameters, for example according to whether or not they have duration, an occurrent quality, phenomenal properties, degrees, a characteristic behavioural or verbal expression, require a historical context, are subject to the will. He continued to characterize psychological terms through the first/third-person asymmetry. But he also warns that categorial terms like 'act', 'event', 'state' or 'process' do not provide a sharply defined basis for philosophical psychology. 'These extremely general terms have an extremely blurred meaning. They relate in practice to innumerable special cases, but that does not make them any *solider*; no, it rather makes them more fluid.' Squeezing psychological concepts into categorial pigeon-holes leads only to distortion (RPP I §§257, 648; MS167 6).

philosophy No philosopher since Kant has thought as hard about the nature of the subject as Wittgenstein. His interest goes back to 1912, when he gave a paper 'What is Philosophy?' In the Preface of the *Tractatus* he claimed to have provided a 'definitive solution' to 'the problems of philosophy'. In 1930 he maintained that his 'new method' of philosophizing was a 'kink' in the 'development of human thought' comparable to the Galilean revolution in science. To the end of his career he insisted that what mattered about his work was not its specific results but its new way of philosophizing, a method or skill which would enable us to fend for ourselves (M 113–14; PI II 206; MS155 73–4; ML 17.6.41). Wittgenstein was right to think of his methodological views as novel and radical. They run up not just against the scientific spirit of the twentieth century (CV 6–7) but against the whole history of philosophy. Ever since its inception, philosophy has been regarded as akin to science in being a cognitive discipline which aspires to provide knowledge about reality. For Platonists, philosophy is an a priori discipline which describes not empirical reality, but a world of abstract entities, and grounds our knowledge by deducing all truths from ultimate principles. For Aristotelians, it is continuous with the special sciences because it describes more-general features of reality – it is either the queen of the sciences or their underlabourer, removing obstacles from their path. (Radical empiricists (Mill, Quine) contend, furthermore, that all disciplines, including philosophy, mathematics and logic, describe reality on the basis of empirical evidence.)

Kant's 'Copernican Revolution' challenged this consensus. He claimed that philosophy should be 'occupied not so much with objects as with the mode of our knowledge of objects' (B25). While science describes reality, philosophy is not concerned with objects of any kind, not even the abstract entities postulated by Platonism. Instead, it reflects on the preconditions of our knowing or experiencing the objects of the material world. Yet, in spite of his reflective turn, Kant insisted that philosophy results in true (synthetic a priori) propositions, those which express necessary preconditions of experience, and to that extent remains within the cognitivist tradition.

The early Wittgenstein stands in the tradition of Kant's critical philosophy. Firstly, both he and Kant hold that philosophy is primarily a critical activity which curbs the excesses of metaphysics and clarifies non-philosophical thoughts (TLP 4.112, 6.53; A11, 735, 851). Secondly, inspired by Schopenhauer and Hertz, he draws a Kantian contrast between science, which pictures or represents the world, and philosophy, which reflects on the nature and preconditions of this representation (TLP 4.11ff.). This contrasts sharply with Frege and Russell. Frege never propounded a general conception of philosophy, but his views on the nature of logic and mathematics imply that in these two areas philosophy is a science of abstract entities. Russell, throughout his evolutions, held fast to the 'scientific conception of philosophy', according to which it shares the tasks of science and should emulate its methods. While the early Wittgenstein took over Frege's separation of logic from psychology (TLP 4.1121, 6.3631, 6.423; *Foundations* Introd.; *Laws* I Pref.) and accepted Russell's identification of philosophy and LOGIC (TLP 4.003f.; *External* ch. II; *Mysticism* ch. 8), he argued against both that philosophy/logic describes neither abstract objects nor the most general features of reality, but concerns the essential preconditions of thinking about or representing reality. He modified this Kantian idea in two respects. Firstly, thoughts are intrinsically linked to their linguistic expression, representation is symbolic representation, and its preconditions are linguistic rules – LOGICAL SYNTAX. Secondly, the bounds of sense drawn by philosophy separate not possible knowledge from idle speculation, but meaningful from nonsensical combinations of signs. This has drastic methodological consequences. In his earliest discussion, Wittgenstein had claimed that philosophy consists of logic (its basis) and metaphysics, and that it differs from science in being the 'doctrine of the logical form of scientific propositions' (NL 106). Later, he labels as 'metaphysics' exclusively the illegitimate philosophy of the past. Legitimate philosophy is a 'critique of language'. 'Most of the propositions and questions to be found in philosophical works are not false but nonsensical' (TLP 4.003f., see Pref., 3.323–3.325, 6.51–7; NB 1.5.15, 2.12.16). They stem from the failure to understand the logic of language, a failure which results in the asking of pseudo-questions that admit of no answer. The task of philosophy is not to try to answer these questions but to show that they violate the bounds of sense.

The reason for this sweeping indictment is that philosophy has always striven to uncover necessary truths about the essential nature of the world. But any attempt to state such necessary truths about kinds of things in the world attributes to them formal or INTERNAL properties (e.g., that the essence of matter/mind is extension/thinking, that only what is extended can be coloured, etc.). According to the SAYING/SHOWING distinction, such formal concepts cannot significantly occur in genuine propositions, since what they exclude is not a possibility but a piece of nonsense. The only expressible necessary truths are 'senseless' TAUTOLOGIES; metaphysical propositions would not be BIPOLAR and are therefore nonsensical. But what such pseudo-propositions try to say shows itself in the logico-syntactic features of non-philosophical propositions (e.g., by the fact that all names of coloured things are values of a variable which ranges over extended things).

The propositions of the *Tractatus* employ formal concepts to make claims about the essential features which language must share with reality, hence they are themselves nonsensical (TLP 6.53). The only legitimate task of philosophy is analytic and elucidatory. It neither aims at the discovery of new truths, nor shares the piecemeal methods of the sciences. For there are no 'philosophical propositions'. Philosophy, unlike science, is not a body of doctrine, but an activity of clarifying non-philosophical propositions through logical analysis (TLP 4.112). Its goal is the attainment of a 'correct logical point of view', an understanding of what can be said (viz., empirical propositions), and of its limits. Philosophy sets 'limits to the disputable sphere of science', 'to what cannot be thought by working outwards through what can be thought'. Without propounding any propositions of its own, it clarifies meaningful propositions, and demonstrates that metaphysical propositions violate the rules of logical syntax (TLP 4.112, 4.113ff., 4.1213, 6.53).

Wittgenstein later developed this 'linguistic turn' in a different direction. The core of his method remained the 'transition from the question of truth to the question of meaning' (MS106 46). The connection between philosophy and language is twofold. Firstly, there is an internal connection between THOUGHT and its linguistic expression: philosophy is interested in language because of its 'paramount role in human life' (BT 194–5, 413); HUMAN BEINGS are essentially language-using animals, an idea shared by Aristotelianism and hermeneutics. The second connection, which inspired logical positivism, is that the a priori nature of philosophical problems and propositions is rooted in linguistic rules: 'philosophy is the grammar of the words "must" and "can", for that is how it shows what is a priori and what a posteriori' (CE 411). Philosophy is not a cognitive discipline, but an activity which aims at clarity (LWL 1; AWL 225; RPP I §115). All this remains. But the ineffable metaphysics is dropped, and the mere promise of critical analysis is replaced by a therapeutic practice: philosophy dissolves the conceptual confusions to which philosophical problems are alleged to owe their existence.

This picture seems to impoverish philosophy, and is generally considered to be the weakest part of Wittgenstein's later work – slogans unsupported by argument and belied by his own 'theory construction', which can be isolated from the rest. Wittgenstein's methodological views must ultimately be judged by their results. But it is important to note that they are inextricably inter-woven with the other parts of his work, especially his conception of logical necessity and of language, and that they arise from a coherent line of thought:

(a)   Philosophy differs in principle from the sciences because of its a priori character.

(b)   Because the a priori is to be explained by reference to linguistic rules, it is concerned not with objects but with our way of talking about objects according to 'grammatical rules'.

(c)   These rules are not responsible to an 'essence of reality', therefore philosophy should neither justify nor reform but only describe them.

(d)   As competent speakers we are already familiar with our grammar, but tend to ignore or distort it in philosophical reflection. Hence, describ-ing grammar cannot lead to discoveries or theory construction; it reminds us of how we speak, for the sake of dissolving conceptual confusions.

(e)   This conceptual clarification cannot be systematic or make progress in the way in which science does (*see* METALOGIC; OVERVIEW).

(a) What links Wittgenstein's philosophizing with the metaphysical tradi-tion is that both aim to resolve the problems which constitute the subject-matter of philosophy (PG 193; BT 416, 431; BB 62; Z §447; PLP 5–6). Wittgenstein suggests his 'new method' as a new way of dealing with these problems, one which is superior because it is based on a better under-standing of the character of the problems (LWL 1; AWL 27–8; M 113–14). In the main, the problems concerned are those of theoretical philosophy (logic, metaphysics, epistemology, philosophy of mind) (RW 160; M 105–6; CV 25). Wittgenstein illustrates their peculiar nature by reference to Augus-tine's question 'What is time?' They are a priori, and hence cannot be solved by empirical observation or scientific experiment (AWL 3, 97, 205); their intractable character is itself enigmatic, since they concern not the arcane, but concepts we are familiar with in non-philosophical (everyday and specialized) discourse; indeed, understanding these concepts is a pre-condition of establishing new empirical facts (PI §89, see §§95, 428; BB 30–1; BT 434–5; RPP II §289; Z §452; CV 4). One might protest with Russell that philosophy is a proto-science, dealing with questions not yet amenable to empirical methods (*Problems* 90; *Logic* 281). But the fact that the special sciences developed out of philosophy does not entail that questions which antecede experience are after all empirical. Wittgenstein argues (powerfully) against the attempt to reduce the necessary propositions of logic, mathe-matics and metaphysics to empirical generalizations. This is why he insists against empiricism that philosophy is a priori (LWL 79–80). He has often been accused of engaging in a priori armchair science, but would respond that it is scientistic philosophers who engage in an incoherent discipline – empirical metaphysics.

(b) Wittgenstein's demarcation between philosophy and SCIENCE does not express a form of irrationalism. His prohibition of theories, hypotheses and explanations (PI §§109, 126, 496; RFM 333) bans from philosophy CAUSAL explanations of empirical phenomena, explanations which are irrelevant to the solution of problems that are conceptual rather than factual (Z §458; CV 79). Socratic 'What is X?' questions, in so far as they concern essential rather than contingent features of X, arise not from ignorance about empirical reality or about a Platonist world behind appearances, but from unclarity about GRAMMAR. Therefore, philosophy is not concerned with describing or explaining reality, but with clarifying our FORM OF REPRESENTATION, which lays down what counts as an intelligible description of reality, and, more generally, determines what it makes sense to say.

(c) According to the *Tractatus* there are metaphysical truths about the structures shared by language and reality, but they are ineffable. By contrast, the later Wittgenstein demythologizes metaphysics (LWL 21; MS157(b) 4). It is constitutive of metaphysics that it confuses factual and conceptual issues, scientific theories/hypotheses and norms of representation (Z §458; BB 18,35). Metaphysics claims to establish true propositions about the essence of reality. Its propositions have the form of statements of fact. Science teaches us that no human being can run faster than 40 km/h, or that there is no intra-mercurial planet – the metaphysician that no human being can have the pains of another, Kant that there is no uncaused event. According to Wittgenstein, the pronouncements of such 'descriptive' metaphysics are grammatical rules – often distorted – in propositional disguise (AWL 18, 65–9; WVC 67). 'Every event has a cause' is a grammatical rule which partly determines what counts as an 'event' (*see* CAUSATION). By contrast, 'revisionary metaphysics', such as the solipsist's 'Only my present experiences are real!', is not disguised grammar, but either nonsense or 'expressions of discontent with our grammar' (BB 55–7). Yet, grammar is AUTONOMOUS, not responsible to a putative essence of reality. Consequently, there are no metaphysical grounds for defending or reforming our grammar.

> Philosophy may in no way interfere with the actual use of language; it can in the end only describe it. For it cannot give it any foundation either. It leaves everything as it is. (PI §124)

This dictum does not promote an intellectual quietism: Wittgenstein does not leave *philosophy* as it is, but tries to reveal it as 'plain nonsense' and 'houses of cards' (PI §§118–19; BT 413, 425). Nor does it deny that language changes (PI §18). There are non-philosophical grounds for conceptual change (e.g., in science). The point is that it is not philosophy's business to bring about such reform by introducing an ideal language.

(d) For the *Tractatus*, language must be governed by a '*super*-order' of rules, to be discovered by LOGICAL ANALYSIS. Now Wittgenstein rejects this CALCULUS MODEL as 'dogmatic' (PI §§81, 92, 108, 131). There are no discoveries or surprises in grammar. 'If one tried to advance *theses* in philosophy, it would never be possible to debate them, because everyone would agree to them' (PI §128, see §599). Philosophical remarks are 'homely', 'stale truisms' (TS213 412; MS109 212; TS220 89–90; TS219 6). Indeed, Wittgenstein professes not to rely on 'opinions' anybody could dispute (AWL 97; LFM 22; RFM 160; LC 72). This seems to lead to a dilemma. Either his remarks conform to his 'no opinion'-methodology, then they cannot amount to a genuine contribution to philosophical debate. Or they do not, then his practice belies his stated methodological views – he would be propounding the non-obvious thesis that there are no non-obvious philosophical theses.

Some commentators believe that Wittgenstein opted for incommensurability with the philosophical tradition. According to this 'no position'-position, his work does not contain arguments which satisfy the standards of philosophical discourse. He is not even in the business of attacking traditional positions or correcting philosophical mistakes. His attempts to provide a surview of grammar are therapeutic attempts to make us abandon philosophical questions for the sake of intellectual tranquillity (CV 43). It is correct that Wittgenstein did not take sides in traditional disputes, but rather tried to undermine the assumptions common to the participants – a strategy pioneered by Kant's 'Transcendental Dialectic' and embraced by Ramsey (*Mathematics* 115–16). He also tried to 'dissolve' questions which lead to such misguided alternatives – an idea intimated in the Preface of Moore's *Principia Ethica*. But in doing so, he seeks the 'right question' (see PI §§133, 189, 321; RFM 147; RPP I §600; MS130 107; WAM 27–8). And he did provide answers to Socratic questions like 'What is understanding?', since doing so is a prerequisite of dissolving misguided questions. What he rejects here is merely the insistence that these questions can be answered only by analytic definitions (*see* EXPLANATION). Wittgenstein was fond of comparing his philosophical critique to a kind of psychotherapy (PI §§133, 254–5; BT 407–10; Z §382). Moreover, he occasionally professed to convert us to a new point of view (LC 27–8; CV 61). Nevertheless, his philosophical critique is an argumentative rather than a medical or missionary enterprise; it should provide arguments that are 'absolutely conclusive' (MS161 3; BT 408, 421). Wittgenstein does not rely on 'opinions', because he provides grammatical reminders of how we use words outside philosophy ('It makes sense to say "I know that she has toothache"' or 'A dog cannot be said to believe that its master will return in a week'). Their point is to draw attention to the violation of grammar by philosophers. They are part of a dialectical critique of sense, an 'undogmatic procedure' (WVC 183–6; see PR 54–5; PI §§89–90,

127; BT 419, 424–5; LPP 45; *see also* NONSENSE). Wittgenstein tries to show that his opponents use words according to conflicting rules. Some of his remarks (e.g., 'An "inner process" stands in need of outward criteria' – PI §580) are synoptic descriptions in which grammatical truisms are drawn together and related to a particular philosophical problem. But even they do not function as premises of deductive arguments. Philosophy is 'flat', without the proofs of the deductive-nomological sciences and formal disciplines like mathematics or logic (PI §§126, 599). Deduction establishes the consequences of premises, but a dialectical critique of sense proceeds by *elenchos*, not demonstration: it scrutinizes the meaning of those premises and the intelligibility of the questions.

pictorial relation   *see* METHOD OF PROJECTION

picture theory   The German term *Bild* is ambiguous between paintings and abstract models. 'I have inherited this concept of a picture from two sides: first from a drawn picture, second from the model of a mathematician, which already is a general concept. For a mathematician talks of picturing (*Abbildung*) where a painter would no longer use this expression' (WVC 185). Hertz had claimed that science forms models of reality such that the possible variations of the model faithfully mirror the different possibilities of the physical system in question (*Mechanics* 1). Wittgenstein turned Hertz's brief remarks about scientific representation into a detailed account of the preconditions of symbolic representation in general. 'We picture facts to ourselves' (TLP 2.1). The essence of language – the GENERAL PROPOSITIONAL FORM – lies in depicting how things are. All meaningful propositions are truth-functions of elementary propositions; all logical relations are due to truth-functional composition. By accounting for elementary propositions, the picture theory explains the basis of representation and of logic.

For this purpose, it must solve two major problems. One, which Wittgenstein noted (as did Frege in his latest writings), is now known as the 'creativity of language': the number of propositions is indefinite, although the number of words is finite (NL 98; TLP 4.02, 4.027; 'Compound' 36; *Posthumous* 225, 243; *Correspondence* 79). The other is the venerable puzzle of intentionality, especially of explaining the possibility of falsehood. If a proposition is true, it corresponds to a fact, depicts how things are in the world. But if it is false, it remains nevertheless meaningful, although no fact corresponds to it. Russell's dual-relation theory of judgement fell foul of this puzzle: A's BELIEF that aRb cannot be a dual relation between a subject and an object, for if it is false nothing in reality corresponds to it, which would leave it bereft of meaning (*Problems* 72–3; NL 95). His multiple-relation theory avoids the problem by holding that A is related to, 'acquainted with', the constituents of the proposition, a, R and b, rather than the proposition as a whole. Wittgenstein pointed out that this would allow A to judge a nonsense, since it is no longer guaranteed that these constituents are combined in a meaningful way. Russell tried to pluck the whole by holding that A is acquainted not just with the constituents of the proposition, but also with a LOGICAL FORM $x \Phi y$, a completely general fact. Wittgenstein showed that this conception of logical forms is inconsistent: on the one hand they are facts, that is, complex, on the other they are objects of acquaintance, that is, simple (NL 100–1). The first alternative creates a third-man regress: it explains why a, R and b can combine to form certain facts (aRb, bRa) but not others (RRb, abR) by reference to a further fact. The second simply adds a further constituent to the proposition, without ensuring that its constituents, including the additional one, are combined in a licit way.

When Wittgenstein developed the picture theory out of the ruins of Russell's theory of judgement, several points were already in place. PROPOSITIONS, unlike names, are (a) essentially composite, (b) FACTS: what represents is the fact that the proposition's components are related to each other in a certain way, (c) BIPOLAR: they represent reality not by standing for something, but through depicting, either truly or falsely, how things are. What remained unsolved was the 'mystery of negation': we can say how things are not, and the problem of the possibility of falsehood: a proposition depicts something even if what it depicts does not obtain (NB 15.11.14). Wittgenstein's solution of these puzzles was that what a proposition depicts is a possibility. It does so not with the help of an additional logical form, or of additional relations between its constituents, but simply through the fact that its components are combined in a certain way. The possibility of that combination is guaranteed not by an additional logical form, but by the combinatorial possibilities of the components mirroring those of the things they stand for.

> One name is the representative of one thing, another of another thing and they themselves are connected; in this way the whole images the situation – like a *tableau vivant*... 'The connection must be possible' means: The proposition and the components of the situation must stand in a particular relation ... in order for a proposition to present a state of affairs it is only necesssary for its components to represent those of the situation and for the former to stand in a connection which is possible for the latter. (NB 4.–5.11.14)

For a propositional sign to depict, no fact need correspond to it as a whole. But two things are required. First, something must correspond to its elements. There must be a one-to-one correlation between these elements and the elements of the situation it depicts. Second, it must be determined what relationships between the propositional elements depict what relationships between things. If both are in place, the fact that the elements of the picture are related to each other in a determinate way represents that the corresponding things are related to each other in the same way, whether or not they actually are. To depict falsely is to depict a non-existing combination of existing elements. 'In a proposition a situation is, as it were, assembled by way of experiment' (TLP 4.031f.; NB 20.–21.11.14; BB 31).

Proposition and situation must differ in some respects, and be identical in others (NB 19.–22.10.14). On the one hand, the proposition must make sense independently of whether the situation is actual. On the other, they must share a possibility which is actualized if the proposition is true, and otherwise not. The proposition literally 'contains' that possibility (TLP 2.203, 3.02). It does not contain the content of its sense, the configuration of things it depicts, but does contain its form, the possibility of that combination, which is guaranteed by the logical isomorphism between the combination of signs in the proposition and the possible combination of things in the situation (TLP 3.13, 3.34). Representation is possible through a logical isomorphism, an agreement in form between what represents – whether it be diorama, painting, musical score, proposition or thought – and what is represented (this recalls Aristotle's idea that in thought the mind and its object, although made of different matter, take on the same form).

The pictorial nature of propositions first occurred to Wittgenstein when he learnt about the practice of representing traffic accidents in a law court by means of a model. We can represent a specific course of events (which may or may not have occurred) with the aid of toy cars and dolls. To do so we must lay down both what toy corresponds to what actual thing, and which relations between the toys represent actual relations between objects (e.g., their spatial relations, but not those between their weights). Thus the *Tractatus*'s account of propositional representation (TLP 3–4.0641) is an application of a prior account of representation in general (TLP 2.1–2.225). Any model or 'picture' must be composite, composed of a multiplicity of elements going proxy for elements of the situation depicted. It must have structure and form. The structure is the conventionally determined way in which its elements are arranged for the purposes of depiction. The possibility of this structure is the 'pictorial form' (e.g., the three-dimensionality of a diorama, the two-dimensionality of a painting, or the linear order of a musical score). A picture must share with what it depicts this pictorial form: it must have the same logico-mathematical multiplicity, that is, the same number of distinct elements, and it must be capable of combining these elements in a way mirroring the possible combinations of the objects (TLP 2.161, 4.04). Models of the same situation in different media have different 'representational forms' but the same logical form, a bare minimum of pictorial form.

Propositional representation shares these features. A proposition is 'a picture of reality', it describes a state of affairs by depicting it (TLP 4.016–4.021). Elementary propositions must be composite, composed of unanalysable NAMES. The 'meanings' of these names are the simple 'objects' for which they stand, and with which they are correlated by the lines of projection. The 'sense' of the proposition is the 'state of affairs it depicts', a possible combination of objects. Only facts can represent facts, only simple names can represent simple objects, and only relations (viz., that 'R' stands in a conventionally determined relation to 'a' and 'b') can represent relations. A proposition consists of structure plus pictorial relation; that is, of two relations, one between its names, and one between the latter and objects in reality. Both of these relations are conventional: we determine not only what names go proxy for what objects, but also what about the names says what about the objects, that is, which relations between the names have symbolic significance and are thereby part of the proposition's 'structure' (TLP 3.322, 3.342, 5.473ff.). On the other hand, these conventions are restricted by the necessary preconditions of representation, the need for a logical isomorphism. Structure and pictorial relation are not on an equal footing. Selecting toys as three-dimensional proxies for three-dimensional objects is *ipso facto* to make their three-dimensional spatial relations the representational form of the picture (although spatial relations between the toys might depict, for example, relations of weight between the objects). Moreover, the combinatorial possibilities of names must mirror those of objects. Correlating a name with an object determines the former's combinatorial possibilities (TLP 3.334). Finally, once both sets of conventions are in place, 'the proposition represents the situation, as it were, off its own bat' (NB 5.11.14; see TLP 3.318, 4.024), irrespective of human activities. This also solves the problem of the creativity of language: with a finite stock of simple names and the rules of LOGICAL SYNTAX which guide their combination in elementary propositions and also the truth-functional combination of the resulting elementary propositions, we can form indefinitely many propositions.

The picture theory has been understood as assimilating propositions to pictures. That suggestion cannot be rejected by insisting that propositions are purely 'logical pictures', whose only pictorial form is logical form. For that holds only of thoughts, not for the propositional signs which express them (TLP 3). The latter rely on combining signs in a particular medium (speech, writing). One might also protest that unlike a proposition, which says that something is the case, a picture does not say anything, but can only be used to do so. However, this ignores that the picture theory is concerned with the unasserted proposition, 'the real picture in the proposition.' Wittgenstein acknowledged that something must be added to turn such a picture into an assertion. 'A proposition shows its sense', that is, 'how things stand *if* it is true. And it *says* *that* they do so stand' (TLP 4.022; NB 26.11.14). What is crucial to the picture theory is that even an unasserted proposition depicts how things stand if it is true, once we have correlated its elements with things, that is, given a method of projection. But although the *Tractatus* is dominated by spatial metaphors, a proposition is a picture not in the literal sense of relying on a spatial (or acoustic) resemblance with what it depicts. ELEMENTARY PROPOSITIONS could not, and are not meant to, represent relations between objects solely through the spatial arrangement of signs, without the help of relation-names. Moreover, the 'pictorial character' (*Bildhaftigkeit*) of propositions is based not on resemblance between their elements and those of reality, but on the 'logic of depiction' (TLP 4.011ff.) – the rules of logical syntax – just as the pictorial relation between phonetic signs and sounds consists in the existence of conventions for deriving one from the other. A proposition *is* a logical picture (TLP 4.03) – albeit not a pure one. Its pictorial nature consists in its being INTERNALLY RELATED to what it depicts; its sense is *in* the proposition as the scene portrayed by a painting is *in* the painting. The only respect in which LOGICAL ANALYSIS will reveal that, appearances notwithstanding, propositions are pictorial, is that there is after all a one-to-one correlation between names and objects, and more generally, that there is a logico-mathematical isomorphism between proposition and state of affairs (TLP 4.04). That is why Wittgenstein speaks of propositions as 'similes' or 'models', which 'construct' a world, rather than reflecting it like a photograph (TLP 4.01, 4.023). Their pictorial nature is illustrated not just by the literal analogy with paintings, but also by a proposition's being a point in LOGICAL SPACE, which is determined by its constituent names just as a point in space is determined by its coordinates (TLP 3.4ff.; NB 29.10./ 1.11.14). This suggests that Wittgenstein would have resisted not only the idea that propositions are just as realistic as paintings, but also the opposite idea, which he helped to inspire among semioticians like Goodman, namely that pictorial representation is just as conventional as linguistic representation.

The picture theory is a poor theory of pictures. But is it a good theory of propositions? There has been a controversy on whether Wittgenstein later answered this question in the negative. Some have held that the picture theory collapses with the atomistic metaphysics with which the *Tractatus* combined it. Others have insisted that there is a logico-semantical core of the picture theory which survives into the later work. The dispute is partly terminological, since it turns on what one includes under the labels 'picture theory', 'logical atomism', etc. Thus, if one identifies the picture theory with the *Tractatus*'s overall theory of symbolism, then it collapses with the doctrine of the general form of the proposition.

However, a pictorial conception of elementary propositions does not essentially depend on that doctrine. This is less obvious for the doctrines of logical atomism. Thus, it may seem that a commitment to absolutely simple, sempiternal objects is essential to the picture theory. Now it is indeed essential to the theory that there is an object corresponding to each and every one of a proposition's constituent names, for only then can it represent a possibly non-existing state of affairs. However, this only yields the idea of sempiternal and absolutely simple OBJECTS if one adds further requirements, such as the idea that the sense of a proposition must not depend on the contingent existence of referents for its components (autonomy of sense) or the insistence that elementary propositions must depict definite (possible) combinations of indestructible elements (*see* DETERMINACY OF SENSE).

These requirements are intimately linked to the picture theory, they provide part of its motivation, but they can nevertheless be severed from it *in principle*. But even this does not hold of several ideas which Wittgenstein's later work rightly criticizes. One is the metaphysics of facts: facts are not composed of objects, nor are they items in the world to which TRUE propositions correspond. Moreover, the picture theory is flawed as a semantic theory. Representation does not presuppose a one-to-one relation between words and things. By identifying the meaning of a name with the object it stands for, and by making a proposition's making sense dependent upon the 'meanings' of its constituent names, the picture theory subscribes to the AUGUSTINIAN PICTURE OF LANGUAGE. Furthermore, it presupposes that a proposition can represent 'off its own bat', once the structure and pictorial relation are in place. But a propositional sign cannot contain its own METHOD OF PROJECTION. And if a proposition is identified with propositional sign *plus* method of projection, depiction is guaranteed no longer by a logical form pinned onto reality, but by our USE of the sign.

Finally, Wittgenstein attacks the core of the picture theory, the doctrine of isomorphism. The idea that a proposition and the possible state of affairs it depicts share a definite logical form collapses with the atomistic idea that either of them has ultimate constituents. But without that specification, to say that a proposition and what it depicts 'have something in common' is merely to state that they are internally related. It is this internal relation which Wittgenstein continues to uphold by speaking of the 'pictoriality' of propositions (PR 57, 63–71; PG 163, 212; PI §§519–21). But this is merely to restate the INTENTIONAL character of propositions. The explanation provided by the picture theory is rejected. The 'harmony between thought and reality' is not a metaphysical relation between a proposition and a worldly item (or a shadow of a worldly item – a possible state of affairs), but orchestrated in language. It boils down to grammatical propositions like 'The proposition that p' = 'the proposition which is verified by the fact that p'.

Apart from the newly explained pictoriality, what remains of the picture theory is a comparison of propositions with pictures, but with literal pictures, not logical pictures (thoughts). Understanding or acting upon a proposition is akin to understanding or acting upon a picture. The difference between fictional and factual propositions is akin to that between genre and historical paintings (PG 42, 163–4; WVC 185; PI §§522–3; Z §444; MS107 155; MS109 26–7). A genre picture tells us something, but precisely not about how things are in reality.

privacy An essential part of the INNER/OUTER picture of the mind which has dominated modern philosophy is the idea that mental phenomena – ideas, sense-data, representations, experiences, etc. – are private in two respects:

> *privately owned* or *inalienable*: no one else can have *my* pain; other people can at most have a pain that is similar to mine;
> *epistemically private*: only I can know that I am in pain, since only I feel it, others can only surmise that I am, on the basis of my behaviour.

This picture fuels scepticism about other minds: since pretence and deceit seem always possible, one can never be sure whether other people are really in the mental states they appear to be in according to their behaviour. It may even lead to SOLIPSISM: if all experiential terms are defined by reference to my inalienable experiences, it is difficult to see how there could be said to be other subjects of experience. Wittgenstein's methodological solipsism of the early thirties adumbrates this consequence (PR ch. VI; M 97–103). But it avoids the idea of an ego, and opts for a no-ownership theory. Although first-person present tense propositions about subjective experiences are semantically basic, the first-person pronoun can be eliminated (*see* I/SELF). 'I have a toothache' should read, following Lichtenberg, 'There is a toothache.' No ego or self owns these private experiences, there is only a contingent causal relationship between primary experiences and a particular body. The owner is abolished because it cannot be encountered in introspection (Hume) and because of the inalienable nature of the experiences. It is logically impossible that someone else should have what I have when I suffer from toothache. Consequently, the 'I' in 'I have a toothache' is redundant. 'Toothache' simply means a cluster of properties which include 'being had by me'; to ascribe it to *me* adds nothing. And if it is nonsense to say that someone else has my toothache it is also nonsensical to deny it. The Cartesian

> (1)   All my experiences are logically (inalienably) owned by an ego

is the product of an illusion. What we can legitimately say is empirical, namely

> (2)   All my experiences are causally dependent upon a single body *B*.

According to Strawson, this position is incoherent, since it is forced to employ the notion of possession by a self or an ego which it officially rejects. For if we drop the term 'my' from (2) we end up with something which is simply false:

(2′)   All experiences are causally dependent upon a single body B.

However, for the middle Wittgenstein (2′) is both *true* – he is a solipsist, albeit an ego-less one – and *contingent*. That the pain which I call 'mine' occurs in this body is an empirical fact, because it is conceivable that I should suffer a pain located in someone else's body (WVC 49; BB 49–52). The person who has a pain is the one who manifests it, and the location of the pain is where the sufferer says it is. It is conceivable that I should locate a toothache in someone else's mouth, for example if I flinch when his tooth is touched, etc. But this claim falls apart in other cases. I cannot intelligibly point to the door and say 'That's where it hurts', if the person in whose body I locate my pain were to leave the room; or explain my limping by saying that I have a pain in someone else's leg (PI II 222; LW II 36).

After abandoning methodological solipsism, Wittgenstein first settled for a deflation of privacy of ownership. 'The proposition "Sensations are private" is comparable to: "One plays patience by oneself" ' (PI §248; BB 54; LW II 56). What the inner/outer picture takes to be a metaphysical truth

(3)   Another person cannot have my pain

is a disguised grammatical proposition which explains the linguistic convention

(3′)   My pain = the pain I have.

Whereas it makes sense to wonder whether a book belongs to me or to someone else, it makes no sense to wonder whether the pain I feel belongs to me or to someone else. But Wittgenstein also came to hold that there is a sense in which (3) is confused. One argument against (3) harks back to the no-ownership theory: 'if as a matter of logic you exclude other people's having something, it loses its sense to say that you have it' (PI §398, see §§253–4; MS129 40). Another argument is that (3) is at variance with our ascriptions of pain. Two people can have the *same* pain, if their pains have the same location, intensity and phenomenal characteristics.

Nevertheless, a proponent of the inner/outer picture like Frege may reply 'Surely, another person cannot have THIS pain!' Although others can have the same pain, that is, an exactly similar one, they cannot have a pain which is *identical* with mine ('Thought' 66–8; *Foundations* §27). The respective sensations are numerically distinct, although qualitatively identical. Your headache is in your head and mine is in my head, and by Leibniz's law, difference in location implies numerical difference. Still, Wittgenstein insists, even by that reasoning Siamese twins who each suffer a pain at the point of juncture have the same pain. But this rejoinder is at odds with another point he makes, one which provides a stronger reply to Frege's position. We locate pains *not* by reference to spatial coordinates but by reference to parts of the sufferer's body. If the head of one of the Siamese twins is conjoined with the back of the other, they have different pains – the one has a headache, the other a back-ache. But if you and I both have a throbbing headache in the temples, we have the same pain in the same place, even though your head is in a different place from mine.

Another response is that the insistence that my pain is mine and your pain is yours turns the alleged owner of the pain into a distinguishing property of the pain, and hence makes a nonsense of the model of ownership. Wittgenstein makes the same point against the idea of particularized qualities, according to which no two objects have the same colour, since we must distinguish the green of your chair from the green of my chair: this turns the object into a distinguishing property of its property, and implies that instead of saying 'This☞ chair is green' one should say 'This green is here☞' (PR 90–1; LSD 4–5). Privacy of ownership projects onto the mental the distinction between numerical and qualitative identity which applies only to particulars. All we have in the mental case is the difference between *A* and *B*'s having similar pains (*A*'s stomach-ache lacks the throbbing character of *B*'s) and their having the same pain.

One might protest that pains do allow of a distinction between qualitative and numerical identity, inasmuch as if I have a pain in my foot, and a qualitatively indistinguishable one in my hand, I have two pains, not one. Difference of location in the subject's body indeed implies different pains. However, this countability of pains is restricted to each person. If two people in a room suffer from the 'same' headache, we might say that there are two people with headaches in the room. But it is senseless to say either that there are two headaches in the room or that there is one. Headaches do not have spatial locations other than their location in the body of the sufferer.

There is one way of distinguishing qualitative and numerical identity of pains (which *Blue and Brown Books* 54–5 mentions but fails to address): even if *A* and *B* have the 'same' pain, it is possible to destroy (anaesthetize) one of them without destroying the other. Yet this does not derogate from the grammatical difference between substances on the one hand, and pains and particularized qualities on the other. Owning physical objects and owning pains are categorially distinct: only in the former case can what is owned be independent of the owner, and be shared between different owners.

Wittgenstein questions both aspects of *epistemic privacy*: 'I can know what someone else is thinking, not what I am thinking' (PI §§246–7, II 222–4). Third-person psychological propositions are justifiably asserted on the basis of behavioural CRITERIA. Obviously, one can fail to manifest, or can even conceal, one's inner states. But these are then only *de facto* unknown to others, and can be revealed through appropriate behaviour in certain circumstances. Again, there may be individuals or communities whose emotions and motives are opaque to us. Yet, we can alleviate the enigma by learning about their biographies or way of life. Finally, there is a constitutional indeterminacy of the inner, since our mental concepts do not connect behaviour, situation and inner phenomenon in a rigid way. However, none of these points amounts to an absolute metaphysical barrier to knowledge of other minds (PG 82–4; LPE 314; LW II 22–31, 61–73).

The other prong of Wittgenstein's attack challenges the venerable idea that introspection provides a privileged, immediate and incorrigible knowledge of our own minds. His complaint is not that introspection is after all indirect and fallible.

(4)   I know that I am in pain

is not open to ignorance or doubt. Nor does it resemble a proposition like 'N.N. is breathing' which, in normal circumstances, is simply too obvious to have a point. For its negation is not simply false, but nonsensical. It makes no sense to say 'I doubt whether I am in pain' or 'I have a sensation, but don't know whether it's a pain or a tickle.' We could give sense to such locutions, and to terms like 'unconscious pain', but only by introducing new criteria for the use of sensation-words (BB 55).

The grammatical exclusion of grounds for the self-ascription of experience does not show that we have an immediate and infallible access to the mind through introspection. Equally, the unintelligibility of doubt or ignorance does not amount to certainty or infallible knowledge – it precludes their intelligibility likewise. For it makes sense to say 'I know' only where it makes sense to say 'I don't know (doubt/found out).' Like the claim that one can only own what one could lack, this may sound like a dogmatic application of the principle of BIPOLARITY: no knowledge without the possibility of ignorance (doubt/misrecognition or misidentification), and indeed that principle does here soldier on. However, Wittgenstein does not simply condemn (4) as a misuse of language; he explicitly grants that it can be used. Originally he claimed that (4) is either nonsensical, or means the same as 'I am in pain' (BB 55; LPE 309). (4) can be used, for example, to emphasize or concede that one is in pain, along the lines of 'I really am in pain' or 'Of course I am in pain.' Moreover, propositions similar to (4), such as '*Only I* can know...', or 'I *must* know...', can be used as GRAMMATICAL propositions, which express rules for the use of psychological terms, for example that there is no room for doubt or that the speaker's sincere expressions have an authoritative status, or that he can hide his sensations if he chooses (PI §§246–8, 251–2, II 224; RPP I §§564–73).

But these same rules preclude (4) from expressing a genuine knowledge claim (LPE 304–7; LSD 13, 112). There is no such thing as recognizing or perceiving the sensation – it does not make sense to say 'From observing myself I can tell that I am in agony.' Moreover, one does not employ criteria to decide whether one has a headache or an itching sensation. Finally, while cognitive claims exclude a possibility – doubt, ignorance or error – (4) does not, and hence says nothing. Wittgenstein here ignores that while (4) does not exclude as a possibility 'I do *not* know whether I am in pain' (which is nonsensical, not false), it nevertheless does draw a *contrast* in line with cognitive claims: '*I* know that I am in pain, but *she* is ignorant of it.' By contrast, 'I have my pain' does not, since both 'I do *not* have my pain' and '*She* has my pain' are nonsensical (provided the latter is construed along the lines of privacy of ownership). This suggests that Wittgenstein's 'bipolar' line of argument works against privacy of ownership, but not against epistemic privacy.

He is right, however, that there is no gap between my putative knowledge and my simply being in pain: 'I know what I feel' = 'I feel what I feel.' ' "I know..." may mean "I do not doubt...", but does not mean that the words "I doubt" are *senseless*, that doubt is logically excluded' (PI II 221). This does not entail that in cases in which doubt is nonsensical, it makes no sense to speak of knowledge (one might speak of knowledge whenever someone is in a position to make a claim). But it shows that doing so employs 'know' in a way which lacks conceptual connections (with ways of finding out) and contrasts (with doubt, ignorance and error) which characterize standard uses (Z §§22, 549; LW I §51).

There remain two major lines of objection. The first denies that doubt and ignorance are unintelligible. After all, we say things like 'While I was running, I didn't feel the pain.' But we might as well say 'While I was running, it didn't hurt', and one could not reply 'It did, but you failed to notice.' This equivalence is absent from ordinary epistemic claims. Again, I may not be quite certain whether what I have is a pain or just an ache, or whether I am really hungry. But this kind of uncertainty could not be remedied by further evidence. Similarly, 'I don't know what I think (intend/want)' does not mean that I think so-and-so but am ignorant of what it is, but rather that I have not yet made up my mind. Next, one might think that it is possible to mislocate sensations. My dentist may show me that the tooth which hurts is the one next to the one I thought. Someone who locates a pain in an amputated foot seems even further off the mark. But the first case is marginal and the second anomalous – our concept of pain-location would break down if it became the rule. Finally, it may seem that someone who screams when a piece of ice is put down his back falsely believes that he has a pain. But he screamed either because the ice did pain him, or because he thought it was going to. In neither case did he mistake one sensation for another.

The second remaining major line of objection focuses on logical transformations. There are meaningful propositions which imply that (4) expresses a genuine knowledge claim, for example

(5) I lied when I said that I was free of pain

(one can lie that not-p only if one knows or believes that p), or

(6) I know that everyone in this room – including myself – is in pain.

Similarly, 'I am in pain' is a base for sentence-forming operators which result in propositions that definitely express something I can know, such as

(7) I was in pain.

But these transformations cannot be items of knowledge, unless the base is as well.

Wittgenstein's rejoinder to this line of objection (LPE 280, 293–4; LW II 33) is based on the idea that the possibility of such transformations does not settle the status of (4). Granted that (5)–(7) involve knowledge claims, the question is what that knowledge amounts to. And the answer must partly refer back to the status of (4). Thus, Wittgenstein insists that (5), unlike lying about one's height, does not presuppose knowledge. He could also insist that (6) should be explicated as

(6′) I am in a position to say that everyone in this room is in pain, since I *am* in pain and I *know* that everyone else is in pain.

The kernel of truth in epistemic privacy is first-person authority: I am in a position to say what I feel, experience, think, not because I have infallible access to a private peep-show, but because what I say, unlike what others say about me, is (typically) an AVOWAL, a groundless expression or manifestation of the inner.

private language argument In a wide sense, this expression refers to the investigation of the relationship between the mental and behaviour in *Philosophical Investigations* §§243–315. More narrowly, it refers to a line of argument which discusses the idea of a 'private language' (MS165 101–2). Such a language is not a personal code (as the one used in some of Wittgenstein's notebooks), nor a language which is used only in soliloquy (as the one canvassed in §243), nor even a language spoken by only one person (as that of the Robinson Crusoe envisaged in MS124 221). It is not a language which is unshared as a matter of fact, but one which is unsharable and unteachable in principle, because its words refer to what can only be known to the speaker, namely his immediate private experiences. §§243–55 introduce the idea of a private language and show that our psychological vocabulary is not private in this sense, while §§256–71 argue that the very notion is incoherent, and §§272–315 that this does not imply that the mental is unreal.

The possibility of a private language is tacitly presupposed by the mainstream of modern philosophy from Descartes through classical British empiricism and Kantianism to contemporary cognitive representationalism. It is the result of two natural assumptions. Firstly, the meaning of words is given by what they stand for – this is part of the AUGUSTINIAN PICTURE OF LANGUAGE. Secondly, in the case of psychological terms, what they stand for are phenomena in a mental theatre which is accessible only to the individual. Sensations, experiences, thoughts are inalienable and epistemically private (see PRIVACY). No one else can have my pain, or know what I have when I am in pain – this is the INNER/OUTER picture of the mind. It follows immediately that no one else can know what I mean by 'pain'. Moreover, if ideas, impressions or intuitions provide not just the evidence for all our beliefs, but also the content of all our words – a view shared by representationalists and idealists, rationalists, empiricists and Kantians – our whole language is private in this sense.

The idea that meanings are private experiences raises Locke's spectre of the inverted spectrum (*An Essay concerning Human Understanding* II.32.15): for all we know, what I mean by 'red' is what you mean by 'green'. The first to accept this conclusion was Russell (*Logic* 195). So possessed was he by the idea that the meanings of our words must be sense-data with which we are acquainted, that he declared it to be a precondition of intersubjective UNDERSTANDING that no two people mean the same by their words. The *Tractatus* moved along similar lines. Although the OBJECTS which are the meanings of simple NAMES are not sense-data, they are objects of acquaintance – shades of colours, points in the visual field. In his VERIFICATIONIST phase, Wittgenstein, in step with Carnap and Schlick, held that there is a primary 'phenomenological' language which refers to immediate experiences. Between 1932 and 1935, he first relinquished the idea of a primary language, and next attacked idealism and SOLIPSISM. The notion of a private language first appears in lectures of 1935–6 (LPE; LSD); the argument against it is developed in manuscripts of 1937–9 and completed in 1944–5.

The final version, polished but condensed, is *Investigations* §§243–315. This has been denied by some adherents of a community-view of RULE-FOLLOWING, who claim that the 'real' private language argument is completed by §202, which states that 'it is not possible to follow a rule "privately": otherwise thinking one was obeying a rule would be the same thing as obeying it.' On this view, §§243–315 merely defend the idea that meaningful discourse requires an actual community of speakers against a potential counter-example, sensation-terms. But in the original drafts (MS180a 68–72; MS129 116–17), §202 follows and presupposes §§243–315. Moreover, the discussion of a private language in §§243–315 is not concerned with soliloquists who do not communicate their sensations. Finally, it does not just apply a lesson about rule-following to sensations, but attempts to dispel general misconceptions about the mind (mental states and processes) and its relationship to behaviour. Although its main focus is on sensations (*Empfindungen*), and in particular on pain, it is equally concerned with experience, notably with visual experiences (PI §§273–80, 290, 305–6, 312).

On the other hand, the private language argument does presuppose the antecedent discussion of rule-following. A discussion of the coherence of the notion of a private language presupposes a conception of language, and Wittgenstein regards language as an activity guided by GRAMMATICAL rules. But he did not reach the conclusion that a private language is impossible simply by defining language as a means of communication (*see* FAMILY RESEMBLANCE), or by applying a previously established 'community-view' of rules. The connection is rather that rules are standards of correctness, and that for a sign like 'pain' to be the name of a sensation, and not just a squiggle or noise, it must be determined how it is to be used (LPE 291). In a putative private language no such standard of correctness could be set up or employed, and hence its signs would be meaningless. A language which is in principle unintelligible to anyone but its speaker is not just (trivially) unsuited to communication, it is unintelligible even to the private linguist himself. The private linguist claims in our public language that he is using a sign 'S' as part of a language, that is, according to rules, albeit rules only he understands (PI §§261, 270). But it transpires that he cannot explain how this is done without connecting 'S' to communicable rules of a public language.

The private linguist maintains that one can give meaning to 'S' independently of any public language, by means of a private ostensive definition. I have a sensation, and baptize it by concentrating my attention on it and saying 'S' to myself. Subsequently, I keep a diary in which I record an 'S' whenever I have the same sensation again. Wittgenstein denies that this amounts to a meaningful employment of 'S'.

> 'I impress [the sensation] on myself' can only mean: this process brings it about that I remember the connection *right* in the future. But in the present case I have no criterion of correctness. One would like to say: whatever is going to seem right to me is right. And that only means that here we can't talk about 'right'. (PI §258)

This remark has been interpreted as resting on scepticism about memory: I cannot be certain that I use 'S' only when I have S, because my memory is fallible. Understood thus, the passage invites the reply that the fallibility of memory is just as much of a problem in the case of a public language, so that the argument is either unsound or threatens the possibility of language in general. Wittgenstein's defenders have retorted that such fallibility is harmless if mistakes can be corrected, but that this is excluded in the private case.

Both criticism and defence are right to focus on checkability, but wrong to link the latter to scepticism about memory. What is at issue is not the truth of my utterance 'There's S again', but its meaningfulness. 'There is no question of my memory's playing me a trick – because (in such cases) there can be no criterion for its playing me a trick' (LSD 8, see 38–9, 114; PI §260; MS166 21), since the original ceremony failed to establish a rule for the use of 'S'. Stated in general terms, there is no such thing as a private rule, because a standard of correctness must be checkable (LPP 247). But in the case of a private standard this is *ex hypothesi* not the case. It has been objected that this relies on an indefensible verificationism, since it confuses the question of whether the private linguist employs a standard of correctness with the question of whether we can know that he does. However, Wittgenstein argues not that we could not possibly know whether the private linguist is applying the rule correctly, but that even for him no rule for the use of 'S' has been laid down. For there is no such thing as a non-operational standard of correctness, one which cannot even in principle be used to distinguish between correct and incorrect applications. One might grant this but insist that while the private linguist's application of 'S' at t_1 is incorrigible at t_1, it can be corrected by him at t_2. However, justification consists in 'appealing to something independent' (PI §265). Since *ex hypothesi*, this is excluded, at t_2 nothing distinguishes the private linguist's rectifying a mistake by reference to a prior rule from his adopting a new rule. Hence, there was in fact no rule to begin with, but only '*impressions* of rules' and a 'pseudo-practice' (PI §259; MS180a 76).

Wittgenstein elaborates this general line of argument by arguing that there cannot be a private ostensive definition, since there are no mental analogues to the essential features of public OSTENSIVE DEFINITIONS. The logical category of the definiendum needs to have been determined, that is, 'S' must be the name of a sensation. However, 'sensation' is a word in our public language which is defined by reference to behavioural CRITERIA. Since the private linguist denies or severs this connection, he must explain the category or 'post' of 'S' afresh. However, simply muttering 'This is S' does not make 'S' the name of a sensation, since it leaves undetermined what 'this' is. Concentrating one's attention cannot establish criteria of IDENTITY for subsequent uses of 'S'. Such criteria can be provided only by specifying what kind of thing is at issue through a sortal term. But the private linguist has not established what it is he is concentrating on. He cannot say that it is a certain 'experience' or 'phenomenon', since he lacks the resources for explaining those terms provided by our public language. He cannot even say that 'S' refers to something he has, since 'has' and 'something' are likewise terms from our public language with a determinate grammar. Thus, an elenctic argument forces the private linguist to the point where he 'would like just to emit an inarticulate sound' (PI §§257, 261–3; LSD 42, 105; LPE 290). In this vein, Schlick professed his inability even to talk about the 'private content' which each person allegedly associates with words (*Papers* II 306–7). But this is to admit that Wittgenstein is right: one cannot invoke a private content in philosophical debate.

Even if one granted the putative sample of the private ostensive definition, there are no ways of checking subsequent employments of 'S' by reference to it, since nothing determines identity or difference between sample and described item. There is no established method for comparing sensations in the way in which there is a method for comparing the lengths of objects by reference to measurements by a ruler. Moreover, one cannot preserve a sensation for future use as a sample (LSD 42, 110). *Investigations* §265 considers the suggestion that for such a reproducible sample one might substitute a mnemonic image of the original sensation. But this procedure is not like calling up a mnemonic image of a colour-chart. In that case, there is an independent standard for remembering correctly. All the private linguist can appeal to in checking whether he can remember what sensation he associated with 'S' is his mnemonic image, which is simply his remembering what sensation he associated with 'S'. He is checking his memory against itself, which is as if he tried to measure a ruler against itself or 'to buy several copies of the morning paper to assure himself that what it said was true'. Even if one grants the private linguist the use of the term 'sensation', all he could mean by 'S' is 'the sensation I'm now experiencing' – not 'such-and-such a sensation I've experienced before'. Consequently, his 'There's S again' does not apply 'S' according to a norm of correctness, and cannot be a description of something private (PI §§222, 232, 265).

If a private ostensive definition cannot provide a standard of correctness, its putative sample, the inner object, drops out of the picture as an 'idle wheel'. In a language-game in which everyone has a box and refers to its contents as a 'beetle', but in which no one has access to the contents of others' boxes, the contents of the box and their nature are irrelevant to the meaning of 'beetle'. The same holds if we imagine the inner object (the sensation S, the inverted colour-spectrum) changing constantly without our noticing. The reason is not that the private object is unknowable, but that it is semantically irrelevant (PI §§271–3, 293, II 207; BB 72–3; LPP 281).

It is tempting to suspect that this leaves us with a kind of BEHAVIOURISM which denies that there is anything behind the outer behaviour. Wittgenstein denies that charge. ' "And yet you again and again reach the conclusion that the sensation itself is a *nothing*." – Not at all. It is not a *something*, but not a *nothing* either!' The sensation is a semantically irrelevant 'grammatical fiction' only if we construe the grammar of 'pain' on the model of object and name (PI §§304–8). If we treat 'pain' as the name of a private object, the question of the identification or misidentification of its referent must arise, since the sensation is supposed to be an object, but cannot be solved, because it is supposed to be private. There are no criteria of identity for private mental entities. That does not imply that there are no such objects, only that even the private linguist himself cannot keep track of them. Nor does it imply that there are no sensations, but rather that sensations cannot be understood as private entities. (Equally, the Kant–Strawson argument that there are no criteria of identity for Cartesian soul-substances implies neither that for all I know my thoughts might be those of a thousand souls, nor that I do not exist, but only that I cannot conceive of myself as a soul-substance.)

Words like 'pain', 'itch' or 'tickle' are names of sensations, but not in the way in which 'table', 'chair' and 'sofa' are names of pieces of furniture. One can point at a table and say that 'table' is the name of this☞ piece of furniture, but one cannot point at a sensation and say that 'pain' is the name of this☞ sensation. Instead, to say that 'pain' is the name of a sensation is to say that there are characteristic behavioural manifestations of pain which provide criteria for statements like 'She is in pain', and that a sentence like 'I am in pain' is (typically) an AVOWAL – not the report of an inner object but an expression of pain. In the case of genuine sensations, the problem about criteria of identity does not arise, since there is no such thing as either identifying or misidentifying one's own sensations (this is arguably the point of *Investigations* §270, which envisages a use for 'S' by treating 'There's S again' not as a description of private goings-on, but as an avowal).

Even if one does not accept Wittgenstein's alternative account of sensation-terms, the private language argument undermines the idea that private experiences provide the foundations of language and of knowledge. It also implies that to know the meaning of psychological terms we do not need to have the corresponding sensation or experience. To state meaningfully that another person is in pain, we do not need a pain, but the concept of pain. Having the experience does not guarantee mastery of the use of the term. Equally, someone who applies and explains the term 'toothache' correctly, but has never had a toothache, knows what 'toothache' means. One might object that we have no reason to believe that such a person has mastered its first-person use. But we have if he can say of himself 'I haven't got a toothache.' The only type of case in which he could be said not to have mastered the first-person use is if he suddenly screams out in agony holding his cheek, but insists that he hasn't got a toothache (Z §§332–3, 547–8; LSD 9–16). This in turn implies the untenability of abstractionism: we could not, and need not, derive concepts by concentrating on certain features of experiences and disregarding others. It also reinforces the Kantian attack on the myth of the given (not always adhered to by Kant himself, but since urged by Sellars): the 'preconceptual intuitions' or 'nonconceptual contents' brandished by empiricists from Locke through the Vienna Circle to Quine and contemporary theorists of content are at best part of the causal mechanism underlying speech, and do not feature in the rules which give meaning to our words. They are semantically and epistemically irrelevant in that they provide neither the sense of, nor the evidence for, our statements.

proposition *Satz* means both 'sentence' and 'proposition', a term which has been variously used to signify what sentences express, the bearers of truth and falsity, and the objects of propositional attitudes. Wittgenstein's immediate predecessors all repudiated the idea, shared by idealism and psychologistic logic, that judgements are operations performed on ideas. Frege distinguished sharply between the sentence, the ideas (*Vorstellungen*) accompanying it, and what it expresses. Every sentence expresses its 'sense', a 'thought', which is neither physical nor mental but part of a Platonic 'third realm', and is the name of its meaning, which is its truth-value, the True or the False. Moore treated a proposition as a complex of concepts, which subsists eternally, and is true or false, regardless of whether it is thought by anyone. Russell replaced 'concept' by 'term' and held that propositions are timeless complexes of terms. All three identified true propositions with facts. But Russell soon came to treat propositions as the complex symbols which correspond to facts, and the latter as complexes consisting of 'individuals', the ultimate constituents of reality ('Thought'; *Writings* ch. 1; *Principles* ch. 4; *Logic* 178–89).

Wittgenstein maintained, against Frege and Russell, that the assertion-sign is of merely psychological importance (*see* BELIEF). Logic is concerned only with the *unasserted* proposition, which may be a constituent of an assertion, a question or a command. All propositions can be analysed into elementary propositions which depict reality by depicting possible states of affairs; the GENERAL PROPOSITIONAL FORM is: 'Things are thus-and-so' (TLP 4.5). The *Tractatus* distinguishes between the propositional sign (*Satzzeichen*) and the proposition (*Satz*): the former is a 'SIGN', a perceptible token-inscription or -utterance; the latter a 'symbol', a type which is common to all propositional signs which have the same sense (TLP 3.31–3.32). *Tractatus* 3.1 states that a sequence of signs is a meaningful proposition which truly or falsely depicts reality only if it *expresses* a thought (*Gedanke*). *Tractatus* 4, on the other hand, states that a proposition with a sense *is* a thought. The inconsistency is merely terminological, however. A sentence expresses a thought by virtue, not of being correlated with an abstract or mental entity, but of having a projective relation to reality. A thought is simply a sentence-in-use, a propositional sign in its projective relation to reality (TLP 3.1ff., 3.32ff., 3.5, 4). The relationship between a propositional sign and a proposition is anal-

315

ogous to that between a dollar bill and a dollar. The bill does not name a dollar, but to present the bill is to present a dollar. However, another tension remains, since the *Tractatus* is committed to a closet mentalism. The METHOD OF PROJECTION requires that the sense be thought into the proposition, that is, that the use of the propositional sign be accompanied by a process of thinking, more specifically by a THOUGHT, a psychic fact, which is not identical but isomorphic with the sentence uttered.

'Frege said "propositions are names"; Russell said "propositions correspond to complexes". Both are false, and especially false is the statement "propositions are names of complexes"' (NL 97). Propositions do not refer to either a truth-value (Frege) or a complex object (Russell). They have a different relation to reality. NAMES have MEANING, that is, stand for objects, propositions have sense, that is, depict a possible state of affairs: 'Names are points, propositions arrows' (NL 101; TLP 3.143–3.144). In order to understand a name one must know what it stands for, in order to understand a proposition one need not know whether it is true (or false), but only what would be the case if it were true. Wittgenstein connected this insight with the claim that propositions must be not just bivalent but also BIPOLAR – capable of being true *and* capable of being false – which excludes the possibility of a proposition's being necessarily true.

Traditional logic maintained that a proposition like 'Plato is the teacher of Aristotle' consists of a *subject* 'Plato' and a *predicate* 'is the teacher of Aristotle', school-grammar further distinguishes the *copula* 'is'. Frege and Russell, by contrast, analyse it into two argument-expressions ('Plato', 'Aristotle') and a two-place concept-word or propositional function 'x is the teacher of y'. Both Frege's 'concepts' and Russell's 'propositional functions' are patterns of correlation. The former map arguments onto truth-values, the latter onto propositions. Having abandoned the view that the subject is united with the predicate by a mental act (being subsumed under it), Frege and Russell were at pains to explain what holds together the components of propositions and facts. Frege accounted for this unity of propositions through a chemical analogy: concept-words (concepts) are 'unsaturated' – they contain a variable – and hence combine with 'saturated' argument-expressions (objects) to form a saturated proposition. Russell maintained that among the components of facts are LOGICAL FORMS, which hold together the components of the complex. But he faced a problem in that aRb and bRa have the same logical form. His solution was that a and b are linked to R through further relations, which differ in these two cases, a proposal which invites Bradley's regress argument against the reality of relations ('Function' 15–17; 'Concept' 197–205; 'Theory' 80–8).

The *Tractatus* substantially modifies this picture:

(a) Propositions are composed of function and argument (TLP 3.141, 5.47).

316

Wittgenstein sided with Russell, in holding that the values of a propositional function '*fx*' are propositions ('*fa*', '*fb*', etc.), not truth-values. In contrast to Russell, its arguments are held to be names, not the objects they stand for (TLP 4.24).

(b) A proposition is a function of the expressions contained in it. In Frege, the sense (content) of a sentence is a function of the senses of its constituents; in Russell, the proposition itself is the value of the propositional function. For Wittgenstein, the sense of a proposition is a function of the meanings of its constituent names (TLP 3.318, 4.024–4.026).

(c) A proposition is 'logically articulated' or composite. It contains two or more constituents, but is not a mere list of names, since what represents is not just the assembly of constituents. '*Not:* "The complex sign '*aRb*' says that *a* stands in the relation *R* to *b*"; but that "*a*" stands in a certain relation to "*b*" says *that aRb*' (NL 105–6, 96–7; TLP 3.14ff., 4.024–4.032; NB 3.10.14, 28.5./22.6.15). A proposition is a FACT which constitutes a description of a possible state of affairs.

(d) That propositions are facts also provides Wittgenstein's explanation of 'how the propositional union comes about'. In a sense, all components (names) are unsaturated, have meaning only in the context of a proposition. But names combine immediately, without the help of logical glue, just as the components of states of affairs fit into one another like links in a chain, without the need of mediating entities or relations (TLP 2.03f., 4.22f.; LWL 120).

According to the PICTURE THEORY, propositions are 'logical pictures' of reality (TLP 2.18–2.19, 3, 4.03). Their elements – names – stand for elements of the depicted situation. But what represents is not the propositional sign itself, but the fact that these names are arranged in a way which, given a method of projection and the rules of LOGICAL SYNTAX, represents an arrangement of objects. After the *Tractatus* the claim that propositions are facts disappears, and so it should. Like the identification of facts with true propositions it is a category mistake: unlike facts, propositions can be true or false, implausible, etc., and are intensional (the proposition that Berkeley was buried in Christchurch chapel differs from the proposition that the author of the *Principles* was buried in Oxford cathedral). What enables a propositional sign to represent is not the fact that its constituents are combined in a certain way, but rather that, according to the rules of our GRAMMAR, this combination can be used to say that such-and-such is the case.

Wittgenstein also came to question the function-theoretic analysis. (i) The argument/function distinction is merely a sublimation of the subject/

predicate distinction. (ii) Like the latter, it does not indicate a hidden depth-structure discovered by LOGICAL ANALYSIS, but merely a FORM OF REPRE-SENTATION, a uniform theoretical mould which we impose on the motley of language, thereby concealing the fact that 'there are countless different logical forms' (PR 119). (iii) Frege's distinction between objects and concepts is too coarse. It papers over the categorial differences between particulars, numbers, truth-values, circles, places, instants, etc. (PR 120–1, 137). (iv) It is mistaken to insist that propositions must be complex. One can imagine language-games in which expressions cannot be classified into words and sentences – it is mistaken to suppose, for example, that 'Slab!' of *Philosophical Investigations* §2 must mean the same as the elliptical sentence 'Slab!' in our language. Moreover, a non-complex symbol (i.e., name) may be used as a description (PI §§19–20, 49; BB 77–8). (v) The sense of a token-sentence is not determined simply by the meanings of its constituents plus its logical form, but also by how it is used on a particular occasion (*see* CONTEXTUALISM).

Wittgenstein continued to hold that something like bipolarity defines the notion of a proposition. Thus, he castigated intuitionism for ignoring that the law of excluded middle (a precondition of bipolarity) is partly constitutive of what we call a 'proposition' (*see* MATHEMATICS). However, in other passages Wittgenstein realized that there is no warrant for restricting the notion of a proposition to bipolar descriptions of possible states of affairs. It is legitimate to speak of necessary propositions in mathematics and logic, as long as one keeps in mind the differences between them and empirical propositions. Not even all empirical propositions fit the narrow picture: the *Weltbild* propositions of *On Certainty* (*see* CERTAINTY) could not simply turn out to be false; and the law of excluded middle does not hold for certain counterfactual conditionals, or statements like 'He has stopped beating his wife' (Z §§677–83; RPP I §§269–74).

In his VERIFICATIONIST phase, Wittgenstein held that only statements about our immediate experiences qualify as 'genuine' propositions. Later he abandoned the idea that propositions display a single general form, and treated 'proposition' as a FAMILY-RESEMBLANCE concept (PI §§23, 65). But from his discussion of LANGUAGE-GAMES, there also emerges a new uniform conception of a proposition, albeit a less rigid one. A sentence is a minimal unit for making a move in the language-game. This conception may have been partly inspired by Bühler, but starts out from the earlier view that only propositions, not individual words, say or communicate something (a view shared by Plato, Aristotle, Bentham and Frege). It adds the idea that sentences are defined by their role in linguistic activities. Whether or not a given linguistic form constitutes a proposition does not depend on a certain structure, but on whether, on a particular occasion, it has been used to perform an intelligible linguistic act (PI §50; PLP 317–20, ch. XIII). By this token, 'Shame!' or 'Ouch!' are propositions, in spite of the fact that they lack subject and predicate and are not expressed through a propositional clause. This is at odds with what we ordinarily call a 'proposition' or 'sentence'. But it is noteworthy that our punctuation treats such utterances as sentences. Wittgenstein's account has the merit of illuminating the most important roles of propositions in our linguistic activities.

R

realism   *see* ELEMENTARY PROPOSITION; TRUTH

relativism   *see* AUTONOMY OF LANGUAGE; FORM OF LIFE

religion   Wittgenstein was a pious man in search of a religion. The young Wittgenstein seems to have held religion in contempt. A profound change was brought about by his experiences during World War I. Wittgenstein tried to prevent 'losing himself' by resigning himself to God's will, and Christianity is declared to be 'the only safe way to happiness' (GT 16./ 25.8./12.11./8.12.14). But this is not conventional theism. Wittgenstein recognizes that Nietzsche would resist such resignation even at the price of misery. Moreover, his God is not a personal one, but identical with the meaning of life, which is also the meaning of the world, and with fate, the 'world which is independent of our will', which is identical with 'how things stand'. There are 'two godheads: the world and my independent I' (NB 11.6./8.7./1.8.16). One way of reconciling these diverse specifications is this. Grasping the meaning of life consists in the one godhead – the metaphysical self – accepting the other godhead – how things are – with Spinozistic equanimity, because it realizes that how things are has no bearing on the meaning of life. Hence the resolution to the 'problem of life' is its disappearance (TLP 6.52f.). 'God does not reveal himself *in* the world' (TLP 6.432), that is, in *how* the world is, but in *that* it is. Religion is part of the MYSTICAL realm of value, and hence ineffable. Unlike contingent facts, religion cannot be expressed in meaningful propositions, it can only be shown. Unlike the logic of language, but like ethics, it is shown not by meaningful propositions, but by one's actions and attitudes (*see* SAYING/SHOWING).

Religion does not occupy an important role in Wittgenstein's later work. But in his occasional remarks, as well as in lectures and conversations, he intimates a picture which has been highly influential, and has given rise to what has been labelled Wittgensteinian fideism (CV *passim*; LC 53–72; LE 9–10; RW 76–171). He abandoned the idea that religious propositions are ineffable, and instead made suggestions about their GRAMMAR, the role terms like 'God', 'sin' or 'Last Judgement' occupy in a form of life (M 103–4; LC 71–2; CV 50, 82; PI §373; AWL 32). His reflections deserve the label fideism, since they maintain that religious faith is neither rational nor irrational, but rather prerational (LC 58–9); and is not assent to a doctrine, but the expression of 'a passionate commitment to a system of reference' or of a certain attitude towards life (CV 64, 85).

On the other hand, by contrast to fideists like Pascal or Kierkegaard, Wittgenstein is not a Christian apologist. 'I am not a religious man but I cannot help seeing 'every problem from a religious point of view' (RW 79, see 93; CV 32–3, 45, 56; LC 63, 70). Wittgenstein does not set out to endorse a particular religious frame of reference, and repeatedly states that he does not share any such framework. What he offers instead is a theology for atheists, an understanding of religion from the outside (as an anthropological phenomenon) which does not accuse it of being either mistaken, unfounded or nonsensical. This theology involves the following points.

The non-descriptive and non-cognitive nature of religion Religious statements do not describe any kind of reality, empirical or transcendent, and do not make any knowledge claims (LC 59–63). Someone who believes in a Last Judgement does not use expressions like 'Such and such will happen' to make a prediction, but rather to express a commitment to a 'form of life', for example one in which people feel constantly admonished by God's approval or disapproval. Indeed, if he were making a prediction, it would not count as a religious belief (LC 56–8; CV 87). Someone who believes in an afterlife is not committed to the Cartesian notion of a soul-substance, but only to a certain picture, although Wittgenstein sometimes admits that he does not have 'any clear idea' of what the picture amounts to (LC 70–1; PI II 178; RPP I §586). The belief in miracles is a propensity to be impressed by certain coincidences. Someone who says 'It is God's will' may be uttering something similar to a command like 'Don't complain!' (CV 61).

The existence of God By the same token, religious terms like 'God' do not refer to entities, and to state that God exists is not to make a statement about the existence of a certain entity (LC 63; CV 50, 82). It expresses a commitment to a certain frame of reference or a form of life, a commitment which is brought about not by argument but by a certain upbringing or certain experiences.

No need for proof Wittgenstein regarded attempts to prove the existence of God or the immortality of the soul as based on misunderstandings of religious belief, and of the roles of statements concerning God or the afterlife in the form of life of religious believers (RW 107–8; CV 82–5; GB 119). This holds not just for proof by a priori argument, but also for proof by revelation or divine inspiration. To say that something has been 'revealed' to me by God is not to specify a source of knowledge, but to state a decision (OC §§361–2). Equally, Christian belief does not rest on the historical truth of the Gospels; our attitude towards these stories is different to our attitude towards a historical account (CV 32).

Religion as a sui generis *form of discourse* Although he characterizes praying as a language-game (PI §23), Wittgenstein nowhere states that religion constitutes a separate form of life. But the idea that it constitutes a *sui generis* grammatical system is implicit in the idea of the non-descriptive and non-cognitive nature of religion. Like any such system, religious discourse is AUTONOMOUS, it neither corresponds nor fails to correspond to an 'essence of reality'. Scientific discourse shows neither that religious discourse is epistemically unfounded, nor that it is meaningless, it merely expresses a different attitude towards the world and life (CV 5; MS134 143–6). Like Kant, Wittgenstein tries to preserve religion from the encroachment of science and metaphysics. Unlike Kant, he suggests that it is also independent of ETHICS.

Faith vs. superstition Wittgenstein distinguished between religious faith on the one hand, and superstition on the other. Throughout his career, Wittgenstein characterized superstition as the false belief in supernatural causal mechanisms, 'a sort of false science' (TLP 5.1361; OL 31; CV 72; GB 111–31). However, he also uses the term 'superstition' for any attempt to justify religious beliefs through some kind of evidence. He condemns both 'Russell and the parsons' for having tried to assess the rational credentials of religion, and contrasts the grey wisdom of philosophy with the colour of life and religion (LC 57–9; RW 102; CV 22, 62, 86). Just as metaphysics is misguided philosophy, superstition is misguided religion, in both cases because non-factual propositions are understood as statements of super-empirical facts. Genuine religious beliefs and rituals are expressive rather than instrumental (*see* ANTHROPOLOGY). What gives them their meaning is not empirical or metaphysical beliefs, but their role in the practice of the believer (CV 85).

While these points contain important insights into the workings of religious language, it is doubtful whether Wittgenstein's conclusions are justified. It is difficult to avoid the impression that double-standards are being employed when one is told, for example, that while '1 = 1' is a 'perfectly useless' proposition (*see* IDENTITY), '1 person + 1 person + 1 person = 1 personal God' makes perfectly good sense in the mouth of a trinitarian Christian. Wittgenstein's reply would be that by contrast to metaphysical pronouncements, religious propositions have a genuine use. However, even the pronouncements of revisionary metaphysics are used in a form of discourse. Wittgenstein would reply that unlike religious propositions, they are not embedded in a form of life, that is, make no difference to our extralinguistic activities. But some philosophical views (e.g., those of Marxism) have had a profound influence on the practice of their adherents. Furthermore, it is unclear how a doctrine like that of the Trinity can be given a sense simply by being uttered as part of religious practices. Finally, it is problematic to say that it is the religious practice, for example in a rite, which gives content to religious doctrines, because the doctrines themselves are supposed to underpin the practice. Although a belief in the existence of God may differ from a belief in, say, the existence of quarks, it cannot simply amount to committing oneself to a religious life, since the belief will typically be part of the reason for making such a commitment.

There are two replies to this attack. First, the fact that believers justify their beliefs by reference to evidence or religious experience no more shows that the former rest on the latter than the fact that people speak of thinking as a brain state confirms materialism. What counts is not believers' philosophical prose, but their practice, and 'the religious practices of a people' are not abandoned when their evidence is shown to be inadequate (LC 60–2; GB 121). But while a people as a whole rarely abandon their religious beliefs, reflective individuals certainly do, if they come to the conclusion that their justifications have been inadequate. Wittgenstein is committed to the view that such individuals are confused, while those who persist in citing what he (without argument) regards as flimsy justifications are not. He is also committed to the view that rationalist philosophers of religion (such as Aquinas, Kant, and Kenny) are superstitious. What implies these unpalatable conclusions is the following line of reasoning: if religious beliefs were based on evidence or metaphysical doctrines, they would be 'stupid'; religious beliefs are not stupid; hence they cannot rest on evidence or metaphysical doctrines (GB 119, 125). But religious beliefs, like philosophical doctrines, may not simply be stupid (may reflect deep-rooted human aspirations and be based on profound reflections) and yet involve irrational or incoherent beliefs.

The second reply is that whereas causal beliefs explain and justify certain instrumental practices, religious doctrines do not explain or justify the ritual practices, since the explanations make sense only within the context of those practices (see GB 121–3, 129) – for example, the doctrine of the Apostolic succession belongs to, rather than explains, the Catholic Mass. But while the doctrine may not provide a reason for participating in the Mass for someone who does not share the religious way of life, it is nevertheless the believer's justification, and it explains the Mass: we can understand why a belief in the Apostolic succession provides a reason for participating in the Mass, even if we find the doctrine incoherent and the practice irrational.

rule-following Rules play a crucial role in Wittgenstein's philosophy because of two abiding convictions: firstly, language is a rule-guided activity; secondly, the a priori status of logic, mathematics and philosophy derives from such rules. In the *Tractatus*, linguistic rules form LOGICAL SYNTAX, a complex calculus of inexorable norms hidden behind the surface of natural languages. By the mid-thirties, Wittgenstein had moved away from this CALCULUS MODEL of language. In particular, he had rejected the idea of rules which guide linguistic behaviour and determine what it makes sense to say without being known to us. To clarify the way in which rules guide our behaviour and determine the meaning of words is the strategic role of his celebrated discussion of rule-following. Because of the connection with linguistic meaning, understanding and logical necessity, the topic is central to his philosophy of language, philosophical psychology and philosophy of mathematics (it pervades *Remarks on the Foundations of Mathematics*).

Wittgenstein did not try to provide an analytic definition of 'rule', since he considered it a FAMILY-RESEMBLANCE concept best explained by reference to examples. But several points can be culled from his remarks (WVC 153–4; AWL 153–5; BT 241; PG 117–18; BB 90–8; RFM 321; SDE 24; PLP 82, 137–44).

(a) Rules are standards of correctness; they do not describe, for example, how people speak, but rather define what it is to speak correctly or meaningfully.

(b) There is a difference between a rule and its expression, a rule-formulation, just as between a number and a numeral (e.g., the same rule can be expressed in different languages). But the difference is not one between an abstract entity and its concrete name, but one between a normative function, and the linguistic form used to perform that function. We can clarify the notion of a rule by investigating the role of rule-formulations.

(c) Unlike commands or orders, rules are inherently general in that they govern an often unlimited multiplicity of occasions.

(d) Features like (a) or (c) are not tied to particular forms of words – a GRAMMATICAL proposition expressing a linguistic rule need not be a meta-linguistic statement about the employment of words, or contain expressions of generality. Rather, they depend on whether an expression has a normative function on a given occasion.

(e) 'Rule-following' is an achievement-verb: there is a difference between believing that one is following the rule and actually following it.

(f) The crucial point for the change in Wittgenstein's conception of linguistic rules is that there is a difference between following a rule and merely acting in accordance with a rule. Although rule-following presupposes a regularity in behaviour, this does not distinguish it from natural regularities like the movement of planets or human acts which happen to conform to a rule

324

unintentionally. If an agent follows a rule in Φing, the rule must be part of his reason for Φing, and not just a CAUSE. He must intend to follow the rule. However, this intentionality is only virtual. He does not have to think about or consult the rule-formulation while Φing, it is only required that he would adduce it to justify or explain his Φing. This excludes the idea of rules which are completely unknown to the agent (as those invoked by the calculus model). It also sets rule-following apart from 'inspiration'. These are cases in which the agent is guided passively, without being able to explain why he acts as he does, or to teach others the technique of following this guidance (PI §§207–8, 222, 232; BB 12–14; RFM 414–22).

The notion of rule-following thus explained poses two interrelated problems. One concerns our UNDERSTANDING of rules, the other the normativity of rules. In *Philosophical Investigations* §§143–84, Wittgenstein attacks the idea that understanding is a mental state or process from which our application of words flows. In §§185–242, he turns to the question of how a rule determines what counts as a correct or an incorrect application. We distinguish between rules which do determine an answer at each step (e.g., $y = 2x$) and those which do not (e.g., $y \neq 2x$) (PI §189; RFM 35–6). But even in the former case a puzzle arises. I teach a pupil the arithmetic series '+2'. But when he first proceeds beyond 1,000, he says '1,000, 1,004, 1,008'. The question is, what are our grounds for saying that he has misunderstood the rule? A rule like '+2' covers an unlimited number of steps. But all the pupil has to go by is a rule-formulation, and a few steps as exemplification. How does the rule-formulation, a mere sign, manage to determine in advance an unlimited number of steps? Wittgenstein considers four different answers to these puzzles.

Mechanism   Understanding a rule is a disposition, and statements about dispositions are ultimately statements about a mechanism (AWL 83–4, 91), in this case a mental or neurophysiological one which produces the right actions in the appropriate circumstances. This picture turns the rule from a reason for action into a cause, and, as a result, violates the normative nature of rules. The relationship between a mechanism and its causal consequences is merely external, at the mercy of contingent facts. To say that '1,002' is the next correct step is not to say that it is one which, say, a computer will take, or the one which I am predisposed to take. Indeed, we judge rather by reference to the rule whether the computer has broken down, or whether I am inclined to give the right answer (see PI §§149, 220; RFM 332). Equally, that I meant the pupil to write '1,002' is not a counterfactual 'Had you asked me which number he should write,...'; unlike the former, the latter is an empirical hypothesis.

325

Platonism The rule, unlike its linguistic expression, is an abstract entity which somehow already contains the whole series of even numbers. This replaces a puzzle by a mystery. It is unclear how the mind grasps such entities. To do justice to the normative nature of rules, Platonism invokes a 'super-strong connexion' which is not just causal. The rule is a 'logical machine', an 'ethereal mechanism' which is immune to break-downs and churns out an infinite totality of applications independently of us, or a set of rails which drag us along inexorably. But this illegitimately 'crosses different pictures'. Both mechanism and Platonism run together 'being determined by a matter of fact' with 'being determined by a stipulation'. In claiming that '1,002' is the next correct step, we do not *predict* that people or machines will arrive at this result, but rather stipulate that the rule has not been followed if they don't (PI §§191–7, 218; RFM 83; LC 14–15; AWL 83–4; Z §375; MS129 176; TS219 33).

Mentalism The pupil's going wrong consists in his failing to intuit what I meant by my instruction. In a way, this is correct (PI §190). But I did not think in advance of this particular step, and could not have thought in advance of the infinite number of steps which constitute the series (PI §186). Even if the rule were a mental state or an abstract entity, that would not explain rule-following, since the question remains of how that rule is to be applied, what the METHOD OF PROJECTING it onto reality or translating it into action is. The idea of a self-applying rule which already 'contains' all the steps to be taken in advance is simply mythological (PI §§195–7; BB 142; AWL 89–90, 131–5).

Hermeneutics How I meant the instruction is expressed in how I interpret it. This suggests that while the rule-formulation by itself does not determine the next correct step, its interpretation does. Against this, Wittgenstein invokes a regress argument which goes back to Kant (A133–4). An 'interpretation' is 'the substitution of one expression of the rule for another' (PI §201), and hence does not get us closer to the correct application. One might think that this definition of interpretation is too narrow (one can interpret without actually substituting one expression for another). But this would not impugn the regress argument. If an interpretation is supposed to provide the symbolic content missing from the mere rule-formulation, it must be 'something given in signs', 'a new symbol added to the old one', which leaves rule plus interpretation 'hanging in the air' (see LWL 24; PG 47; BB 4–5, 33–5, 124; Z §§229–35; PI §§84–7, 198). Rule-following cannot be explained by invoking rules on how to apply rules.

To some commentators, Wittgenstein's rejection of these explanations has suggested that he adopted a rule-scepticism. There is no such thing as objectively following or violating a rule, since any action is, on some interpretation, in accord with the rule. Even I myself cannot know what I meant by the instruction 'Add 2.' It would follow that there is no such thing as linguistic meaning. But since this semantic nihilism is obviously self-refuting, some difference between correct and incorrect proceeding is reintroduced through a Humean 'sceptical solution': what makes the pupil's proceeding incorrect is that it is rejected by the linguistic community. Alas, this is no solution, sceptical or other. If I cannot know what *I mean* by 'Add 2', the pupil has no chance of knowing whether in saying 'Carry on!' or 'Look what you've done!' (PI §185) the community means to accept or reject his steps.

Wittgenstein struggled hard to steer a line between the Scylla of rule-scepticism, and the Charybdis of pseudo-explanations like the four noted above. There are occasional hints of rule-scepticism in his reflections on FAMILY RESEMBLANCE and on MATHEMATICAL PROOF. Furthermore, some passages agonize over the 'gap' between a rule and its application, and contemplate whether a new decision is required at each step (PI §§186, 198; MS180a 68–75; MS129 117, 182). But he also stated that the sceptical 'paradox' according to which 'no course of action could be determined by a rule', because there is always another possible interpretation, is based on a 'misunderstanding'; it shows not that the rule leaves its applications undetermined, but that 'there is an understanding of the rule which is *not* an *interpretation*, but which is exhibited in what we call "obeying the rule" and "going against it" in actual cases' (PI §201). Some passages suggest that the gap between a rule and its application is crossed in our practice (TS211 112). This is correct in so far as rule-following is essentially a practice (PI §202; RFM 335, 344–6). But to think that 'a gap exists between a rule and its application' is a 'mental cramp' in the first place (AWL 90; LSD 24). The relation between a rule and its correct application, like other INTENTIONAL relations, is INTERNAL. To understand the rule *is* to know how to apply it, to know what counts as acting in accord with it and what violating it (RFM 331–2).

Any finite sequence of numbers (e.g., 1, 4, 9, 16, 25) is compatible with an infinite number of mathematical series. By the same token, any finite array of behaviour is compatible with 'any number' of rules (BB 13). It follows that extrapolating a rule from its extension, that is, behaviour described without reference to the rule, is underdetermined (this converges with Quine's thesis of the indeterminacy of translation). But it does not follow that the rule leaves its application underdetermined, as rule-scepticism has it. Internal relations are *de dicto*, they depend on how we describe things: if the rule-formulation 'Add 2' and the utterance '1,000, 1,002, 1,004' are described phonetically, it is no more possible to tell whether the latter is a correct application of the former than to derive the age of a ship's captain from its

327

dimensions (TS211 494). But the rule provides a standard for describing actions as 'obeying' or 'going against it'. Between the rule and its application there is a category difference (as between an ability and its exercise), but no gap to be bridged: if '1,002' were not the next correct step, this series would not be what we *call* 'the series of even numbers'.

This seems to reintroduce the sceptical solution. But by contrast to the latter, what counts as a correct application of a word or rule is precisely not determined 'by the agreement of human beings' but rather by reference to the rule itself. Communal agreement in judgements is a FRAMEWORK condition: unless we could agree on how to apply a rule, we would not engage in that practice (RFM 406; Z §§319, 428–31; PI §§219, 241; RPP II §414). But 'applying the rule correctly' does not mean 'doing what most people do' (rules can be misapplied by a whole group, as with the first Newtonian calculations of the moon's orbit). The rule is our standard of correctness. But nothing is such a standard unless it is used as such. There is no rule unless there is a practice of calling such-and-such 'obeying' or 'going against it'. Internal relations are effected by our normative activities – we teach and explain rules, and criticize, justify or characterize actions by reference to them (PI §§197–202; PG 213–14; RFM 344–5; LFM 83).

Unlike the connection between the proposition that *p* and the fact that *p*, that between an arithmetic formula and its application is not directly visible. So how does the pupil know what we mean? Through our explanations and instructions! If 'Add 2' meant 'Add 2 up to 1,000, 4 from 1,000 up to 2,000, etc.', it would not be correctly explained by '0, 2, 4, 6, and so on'. Given our arithmetic techniques, there is an onus to specify that the pattern changes after 1,000. But 'who says what "change" and "remaining the same" mean here?' (RFM 79–81). Appearances notwithstanding, such passages do not express a rule-scepticism, but make two other points. Firstly, although the rule does not leave us in the lurch, we are not logically compelled to follow one rule rather than another. The rule does not grab the pupil by the throat. If he continues '1,004', he is simply not playing our game. What he does is not what we call 'adding 2', but again there is no *logical* compulsion why we must use the signs 'adding 2' in this way (AWL 88–9; RFM 35–8, 328–9, 414; LFM 108, 183–7). Secondly, the notions of IDENTITY ('doing the same') or of 'accord' do not provide us with an independent ground for reprimanding a deviant pupil (PI §§214–16, 223–7; BB 140; Z §305; RFM 348–9, 392–3, 405). The concepts of 'rule-following' and of 'doing the same' are interwoven. It is a grammatical proposition that doing the same thing as before is correct if what was previously done is correct. But what counts as 'doing the same' can only be determined by reference to a particular rule. Our deviant pupil *is* doing the same as before relative to the rule 'Add 2 up to 1,000, 4 up to 2,000, 6 up to 3,000, etc.'

We can interpret any rule-formulation in different ways, and have to interpret it in some way if it is ambiguous or unclear. Yet this means not that interpretation goes on for ever, but only that what for us is the last interpretation need not be. 'Interpretation comes to an end' (RFM 341–2; PG 147; BB 34; PI §201). I can justify my writing '1,002, 1,004,...' by reference to my instructions (e.g., by counting '1,001, 1,002 – that's adding 2 to 1,000'). Asked why I understand the latter in this way I can only say 'This is simply what I do', because I have exhausted the justifications and reached 'bedrock'. But the brute factuality of our practice does not provide room for scepticism. Acting 'without justification' after all justifications have been given is not acting 'wrongfully' (PI §§211, 217, 289, 381; RFM 199, 406; Z §§300–2). If a sceptic doubts that the rule-formulation 'Add 2' as we use it demands '1,002' at the 501st step, he cannot be talking about those relata, which are defined by this fact. His doubt cannot even address the grammatical proposition it purports to address.

Wittgenstein describes rule-following as a social practice, speaking of 'customs', 'habits' and 'institutions' (PI §199). The question is whether he held a community-view, according to which rule-following is possible only within a social community. This is suggested by the claim that 'it is not possible to follow a rule "privately"' (PI §202), but the scare-quotes may indicate that what is meant is not rules which are unshared but only those which are unsharable in the sense of the PRIVATE LANGUAGE ARGUMENT (PI §256), in which this passage originally occurred. *Investigations* §199 denies that there could be 'only a single occasion' (*nur einmal*) on which 'only a single person' (*nur ein Mensch*) followed a rule. But it has been replied that this is due to the fact that the *Investigations* discusses rules which are communal; while insisting that what is essential to rule-following is only a multiplicity of occasions, not a multiplicity of speakers (PI §§204–5; RFM 334–6, 346; Z §568). Both parts of this reply would be contrived were it not for two facts: firstly, there is no plausible rationale for restricting rule-following to a community; secondly, the *Nachlass* explicitly condones the possibility of a solitary person like Robinson Crusoe following and inventing rules. Proponents of the community-view respond that this is possible only because Crusoe had been a member of a community. But Wittgenstein rightly insists that whether someone follows rules depends on what he is capable of doing, not on how he acquired that capability (MS124 213–21; MS165 103–4; MS166 4; PG 188; BB 12, 97; PI §495). Yet, Wittgenstein also suggests that rule-following is *typically* social, and that *some* rule-guided activities – including not just those which are communal by definition like buying and selling, but also doing mathematics – require the context of a social and historical 'way of living' (RFM 335–50; PI §§200–5, 337). One can play even patience only if the institution of the game exists.

S

saying/showing   The distinction between what can be said by meaningful propositions and what can only be shown pervades the *Tractatus* from the Preface to the famous final admonition 'Whereof one cannot speak, thereof one must remain silent.' To Russell, Wittgenstein wrote that it was 'the main point' of the book, and 'the cardinal problem of philosophy' (RUL 19.8.19). In a letter to von Ficker (FL 10./11.19), he proclaimed that the *Tractatus* 'consists of two parts: of the one which is here, and of everything which I have *not* written. And precisely this second part is the important one. For the Ethical is delimited from within... by my book; and I'm convinced that, *strictly* speaking, it can ONLY be delimited in this way.'

There are reasons for regarding this as a slightly hysterical piece of self-promotion *vis-à-vis* a potential publisher. Although Wittgenstein harps on the existential insignificance of the sayable (TLP Pref., 6.41–6.522), his work before and after concerns not what the *Tractatus* leaves unsaid, but what it *tries to say*. The *Tractatus* has indeed two parts, a logical one (atomistic ontology, picture theory, tautologies, mathematics, science), and a mystical one (solipsism, ethics, aesthetics). The real significance of the saying/showing distinction lies in the fact that it holds the two together by proscribing both propositions about the essence of symbolic representation and mystical pronouncements about the realm of value. It is the cardinal problem of philosophy because it transformed Wittgenstein's conception of the subject: it can no longer be the doctrine of the logical form of propositions (NL 106), since logical form cannot be stated. Instead, it is a clarificatory activity which signifies 'what cannot be said, by presenting clearly what can be said' (TLP 4.115).

Wittgenstein's index of ineffabilia includes the pictorial form common to picture and what is depicted (TLP 2.172–2.174), the meaning of signs and that two signs have the same meaning (TLP 3.33ff., 6.23), that a given symbol signifies an object or a number (TLP 4.126), the sense of a proposition (TLP 4.022, see 2.221, 4.461), the logic of facts (TLP 4.0312), the logical multiplicity or form of a proposition and of reality (TLP 4.041, 4.12f.), that a proposition is about a certain object (TLP 4.1211, 5.535), that something falls under a formal concept (TLP 4.126), that logical propositions are

TAUTOLOGIES and do not refer to LOGICAL CONSTANTS (TLP 4.0621, 4.461), that one proposition follows from another (TLP 5.12–5.132, 6.1221), the limits or scaffolding of language and the world (TLP 5.5561, 5.6f., 6.124), that there is no soul (TLP 5.5421), the truth in SOLIPSISM – that the 'world is *my* world' (TLP 5.62), that there are laws of nature (TLP 6.36), the ethical and everything that is 'higher' (TLP 6.42f.), the meaning of life – the mystical (TLP 6.52ff.), the pronouncements of the *Tractatus* itself (TLP 6.54). One can distinguish the following clusters:

(a)   the logical form common to propositions and what they depict (inexpressibility of the harmony between thought and reality);
(b)   the meaning of signs and the sense of propositions (prohibition of semantics);
(c)   the logical relations between propositions (no rules of LOGICAL INFERENCE);
(d)   the logico-syntactical category of signs (formal concepts are pseudo-concepts);
(e)   the structure of thought and world (limits to thought are set from within);
(f)   the mystical (the ineffability of value).

Expressions which try to state any of the above are 'pseudo-propositions'. What unites them is the contrast with the BIPOLAR propositions of science. While the latter make factual statements, depict combinations of objects that may or may not obtain, the former attempt to say things that could not be otherwise. It might seem that being necessary is not a sufficient condition for being a pseudo-proposition, since tautologies and contradictions are not pseudo-propositions. But this is due to the fact that the latter are degenerate propositions produced by licit combinations of genuine propositions (NM 118). Pseudo-propositions do not depend on how things are, since they concern 'transcendental' preconditions of representation and the world (NB 24.7.16; TLP 6.13, 6.421). It is unclear why (f) should have this transcendental status. Moreover, what can be shown cannot be said (TLP 4.121ff.). And in the case of (a)–(e) the reverse also holds. What such propositions try to say is shown by bipolar propositions and their limiting cases – tautologies and contradictions. But there are no meaningful propositions which even show, for example, ETHICAL value. Unlike the logical, the mystical is transcendent, not just transcendental.

Leaving aside this special case, the underlying idea is that the preconditions of symbolic representation, the rules of LOGICAL SYNTAX, cannot themselves be represented (NM 108–9). They cannot be represented by bipolar propositions, because they concern essential features which language and reality must share for the former to represent the latter. Yet the saying/

showing distinction is not simply based on a dogmatic stipulation that only bipolar propositions make sense. Rather, the principle of bipolarity is itself informed by insights into the peculiar nature of attempts to state essential features of symbolism. For one thing, unlike bipolar propositions, such propositions exclude not a genuine possibility, but rather something which contravenes logic, and hence the bounds of sense. But the attempt to refer to something illogical, even for the purpose of excluding it as NONSENSE, is itself nonsensical – this is the point of (e). For another, no proposition can say something about the logical properties of language: either such a proposition itself conforms to logic, then those logical properties must already be understood (circularity), or it does not, then it cannot be a meaningful proposition (an illogical language is impossible) (TLP 3.031, 4.12, 5.4731).

This general point is applied by (a) to the picture theory. It is not a dogmatic exclusion of self-referential propositions. Nor is it a matter of the impossibility of a proposition or model's depicting how it depicts. If a fixed map, for example, depicted itself (on a smaller scale), together with its key, this would lead to a regress, since the key to reading the key would have to be provided as well. But this is the impossibility of a picture's depicting its own METHOD OF PROJECTION. A picture cannot depict its own 'pictorial form', the possibility of structure which it must share with what it depicts, for a different reason, namely that it cannot represent it *as a possibility*. For the pictorial form of a proposition is one of its 'internal properties' (TLP 4.122–4.1241) – it could not lack that pictorial form without ceasing to be the picture it is. By the same token, no *other* proposition could represent it as a possibility, which means that there can be no bipolar propositions about the pictorial forms of propositions.

It has been suggested that the saying/showing distinction derives from Frege's paradox of concepts. Frege distinguished sharply between objects or arguments, which are saturated, and concepts or functions, which are unsaturated – i.e., cannot stand on their own but demand completion through an argument. This led Frege to make the paradoxical statement that 'the concept *horse* is not a concept.' For in attributing properties to a concept we have to use a name ('the concept *horse*') to refer to something which is unsaturated, although names can only refer to saturated entities. Frege's paradox arises out of the untenable idea that concept-words ('is a horse') *name* unsaturated entities and that proper names ('the concept (of a) horse') cannot perform that role because they do not reflect the unsaturated nature of what they try to refer to. It involves a profession of linguistic impotence, since the attempt to refer to concepts through names is a mistake forced on us by language ('Concept' 195–9; *Posthumous* 193). But it is not the seed of the saying/showing doctrine. Even (d), which deals with 'concepts', prohibits, not referring to unsaturated functions by names, but any use of formal (i.e., categorial) concepts, which include 'name', 'object',

'colour' and 'number', as in '*A* is an object' or '1 is a number' (TLP
4.126–4.1274).

One might respond that the *Tractatus* extends Frege's point because it
holds that *all* NAMES, including those of objects, are unsaturated. But while
Frege is worried about referring to unsaturated entities, the *Tractatus* is worried about predicating of a symbol that it belongs to a logico-syntactic category. This worry arose out of reflections on Russell's theory of types (RUL
1.13; NL 96–101). Russell prevents the set-theoretic paradoxes by prohibit-
ing sentences which predicate of a thing of one logical type (e.g., classes)
properties which can be predicated only of things of a different type (e.g.,
individuals). It might prohibit, for example

(1)   The class of lions is a lion

through a rule like

(1′)   'The class of lions is a lion' is nonsensical.

According to Wittgenstein, such a theory is neither possible nor necessary.
(1′) is either about SIGNS – in which case it states a contingent fact about
arbitrary conventions, not a logical rule. Or it is about symbols. In that case
it must refer to the sense or meaning of expressions. But it cannot refer to
the sense of (1), which is *ex hypothesi* nonsensical. Nor can it refer to the
meaning of the names which ultimately constitute (1). For those constituents
do not have a meaning in advance of their logical syntax being fixed.
Therefore the rules of logic cannot be expressed through propositions of the
form ' "*A*" must have such-and-such rules because it refers to an object of
such-and-such a type' (TLP 3.33ff.) – this is the point of (b).

The point of (d) is that we cannot talk about either the logico-syntactical
category of a name or the ontological category of an object with the help of
formal concepts. The ontological category of an object is determined by its
LOGICAL FORM, that is, by what other objects it can combine with in a state of
affairs. That *A* is a visual object means that it can combine with colours but
not with a pitch (TLP 2.0251; PT 2.0252). But the form of an object can
neither be named (it is not itself an object) nor be described through a
formal concept like 'colour'. Rather, it is shown by the fact that its name is
a substitution instance of a given kind of 'propositional variable' (TLP
4.127ff.). If we replace one of the 'constituents' of

(2)   *A* is red

by a placeholder, we get a propositional variable, or propositional function
(Russell)

(2′)   *X* is red.

The variable is given by the determination of its values, that is, by stipulating what sort of propositions can be constructed through filling the argument-place (TLP 3.31ff.). The values of (2′) are all those propositions we get by substituting a name for X; the variable 'collects' all the propositions of the form – 'A is red', 'B is red', etc. The formal concept of a visible object is given by this variable; it is the constant form of all expressions which can be meaningfully substituted in (2′). In an ideal notation there would be a distinct variable and a distinct style of names for each logical category.

A material concept like 'red' can occur in a genuine proposition like (2), but a formal concept like 'visible object' cannot. For it is in effect a variable, and a proposition can contain only apparent (i.e., bound) variables (*see* TAUTOLOGY). The second step above is trivial – (2′) is not a proposition but a propositional function. But the insistence that a formal concept is in effect a variable is once more based on the idea that there can be no propositions ascribing INTERNAL properties to things. 'A is an object' or 'Red is a colour' are pseudo-propositions, but what they try to say is shown by properly analysed empirical propositions in which 'A' or 'red' occur. This is the logical core of the saying/showing distinction: although the rules of logical syntax cannot be expressed in philosophical propositions, they show themselves in the logical structures of non-philosophical propositions.

Wittgenstein claims that his theory of symbolism can replace the theory of types because Russell's paradox concerning the set of all sets which are not members of themselves is disposed of by realizing that a propositional function cannot be its own argument (TLP 3.332f.; NL 96, 107). That last claim follows from Wittgenstein's conception of a propositional function (which in this respect resembles Frege's conception of concepts). If a function could be its own argument, there would be a proposition '$f(fx)$'. However, in such a construction the inner 'f' must refer to a function of the form Φx, the outer to one of the form $\Psi(\Phi x)$. The two have the sign 'f' in common, but necessarily different meanings, that is, are different symbols, simply because nothing can be a proper part of itself. It follows that one and the same propositional function cannot occur twice in a proposition, and hence that self-predication is impossible. Ruling out self-predication prevents the propositions which yield Russell's paradox – '$x \in x$' and '$x \notin x$' – if classes are (as Russell held) logical fictions such that '$\in$' is explained through predication: self-membership is a case of self-predication, and hence ruled out.

An immediate consequence of the saying/showing distinction is that the propositions of the *Tractatus* itself are nonsensical, since they employ formal concepts ('fact', 'proposition', 'object') to make claims about the essence of representation. *Notebooks* 20.10.14 suggests that such pseudo-propositions at least show what they try to say. But unlike tautologies, which show the structure of the world, philosophical pseudo-propositions cannot show anything, since they do not employ symbols in a meaningful way. The *Tractatus*'s penultimate remark accepts this conclusion:

> My propositions serve as elucidations in the following way: anyone who understands me eventually recognizes them as nonsensical ... (He must, so to speak, throw away the ladder after he has climbed up it.) He must transcend these propositions, and then he will see the world aright. (TLP 6.54; for the ladder-image see Mauthner, *Beiträge* I 2 and Schopenhauer, *World* II ch. 7; it is later repudiated, see MS109 207)

The *Tractatus* is committed to distinguishing nonsense which is based on mis-understanding logical syntax from 'important nonsense' (Ramsey, *Mathematics* 263) which is based on a correct insight into logical syntax, and tries to say what can only be shown. If, as some have claimed, its pronouncements were meant to be nonsense in the first sense, it would be neutral between, for example, Frege's and Russell's idea that propositions are names of objects and Wittgenstein's own idea that they are facts, which is obviously not the case. The *Tractatus* is neither an existentialist joke, nor a protracted nonsense poem with a numbering system. It was intended as the swansong of meta-physics and violates the bounds of sense only to attain the correct logical point of view which allows one to engage in critical logical analysis without any further violations (TLP 4.1213, 6.53).

The saying/showing distinction is a response to a problem facing any attempt to identify the bounds of sense with the limits of empirical knowl-edge, namely that establishing such bounds is not itself empirical (note Kant's difficulties in avoiding knowledge claims about things as they are in themselves). It is heroic, but self-defeating. As Ramsey pointed out, it resem-bles the child's remarks in the dialogue: A: Say 'breakfast'!; C: I can't. A: What can't you say? C: Can't say 'breakfast'. One may therefore sym-pathize with Russell's suggestion that this impasse might be overcome by talking about the logical properties of our language in a meta-language ('Introduction'). In *The Logical Syntax of Language*, Carnap elaborated this idea. He suggested that the limits of language can be expressed by switching from propositions in material mode, like

(3)   Red is a colour

to propositions in formal mode, like

(3')   'Red' is a colour-word

which is a bipolar proposition about a physical object, namely the word 'red'. This move does not escape Wittgenstein's strictures, since the *Tractatus* treats as formal concepts not just ontological but also logico-linguistic cate-gories like 'name' and 'proposition'. But the moot question is whether these

335

strictures are justified. The real shortcoming with Carnap's suggestion is that (3') only captures the necessary status which is essential to (3) if it is about a symbol, a SIGN which means a particular object. But the ontological category of that object, and hence the logico-syntactic category of the symbol, is once more an internal property. It follows that (3') could no more be bipolar than (3).

Wittgenstein's own later solution is to abandon the idea that only empirical propositions are meaningful. The *Tractatus*'s arguments show only that propositions employing formal or 'logical concepts' (OC §§36–7) do not provide us with insights into the essence of reality, or with new information (a point preserved in the idea that language is AUTONOMOUS). It does not follow that such propositions are nonsensical pseudo-propositions (RFM 395–6, 402–3). Formal concepts have legitimate uses in GRAMMATICAL propositions, as explanations of meaning or philosophical reminders. (3') *and* (3) can be used to express the rule that whatever can be said to be red can also be said to be coloured. One use of such grammatical propositions is to exclude as nonsensical the sentences which generate paradoxes like Russell's, Grelling's or the Liar. Like the *Tractatus*, the later Wittgenstein holds that these paradoxes can be dispelled not through a consistency proof, but through an analysis of the terms used in constructing them (WVC 121–4). His own analysis resembles Ryle's. Paradoxical sentences have no application in the language-game, they resemble a game like 'thumb-catching' (RFM 120–3, 367; LFM 206–9). This means that they make no statement, and hence cannot be used to derive a contradiction.

(4)   This statement is false

makes a statement only if 'this' refers to a form of words which make a true or false statement. But if 'this' refers to (4) itself, the question of what statement, if any, is made cannot be solved without vicious circularity. One can imagine a use for paradoxical sentences in a logical exercise. But (4) cannot be used to make a self-referential statement about which we can raise the unanswerable question of whether it is true or false (RFM 404; RPP I §§65, 565; Z §691; *see* CONTRADICTION).

scepticism   This is the view that knowledge is impossible, either in general or with respect to a particular domain. Modern scepticism derives from Descartes. It is based on the assumption that for a proposition to be known it must either be evident, that is, self-evident or evident to the senses, or be adequately supported by evident propositions. For the Cartesian and empiricist traditions evident propositions are those about subjective appearances ('It seems to me just as if I were perceiving such and such'), which are supposed to be immune to doubt. The sceptic challenges our right to pass from such statements to propositions about mind-independent things ('I perceive such and such'). Various foundationalist responses try to meet this challange: inductivism (inference to the best explanation), reductivism (idealist or phenomenalist), transcendental philosophy and the defence of common sense (Reid). There have also been indirect responses, which try to defuse the sceptical challenge, by rejecting the very questions it poses. The 'scandal of philosophy' is not that a proof of the existence of the external world is yet to be given (Kant), but that 'such proofs are expected and attempted again and again' (Heidegger).

One indirect response is Humean naturalism: our beliefs cannot be justified, because the sceptic's reasoning itself is perfectly legitimate and correct. But due to our natural dispositions we cannot help holding the beliefs attacked by scepticism, which hence need not be taken seriously outside the realm of philosophy. Wittgenstein agreed that sceptical doubts cannot be refuted in the sense of being shown to be false. But he insisted that scepticism is flawed in a way which can be exposed by rational argument, namely by virtue of being nonsensical. Against Russell's Humean stance that scepticism is 'practically barren' though 'logically irrefutable', he remarked 'Scepticism is *not* irrefutable, but obviously nonsensical, when it tries to raise doubts where no questions can be asked. For doubt can exist only where a question exists, a question only where an answer exists, and an answer only where something *can be said*' (TLP 6.51; NB 1.5.15).

The work leading up to and including *Philosophical Investigations* provides glimpses of such a critique of sense, a critique that helped to inspire the anti-sceptical arguments of linguistic philosophy. 'If we are using the word "to know" as it is normally used (and how else are we to use it?), then other people very often know when I am in pain' (PI §246). According to the rules of our grammar, it makes perfectly good sense to say that I know that others are in pain. This suggests that the sceptic is like someone who claims that there are no physicians in Reading, since by 'physician' he understands someone who can cure any disease within twenty minutes. His doubts either amount to an *ignoratio elenchi*, since they employ 'knowledge' according to other rules than the knowledge claims they purport to attack, or express the sceptic's rejection of those rules (BB 55–61). But according to the AUTONOMY OF LANGUAGE that rejection cannot be justified by reference to the essence of reality. Nor could it be argued that our rules are pragmatically inferior to those implicit in the sceptic's position. Our concepts draw important distinctions (e.g., between more or less well-established beliefs) which he obliterates.

Both the Cartesian sceptic and his foundationalist opponent assume that we at any rate *know*, incorrigibly, how things appear to us on the basis of introspection. Wittgenstein's attack on the INNER/OUTER picture of the mind turns the sceptic's picture on its head. We can know about the material world, but not about the postulated mental realm: first-person present tense psychological statements are (typically) AVOWALS rather than descriptions of an inner realm based on infallible introspection. Moreover, Wittgenstein suggested that the language of subjective appearances is semantically parasitic on the language of perceptual objects and qualities. We learn it later, and the sense of 'It is raining' is presupposed by that of 'It looks to me as if it is raining.' The expression of what is subjectively seen is not a description of private objects from which we precariously infer descriptions of public objects, but a new linguistic technique, namely of making *tentative* judgements about material objects (Z §§420–35). These ideas also undermine egocentric foundationalism (inductivism, reductivism). But they resemble Kant's transcendental argument that the possibility of ascribing perceptual qualities to mind-independent objects is a precondition of the possibility of ascribing mental states to oneself, except that Wittgenstein would deny that the latter are descriptions or cognitive claims.

Wittgenstein's most substantial discussion of scepticism is contained in *On Certainty*. Its inspiration was Moore's defence of common sense. Moore claimed that there are empirical truths which we can know with certainty – for example, 'The earth has existed for a great many years.' Moreover, he maintained that these common-sense truisms provide a rigorous proof of the existence of the external world, since the premises are known for certain and entail the conclusion. He held up his two hands and said 'Here is one hand and here is another, so there exist at least two material things.' *On Certainty* conducts a three-cornered argument with Moore and the sceptic. Wittgenstein grants that Moore is CERTAIN of these common-sense truisms, but denies that he *knows* them. He also rejects Moore's claim to have *proven* the philosophical proposition 'There are physical objects', since his common-sense premise begs the question. For the sceptic, a doubt remains, namely why should looking at my hands guarantee anything? After all, he is not challenging a move within our established LANGUAGE-GAMES, for example that Pluto exists. That sort of doubt can be resolved by observations and calculations. By denying that there are *any* ways of making sure, he is challenging the whole language-game of physical-object discourse (OC §§19, 23, 83, 617). In claiming to know that he has two hands, Moore takes for granted the conceptual framework which the sceptic attacks.

Wittgenstein tries to undermine both positions by impugning the sense of the very proposition 'There are physical objects' (OC §§35–7, 57). It is not an *empirical* proposition: on the sceptic's view, whether there are physical objects makes no difference to the course of our experience, which is correct in so far as we cannot even specify what it would be for there to be no physical objects. Unlike, say, 'A chair is a physical object' it is not a *grammatical* proposition either, since it is not used to explain the meaning of 'chair' or 'physical object', and does not stipulate, for example, that one can proceed from 'A chair is in the room' to 'A physical object is in the room.'

At best, like 'There are colours', it means that there is a category of words, namely 'physical-object words'. This position is heir to the *Tractatus*: like the formal concepts of the SAYING/SHOWING distinction, 'logical concepts' like that of a physical object cannot be used in empirical propositions, but are evident from the logical behaviour of physical-object words. It is also close to Carnap's proposal that the question of whether there are physical objects is an external one which, unlike internal questions ('Are there dodos?'), boils down to the question of whether to adopt a certain conceptual framework (although Carnap's idea that we might instead opt for a sense-datum language is incompatible with Wittgenstein's claim that the latter is parasitical on our physical-object language). Both philosophers also hold that doubting makes sense only if something could speak for or against the doubt, and that hence a sceptical challenge like 'Things may change when unobserved and change back when observed' is meaningless (OC §§117, 214–15; *see* VERIFICATIONISM)

Scepticism and foundationalism alike ignore that doubt and the allaying of doubt (justification) make sense only within a language-game. The language-game itself can be neither justified nor doubted, is neither reasonable nor unreasonable (OC §§559, 609–12). What kind of ground it makes sense to require or adduce in favour of a claim is part of the meaning of that claim, and hence subject to grammatical rules. These rules set limits to meaningful doubt, by determining what could possibly count as questioning or vindicating a claim of a particular kind. Doubt and justification make sense only relative to the rules guiding the use of the expressions involved. They come to an end when, after going through the ordinary procedures for assessing a claim, we are confronted with doubts which are not provided for by our rules, that is, which do not count as legitimate moves in the language-game (OC §204; PG 96–7, 101). If I have justified a claim in the ways licensed by these rules, I can only react to further challenges by rejecting them.

When challenged to show that the ripe tomato I look at in plain daylight is red my only reply is that this☞ is simply what we call 'red'. If pressed further I could only point out that this is how we speak, that is, reject the challenge as meaningless. 'It is part of the grammar of the word "chair" that *this* is what we call "to sit on a chair"' (BB 24; OC §§624–5; PI §§380–1). Such claims were one source of the paradigm-case argument employed by linguistic philosophers in the fifties: if this (pointing to the chair) is what we call 'a chair', then in stating that it is a chair we could not fail to state the truth. However, Wittgenstein insisted that 'This is a chair' is exempt from doubt only as an OSTENSIVE DEFINITION which uses the chair as a sample. In that case we have not refuted the sceptic by proving an indubitable truth, but have excluded his doubts as nonsensical through a grammatical stipulation. Equally, if a sceptic about INDUCTION remonstrates that it is only in the past that such and such a regularity has been observed, he ignores that there is no such thing as *now* having evidence from the future. What we *call* 'evidence that something will happen' is past observations (OC §275).

Moore's common-sense truisms mark points at which doubt looses its sense. They are the background against which we distinguish between true and false, and therefore 'hinges' on which even our doubts turn (OC §§94, 341–3, 401–3, 514–15, 655). At least some of them are empirical in that they state contingent facts, that is, their negation is not ruled out as nonsensical by GRAMMAR. Nevertheless, the possibility of their being false is restricted by the fact that not only our web of beliefs, but also our language-games depend on them. If they should turn out to be false, other propositions would loose their sense. For we can distinguish between true and false only against this backcloth. Consequently, we can call these propositions into question only by doubt which calls itself into question, rather like cutting off the branch on which one is sitting. As the scope of the sceptic's doubt increases, its sense contracts. 'Doubt gradually loses its sense. This language-game just *is* like that' (OC §56, see §§494, 498).

This strategy is reminiscent of the elenctic or transcendental arguments envisaged by Aristotle and Strawson: the sceptic's doubts are incoherent, since their making sense tacitly presupposes the conceptual framework which they explicitly attack. It is conclusive when directed against the idea of universal doubt, or scepticism concerning the laws of logic. But Wittgenstein extends it to sceptical attacks on empirical knowledge. The 'hypothesis' that nothing around us exists is like the hypothesis that all our calculations might be wrong, or that all moves we make in playing chess might be wrong – it removes the grounds for speaking about 'hypotheses', 'calculations' or 'playing chess'. If one is asked to bring a book, and doubts that the thing over there really is a book, one must either know what people mean by 'book' or be able to look it up or ask someone – which itself presupposes knowledge of what other words mean. But that a given word means what it does is itself an empirical fact. Hence, to engage in doubt, some empirical facts must be beyond doubt (OC §§55, 514–19).

Wittgenstein also applies this strategy to Descartes' dreaming-argument. He claims that dream-reports are AVOWALS rather than descriptions (PI §448, II 184, 222–3; see LC 41–52 for a discussion of Freud's theory of dreams). In *On Certainty*, he intimates that the dreaming-argument ignores that one cannot entertain occurrent thoughts while dreaming (OC §§675–6). This argument, elaborated by Malcolm and Kenny, is better than its reputation. Wittgenstein has a reasonable case for holding that the possibility of occurrent THOUGHTS is linked to the possibility of avowing these thoughts, and hence incompatible with sleep (he would argue that although things can occur to one during sleep, these are not beliefs one holds). Accordingly, whenever I entertain the question 'Am I awake?' I can answer it affirmatively, and without having to rely on any evidence. One might think that even if the sceptic grants the difference between dreaming that p and believing that p, he can challenge me to show that I actually believe that I am awake, as opposed to merely dreaming it. But this ignores that I can only be challenged, etc., if I am awake, otherwise I shall merely dream that I am being challenged. 'The argument "I may be dreaming" is senseless for this reason: if I am dreaming, this remark is being dreamed as well – and indeed it is also being dreamed that these words have any meaning' (OC §§383, 642). To dream that a certain string of words makes sense does not entail that it does make sense ('Dap' never entails 'p'). To be sure, it does not exclude the possibility of their making sense either, since not everything that is dreamed is false. But Wittgenstein's point is that we cannot even entertain a *doubt* whether we understand our own language, without standing 'before the abyss' (OC §§369–70, see §§114, 126), that is, without meaningful discourse coming to an end.

It has been maintained that the sceptic could cheerfully accept that his doubts violate preconditions of the possibility of language, since he rejects the possibility of semantic knowledge as well. Cheerfully perhaps, but not coherently. A claim like 'I cannot know what these words mean' is self-refuting: if it is true it must be meaningless. *If* Wittgenstein can drive the sceptic into this corner, he has prevented him from making a coherent contribution to the debate. That is not the same as refuting the sceptic, but it is not a second-best: to silence a doubt by means of argument is to resolve the philosophical problem.

science While Wittgenstein had an abiding interest in engineering and certain kinds of scientific investigation, his cultural attitudes were inimical to the scientific spirit of the twentieth century. But this ideological stance can be separated from his methodological position. The latter rejects not science but scientism, the imperialist tendencies of scientific thinking which result from the idea that science is the measure of all things. Wittgenstein insists that PHILOSOPHY cannot adopt the tasks and methods of science. His early work was influenced by the Neo-Kantian philosopher-scientists Hertz and Boltzmann. They reflected on the nature of science in order to free it from metaphysical elements, sharply distinguished between its empirical and a priori elements, and linked the latter to the nature of representation. Science forms pictures or models (*Bilder*) of reality, whose logical consequences correspond to the actual consequences of the situations depicted. Its theories are not only determined by experience, but actively constructed within the framework of a 'form of representation'. Within limits set by logic, these forms are subject only to pragmatic constraints – simplicity and explanatory power (*Mechanics* Introd.).

The *Tractatus* makes explicit this Kantian contrast between science, which represents the world, and philosophy, which 'sets' the logical 'limits' to the 'sphere of natural science'. Science explores the accidental and consists of the 'totality of true propositions' (TLP 4.11ff.). The more specific discussion of the nature of scientific theory (TLP 6.3ff.) distinguishes the following phenomena:

(a) Empirical generalizations are molecular propositions, truth-functions of ELEMENTARY PROPOSITIONS. They describe objects, and their totality is an all-inclusive description of the world.

(b) 'Laws of nature', by contrast, depict reality only indirectly. Newtonian mechanics, for example, describes all physical facts through differential equations, and in terms of forces acting upon point-particles. Its natural laws provide the 'building blocks' of empirical science, by determining a 'form of description'. They lay down how scientific propositions can be derived from 'axioms', and hence what form specific generalizations and descriptions can take. But they do not themselves describe particular point-masses. Natural laws do not describe necessities in the world, since the only necessity is logical. Indeed, they do not even provide EXPLANATIONS of why things happen as they do. In the absence of physical necessities, what happens in the world is a matter of brute contingency; it can no more be explained by reference to the operation of inviolable natural laws than by invoking fate (TLP 6.341, 6.343ff., 6.37ff.).

(c) The principles of specific scientific systems like Newtonian mechanics differ from the a priori principles of scientific theorizing in general, notably the laws of causation, induction, least action and conservation, which are themselves a mixed bag. The law of CAUSATION signifies the insistence that any event must be explicable through a natural law of *some* kind; the law of INDUCTION, by contrast, expresses an empirical proposition, namely that our forms of description will continue to fit future facts in the way they have done in the past (TLP 6.31–6.321, 6.36f., 6.362–6.372; RUL 1.14).

In formulating natural laws within the constraints of a chosen physical theory, we proceed through the 'process of induction', which means that we opt for the *simplest* law that can be reconciled with our experience. This law is then employed as the basis for predictions, on the assumption of the 'principle of induction'. We assume that nature is simple and uniform – but there can be no *logical* justification for this assumption (TLP 6.31, 6.363f.). Accordingly, laws of nature are rules for the derivation of predictions; and the principles which underlie particular scientific theories are conventions. There is only *one* LOGICAL SYNTAX. However, within its limits, different scientific theories (Newtonian vs. relativistic mechanics) are guided by different 'systems' or 'forms of describing the world' (*Formen der Weltbeschreibung*). These determine how empirical phenomena can be depicted within their framework, and hence are not themselves accountable to experience. Wittgenstein illustrates this through the analogy of describing irregular spots on a surface with the aid of a 'network' (TLP 6.341f.; NB 6.12.14, 17.1./25.4./20.6.15). On the one hand, any figure can be recorded to any degree of precision by a sufficiently fine mesh (if necessary, by moving the points of origin of the grids); the shape of the mesh (e.g., square or triangular) is 'optional'; and the use of a network brings the description into a 'unified form', which is given a priori. On the other hand, it is a posteriori, and shows something about reality, that a given figure can be described most simply by a net of a specific shape and fineness.

This picture of science is conventionalist, in the vein of Hertz and Boltzmann. In spite of its cryptic style, and the scarcity of illustrations, it became one of the major inspirations of instrumentalist conceptions of science. Unlike the *Tractatus*, Ramsey and Schlick held that laws of nature are generalizations; but they tried to distinguish them from accidental generalizations by treating them as rules rather than propositions. Wittgensteinian instrumentalism improves on earlier versions in that it does not regard scientific theories as premises of scientific predictions – which would mean that they must be true or false, and hence descriptions – but rather as rules which license scientific inferences. Nevertheless it remains open to serious objections. For one thing, the denial that natural laws provide explanations seems guided by a rationalist ideal of explanation, according to which *A* explains *B* only if *A* logically entails *B*. For another, the fact that scientific theories can be used to construct predictions does not entail that they are not descriptions. Why not say that Newton's laws describe, or are propositions about, how bodies move in the absence of friction?

The later Wittgenstein would have accepted this reply, because he adopted a more catholic conception of PROPOSITIONS (neither is there a trace of rationalist prejudices concerning explanation). But he continues to insist that scientific theories or laws of nature differ from straightforward descriptions of particular objects – by virtue of the *role* they play within scientific belief formation. His scattered remarks prefigure Kuhn (AWL 16, 39–40, 70–1, 98; BB 23, 56–7; RPP I §225; OC §§512–16): what the latter calls a scientific 'paradigm', which informs the way a scientific theory responds to evidence, Wittgenstein calls a FORM OF REPRESENTATION. For example, Newton's first law of motion is not an empirical proposition which is up for grabs, but a 'norm of representation', which guides the physicist's reaction to recalcitrant evidence. If a body does not rest or move with constant motion along a straight line, we postulate that some mass acts upon it; and if there are no visible masses, we postulate 'invisible masses', as did Hertz. The introduction

343

of a new form of representation (e.g., the Copernican revolution or Freud's idea of 'unconscious desires') may result from an empirical discovery, but is not itself a discovery forced upon us by facts. Rather, it is to adopt a new 'notation' for reasons of simplicity, explanatory power, etc.

Whether or not it is correct, this conventionalist account does not reduce scientific revolutions to attaching old labels ('desire') to new things (as is often claimed). A form of representation determines the meaning of key scientific expressions. But it does more than simply label things; it provides a way of making sense of experience, of making predictions and thus informs complex scientific practices. Changes to our form of representation are far from trivial as concerns their grounds and consequences: they result not in mere re-naming, but in a new way of theorizing about the world. Indeed, some elementary scientific propositions ('Water boils at 100° C') are so central that although they can in principle be refuted by experience, this would in effect be to 'change our whole way of looking at things' (OC §292, see §§108, 293, 342, 599–608).

The later Wittgenstein's main aim is not to provide an account of science itself, but to contrast it with PHILOSOPHY, AESTHETICS and psychoanalysis (PI §§109, 126; AWL 37–40; LC 11–29). This contrast is independent of the tenability of his conception of science, since it presupposes only that scientific theories and hypotheses try to provide causal explanations of empirical phenomena. Philosophical problems, by contrast, cannot be solved by experience or causal explanation, since they are conceptual, not factual. They require not new information or discoveries, but greater clarity about GRAMMAR. This means that there should be a division of labour between science and philosophy's second-order reflection on our conceptual apparatus. Alas, the twentieth century obsession with science makes it difficult to uphold this division, and thereby obstructs philosophy (CV 16; PR Pref.; BB 17–18):

The scientific procedure of explaining diverse phenomena by reference to a small number of fundamental laws induces a 'craving for generality' and a 'contemptuousness for the particular case': we seek analytic definitions when we should be mapping the various uses of words.

Science tries to make phenomena intelligible through causal explanations, while Wittgenstein thought that philosophical problems should be solved through an OVERVIEW of phenomena in the spirit of Goethe and Spengler (although occasionally he extends the idea of an overview to scientific problems).

The scientific obsession with progress leads us to believe that philosophical achievement must lie in the construction of ever grander theories, not in the clarification of concepts.

We are prone to believe that only science, especially physics, can tell us what is real, and that, for example, secondary qualities are merely subjective. Wittgenstein regards such claims on behalf of science as conceptual confusions which must be subjected to a philosophical critique.

In addition to this methodological resistance to scientism, Wittgenstein also developed an ideological contempt for the 'idol worship' of science, which he regarded as both a symptom and a cause of cultural decline (RW 112, 202–3; CV 6–7, 49, 56, 63). Partly, this reaction indicates his cultural conservativism. However, it also expresses a humanistic worry that the predominance of science and the advance of technology and industrialization marginalize ETHICS and art, and thus endanger the human spirit. Yet, even while regretting the pernicious influence of the scientific spirit, Wittgenstein distinguished between good and bad scientific works (RW 117; LE 4; LC 27–8; CV 42). The former follow ideals of clarity and intellectual honesty, and involve detailed empirical investigations, like Faraday's *Chemical History of a Candle*. The latter, like Jean's *Mysterious Universe*, pander to a craving for mystery, and engage in speculation.

sense (Sinn)   *see* MEANING

sign/symbol   The *Tractatus* distinguishes between signs (*Zeichen*), perceptible sounds or inscriptions, and symbols, signs which have been projected onto reality. A PROPOSITION is a 'propositional sign in its projective relation to the world' (TLP 3.12), it has a sense because it has been correlated with a situation; similarly a name is a sign which has meaning because it has been correlated with an object. At one level this distinction between a mere sign (sound or squiggle) and a significant sign or symbol is straightforward, but it is linked to several complex issues.

(a) According to the *Tractatus*'s initial explanation, a sign is 'what can be perceived of a symbol'; a 'symbol' or 'expression' is a proposition or part of a proposition which 'characterizes' or is 'essential to' the sense of the proposition, and can be shared by different propositions (TLP 3.31ff., 3.32). Accordingly, if there is something which different propositions all say, then there is an expression which characterizes this class of propositions – for example, '*A* is red', '*A* is green', etc. all say that *A* is coloured. This cannot be expressed by a bipolar proposition, since it involves a formal concept like 'colour', but only through the use of a propositional variable whose values are all propositions ascribing a colour to *A* (*see* SAYING/SHOWING).

(b) There are puzzles about the criteria of identity for symbols. (a) suggests that all signs with the same logical function, that is, all names with the same meaning and all propositional signs with the same sense (e.g., '$p \lor q$' and

345

'$\sim(\sim p . \sim q)$') express the same symbol. That is why in an ideal notation, which reveals 'the symbol in the sign' (TLP 3.325f.), every object will only have one name and every name will name only one object (*see* IDENTITY), and all propositions with the same truth-conditions will be expressed by the same T/F symbol (*see* TRUTH-TABLES). This suggests that signs are tokens (inscriptions or utterances), while symbols are types which are expressed through these tokens. But that suggestion conflicts with two other points: (i) a symbol *is* a sign in its projective relation to reality; (ii) the *Tractatus* distinguishes between 'accidental' or arbitrary, and 'essential' features of *symbols*. The latter constitute 'what signifies in a symbol', namely what all symbols that fulfil the same logical function (and hence are substitutable according to the rules of logical syntax) have in common (TLP 3.34ff.). For example, the 'real name' is what is common to all symbols which signify the same object (TLP 3.3411). Wittgenstein deliberately changed a distinction between accidental and essential features of signs into one concerning symbols (PT 3.24ff.). Presumably, his reason was that while every symbol is a sign, namely one projected onto reality, a 'mere sign' does not include its method of projection, and hence lacks essential logical features. Accordingly, we have to distinguish mere signs, symbols, and real symbols. Thus, '$p \vee q$' and '$\sim(\sim p . \sim q)$' are two different symbols, with different methods of projection; the real symbol is what they have in common in the T/F notation, namely '(TTTF)(p,q)'.

(c) The idea of a symbol is linked to that of a 'mode of signification'. *Tractatus* 3.321–3.323 states that a single sign may be 'common' or 'belong to' two different symbols, in which case they 'signify in different ways' (thereby creating philosophical confusions). It has been argued that this idea of a 'mode of signification' (*Bezeichnungsweise*) corresponds to Frege's idea of sense, a mode of presentation of a meaning. *Tractatus* 3.317 suggests that a meaning (*Bedeutung*) is what is signified by a symbol; 3.3411 that a single object may be signified by different symbols. If one assumes that these symbols differ in their mode of representing the object, it seems to follow that unlike their Russellian counterparts, Tractarian NAMES are correlated with objects not directly, but via a Fregean sense.

Against this speaks the fact that *Tractatus* 3.321 states only that any difference in mode of signification is always a difference in symbol, not that any difference in symbol is always a difference in mode of signification. Following the idea that symbols are projected signs, different symbols referring to the same object may differ not in their mode of signification, but simply in being different signs. But even if one accepts instead the idea that symbols are types, it is clear that there cannot be two names which refer to the same object through different modes of signification, simply because in an ideal notation there will be only one name for each object, which means that modes of signification do not play a role in the logical functioning of a name. Moreover, words signifying in different ways is a matter not of names referring to a single object in different ways, but of words belonging to different logical categories, as 3.323 makes clear: it applies not to logically proper names '*a*' and '*b*', but to 'is' in its capacity as copula, identity-sign, and expression of existence. It has been objected that charity demands that 3.3411 be interpreted as allowing that co-referential names can have different senses (modes of signification), since otherwise it boils down to the trivial point that we can use different signs to refer to the same object. In fact, this interpretation is extremely uncharitable, since it makes Wittgenstein's discussion of symbols contradict his explicit insistence that 'Only propositions have sense' (TLP 3.3) and that names are *directly* correlated with their meanings (TLP 3.221) and hence immune to referential failure.

(d) In the notation of the *Tractatus*, '*aRb*' is a (propositional) symbol (it depicts *a*'s standing-in-relation-*R* to *b*), while '*x-0*' is a mere sign. It could be turned into a symbol, by laying down a METHOD OF PROJECTION for its elements, that is, correlating them with elements of reality. This is something human beings do – and only human beings, since it involves a process of thinking: the noises made by a parrot could never be anything more than mere signs (*see* THOUGHT/THINKING). In this respect, signs are conventional, as the existence of different languages and notations shows. It is 'arbitrary' what signs we use as symbols, and what differences in signs mark a difference in what is symbolized (TLP 3.322). But the rules of symbolism are not arbitrary. Once we have laid down that a certain sign is to stand for a certain object, the combinatorial rules of the former are determined by the LOGICAL FORM of the latter. The possibility of adopting a certain 'notation', of projecting a system of signs in a coherent manner, 'discloses something about the essence of the world' (TLP 3.342f.). It is arbitrary whether we express negation through the presence or absence of '~', but not that any sign expressing negation must reverse the sense of what it applies to. It does not matter whether we use the *N*-operator or the standard set of LOGICAL CONSTANTS, but it does matter that the latter are replaceable by the former. It does not matter whether we call a complex 'Tully' or 'Cicero', but both signs must be analysable in the same way into ELEMENTARY PROPOSITIONS consisting of logically proper names.

The later Wittgenstein does not use the *Tractatus*'s complex contrast between signs and symbols. He continues to discuss the question of what gives MEANING to signs, but in a way which diverges from the *Tractatus*. The latter acknowledged that in order to 'recognize the symbol in the sign', that is, in order to recognize its logical role, one must pay attention to its 'significant use' (TLP 3.326). But what makes for the significant use is a mental process of thinking which accompanies the use of signs. By contrast, the later Wittgenstein rejects the search for 'the *real* sign' in our words (PI §105; OC §601). What gives life to signs is not an entity or a process associated with them, but their USE.

solipsism This is the view that nothing exists apart from oneself and the contents of one's mind. Although this idea has rarely been endorsed explicitly, idealists or phenomenalists have been tempted by or even implicitly committed to it. The discussion of solipsism (TLP 5.6–5.641) marks the intersection of the logical and mystical parts of the *Tractatus*. The 'key to the problem, how much truth there is in solipsism' is that '*the limits of my language* mean the limits of my world.' What the solipsist *means* is that 'the world is *my* world.' This inexpressible truth manifests itself in 'the fact that the limits of *language* (of the only language which I understand) mean the limits of *my* world' (TLP 5.62 refers to 5.6, see NB 23.5.15).

Russell had linked solipsism not just to the limits of knowledge, but also to those of language. According to his principle of acquaintance, every meaningful word must stand for something within the individual's immediate present experience. This suggests a semantic 'solipsism of the present moment' according to which only the sense-data I am presently aware of are real. Russell escapes this conclusion by an inductive inference to the conclusion that there probably are other minds (*Logic* 130–4; *Problems* 8–9). Wittgenstein repudiated this approach to SCEPTICISM, but developed the linguistic perspective on solipsism. His main source, however, was transcendental idealism. Kant had refuted the Cartesian doctrine of a soul-substance, but introduced two other notions: the 'transcendental unity of apperception', a formal feature of judgements, namely that they can be prefixed by 'I think'; and a 'noumenal self', the locus of free will and the moral law. Schopenhauer elaborated the former notion by claiming that the 'subject of knowledge' to which the world as representation appears is merely an 'indivisible point'. It cannot be encountered in experience, just as the eye 'sees everything except itself'. Nevertheless, it is a 'centre of all existence' and determines the limits of the world. For 'the world is my representation', and the idea of a world without a representing subject is a contradiction in terms (*World* I 3–5, 15, 332, II 277–8, 491). Schopenhauer replaced the noumenal self by a superindividual cosmic will which underlies the world as representation. I know my body as the embodiment of this will, because I am directly aware of my actions. As regards both cognition and volition, the individual, the 'microcosm', is identical with the 'macrocosm' (*World* I 103–6, 162, II 486 – an idea taken up by Weininger). Schopenhauer disavows the solipsistic implications of this identification. But, like Russell, he grants that solipsism is irrefutable, and departs from it only through insisting that the subject of experience is not a mental substance, and that everything is a manifestation of the superindividual will.

The early Wittgenstein disregarded this facile disclaimer. He developed a transcendental solipsism through metaphors and topics (MYSTICISM, ETHICS, WILL) derived from Schopenhauer. Russell had insisted that acquaintance requires a subject, with which we are acquainted, or which we know by description. Wittgenstein, by contrast, rejects the idea of the 'thinking, presenting subject'. In a book entitled *The World as I found it* no self would (Hume) or could (Schopenhauer) be mentioned. Like the eye of the visual field, the self is not a possible object of experience; and it cannot be inferred from the content of experience either. There is a 'human soul' which is the legitimate subject-matter of psychology, but it is not a unitary self or subject, but only an array of mental episodes (TLP 5.631–5.641; NB 7.8./11.8.16; cp. *Problems* 27–8; *Mysticism* ch. X; 'Theory' 36–7; *Logic* 125–74).

Like Kant and Schopenhauer, Wittgenstein combines this rejection of the Cartesian soul with accepting a 'metaphysical subject' or 'philosophical I' which enters philosophy through the fact that 'the world is my world.' This metaphysical subject is not a part of the world, but is nevertheless its 'centre', being both 'a presupposition of its existence' and its 'limit'. The relation of what we experience, our field of consciousness, to the subject of experience is analogous to that of the visual field to the eye – not the sense-organ, but what he later called the 'geometrical eye'. This self is an 'extensionless point', and the human individual a 'microcosm' (NB 11.6./4.8./12.8./2.9./12.10.16; TLP 5.63, 5.633–5.64; LPE 297–9; BB 63–5). Arguably, this metaphysical subject is identical with the 'willing subject', which is the bearer of good and evil (TLP 5.633, 5.641; NB 21./24./29.7./2.8./2.9.16).

The prima facie case for detecting *some* version of solipsism in the *Tractatus* is overwhelming. Wittgenstein concedes not only that solipsism contains a kernel of truth, as 'anti-solipsist' interpreters have it, but that 'what the solipsist *means* is quite correct' – namely that the world is my world. The only criticism is that the solipsist tries to say what can only be shown, which is the predicament of the whole *Tractatus* (*see* SAYING/SHOWING). Moreover, Wittgenstein writes *in propria persona* about the metaphysical self, that 'world and life are one' and 'that I am identical with my world'. Finally, the *Notebooks* are full of purple passages which identify the world with life, life with consciousness in general, and consciousness with the metaphysical self, and judge philosophical views by their compatibility with the 'strictly solipsistic point of view' (TLP 5.621f.; GT 8.12.14; see NB 11.6./1.–2.8.16).

On the other hand, Wittgenstein claims to have travelled from 'idealism' through 'solipsism' to 'pure realism', because 'I too belong with the rest of the world.' Wittgenstein attacks Schopenhauer's view that while the rest of the world is mere representation, the human body is a direct embodiment of the will. Moreover, in contrast to the self of traditional solipsism, both the willing and the metaphysical subject seem impersonal, a 'world soul' stripped of all individuality. However, Wittgenstein wavers on this point: the 'ethical will' is linked to individuals, and 'in a higher sense' the Schopenhauerian 'world-will' is '*my* will', just as my representations are the world (NB 2.9./ 12.–17.10./4.11.16; TLP 5.64f.). Moreover, the 'pure realism' into which solipsism collapses is compatible with an austere version of transcendental solipsism in which the analogy of the visual field takes the place of the transcendental unity of apperception. Although the subject of experience cannot be part of experience, it is a logical feature of my experiences that they belong to me. 'The subject – we want to say – does not drop out of the experience but is so much involved in it that it cannot be described' (PG 156). Any representation of the world occurs from a perspective which is uniquely mine. Because representation is linguistic, transcendental solipsism takes a linguistic turn. The 'connection between solipsism' and 'the way a sentence signifies' is that 'the I is replaced by the sentence and the relation between the I and reality is replaced by the relation between the sentence and reality' (BT 499). And that relation depends on the metaphysical subject, a linguistic soul which breathes life into mere signs:

(a) Language is *my* language, because mere SIGNS turn into symbols through *my* 'thinking the sense of the proposition' (TLP 3.11).
(b) The method of projection which underlies this language of thought links names with objects through acts of meaning (*see* OSTENSIVE DEFINITION).
(c) These acts are arguably performed by the will of the metaphysical self: 'Things acquire "meaning" only in relation to my will'; and a Schopenhauerian will is invoked to explain intentionality (NB 15.10.16; PG 144–56).
(d) I can correlate with names only objects I experience, and what I cannot project is not language. '*I* have to judge the world, to measure things' (NB 2.9.16), namely by injecting contents into logical forms.

Transcendental solipsism is compatible with empirical realism: it does not assert that 'I am the only person that exists' or reject empirical propositions about the external world or 'other minds'. The truth of solipsism manifests itself in the very possibility of representation, and more specifically, the logical form of all empirical propositions: fully analysed '*A* is in pain' refers only to pain-behaviour of which *I* am aware, while 'I am in pain' directly refers to my experience.

In his later work, Wittgenstein's perspective is 'the diametrical opposite of solipsism', and he compares the solipsist to a fly in a fly-bottle (LPE 282, 300; PI §309). His first attempt to find a way out was the methodological solipsism of his VERIFICATIONIST phase, which he shared with Carnap and Schlick (PR ch. VI; WVC 49–50; M 100–3). He abandons the metaphysical subject of transcendental solipsism, but retains the idea of a mono-centred language. First-person present tense propositions referring to immediate experiences constitute the basis of language. Although such a language can have anyone as its centre, a language with *me* as its centre is particularly adequate. Third-person psychological propositions such as

(1)   *A* feels pain

are analysed by reference to me, namely as

(1′)   *A* behaves as I do when I'm in pain.

Curiously, however, the 'I' here does not signify an ego which owns these experiences, but only an ineffable centre of language. In

(2)   I feel pain

'I' is redundant, because 'pain' is defined as something *I* have, and no one else could have (*see* I/SELF; PRIVACY). This position makes it difficult to draw a contrast between *A*'s displaying pain-behaviour, and *A*'s being in pain; BEHAVIOURISM is the flipside of solipsism. Moreover, private experiences enter into the verification of (2), but not of (1). Because of this difference in verification, mental terms do not mean the same in first- and third-person utterances.

This exotic conclusion follows not just from methodological solipsism, but from any approach to the problem of other minds based on the INNER/OUTER picture. That picture accepts that statements like (1) are conjectures based on behavioural evidence, while those like (2) are infallible, since they refer to our own private experiences. It attempts to resist the sceptical conclusion that we can never know that there are other minds through the argument from analogy: I infer that when other people behave in the way I do when I am in pain, they are also in pain. But if 'one has to imagine someone else's pain on the model of one's own, this is none too easy a thing to do; for I have to imagine pain which I *do not feel* on the model of pain which I *do feel*' (PI §302, see §398; BB 46). If a given psychological term means THIS, which I have and no one else could conceivably have, then the belief that there are other subjects of experience is not just uncertain, as the sceptic has it, but does not even make sense.

If this is correct, the 'semi-solipsism' of the inner/outer picture ultimately collapses into the solipsism of the present moment which Wittgenstein discussed in the early thirties, which claims, firstly, that whenever anything is *really* perceived it is always I who perceive it, and it is *this*, my present experience, that is perceived; and secondly, that I am the 'centre of the world' and 'the vessel of life' in that the only reality is my present experience (LPE 299; BB 61–5). The solipsist purports to have discovered that the world is *really* identical with his experiences, when all he has done is to recommend a new form of expression, namely one in which attributions of 'real' experiences to anybody other than the solipsist are meaningless, and in which we might say, for example, 'There is a real toothache' instead of 'N.N. (the solipsist) has a toothache' (BB 58–9; PI §§401–2). That way of speaking has no practical advantage, since it is not supposed to make a difference to the solipsist's behaviour. It cannot have a philosophical advantage either since it cannot be justified by reference to an 'essence of reality' (*see* AUTONOMY OF LANGUAGE).

Wittgenstein's other arguments against solipsism, which are not included in *Philosophical Investigations*, have a Kantian flavour. The solipsist invokes our ordinary concepts, but without the contrasts (e.g., between one's own present experiences and what they are experiences of) which are essential to these concepts. Thus, not only does he oscillate between different grammatical systems, but also, without these contrasts, terms like 'mine' or 'present' are vacuous. (a) In the solipsist's mouth the term 'present' has no 'neighbours'; it does not stand in contrast with past or future, and is hence redundant. Equally, 'my pain' can be used to make a significant claim only in a system in which it contrasts, for example, with 'her pain', not in one in which it reduces to 'there is pain' (PR 84–6; WVC 50, 107; M 100–3; LPE 297; BB 71–2). The sense of the solipsist's proclamation 'Only my pain is real' presupposes the grammatical system he purports to reject. (b) The first-person pronoun 'I' does not refer to, or trace, a continuous immaterial substance since the purported referent could constantly change without its use being affected at all. Nor can it express the solipsist's allegedly unique perspective, since what *he* perceives simply is *what is perceived*. It merely indicates the formal feature – the transcendental unity of apperception – that propositions can be prefixed by 'I think that' (LPE 283, 298–300; BB 60–9). Unique ownership loses its sense with the disappearance of a unique self: to be had by me is simply to be an experience. These arguments rule out anything but a methodological, ego-less solipsism which insists that language derives its meaning through private ostension to private experiences. By demonstrating the incoherence of that view, the PRIVATE LANGUAGE ARGUMENT pulls the carpet from underneath all forms of solipsism and idealism.

state of affairs   *see* FACT

surveyability   *see* MATHEMATICAL PROOF

symbol   *see* SIGN/SYMBOL

T

tautology   'Tautology' is a Greek term which means 'repetition of what has been said'. Its use in logic goes back at least to Kant (*Logik* §§36–7). Kant characterized formal logic as analytic, but distinguished between two types of analytic propositions, those in which the containment of the predicate in the subject-concept is implicit, as in 'All bodies are extended', and those in which it is explicit, as in 'All extended things are extended.' The latter he labels 'tautological', and insists that unlike the former they are 'virtually empty or devoid of consequences', since they do not even explicate the subject. This corresponds to Leibniz's distinction between 'necessary' and 'identical' truths, and to the contemporary distinction between analytical truths proper and logical truths, the former being propositions which can be reduced to logical truths through the use of definitions. In the nineteenth century, 'tautological' was used pejoratively to indicate that formal logic, in particular the law of identity '$a = a$', is trivial and pointless, since it does not extend our knowledge. Wittgenstein would have encountered the term in Coffey (see RCL) and Mauthner, who claimed that not just logical and mathematical, but even empirical truths are tautological once known (*Beiträge* III 301, 324–5). And although Russell passionately denied that logical truths are tautological or purely analytic, *Principia Mathematica* (*1.2) labels '$(p \lor p) \supset p$' the 'principle of tautology'. Even Frege admitted that a logical truth like '$p \supset p$' seems 'almost without content' ('Compound' 50).

Although the early Wittgenstein was not the first to characterize logic as tautological, he was the first to use the term in a way which is both precise and general, that is, not confined to either the principle of identity or propositions involving literal repetitions. Moreover, he used it to distinguish different types of propositions that had been treated indiscriminately as belonging to LOGIC. And he made out a convincing case for the idea that logical propositions do not describe reality, but reflect linguistic rules.

According to Frege, the truths of logic are analytic in the sense of being deducible from definitions and self-evident axioms. However, the axioms, and hence indirectly the theorems, are characterized as truths which unfold timeless relations between entities (thoughts and truth-values) inhabiting a 'third realm' beyond space and time (*Foundations* Introd., §§3, 26; *Laws* I

Pref.; 'Thought'). Russell's position was more Aristotelian than Platonist. He treated logical truths as descriptions of the most general and pervasive features of reality, and insisted that they contain only logical constants and unbound variables. Thus, 'Whatever x, α and β may be, if all αs are βs, and x is an α, then x is a β' is a logical proposition, but not 'If all men are mortal, and Socrates is a man, then Socrates is mortal' (*Principles* 11; *Principia* 93; 'Theory' 98–101; *External* 66). But he and Frege share the conviction that logic makes statements about entities or forms of some kind, just as the empirical sciences make statements about physical objects.

Rejecting this assumption is the starting-point of Wittgenstein's philosophy of logic. 'Logic must turn out to be of a TOTALLY different kind than any other science.' The first step in delivering this promise is realizing that the propositions of logic 'contain ONLY APPARENT variables', and that there are no LOGICAL CONSTANTS (RUL 22.6.12, 22.7.13; NL 107; TLP 6.112). The latter claim is directed against the idea that the terms of logic – propositional connectives and quantifiers – are names of entities, the former against the ensuing idea that the propositions of logic are statements about these entities.

Both Frege and Russell expressed the universal character of logical truths through the use of 'real' variables, that is, variables which unlike 'apparent' variables are not bound by quantifiers (*Notation* §§1, 14; *Laws* I §§17–18; *Principia* ch. I). By this token, '$p \lor \sim p$' and '$(x)fx \supset fa$' are implicit generalizations over propositions, concepts and objects. Initially, Wittgenstein agreed that logical propositions are general, but he insisted that unlike empirical generalizations they are essentially rather than accidentally true, and hence cannot be expressed through signs containing real variables (RUL 11.–12.13; NL 100). Unlike

(1) It is either raining or not raining

signs like '$p \lor \sim p$' are not themselves meaningful propositions, but only 'schemas of propositions' which use sentence-letters as dummies to indicate the logical form of those propositions which are created by replacing the dummies by meaningful sentences (this is close to Quine's account of the role of sentence-letters in such schemas). Consequently, the complete generality of the law of excluded middle can only be expressed with the help of quantifiers, namely as

(2) $(p)(p \lor \sim p)$

and logical propositions are generalizations of tautologies like (1).

'Notes dictated to Moore' substantially modifies this position, rejecting propositions like (2) as nonsensical. Three reasons are implicit in Wittgenstein's new account. First, by quantifying over propositions, (2) assimilates propositions to NAMES standing for objects, contrary to the sharp contrast

Wittgenstein elsewhere draws between the two. Second, the emerging SAYING/SHOWING distinction puts on the index both (2) and its non-formal equivalent 'Every proposition is either true or false', since they employ a formal concept to characterize essential properties of propositions. Third and most important, being general is neither necessary nor sufficient for being a logical truth. *Pace* Russell, an ungeneralized proposition like (1) is essentially true, and hence part of logic. On the other hand, general principles like the axioms of reducibility and of infinity or the law of induction are contingent and have no place in logic (NM 108–9; TLP 5.535, 6.1231ff., 6.31). The propositions of logic are not generalizations of tautologies, but themselves tautologies, that is, represented by schemas like '$p \lor \sim p$'.

Wittgenstein gives 'tautology' a precise meaning through the idea of truth-functional composition. The truth-value of a molecular proposition depends on those of the ELEMENTARY PROPOSITIONS of which it is a truth-function. Among the truth-functional combinations of propositions there are two 'limiting cases'. Tautologies are combinations which are true (contradictions like '$p . \sim p$' false) no matter what the facts are, and this is displayed by their TRUTH-TABLE taking a T (or F) for all truth-possibilities (assignments of truth-values). Ordinary truth-functions have sense, since they depict possible states of affairs truly or falsely. By contrast, tautologies and contradictions say nothing. They do not delimit the world in any way, since the former are compatible with all possible situations, the latter with none. They are not 'nonsensical', since they are licit combinations of propositions, but 'senseless' in a quantitative way, that is, they have zero sense. Unlike 'It is raining', (1) says nothing about the weather. Tautologies 'give no information': 'If fifteen, then fifteen!' is no more an answer to the question 'How many people will be present?' than 'Take it or leave it' is an order (TLP 4.46ff., 5.101; NM 118; BB 161; RFM 231; LFM 280).

Frege resisted the idea that logical truths are vacuous by pointing out that they are 'undeniably true'. Wittgenstein would grant that they are 'on the side of truth', but insist that they are 'degenerate propositions' in the sense in which a point is a degenerate conic section. For they are *made* so as to be true, since they combine BIPOLAR propositions in such a way that all factual information cancels out, and it is for this reason that they can be neither confirmed nor refuted by experience (RFM 167; see LFM 177–8; TLP 4.461, 4.465f., 6.121; NB 3./29.10.14, 6.6.15; 'Compound' 50). Again, it has been objected that at least complex logical propositions are far from vacuous. But the crucial point is that while the truth of bipolar propositions can be determined only by comparing them to reality, even complex tautologies can be recognized to be true 'from the symbol alone', namely through calculations which use 'only *rules that deal with signs*' (TLP 6.113, 6.126).

Logical propositions are not truths about an ultimate reality, nor do they express a special type of knowledge, as had traditionally been assumed; for they differ from all other propositions by virtue of being vacuous (TLP 5.1362, 6.111). Wittgenstein's account also casts more specific doubts on Frege's and Russell's axiomatic representation of logic. There are no privileged logical propositions ('axioms' or 'basic laws') from which all others ('theorems') are derived. It is a matter of indifference from which logical proposition one commences; they are all of equal status, namely tautologies, and they all say the same, namely nothing (TLP 5.43, 6.127f.; NB 10.6.15). The T/F notation reveals that '$p \vee {\sim}p$', '${\sim}(p\,.{\sim}p)$', '$p \supset p$', etc., are merely different ways of expressing one and the same tautology, namely $(TT)(p)$. For any number n of elementary propositions, there are only two limiting cases of truth-functional combination, and these are represented respectively by formulae with 2^n T's and 2^n F's. Moreover, in an ideal notation all propositions are expressed as truth-functions of the entire set of elementary propositions. This threatens to collapse logic into a single immense tautology (hence Sheffer's remark, 'There is but one Tautology and Wittgenstein is its prophet' – WAM 86). Finally, to Moore the idea that all tautologies say the same appeared as a *reductio* of the claim that they say nothing (M 61-6). Wittgenstein tries to avoid both problems by maintaining that although all tautologies *say* the same, they *show* different things about the logical properties of their constituent propositions (NM 114-17; TLP 6.12ff.). Thus, '${\sim}(p\,.{\sim}p)$' shows that 'p' and '${\sim}p$' contradict each other, '$((p \supset q)\,.p) \supset q$' shows that '$q$' follows from '$p \supset q$' and '$p$'. He thereby also provides room for LOGICAL INFERENCE: being vacuous, tautologies cannot state that one proposition follows from others, but *that* '$((p \supset q)\,.p) \supset q$' is tautological (or '$((p \supset q)\,.p)\,.{\sim}q$' a contradiction) provides 'the form of a proof' (*modus ponens*).

The *Tractatus* contends that the only logically necessary propositions are analytical, that is, vacuous tautologies (TLP 6.1f., 6.3, 6.375). All propositions which seem to be true whatever the circumstances but do not fit that bill must, on analysis, turn out to be either (a) empirical after all; (b) tautological truth-functions; (c) nonsensical, attempts to say what can only be shown. (c) holds not only of metaphysical propositions, but also of MATHEMATICAL equations. Like tautologies, they do not express a thought, but unlike tautologies they are pseudo-propositions (TLP 6.2f.). (b) applies to logical truths of the predicate calculus, for example '$(x)fx \supset fa$', because 'fa' expresses one of the possibilities which make up the possibly infinite conjunction abbreviated by '$(x)fx$' – '$fa\,.fb\,.fc$, etc.' It also applies to '${\sim}(A$ is red. A is green)', which allegedly can be analysed into a truth-functional tautology (TLP 6.1201-6.1203, 6.3751). The treatment of the former case is undermined by Wittgenstein's realization that GENERALITY cannot be explained in terms of infinite logical products, that of the latter by his subsequent discussion of COLOUR-exclusion.

For a while, Wittgenstein tried to retain the idea that such propositions are tautological by introducing into the truth-table notation rules which exclude certain truth-possibilities, such as 'TT' for '$\mathcal{A}$ is red' and 'A is green' (RLF 34–7; WVC 73–4, 91–2). However, this amounts to abandoning the idea that all necessity is analytical, based on the *truth-functional* combination of logically independent propositions. It has been maintained that in response to this difficulty Wittgenstein extended the notion of tautology to *all* necessary truths. In fact, Wittgenstein continues to reserve that label for the propositions of logic (BB 71; LPE 283; NPL 449; LFM 272–85). However, other necessary propositions resemble them in one respect. They are not compared with reality, and hence are not descriptions of anything, and *a fortiori* not of logical entities, but are to be explained by reference to linguistic rules. '$p \vee {\sim}p$' is a vacuous tautology; but *that it is* a tautology gives rise to a rule of inference which is neither ineffable nor tautological, but part of our FORM OF REPRESENTATION in that it specifies how empirical propositions can be transformed (AWL 137–40; LFM 277–80; RFM 123, 231, 245–7; WVC 35, 106, 158–9; PR 125–30). Wittgenstein also abandoned the idea that the fact that certain truth-functional combinations of elementary propositions are tautologies shows the essence of the world (TLP 6.124, 6.13; NM 108–11; *see* BIPOLARITY).

Due to the *Tractatus*, the truths of the propositional calculus are commonly characterized as tautologies. The claim that logical propositions are vacuous was accepted reluctantly by Russell, and enthusiastically by Ramsey and by the logical positivists. The logical positivists used it against Kant's idea that some a priori truths are synthetic. But they ignored Wittgenstein's distinction between tautologies and mathematical equations, and his mythology of symbolism. For them tautologies are consequences of arbitrary conventions (the truth-tabular definitions of logical constants).

thought/thinking　In the mentalist tradition, thoughts (cogitations, ideas) were understood as psychic entities or occurrences which inhabit the minds of individuals. In reaction, the anti-psychologistic and anti-idealistic movement (Frege, Moore, Russell) reverted to a Platonic picture. Thus, Frege distinguished between private ideas (*Vorstellungen*), and thoughts, which are abstract entities inhabiting a Platonic third realm. His grounds were (a) a thought, that is, what someone thinks, is true or false independently of someone's thinking it; (b) two people can have the same thought; (c) thoughts can be communicated ('Sense' 29–32; 'Thought').

Wittgenstein's early position seems to eschew both mentalism and Platonism, but the issue is obscured by the fact that he uses 'thought' (*Gedanke*) in two different roles. In its primary, Fregean use it signifies a proposition (*Satz*). A thought is a 'logical picture of facts', that is, an optimally abstract picture whose only pictorial form is its LOGICAL FORM and which does not rely on any specific medium of representation. 'In a proposition a thought finds an expression that can be perceived by the senses.' However, a thought is neither an abstract nor a mental entity correlated with a sentence. Rather, it is an 'applied, thought (*gedachte*), propositional sign', a 'proposition with a sense' (TLP 3, 3.1, 3.5, 4). This means that a thought is a sentence-in-use, a propositional sign which has been projected onto reality.

At the same time, the 'method of projection' which projects the propositional sign onto a state of affairs is 'to think the sense of the proposition' (TLP 3.11; PT 3.12f.). In its second use, *Gedanke* signifies a mental entity which has 'psychical constituents' that stand in the same sort of relation to reality as the words which are the constituents of the propositional sign (RUL 19.8.19). This suggests that a thought is a psychic fact which is not identical but isomorphic with the propositional sign on the one hand, and the depicted state of affairs on the other.

Perhaps Wittgenstein failed to notice the inconsistency because he held that the mental process of 'thinking is a kind of language' (NB 12.9.16). A thought is itself a proposition in the language of thought, and intimately tied to the propositional sign. Just as a propositional sign is a significant proposition only if it is projected by a thought onto the world, so a relation between psychical elements is a thought (rather than, say, a headache) only if it is a projection of a propositional sign. Accordingly, it is essential to thoughts that they can be completely expressed in language. This breaks with the venerable view, shared by Frege and Russell, that the relationship between thought and language is external. Thoughts are not entities beyond language, and language is not merely a medium for transmitting a prelinguistic process of thinking. At the same time, the *Tractatus* holds that the LOGICAL ANALYSIS of a proposition of sign-language (*Zeichensprache*) will reveal the structure of the underlying proposition in the language of thought. Moreover, it remains wedded to the doctrine that it is the mind which gives meaning to language by breathing life into sounds and inscriptions that would otherwise be 'dead' (BB 3–5). While the precise nature of thinking is relegated to empirical psychology, the production of thoughts is conceived of as a process which must accompany speaking, and distinguishes it from the squawkings of a parrot.

Wittgenstein later contended that the idea of a language of thought faces a dilemma. On the one hand, thought must be intrinsically representational: while my words can be interpreted by reference to what I think, my interpreting my own thoughts (save in the sense of asking myself why I have a particular thought) makes no sense; unlike speech, 'thought is the last interpretation' (BB 34–5; PG 144–5). On the other hand, this means that the psychic elements do *not* stand in the same sort of relation to reality as words. More generally, Wittgenstein criticized the view that thinking is a mental process which accompanies speech and endows it with meaning (BT ch. 6; PG ch.V; PI §§316–62). If thoughts are to give meaning to sentences they must themselves have symbolic content. Yet this leads to a vicious regress (*see* METHOD OF PROJECTION). This is obvious if one replaces the mental accompaniment by a physical one: a sentence plus a painting is no less capable of different interpretations than the sign by itself. To suppose that the mind 'could do much more in these matters' because of its occult qualities is a mythology of psychology (PG 99; Z §211).

Wittgenstein's second argument against the accompaniment conception of thinking is that what distinguishes speaking with UNDERSTANDING from the mechanical utterances of a machine or parrot is not an accompanying process (he often – PI §§330–2, 341 – speaks of the difference between 'thinking speech' (*denkendes Sprechen*) and 'thoughtless speech' (*gedankenloses Sprechen*), which wrongly suggests that he is concerned with the contrast of well-considered and careless utterances, although that topic is broached in RPP II §§250–67). Firstly, such processes are neither necessary nor sufficient for meaningful speech. Secondly, one cannot subtract the linguistic expression to distil a separate process of thinking. Speaking with understanding or thought is not like singing and accompanying it by playing the piano, but like 'singing with expression' (PI §332). The difference lies in how it is done, and in what the speaker is capable of doing (by way of explaining or defending his utterance). 'Thinking' has an adverbial character.

For a while, Wittgenstein had continued to identify thought with language, albeit 'sign-language' rather than the language of thought: philosophy is a 'descriptive science ... of thought'; but thoughts and their logical relations 'must be examined through the expressions conveying them'; thought is a 'symbolic process', and thinking 'the activity of operating with signs', which is performed by the hand, in writing, or the mouth and larynx, in speaking (LWL 4, 25; BB 6; BT 408). But while we write *with* our hands, we only *think* with them in the sense of accompanying our speech by gestures. And Wittgenstein himself came to realize that while thinking and speaking are conceptually related, they are 'categorially distinct' (RPP II §§6–8, 183–93, 238, 248, 266–7; Z §§100–3). His mature discussion undermines the assumption behind both mentalism (*Psychology* II ch. XVIII) and his own earlier lingualism (of which traces remain in *Philosophical Investigations* §§329–30), namely that thought requires a medium or vehicle.

His first step was to abandon the catholic use of 'thought', which, like the mentalist use of 'idea' and 'representation', skates over the differences between different mental concepts. He treats 'thinking' as a 'widely ramified concept', and discusses four major employments (Z §§110–12, 122; RPP II §§194, 216): (a) thinking about or meaning something; (b) reflecting on a problem; (c) believing or opining that *p*; (d) occurrent thoughts which cross one's mind at a particular moment. None of them *consist* in physical or mental processes, either words or images crossing one's mind, since such goings-on are neither necessary nor sufficient.

Clearly, long-standing 'convictions' could not consist in images or words constantly crossing one's mind (*see* PHILOSOPHICAL PSYCHOLOGY). The point holds also for (b). It would be foolish to deny, as some behaviourists have done, that when one is thinking mental images may cross one's mind. However, such inner goings-on are neither sufficient nor necessary for me to think. In a delirium I may have mental images but do not think; and I may think about a problem without any images crossing my mind. Not all of our thinking can be characterized as having mental images (a point Berkeley and Kant made *vis-à-vis* 'general ideas' or concepts).

The 'linguistic' alternative fares no better. Saying that *p* and thinking that *p* are obviously not the same. Fortunately, we do not express all of our thoughts in words; and we sometimes say that *p* when we think that *q*. One might reply that in such cases we talk to ourselves *in foro interno*, and that thinking is a kind of internal monologue, as Plato had suggested (*Theaetetus* 189e). But speaking to oneself in the imagination is no more sufficient or necessary for thinking than is having mental images. When I count sheep in order to induce sleep, I talk inwardly but I don't think; and one can perform even the most complex intellectual tasks without talking to oneself in the imagination.

This holds even for 'lightning-like thoughts' (PI §§318–21). It is implausible to insist that when it suddenly occurs to a motorist: 'You fool; there's a radar control behind the bridge, you had better slow down to 50!', his mind runs through that string of words (or of mental images) within a split second. Mental images and inner speech may be accompaniments of thinking, and may be 'logical germs' of thoughts (LW I §843). As psychological studies in the wake of Vygotsky have shown, they give rise to thoughts and serve as heuristic or mnemonic devices. However, this dependency is contingent. Inner goings-on do not determine what I think, and are not logically necessary for me to think. What we think is determined by what we would sincerely say and do, not by what images or words may flit across our minds. A motorist can be credited with the aforementioned thought if he sincerely AVOWS it, either then or later (PI §343; BB 147). Equally, whether I thought about a problem on a given occasion is determined not by internal accompaniments, but by what I am capable of doing and by the way I speak and act, and it may well depend on what went on before or after.

Wittgenstein also intimates doubt about the idea that when I speak, I must first think in some inner symbolism, linguistic or mental, and then transpose my thoughts into utterances of a different, public symbolism (BB 41; LPP 247–8). That picture has the absurd consequence that I might always be mistaken about my own thoughts. For I might read them off incorrectly from my internal display of words or images, or mis-translate them into the sign-language. One can *talk* inwardly in a particular language, but this is not the same as to *think* in a particular language. The question of whether I think in a certain language is simply the question of whether I need to translate from another language in order to speak this one.

There *are* essential links between thought and language, but they do not require any actual inner vocalization. For one thing, we identify thoughts/ beliefs by identifying their linguistic expressions (see BB 4–5, 161; PI §§501– 2; MS108 237). The answer to the question 'What are you thinking?' is not a description of an inner process, but an expression of my thoughts in words (e.g., 'I think that it will rain'). If I am challenged by a Platonist or mentalist to express the thought behind that utterance, I do not re-examine some inner process to see whether I can describe it better. Instead, I para- phrase my utterance into other symbols. Consequently, language is not just the only, if distorting, expression of thought, as Frege had it (*Posthumous* 225, 269–70), it is its ultimate expression. Equally, it is the expression of thoughts which allows one to speak of their having constituents, as Fregeans do.

The second essential link between thought and language is that the capa- city for having thoughts or beliefs (c) requires the capacity to manipulate symbols, not because unexpressed thoughts must be in a language, but because the *expression* of thoughts must be. The reason is that ascribing thoughts makes sense only in cases where we have criteria for identifying thoughts. Something must count as thinking that p rather than that q. This means that thoughts, although they need not actually be expressed, must be capable of being expressed. And only a restricted range of thoughts can be expressed in non-linguistic behaviour. A dog can think that its master is at the door, but not that its master will return in a week's time. For it could not display such a thought in its behaviour (PI §§344, 376–82, 650, II 174; Z §§518–20). Equally, we can ascribe thinking to, for example, chimpanzees only because of their problem-solving *activities*.

James mentions the case of Ballard, a deaf-mute who, having learnt sign- language, claimed that as a child he had had thoughts like 'What is the origin of the world?' (*Psychology* I 266–9). Wittgenstein challenges the idea that this story provides an empirical proof that thought is possible without speech. The thrust of his tentative reply (PI §§288, 342; LPP 43) is this. By contrast to normal cases, whether Ballard thought about the origin of the world or, for example, about dinner, is not determined by what he could have said at the time, since *ex hypothesi* he lacked the ability to use language. But, Wittgenstein has argued, neither is it straightforwardly determined by anything which may have crossed his mind. The only possible ground for attributing a particular thought to him is that he is now translating his pre- vious wordless thoughts into words. As we have seen, however, in normal cases there can be no question of having mistranslated one's thoughts, since there is no such thing as *translating* one's thoughts into language. But in Bal- lard's case the question arises whether he has translated his alleged thoughts correctly, and this casts doubt on the idea that there was anything to trans-

361

late to begin with. Ascriptions of thought make sense only on the assumption of expressive abilities, although of course one can be temporarily prevented from exercising them.

Wittgenstein thus links the notion of thinking to potential behaviour rather than to actual mental goings-on. In some passages, he goes so far as to question whether thinking is a mental *activity* (PI §339; RPP II §193; MS124 215). Reflection is not an activity one performs with the brain, since the latter is not an organ over which one has control. Nevertheless, (a) it is a voluntary exercise of an acquired mental capacity, just as running is an exercise of an acquired physical capacity; (b) it can take time, be interrupted and involve stages; (c) it can be performed in various ways, for example, with more or less effort; (d) one answer to the question 'What is she doing' is 'She is thinking about Wittgenstein.' It has been suggested that thinking *per se* (rather than thinking about arithmetic, etc.) cannot be taught and does not consist in anything. But this is equally true of an activity like moving one's arm. What underlies Wittgenstein's qualms is rather that the different stages of a thought-process can be identified only by what thoughts the thinker would vent from one moment to the next, and not by any inner goings-on. However, this lesson is better expressed by pointing out the differences between thinking and physical activities (e.g. BB 6–7; RPP II §217).

Wittgenstein's attack on the language of thought threatens a pillar of contemporary cognitive science. It anticipates Ryle's account of the adverbial nature of thinking, and his attack on the idea that we must always 'think in' something (words or images). While avoiding the pitfall of insisting on language as the universal medium of thought, Wittgenstein rehabilitates and radicalizes the Aristotelian idea that HUMAN BEINGS are essentially language-using animals. Those features that have, at various times, been thought to distinguish human beings from all other creatures – a capacity for knowing necessary truths, the possession of a moral sense, self-consciousness or a sense of history – are all derivative from our distinctive language-using abilities.

Tractatus Logico-Philosophicus (*Logisch-Philosophische Abhandlung*) Wittgenstein always referred to the only philosophical book he published during his lifetime as *Logisch-Philosophische Abhandlung*. Nevertheless, the title Moore suggested for the English edition, *Tractatus Logico-Philosophicus*, has carried the day and is now an academic household name. Unfortunately, the work itself has remained obscure. Part of the difficulty, and the appeal of the book, lies in the fact that it discusses problems like linguistic meaning, the nature of logic, the aim of philosophy and the place of the self, in a way that combines the formal with the Romantic. 'The work is strictly philosophical and at the same time literary, but there is no babbling in it' (FL 10.19). Another obstacle is that the marmoreal remarks of the *Tractatus* are extremely condensed. They are not aphorisms, since they are rigidly fitted into a tight structure. But in his attempt to avoid babbling, Wittgenstein adopted a laconic tone and compressed his remarks into what Broad called 'syncopated pipings'. Wittgenstein himself later acknowledged the justice of that remark, admitting that every sentence in the *Tractatus* should be read as the heading of a chapter, needing further exposition (the background of the *Tractatus*'s sibylline pronouncements is sometimes provided by the *Notebooks*). Finally, the 'decimal numbers assigned to the individual propositions indicate the logical importance of the propositions, the stress laid on them in my exposition. The propositions $n.1$, $n.2$, $n.3$, etc. are comments on proposition no. n; the propositions $n.m1$, $n.m2$, etc. are comments on proposition no. $n.m$; and so on' (TLP 1n). Wittgenstein considered this system essential to the book (FL 5.12.19), but it has struck many as misleading. Wittgenstein first used it in the so-called 'Prototractatus', a typescript which he composed from his *Notebooks* in 1917–18. Originally, it served as an aid for composition; but later it turned into a system of signposting. The *Tractatus* does not apply it consistently. What Wittgenstein called his 'basic thought' is tucked away as 4.0312. Propositions 1–7 are best seen as chapter headings, although 4 is elucidated not by what follows but by what precedes it.

Wittgenstein had great difficulties finding a publisher for the *Tractatus* (he unsuccessfully approached Frege and von Ficker to facilitate publication). It was eventually published in 1921 in Ostwald's *Annalen der Naturphilosophie*, and a year later in an English–German parallel edition. This was thanks to Russell's generous support. To ensure publication, Russell wrote an Introduction which Wittgenstein condemned as superficial and misleading (RUL 6.5.20), with partial justification.

The work which culminated in the *Tractatus* started in 1912 as an attempt to clarify the nature of 'the propositions of logic' and of the LOGICAL CONSTANTS. Since Wittgenstein explains LOGIC by reference to the nature of representation, this immediately led on to a 'theory of symbolism' which elucidates the nature of significant propositions in general (RUL 22.6.12, 26.12.12). The result of the discussion of logic was reached in 'Notes dictated to Moore' (1914), namely that logical propositions are TAUTOLOGIES which say nothing about reality. Wittgenstein's eventual theory of symbolism is the PICTURE THEORY (NB 29.10.14), which furnishes the background against which logical propositions occupy their unique status. Unlike tautologies, ordinary propositions depict possible states of affairs.

The picture theory draws in its wake an elaborate atomistic ontology of indestructible OBJECTS. By explaining the essence of the proposition, it explains the 'essence of being' (NB 22.1.15). This has given rise to a controversy between 'linguistic' interpretations, for which the objects of the *Tractatus* are mere posits, and 'ontological' interpretations, for which

363

language is prior only as regards the *ordo cognescendi*, not as regards the *ordo essendi*. The former is correct in that Wittgenstein's metaphysics is the fallout of his logic (NL 106): the existence of objects is deduced from a theory of linguistic representation. However, it is crucial to that theory that language is not AUTONOMOUS, but must mirror the essential nature of reality in order to be capable of depicting it. Yet later, Wittgenstein declared that his work had 'extended from the foundations of logic to the nature of the world' (NB 2.8.16). This not only fits the move from logic to ontology, but also heralds the emergence of a linguistic version of Schopenhauer's transcendental idealism (*see* SOLIPSISM), and of MYSTICAL themes.

The *Tractatus* comprises four parts, which correspond to stages of its rocky development: the theory of logic (1912–14), the picture theory (1914), the discussion of science and mathematics (1915–17), and the discussion of the mystical (1916–17). The structure of the book is as follows:

Ontology (1–2.063): although the *Tractatus* is concerned with symbolic representation (Pref.), it starts with ontology, since the nature of representation, and of what represents (thought/language), is isomorphic with the nature of what is represented (reality).

Depiction (2.1–3.5): having claimed that the world is the totality of facts, the *Tractatus* proceeds to investigate a subset of that totality, namely pictures, in particular PROPOSITIONS, that is, facts which are capable of representing other facts.

Philosophy (4–4.2): unlike science, philosophy does not consist of propositions, since the logical form shared by language and reality cannot be expressed in meaningful propositions, but shows itself in empirical propositions (*see* SAYING/SHOWING).

Theory of logic (4.21–5.641, 6.1–6.13): Wittgenstein uses truth-func-tional operations to explain the construction of molecular propositions out of elementary ones – thereby providing an account of the GENERAL PRO-POSITIONAL FORM – and to establish that logical propositions are tautologies.

Mathematics (6–6.031, 6.2–6.241): mathematics is also explained as an aspect of the logical operations by which propositions are derived from each other.

Science (6.3–6.372): science is treated along Hertzian lines as containing a priori elements, the network of our description of the world.

Mysticism (6.373–6.522): ETHICAL and AESTHETICAL value is ineffable.

Kicking away the ladder (6.53f.): the *Tractatus* aims to indicate the limits of the sayable, but acknowledges that its own pronouncements are on the far side of the limit. They should be used as a ladder which can be kicked away once climbed. 'Whereof one cannot speak, thereof one must be silent' (7).

Part of the *Tractatus*'s fascination lies in its elusive unity. A theory of representation, the picture theory of meaning, delivers an atomistic on tology; a theory of logic, an account of mysticism and a fascinating picture of philosophy itself. But some of the links are tenuous. Mysticism is not ineffable in the same way as logic, and it is not easy to see how the abstract account of scientific theories fits in with the overall picture of language.

training (*Abrichtung*) *see* EXPLANATION

truth There is no theory of truth which has not been ascribed to Wittgenstein. He has been 'credited' with a coherence theory, a pragmatic theory, a consensus theory. The truth of the matter is straightforward. The early Wittgenstein developed a sophisticated version of the correspondence theory, while the later Wittgenstein, together with Ramsey, pioneered the redundancy theory. According to the correspondence theory, truth is a relation between a truth-bearer (judgement, sentence, proposition) and something in reality which makes it true (a fact). A difficulty for proponents of the theory, such as Locke, Moore and Russell, is to give a clear account of the notions of truth-bearer, truth-maker and relation of correspondence. Frege despaired over specifying a relation of correspondence which would not collapse truth-bearer and truth-maker. He concluded that truth is *sui generis* and indefinable ('Thought' 59–60).

Wittgenstein tried to meet the challenge. Truth and falsity are not two abstract entities which the proposition names, as Frege had it (TLP 4.441; NL 107; *see* LOGICAL CONSTANTS). Nor are they two properties which propositions happen to possess, just as roses might happen to be either red or white, as Russell suggested. Being true and being false are two relations in which a proposition can stand to reality; and it is an essential feature of propositions to be BIPOLAR, that is, to be capable of standing in either relation to reality: a proposition must be capable of being true and capable of being false. Wittgenstein's positive account starts with observations which anticipate the redundancy theory and Tarskian theories of meaning and truth:

(1) '*p*' is true ≡ *p*.

But to understand the proposition that *p* we need to know more than (1), namely the logical form of the fact which constitutes the proposition '*p*' (NL 104; NM 113).

The PICTURE THEORY provides an account of how a PROPOSITION, which is a fact, represents other facts truly or falsely. 'A proposition is a picture of reality: for if I understand a proposition, I know the situation that it represents

... A proposition *shows* how things stand *if* it is true. And it *says that* they do so stand' (TLP 4.021f.).

Propositions can depict reality either truly or falsely only by being pictures or models which are compared with reality, as a ruler is laid next to an object of measurement (TLP 2.1512f., 4.05–4.062; NL 95; NB 24.11.14, 11.1.15). Molecular propositions are truth-functions of ELEMENTARY PROPOSITIONS. The truth or falsity of a molecular proposition is determined by the truth or falsity of its constituent elementary propositions. A molecular proposition is true if and only if one of its truth-grounds is fulfilled, that is, if and only if one of the possible combinations of truth-values under which it comes out as true in a TRUTH-TABLE actually obtains. Thus, '$p \cdot q$' is true if and only if one of its truth-possibilities obtains, namely the one in which both 'p' and 'q' are assigned a T in the truth-table.

Elementary propositions are composed of unanalysable NAMES which stand for simple OBJECTS in reality. Given an appropriate METHOD OF PROJECTION, the fact that these names are combined in a certain way depicts a state of affairs, a possible combination or configuration of objects in reality. An elementary proposition 'p' is true if and only if the state of affairs it depicts exists, that is, is a fact. This in turn means that the objects for which its names stand are combined in the way that the combination of names in the proposition says they are. 'A picture agrees with reality or fails to agree; it is correct or incorrect, true or false ... The agreement or disagreement of its sense with reality constitutes its truth or falsity' (TLP 2.21–2.222).

The demise of the ontology of logical atomism in 1929 removed the main elements of this account. For Austin, this was the stimulus to develop a version of the correspondence theory that does not rely on simple objects etc. For Wittgenstein it was the signal to go back to his starting-point. Having abandoned the idea that propositions are facts which combine unanalysable elements, he was left with the simple logical equivalence (1). Ramsey, perhaps stimulated by Wittgenstein, drew the conclusion that 'It is true that it is raining' says no more than 'It is raining.' The extra words have no assertive content (*Mathematics* 138–55). Unlike the early Wittgenstein, he did not formulate this equivalence through a disquotational statement like (1), but as

(1′) 'It is true that p' $\equiv$ 'p'

Wittgenstein followed suit. He insisted that ' "p" is true' can be understood only if one treats the sign 'p' as a propositional sign rather than as the name of a particular ink mark. In contrast to Tarskian theories, Wittgenstein rightly denied that 'is true' applies to sentences. Like Ramsey, he had no qualms about quantifying over propositions, which is necessary to account for statements that would otherwise defy the redundancy theory. Thus, 'Whatever the Pope says is true' is rendered as '(p)((the Pope says that

$p) \supset p)$'; 'What he says is true' is rendered as 'Things are as he says', that is, '(He says that p). p' (PG 123–4). However, Wittgenstein later reverted to a disquotational account similar to that adopted by Quine, stating that ' "p" is true = p' (PI §136; RFM 117). In either version, 'true' does not provide a peg on which to hang metaphysical disputes, since 'is true' does not state a relation, either between a proposition and a fact (as realist correspondence theorists hold), or between a proposition and a set of beliefs (as idealist coherence theorists have it). But this is not to say that (1) is all there is to the notion of truth. Wittgenstein discusses at length what it is for different types of propositions to be true, and what counts as VERIFYING them (OC §200).

In the course of abandoning logical atomism, Wittgenstein also intimated a critique of the correspondence theory which prefigures Strawson's later attack. The correspondence theory treats FACTS as inhabitants of the world. But facts are not located in space and time, they are neither here nor there. The fact that the Battle of Hastings was fought in 1066 did not happen in 1066, nor could it have been found on the battle-site. Accordingly, to say that the proposition that p is made true by the fact that p is misleading, for there is no extralinguistic item which could do anything to the proposition, or correspond to it in the way in which a statue and its replica can correspond.

Wittgenstein also denied that one can justify a proposition by pointing to the fact which, if it obtains, verifies it. One cannot point to (or describe) a fact, since a fact is not an object or a complex of objects (PR 301–3). All one can do is to point out a fact. But this is nothing other than to state it. This means, however, that the verifying fact cannot be invoked as a justification, for one would simply be repeating the proposition one was seeking to justify. One can empirically justify the proposition that p by reference to the proposition that q. One can also justify it by applying the appropriate methods of justification successfully. But one cannot justify it simply by stating that it is a fact that p. 'The limit of language is shown by its being impossible to describe the fact which corresponds to ... a sentence, without simply repeating the sentence. (This has to do with the Kantian solution of the problem of philosophy)' (CV 11; there is indeed a striking parallel with Kant's 'diallelus' argument, *Logik* Introd.).

This is not linguistic idealism. Empirical statements are verified or falsified by the way things are, which is independent of how we say they are. The truth-value of a proposition is completely independent of grammatical conventions. Yet, to say that propositions are made true by the facts, suggests a correlation of items like 'Dropping crockery makes it break.' In fact, it is more akin to saying 'Being a female fox makes one a vixen.' For Wittgenstein, it is simply a misleading way of expressing a grammatical proposition, which is, the kernel of truth in the correspondence theory: the proposition that p is true if things in fact are as it says they are (BB 30–8; PI §§134, 444).

Wittgenstein does claim that grammar is AUTONOMOUS. But that is a claim not about truth but about concepts. We must distinguish between empirical propositions, which are verified or falsified by how things are, and GRAMMATICAL propositions, which express rules for the use of words. Rules do not mirror reality, precisely because they cannot be said to be true or false. Our linguistic practice determines what empirical statements we can meaningfully make, but not whether these are true or false. Our conceptual net determines what fish we can catch, but not what, if any, fish we do catch.

Wittgenstein explicitly denies that a proposition is true if we accept it or if we find it useful (RFM 406; Z §§319, 428–31; RPP I §266).

'So you are saying that human agreement decides what is true and what is false?' – It is what human beings *say* that is true and false ... (PI §241)

Only in thinking do correct·and incorrect exist, and hence in the expression of thoughts: and the expression of thoughts, the language, is common to men. (MS124 212–13, quoted by G. P. Baker and P. M. S. Hacker, *Wittgenstein: Rules, Grammar and Necessity* (1985), 257)

The words 'is true' have a meaning or role only because human beings make, dispute and verify assertions; the concept of truth does not exist independently of our linguistic behaviour. But whether or not these assertions are true depends on how things are, because that is how we use the term 'true'.

truth-tables These are tabular representations of the way in which the truth-values of molecular propositions depend on the truth-values of their constituents (ELEMENTARY PROPOSITIONS in the *Tractatus*). The truth-table is Wittgenstein's only formal device to have found its way into logic textbooks. He himself suggests that Frege used truth-tables to explain the logical connectives, but also to make statements about truth-functions. In fact, the idea goes back to Boole, and the suggestion of using truth-tables as a mechanical decision procedure was mooted by Peirce and Schröder. It came to technical maturity simultaneously in Post and the *Tractatus* (TLP 4.31–4.45, 5.101). What is unique about the latter is the idea of using truth-tables, not as definitions of truth-functional connectives, nor exclusively as a decision procedure for the propositional calculus, but as 'propositional signs', a way of symbolizing molecular propositions, as an alternative to writing them down as '$p.q$' or '$p \lor q$', for example (TLP 4.431, 4.442; AWL 135–6; LFM 177; cp. *Notation* §7).

Truth-tables are a crucial part of the early Wittgenstein's theory of symbolism, his attempt to devise an ideal notation or 'sign-language' (*Zeichensprache*) which would reveal the LOGICAL SYNTAX underlying any possible language. In such a notation, the identity and difference of symbols would correspond precisely to the identity and difference of things symbolized (TLP 3.325, 3.342ff., 5.533). Consequently, it would show that sentences which Frege and Russell had treated as different, are one and the same symbol, alternative ways of writing the same proposition.

Wittgenstein's first attempt to replace what he calls the 'truth-function notation' of Frege and Russell was the '*ab*-notation' (NL 93–6, 102–3; NM 113–15; LWL 52). A proposition '*p*' is written as 'a-*p*-b', and '~*p*' as 'b-a-*p*-b-a', a and b being the 'two poles' of the proposition, corresponding to T and F in the *Tractatus*. What symbolizes in such a formula is the correlation of the innermost and outermost poles. This shows that 'a-b-a-*p*-b-a-b' ('~~*p*') is the same symbol as 'a-*p*-b' ('*p*'), contrary to Frege. Wittgenstein tried to extend this notation to quantifiers: 'a-(x)-a-Φx-b-(∃x)-b' corresponds to '(x)Φx', 'a-(∃x)-a-Φx-b-(x)-b' to '(∃x)Φx'. This notation symbolizes internal negation ('(x)~Φx') by reversal of the inner *ab* poles, external negation ('~(x)Φx') by reversal of the outer *ab* poles. It also shows that the arguments of the quantifiers are propositions with a sense (they have two poles), rather than names of first-level functions as in Frege. But he encountered insurmountable obstacles in extending it to IDENTITY (RUL 17.10.13).

In a two-dimensional variation of the *ab*-notation, one can display the connections between the poles of molecular propositions and those of their constituent atomic propositions (RUL 11.–12.13; NM 115). This provides a decision procedure for the propositional calculus ('*one* method'), a mechanical algorithm for distinguishing tautologies, contradictions and contingent propositions. This cumbersome procedure is included in the *Tractatus* (TLP 6.1203), but the *ab*-notation gives way to the truth-table notation (TLP 4.27–4.45, 5.101). A truth-table displays the truth-value, T or F, of a compound proposition for every possible combination of the truth-values of its constituents (elementary propositions). For a set of n elementary propositions, there are 2^n 'truth-possibilities' or 'truth-combinations', that is, possible combinations of their truth-values, each represented by a row of the truth-table. Those truth-possibilities which verify a molecular proposition are its 'truth-grounds'. And there are $(2^n)^n$ 'groups of truth-conditions', one for every possible truth-function of n propositions. The truth-conditions of a molecular proposition are its 'agreement and disagreement with the truth-possibilities of elementary propositions' (TLP 4.431), that is, its truth or falsity for the various truth-possibilities, which is recorded by the last column of a truth-table. For a pair of propositions p and q there are thus four truth possibilities, namely TT (both true), FT, TF, FF. Their truth-functions '$p . \sim q$' and '$p \supset q$', for example, are represented respectively as:

' p q	'
T T	F
F T	F
T F	T
F F	F

' p q	'
T T	T
F T	T
T F	F
F F	T

'p. ~q' has a single truth-ground, represented by the third line, (TF), and its truth-conditions are (FFTF); '$p \supset q$' has three truth-grounds, (TT, (FT), (FF), and its truth-conditions are (TTFT). Unlike their contemporary successors, Wittgenstein's truth-tables appear in inverted commas, and without the proposition at the top of the right-hand column. This indicates that they neither define the propositional connectives, nor specify the truth-conditions of molecular propositions, but are themselves propositional signs which express molecular propositions like 'p. ~q' or '$p \supset q$' without recourse to logical 'constants' or connectives.

Once the order of T's and F's in the first two columns is fixed (it is the reverse of that in modern textbooks), this notation can be simplified by writing down the last column as '(FFTF)(p,q)' or '(TTFT)(p,q)' respectively. Moreover, the elementary proposition 'p' can be represented not just by '(TF)(p)', but also by '(TFTF)(p,q)', that is, as a conjunction of itself with a tautology involving 'q', for example 'p.($q \lor$ ~q)'. The T/F column under this conjunction is identical with the T/F column under 'p' as it occurs in a table with 2^2 rows (TLP 4.442, 4.465, 5.101, 5.513; NB 3.10.14, 10.6.15). Accordingly, every proposition can be, and in an ideal notation is, represented as a truth-function of the entire set of elementary propositions, namely in a truth-table which, if there are n elementary propositions, has 2^n rows.

For Wittgenstein, the technical innovation of providing a decision procedure was only a means for revealing essential features of logic and symbolism which had been distorted by the formal languages of Frege and Russell. In particular, the truth-table notation reveals the following essential features of language:

(a) While genuine propositions have two poles, are BIPOLAR, the propositions of logic are TAUTOLOGIES which combine bipolar propositions so that their truth-values cancel each other out.

(b) Molecular propositions are represented through their truth-conditions, which shows that every proposition is a truth-function of elementary propositions.

(c) The logical properties of propositions can be calculated (or even literally seen) from the symbol alone. This replaces the dubious appeal to the self-evidence of logical propositions by a method for calculating

370

the formal properties of symbols. Logical propositions and rules of LOGICAL INFERENCE become superfluous, since the logical relations between (non-logical) propositions can be seen from their T/F representation (TLP 6.122).

(d) 'p', '$\sim\sim p$' and '$\sim\sim\sim\sim p$' are shown to be the same proposition, namely '(TF)(p)', which shows that truth-functional connectives do not stand for functions, but rather express operations (NL 93–4; *see* LOGICAL CONSTANTS). In the same manner, '$p \vee \sim p$', '$\sim(p . \sim p)$', '$p \equiv \sim\sim p$' and '$p \supset p$' turn out to be one and the same tautology, '(TT)(p)'; and '$(p.(p \supset q)) \supset q$' and '$(p.(\sim q \supset \sim p)) \supset q$' are similarly both expressed by '(TTTT)(p,q)'. This shows that it is impossible to distinguish between axioms (primitive logical propositions) and theorems.

Although Wittgenstein initially tried to extend the truth-table method to the predicate calculus, the *Tractatus*, unlike the Vienna Circle, is perfectly aware of the fact that the method is restricted to 'cases in which no generality-sign occurs', since it cannot be applied to infinite logical sums or products (TLP 6.1203; cf. RUL 11.–12./13). For this reason, Church's theorem, which shows that there can be no decision procedure for the polyadic predicate calculus, does not directly refute the *Tractatus*. Wittgenstein's claim that the logical truths of the predicate calculus are tautologies in the same sense as those of the propositional calculus was a claim about the nature of logical truth, not about the scope of a decision procedure. However, since the idea of a tautology is explained by reference to truth-tables, the limitations of truth-tables limit the scope of the *Tractatus's* account. Two such limitations dawned on Wittgenstein, namely the problem of explaining GENERALITY in terms of logical products, and the problem of COLOUR-exclusion. The latter made him realize that not all necessity is tautological, since there are non-truth-functional logical relations, and he soon abandoned an attempt to adapt the truth-table notation to such relations (RLF; WVC 73–4, 91–2). It also forced him to abandon the idea that elementary propositions are logically independent, which destroys the claim of the T/F notation to display all meaningful propositions as truth-functions of elementary propositions, a claim which presupposes that every one of the 2^n rows of the truth-table presents a separate truth-possibility. As a result, in Wittgenstein's later work, truth-tables lose their paramount role of displaying the structure of propositions and the nature of logical necessity.

U

understanding   According to the mentalist theory of meaning epitomized
by Locke, the meaning of a word is an idea, an image in the mind of the
speaker. A similar picture is at work in Russell, for whom understanding a
proposition is being acquainted with what its ultimate consituents stand for,
namely sense-data, and with its logical form. For mentalism, communication
is either a causal process by which speakers induce in their hearers ideas
which are similar to the ones they associate with a word, or a matter of
translation, with speakers translating their internal mental vocabulary into
sounds which their hearers retranslate into their own PRIVATE LANGUAGES.
This position implies that we can never know whether communication has
been successful. Since people are *ex hypothesi* acquainted with different sense-
data or ideas, they attach 'quite different meanings to their words' (*Logic*
195; 'Theory' 105–35). So presumably, communication requires only that a
similar idea is produced in the hearer. However, we could never know whether the speaker manages to do so, since each one of us is acquainted only
with his own ideas.

The Frege showed against mentalism that the sense of a sentence, the thought
it expresses, cannot be private, and he concluded that it is an abstract entity
which can be apprehended by different people. However, he was forced to
supplement this Platonist conception of meaning by a mentalist account of
understanding. To understand a sentence is to 'grasp its sense', that is to
latch on to this abstract entity. In communication the speaker does not
induce in the hearer a qualitatively identical idea, but brings him to grasp a
numerically identical thought. Understanding is a 'mental process', albeit
one at the 'very confines of the mental', since it has to cross the ontological
gap between the mental and the abstract. The nature of this process
remains a mystery. It is equally mysterious how we can check whether
speaker and hearer have indeed latched on to the same abstract entity, since
Frege accepts the received idea that the contents of the mind are private
('Sense' 29–30; 'Thought' 68; *Posthumous* 137–45).

The early Wittgenstein combined Frege's anti-psychologistic evasiveness
with Russell's logical atomism. We are capable of constructing and understanding an unlimited number of propositions because we tacitly calculate

their senses from their constituents and their mode of combination. The sense of a molecular proposition is derived from those of its constituent elementary propositions according to the rules of truth-functional combination. The sense of an elementary proposition is derived from the meanings of its unanalysable elements, logically proper NAMES. The process of calculation presupposes a process of analysis, since the constituents and logical forms of ordinary propositions are hidden behind their grammatical surface (TLP 3.318, 4.002, 4.024–4.026). Both processes must be unconscious: we are usually not aware of them, and they will only be made explicit by a successfully completed LOGICAL ANALYSIS of the propositions of natural languages. The result of calculating the sense of a proposition is a string of 'thoughts' which accompany communication. Thoughts are psychic facts which consist of thought-constituents that correspond to the names in the propositional sign. The relation of these constituents to the objects of the depicted situation 'would be a matter for psychology to find out'. More generally, the study of 'thought-processes' is irrelevant to logic (TLP 4.1121; RUL 19.8.19; NB 10.11.14).

Wittgenstein's later approach is radically different. Instead of sweeping the problem of how we explain and understand words and sentences under the carpet in the name of anti-psychologism, he develops a non-psychologistic account of understanding. He rejects the assumption, shared by mentalism and Platonism, that sentences merely provide the perceptible clothing of language-independent THOUGHTS. Frege and the *Tractatus* were right to regard mental processes and images as irrelevant to sentence-meaning, but wrong to think that the notion of meaning can therefore be explained without reference to the notion of understanding. Communication is not a matter of making something happen in the hearer's mind, the grasping of a sense, such that it is irrelevant what happens thereafter. Understanding an utterance is not having an experience, nor is it anything else which happens in the hearer's mind. Rather, it is an ability, which is manifest in how the hearer reacts to the utterance (PI §§317, 363, 501–10). Understanding a word is also an ability, which manifests itself in three ways: in how one uses the word, in how one responds to its use by others, and in how one explains what it means when asked (PI §75; AWL 48–50; LFM 19–28). These three CRITERIA of understanding a word can in principle come apart (someone might use a word correctly without reacting appropriately or being able to explain it), but it is crucial to our concept that they commonly coincide. Understanding is a 'correlate' of EXPLANATION and meaning, and instead of asking 'What is the meaning of "*X*"?' we should ask 'How is "*X*" explained?' and 'What are our criteria for someone's understanding "*X*"?' (PG 45, 60; BT 11).

During his transition period, Wittgenstein regarded 'understanding' as a FAMILY-RESEMBLANCE term denoting a variety of interconnected processes (PG

49, 74; PLP 347–8). His rationale was that there are diverse behavioural manifestations of understanding. Later, this claim recedes into the background, presumably because he realized that a term may be applied on the basis of diverse criteria without signifying a family of cases. But he may have continued to hold that linguistic understanding and *other* types of understanding, like understanding people or AESTHETIC understanding, are connected only by overlapping similarities. For example, one can understand a piece of music without being able to provide a paraphrase. By contrast, the understanding of a poem involves a higher degree of linguistic understanding: one knows how to paraphrase expressions occurring in a poem, but also why they cannot be replaced by a paraphrase in this context (PI §§522–35; PG 69; M 105).

Wittgenstein also came to reject the idea that 'understanding' signifies a family of *phenomena* (PI §§143–84). Understanding is neither a mental nor a physical event, process or state. This is not to deny that there may be characteristic mental or physiological 'accompaniments' of understanding, it is to deny only that these *constitute* our understanding (PI §152, II 181). Wittgenstein adduces three different arguments in favour of this claim. The first is that no mental or physiological phenomena are logically *necessary* for understanding. Although a variety of images or feelings may cross my mind when I understand a proposition, none of them are essential to understanding. Mentalist theories of meaning assume that having a mental image is necessary for connecting an expression and the object it refers to. But this cannot be a general precondition: otherwise it would be impossible to understand the order 'Imagine a yellow patch!' without first executing it (PI §§35, 172–9; BB 12, 149–50). There are physiological prerequisites of understanding – for example having a brain of a certain size and complexity, or even the occurrence of specific neural processes. But these are empirical necessities which tell us nothing about the concept of 'understanding' (BB 7, 118–20; PI §§149–58, 339, 376; RPP I §1063). Wittgenstein has been accused of ignoring that neural processes are necessary for understanding, in a metaphysical rather than an empirical or a conceptual sense. But Wittgenstein explicitly rejected metaphysical necessities of this kind (*see* AUTONOMY OF LANGUAGE). Neither 'Now she understands' (e.g., a word) nor 'Now I can go on' (e.g., continue an arithmetical series) is a claim about neural goings-on. The former is based on behavioural criteria, that is, on performance. The latter is not a description or a report, but an AVOWAL of understanding, which is not based on evidence of any kind (PI §§151, 179–81, 323). For others, my sincere avowal is a criterion of my understanding: it usually creates a presumption that I in fact understand, although that presumption can be overturned by my failure to manifest this understanding in appropriate circumstances.

Wittgenstein's second argument is that such phenomena are not *sufficient* –

their presence does not guarantee understanding. It is tempting to suppose that having an appropriate mental image guarantees understanding. But if I am told to fetch a yellow flower, an image of a yellow flower may cross my mind, without my understanding the order. After all, any mental image which occurs to me remains to be applied, and there are different METHODS OF PROJECTING it. Equally, the fact that the correct formula occurs to a pupil who is taught an arithmetical series does not guarantee that he will be able to continue the series. This lesson also applies to the Fregean picture. Even if we grant the mysterious grasping of the sense, how can such an abstract entity be a 'mode of determining' what the expression stands for? How can it determine the use of a word over time? It could do so only if it were a 'logical machine', an entity in which all the possible applications were already laid up in such a way that grasping it takes one through an infinite number of steps. But this 'philosophical superlative' is sheer mystery-mongering (PI §§139, 192; PG 40; BB 32–6; LSD 136; *see* RULE-FOLLOWING).

One might protest that the pupil's understanding consists not in the formula's simply flitting through his mind, but in the fact that he derives his steps from the formula. Wittgenstein tackles this reply in his discussion of reading (PI §§156–78). He concedes that the difference between a person who reads and one who merely pretends to read is that the former derives what he says from the text. The text is not the cause but the reason for my reading aloud as I do. Reading is a rule-guided activity. But the attempt to identify an essence of 'deriving' among the multiplicity of circumstances surrounding it fails. Such failures led James to exclaim that understanding is a mysterious phenomenon which eludes our coarse psychological vocabulary. However, this is because we have stripped the onion of its skin in search of its heart (PI §164; *Psychology* I 244, 251; this metaphor stems from Ibsen's *Peer Gynt*). For whether or not I have derived my words from the text does itself depend not on anything which went through my mind at the time, but on what I am capable of doing with the text. Reading is the exercise of an ability, not the manifestation of a mechanism, mental or biological.

This conclusion is reinforced by Wittgenstein's third argument. Linguistic understanding is not an act: it is not something we do, either voluntarily or involuntarily. Nor is it an event or a process (PI §154; PG 85), since it is not something which happens or goes on. 'Understanding' signifies an abiding condition. The moot question is whether it signifies a state, not just in the sense of being a static verb, but as regards its overall GRAMMAR. *Philosophical Investigations* 59n suggests that understanding a word is a state, but not a mental one, presumably because it is the state of a person rather than a mind. But other passages repudiate this suggestion (BB 117–18; Z §§71–87) on grounds Wittgenstein also rehearsed concerning INTENDING AND MEANING SOMETHING. Unlike mental states (e.g., having a headache), understanding lacks 'genuine duration': one cannot by checking ascertain whether it is still

375

going on, and it is not interrupted by, for example, sleep. Moreover, there are no criteria for this state which are independent of its manifestations (PI §149; see Z §§21, 26, 78, 669; BB 5, 20, 32, 78, 143). This suggests that understanding is a potentiality rather than an actuality. Moreover, it is not a disposition, since I do not avow understanding on the basis of observing my past behaviour under similar circumstances. Rather, linguistic understanding is an ability (*Können*), the mastery of the techniques of using words in countless speech activities (PI §150; BT 149; PG 47–51).

The phenomenon of understanding 'in a flash' raises a puzzle for Wittgenstein's position (PI §§138, 197, II 175–6, 181). The use of a word is spread out over time and hence it is difficult to see how it could be grasped in an instant. Wittgenstein replies that the fact that we can understand a word in an instant is no more mysterious than the fact that in intending to play chess we do not need to run through all of its rules to ensure that it is chess and not some other game that we intend to play. 'Now I can go on' is not the report of an infinitely condensed process (going through the whole of an arithmetical series), but a reaction. But of course it is not incorrigible. Whether and what I understand in an instant is determined not by anything going on at the time, but by what I am capable of doing subsequently, which has to conform to an established practice of using the term or continuing the arithmetical series. And if such reactions of understanding were generally not followed by successful performance, they would lose their role in our language-game.

use According to what Wittgenstein called the AUGUSTINIAN PICTURE OF LANGUAGE, the meaning of an expression is the object to which it refers. While the early Wittgenstein, along with Russell and Frege, subscribed to a version of this picture, the later Wittgenstein was the first to subject it to sustained criticism. Failure to stand for an object does not render an expression meaningless, and it is a category mistake to treat the object a word refers to as its meaning. Wittgenstein also presented a famous alternative to the referential conception. His early work had already given prominence to the *use* of signs. However, for the *Tractatus* the use of a sign merely *displays* its combinatorial possibilities, which are *determined* by the combinatorial possibilities of the object it stands for. It is up to us what NAMES to project onto what objects, but once we have done so, our use has to mirror the essence of those referents (TLP 3.326ff., 6.211; NB 11.9.16; *see* MEANING-BODY).

Wittgenstein's later position is radically different. The meaning of a sign is not a meaning-body, an entity which determines its use. A sign becomes meaningful not through being associated with an object, but through having a rule-governed use (PI §§432, 454; AWL 3, 30). Whether a sign is meaningful depends on whether there is an established use, whether it can be employed to perform meaningful linguistic acts; what meaning it has depends on how it can be used. 'For a *large* class of cases – though not for all – in which we employ the word "meaning" it can be defined thus: the meaning of a word is its use in the language' (PI §43, cp. §30; BB 69). Given that Wittgenstein had no qualms about ascribing meaning in this sense to, for example, proper names, the qualification probably excludes not certain types of expressions, but a certain sense of 'meaning', namely natural significance, as in 'These clouds mean rain.'

Wittgenstein's suggestion that meaning is use not only informs the linguistic philosophy of Ryle, Austin and Strawson, but is also accepted by some of their adversaries (Quine, Dummett), and taken for granted by lexicographers and field-linguists. It is also plausible: we learn the meaning of words by learning how to use them, just as we learn how to play chess, not by associating the pieces with objects, but by learning how they can be moved. Nevertheless, it has come in for severe criticism from formal semanticists. Sometimes, Wittgenstein's followers try to bypass the latter *ab initio*. Thus, it is pointed out that he does not proffer a *theory* of meaning. This is correct, but does not immunize his position. Wittgenstein elucidates the meaning of words by describing their use. This presupposes an *account* of meaning – all the more so if such investigations are contrasted with systematic theories. Whether meaning is the sort of thing one should have a theory of depends on the concept of meaning. On the other hand, Wittgenstein's critics often ignore that what is at issue here is the ordinary concept of meaning, not technical notions which formal semanticists might devise.

Another evasive move is to insist that Wittgenstein does not provide even an account of meaning, but was simply giving a piece of methodological advice: 'Don't ask for the meaning, ask for the use!' In our investigations of philosophically contentious terms, the very notion of 'the meaning' misleads us, since its nominal form suggests an object beyond the sign (this is even more obvious for *Bedeutung*, which derives from *deuten*, i.e. 'pointing'). The concept of meaning is obsolete save for expressions such as 'means the same' or 'has no meaning' (M 51–2; AWL 30; PG 56; PI §120). The same line is taken by Quine. However, unlike Quine, Wittgenstein is committed to the view that philosophical problems about meaning cannot be solved simply by expunging the term from philosophical vocabulary (*see* METALOGIC). Wittgenstein's methodological maxim must be based on a clear understanding of the concept of meaning.

Wittgenstein has been blamed for disregarding the fact that the meaning of a word cannot be identified with particular utterances, or even all actual utterances, since they include misuses. It has also been objected that we should be concerned not with how we use words, but with why we use them the way we do. Both points ignore the normative dimension of Wittgenstein's conception of linguistic meaning. Wittgenstein elucidates the notion of meaning by establishing its conceptual connections with other notions, such as UNDERSTANDING and EXPLANATION. The meaning of a word is what is explained by an explanation of meaning, namely how a word can be used meaningfully in a particular language. Such explanations are what Wittgenstein calls GRAMMATICAL rules. They cover an unlimited number of occasions, and are standards for the *correct* use of expressions. We invoke them to justify and criticize our employment of words, which means that they are our rationales for using words the way we do. And if the question of why we use words is aimed at establishing the causes of our adopting certain rules, it is irrelevant to the meaning of the words concerned (although it may be relevant to their etymology). Meaning is use in accordance with grammatical rules (AWL 44–8, 85; OC §§61–3).

However, although the notions of meaning and rule-guided use overlap, they diverge in important respects. First, there are expressions which have a use, but no meaning, such as 'tally-ho' and 'abracadabra'. Second, unlike its meaning, the use of a word can be fashionable, accompanied by gestures and reveal something about the speaker, etc. Third, two expressions may have the same meaning without having the same use (e.g., 'cop'/'policeman'). Someone who identifies meaning and use cannot discard these points as minor details. For they reveal that the use of 'the use of a word' differs from the use of 'the meaning of a word', and if the identification-slogan were correct, this would demonstrate that the two words do *not* mean the same. The first divergence shows that the notion of use has a wider extension than that of meaning; the second that there is a category difference between 'meaning' and 'use'; the third that not all aspects of the use of a term are relevant to its meaning.

While some passages simply identify meaning and use, others are compatible with the above qualifications (PG 60; LFM 192 vs. PI §139, II 212, 220). Although meaning does not determine use, use determines meaning, not causally, but logically (just as for Frege sense determines 'meaning', what a word stands for). While sameness of meaning co-exists with difference of use, every difference in meaning is a difference in use. Given the use of a word, we can infer its meaning without further evidence, but not vice versa. One cannot tell from a dictionary explanation of 'cop' whether the term is frequently used by British academics, but one can write the dictionary entry on the basis of a full description of the term's employment. We can learn from the use of a word everything there is to its meaning; which means that conceptual analysis remains a matter of investigating linguistic use. Unfortunately, this does not solve the problem that the term 'use' *in vacuo* is too nebulous to be helpful. But it brings the difficulty into focus: what aspects of use are relevant to meaning? Wittgenstein was aware of this problem. Commenting on a fictional language-game in which one and the same type of tool has a different name on different days of the week, he claims 'not every *use* is a meaning' (LW I §289). One suggestion, which seems to take us back to a referential conception, is that what matters about the use of an expression to its meaning is what it is used of or signifies. However, not all expressions stand for an object. It has been replied that even non-referring expressions like 'and' signify something: there are 'features' or 'conditions' that warrant their application. But this amounts to no more than saying that they are meaningful. The meaning of expressions is a matter of the conditions of their correct use. But that is not disputed by a use-oriented conception of meaning. We use signs in the world, whether or not we use them to refer to objects in the world.

Wittgenstein himself suggests that those aspects of the use of a word which determine its meaning are its role or function, but admits that this idea is itself imprecise (LW I §§278–304; LPP 291). Elsewhere, he links the meaning of a word to its purpose or aim, and compares words and propositions to tools. Important logical differences between words are disguised by the similarity in their linguistic appearance or form ('2', 'pain', 'table' are all nouns; 'to swim', 'to mean' verbs) but are revealed by their function, just as the differences between a hammer and a chisel are revealed in the way they operate (PI §§5, 11–14, 421, 489; BB 67). However, Wittgenstein did not hold an instrumentalist conception of meaning according to which the meaning of a word, like that of a tool, is its effect, namely on the behaviour of others. Such causal theories had been developed in the twenties by Russell on the one hand, and Ogden and Richards on the other. For Russell, speech is a means of producing in our hearers the images which are in us. The connection between a word and its meaning (an object, or a mental image of it in the case of memory statements) is a causal one. One understands⁻ a word actively if suitable circumstances make one use it, passively if hearing the word causes one to behave in suitable ways (*Analysis* ch. X). Ogden and Richards held a similar theory: the meaning of a symbol is the thought which hearing it causes or which causes the uttering of it. Whether the use of a symbol is correct depends on whether it produces in the hearer a thought similar to that of the speaker.

Both theories were *inter alia* meant to fill the lacuna left by the *Tractatus*'s refusal to specify how signs are connected with what they signify. But when Wittgenstein turned to this problem after his return to philosophy, he criticized Russell, and Ogden and Richards, through arguments which apply to causal and behaviourist theories in general, and developed his own account of meaning in direct contrast to them. (For this reason, Quine is wrong to hold that the idea of meaning as use was anticipated by Dewey, who merely resisted mentalist theories of meaning in the name of behaviourism.) Just as causal accounts cannot do justice to the logical nature of INTENTIONALITY, they cannot do justice to the normative aspect of meaning, and obliterate the distinction between sense and nonsense. Whether a sign is meaningful or

379

meaningless does not depend on whether its utterance has the desired effect, either on a particular occasion or in general. 'This sign means X' does not mean 'When I utter this sign I get X.' Even if the regular result of my uttering 'Bring me sugar!' is that people stare at me and gape, this does not mean that my utterances mean 'Stare at me and gape!' The meaning of a word is determined by general conventions governing its use, while its effect depends on contingent conditions pertaining to specific circumstances.

On the causal theory, there can be no such thing as understanding an order, and yet disobeying it, since in this case the order does not have the desired effect. A causal theorist might reply that the theory does allow that an order can be disobeyed, because it is only one part of the causal chain which leads to its execution. In particular, the addressee must be so conditioned as to be willing to obey it. But this reply does not remove the difficulty. It is logically possible that the order will be disobeyed even if all the other links of the chain, including a disposition of the addressee, are functioning. A dog, however well trained, may disobey, and a mechanism, however well constructed, may break down. To explain the sense of an order is not to predict its consequences, not even with the proviso that the causal chain should not be deviant. For it is only by reference to norms of expression (grammatical rules) that we can distinguish between deviant and non-deviant causal chains, since only the rules determine *what counts* as complying with the order or understanding an utterance (PI §§493–8; PR 64; BT 193–4; PG 68–9, 187–92; PLP ch. IV; FW 97).

During the transition period, Wittgenstein claimed that while the meaning of a word is not identical with its effect, language can be seen as a causal mechanism linking stimuli and responses. Later, he rejected this claim, presumably because it is incompatible with the idea that mechanistic behaviour which merely happens to accord with a rule does not constitute RULE-FOLLOWING: if utterances were merely part of a mechanism, they would not count as moves in a language-game (PI §493; LPP 17, 135, 257). This is not to deny that language involves causal mechanisms, but rather to say that its meaningfulness cannot be made intelligible by reference to them.

Even if Wittgenstein did not hold a causal theory, he might have held a 'communication-intention' theory of the kind developed by G. H. Mead and Grice, according to which the meaning of a word is the effect the speaker *intends* to produce by it. But for Wittgenstein what matters to meaning is the purpose or role of expressions, not speakers (PI §§6, 8, 317, 345). It is not the intention of speakers to produce a particular effect in their audience by uttering a form of words in a particular situation (the intention to perform what Austin calls the perlocutionary act) that matters, but the function an expression has as a matter of linguistic convention, its role or place in grammar (PG 59, 189–90). Moreover, he would claim that my intention to produce in hearers a particular effect can itself be understood only by reference to its linguistic expression, and hence cannot explain the latter's meaning (*see* INTENDING AND MEANING SOMETHING).

The conventional or grammatical role of an expression does not just include the speech acts which can be effected by uttering it (as has been suggested by those assimilating Wittgenstein to speech-act analysis); it includes also its combinatorial possibilities, the logical relations of propositions in which it occurs, and the way in which its employment can be criticized or justified (*see* VERIFICATIONISM). Sometimes, Wittgenstein conceives it *too wide*, by holding that the meaning of a word is determined by its 'role in the whole life of a tribe' (EPB 149). 'Indigestion' has the same role in English as *Kreislaufbeschwerden* (circulatory disturbance) in German, namely of expressing the default complaint of hypochondriacs. Yet this does not indicate sameness of meaning, but rather divergence in form of life (paralysis here, *Angst* there). He is on safer ground in suggesting that the notion of sameness or difference in meaning is no more an all or nothing affair than sameness or difference in role (PI §§547–70). If this is correct, one should not try to make the former more precise by invoking the latter, but rest content with distinguishing the conventional role of a word in a language from its perlocutionary one on a given occasion.

V

vagueness   *see* DETERMINACY OF SENSE

variable   *see* PROPOSITION; SAYING/SHOWING; TAUTOLOGY

verificationism   This is the view that the meaning of a proposition is its method of verification (the principle of verification), and that a proposition is meaningless if it cannot be verified or falsified (the verificationist criterion of meaningfulness). The principle was first espoused by the Vienna Circle, but they attributed it to Wittgenstein, who seems to have transmitted it to Waismann in conversations. According to some commentators, the basic contrast between Wittgenstein's earlier and later work is that between a realist semantics based on truth-conditions, and an anti-realist semantics which rejects the notion of verification-transcendent truth and instead settles for assertability- or justifiability-conditions. The *Tractatus* indeed states that to understand a proposition is to know what is the case if it is true (TLP 4.024; *see* MEANING). However, this does not mark a simple contrast with verificationist ideas. Indeed, when Waismann attempted to summarize the *Tractatus* in 1930, he moved swiftly from the idea that to understand a proposition is to know under what conditions one would *call* it true to the principle of verification and the verificationist criterion of meaningfulness (WVC 243–5). This move is at least compatible with the *Tractatus*: to know whether a proposition is true one must *verify* it, hold it against reality like a ruler (TLP 2.1512f., 2.223). And to understand a proposition is to know what possible combination of objects *would* verify it, but not whether that combination actually obtains. Thus, the *Tractatus* is tacitly committed to a verificationist criterion of meaningfulness, although not to the principle of verification.

Wittgenstein started paying attention to the method of comparing a proposition with reality in 1929–30, once he realized that a proposition and what it depicts are not linked through a logico-metaphysical isomorphism (*see* INTENTIONALITY). As a result, he espoused a full-blown verificationism. A proposition is meaningful only if it can be verified or falsified completely; its meaning or sense is the method of verification; a difference of verification is a difference in meaning; and to understand a proposition is to know how to decide its truth or falsity; verification constitutes the *whole* sense of the proposition (WVC 47, 53, 79; PR 66–7, 77, 89, 174, 200; AWL 20; MS107 143). On this basis, he distinguished between three types of propositions, according to how they are verified. 'Genuine propositions' (*Aussagen*) can be conclusively verified or falsified by being compared with reality, because they describe 'primary experience' or sense-data, as in 'It seems as if there is a sphere in front of me.' They are either true or false. By contrast, 'hypotheses', statements about material objects and the mental states of others, are not propositions in the same sense, because they are not really true or false, but only more or less probable. Occasionally, Wittgenstein characterizes them as laws or rules for constructing genuine propositions (an idea which he may have got from Weyl): propositions about material objects ('There is a sphere in front of me') connect multiple propositions about what we see when looking at them (WVC 100–1, 159, 210–11; PR 282–97). Finally, the sense of mathematical propositions is given by their proofs. At first, Wittgenstein called this a verification of a different kind. Later, he insisted that proof and experience are not two comparable methods of verification, since a MATHEMATICAL PROOF does not establish the truth of a statement of fact, but rather the acceptability of a rule (PR 192, 200; M 60–1; PG 361).

'Genuine propositions' are the successors of the *Tractatus*'s ELEMENTARY PROPOSITIONS. They constitute a 'phenomenological language' which is semantically 'primary'. It is segmented into 'perceptual modality spaces' such as visual space, auditory space, etc. Hypotheses, that is, everyday propositions about physical objects and other minds, constitute a 'secondary' language, since they are constructed out of phenomenological propositions (*see* CRITERIA). The *Tractatus* had left open the precise nature of elementary propositions, although it suggested that they are about OBJECTS of acquaintance. Now Wittgenstein adopts an unequivocal phenomenalism. However, he soon abandoned this position. Initially, a 'phenomenological language' is semantically primary because it refers to what is immediately given to the senses (PR 88, 100–4, 267). This is superseded by the idea that what distinguishes 'phenomenology' from 'physics' is not reference to something inner, but that it is purely descriptive, that is, does not provide causal explanations. Thus understood, 'phenomenology is grammar', the investigation of linguistic rules (BT 437–86; PR 58, 84; WVC 63–8) (although in *Remarks on Colour* 'phenomenology' refers to a putative subject that claims to stand between grammar and physics, such as Goethe's theory of COLOURS).

In 1932, Wittgenstein realized that what he had conceived of as the only genuine propositions are in fact not *descriptions* of experiences, but AVOWALS. He also came to reject the idea that hypotheses can never be certain. First, a proposition can be *probable* only if it is logically possible for it to be certain. Secondly, the myth of the given, of private experiences providing the foundation of knowledge, is undermined by the PRIVATE LANGUAGE ARGUMENT.

Thirdly, unlike scientific statements of laws of nature, humdrum propositions about material objects are not rules for the construction of descriptions, but themselves descriptions.

During the thirties, both Wittgenstein and the Vienna Circle modified the principle of verification, the latter by conceding that verifying or falsifying a meaningful proposition need be possible only in principle, and need not be conclusive, the former by holding that the method of verification is only one aspect of the sense of a proposition (*see* USE), and, moreover, that it is one which does not apply in the case of first-person present tense psychological propositions. 'Asking whether and how a proposition can be verified is only a particular way of asking "How d'you mean?" The answer is a contribution to the grammar of the proposition' (PI §353; BT 265–70; AWL 28–9; Z §437). Moreover, Wittgenstein gradually realized that not all aspects of the method of its verification are part of the sense of a proposition, but only those which are linked to the way the relevant concepts are explained. In 1932–3, he argued that the fact that we can learn about who won the boat race by reading a newspaper goes some way to explaining the meaning of 'boat race'. Later, he insisted that to say that the length of playing fields is measured with the help of tripods is a matter of physics, while to say that measuring involves the possibility of comparing the lengths of different objects is partly constitutive of the meaning of 'length' (M 59–60; PI II 225).

Unlike contemporary anti-realism, Wittgenstein never cast doubt on the intelligibility of empirical propositions which are verification-transcendent but for which there can be evidence of some sort, such as propositions about the past (e.g., concerning Rosa Luxemburg's last thoughts) or the future ('A city will never be built here'). But he questioned the intelligibility of metaphysical propositions which are such that nothing would count as evidence for or against them. This holds, for example, for the sentence 'There is a white rabbit between the chairs whenever no one observes them', but equally for Russell's suggestion that 'The world might have been created five minutes ago, complete with records of the past' (LWL 111; AWL 25–6; BB 45–6; PI II 221). However, this is not a lazy philistinism which accepts only problems for which we have answers. Wittgenstein's point is not epistemological, namely that we could never know, but logical, namely that such propositions are 'idle wheels'. These strings of words cannot be used to make a move in the language-game, if they are taken in the way intended by the metaphysician. Metaphysical uses of words like 'flux', 'vagueness' or 'appearance' are without 'antithesis'. The metaphysician is not prepared to *count* anything as stable, accurate or real. That means, however, that he has not explained what his contrast between apparent and real amounts to. There are no standards of correctness for his metaphysical use of these terms, and hence his employment of them is meaningless. Whether or not this verdict can be sustained, it cannot be dismissed on the popular grounds that we must, rather, distinguish the onto-logical question of whether there are verification-transcendent rabbits from the epistemological question of how we could know about them. For Witt-genstein is concerned with the question of whether the purported ontologi-cal statement makes sense. Only if that question can be answered affirmatively, can the question of whether it is true or can be known arise. Logic is prior to both ontology and epistemology.

W

will Wittgenstein's early treatment is influenced by Schopenhauer's idea that the world as it appears to us is a manifestation of an underlying reality, an impersonal, cosmic will. We can know this noumenal reality, since our bodies are direct manifestations of it (not mere phenomena), and since we have access to our own willing, the only event we understand 'from within', not merely as a phenomenon (*World* I §19, II ch. 18).

Wittgenstein's discussion of SOLIPSISM is based on a Schopenhauerian distinction between the illusory 'thinking subject', and a metaphysical self which is not only the ineffable subject of experience, but also the 'willing subject' (NB 2.–5.8.16; TLP 5.631). He also distinguishes between 'the will as a phenomenon ... of interest only to psychology' and 'the will as the subject of ethical attributes'. The former is part of the episodes which constitute an individual's mental life, the latter is housed in the metaphysical self, and hence ineffable (TLP 6.423; NB 21.7.16). Like Schopenhauer, Wittgenstein views the world as morally inert and locates ETHICS in this metaphysical will. But for Schopenhauer salvation lies in overcoming the dictates of this blind force, while Wittgenstein regards the will as the 'bearer' of both 'good and evil' (NB 21./24./29.7.16). As in Schopenhauer, the metaphysical will is impersonal and 'permeates' the world, although this 'world-will' is 'in a higher sense *my* will' (NB 11.6./17.10.16). At the same time, Wittgenstein rejects Schopenhauer's metaphysics of the will as a thing in itself of which the phenomenal world is a manifestation. The metaphysical will is not a primordial force operating in the world, but an ethical 'attitude of the subject to the world'. It does not alter the facts but rather 'the limits of the world' (NB 5.7./4.11.16), namely the metaphysical self's attitude towards the facts which constitute the world – an idea reminiscent of Kierkegaard.

Underlying this position is the view that 'the world is independent of my will', that I am 'completely powerless' to bend events to my will (TLP 6.373; NB 11.6./8.7.16). One possible reason is that my only relation to the world which matters to logic is my depicting it in propositions. Yet, according to *Tractatus* 6.423, there is a psychological difference between different propositional attitudes like thinking and willing that *p*. As an empirical phenomenon, however, the will is impotent in a sense which is crucial to Wittgenstein's early position. There is no *logical* relation between the occurrence of any two empirical events, but only a contingent one (*see* CAUSATION), and this holds equally for my willing that p and p's coming about. This has three important consequences. First, the freedom of the will consists merely in the fact that we cannot know, that is, logically infer, our own future actions (TLP 5.135–5.1362). Second, if what we 'wish' happens, this is only a contingent 'physical connection', which itself is not under my control (TLP 6.374). By the same token, although there is a difference between those parts of my body which are and those which are not under my control (TLP 5.631), that control is merely a contingent one. This means, finally, that, *pace* Schopenhauer, I do not have an intuitive certainty of my intentional actions; my body is a mere phenomenon, on a par with all other parts of the world (TLP 5.641; NB 2.9./12.10./4.11.16).

Thus, the *Tractatus* presents a contemplative conception of the will: the phenomenal will is an ordinary empirical event, which merely happens to us, and is only contingently related to our actions; the metaphysical will is a mere ethical perspective. Certain passages in the *Notebooks* put pressure on this paradoxical position. Firstly, thinking itself involves an exercise of the will, and may be impossible without our controlling at least certain mental events (NB 21.7.16). This intimates a major difficulty in Wittgenstein's position, which insists on the impotence of the will while relying on the transcendental will for connecting language with reality through something akin to mental ostension. Secondly, there is a difference between wishing and willing. The former is indeed merely a mental phenomenon that may or may not be followed by a bodily movement. The latter, however, is not contingently related to action, it 'is acting', the volition *is* 'the action itself'. Hence it can involve certainty (I can predict that I shall raise my arm in five minutes) and a feeling of responsibility. By the same token, the relationship between volition and act is not that of cause and effect. This is precisely Schopenhauer's position, as is the claim that 'the act of will is not an experience' (NB 4.–9.11.16; see *World* I §18).

When Wittgenstein later developed this point it was first through the idea that representation itself involves INTENTIONALITY. Like thinking, willing is not a phenomenon that 'simply *happens*' and which we observe 'from outside', but something 'we *do*'; it consists in our being 'in the action', as its true 'agent' (PG 143–50). *Philosophical Investigations* moves on to discuss in its own right the concept of willing, perhaps because of the importance it attaches to human practice, but also because of conflicting philosophical pressures. Wittgenstein's aim is to undermine both the empiricist idea that 'willing too is merely an experience', and the 'transcendental' idea of willing as an 'extensionless point', an ineffable mental force (PI §§611, 620; EPB 236). The conflict has two interrelated dimensions, the question of whether willing is something beyond our control, and the question of whether willing is a mental accompaniment of action, as wishing is.

The empiricist position attacked is that of the *Tractatus*, but also of Russell (*Analysis* ch. XIV), and especially James (*Psychology* I), whose ideo-motor theory conceives of willing an act as the occurrence of prior kinaesthetic sensations, and assimilates willing to wishing. In both James and the early Wittgenstein the idea that willing is a phenomenon over which we lack control is fuelled by experiments like the intertwining of fingers or drawing from a mirror image. They suggest that one cannot produce the requisite experience of willing prior to the action. It seems that willing 'comes when it comes; I cannot bring it about', that 'one can't will whenever one wants. It just happens' (EPB 235–6; cf. NB 4.11.16; BB 153–5; PI §§612, 617). But if I am unable to bring about my willing, I would be powerless even if the connection between volition and action were one of necessity.

Against the view that willing is an experience which I cannot bring about, Wittgenstein makes the following points: (a) it is only in special cases, for example in the absence of muscular effort, that we say of an action that 'it comes when it comes'; (b) in the ordinary sense of 'bring about' it is possible for me to bring about, say, my willing to swim, namely by jumping into the water – we learn how to will to Φ by learning to Φ; (c) the finger-intertwining and mirror-drawing experiments suggest that willing is an experience only on the assumption that a voluntary movement is a movement that is brought about by the will, an assumption that Wittgenstein goes on to question; (d) the relation between willing and bodily movement is *not* merely contingent, as the *Tractatus* had it: 'when "I raise my arm", my arm goes up' (PI §§612–21; EPB 236).

However, the empiricist position need not stress the idea of impotence. It may be looking in experience precisely for the real doing, the real agent. This search lies behind the famous question 'what is left over if I subtract the fact that my arm goes up from the fact that I raise my arm?' (PI §621). That the exercise of the will is phenomenally distinguishable in experience is suggested by the fact that I can be certain as to whether I am willing, and if so, what I am willing (NB 4.11.16): how could I know this unless the willing and its content could be read off from my experience? Wittgenstein discusses two candidates for the experience constituting the real volition or doing (PI §§621–6; BB 51). James suggested that a voluntary physical action feels different from an involuntary movement, since it involves KINAESTHETIC sensations of action. Wittgenstein retorts that much of our authority to pronounce about ourselves does not involve kinaesthetic feelings, and even when it does they do not underpin judgements of having acted voluntarily, since we identify those feelings by reference to the voluntary movements of our limbs.

The second candidate for a phenomenal doing has been popular in recent action theory, namely, trying. Wittgenstein rejects this candidate on the grounds that not all actions involve trying. He suggests that it is false to say that I try to Φ if my Φing involves neither an effort nor a possibility of failure. To this Griceans have objected that although we are reluctant to speak of 'trying' in such cases, the reason is not that this would be false, but that it would be too obvious to be worth stating. But their position does not accord with the linguistic facts. It is committed to the mystifying claim that it is *less* obvious (and hence more worth saying) that I am trying to Φ when my Φing involves an effort. Moreover, if an interlocutor were to tell one 'Graf is trying to play tennis' in a situation in which Graf is effortlessly applying her forehand, one would not respond 'No need to tell me, I can see that she is.' Rather, one would react to the statement as a misapplication of a word: 'What do you mean "She's trying", can't you see how effortlessly she is playing?'

For Wittgenstein, the failure of these attempts to identify a phenomenon of willing is no coincidence. As soon as we try to identify the real doing with something in experience, it will appear as a mere phenomenon, something itself produced, not the unmoved mover behind the action. 'The will can't be a phenomenon, for whatever phenomenon you take is something that *simply happens*, something we undergo, not something we *do*' (PG 144). But the idea that the empiricist picture makes a nonsense of agency is the sole motive behind this transcendental alternative, which locates the real agent beyond experience.

Wittgenstein rejects this picture as equally awry. There *are* experiences involved in voluntary action (e.g., our seeing and feeling that we raise our arm). When we try to 'distinguish between *all the experiences* of acting plus the doing (which is not an experience) and *all* those experiences without the element of doing', the element of doing appears 'redundant' (PG 145). Nothing is left over in experience when we subtract the experience of our arm rising from the experience of our raising our arm. But this does not show that there is a real doing left over which is *not* in experience. Willing, unlike wishing, is not a mental event prior to or accompanying the bodily action. It *is* the action, as the *Notebooks* suggested, not, however, in a mysterious Schopenhauerian sense, but in 'the ordinary sense' of speaking, writing, walking, etc. And in cases in which I try but fail to Φ, it *is* the trying to Φ (PI §§614–16).

This denial that willing is a mental accompaniment of action parallels Wittgenstein's account of thinking (*see* THOUGHT/THINKING). The difference between voluntary and non-voluntary movement does not lie in mental goings-on, but in the context, and in what the agent is capable of doing on this occasion. Wittgenstein mentions the following features of voluntary action (Z §§577–99; PI §§611–28; BB 157): (a) susceptibility to orders, and the manner of this susceptibility – orders are normally not obeyed automatically; (b) the possibility of deciding whether or not to Φ; (c) the character of the movements and their relations to other surrounding events and circumstances; (d) different conclusions we draw from them, notably concerning responsibility; (e) while one can wish for anything, one can will only what is, or what one believes to be, within one's powers.

If the distinction between the voluntary and the involuntary does not lie in the presence or absence of an extra element of willing, willing is not the source of our voluntary actions. This undermines the idea that willing is our executive relation to our physical acts, an idea shared by both empiricism and transcendentalism. There are two important consequences. First, we do not use any means to bring about our action, for example an act of wishing (PI §614). Second, the conflict between empiricism and transcendentalism is based on a wrong assumption. Willing is neither a caused event which happens to me, beyond my control, nor 'an immediate, non-causal bringing-about' (PI §613). Wittgenstein reinforces this conclusion by arguing that willing is neither voluntary nor involuntary: (a) it makes no sense to speak of 'willing willing'; (b) if it did, 'willing' would be the name of an act, the act of willing, but it is not – one cannot, for example, obey the command to will, as nothing is specified thereby; (c) it makes sense to say that my body does not obey my will, but not that my will does not.

This line of thought is reminiscent of Ryle's argument against volitions and causal conceptions of the will. The insight that we don't usually cause our own actions has echoes in Davidson. But the claim that the empiricist position makes a nonsense of voluntary action by turning the will into a mere phenomenon, and the denial that particular actions are inherently voluntary due to a special origin, run counter to the causal accounts of the mind forcefully developed by Davidson. Regarding the problem of free will, Wittgenstein, like Schopenhauer, denied that libertarianism is vindicated by an experience of free volitions. He tried to avoid determinism by claiming that the fact that our actions follow natural laws does not show that we are in any way 'compelled', but his cursory reflections on this matter (LFW) are themselves uncompelling.

Bibliography of secondary sources

This survey of the secondary literature is extremely selective. For further bibliographical assistance see

Frongia, G. and McGuinness, B., *Wittgenstein: A Bibliographical Guide* (Oxford: Blackwell, 1990).
Shanker, V. A. and Shanker, S. G., *A Wittgenstein Bibliography* (Beckenham: Croom Helm, 1986).
[The latter is more comprehensive, the former features useful abstracts.]

HISTORICAL BACKGROUND

Hacker, P. M. S., *Wittgenstein's Place in Twentieth-Century Analytical Philosophy* (Oxford: Blackwell, forthcoming). [A magisterial if partisan treatment.]
Haller, R., *Questions on Wittgenstein* (London: Routledge, 1988). [Sheds valuable light on the Germanophone context of Wittgenstein's work.]
Janik, A. and Toulmin, S., *Wittgenstein's Vienna* (New York: Simon & Schuster, 1973). [Illuminates Wittgenstein's intellectual milieu, although many of its exegetical claims are problematic.]
Monk, Ray, *Wittgenstein: the Duty of Genius* (London: Cape, 1990).
McGuinness, B., *Wittgenstein, a Life: Young Ludwig 1889–1921* (London: Penguin, 1988). [Both biographies are excellent, McGuinness is stronger on Wittgenstein's intellectual background, Monk on his character.]
Nedo, M. and Ranchetti, M., *Wittgenstein: Sein Leben in Bildern und Texten* (Frankfurt: Suhrkamp, 1983). [A lavish and well-documented collection of photographs].
Passmore, J., *A Hundred Years of Philosophy* (London: Duckworth, 1966). [The most comprehensive history of analytic philosophy – a masterpiece.]
Skorupski, J., *English-Speaking Philosophy 1750–1945* (Oxford: OUP, 1992). [The title notwithstanding, the book deals with the development of philosophical modernism in Frege, Russell and Wittgenstein.]
Urmson, J. O., *Philosophical Analysis* (Oxford: OUP, 1956). [A bit dated on TLP, but strong on Cambridge between the wars.]
Wedberg, A., *A History of Philosophy*, Vol. 3: *From Bolzano to Wittgenstein* (Oxford: OUP, 1984).

GENERAL INTRODUCTIONS

Fogelin, R. F., *Wittgenstein* (London: Routledge, 1987; 1st edn. 1976). [Excellent on TLP; contains the first statement of the rule-sceptical interpretation of PI. The diagram on p. 109 and the list on p. 153 are derived from this book.]

Grayling, A. C., *Wittgenstein* (Oxford: Oxford University Press, 1988). [A brief introduction to the main themes.]

Hacker, P. M. S., *Insight and Illusion* (Oxford: Clarendon Press, 1986; 1st edn. 1972). [Arguably the best single book on Wittgenstein; traces the development of his views on philosophy and the mind.]

Kenny, A., *Wittgenstein* (Harmondsworth: Penguin, 1973). [Still the best first introduction; excellent on TLP; stresses the continuity between the early and later work.]

Malcolm, N., *Nothing is Hidden: Wittgenstein's Criticism of his Early Thought* (Blackwell, Oxford, 1986). [An excellent account of the contrast between the early and later views.]

Pears, D., *Wittgenstein* (London: Fontana, 1971). [Places Wittgenstein in the tradition of critical philosophy.]

Schulte, J., *Wittgenstein: an Introduction* (New York: State University of New York Press, 1992; German edn. Stuttgart: Reclam, 1989). [Covers a wide range of topics in a very accessible manner.]

COMMENTARIES

Black, M., *A Companion to Wittgenstein's 'Tractatus'* (Cambridge: Cambridge University Press, 1964). [Provides a wealth of background material; less good at shedding light on difficult passages.]

Baker, G. P. and Hacker, P. M. S., *Wittgenstein: Understanding and Meaning* – Vol. 1 of *An Analytical Commentary on the Philosophical Investigations* (Oxford: Blackwell, 1980).

—— *Wittgenstein: Rules, Grammar and Necessity* – Vol. 2 of *An Analytical Commentary on the Philosophical Investigations* (Oxford: Blackwell, 1985).

Hacker, P. M. S., *Wittgenstein: Meaning and Mind* – Vol. 3 of *An Analytical Commentary on the Philosophical Investigations* (Oxford: Blackwell, 1990).

—— *Wittgenstein: Mind and Will* – Vol. 4 of *An Analytical Commentary on the Philosophical Investigations* (Oxford: Blackwell, 1996). [The best commentaries on PI; combine scholarship with rigorous argument.]

Hallett, G., *A Companion to Wittgenstein's 'Philosophical Investigations'* (Ithaca: Cornell University Press, 1977). [Unlike the other commentaries, Hallett also covers PI Part II.]

Savigny, E. von, *Wittgensteins Philosophische Untersuchungen: Ein Kommentar für Leser* (Frankfurt: Klosterman, 1988). [Interprets PI without recourse to the *Nachlass*; close scrutiny of linguistic details.]

COLLECTIONS OF ESSAYS

Arrington, R. L. and Glock, H.-J. (eds), *Wittgenstein's Philosophical Investigations: Text and Context* (London: Routledge, 1991). [Essays devoted to particularly difficult passages in PI.]

—— (eds), *Wittgenstein and Quine* (London: Routledge, 1996). [Discussions of the similarities and differences between the two.]

Block, N. (ed.), *Perspectives on the Philosophy of Wittgenstein* (Oxford: Blackwell, 1981). [An excellent collection.]

Canfield, J. (ed.), *The Philosophy of Wittgenstein: A Fifteen Volume Collection* (New York: Garland, 1986). [The most comprehensive collection of critical essays.]

Copi, I. M. and Beard, R. W. (eds), *Essays on Wittgenstein's Tractatus* (London: Routledge, 1966). [Collects the best of the early essays on TLP.]

Fann, K. T. (ed.), *Ludwig Wittgenstein, the Man and his Philosophy* (Hassocks: Harvester, 1967). [Contains assessments by contemporaries.]

Glock, H.-J. (ed.), *Wittgenstein – A Critical Reader* (Oxford: Blackwell, forthcoming). [These essays are intended to accompany the selections in A. Kenny, *The Wittgenstein Reader.*]

Griffiths, A. P. (ed.), *Wittgenstein: Centenary Essays* (Cambridge: CUP, 1991). [Contains some essays on unusual topics.]

Heringer, H. J. and Nedo, M. (eds) *Wittgenstein and his Times* (Oxford: Blackwell, 1982; German edn. 1979). [Essays on Wittgenstein's perspective on modernity.]

Hintikka, J. (ed.), *Essays on Wittgenstein in Honour of G. H. von Wright* (Amsterdam: North-Holland, 1976). [Contains important essays, including Cioffi on aesthetic explanation.]

Kenny, A., *The Legacy of Wittgenstein* (Oxford: Blackwell, 1984). [Incisive and profound essays on Wittgenstein's work and its impact.]

Klemke, E. D. (ed.), *Essays on Wittgenstein* (Urbana: University of Illinois Press, 1971).

Luckhardt, G. (ed.), *Wittgenstein: Sources and Perspectives* (Ithaca: Cornell University Press, 1979). [A valuable source for scholars.]

Malcolm, N., *Wittgensteinian Themes* (Cornell: Cornell University Press, 1995).

Pitcher, G. (ed.), *The Philosophical Investigations* (London: Macmillan, 1968). [Seminal essays from the early period of Wittgenstein interpretation.]

Schulte, J., *Chor und Gesetz* (Frankfurt: Suhrkamp, 1990). [Highly informative essays on topics which are usually neglected.]

Shanker, S. (ed.), *Wittgenstein: Critical Assessments*, 4 vols (London: Croom Helm, 1986). [Contains most important exegetical essays.]

Teghrarian, S. (ed.), *Wittgenstein and Contemporary Philosophy* (Bristol: Thoemmes, 1994). [Most of the essays discuss Wittgenstein's relationship with contemporary philosophy.]

Vesey, G. (ed.), *Understanding Wittgenstein* (Ithaca: Cornell University Press, 1974). [An important collection of essays.]

Winch, P. (ed.), *Studies in the Philosophy of Wittgenstein* (London: Routledge & Kegan Paul, 1969). [Cook's 'Human Beings' is particularly valuable.]

von Wright, G. H., *Wittgenstein* (Oxford: Blackwell, 1982). [An invaluable collection, features essays on the origin of TLP and PI, as well as a catalogue of the *Nachlass*.]

THE EARLY WORK

Anscombe, G. E. M., *An Introduction to Wittgenstein's Tractatus* (London: Hutchinson, 1959). [Difficult, but vigorous and stimulating.]

Baker, G. P., *Wittgenstein, Frege and the Vienna Circle* (Oxford: Blackwell, 1988). [A thorough and subtle treatment of the development of Wittgenstein's account of logical necessity.]

Carruthers, P. *Tractarian Semantics* (Oxford: Blackwell, 1989).

—— *The Metaphysics of the Tractatus* (Cambridge: CUP, 1990).

[Both books assimilate TLP to Frege in a problematic fashion, but feature interesting criticisms of orthodox interpretations.]

Griffin, J. P., *Wittgenstein's Logical Atomism* (Oxford: Clarendon Press, 1964).

Lange, E. M., *Wittgenstein und Schopenhauer* (Cuxhaven: Junghans, 1989). [Sheds light on the background of TLP's treatment of solipsism.]

McDonough, R. M., *The Argument of the Tractatus* (Albany: State University of New York Press, 1986).

Mounce, H. O., *Wittgenstein's Tractatus: an Introduction* (Oxford: Blackwell, 1981). [The most accessible introduction to TLP.]

Pears, D., *The False Prison, Vol. I* (Oxford: Clarendon Press, 1987). [Features an illuminating account of the emergence of the picture theory from Russell's theory of judgement.]

Stenius, E., *Wittgenstein's Tractatus* (Oxford: Blackwell, 1960). [The first realist interpretation of TLP; stresses Kantian aspects.]

THE LATER WORK

Baker, G. P. and Hacker, P. M. S., *Scepticism, Rules and Language* (Oxford: Blackwell, 1984). [A vehement attack on the rule-sceptical interpretation.]

Barrett, C., *Wittgenstein on Ethics and Religious Belief* (Oxford: Blackwell, 1991). [A survey of Wittgenstein's views.]

Budd, M., *Wittgenstein's Philosophy of Psychology* (London: Routledge, 1989). [Meticulous and level-headed account.]

Canfield, J., *Wittgenstein: Language and World* (Amhurst: University of Massachusetts Press, 1981. [A painstaking discussion of the notions of grammar and of criteria.]

Diamond, C., *The Realistic Spirit* (Cambridge, Mass: MIT Press, 1991). [Difficult but interesting, especially on the topic of nonsense.]

Fann, K. T., *Wittgenstein's Conception of Philosophy* (Oxford: Blackwell, 1969).

Frascolla, P., *Wittgenstein's Philosophy of Mathematics* (London: Routledge, 1994). [Identifies unifying themes in Wittgenstein's early and later philosophy of mathematics.]

Hanfling, O., *Wittgenstein's Later Philosophy* (London: Macmillan, 1989). [Lucid and level-headed, focuses on the idea that explanations come to an end; the diagram on p. 121 is taken from Hanfling.]

Hark, M. ter, *Beyond the Inner and the Outer* (Dordrecht: Kluwer, 1990).

Hilmy, S., *The Later Wittgenstein* (Oxford: Blackwell, 1987). [An immensely scholarly investigation of the emergence of Wittgenstein's later views.]

Hintikka, M. B. and Hintikka, J., *Investigating Wittgenstein* (Oxford: Blackwell, 1986). [Interprets the private language argument as the result of Wittgenstein's abandonment of phenomenalism.]

Hunter, J., *Understanding Wittgenstein* (Edinburgh: Edinburgh University Press, 1985). [Short but highly illuminating essays on specific passages of PI.]

Johnston, P., *Wittgenstein and Moral Philosophy* (London: Routledge, 1989). [A sympathetic account of Wittgenstein's views on ethics and moral psychology.]

—— *Wittgenstein: Rethinking the Inner* (London: Routledge, 1993).

Kripke, S. A., *Wittgenstein on Rules and Private Language* (Oxford: Blackwell, 1982). [A powerful presentation of rule-scepticism and the community-view of rule-following.]

Marion, M., *Wittgenstein and Finitism* (Oxford: Clarendon Press, forthcoming).

McGinn, C., *Wittgenstein on Meaning* (Oxford: Blackwell, 1984). [A good discussion of rule-following and understanding.]

Mulhall, S., *On Being in the World* (London: Routledge, 1990). [An illuminating comparison of Heidegger and the later Wittgenstein.]

Pears, D., *The False Prison, Vol. II* (Oxford: Clarendon Press, 1988). [Focuses on the private language argument and rule-following; difficult.]

Phillips, D. Z., *Wittgenstein and Religion* (Basingstoke: St Martin's, 1993). [Essays by the most eminent proponent of a Wittgensteinian philosophy of religon.]

Rundle, B., *Wittgenstein and Contemporary Philosophy of Language* (Oxford: Blackwell, 1990). [Incisive and subtle criticisms of Wittgenstein's later philosophy of language.]

Schulte, J., *Experience and Expression* (Oxford: Clarendon Press, 1993; German edn. 1987). [Discusses Wittgenstein's philosophical psychology after PI; the diagrams on pp. 290–1 are developed from Schulte.]

Shanker, S., *Wittgenstein and the Turning Point in the Philosophy of Mathematics*

(London: Croom Helm, 1987). [The best defence of Wittgenstein's philosophy of mathematics.]

Stroll, A., *Moore and Wittgenstein on Certainty* (Oxford: Oxford University Press, 1994). [Stresses that for OC the basis of certainty lies in actions rather than propositions.]

Wright, C., *Wittgenstein on the Foundations of Mathematics* (London: Duckworth, 1980). [The first book to examine the implications of the rule-following considerations for the account of logical necessity.]

WITTGENSTEIN'S IMPACT ON OTHER DISCIPLINES

Baker, G. P. and Hacker, P. M. S., *Language, Sense and Nonsense* (Oxford: Blackwell, 1984). [Uses Wittgenstein's ideas to criticize theories of meaning in contemporary philosophy and linguistics.]

Bloor, D., *Wittgenstein: A Social Theory of Knowledge* (New York: Columbia University Press, 1983). [Exploits Wittgenstein for the sociology of knowledge.]

Bouveresse, J., *Wittgenstein Reads Freud* (Princeton: Princeton University Press, 1995). [An evenhanded account of the implications of Wittgenstein's remarks for our understanding of the unconscious.]

Chapman, M. and Dixon, R. A. (eds.), *Meaning and the Growth of Understanding: Wittgenstein's Significance for Developmental Psychology* (Berlin/New York: Springer, 1992).

Dilman, I., *Freud and the Mind* (Oxford: Blackwell, 1984). [Features many illuminating comparisons with Wittgenstein.]

Harris, R., *Language, Saussure and Wittgenstein* (London: Routledge, 1988).

Hyman, J. (ed.), *Investigating Psychology* (London: Routledge, 1991). [Contains articles about the implications of Wittgenstein's thought for contemporary psychology.]

Kerr, F., *Theology after Wittgenstein* (Oxford: Blackwell, 1986). [Spells out various implications for theology.]

Langer, S. K., *Philosophy in a New Key* (Cambridge, Mass: Harvard University Press, 1948). [Applies a theory of symbolism influenced by TLP to problems in aesthetics.]

Pitkin, H. F., *Wittgenstein and Justice* (Berkeley: University of California Press, 1972). [Draws implications for social and political thought.]

Tilghman, B. R., *But is it Art?* (Oxford: Blackwell, 1984). [Discusses whether art can be defined from a Wittgensteinian perspective.]

Winch, P., *The Idea of a Social Science and its Relation to Philosophy* (London: Routledge, 1958). [*Locus classicus* for a Wittgensteinian approach to the explanation/understanding debate.]

Index

Entry titles are printed in small capitals. Bold page-numbers indicate a sustained discussion of a topic, whether or not it features as an entry.